The Complete Works Of William Makepeace Thackeray

Standard Library Edition

THE COMPLETE WORKS

OF

WILLIAM MAKEPEACE THACKERAY

*WITH ILLUSTRATIONS BY THE AUTHOR AND OTHERS, AND
WITH INTRODUCTORY NOTES SETTING FORTH THE
HISTORY OF THE SEVERAL WORKS*

IN TWENTY-TWO VOLUMES

VOLUME XXII

Thackeray
From a photograph about 1851

MISCELLANEOUS PAPERS
AND SKETCHES

Hitherto Uncollected

BY

WILLIAM MAKEPEACE THACKERAY

WITH THE ORIGINAL ILLUSTRATIONS

BOSTON AND NEW YORK
HOUGHTON, MIFFLIN AND COMPANY
The Riverside Press, Cambridge

The Riverside Press, Cambridge, Mass., U. S. A.
Printed by H. O. Houghton and Company.

INTRODUCTORY NOTE.

AFTER Thackeray's death a definitive edition of his works was issued in London, of which the present edition is substantially a reprint. The penultimate volume of that edition was entitled *Miscellaneous Essays, Sketches, and Reviews,* and contained papers not previously reprinted. In making up the present edition, the contents of that volume have been distributed in volumes xix., xx., and this final volume; but in addition, use has been made of another posthumous collection of Thackeray's writings, entitled *Sultan Stork and other Stories and Sketches,* published in 1887 by George Redway.

The articles in this final volume of the American reissue have been grouped with some reference to their association, and the original date and place of publication have been prefixed to the several numbers. A few scattered papers not in any collected edition of Thackeray have been interspersed, and the opportunity has been taken to add such few speeches as had been reported, and the few letters scattered in the volumes of correspondence of Thackeray's contemporaries. This edition, therefore, makes good its claim to be the fullest, most exhaustive edition of Thackeray's writings which has appeared either in England or America.

In drawing from the two principal sources of this compilation, the editor has availed himself of the occasional footnotes supplied by the English editors. It would have been a feeble and most idle evasion to have used the material and merely changed the form so as to give the appearance of original investigation. His work as an editor has been confined to searching for the few pieces not in the two main books from which this volume is drawn, and to the orderly arrangement of material. The sources from which he has drawn the facts set forth in the several introductions are many, but he would chiefly specify as aiding him, not perhaps so much in specific passages, since the scope of the volume is limited bibliographically, as in its general illustration of Thackeray's personality, the volume *A Collection of Letters of Thackeray* published by Charles Scribner's Sons.

At the close of the present volume will be found an alphabetical index of titles of all works and articles.

BOSTON, *October*, 1889.

CONTENTS.

CONTRIBUTIONS TO "THE SNOB."

OUR "SNOB'S" BIRTH, PARENTAGE AND EDUCATION.

"Never shall I forget," said an old crone to me the other day, who, as far as we know, is contemporary with the alley in which we live — "Never shall I forget the night, in which you, Mr. Tudge, made your first appearance among us. Your father had, in his usual jocular manner, turned every one from the fireside, and putting a foot on each hob, with a pot in one hand, and a pipe in the other, sat blowing a cloud." "Ay, Mrs. Siggins," said I, "νεφεληγερέτα Ζεύς,* I suppose, as the blind bard has it." "Keep your Latin for the collegers," said she; "I know nothing on 't. Well, lo and behold, as I was saying, we were all sitting quiet as mice, when just as I had turned over the last page of the 'Skeleton Chief, or Bloody Bandit,' a sound, like I don't know what, came from overhead. Now, no one was upstairs, so, as you may well suppose, the noise brought my heart into my mouth, — nay more, it brought your dad to his legs, and you into the world. For your mother was taken ill directly, and we helped her off to bed." "*Parturiunt montes, nas* "† — said I, stopping short in confusion, — thank Heaven, the old woman knew not the end of the proverb, but went on with her story. "'Go, Bill,' says your father, 'see what noise was that.' Off went Bill, pale as a sheet, while I attended to your mother. Bill soon came laughing down. 'The boot-jack fell off the peg,' says he. 'It's a boy,' screams I. 'How odd!' says your dad. 'What's odd?' says I. 'The

---

* [νεφεληγερέτα Ζεύς. (Hom. *Iliad.*, a. 511, 517, *et sæpius*), i.e. "cloud-compelling Jove." — Ed.]

† [*Parturiunt montes, nascetur ridiculus mus.* — Hor. De Art. Poet. — 139. — Ed.]

1

child and the jack—it's ominous,' says he. 'As how?' says I. 'Call the child Jack,' says he." And so they did, and that's the way, do you see, my name was Jack Clypei Septemplicis Ajax.

Early in life I was sent to a small school in the next street, where I soon learned to play at marbles, blow my nose in my pinafore, and bow to the mistress. Having thus exhausted her whole stock of knowledge, I migrated to Miss G——'s, in Trumpington Street, and under the tuition of the sisters, became intimately acquainted, before I was nine years of age, with the proper distribution of letters in most three-syllable words of the British tongue, i.e. I became an expert speller.

(To be continued.)

Mrs. RAMSBOTTOM IN CAMBRIDGE.

RADISH GROUND BUILDINGS.

Dear Sir, — I was surprised to see my name in Mr. Bull's paper, for I give you my word I have not written a syllabub to him since I came to reside here, that I might enjoy the satiety of the literary and learned world.

I have the honor of knowing many extinguished persons. I am on terms of the greatest contumacy with the Court of Aldermen, who first recommended your weekly dromedary to my notice, knowing that I myself was a great literati. When I am at home, and in the family way, I make Lavy read it to me, as I consider you the censure of the anniversary, and a great upholder of moral destruction.

When I came here, I began reading Mechanics (written by that gentleman whose name you whistle). I thought it would be something like the Mechanics Magazine, which my poor dear Ram used to make me read to him, but I found them very foolish. What do I want to know about weights and measures and bull's-eyes, when I have left off trading? I have therefore begun a course of ugly-physics, which are very odd, and written by the Marquis of Spinningtoes.

I think the Library of Trinity College is one of the most admirable objects here. I saw the busks of several gentlemen whose statutes I had seen at Room, and who all received their edification at that College. There was Aristocracy who wrote farces for the Olympic Theatre, and Democracy who was a laughing philosophy.

I forgot to mention that my son George Frederick is entered at St. John's, because I heard that they take most care of their morals at that College. I called on the tutor, who received myself and son very politely, and said he had no doubt my son would be a tripod, and he hoped perspired higher than polly, which I did not like. I am going to give a tea at my house, when I shall be delighted to see yourself and children.

Believe me, dear Sir,
Your most obedient and affectionate
DOROTHEA JULIA RAMSBOTTOM.

A STATEMENT OF FAX RELATIVE TO THE LATE MURDER.

BY D. J. RAMSBOTTOM.

"Come I to speak in Cæsar's funeral."
MILTON, JULIUS CÆSAR, *Act III.*

ON Wednesday the 3d of June as I was sitting in my back parlor taking tea, young Frederick Tudge entered the room; I reserved from his dislevelled hair and vegetated appearance, that something was praying on his vittles. When I heard from him the cause of his vegetation, I was putrified! I stood transfigured! His father, the Editor of "The Snob," had been macerated in the most sanguine manner. The drops of compassion refused my eyes, for I thought of him, whom I had lately seen high in health and happiness; that ingenious indivisable, who often and often when seated alone with me has "made the table roar," as the poet has it, and whose constant aim in his weakly dromedary was to delight as well as to reprove. His son Frederick, too young to be acquainted with the art of literal imposition, has commissioned me to excommunicate the circumstances of his death, and call down the anger of the Proctors and Court of Aldermen on the phlogitious perforators of the deed.

It appears that as he was taking his customary rendez-vous by the side of Trumpington Ditch, he was stopped by some men in under-gravy dresses, who put a pitch-plaster on him, which completely developed his nose and eyes, or, as Shakespeare says, "his visible ray." He was then dragged into a field, and the horrid deed was replete! Such are the circumstances of his death; but Mr. Tudge died like Wriggle-us, game to the last; or like Cæsar in that beautiful faction of the poet, with which I have headed my remarks, I mean him who wanted to be Poop of Room, but was killed by two Brutes, and the fascinating hands of a perspiring Senate.

With the most sanguinary hopes that the Anniversary and Town will persecute an inquiry into this dreadful action, I will conclude my repeal to the pathetic reader; and if by such a misrepresentation of fax, I have been enabled to awaken an apathy for the children of the late Mr. Tudge, who are left in the most desultory state, I shall feel the satisfaction of having exorcised my pen in the cause of Malevolence, and soothed the inflictions of indignant Misery.

D. J. RAMSBOTTOM.

P.S. — The publisher requests me to state that the present No. is published from the MS. found in Mr. Tudge's pocket, and one more number will be soon forth-coming containing his inhuman papers.

TIMBUCTOO.

TO THE EDITOR OF "THE SNOB."

Sir, — Though your name be "Snob," I trust you will not refuse this tiny "Poem of a Gownsman," which was unluckily not finished on the day appointed for delivery of the several copies of verses on Timbuctoo. I thought, sir, it would be a pity that such a poem should be lost to the world; and conceiving "The Snob" to be the most widely circulated periodical in Europe, I have taken the liberty of submitting it for insertion or approbation.

I am, Sir, yours, etc., etc., etc.   T.

TIMBUCTOO.

The situation. In Africa (a quarter of the world)
Men's skins are black, their hair is crisp and
curled;
And somewhere there, unknown to public view,
A mighty city lies, called Timbuctoo.

The natural history. There stalks the tiger,—there the lion roars 5
Who sometimes eats the luckless blackamoors;
All that he leaves of them the monster throws
To jackals, vultures, dogs, cats, kites, and
crows.
His hunger thus the forest monarch gluts,
And then lies down 'neath trees called cocoa
nuts. 10

The lion hunt. Quick issue out, with musket, torch, and
brand,
The sturdy blackamoors, a dusky band!
The beast is found, — pop goes the muske-
toons, —
The lion falls, covered with horrid wounds.

Their lives at home. At home their lives in pleasure always flow, 15
But many have a different lot to know!

LINES 1 and 2. See Guthrie's Geography.
The site of Timbuctoo is doubtful; the Author has neatly expressed this in the Poem, at the same time giving us some slight hints relative to its situation.

LINE 5. So Horace — "leonum arida nutrix."
LINE 8. Thus Apollo   ἑλώρια τεῦχε κύνεσσιν.
Οἰωνοῖσί τε πᾶσι

LINE 5–10. How skilfully introduced are the animal and vegetable productions of Africa! It is worthy to remark the various garments in which the Poet hath clothed the Lion. He is called, 1st, the Lion; 2d, the Monster (for he is very large); and 3d, the Forest Monarch, which he undoubtedly is.

LINE 11–14. The Author confesses himself under peculiar obligations to Denham's and Clapperton's Travels, as they suggested to him the spirited description contained in these lines.

LINE 13. "Pop goes the musketoons." A learned friend suggested "Bang" as a stronger expression; but as African gunpowder is notoriously bad, the Author thought "Pop" the better word.

LINE 15–18. A concise but affecting description is here given of the domestic habits of the people, — the infamous manner in which they are entrapped and sold as slaves is described, — and the whole ends with an appropriate moral sentiment. The Poem might here finish, but the spirit of the bard penetrates the veil of futurity, and from it cuts off a bright piece for the hitherto unfortunate Africans, as the following beautiful lines amply exemplify.

Abroad.

They're often caught, and sold as slaves, alas!
Thus men from highest joy to sorrow pass.

Reflections on
the foregoing.

Yet though thy monarchs and thy nobles boil
Rack and molasses in Jamaica's isle!   20
Desolate Afric! thou art lovely yet!!!
One heart yet beats which ne'er shall thee for-
        get.
What though thy maidens are a blackish brown,
Does virtue dwell in whiter breasts alone?
Oh no, oh no, oh no, oh no, oh no!   25
It shall not, must not, cannot, e'er be so.
The day shall come when Albion's self shall
        feel
Stern Afric's wrath, and writhe 'neath Afric's
        steel.
I see her tribes the hill of glory mount,
And sell their sugars on their own account; 30
While round her throne the prostrate nations
        come,
Sue for her rice, and barter for her rum.   32

It may perhaps be remarked that the Author has here "changed
his hand;" he answers that it was his intention so to do. Before it
was his endeavor to be elegant and concise, it is now his wish to be
enthusiastic and magnificent. He trusts the Reader will perceive the
aptness with which he hath changed his style: when he narrated facts
he was calm, when he enters on prophecy he is fervid.

The enthusiasm which he feels is beautifully expressed in lines 25,
26. He thinks he has very successfully imitated in the last six lines
the best manner of Mr. Pope, and in lines 19–26 the pathetic elegance
of the Author of Australasia and Athens.

The Author cannot conclude without declaring that his aim in writing this Poem will be fully accomplished, if he can infuse in the
breasts of Englishmen a sense of the danger in which they lie. Yes
— Africa! If he can awaken one particle of sympathy for thy sorrows, of love for thy land, of admiration for thy virtue, he shall sink
into the grave with the proud consciousness that he has raised esteem
where before there was contempt, and has kindled the flame of hope
on the smouldering ashes of Despair!

CONTRIBUTIONS TO "THE NATIONAL STANDARD."

[1833.]

FOREIGN CORRESPONDENCE.

PARIS, Saturday, June 22.

THIS is a most unfavorable moment for commencing a Parisian correspondence. All the world is gone into the country, with the exception of the deputies, who are occupied in voting supplies; an occupation necessary, but not romantic, and uninteresting to the half million of Englishmen who peruse the "National Standard." However, in all this dearth of political and literary news, the people of France are always rich enough in absurdities to occupy and amuse an English looker-on. I had intended, after crossing the Channel to Boulogne, to have staid there for a while, and to have made some profound remarks on the natives of that town, but of these, I believe, few exist; they have been driven out by the English settlers, one of whom I had the good fortune to see. He did not speak much, but swore loudly; he was dressed in a jacket and a pair of maritime inexpressibles, which showed off his lower man to much advantage. This animal, on being questioned, informed me that the town was d——d pretty, the society d——d pleasant, balls delightful, and cookery excellent. On this hint, having become famished during a long and stormy voyage, I requested the waiter of the hotel to procure some of the delicacies mentioned by the settler. In an hour he returned with breakfast: the coffee was thin, the butter bad, the bread sour, the delicacies, mutton-chops. This was too much for human patience. I bade adieu to the settler, and set off for Paris forthwith.

I was surprised and delighted with the great progress made by the Parisians since last year. Talk of the " march

7

of mind" in England, La jeune France completely distances us : all creeds, political, literary, and religious, have
undergone equal revolutions, and met with equal contempt.
Churches, theatres, painters, booksellers, kings, and poets,
have all bowed before this awful spirit of improvement,
this tremendous "Zeitgeist." In poetry and works of fiction, this change is most remarkable. I have collected one
or two specimens, which I assure you are taken from works
universally read and admired. I have, however, been
obliged to confine ourselves to the terrific ; the tender parts
are much too tender for English readers. In England it
was scarcely permitted in former days to speak of such a
book, as the Memoirs of the celebrated M. de Faublas ; in
France it was only "a book of the boudoir," taken in private
by ladies, like their cherry-brandy ; now the book is public
property. It is read by the children, and acted at the
theatres ; and for Faublas himself, he is an absolute Joseph,
compared to the Satanico-Byronico heroes of the present
school of romance. As for murders, etc., mere Newgate-
Calendar crimes, they are absolute drugs in the literary
market. Young France requires something infinitely more
piquant than an ordinary hanging matter, or a commonplace *crim. con.* To succeed, to gain a reputation, and to
satisfy La jeune France, you must accurately represent all
the anatomical peculiarities attending the murder, or crime
in question : you must dilate on the clotted blood, rejoice
over the scattered brains, particularize the sores and
bruises, the quivering muscles, and the gaping wounds ; the
more faithful, the more natural; the more natural, the
more creditable to the author, and the more agreeable to
La jeune France.

I have before me a pleasing work with the following
delectable title : "Champavert : Immoral Tales. By Petrus
Borel the Lycanthrope !" After having perused this
pretty little book, I give the following summary of it, for
the benefit of English readers.

Tale 1. "M. de L'Argentière," contains a rape, a murder, an
execution.

Tale 2. "Jaquez Barraou," concludes thus :

"Immediately he seized him by the throat — the blood
gushed out, and Juan screamed aloud, falling on one knee
and seizing Barraou by the thigh ; who in turn, fastened on
his hair, and struck him on the loins, while, with a back-
stroke, *il lui étripe le ventre.* (The manœuvre is extraor-

dinary, and the language utterly untranslatable.) They rolled on the ground: now Juan is uppermost, now Jaquez — they roar and writhe!

"Juan lifted his arm, and broke his dagger against the wall. Jaquez nailed his in Juan's throat! Covered with wounds and blood, uttering horrid screams, they seemed a mere mass of blood flowing and curdling! Thousands of obscene flies and beetles might be seen hovering round their mouths and nostrils, and buzzing round the sores of their wounds.

"Towards night a man stumbled over the corpses. 'They are only negroes,' said he; and went his way."

It is, as the reader will see, quite impossible to translate properly this elegant passage; it displays a force, originality, and good taste, which can never be transferred to our language.

Tale 3. "Andréa Vésalius." Three adulteries, four murders. The victims are a wife and her three lovers, murdered first, and dissected afterwards, by Andréa Vésalius.

Tale 4. "Three-fingered Jack." Contains only one suicide, and the death of Jack in fair fight.

Tale 5. "Dina." One rape, one murder, one suicide.

Tale 6. "Passereau." Two murders and some intrigues — very prettily described.

Tale 7. "Champavert." This is the history of Lycanthrope himself. He was an extraordinary and melancholy young man, remarkable for a strong poetical genius and a long beard, both of which he had manifested from the age of seventeen. This history contains a couple of seductions, a child murder, and two suicides. Whether Champavert were a fictitious or real personage, I know not; there is, however, a long circumstantial account of his suicide here given; and I trust, for the honor of France, that the Lycanthrope actually lived and died in the manner described in the book.

My dear young ladies, who are partial to Lord Byron, and read Don Juan slyly in the evening; who admire French fashions, and dishes, and romances, — it is for your profit and amusement that this summary has been made. You will see by it how far this great nation excels us in genius and imagination, even though Bulwer and D'Israeli still live and write.

The costume of Jeune France is as extraordinary as its literature. I have sent a specimen, which I discovered the

other day in the Tuileries. It had just been reading the
Tribune, and was leaning poetically against a tree; it had
on a red neckcloth and a black flowing mane; a stick or
club, intended for ornament as well as use; and a pair of
large though innocent spurs, which had never injured anything except the pantaloons of the individual who wore
them.   Near it was sitting an old gentleman, who is
generally to be seen of a sunny day in the Tuileries, reading
his Crebillon or his prayer-book: a living illustration of
times past, — a strange contrast with times present! *

PARIS, Saturday, June 29.

There is no doubt that the "National Standard," though
the best conducted Journal in the world, has a most senseless, impotent, and unmeaning title: National Standard;
what does it signify ?   It may be a newspaper, or a measure
for brandy; a banner for King William, or a flag for King
Cobbett: you should take advice by the papers of this
country, and fix on a name more striking.   These observations have been inspired by the title of a journal which is
about to appear here, " Le Necrologe: Journal des Morts;"
a pretty romantic and melancholy title, printed on a sentimental paper, handsomely edged with black, and bearing an
urn for a frontispiece.   O death! O life! O *jeune France*,
what a triumph of art and taste is here! Fancy " *The
Mourning Advertiser; the Sexton's Miscellany ; The Raw
Head and Bloody Bones ; the Undertaker's Manual ; the
Pickaxe, or Gravedigger's Vade Mecum*," published every
morning for breakfast, and treating of all the most fashionable deaths, murders, suicides, and executions in Europe.
What a pleasing study for melancholy young men and
tender young ladies !   Then one has the advantage of
swallowing sentiment and history at the same time, and (as
Figaro says), while living, one is a subscriber to it; when
dead, an article.   The November suicides in England used
to be a staple article of French satire ; they used to think
that London Bridge was built for the mere convenience of
throwing one's self from it into the Thames, and that our
lamp-posts were only cast-iron substitutes for gibbets: in
regard to lamp-posts, however, we borrowed our learning from
them ; and, as to suicides, the advantage is now decidedly on

* Here, in *The National Standard*, appears an admirable sketch, which,
indifferently drawn as it is, has much of the spirit and humor of Thackeray's maturer illustration of his own text.

the French side. Half a dozen fellows "asphixient" themselves every morning, and servant maids with low spirits and wages, generally adopt this means of retirement, as one easy, expeditious, and certain. I heard just now of a young gentleman who had arrived at the mature age of sixteen, and of another more venerable by a couple of years, who sometime ago brought their lives to a conclusion in charcoal. They had, together, written a drama, which was represented at the Porte St. Martin, and succeeded; it procured for them, no doubt, a few dozen francs, and an eternity of half a dozen nights, which seemed entirely to answer their hopes and satisfy their ambition. Their enjoyment was complete, their cup of fame was full; and they determined, like young sages as they were, to retire from the world before their happiness should fade, or their glory tarnish, thinking no doubt that their death, their last and noblest action, would establish beyond all question their spiritual immortality.

So they purchased the means of their death (it is very cheap, twopenny worth will kill half a thousand young poets); they retired to their *sixième*, they shut out the world, and closed up the windows; and when, some hours after, the door of their apartment was forced open, their spirits and the charcoal-smoke flew out together, leaving only the two corpses to be admired by the public, and buried by the same. In France they dropped tears on their bodies; they would have employed stakes, instead of tears, in our less romantic country. However, peace be to their ashes! they are now, no doubt, comfortably situated in that heaven where they will find Cato and Addison, and Eustace Budgell, and all the suicidal philosophers; and some day or other, Liston, Talma, and all the great tragedians.

I asked my informer the names of these young unfortunates, and the title of their tragedy. He had forgotten both! So much for their reputation.

The theatres are in a flourishing condition: they have all at this moment some piece of peculiar attraction. At the *Ambigu Comique* is an edifying representation of "Belshazzar's Feast." The second act discovers a number of melancholy Israelites sitting round the waters of Babylon, with their harps on the willows! A Babylonian says to the leader of the chorus, "Sing us one of the songs of Zion;" the chorus answers, "How can we sing in a strange land?" and so on: the whole piece is a scandalous parody of the Scripture, made up with French sentiment and French decency. A large family of children were behind me, looking, with much interest and edification, at the Queen rising from her bath! This piece concludes with a superb imitation of Martin's picture of Belshazzar. Another piece at the *Porte St. Martin*, called "Bergami," vivifies Hayter's picture of the House of Lords, at Queen Caroline's trial. There was a report this morning that a courier had arrived from England, for the express purpose of forbidding this piece; and supposing, from that circumstance, that it must contain something very terrible, I sallied to the *Porte St. Martin* to see it; but I was sadly disappointed: for there was nothing in it but a little Platonic dialogue between Bergami, who is an angel, and the queen, who is an injured woman. Bergami appears first in the character of a post-boy, and makes such delightful remarks on the weather, the scenery, and Italian politics, that the warm-hearted queen is subdued at once, and makes him forthwith her equerry. The first act ends, and the queen gets into a carriage. In the second she gets into a packet (that unlucky packet!); in the third she gets into a balcony; in the fourth she gets into a passion, as well she may, since Bergami is assassinated by Lord Ashley (on which fact we beg to congratulate his lordship); and accordingly, she goes to the House of Lords to make her complaint against him for this act of unpoliteness; here the scene is very animated (it is taken from the picture). *Sir* Brougham makes a speech about injured women, patriotism, and so forth; Lord Eldon replies, the Ministerial bench cheers, the Opposition jeers, and the queen comes in majestically, bowing right and left, and uttering the noblest sentiments. Presently a row is heard in the streets: the mob is in arms for the queen! Lord Eldon motions the Minister of War; he rushes out to quell the disturbance, the queen follows him, but the attempts of both are ineffectual; windows are broken, stones are flung, Lord Eldon disappears, Sir Brougham bolts, and Lord Liverpool (a stout man in a white waistcoat, with a large tin star) falls to the earth, struck violently in the stomach with a leather brick-bat, and the curtain, of course, drops with the Prime Minister. The French nation was exalted by this exhibition to a pitch of immoderate enthusiasm, and called stoutly for the *Marseillaise*. I did not see the fifth act, in which the queen is poisoned (Lord Ashley again!), but returned home to give an account of this strange tragedy. There is a third play, of much more importance than the two former, of which I had wished to give some account, " Les Enfans d'Edouard," by M. Casimir Delavigne, one of the best-acted tragedies I had ever the good fortune to see ; but I have made this letter so long, that I must reserve this for some future day. I could not, however, refrain from sending a little sketch of Ligier,* who performs the part of *Richard*, in this play, in a manner, I think, which Kean never equalled.

Beside Ligier is the admirable Mademoiselle Mars, and that most charming, gay, graceful, *naïve* actress, Madame Anais Aubert. It would be worth an English actor's while to come to Paris, and study the excellent manner of the French comedians ; even Cooper might profit by it, and Diddear go away from the study a wiser and better man. Here is too much about theatres, you will say ; but after all, is not this subject as serious as any other ?

THE CHARRUAS.

PARIS, July 5.

The wondering reader may fancy that the scene here given was designed in the wilds of America, rather than in this gay city of Paris ; but he will see, if he takes the trouble of reading the following article (from the pen of M. Jules Janin), how the figures above † represent three unfortunate Charruas Indians, who have quitted South America to shiver under the cold Parisian sun.

" Allons ! let us go and see the savages ; they are lodged in the Champs Elysées, in one of those half-built houses, those ruins of yesterday, the view of which is sad without being solemn. Here are the heroes of our drama, not taller than the brave Agamemnons and Alexanders of the Theatre Français, but well-built and active, bold cavaliers, and gallant horse-tamers. They are perfidious, idle, revengeful, cruel cannibals, some of them ; perfect dramatic characters, in fact. In truth, they possess all the qualities requisite for the modern drama ; they can ride, fight, betray, revenge, assassinate, and eat raw flesh ; it is true that they don't know a word of French ; but what of that ? it is all the better for the theatre nowadays.

* The sketch appears with the letter in *The National Standard :* we regret to be unable to reproduce it here. — ED.

† A sketch of the Charruas headed this letter in *The National Standard.* — ED.

"When I saw them huddled together in their court, I declare I thought that I was looking at some modern tragedy: these brave savages wore costumes hideous and fanciful; they were all three seated in different solemn attitudes. First, the cacique, with hair uncombed, and fierce and heavy looks; he would have made a capital tyrant for a melodrama: the next, a lean, livid animal, with a sidelong look, and an indefinable smile, reminded me of Cooper's *Magna*; the third was gay, careless, and merry enough: and then came the timid and gentle Guynuya. She sate alone in the corner of the court, with her head on her bosom, bending under the weight of her captivity, like a princess of Ilium of old. This woman is truly sublime: it is true she is fickle and faithless, that she loves pleasure and change, that she has not our ideas of conjugal fidelity; but she has more passion and love than all the heroines of our tragedy; and above all, she has the passion of grief. I was much touched by this woman and her sorrows; her arms are all scarred over with wounds, and each of these wounds is the history of a sorrow. They were inflicted by herself: there is a scar for each friend she has lost; for every child of which she has been deprived there is a finger gone; she has lost two fingers, and there are near eighty scars on her arm; and this woman is not yet eighteen years old!

"Have you, in all the range of your drama, such a heroine as this? Have you, in all your poetry, so profound a grief as hers? And, for heroes, here is one whose shoulder has been laid open by a hatchet; and who, for the last miserable white Frenchwoman, who blunders through your ballets and your choruses, would go gladly to the Bois de Boulogne, and defy a dozen gentlemen at once! You call your heroes cruel, and your heroines tender! Here is a hero who poisons his own arrows, and a woman who gashes her arms with a wicked knife with as much ease as you would flourish a fan. Poor dramatists! See how utterly you are beaten off your ground by the first arrival from the plains of Paraguay. Thus, in fact, it is: as soon as one quits the poetical drama for that of the heart, and literary truth for common truth, one must expect to be vanquished by the first matter-of-fact competitor, whether savage or not; by all which, I mean to say, as Lord Byron has said before, that truth is stranger than fiction.

"Now, these heroes of the Champs Elysées are as poetic

as the heroes of Homer. Vaimaca Peru is a great chief, a veritable cacique, a specimen, in fact, of vagabond royalty, no more called on to uncover his head than are other vagabond royalties. Senaqué is the devoted friend of his chief, a subject faithful and sorrowful, more sorrowful indeed than his destitute master; and this is a common case about ruined thrones. The next, the young man, is careless and brave; and, although conquered, happy still, because he is young, and looks to the future. The woman Guynuya is truly the epic heroine, resigned to her fate; her very smile is full of tears, her sufferings are consoled by her weaknesses. Do you know that these savages have come from the extremity of Southern America? that they were made prisoners after long and bloody battles; that they have come hither to Paris, as a last asylum; and that this is the St. Helena of the vanquished cacique? For a long time they fought under Ribera; a year ago their tribe was destroyed, and they fled into the desert, bearing with them, not their harps, like the Hebrews, but the skulls of their enemies, the ornaments of their cabins. And now, vanquished prisoners, fugitives, they have come so far to find an asylum, and to receive a visit of that amateur of monsters, M. Geoffroy St. Hilaire.

"How times are changed! Formerly, when the grand kingdom of France was a Christian kingdom, the arrival of these savages would have caused a sensation amidst all the Catholicism of Paris. There would have been a tender solicitude evinced for the welfare of their immortal souls. They would have found, most likely, the king's mistress for a godmother, and the king's brother for a godfather; they would have been the objects of infinite dissertations, philosophical and religious: Jansenists and Jesuits would have disputed over these four souls with a ferocity altogether ecclesiastical. Our savages meanwhile would have been baptized, fêted, and amused, and sent back to their country loaded with presents and honors. At present, what is their fate, poor monarchs of the deserts? They have been received by the Academy of Sciences; and next, they will go to St. Cloud, and see the king, that is, if the master of the ceremonies permits it. The director of the opera will give them a box some night when all the boxes are empty; then they will go to the Porte St. Martin, then to Franconi's, and then to some cabaret of the lower order, where the grisette, come out for her Sunday, will scarcely deign

˙to look at them, seeing that she prefers her quadrille to all the savages in the world. Poor fellows! they will be lucky enough if they do not, like their brethren of the North,* die in the hospital, with a sister of charity on each side of them.

"I did not forget to caress the ostrich which gallops about in the court; he is a careless and gentle ostrich, who much pleased me: having nothing to give him, I offered him a piece of money, which he did me the honor of accepting, and which he swallowed and pocketed with the grace of a civilized individual.   JULES JANIN."

I have curtailed this article of M. Janin's, which is, I think, a tolerable specimen of the French style of periodical writing. It concludes with a long paragraph, expressing the writer's joy at escaping from the savages into the Champs Elysées; and some remarks on the civilized world in general. The paragraph proves that M. Janin was in a fright, and no wonder; three cannibals with knives and poisoned arrows are not pleasant companions even for a brave Frenchman. In the sketch given above, the stout man is the chief; the lady Guynuya has her back turned, a piece of unpoliteness in which she persisted during the whole of my visit. They play cards all day, laugh, eat raw beef, and drink all they can get.

PARIS, July 13.

The figure above † is a copy of the statue which shortly is to decorate the column in the Place Vendôme. It is, as everybody knows, to be elevated about the 29th of the month; but his majesty the king of the French, being averse to *emeutes dépenses* of all kinds, has determined that it shall be erected privily in the night season, and shall have no needless extravagance or unnecessary publicity to accompany its elevation.

The statue has been cast of bronze, or brass made of Austrian cannon (the victories of Napoleon are, luckily, not all used up), and represents, as the reader beholds, the little corporal in his habit of war. The column, up to 1814, was surmounted with a representation of the Em-

* The Osages, who were exhibited at Paris some years ago, and died there. '
† A sketch of Napoleon on the Vendôme Column headed this letter in *The National Standard.* — ED.

peror Napoleon, with robes and sceptre imperial; it bore
on its base the following sonorous inscription:

Neapolio Imp. Aug.
Monumentum Belli Germanici
anno MDCCCV.
Trimestre spatio profligati
ex ære capto
Gloriæ exercitus maximi dicavit.

In 1814 the inscription was removed, the statue torn
down, and a dirty white flag replaced it. It seemed a lame
and impotent conclusion to the series of victories which are
carved on the column itself, and wind from the base to the
summit, as if these battles had been fought and won for
the sole purpose of re-establishing the white flag aforesaid.

Next week, however, Napoleon will make his second
appearance on the column. He certainly ought to make
a short speech on the occasion, which, we should think,
would run something in this manner.

The emperor, after having raised his bronze spyglass to
his brazen eye, and regarded the multitude who are waiting
to hear his oration, begins

"Ladies and gentlemen! (*Tremendous applause.*)

"Unaccustomed as I am to public speaking, and overpowered by feelings of the deepest and tenderest nature,
you may readily fancy my inability to address you with
the eloquence demanded by your presence, and by this
occasion.

"Ladies and gentlemen: This is the proudest moment of
my life! (*Bravo, and cheers.*)

"I thank you for having placed me in a situation so safe,
so commanding, and so salubrious: from this elevation I
can look on most parts of your city. I see the churches
empty, the prisons crowded, the gambling-houses overflowing; who, with such sights before him as these, gentlemen,
and *you*, would not be proud of the name of Frenchmen?
(*Great cheers.*)

"The tricolor waves over the Tuileries as it used in my
time. It must be satisfactory to Frenchmen to have re-
established their glorious standard, and to have banished
forever the old white flag; and, though I confess myself
that I cannot perceive any other benefit you have wrought
by your resistance to a late family, you of course can.
(*Applause, mingled with some unseemly groans from the
police.*)

"I apprehend that the fat man * with the umbrella, whom I see walking in the gardens of the Tuileries, is the present proprietor. May I ask what he has done to deserve such a reward from you? Does he found his claim on his own merits, or on those of his father? (*A tremendous row in the crowd: the police proceed to* empoigner *several hundred individuals.*) Go your ways" (said the statue, who was what is vulgarly called a dab, at an impromptu); "go your ways, happy Frenchmen! You have fought, you have struggled, you have conquered: for whom? for the fat man with the umbrella!

"I need not explain what were my intentions and prospects, if I had had the good fortune to remain among you. You were yourselves pleased to receive them with some favor. The rest of Europe, however, did not look on them in the same light, and expressed its opinions so strongly, that we, out of mere politeness, were obliged to give up our own.

"I confess myself that I was somewhat arbitrary and tyrannical: but what is our fat friend below? Is it not better to be awed by a hero than to be subdued by a money-lender? to be conquered by a sword than to be knocked down by an umbrella? (*Here there was an immense cry of* "A bas les Parapluies!" *Some further arrests took place.*)

"Perhaps, if it be not a bore ("*Go on*"), you will allow me to say a word concerning those persons who so strongly voted my own removal, and the re-establishment of the white cloth, now folded up forever.

"The Russians are occupied in strangling, murdering, and banishing; I could not possibly have chosen for them a better occupation.

"The English, with their £800,000,000 of debt, have destroyed their old institutions, and have as yet fixed on no new ones. (*Here a further crowd were marched off by the police.*) I congratulate you. Gentlemen, *they* too have policemen.†

"The Portuguese are fighting about two brothers, both of whom they detest. Heaven preserve the right, whichever he may be.

"From Italy there are delightful accounts of revolts, and deaths thereon consequent.

* Napoleon here makes an irreverent and personal allusion to King Louis Philippe. His stoutness and his umbrella were depicted some two months ago in our paper.
† This struck us as rather a vulgar allusion on the part of the statue.

The Germans are arresting students for want of a better employment. The Spaniards are amusing themselves with sham fights: what a pity they cannot be indulged with real ones!

"And the family! for whom about five hundred thousand lives were sacrificed, — where are they? The king is doting, and the dauphin is mad in a chateau in Germany; and the duchess must divide her attentions between her son and her daughter.

"And yourselves, gentlemen, you have the freedom of the press, — but your papers are seized every morning, as in my time. You have a republic, but beware how you speak of the king! as in my time also. You are free; but you have seventeen forts to keep you in order. I don't recollect anything of the sort in my time.

"Altogether, there is a most satisfactory quantity of bullying, banishing, murdering, taxing, and hanging, throughout Europe. I perceive by your silence " — Here the emperor stopped: the fact was, there was not a single person left in the Place Vendôme; they had all been carried off by the police!

CRITICISMS IN LITERATURE AND ART.

WILLIS'S DASHES AT LIFE WITH A FREE PENCIL.

[*Edinburgh Review, October,* 1845.]

WHATEVER doubt or surprise the details and extracts with which we are about to amuse our readers may seem to attach to the fact, we beg to assure those of them who do not already know it, that Mr. Willis has actually written some rather clever books, occasionally marked by traits of genius. But, with respect to the present publication, we confess we have been frequently at a loss to judge whether his narratives were intended to be taken as serious, or only jocular — as what he himself believed to be truths, or intended only as amusing fancies. True, he writes, as he tells us, with " a free pencil;" but it is also true that he writes as if he wished his readers to think that he is perfectly in earnest; that he speaks in his own proper person, and reveals his own adventures, or what he appears to wish to be taken as such; and we therefore feel it to be quite fair — indeed that we are bound — to take him at his word, and to deal with him accordingly.

The history of these " Dashes at Life," which some of our contemporaries have much extolled, is thus modestly given in the preface: — " Like the sculptor who made toys of the 'fragments of his unsalable Jupiter,' the author, in the following collection of brief tales, gives material, that, but for a single objection, would have been moulded into books of a larger design. That objection is the unmarketableness of American books in America, owing to our (Mr. Willis is an American) defective law of copyright." And he proceeds to show, with pathetic accuracy, that as an American publisher can get all English books for nothing, he will not throw away his money on American writers: hence the only chance of a livelihood for the latter is to contribute to periodical literature, and to transport works of bulk and merit to the English market.

So, after all, if a few authors and publishers grumble at piracy, the public gains. But for the pirates of New York and Boston, we should never have had Mr. Willis's "Dashes." And though the genius which might have perfected the Jupiter has been thus partly balked, though Mr. Willis has been forced to fritter away his marble and intellect in a commerce of toys; still the fragmented Jupiter has, with the frieze of the Parthenon, found an appropriate locality in the capital of the world.

But, to proceed with the history, we may state that it was Mr. Willis's intention to work up some of these sketches into substantial novels, but for the unsatisfactory state of the market for that commodity; and there can be no sort of doubt that the genius which conceived might have enlarged the "Dashes" to any size. In the first half of these volumes, there are some twenty tales illustrative of English and Continental life — true copies, Mr. Willis states, of what he has seen there; and most of them of so strange and diverting a nature, that a man of genius might have made many scores of volumes out of the adventures recorded in only a few hundreds of these duodecimo pages. The Americans, by their piratical system, have robbed themselves of that pleasure; and the Union might have had a novelist as prolific as M. Dumas or Mr. James, had it possessed the common generosity to pay him. The European, as contradistinguished from the American views of society, we take to be by far the most notable of the "Dashes." The judgment of foreigners has been called, by a happy blunder of logic, that of contemporary posterity. In Mr. Willis we have "a republican visiting a monarchical country for the first time, traversing the barrier of different ranks with a stranger's privilege, and curious to know how nature's nobility holds its own against nobility by inheritance, and how heart and judgment were modified in their action by the thin air at the summit of refinement." That Mr. Willis, in his exalted sphere, should have got on in a manner satisfactory to himself, is no wonder. Don Christopher Sly conducted himself, we all remember, with perfect ease in the Ducal chair. Another personage of somewhat humble rank in life, was, as we also know, quite at home at the court of Queen Titania, and inspired her Majesty with a remarkable passion. So, also, our republican stranger appears to have been equally at his ease, when he appeared for the first time in European aristocratical society.

The great characteristic of high society in England, Mr. Willis assures us, is admiration of literary talent. "At the summit of refinement," a natural nobleman, or a popular writer for the magazines, is in all respects the equal of a Duke. As some captain of Free Lances of former days elbowed his way through royal palaces, with the eyes of all womankind after him — so, in the present time, a man, by being a famous "Free Pencil," may achieve a similar distinction. Of such a champion, the ladies don't say, as in the time of the Free Lances, he fought at Hennebon or Pavia, but that he wrote that charming poem in Colburn, that famous article in Blackwood. Before that title to fame, all aristocratic heads bow down. The ladies do not care for rank, or marry for wealth, they only worship genius !

This truly surprising truth forms the text of almost every one of Mr. Willis's "Dashes" at English and Continental life. The heroes of the tales are all more or less alike — all "Free Pencils." Sometimes the tales are related in the first person, as befalling our American; sometimes a flimsy third person veils the author, but you can't but see that it is Cæsar who is writing his own British or Gallic victories, for the "Free Pencil" always conquers. Duchesses pine for his love; modest virgins go into consumptions, and die for him; old grandmothers of sixty forget their families and propriety, and fall on the neck of this "Free Pencil." If this be true, it is wonderful; if it is fiction, it is more wonderful still, that all a man's delusions should take this queer turn, — that Alnaschar should be always courting the Vizier's daughter — courting! What do we say ? It is the woe-worn creature who is always at Alnaschar's feet, and he (in his vision) who is kicking her.

The first of the pictures of London life is called "Leaves from the Heart-book of Ernest Clay." This, but for the unfavorable circumstances before alluded to, was to have been a novel of three volumes; and indeed it would have been hard to crowd such a hero's amours into a few chapters. Ernest is a great "Free Pencil," with whom Jules Janin himself (that famous chieftain of the French "Free Pencils," who translated Sterne, confessing that he did not know a word of English, and "did" his own wedding-day in a *feuilleton* of the *Journal des Débats*) can scarcely compare. The "Heart-book" opens in Ernest's lodgings, in a second floor front, No.—, South Audley Street, Grosvenor Square, where Ernest is writing, before a three-halfpenny inkstand, an article for the next new monthly magazine. It was two o'clock, and the author was at breakfast, — and to show what a killing man of the world poor Ernest was, his biographer tells us that —

"On the top of a small leather portmanteau, near by (the three-halfpenny inkstand, the like of which you may buy "in most small shops in Soho"), stood two pair of varnished-leather boots of a sumptuous expensiveness, slender, elegant, and without spot, except the leaf of a crushed orange blossom clinging to one of the heels. The boots and the inkstand were tolerable exponents of his (the fashionable author's) two opposite but closely woven existences."

A printer's Devil comes to him for his Tale, and as the man of genius has not written a word of it, he begins to indite a letter to the publisher, which we print with what took place subsequently; that the public may be made acquainted with the habits of "Free Pencils" in composition.

[Here follows an extract.]

Both the carriages, the coroneted chariot and the plain coach "out of Grosvenor Square," contain ladies who are wildly in love with the celebrated writer for the Magazines. He is smitten by the chariot; he has offered marriage to the family coach; which of the two vehicles shall carry him off? The rival owners appear in presence (at Mrs. Rothschild's ball!), and after a slight contest between vice and virtue, the well-principled young man of genius finishes the evening by running away with the coronet to a beautiful retreat in Devonshire, leaving his bride-elect to wear the willow. This may be considered as Volume I. of the "Heart-book." Who would not be interested in reading the secrets of such a heart — who would not pardon its poetic vagaries?

In Volume II. the "Free Pencil," seeing in the newspapers the marriage of an old flame, merely in joke writes the lady a letter so thrilling, tender, and impassioned, that she awakens for the first time to a sense of her exquisite beauty, and becomes a coquette forever after. The "Free Pencil" meets with her at Naples; is there kissed by her in public; crowned by her hand, and proclaimed by her beautiful lips the prince of poets; and as the lady is married, he, as a matter of ordinary gallantry, of course wishes to push his advantages further. But here (and almost for the only time) he is altogether checked in his advances, and made to see that the sovereign power of beauty is even paramount to that of "free pencilling" in the genteel world. By way of episode, a story is introduced of a young woman who dies of love for the poet (having met him at several balls in London). He consoles her by marrying her on her death-bed. In Volume III. the "Free Pencil" recovers his first love, whom he left behind in the shawl-room at Mrs. Rothschild's ball, and who has been pining and waiting for him ever since. The constancy of the beautiful young creature is rewarded, and she becomes the wife of the highly-gifted young man.

Such briefly is the plot of a tale, purporting to be drawn from English life and manners; and wondering readers may judge how like the portrait is to the original; how faithfully the habits of our society are here depicted; how Magazine writers are the rulers of fashion in England; how maids, wives, and widows, are never tired of running away with them. But who can appreciate the powers of description adorning this likely story; or the high-toned benevolence and morality with which the author invests his hero? These points can only be judged of by a perusal of the book itself. Then, indeed, will new beauties arise to the reader's perception. As, in St. Peter's, you do not at first appreciate the beautiful details, so it is with Mr. Willis's masterpiece. But let us, for present recreation, make one or two brief extracts: —

A lady arriving at a tea-party. "Quietly, but with a step as elastic as the nod of a water-lily, Lady Mildred glided into the room, and the high tones and unharmonized voices of the different groups suddenly ceased, and were succeeded by a low and sustained murmur of admiration. A white dress of faultless freshness of fold; a snowy turban, from which hung on either temple a cluster of crimson camelias still wet with the night dew; long raven curls of undisturbed grace falling on shoulders of that indescribable and dewy coolness which follows a morning bath (!), giving the skin the texture and the opaque whiteness of the lily; lips and skin redolent of the repose and purity, and the downcast but wakeful eye so expressive of recent solitude, and so peculiar to one who has not spoken since she slept — these were attractions which, in contrast with the paled glories around, elevated Lady Mildred at once into the predominant star of the night."

What a discovery regarding the qualities of the "Morning bath " — how naïvely does the "nobleman of nature" recommend the use of that rare cosmetic! Here follows a description of the triumphs of a "Free Penciller."

[Here follows the extract.]

We shall next notice a wonderful history of foreign life, containing the development of a most wonderful idiosyncrasy. It is that of an author — our "Free Penciller!" His life is but a sleeping and forgetting — the new soul that rises in him has had elsewhere its setting, and cometh again from afar. He has not only a Pythagorean belief, but sometimes a consciousness of his previous existence, or existences — nay, he has not only a consciousness of having lived formerly, but often believes that he is living somewhere else, as well as at the place where at the present moment he may be. In a word, he is often conscious of being two gentlemen at once ; — a miraculous *égarement* of the intellect described in the following manner.

[Here follows an extract.]

This awakening to a sense of previous existence is thus further detailed. "The death of a lady in a foreign land," says Mr. Willis, "leaves me at liberty to narrate the circumstances which follow." Death has unsealed his lips; and he may now tell, that in a previous state of existence he was in love with the beautiful Margaret, Baroness R——, when he was not the present "Free Penciller," but Rodolph Isenberg, a young artist of Vienna. Travelling in Styria, Rodolph was taken to a *soirée* at Grätz, in the house of a "certain lady of consequence there," by "a very courteous and well-bred person, a gentleman of Grätz," with whom Mr. Willis has made acquaintance in the *coupé* of a diligence. No sooner was he at the *soirée* than he found himself on the balcony talking to "a very quiet young lady," with whom he "discoursed away for half an hour very unreservedly," before he discovered that a third person, "a tall lady of very stately presence, and with the remains of remarkable beauty," was earnestly listening to their conversation, with her hand upon her side,

in an attitude of repressed emotion." On this the conversation "languished;" and the other lady, his companion,
rose, and took his arm to walk through the rooms. But he
had not escaped the notice of the elder lady.

Such are the pictures of European society which this
"Free Penciller" has sketched. Of the truth of his descriptions of his own country and countrymen, it is not for
us to speak. We shall only mention, that, in characteriz-
ing them, he remarks that they are much more French than
English in many of their qualities. "They are," says he,
"in dressing, dancing, congregating, in chivalry to women,
facility of adaptation to new circumstances, elasticity of
recuperation from trouble" (a most delicious expression!),
"in complexion and figure, very French!" Had the
"Dashes" been the work of a native genius, we might
have hinted, perhaps, some slight occasional objections,
pointed out a very few blunders, questioned, very diffi-
dently, the great modesty of some statements, and the
truth and accuracy of others. But as the case stands, we
feel that we are bound to excuse much to a young "republican visiting a monarchical country for the first time."

BARMECIDE BANQUETS, WITH JOSEPH BREGION AND ANNE MILLER.

[*Fraser's Magazine, November,* 1845.]

GEORGE SAVAGE FITZ-BOODLE, ESQUIRE, TO THE REVEREND LIONEL GASTER, FELLOW AND TUTOR OF SAINT BONIFACE COLLEGE, OXON.

PALL MALL, October 25, 1845.

My dear Lionel, — There is a comfort to think, that however other works and masterpieces bearing my humble name have been received by the public, namely, with what I cannot but think (and future ages will, I have no doubt, pronounce) to be unmerited obloquy and inattention, the present article, at least, which I address to you through the public prints, will be read by every one of the numerous readers of this Magazine. What a quantity of writings by the same hand have you, my dear friend, pored over ! How much delicate wit, profound philosophy (lurking hid under harlequin's black mask and spangled jacket, nay, under clown's white lead and grinning vermilion), — how many quiet wells of deep gushing pathos, have you failed to remark as you hurried through those modest pages, for which the author himself here makes an apology, not that I quarrel with my lot, or rebel against that meanest of all martyrdoms, indifference, with which a callous age has visited me — not that I complain because I am not appreciated by the present century — no, no ! — he who lives at this time ought to know it better than to be vexed by its treatment of him — he who pines because Smith or Snooks doesn't appreciate him, has a poor puny vein of endurance, and pays those two personages too much honor.

Pardon, dear Lionel, the egotism of the above little disquisition. If (as undoubtedly is the case) Fitz-Boodle is a *grande âme inconnue,* a *génie incompris,* you cannot say that I complain — I don't push cries of distress like my friend Sir Lytton — if I am a martyr, who ever saw me out of temper ? I lie smiling on my rack or gridiron, causing every now and then an emotion of pity in the bystanders at my angelic good-humor. I bear the kicks of the world with smiling meekness, as Napoleon used to say Talleyrand could; no one could tell from the jolly and contented expression of my face what severe agonies were felt — what torturous indignities were inflicted elsewhere.

I think about my own exceedingly select class of readers with a rueful modesty, when I recollect how much more lucky other authors are. Here, for instance, I say to myself, looking upon the neat, trim, tight, little, handsome book, signed by Joseph Bregion and Anne Miller, "Here is a book whereof the public will infallibly purchase thousands. Maidens and matrons will read and understand it. Smith will buy it and present it to his lady; Snooks will fully enter into the merit of it, and recommend its perusal to his housekeeper. Nor will it be merely enjoyed by these worthy humdrum people, but men of learning and genius will find subject of interest and delectation in it. I dare say it will find a place in bishops' libraries, or on the bookshelves of men of science, or on the tables of poets and painters; for it is suited to the dullest and the highest intelligence." And where is the fool or the man of genius that is insensible to the charms of a good dinner? I myself have been so much amused and instructed by the reading of the "Practical Cook" that I have purchased, out of my own pocket, several copies for distribution among my friends. Everybody can understand it and get benefit by it. You, not the least among the number, my reverend and excellent friend; for though your mornings are passed in the study of the heathen classics, or over your favorite tomes of patristic lore — though of forenoons you astonish lecture-rooms with your learning, and choose to awe delighted undergraduates, — yet I know that an hour comes daily when the sage feels that he is a man, when the reverend expounder of Austin and Chrysostom forsakes his study table for another, which is spread in the common-room, whereon, by the cheerful glimmer of wax-tapers, your eye rests complacently upon crystal flasks mantling with the red juices of France and Portugal, and glittering silver dishes, smoking with viands prepared by your excellent college cook.

Do you remember the week I once passed at Saint Boniface College, honored to be your guest and that of the society? I have dined in many countries of Europe and Asia since then — I have feasted with aldermen, and made one at

Soyer's house-dinners — I have eaten the produce of Borel's larder, and drunk Clos-Vougeot at the "Trois Frères " — I have discussed the wine of Capri, and know the difference of the flavor of the oysters of Poldoodie and the Lucrine Lake — I have examined bouillabaisse at Marseilles and pilaff at Constantinople — I have consorted with epicures of all ages and nations, — but I never saw men who relished a dinner better than the learned fellows of Saint Boniface ! How Gaster will relish this book ! I thought to myself a hundred times as I revelled over the pages of Anne Miller and Joseph Bregion.

I do not believe, however, that those personages, namely, Bregion, "formerly cook to Prince Rasumowski " (I knew his Highness intimately), "to Prince Nicholas Esterhazy, the Russian Ambassador at Paris, etc., and Anne Miller, cook in several English families of distinction," are the real authors of this excellent and truly "Practical Cook." A distinguished amateur of cookery and almost every other science, a man whose erudition is as varied and almost as profound as your own, a practical philosopher, who has visited every capital in Europe, their victuals noted and their wines surveyed, is, I have reason to think, the real genius under whose presiding influence Anne and Joseph have labored. For instance, of the Portuguese and Spanish dishes here described, the invaluable collection of Turkish and Indian receipts, the Sicilian and Hungarian receipts, it is not probable that Joseph or Anne should have had much personal experience; whereas it is my firm opinion that the occult editor of the "Practical Cook" has tasted and tested every one of the two hundred and twenty-three thousand edible and potable formulæ contained in the volume. A great genius, he has a great appetite and digestion. Such are part of the gifts of genius. In my own small way, and at a single dinner at Brussels, I remember counting twenty-nine dishes of which I partook. By such a process alone, and even supposing that he did not work at breakfast or supper, a man would get through 10,480 dishes in a year, so that twenty years' perseverance (and oh how richly would that industry be repaid!) would carry you through the whole number above specified.

Such a gormandizing encyclopædia was indeed wanted, and is a treasure now that we have it complete. You may feast with any nation in the world as you turn over the pages of this delightful volume. In default of substantial banquets even imaginary ones are pleasant. I have always relished Alnaschar's dinner, off lamb and pistachio-nuts, with the jolly Barmecide, and could, with an easy and thankful heart, say grace over that light repast. What a fine, manly, wholesome sense of roast and boiled, so to speak, there is in the "Iliad"! In my mind I have often and often cut off great collops of the smoking beeves under Achilles' tent, and sat down to a jovial scrambling dinner along with Penelope's suitors at Ithaca. What appetites Ariosto's heroes have, and the reader with them! (Tasso's Armida dinners are rather theatrical in my mind, gilt pasteboard cups with nothing in them, wooden pullets and pineapples, and so forth.) In Sir Walter Scott, again, there reigns a genuine and noble feeling for victuals. Witness King James's cocka-leekie, those endless admirable repasts in "Ivanhoe," especially that venison pasty in "Quentin Durward," of the flavor of which I have the most distinct notion, and to which I never sit down without appetite, nor quit unsatisfied. The very thought of these meals, as recalling them one by one, I note them down, creates a delightful tickling and longing, and makes one quite hungry.

For these spiritual banquets of course all cookery-books are good; but this of the so-called Miller and Bregion is unrivalled. I have sent you a copy down to Oxford, and would beg you, my dear Lionel, to have it in your dressing-room. If you have been taking too many plovers' eggs, or *foie gras* patty, for breakfast, if you feel yourself a trifle heavy or incommoded after a hot luncheon, you naturally mount your cob, take a gentle breathing for a couple of hours on the Blenheim or Bagley road, and return to dress for dinner at the last minute; still feeling that you have not got your appetite quite back, and, in spite of the exercise, that you are not altogether up to the good things of the fellows' table. In this case (which may often occur), take my advice. Instead of riding for two hours, curtail your exercise, and only trot for an hour and forty minutes. Spend these twenty minutes in your easy-chair over the "Practical Cook." Begin almost at any page. After the first few paragraphs the languor and heaviness begin to disappear. The idea of dining, which was quite disagreeable to you half an hour since, begins to be no longer repulsive — a new interest springs up in your breast for things edible — fancy awakens the dormant appetite, which the coarse remedy of a jolt on horseback had failed to rouse, and, as the

second bell rings, you hasten down to Hall with eagerness,
for you know and feel that you are hungry. For some time
I had the book by my bedside, and used to read it of nights ;
but this is most dangerous. Twice I was obliged to get up
and dress myself at two o'clock in the morning, and go out
to hunt for some supper.

As you begin at the preface of the book it charms you
with its philosophical tone.

" Far are we from saying that a dinner should not be a subject of
morning or mid-day meditation or of luxurious desire; but in the
present advanced state of civilization, and of medical and chemical
knowledge, something more than kneading, baking, stewing, and
boiling are necessary in any nation pretending to civilization. The
metropolis of England exceeds Paris in extent and population: it
commands a greater supply of all articles of consumption, and contains a greater number and variety of markets, which are better
supplied. We greatly surpass the French in mutton, we produce
better beef, lamb, and pork, and are immeasurably superior both in
the quantity and quality of our fish, our venison, and our game, yet
we cannot compare, as a nation, with the higher, the middle, or the
lower classes in France, in the science of preparing our daily food.
The only articles of food in the quality of which the French surpass
us are veal and fowl, but such is the skill and science of their cooks,
that with worse mutton, worse beef, and worse lamb than ours, they
produce better chops, cutlets, steaks, and better made dishes of every
nature and kind whatsoever. In *fricassées, ragoûts, salmis, quenelles,
purées, filets,* and more especially in the dressing of vegetables, our
neighbors surpass us, and we see no good reason why we should not
imitate them in a matter in which they are so perfect, or why their
more luxurious, more varied, more palatable, and more dainty cookery,
should not be introduced among the higher and middle classes to
more general notice."

No Joseph Bregion, though Rasumowski's *chef ;* no
Anne Miller, though cook to ever so many English families of distinction, could write like this. No, no. This
is not merely a practical cook, but a practical philosopher,
whose pen we think we recognize, and who wishes to reconcile ourselves and our Gallic neighbors by the noble means
of a good dinner. There is no blinking the matter here ;
no foolish vainglory and vaporing contempt of Frenchmen, such as some Britons are wont to indulge in, such as
all Frenchmen endeavor to make pass for real. Scotland,
they say, is the best cultivated country of Europe; and
why ? — because it is the most barren. Your Neapolitan
peasant lolls in the sunshine all day, leaving his acres to
produce spontaneous melons and volunteer grapes, with
which the lazy farmer nourishes himself. Your canny

Scot invents manures, rotatory crops, subsoil ploughs, tile-drains, and other laborious wonders of agriculture, with which he forces reluctant Nature to be bountiful to him. And as with the fruits of the field, so it is with the beasts thereof; because we have fine mutton to our hand, we neglect cookery. *The French, who have worse mutton, worse beef, and worse lamb than ours, produce better chops, cutlets, and steaks.* This sentence should be painted up as a motto in all our kitchens. Let cooks blush when they read it. Let housekeepers meditate upon it. I am not writing in a burlesque or bantering strain. Let this truth be brought home to the bosoms of English kitchens, and the greatest good may be done.

The grand and broad principles of cookery or cookics thus settled, the authors begin to dissert upon the various branches of the noble science, regarding all of which they have to say something new, or pleasant, or noble. Just read the heads of the chapters, — what a pleasant smack and gusto they have ! —

RULES NECESSARY TO BE OBSERVED BY COOKS IN THE REGULA-
     TION AND MANAGEMENT OF THEIR LARDER.
OBSERVATIONS AS TO UNDRESSED MEATS.
OBSERVATIONS ON THE KITCHEN AND ITS UTENSILS.
OBSERVATIONS ON AND DIRECTIONS FOR CARVING.
GENERAL OBSERVATIONS ON ENGLISH SOUPS AND BROTHS, AND
     DIRECTIONS CONCERNING THEM.
OBSERVATIONS ON MEAT IN GENERAL.

The mere titles themselves are provocative of pleasant thoughts and savory meditations. I seize on them. I sniff them spiritually. I eye them (with the eyes of the imagination) yearningly. I have seen little penniless boys eying meat and puddings in cookshops so — no pleasant occupation perhaps to the hungry — but good and whole-some for such as have dined to-day and can afford to do so to-morrow. Even after dinner, I say this book is pleasant to read and think over. I hate the graceless wretch who begins to be disgusted with eating so soon as his own appetite is satisfied. Your truly hospitable man loves to see others eating happily around him, though satiety has caused him to lay down his own knife and fork; the spectacle of a hungry fellow-creature's enjoyment gives a benevolent gormandizer pleasure. I am writing this very line after an excellent repast of three courses; and yet this mere account of an English dinner awakens in me an active interest and a manly and generous sympathy.

"*On laying out a table.* — The manner of laying out a table is nearly the same in all parts of the United Kingdom: yet there are trifling local peculiarities to which the mistress of a house must attend. A centre ornament, whether it be a *dormant*, a *plateau*, an *épergne*, or a *candelabra*, is found so convenient, and contributes so much to the good appearance of the table, that a fashionable dinner is now seldom or never set out without something of this kind.

"Utility should be the true principle of beauty, at least in affairs of the table, and, above all, in the substantial first course. A very false taste is, however, often shown in centre ornaments. Strange ill-assorted nosegays and bouquets of artificial flowers begin to droop or look faded among hot steams. Ornamental articles of family plate, carved, chased, or merely plain, can never be out of place, however old-fashioned. In desserts, richly-cut glass is ornamental. We are far, also, from proscribing the foliage and moss in which fruits are sometimes seen bedded. The sparkling imitation of frost-work, which is given to preserved fruits and other things, is also exceedingly beautiful; as are many of the trifles belonging to French and Italian confectionery.

"Beautifully white damask, and a green cloth underneath, are indispensable.

"In all ranks, and in every family, one important art in house-keeping is to make what remains from one day's entertainment contribute to the elegance or plenty of the next day's dinner. This is a principle understood by persons in the very highest ranks of society, who maintain the most splendid and expensive establishments. Vegetables, ragoûts, and soups may be re-warmed; and jellies and blancmange remoulded, with no deterioration of their qualities. Savory or sweet patties, croquets, rissoles, *vol-au-vents*, fritters, tartlets, etc., may be served with almost no cost, where cookery is going forward on a large scale. In the French kitchen, a numerous class of culinary preparations, called *entrées de dessert*, or made-dishes of left things, are served even at grand entertainments.

"At dinners of any pretension, the First Course consists of soups and fish, removed by boiled poultry, ham, or tongue, roasts, stews, etc.; and of vegetables, with a few made-dishes, as ragoûts, curries, hashes, cutlets, patties, fricandeaux, etc., in as great variety as the number of dishes permits. For the Second Course, roasted poultry or game at the top and bottom, with dressed vegetables, omelets, macaroni, jellies, creams, salads, preserved fruit, and all sorts of sweet things and pastry, are employed — endeavoring to give an article of each sort, as a jelly and a cream, as will be exemplified in bills of fare which follow. This is a more common arrangement than three courses, which are attended with so much additional trouble both to the guests and servants.

"Whether the dinner be of two or three courses, it is managed nearly in the same way. Two dishes of fish dressed in different ways — if suitable — should occupy the top and bottom; and two soups, a white and a brown, or a mild and a high-seasoned, are best disposed on each side of the centre-piece; the fish-sauces are placed between the centre-piece and the dish of fish to which each is appropriate; and this, with the decanted wines drunk during dinner, forms the first course. When there are rare French or Rhenish wines, they are placed in the original bottles, in ornamented wine-vases, between the centre-piece and the top and bottom dishes; or if four kinds, they are ranged round the plateau. If one bottle, it is placed in a vase in the centre. ·

"The Second Course at a purely English dinner, when there are three, consists of roasts and stews for the top and bottom; turkey or fowls, or fricandeau, or ham garnished, or tongue for the sides; with small made dishes for the corners, served in covered dishes; as *palates*, currie of any kind, *ragoût* or *fricassée* of rabbits, stewed mushrooms, etc., etc.

" The Third Course consists of game, confectionery, the more delicate vegetables dressed in the French way, puddings, creams, jellies, etc.

" Caraffes, with the tumblers belonging to and placed over them, are laid at proper intervals. Where hock, champagne, etc. etc. are served, they are handed round between the courses. When the third course is cleared away, cheese, butter, a fresh salad, or sliced cucumber, are usually served; and the finger-glasses precede the dessert. At many tables, particularly in Indian houses, it is customary merely to hand quickly round a glass vessel or two filled with simple, or simply per-fumed tepid water, made by the addition of a little rose or lavender water, or a home-made strained infusion of rose-leaves or lavender spikes. Into this water each guest may dip the corner of his napkin, and with this refresh his lips and the tips of his fingers.

" The Dessert, at an English table, may consist merely of two dishes of fine fruit for the top and bottom; common or dried fruits, filberts, etc., for the corners or sides, and a cake for the middle, with ice-pails in hot weather. Liqueurs are at this stage handed round; and the wines usually drunk after dinner are placed decanted on the table along with the dessert. The ice-pails and plates are removed as soon as the company finish their ice. This may be better understood by following the exact arrangement of what is considered a fashionable dinner of three courses and a dessert."

Now what can be finer than this description of a feed? How it recalls old days and old dinners, and makes one long for the return of friends to London and the opening of the dining campaign! It is not far removed, praised be luck. Already the lawyers are coming back (and, let me tell you, some of the judges give uncommonly good din-ners), railroad speculations are bringing or keeping a good number of men of fortune about town : presently we shall have Parliament, the chief good of which institution is, as I take it, that it collects in London respectable wealthy dinner-giving families; and then the glorious operations will commence again; and I hope that you, dear Lionel (on your occasional visits to London), and your humble servant and every good epicure will, six times at least in every week, realize that delightful imaginary banquet here laid out in type. ·

But I wish to offer a few words of respectful remon-strance and approving observation regarding the opinions delivered above. The description of the dinner, as it actually exists, we will pass over; but it is of dinners as they should be that I would speak. Some statements in the Bregion-Miller account I would question; of others I deplore that they should be true.

In the first place — as to central ornaments — have them, as handsome, as massive as you like — but be hanged to flowers! I say; and, above all, no candelabra on the table — no cross-lights; faces are not seen in the midst of the abominable cross-lights, and you don't know who is across the table. Have your lights rich and brilliant overhead, blazing on the sideboard, and gleaming hospitably from as many sconces as you please along the walls, but no lights on the tables. "Roses, bouquets, moss, and foliage," I have an utter contempt for as quite foolish ornaments, that have no right to appear in atmospheres composed of the fumes of ham, gravy, soup, game, lobster-sauce, etc. Away with all poetastering at dinner-parties. Though your friends Plato and Socrates crowned themselves with gar-lands at dinner, I have always fancied Socrates an ass for his pains. Fancy old Noddly, of your college, or your own venerable mug or mine, set off with a wreath of tulips or a garland of roses, as we ladled down the turtle-soup in your hall! The thought is ridiculous and odious. Flowers were not made to eat — away with them! I doubt even whether young unmarried ladies should be allowed to come down to dinner. They are a sort of flowers — pretty little sentimental gewgaws — what can *they* know about eating? They should only be brought down for balls, and should dine upon roast mutton in the nursery.

"Beautiful white damask and a green cloth are indis-pensable." Ah, my dear Lionel, on this head I exclaim, let me see the old mahogany back again, with the crystal, and the wine quivering and gleaming in it. I am sorry for the day when the odious fashion of leaving the cloth down was brought from across the water. They leave the cloth on a French table because it is necessary to disguise it; it is often a mere set of planks on trestles, the meanness of which they disguise as they disguise the poverty of their meat. Let us see the naked mahogany; it means, I think, not only a good dinner, but *a good drink after dinner.* In houses where they leave the cloth down you know they are

going to shirk their wine. And what is a dinner without a
subsequent drink ? A mockery — an incomplete enjoyment
at least. Do you and I go out to dine that we may have
the pleasure of drinking tea in the drawing-room, and hearing Miss Anne or Miss Jane sing ? Fiddlededee ! I can
get the best singing in the world for half a guinea ! Do we
expend money in cabs, kid gloves, and awful waistcoats, in
order to get muffins and tea ? Bah ! Nay, does any man
of sense declare honestly that he likes ladies' conversation ?
I have read in novels that it was pleasant, the refinement
of woman's society — the delightful influence of a female
presence, and so forth ; but say now, as a man of the world
and an honest fellow, did you ever get any good out of
women's talk ? What a bore a clever woman is ! — what a
frightful bore a mediocre respectable woman is ! And every
woman who is worth anything will confess as much. There
is no woman but *one* after all. But mum ! I am getting
away from the dinner-table ; they it was who dragged me
from it, and it was for parsimony's sake, and to pleasure
them, that the practice of leaving on the cloth for dessert
was invented.

This I honestly say as a diner-out in the world. If I accept an invitation to a house where the dessert-cloth practice is maintained (it must be, I fear, in large dinners of
apparat now, but I mean in common *réunions* of ten or
fourteen) — if I accept a dessert-cloth invitation, and a
mahogany invitation subsequently comes, I fling over dessert-cloth. To ask you to a dinner without a drink is to
ask you to half a dinner.

This I say in the interest of every diner-out. An unguarded passage in the above description, too, might give
rise to a fatal error, and be taken advantage of by stingy
curmudgeons who are anxious for any opportunity of saving their money and liquor, — I mean those culpably careless words, " *Where hock, champagne, etc., etc., are served,
they are handed round between the courses.*" Of course they
are handed round between the courses ; but they are handed
round during the courses too. A man who sets you down
to a driblet of champagne — who gives you a couple of beg-
garly glasses between the courses, and winks to John who
froths up the liquor in your glass, and screws up the remainder of the bottle for his master's next day's drinking,
— such a man is an impostor and despicable snob. This
fellow must not be allowed an excuse for his practice — the

wretch must not be permitted to point to Joseph Bregion and Anne Miller for an authority, and say they declare that champagne is to be served only between the courses. No! —no! you poor lily-livered wretch! If money is an object to you, drink water (as we have all done, perhaps, in an angust state of domestic circumstances, with a good heart); but if there is to be champagne, have no stint of it in the name of Bacchus! Profusion is the charm of hospitality; have plenty, if it be only beer. A man who offers champagne by driblets is a fellow who would wear a pinchbeck breastpin, or screw on spurs to his boots to make believe that he kept a horse. I have no words of scorn sufficiently strong to characterize the puny coward, shivering on the brink of hospitality, without nerve to plunge into the generous stream!

Another word should be said to men of moderate means about that same champagne. It is actually one of the cheapest of wines, and there is no wine, out óf which, to speak commercially, you get your returns so directly. The popping, and fizzing, and agreeable nervous hurry in pouring and drinking, give it a prestige and an extra importance — it makes twice the appearance, has twice the effect, and doesn't cost you more than a bottle of your steady, old, brown sherry, which has gathered on ·its head the interest of accumulated years in your cellar. When people have had plenty of champagne they fancy they have been treated liberally. If you wish to save, save upon your hocks, Sauternes, and Moselles, which count for nothing, but disappear down careless throats like so much toast and water.

I have made this remark about champagne. All men of the world say they don't care for it; all gourmands swear and vow that they prefer Sillery a thousand times to sparkling, but look round the table and behold! We all somehow drink it. All who say they like the Sillery will be found drinking the sparkling. Yes, beloved sparkler, you are an artificial, barley-sugared, brandied beverage, according to the dicta of connoisseurs. You are universally sneered at, and said to have no good in you. But console yourself, you are universally drunken — you are the wine of the world, — you are the liquor in whose bubbles lies the greatest amount of the sparkle of good spirits. May I die but I will not be ashamed to proclaim my love for you! You have given me much pleasure, and never any pain — you have stood by me in many hard moments, and cheered me in many dull ones — you have whipped up many flagging thoughts, and dissipated many that were gloomy — you have made me hope, ay, and forget. Ought a man to disown such a friend ?

Incomparably the best champagne I know is to be found in England. It is the most doctored, the most brandied, the most barley-sugared, the most *winy* wine in the world. As such let us hail, and honor, and love it.

Those precious words about *réchauffés* and the art of making the remains of one day's entertainment contribute to the elegance and plenty of the next day's dinner, cannot be too fondly pondered over by housekeepers, or too often brought into practice. What is it, ladies, that so often drives out men to clubs, and leaves the domestic hearth desolate — what but bad dinners ? And whose fault is the bad dinners but yours — yours, forsooth, who are too intellectual to go into the kitchen, and too delicate to think about your husband's victuals ? I know a case in which the misery of a whole life, nay, of a whole series of little and big lives, arose from a wife's high and mighty neglect of the good things of life, where *ennui*, estrangement, and subsequent ruin and suicide, arose out of an obstinate practice of serving a leg of mutton three days running in a small respectable family.

My friend, whom I shall call Mortimer Delamere (for why not give the unfortunate fellow as neat and as elegant a name as possible, as I am obliged to keep his own back out of regard to his family ?) — Mortimer Delamere was an ornament of the Stock Exchange, and married at the age of twenty-five.

Before marriage he had a comfortable cottage at Sutton, whither he used to drive after business hours, and where you had roast ducks, toasted cheese, steaks and onions, wonderful bottled stout and old port, and other of those savory but somewhat coarse luxuries with which home-keeping bachelors sometimes recreate their palates. He married and quitted his friends and his little hospitalities, his punch and his cigars, for a genteel wife and house in the Regent's Park, where I once had the misfortune to take pot-luck with him.

That dinner, which I never repeated, showed me at once that Delamere's happiness was a wreck. He had cold mutton and mouldy potatoes. His genteel wife, when he humbly said that he should have preferred the mutton hashed, answered superciliously that the kitchen was not her province, that as long as there was food sufficient she did not heed its quality. She talked about poetry and the Reverend Robert Montgomery all the evening, and about a quarter of an hour after she had left us to ourselves and the dessert, summoned us to exceedingly weak and muddy coffee in the drawing-room, where she subsequently entertained us with bad music, sung with her own cracked, false, genteel voice. My usual politeness and powers of conversation did not of course desert me even under this affliction; and she was pleased to say at the close of the entertainment that she had enjoyed a highly intellectual evening, and hoped Mr. Fitz-Boodle would repeat his visit. Mr. Fitz-Boodle would have seen her at Jericho first.

But what was the consequence of a life of this sort? Where the mutton is habitually cold in a house, depend on it the affection grows cold, too. Delamere could not bear that comfortless, flavorless, frigid existence. He took refuge in the warmth of a club. He frequented not only the library and coffee-room, but, alas! the smoking-room and card-room. He became a *viveur* and jolly dog about town, neglecting the wife who had neglected him, and who is now separated from him, and proclaimed to be a martyr by her genteel family, whereas, in fact, her own selfishness was the cause of his falling away. Had she but condescended to hash his mutton and give him a decent dinner, the poor fellow would have been at home to this day; would never have gone to the club or played with Mr. Denman, who won his money; would never have been fascinated by Senhora Dolora, who caused his duel with Captain Tufto; would never have been obliged to fly to America after issuing bills which he could not take up — bills, alas! with somebody else's name written on them.

I venture to say that if the "Practical Cook" had been published, and Mrs. Delamere had condescended to peruse it; if she had read pages 30–32, for instance, with such simple receipts as these: —

BILLS OF FARE FOR PLAIN FAMILY DINNERS.

DINNERS OF FIVE DISHES.

Peas or Mulligatawny Soup.

Potatoes browned below the Roast.	Apple Dumpling, or Plain Fritters.	Mashed Turnips or Pickles.

Roast Shoulder of Mutton.

Haddocks boiled, with Parsley and Butter Sauce.
Potatoes.   Newmarket Pudding.   Rice or
                Haricot, Currie, Hash, or Grill,   Pickles.
                of the Mutton of the former day.

———

Knuckle of Veal Ragoût, *or with Rice.*
Stewed Endive.   A Charlotte.   Potatoes.
Roast of Pork, or Pork Chops — *Sage Sauce, or Sauce Piquante.*

———

Boiled Cod, with Oyster, Egg, or Dutch Sauce.
Potatoes.   Mutton Broth.   Carrots or
                Scrag of Mutton, with   Turnips.
                Caper Sauce, or Parsley and Butter.

———

Cod Currie, or a Béchamel, of the Fish of former day.
Scalloped Oysters.   Rice Pudding.   Mashed Potatoes.
                Roast Ribs of Beef.

———

Bouilli, *garnished with Onions.*
                                Beef Cecils, of the
Marrow Bones.   Soup *of the Bouilli.*   Roast Ribs of the
                                former day.
                Lamb Chops, with Potatoes.
                Vegetables on the Side Table.

she would have had her husband at home every day. As
I read them over myself, dwelling upon each, I say inwardly, "Could I find a wife who did not sing, and who
would daily turn me out such dinners as these, Fitz-Boodle
himself would be a family man."   See there how the
dishes are made to play into one another's hands; how the
roast shoulder of mutton of Monday (though there is no
mention made of the onion sauce) becomes the currie or
grill of Tuesday; how the boiled cod of Thursday becomes
the béchamel of Friday, a still better thing than boiled
cod!   Feed a man according to those receipts, and I engage
to say he *never* would dine out, especially on Saturdays, with
that delicious bouilli garnished with onions, — though, to be
sure, there is a trifle too much beef in the *carte* of the day;
and I for my part should prefer a dish of broiled fish in
the place of the lamb-chops with potatoes, the dinner as it
stands here being a trifle too *brown.*

One day in the week a man might have a few friends
and give them any one of these : —

GOOD FAMILY DINNERS OF SEVEN DISHES.

Crimped Salmon.
Lobster Sauce, or Parsley and Butter.
Mashed Potatoes,   Mince Pies, *or Rissoles.*
in small shapes.   Irish Stew.
     (*Remove* — Apple-pie)
Oxford Dumplings.   Mince Veal.
     Pickles.
     Roast of Beef.

Irish Stew, or Haricot of Mutton.
Chickens.   Mashed Potatoes.
     Fritters.
Apple Sauce.   Tongue on Spinach,
     or a Piece of Ham.
     Stubble Goose.

     Fried Soles.
Savory Patties.   Onion Soup.   Salad.
     (*Remove* — A Charlotte.)
Macaroni.   *Sliced Cucumber.* Veal Sweetbreads.
     Saddle of Mutton roasted.

Very moderate means might enable a man to give such a dinner as this; and how good they all are! I should like to see eight good fellows over No. 3, for instance, — six men, say, and two ladies. They would not take any onion soup, of course, though all the men would; but the veal sweetbreads and the remove, a *charlotte*, are manifestly meant for them. There would be no champagne, the dinner is too jolly and *bourgeois* for that; but after they had partaken of a glass of wine and had retired, just three bottles of excellent claret would be discussed by us six, and every man who went upstairs to coffee would make himself agreeable. In such a house the coffee would be good. The way to make good coffee is a secret known only to very few housekeepers, — it is to have plenty of coffee.

Thus do Joseph Bregion and Anne Miller care for high and low. They provide the domestic dinner to be calm in the bosoms of private families; they invent bills of fare for the jolly family party, that pleasantest of all meetings; and they expand upon occasion and give us the magnificent parade banquet of three courses, at which kings or fellows of colleges may dine. If you will ask your cook at Saint Boniface to try either of the dinners marked for January and February, and will send your obedient servant a line, he for one will be happy to come down and partake of it at Oxford.

I could go on prattling in this easy innocent way for hours, my dear Lionel, but the Editor of this Magazine (about whose capabilities I have my own opinion) has limited me to space, and that space is now pretty nearly occupied. I should like to have had a chat with you about the Indian dishes, the chapter on which is very scientific and savory. The soup and broth chapter is rich, learned, and philosophical. French cookery is not, of course, *approfondi* or elaborately described, but nobly *raisonné*, like one of your lectures on a Greek play, where you point out in eloquent terms the salient beauties, sketch with masterly rapidity the principal characters, and gracefully unweave the complications of the metre. But I have done. The "Practical Cook" will triumph of his own force without my puny aid to drag the wheels of his car. Let me fling a few unpretending flowers over it, and sing *Io* to the victor! Happy is the writer, happy the possessor, happy above all the publishers of such a book!

Farewell, dear Lionel; present my respectful remembrances to the Master of your college and our particular chums in the common-room. I am come to town for Christmas, so you may send the brawn to my lodgings as soon as you like.

Your faithful

G. S. F.-B.

ABOUT A CHRISTMAS BOOK.

IN A LETTER FROM MICHAEL ANGELO TITMARSH TO OLIVER
YORKE, ESQ.

[*Fraser's Magazine, December,* 1845.]

THE DEANERY, November 25th.

AT this season of approaching Christmas, when tender
mothers are furbishing up the children's bedrooms, and
airing the mattresses which those little darlings (now counting the days at Dr. Swishtail's Academy, or the Misses
Backboard's Finishing Establishment) are to occupy for
six happy weeks, we have often, dear Mr. Yorke, examined
the beautiful store of gilt books with pretty pictures, which
begin to glitter on Mr. Nickisson's library-table, and selected therefrom a store of presents for our numerous young
friends. It is a pleasant labor. I like the kindly produce
which Paternoster Row sends forth at this season. I like
Christmas books, Christmas pantomimes, mince-pies, snapdragon, and all Christmas fruit; for though you and I can
have no personal gratification in the two last-named deleterious enjoyments, — to eat that abominable compound of
currants, preserves, and puff-paste, which infallibly results
in a blue-pill; or to dip in a dish of inflamed brandy for
the purpose of fishing out scalded raisins, which we don't
like, — yet it gives us pleasure to see the young people so
occupied, a melancholy and tender pleasure. We indulge
in pleasant egotisms of youthful reminiscence. The days
of our boyhood come back again. The holy holidays!
How much better you remember those days than any
other. How sacred their happiness is; how keen even at
this minute their misery. I forget whether I have told
elsewhere the story of my friend, Sir John C——. He
came down to breakfast with rather a disturbed and pallid
countenance. His lady affectionately asked the cause of his
disquiet. "I have had an unpleasant dream. I dreamed I
was at Charter-House, and that Raine flogged me!" He

is sixty-five years old.   A thousand great events may have
happened to him since that period of youthful fustigation.
Empires have waxed and waned since then.   He has come
into twenty thousand pounds a year; Napoleon is dead
since that period, and also the late Mr. Pitt.   How many
manly friends, hopes, cares, pleasures, have risen and died,
and been forgotten!   But not so the joys and pains of boyhood, the delights of the holidays are still as brilliant as
ever to him, the buds of the school birch-rod still tickle
bitterly the shrinking os coccygis of memory!

Do you not remember, my dear fellow, our own joy when
the 12th came and we plunged out of school, not to see the
face of Muzzle for six weeks?   A good and illustrious boy
were you, dear Oliver, and did your exercises, and mine
too, with credit and satisfaction; but still it was a pleasure
to turn your back upon Muzzle.   Can you ever forget the
glories of the beefsteak at the Bull and Mouth, previous to
going home; and the majestic way in which we ordered the
port, and pronounced it to be "ropy" or "fruity;" and
criticised the steak as if we had been Joseph Bregion, cook
to Prince Rasumowski?   At twenty-five minutes past four
precisely, the grays were in the coach, and the guard
comes in and says, "Now, gentlemen!"   We lighted
cigars magnanimously (since marriage — long, long before
His Grace the Duke of Wellington's pathetic orders against
smoking, we gave up the vile habit).   We take up the in-
sides at the office in the Quadrant; and go bowling down
Piccadilly on the road to Hounslow, Snow the guard playing
"Home, Sweet Home," on the bugle.   How clear it twangs
on the ear even now!   Can you ever forget the cold veal-
pies at Bagshot, and the stout waiter with black tights, on
the lookout for the coach as it came in to a minute?   Jim
Ward used to drive.   I wonder where Jim is now.   Is he
gone?   Yes, probably.   Why, the whole road is a ghost
since then.   The coaches and horses have been whisked
up, and are passed away into Hades.   The gaunt inns are
tenantless; the notes of the horn that we used to hear
tooting over Salisbury Plain as the dawn rose and the
wind was nipping cold, are reverberating in endless space.
Where are the jolly turnpike-men who used to come out as
the lamps lighted up the white bars of the gates, and the
horses were in a halo of smoke?   How they used to go over
the six miles between Honiton and Escot Lodge!   And
there — there on Fair Mile Hill is the little carriage wait-

ing, and Home in it, looking out with sweet eyes — eyes, oh, how steadfast, and loving, and tender.

. . . . . .

This sentimentalism may surprise my revered friend and annoy the public, who are not called upon to be interested in their humble servant's juvenile biography; but it all comes very naturally out of the opening discussion about Christmas and Christmas books in general, and of this book in particular, just published by Mr. Burns, the very best of all Christmas books. Let us say this, dear Yorke, who, in other days, have pitilessly trampled on Forget-me-nots, and massacred whole galleries of Books of Beauty. By the way, what has happened to the beauties? Is May Fair used up? One does not wish to say anything rude, but I would wager that any tea-party in Red Lion Square will turn out a dozen ladies to the full as handsome as the charmers with whose portraits we are favored this year. There are two in particular whom I really never — but let us not be too personal, and return to Mr. Burns's "Poems and Pictures."

The charming Lieder und Bilder of the Dusseldorf painters has, no doubt, given the idea of the work. The German manner has found favor among some of our artists — the Puseyites of art, they may be called, in this country, such as Messrs. Cope, Redgrave, Townshend, Horsley, etc.; who go back to the masters before Raphael, or to his own best time (that of his youth) for their models of grace and beauty. Their designs have a religious and ascetic, not a heathen and voluptuous tendency. There is in them no revelling in boisterous nudities like Rubens, no glowing contemplation of lovely forms as in Titian and Etty, but a meek, modest, and downcast demeanor. They appeal to tender sympathies, and deal with subjects of conjugal or maternal love, or charity, or devotion. In poetry, Goethe can't find favor in their eyes, but Uhland does. Milton is too vast for them, Shakespeare too earthy, but mystic Collins is a favorite; and gentle Cowper; and Alford sings pious hymns for them to the mild strains of his little organ.

The united work of these poets and artists is very well suited to the kind and gentle Christmas season. All the verses are not good, and some of the pictures are but feeble; yet the whole impression of the volume is an exceedingly pleasant one. The solemn and beautiful forms of the figures; the sweet, soothing cadences and themes of the

verse, affect one like music. Pictures and songs are surrounded by beautiful mystical arabesques, waving and twining round each page. Every now and then you light upon
one which is so pretty, it looks as if you had put a flower
between the leaves. You wander about and lose yourself
amongst these pleasant labyrinths, and sit down to repose
on the garden-bench of the fancy (this is a fine image),
smelling the springing blossoms, and listening to the chirping birds that shoot about amidst the flickering sunshine
and the bending twigs and leaves. All this a man with
the least imagination can do in the heart of winter, seated
in the arm-chair by the fire, with the "Poems and Pictures"
in his hand. What were life good for, dear Yorke, without
that blessed gift of fancy? Let us be thankful to those
kind spirits who minister to it by painting, or poetry, or
music. When Mrs. Y. has sung a song of Haydn's to you,
I have seen the tears of happiness twinkle in your eyes;
and at certain airs of Mozart, have known the intrepid, the
resolute, the stern Oliver to be as much affected as the soft-
hearted Molly of a milkmaid mentioned by Mr. Wordsworth, who, moved by the singing of a blackbird, beheld a
vision of trees in Lothbury, and a beautiful, clear Cumber-
land stream dashing down in the neighborhood of St. Mary
Axe.

And this is the queer power of Art; that when you wish
to describe its effect upon you, you always fall to describing something else. I cannot answer for it that a picture
is not a beautiful melody; that a grand sonnet by Tennyson is not in reality a landscape by Titian; that the last
pas by Taglioni is not a bunch of roses or an ode of Horace;
but I am sure that the enjoyment of the one has straightway brought the other to my mind, and vice versâ. Who
knows that the blind man, who said that the sound of a
trumpet was his idea of scarlet, was not perfectly right?
Very likely the sound of a trumpet is scarlet. In the matter of this book of "Poems and Pictures," I have never
read prettier pictures than many of these verses are, or
seen handsomer poems hung up in any picture-gallery.
Mrs. Cope's poem of the "Village Stile" is the first piece
as you enter the gallery: —

"Age sat upon't when tired of straying,
And children that had been a-maying
There twined their garlands gay:
What tender partings, blissful meetings,
What faint denials, fond entreatings,
It witnessed in its day!

The milkmaid on its friendly rail
Would ofttimes rest her brimful pail,
  And lingering there a while,
Some lucky chance — that tell-tale cheek
Doth something more than chance bespeak! —
    (The sly rogue!)
  Brings Lubin to the stile.

But what he said or she replied,
Whether he asked her for his bride,
  And she so sought was won,
There is no chronicle to tell;
For silent is the oracle,
  The village stile is gone."

In the very midst of these verses, and from a hedge full of birds, and flowers, and creeping plants tangling round them, the village stile breaks out upon you. There is Age sitting upon it, returning home from market; on t'other side the children, who have been maying, are twining their garlands. The cottage chimney is smoking comfortably; the birds in the arabesque are making a great chirping and twittering; the young folks go in, the old farmer hobbles over the stile and has gone to supper; the evening has come, it is page 3. The birds in the arabesque have gone to roost; the sun is going down; the milkmaid is sitting on the stile now — beautiful, sweet, down-eyed, tender milkmaid! — and has her hand in Lubin's, somehow. Lubin is a capital name for him; a very meek, soft, handsome, young fellow; just such a sentimental-looking spooney as a perverse lass would choose; and at page 4, the village stile is gone. And what is it we have in its stead, lackaday? What means that broken lily? How comes that young lady in the flowing bedgown to be lying on the floor, her head upon the cushion of her praying-stool? Alas, the lily is the emblem of the young lady! *Jeune fille et jeune fleur,* they are both done for. Woe is me, that two so young and beautiful should be nipped off thus suddenly, the Lady Lys and Fleur de Marie! *Sic jacent,* and Mr. Alford comes like a robin and pipes a dirge over the pair: —

"Thou wert fair, Lady Mary,
  As the lily in the sun;
And fairer yet thou mightest be,
  Thy youth was but begun.

Thine eye was soft and glancing,
  Of the deep bright blue,
And on the heart thy gentle words,
  Fell lighter than the dew.

> They found thee, Lady Mary,
>   With thy palms upon thy breast,
> Even as thou hadst been praying
>   At thy hour of rest.
>
> The cold pale moon was shining
>   On thy cold pale cheek,
> And the Morn of thy Nativity
>   Had just begun to break."

A sad Christmas this, indeed! but the friends of Lady Mary must be consoled by the delightful picture which Mr. Dyce has left of her. How tenderly she lies there with folded palms, the typical lily bending sadly over her! Pretty, prim, and beautified, it would be almost disrespectful to mourn over such an angel.

But when we get to a real character — a real woman — (though no great beauty, if Mr. Horsley's portrait of her be a true one) — where we have a poet speaking of genuine feeling — Cowper writing on receipt of his mother's picture out of Norfolk — a man's heart is very differently moved:—

> "'Oh that those lips had language.' Life has passed
> With me but roughly since I heard thee last.
> Those lips are thine — thine own sweet smile I see,
> The same that oft in childhood solaced me;
> Voice only fails, else how distinct they say,
> 'Grieve not, my child, chase all thy fears away!'
> The meek intelligence of those dear eyes
> (Blessed by the art that can immortalize, —
> The art that baffles Time's tyrannic claim
> To quench it) here shines on me still the same.
>
> Faithful remembrancer of one so dear,
> O welcome guest, though unexpected here!
> Who bidd'st me honor with an artless song,
> Affectionate, a mother lost so long;
> I will obey, not willingly alone,
> But gladly, as the precept were her own:
> And, while that face renews my filial grief,
> Fancy shall weave a charm for my relief;
> Shall steep me in Elysian reverie,
> A momentary dream that thou art she."

How tender and true the verses are! How naturally the thoughts rise as the poet looks at the calm portrait; and the sacred days of childhood come rising back again to his memory. The very trivialities in subsequent parts of the poem betoken its authenticity, and bear witness to the naturalness of the emotion: —

"Where once we dwelt our name is heard no more,
Children not thine have trod my nursery floor;
And where the gardener Robin, day by day,
Drew me to school along the public way,
Delighted with my bauble coach, and wrapped
In scarlet mantle warm, and velvet cap:
'Tis now become a history little known,
That once we called the pastoral house our own.
Short-lived possession! but the record fair,
That memory keeps of all thy kindness there,
Still outlives many a storm, that has effaced
A thousand other themes less deeply traced.
Thy nightly visits to my chamber made,
That thou mightst know me safe and warmly laid·
Thy morning bounties ere I left my home,
The biscuit or confectionery plum;
The fragrant waters on my cheeks bestowed
By thy own hand, till fresh they shone and glowed;
All this, and more endearing still than all,
Thy constant flow of love, that knew no fall,
Ne'er roughened by those cataracts and breaks,
That humor interposed too often makes; —
All this, still legible in memory's page,
And still to be so to my latest age,
Adds joy to duty, makes me glad to pay
Such honors to thee as my numbers may!
Perhaps a frail memorial, but sincere,
Not scorned in heaven, though little noticed here."

Even that twaddling about biscuit and confectionery plum
has a charm in it. You see the gentle lady busied in her
offices of kindness for the timid, soft-hearted boy.

"Wretch even then, life's journey just begun,"

conscience comes even there to disturb that delicate spirit,
and imbitter the best and earliest memorials of life. Mr.
Horsley follows the painter down the text with delightful
commentaries; he has illustrated the lines which a certain
chair-maker has rendered abominably common, and shows
us the gardener Robin leading the boy to school in scarlet
mantle and warm velvet cap. The kind mother is peering
from the garden-gate before the parsonage, and the old
church in the quiet village.

One great charm in the verses has always been to me,
that he does not grieve too much for her. The kind, humble heart follows her up to heaven, and there meekly acknowledges her. "The son of parents passed into the
skies," says the filial spirit, so humble that he doubted of
himself only. The little churchyard sketch with which

Mr. Horsley closes this sweet elegy is a delightful comment on it, — the poem in the shape of a picture it seems to me. One may muse over both for hours, and get nothing but the sweetest and kindest thoughts from either.

Whether it is that where the verses fail, the artists are feeble, or that a poor poem makes a discord, as it were, and destroys the harmony which the concert of poet and painter ought to produce, I don't know : but if the verses are feeble, the pictures look somehow unsatisfactory by their side; and one believes in neither. Thus the next illustrated poem, "The Tale of the Coast Guard," is too fine and pompous, and the accompanying picture by Redgrave equally unreal. "Sir Roland Graeme," with illustrations by Selous, very clever and spirited, affects me no way. I do not care if I see those theatrical fellows plunging and fighting with harmless broadswords again. Whereas, at the next page, you come to some verses about a snowdrop, and a picture overhead of that small bulbous beauty — to look at both, which causes the greatest pleasure ? All the pages adorned with natural illustrations are pleasant; such as the holly which figures by the famous old song of "When this Old Cap was New;" some buttercups which illustrate a subject as innocent, etc. Where there is violent action requisite the artists seem to fail, except in one, or couple of instances. Mr. Tenniel has given a gallant illustration of the ballad of "War comes with manhood, as light comes with day," in which drawing there is great fire and energy; and Mr. Corbould's "Wild Huntsman" has no little vigor and merit. His illustrations to the legend of Gilbert à Beckett are quite tame and conventional. Mr. Tenniel's "Prince and Outlaw" represent a prince and outlaw of Astley's — the valorous Widdicomb and the intrepid Gomersal. The truth is that the ballads to which the pictures are appended are of the theatrical sort, and quite devoid of genuineness and simplicity.

But set them to deal with a real sentiment and the artists appreciate it excellently. Witness Cope's delightful drawings to "The Mourner," his sweet figures to the sweet and plaintive old ballad of "Cumnor Hall." Townshend's excellent compositions to the "Miner;" Dyce's charming illustration of the "Christ-Cross Rhyme," — in which page both poet and painter have perfectly reproduced the Catholic spirit: —

"Christ his Cross shall be my speed !
Teach me, Father John, to read,
That in church on holy-day
I may chant the psalm, and pray.

Let me learn, that I may know
What the shining windows show,
With that bright Child in her hands,
Where the lovely Lady stands.

Teach me letters one, two, three,
Till that I shall able be
Signs to know, and words to frame
And to spell sweet Jesu's name.

Then, dear master, will I look
Day and night in that fair book
Where the tales of saints are told,
With their pictures all in gold.

Teach me, Father John, to say
Vesper-verse and matin-lay;
So when I to God shall plead,
Christ his Cross will be my speed."

A pretty imitation, indeed. Copes and censers, stained glass and choristers, — all the middle-age paraphernalia, produced with an accuracy that is curiously perfect and picturesque. But, O my dearly beloved Oliver! what are these meek canticles and gentle nasal concerts compared to the full sound which issues from the generous lungs when A Poet begins to sing ! —

"And bring the lassie back to me
That's aye sae neat and clean ;
Ae blink o' her wad banish care,
Sae charming is my Jean.

What sighs and vows, amang the knowes,
Hae passed atween us twa!
How fond to meet, how wae to part,
That night she gaed awa!"

Heaven bless the music! It is a warm, manly, kindly heart that speaks there, — a grateful, generous soul that looks at God's world with honest eyes, and trusts to them rather than to the blinking peepers of his neighbor. Such a man walking the fields and singing out of his full heart is pleasanter to hear, to my mind, than a whole organ-loft full of Puseyites, or an endless procession of quavering shavelings from Littlemore.

But every bird has its note, from the blackbird on the thorn to the demure pie that haunts cathedral yards, and, when caught, can be taught to imitate anything. Here you have a whole aviary of them. Cowper, that coos like a dove; Collins, that complains like a nightingale; with others that might be compared to the brisk bulfinch, the polite canary, or the benevolent cock-robin; — each sings, chirps, twitters, cock-a-doodledoos in his fashion — a pleasant chorus. And I recommend you, dear Yorke, and the candid reader, to purchase the cage.

A BROTHER OF THE PRESS ON THE HISTORY OF A LITERARY MAN, LAMAN BLANCHARD, AND THE CHANCES OF THE LITERARY PRO-FESSION.

IN A LETTER TO THE REVEREND FRANCIS SYLVESTER AT ROME, FROM MICHAEL ANGELO TITMARSH, ESQUIRE.

[*Fraser's Magazine, March,* 1846.]

LONDON, February 20, 1846.

My dear Sir, — Our good friend and patron, the publisher of this Magazine, has brought me your message from Rome, and your demand to hear news from the *other* great city of the world. As the forty columns of the *Times* cannot satisfy your Reverence's craving, and the details of the real great revolution of England which is actually going on do not sufficiently interest you, I send you a page or two of random speculations upon matters connected with the literary profession : they were suggested by reading the works and the biography of a literary friend of ours, lately deceased, and for whom every person who knew him had the warmest and sincerest regard. And no wonder. It was impossible to help trusting a man so thoroughly generous and honest, and loving one who was so perfectly gay, gentle, and amiable.

A man can't enjoy everything in the world; but what delightful gifts and qualities are these to have ! Not having known Blanchard as intimately as some others did, yet, I take it, he had in his life as much pleasure as falls to most men; the kindest friends, the most affectionate family, a heart to enjoy both; and a career not undistinguished, which I hold to be the smallest matter of all. But we have a cowardly dislike, or compassion for, the fact of a man dying poor. Such a one is rich, bilious, and a curmudgeon, without heart or stomach to enjoy his money, and we set him down as respectable : another is morose or passionate, his whole view of life seen bloodshot through

passion, or jaundiced through moroseness; or he is a fool
who can't see, or feel, or enjoy anything at all, with no ear
for music, no eye for beauty, no heart for love, with
nothing except money : we meet such people every day, and
respect them somehow. That donkey browses over five
thousand acres; that madman's bankers come bowing him
out to his carriage. You feel secretly pleased at shooting
over the acres, or driving in the carriage. At any rate,
nobody thinks of compassionating their owners. We are a
race of flunkeys, and keep our pity for the poor.

I don't mean to affix the plush personally upon the kind
and distinguished gentleman and writer who has written
Blanchard's Memoir; but it seems to me that it is couched
in much too despondent a strain; that the lot of the hero of
the little story was by no means deplorable; and that there
is not the least call at present to be holding up literary men
as martyrs. Even that prevailing sentiment which regrets
that means should not be provided for giving them leisure,
for enabling them to perfect great works in retirement,
that they should waste away their strength with fugitive
literature, etc., I hold to be often uncalled for and dangerous. I believe, if most men of letters were to be pensioned,
I am sorry to say I believe they wouldn't work at all; and
of others, that the labor which is to answer the calls of the
day is the one quite best suited to their genius. Suppose
Sir Robert Peel were to write to you, and, enclosing a
check for 20,000*l.*, instruct you to pension any fifty deserving authors, so that they might have leisure to retire
and write "great" works, on whom would you fix ?

People in the big-book interest, too, cry out against the
fashion of fugitive literature, and no wonder. For instance, —

The *Times* gave an extract the other day from a work by
one Doctor Carus, physician to the King of Saxony, who
attended his royal master on his recent visit to England,
and has written a book concerning the journey. Among
other London lions, the illustrious traveller condescended
to visit one of the largest and most remarkable, certainly,
of metropolitan roarers — the *Times* printing-office; of
which, the Doctor, in his capacity of a man of science,
gives an exceedingly bad, stupid, and blundering account.

Carus was struck with "disgust," he says, at the prodigious size of the paper, and at the thought which suggested itself to his mind from this enormity. There was as

much printed every day as would fill a thick volume. It required ten years of life to a philosopher to write a volume. The issuing of these daily tomes was unfair upon philosophers, who were put out of the market; and unfair on the public, who were made to receive (and, worse still, to get a relish for) crude daily speculations, and frivolous ephemeral news, when they ought to be fed and educated upon stronger and simpler diet.

We have heard this outcry a hundred times from the big-wig body. The world gives up a lamentable portion of its time to fleeting literature; authors who might be occupied upon great works fritter away their lives in producing endless hasty sketches. Kind, wise, and good Doctor Arnold deplored the fatal sympathy which the "Pickwick Papers" had created among the boys of his school; and it is a fact that *Punch* is as regularly read among the boys at Eton as the Latin Grammar.

Arguing for liberty of conscience against any authority, however great — against Doctor Arnold himself, who seems to me to be the greatest, wisest, and best of men, that has appeared for eighteen hundred years; let us take a stand at once, and ask, Why should not the day have its literature? Why should not authors make light sketches? Why should not the public be amused daily or frequently by kindly fictions? It is well and just for Arnold to object. Light stories of Jingle and Tupman, and Sam Weller quips and cranks, must have come with but a bad grace before that pure and lofty soul. The trivial and familiar are out of place there; the harmless joker must walk away abashed from such a presence, as he would be silent and hushed in a cathedral. But all the world is not made of that angelic stuff. From his very height and sublimity of virtue he could but look down and deplore the ways of small men beneath him. I mean, seriously, that I think the man was of so august and sublime a nature, that he was not a fair judge of us, or of the ways of the generality of mankind. One has seen a delicate person sicken and faint at the smell of a flower; it does not follow that the flower was not sweet and wholesome in consequence; and I hold that laughing and honest story-books are good, against all the doctors.

Laughing is not the highest occupation of a man, very certainly; or the power of creating it the height of genius. I am not going to argue for that. No more is the blacking of boots the greatest occupation. But it is done, and well and honestly, by persons ordained to that calling in life, who arrogate to themselves (if they are straightforward and worthy shoeblacks) no especial rank or privilege on account of their calling; and not considering boot-brushing the greatest effort of earthly genius, nevertheless select their Day and Martin, or Warren, to the best of their judgment; polish their upper-leathers as well as they can; satisfy their patrons; and earn their fair wage.

I have chosen the unpolite shoeblack comparison, not out of disrespect to the trade of literature; but it is as good a craft as any other to select. In some way or other, for daily bread and hire, almost all men are laboring daily. Without necessity they would not work at all, or very little, probably. In some instances you reap Reputation along with Profit from your labor, but Bread, in the main, is the incentive. Do not let us try to blink this fact, or imagine that the men of the press are working for their honor and glory, or go onward impelled by an irresistible afflatus of genius. If only men of genius were to write, Lord help us! how many books would there be? How many people are there even capable of appreciating genius? Is Mr. Wakley's or Mr. Hume's opinion about poetry worth much? As much as that of millions of people in this honest stupid empire; and they have a right to have books supplied for them as well as the most polished and accomplished critics have. The literary man gets his bread by providing goods suited to the consumption of these. This man of letters contributes a police-report; that, an article containing some downright information; this one, as an editor, abuses Sir Robert Peel, or lauds Lord John Russell, or *vice versâ;* writing to a certain class who coincide in his views, or are interested by the question which he moots. The literary character, let us hope or admit, writes quite honestly; but no man supposes he would work perpetually but for money. And as for immortality, it is quite beside the bargain. Is it reasonable to look for it, or to pretend that you are actuated by a desire to attain it? Of all the quill-drivers, how many have ever drawn that prodigious prize? Is it fair even to ask that many should? Out of a regard for poor dear posterity and men of letters to come, let us be glad that the great immortality number comes up so rarely. Mankind would have no time otherwise, and would be so gorged with old masterpieces, that they could not occupy themselves with new, and future literary men would have no chance of a livelihood.

To do your work honestly, to amuse and instruct your reader of to-day, to die when your time comes, and go hence with as clean a breast as may be; may these be all yours and ours, by God's will. Let us be content with our *status* as literary craftsmen, telling the truth as far as may be, hitting no foul blow, condescending to no servile puffery, filling not a very lofty, but a manly and honorable part. Nobody says that Doctor Locock is wasting his time because he rolls about daily in his carriage, and passes hours with the nobility and gentry, his patients, instead of being in his study wrapped up in transcendental medical meditation. Nobody accuses Sir Fitzroy Kelly of neglecting his genius because he will take anybody's brief, and argue it in court for money, when he might sit in chambers with his oak sported, and give up his soul to investigations of the nature, history, and improvement of law. There is no question but that either of these eminent persons, by profound study, might increase their knowledge in certain branches of their profession; but in the mean while the practical part must go on — causes come on for hearing, and ladies lie in, and some one must be there. The commodities in. which the lawyer and the doctor deal are absolutely required by the public, and liberally paid for; every day, too, the public requires more literary handicraft done; the practitioner in that trade gets a better pay and place. In another century, very likely, his work will be so necessary to the people, and his market so good, that his prices will double and treble; his social rank rise; he will be getting what they call "honors," and dying in the bosom of the genteel. Our calling is only sneered at because it is not well paid. The world has no other criterion for respectability. In Heaven's name, what made people talk of setting up a statue to Sir William Follett? What had he done? He had made 300,-000*l*. What has George IV. done that he, too, is to have a brazen image? He was an exemplar of no greatness, no good quality, no duty in life; but a type of magnificence, of beautiful coats, carpets, and gigs, turtle-soup, chandeliers, cream-colored horses, and delicious Maraschino, — all these good things he expressed and represented: and the world, respecting them beyond all others, raised statues to "the first gentleman in Europe." Directly the men of letters get rich, they will come in for their share of honor too; and a future writer in this miscellany may be getting ten guineas where we get one, and dancing at Buckingham Palace while you and your humble servant, dear Padre Francesco, are glad to smoke our pipes in quiet over the sanded floor of the little D——.

But the happy *homme de lettres*, whom I imagine in futurity kicking his heels *vis-à-vis* to a duchess in some fandango at the Court of her Majesty's grandchildren, will be in reality no better or honester, or more really near fame, than the quill-driver of the present day, with his doubtful position and small gains. Fame, that guerdon of high genius, comes quite independent of Berkeley Square, and is a republican institution. Look around in our own day among the holders of the pen : begin (without naming names, for that is odious) and count on your fingers those whom you will back in the race for immortality. How many fingers have you that are left untold ? It is an invidious question. Alas ! dear ——, and dear * *, and dear † †, you who think you are safe, there is futurity, and limbo, and blackness for you, beloved friends ! *Cras ingens iterabimus æquor :* there's no use denying it, or shirking the fact ; in we must go, and disappear for ever and ever.

And after all, what is this Reputation, the cant of our trade, the goal that every scribbling penny-a-liner demurely pretends that he is hunting after ? Why should we get it ? Why can't we do without it ? We only fancy we want it. When people say of such and such a man who is dead, "He neglected his talents ; he frittered away in fugitive publications time and genius, which might have led to the production of a great work ; " this is the gist of Sir Bulwer Lytton's kind and affecting biographical notice of our dear friend and comrade Laman Blanchard, who passed away so melancholily last year.

I don't know anything more dissatisfactory and absurd than that insane test of friendship which has been set up by some literary men —viz. admiration of their works. Say that this picture is bad, or that poem poor, or that article stupid, and there are certain authors and artists among us who set you down as an enemy forthwith, or look upon you as a *faux-frère*. What is there in common with the friend and his work of art ? The picture or article once done and handed over to the public, is the latter's property, not the author's, and to be estimated according to its honest value ; and so, and without malice, I question Sir Bulwer Lytton's statement about Blanchard — viz. that he would have been likely to produce with leisure, and under favorable circumstances, a work of the highest class. I think his education and habits, his quick easy manner, his sparkling hidden fun, constant tenderness, and brilliant good-humor were best employed as they were. At any rate he had a duty, much more imperative upon him than the preparation of questionable great works, — to get his family their dinner. A man must be a very Great man, indeed, before he can neglect this precaution.

His three volumes of essays, pleasant and often brilliant as they are, give no idea of the powers of the author, or even of his natural manner, which, as I think, was a thousand times more agreeable. He was like the good little child in the fairy tale, his mouth dropped out all sorts of diamonds and rubies. His wit, which was always playing and frisking about the company, had the wonderful knack of never hurting anybody. He had the most singular art of discovering good qualities in people; in discoursing of which the kindly little fellow used to glow and kindle up, and emphasize with the most charming energy. Good-natured actions of others, good jokes, favorite verses of friends, he would bring out fondly, whenever they met, or there was question of them; and he used to toss and dandle their sayings or doings about, and hand them round to the company, as the delightful Miss Slowboy does the baby in the last Christmas book. What was better than wit in his talk was, that it was so genial. He *enjoyed* thoroughly, and chirped over his wine with a good-humor that could not fail to be infectious. His own hospitality was delightful: there was something about it charmingly brisk, simple, and kindly. How he used to laugh! As I write this, what a number of pleasant hearty scenes come back! One can hear his jolly, clear laughter; and see his keen, kind, beaming Jew face, — a mixture of Mendelssohn and Voltaire.

Sir Bulwer Lytton's account of him will be read by all his friends with pleasure, and by the world as a not uncurious specimen of the biography of a literary man. The memoir savors a little too much of the funeral oration. It might have been a little more particular and familiar, so as to give the public a more intimate acquaintance with one of the honestest and kindest of men who ever lived by pen; and yet, after a long and friendly intercourse with

Blanchard, I believe the praises Sir Lytton bestows on his character are by no means exaggerated: it is only the style in which they are given, which is a little too funereally encomiastic. The memoir begins in this way, a pretty and touching design of Mr. Kenny Meadows heading the biography : —

"To most of those who have mixed generally with the men who, in our day, have chosen literature as their profession, the name of Laman Blanchard brings recollections of peculiar tenderness and regret. Amidst a career which the keenness of anxious rivalry renders a sharp probation to the temper and the affections, often yet more imbittered by that strife of party, of which, in a representative Constitution, few men of letters escape the eager passions and the angry prejudice — they recall the memory of a competitor, without envy; a partisan, without gall; firm as the firmest in the maintenance of his own opinions; but gentle as the gentlest in the judgment he passed on others.

"Who, among our London brotherhood of letters, does not miss that simple cheerfulness — that inborn and exquisite urbanity — that childlike readiness to be pleased with all — that happy tendency to panegyrize every merit, and to be lenient to every fault ? Who does not recall that acute and delicate sensibility — so easily wounded, and therefore so careful not to wound — which seemed to infuse a certain intellectual fine breeding, of forbearance and sympathy, into every society where it insinuated its gentle way ? Who, in convivial meetings, does not miss, and will not miss forever, the sweetness of those unpretending talents — the earnestness of that honesty which seemed unconscious it was worn so lightly — the mild influence of that exuberant kindness which softened the acrimony of young disputants, and reconciled the secret animosities of jealous rivals ? Yet few men had experienced more to sour them than Laman Blanchard, or had gone more resolutely through the author's hardening ordeal of narrow circumstance, of daily labor, and of that disappointment in the higher aims of ambition, which must almost inevitably befall those who retain ideal standards of excellence, to be reached but by time and leisure, and who are yet condemned to draw hourly upon unmatured resources for the practical wants of life. To have been engaged from boyhood in such struggles, and to have preserved, undiminished, generous admiration for those more fortunate, and untiring love for his own noble yet thankless calling; and this with a constitution singularly finely strung, and with all the nervous irritability which usually accompanies the indulgence of the imagination; is a proof of the rarest kind of strength, depending less upon a power purely intellectual, than upon the higher and more beautiful heroism which woman, and such men alone as have the best feelings of a woman's nature, take from instinctive enthusiasm for what is great, and uncalculating faith in what is good.

"It is, regarded thus, that the character of Laman Blanchard assumes an interest of a very elevated order. He was a choice and worthy example of the professional English men of letters, in our day. He is not to be considered in the light of the man of daring and turbulent genius, living on the false excitement of vehement calumny and uproarious praise. His was a career not indeed obscure, but sufficiently quiet and unnoticed to be solaced with little of the pleasure with which, in aspirants of a noisier fame, gratified and not ignoble vanity rewards the labor and stimulates the hope. For more than twenty years he toiled on through the most fatiguing paths of literary composition, mostly in periodicals, often anonymously; pleasing and lightly instructing thousands, but gaining none of the prizes, whether of weighty reputation or popular renown, which more fortunate chances, or more pretending modes of investing talent, have given in our day to men of half his merits."

Not a feature in this charming character is flattered, as far as I know. Did the subject of the memoir feel disappointment in the higher aims of ambition? Was his career not solaced with pleasure? Was his noble calling a thankless one? I have said before, his calling was not thankless; his career, in the main, pleasant; his disappointment, if he had one of the higher aims of ambition, one that might not uneasily be borne. If every man is disappointed because he cannot reach supreme excellence, what a mad misanthropical world ours would be! Why should men of letters aim higher than they can hit, or be "disappointed" with the share of brains God has given them? Nor can you say a man's career is unpleasant who was so heartily liked and appreciated as Blanchard was, by all persons of high intellect, or low, with whom he came in contact. He had to bear with some, but not unbearable poverty. At home he had everything to satisfy his affection: abroad, every sympathy and consideration met this universally esteemed, good man. Such a calling as his is *not* thankless, surely. Away with this discontent and morbid craving for renown! A man who writes (Tennyson's) "Ulysses," or "Comus," *may* put in his claim for fame if you will, and demand and deserve it: but it requires no vast power of intellect to write most sets of words, and have them printed in a book: — To write this article for instance, or the last novel, pamphlet, book of travels. Most men with a decent education and practice of the pen could go and do the like, were they so professionally urged. Let such fall into the rank and file, and shoulder their weapons, and load and fire cheerfully. An every-day writer has no more right to repine because he loses the great prizes, and can't write like Shakespeare, than he has to be envious of Sir Robert Peel, or Wellington, or King Hudson, or Taglioni. Because the sun shines above, is a man to warm himself and admire; or to despond because he can't in his person flare up like the sun? I

don't believe that Blanchard was by any means an amateur
martyr, but was, generally speaking, very decently satisfied with his condition.

Here is the account of his early history — a curious and
interesting one : —

"Samuel Laman Blanchard was born of respectable parents in the
middle class at Great Yarmouth, on the 15th of May, 1803. His
mother's maiden name was Mary Laman. She married first Mr.
Cowell, at St. John's Church, Bermondsey, about the year 1796; he
died in the following year. In 1799, she was married again, to
Samuel Blanchard, by whom she had seven children, but only one
son, the third child, christened Samuel Laman.

"In 1805, Mr. Blanchard (the father) appears to have removed to
the metropolis, and to have settled in Southwark as a painter and
glazier. He was enabled to give his boy a good education — an education, indeed, of that kind which could not but unfit young Laman
for the calling of his father; for it developed the abilities and bestowed the learning, which may be said to lift a youth morally out of
trade, and to refine him at once into a gentleman. At six years old
he was entered a scholar of Saint Olave's School, then under the direction of the Reverend Doctor Blenkorm. He became the head Latin
scholar, and gained the chief prize in each of the last three years he
remained at the academy. When he left it, it was the wish of the
master and trustees that he should be sent to College, one boy being
annually selected from the pupils, to be maintained at the University,
for the freshman's year, free of expense; for the charges of the two
remaining years the parents were to provide. So strong, however,
were the hopes of the master for his promising pupil, that the
trustees of the school consented to depart from their ordinary practice,
and offered to defray the collegiate expenses for two years. Unfortunately, the offer was not accepted. No wonder that poor Laman
regretted in after life the loss of this golden opportunity. The advantages of a University career to a young man in his position, with
talents and application, but without interest, birth, and fortune, are
incalculable. The pecuniary independence afforded by the scholarship
and the fellowship is in itself no despicable prospect; but the benefits
which distinction, fairly won at those noble and unrivalled institutions,
confers, are the greatest where least obvious: they tend usually to bind
the vagueness of youthful ambition to the secure reliance on some
professional career, in which they smooth the difficulties and abridge
the novitiate. Even in literature a College education not only tends
to refine the taste, but to propitiate the public. And in all the many
walks of practical and public life, the honors gained at the University
never fail to find well-wishers amongst powerful contemporaries, and
to create generous interest in the fortunes of the aspirant.

"But my poor friend was not destined to have one obstacle
smoothed away from his weary path.*   With the natural refinement

* "The elder Blanchard is not to be blamed for voluntarily depriving
his son of the advantages proffered by the liberal trustees of Saint
Olave's; it appears from a communication by Mr. Keymer (brother-in-
law to Laman Blanchard) — that the circumstances of the family at that
time were not such as to meet the necessary expenses of a student — even
for the *last* year of his residence at the University."

of his disposition, and the fatal cultivation of his intellectual susceptibilities, he was placed at once in a situation which it was impossible
that he could fill with steadiness and zeal. Fresh from classical
studies, and his emulation warmed by early praise and schoolboy
triumph, he was transferred to the drudgery of a desk in the office of
Mr. Charles Pearson, a proctor in Doctors' Commons. The result
was inevitable; his mind, by a natural reaction, betook itself to the
pursuits most hostile to such a career. Before this, even from the
age of thirteen, he had trifled with the Muses; he now conceived in
good earnest the more perilous passion for the stage.

"Barry Cornwall's 'Dramatic Scenes' were published about this
time — they exercised considerable influence over the taste and aspirations of young Blanchard — and many dramatic sketches of brilliant promise, bearing his initials, S. L. B., appeared in a periodical
work existing at that period called *The Drama.* In them, though the
conception and general treatment are borrowed from Barry Cornwall,
the style and rhythm are rather modelled on the peculiarities of
Byron. Their promise is not the less for the imitation they betray.
The very characteristic of genius is to be imitative — first of authors,
then of nature. Books lead us to fancy feelings that are not yet genuine. Experience is necessary to record those which color our own
existence: and the style only becomes original in proportion as the
sentiment it expresses is sincere. More touching, therefore, than these
'Dramatic Sketches,' was a lyrical effusion on the death of Sidney
Ireland, a young friend to whom he was warmly attached, and over
whose memory, for years afterwards, he often shed tears. He named
his eldest son after that early friend. At this period, Mr. Douglas
Jerrold had written three volumes of Moral Philosophy, and Mr.
Buckstone, the celebrated comedian, volunteered to copy the work for
the juvenile moralist. On arriving at any passage that struck his
fancy, Mr. Buckstone communicated his delight to his friend Blanchard, and the emulation thus excited tended more and more to sharpen
the poet's distaste to all avocations incompatible with literature. Anxious, in the first instance, to escape from dependence on his father
(who was now urgent that he should leave the proctor's desk for the
still more ungenial mechanism of the paternal trade), he meditated
the best of all preparatives to dramatic excellence; viz. a practical
acquaintance with the stage itself: he resolved to become an actor.
Few indeed are they in this country who have ever succeeded eminently in the literature of the stage, who have not either trod its boards,
or lived habitually in its atmosphere. Blanchard obtained an interview
with Mr. Henry Johnston, the actor, and recited, in his presence,
passages from Glover's 'Leonidas.' He read admirably — his elocution
was faultless — his feeling exquisite; Mr. Johnston was delighted
with his powers, but he had experience and wisdom to cool his professional enthusiasm, and he earnestly advised the aspirant not to think
of the stage. He drew such a picture of the hazards of success — the
obstacles to a position — the precariousness even of a subsistence, that
the young boy's heart sunk within him. He was about to resign himself to obscurity and trade, when he suddenly fell in with the manager of the Margate Theatre; this gentleman proposed to enroll him in
his own troop, and the proposal was eagerly accepted, in spite of the
warnings of Mr. Henry Johnston. 'A week,' says Mr. Buckstone
(to whom I am indebted for these particulars, and whose words I
now quote), 'was sufficient to disgust him with the beggary and

drudgery of the country player's life; and as there were no "Harle-quins" steaming it from Margate to London Bridge at that day, he performed the journey back on foot, having, on reaching Rochester, but his last shilling — the poet's veritable last shilling — in his pocket.

"'At that time a circumstance occurred, which my poor friend's fate has naturally brought to my recollection. He came to me late one evening, in a state of great excitement; informed me that his father had turned him out of doors; that he was utterly hopeless and wretched, and was resolved to destroy himself. I used my best endeavors to console him, to lead his thoughts to the future, and hope in what chance and perseverance might effect for him. Our discourse took a livelier turn; and after making up a bed on the sofa in my own room, I retired to rest. I soon slept soundly, but was awakened by hearing a footstep descending the stairs. I looked towards the sofa, and discovered he had left it; I heard the street door close; I instantly hurried on my clothes, and followed him; I called to him, but received no answer; I ran till I saw him in the distance also running; I again called his name; I implored him to stop, but he would not answer me. Still continuing his pace, I became alarmed, and doubled my speed. I came up with him near to Westminster Bridge; he was hurrying to the steps leading to the river; I seized him; he threatened to strike me if I did not release him; I called for the watch; I entreated him to return; he became more pacified, but still seemed anxious to escape from me. By entreaties; by every means of persuasion I could think of; by threats to call for help, I succeeded in taking him back. The next day he was more composed, but I believe rarely resided with his father after that time. Necessity compelled him to do something for a livelihood, and in time he became a reader in the office of the Messrs. Bayliss, in Fleet Street. By that employ, joined to frequent contributions to the *Monthly Magazine*, at that time published by them, he obtained a tolerable competence.

"'Blanchard and Jerrold had serious thoughts of joining Lord Byron in Greece; they were to become warriors, and assist the poet in the liberation of the classic land. Many a nightly wandering found them discussing their project. In the midst of one of these discussions they were caught in a shower of rain, and sought shelter under a gateway. The rain continued; when their patience becoming exhausted, Blanchard, buttoning up his coat, exclaimed, "Come on, Jerrold! what use shall we be to the Greeks if we stand up for a shower of rain?" So they walked home and were heroically wet through.'"

It would have been worth while to tell this tale more fully; not to envelop the chief personage in fine words, as statuaries do their sitters in Roman togas, and, making them assume the heroic-conventional look, take away from them that infinitely more interesting one which Nature gave them. It would have been well if we could have had this stirring little story in detail. The young fellow, forced to the proctor's desk, quite angry with the drudgery, theatre-stricken, poetry-stricken, writing dramatic sketches in Barry Cornwall's manner, spouting "Leonidas" before a manager, driven away starving from home, and, penniless and full of romance, courting his beautiful young wife. *" Come on, Jerrold! what use shall we be to the Greeks if we stand up for a shower of rain? "* How the native humor breaks out of the man! Those who knew them can fancy the effect of such a pair of warriors steering the Greek fire-ships, or manning the breach at Missolonghi. Then there comes that pathetic little outbreak of despair, when the poor young fellow is nearly giving up; his father banishes him, no one will buy his poetry, he has no chance on his darling theatre, no chance of the wife that he is longing for. Why not finish with life at once? He has read " Werther," and can understand suicide. "None," he says, in a sonnet, —

> " None, not the hoariest sage, may tell of all
>   The strong heart struggles with before it fall."

If Respectability wanted to point a moral, isn't there one here? Eschew poetry, avoid the theatre, stick to your business, do not read German novels, do not marry at twenty. All these injunctions seem to hang naturally on the story.

And yet the young poet marries at twenty, in the teeth of poverty and experience; labors away, not unsuccessfully, puts Pegasus into harness, rises in social rank and public estimation, brings up happily round him an affectionate family, gets for himself a circle of the warmest friends, and thus carries on for twenty years, when a providential calamity visits him and the poor wife, almost together, and removes them both.

In the beginning of 1844, Mrs. Blanchard, his affectionate wife and the excellent mother of his children, was attacked with paralysis, which impaired her mind and terminated fatally at the end of the year. Her husband was constantly with her, occupied by her side, whilst watching her distressing malady, in his daily task of literary business. Her illness had the severest effect upon him. He, too, was attacked with partial paralysis and congestion of the brain, during which first seizure his wife died. The rest of the story was told in all the newspapers of the beginning of last year. Rallying partially from his fever at times, a sudden catastrophe overwhelmed him. On the night of the 14th February, in a gust of delirium, having his little boy in bed by his side, and having said the Lord's

Prayer but a short time before, he sprang out of bed in the absence of his nurse (whom he had besought not to leave him), and made away with himself with a razor. He was no more guilty in his death than a man who is murdered by a madman, or who dies of the rupture of a blood-vessel. In his last prayer he asked to be forgiven, as he in his whole heart forgave others; and not to be led into that irresistible temptation under which it pleased Heaven that the poor wandering spirit should succumb.

At the very moment of his death his friends were making the kindest and most generous exertions in his behalf. Such a noble, loving, and generous creature is never without such. The world, it is pleasant to think, is always a good and gentle world to the gentle and good, and reflects the benevolence with which they regard it This memoir contains an affecting letter from the poor fellow himself, which indicates Sir Edward Bulwer's admirable and delicate generosity towards him. "I bless and thank you always," writes the kindly and affectionate soul, to another excellent friend, Mr. Forster. There were other friends, such as Mr. Fonblanque, Mr. Ainsworth, with whom he was connected in literary labor, who were not less eager to serve and befriend him.

As soon as he was dead, a number of other persons came forward to provide means for the maintenance of his orphan family. Messrs. Chapman & Hall took one son into their publishing-house, another was provided for in a merchant's house in the City, the other is of an age and has the talents to follow and succeed in his father's profession. Mr. Colburn and Mr. Ainsworth gave up their copyrights of his Essays, which are now printed in three handsome volumes, for the benefit of his children.

Out of Blanchard's life (except from the melancholy end, which is quite apart from it) there is surely no ground for drawing charges against the public of neglecting literature. His career, untimely concluded, is in the main a successful one. In truth, I don't see how the aid or interposition of Government could in any way have greatly benefited him. or how it was even called upon to do so. It does not follow that a man would produce a great work even if he had leisure. Squire Shakespeare of Stratford, with his lands and rents, and his arms over his porch, was not the working Shakespeare; and indolence (or contemplation, if you like) is no unusual quality in the literary man. Of all the squires who have had acres and rents, all the holders of lucky easy Government places, how many have written books, and of what worth are they? There are some persons whom Government, having a want of, employs and pays — barristers, diplomatists, soldiers, and the like; but it doesn't want poetry, and can do without tragedies. Let men of letters stand for themselves. Every day enlarges their market, and multiplies their clients. The most skilful and successful among the cultivators of light literature have such a hold upon the public feelings, and awaken such a sympathy, as men of the class never enjoyed until now: men of science and learning, who aim at other distinction, get it; and in spite of Dr. Carus's disgust, I believe there was never a time when so much of the practically useful was written and read, and every branch of book-making pursued, with an interest so eager.

But I must conclude. My letter has swelled beyond the proper size of letters, and you are craving for news : have you not to-day's *Times'* battle of Ferozeshah? Farewell.

M. A. T.

ON SOME ILLUSTRATED CHILDREN'S BOOKS.

BY MICHAEL ANGELO TITMARSH.

[*Fraser's Magazine, April,* 1846.]

THE character of Gruff-and-Tackleton, in Mr. Dickens's
last Christmas story, has always appeared to me a great and
painful blot upon that otherwise charming performance.
Surely it is impossible that a man whose life is passed in
the making of toys, hoops, whirligigs, theatres, dolls, jack-
in-boxes, and ingenious knick-knacks for little children,
should be a savage at heart, a child-hater by nature, and an
ogre by disposition.   How could such a fellow succeed in
his trade ?   The practice of it would be sufficient to break
that black heart of his outright.   Invention to such a person would be impossible; and the continual exercise of his
profession, the making of toys which he despised, for little
beings whom he hated, would, I should think, become so
intolerable to a Gruff-and-Tackleton, that he would be sure
to fly for resource to the first skipping-rope at hand, or to
run himself through his dura ilia with a tin sabre.   The
ruffian! the child-hating Herod! a squadron of rocking-
horses ought to trample and crush such a fellow into
smaller particles of flint.   I declare for my part I hate
Gruff-and-Tackleton worse than any ogre in Mother Bunch.
Ogres have been a good deal maligned.   They eat children,
it is true, but only occasionally, — children of a race which
is hostile to their Titanic progeny; they are good enough
to their own young.   Witness the ogre in Hopomythumb,
who gave his seven daughters seven crowns, the which
Hopomythumb stole for his brothers, and a thousand other
instances in fairy history.   This is parenthetic, however.
The proposition is, that makers of children's toys may
have their errors, it is true, but must be, in the main,
honest and kindly-hearted persons.

I wish Mrs. Marcet, the Right Honorable T. B. Macaulay.
or any other person possessing universal knowledge, would
take a toy and child's emporium in hand, and explain to

us all .the geographical and historical wonders it contains. That Noah's ark, with its varied contents, — its leopards and lions, with glued pump-handled tails; its light-blue elephants and ⊥ footed ducks; that ark containing the cylindrical family of the patriarch was fashioned in Holland, most likely, by some kind pipe-smoking friends of youth, by the side of a slimy canal. A peasant, in a Danubian pine-wood, carved that extraordinary nut-cracker, who was painted up at Nuremberg afterwards in the costume of a hideous hussar. That little fir lion, more like his roaring original than the lion at Barnet, or the lion of Northumberland House, was cut by a Swiss shepherd boy tending his goats on a mountain-side, where the chamois were jumping about in their untanned leather. I have seen a little Mahometan on the Etmeidan at Constantinople, twiddling about just such a whirligig as you may behold any day in the hands of a small Parisian, in the Tuileries Gardens. And as with the toys so with the toy-books. They exist everywhere; there is no calculating the distance through which the stories come to us, the number of languages through which they have filtered, or the centuries during which they have been told. Many of them have been narrated, almost in their present shape, for thousands of years since, to little copper-colored Sanscrit children, listening to their mother under the palm-trees by the banks of the yellow Jumna — their Brahmin mother, who softly narrated them through the ring in her nose. The very same tale has been heard by the Northern Vikings as they lay on their shields on deck; and by the Arabs, couched under the stars on the Syrian plains when the flocks were gathered in, and the mares were picketed by the tents. With regard to the story of Cinderella, I have heard the late Thomas Hill say that he remembered to have heard, two years before Richard Cœur de Lion came back from Palestine, a Norman jongleur — but, in a word, there is no end to the antiquity of these tales, a dissertation on which would be quite needless and impossible here.

One cannot help looking with a secret envy on the children of the present day, for whose use and entertainment a thousand ingenious and beautiful things are provided, which were quite unknown some few scores of years since, when the present writer and reader were very possibly in the nursery state. Abominable attempts were made in those days to make useful books for children, and cram science down their throats as calomel used to be, administered under the pretence of a spoonful of currant jelly. Such picture-books as we had were illustrated with the most shameful, hideous, old woodcuts which had lasted through a century, and some of which may be actually seen lingering about still as head-pieces to the Catnach ballads, in those rare corners of the town where the Catnach ballads continue to be visible. Some painted pictures there were in our time likewise, but almost all of the very worst kind; the hideous distortions of Rowlandson, who peopled the picture-books with bloated parsons in periwigs, tipsy aldermen and leering salacious nymphs, horrid to look at. Tom and Jerry followed, with choice scenes from the Cockpit, the Round House, and Drury Lane. Atkins's slang sporting subjects then ensued, of which the upsetting of Charleys' watch-boxes, leaping five-barred gates, fighting duels with amazing long pistols, and kissing short-waisted damsels in pink spencers, formed the chief fun. The first real, kindly, agreeable, and infinitely amusing and charming illustrations for a child's book in England which I know, were those of the patriarch George Cruikshank, devised for the famous German popular stories. These were translated by a certain magistrate of Bow Street, whom the Examiner is continually abusing, but whose name ought always to be treated tenderly on account of that great service which he did to the nation. Beauty, fun, and fancy, were united, in these admirable designs. They have been copied all over Europe. From the day of their appearance, the happiness of children may be said to have increased immeasurably. After Cruikshank, the German artists, a kindly and good-natured race, with the organ of philoprogenitiveness strongly developed, began to exert their wits for children. Otto Speckter, Neureuther, the Dusseldorf school, the book-designers at Leipzig and Berlin, the mystical and tender-hearted Overbeck, and numberless others, have contributed to the pleasure and instruction of their little countrymen. In France the movement has not been so remarkable. The designers in the last twenty years have multiplied a hundred-fold: their talent is undeniable: but they have commonly such an unfortunate penchant for what is wrong, that the poor little children can hardly be admitted into their company. They cannot be benefited by voluptuous pictures illustrative of Balzac, Beranger, Manon-Lescaut, and the like. The admirable Charlet confined himself to war and battle, and *les gloires de la France* chiefly : the brilliant designs of Vernet and Raffet are likewise almost all military. Gavarni, the wittiest and cleverest designer that ever lived probably, depicts *grisettes* Ste. Pélagie, *bals-masqués,* and other subjects of town-life and intrigue, quite unfit for children's edification. The caustic Granville, that Swift of the pencil, dealt in subjects scarcely more suited to children than the foul satires of the wicked old Cynic of St. Patrick's, whose jokes to my mind are like the fun of a demon; and whose best excuse is Swift's Hospital.

In England the race of designers is flourishing and increasing, and the art as applied to the nursery (and where, if you please, you who sneer, has our affectionate Mother Art a better place ?) has plenty of practitioners and patronage. Perhaps there may be one or two of our readers who have heard of an obscure publication called Punch, a hebdomadal miscellany, filled with drawings and jokes, good or bad. Of the artists engaged upon this unfortunate periodical, the chief are Messrs. Leech and Doyle, both persons, I would wager, remarkable for love of children, and daily giving proofs of this gentle disposition. Whenever Mr. Leech, "in the course of his professional career," has occasion to depict a child by the side of a bottle-nosed alderman, a bow-waistcoated John Bull, a policeman, a Brook-Green Volunteer, or the like, his rough, grotesque, rollicking pencil becomes gentle all of a sudden, he at once falls into the softest and tenderest of moods, and dandles and caresses the infant under his hands, as I have seen a huge whiskered grenadier do in St. James's Park, when mayhap (but this observation goes for nothing), the nursemaid chances to be pretty. Look at the picture of the Eton-boy dining with his father, and saying, "Governor, one toast before we go — the ladies !" This picture is so pretty, and so like, that it is a positive fact, and every father of an Eton-boy declares it to be the portrait of his own particular offspring. In the great poem of "the Brook-Green Volunteer," cantos of which are issued weekly from the Punch press, all the infantine episodes, without exception, are charming; and the volunteer's wife such a delightful hint of black-eyed smiling innocence and prettiness, as shows that beauty is always lying in the heart of this humorist, — this good humorist, as he assuredly must be. As for Mr. Doyle, his praises have been

sung in this Magazine already; and his pencil every day
gives far better proofs of his genuine relish for the grotesque and beautiful than any that can be produced by the
pen of the present writer.

The real heroes of this article, however, who are at
length introduced after the foregoing preliminary flourish,
are, Mr. Joseph Cundall, of 12 Old Bond Street, in the
city of Westminster, publisher; Mr. Felix Summerly, of
the Home Treasury-office; Mrs. Harriet Myrtle; Ambrose
Merton, Gent., the editor of "Gammer Gorton's Story-
Books;" the writer (or writers) of the "Good-natured
Bear," the "Story-Book of Holiday Hours," etc., and the
band of artists who have illustrated for the benefit of
youth these delightful works of fiction. Their names are
Webster, Townshend, Absolon, Cope, Horsley, Redgrave,
H. Corbould, Franklin, and Frederick Tayler,—names all
famous in art; nor surely could artists ever be more amia-
bly employed than in exercising their genius in behalf of
young people. Fielding, I think, mentions with praise the
name of Mr. Newberry, of Saint Paul's Churchyard, as the
provider of story-books and pictures for children in his
day. As there is no person of the late Mr. Fielding's
powers writing in this Magazine, let me be permitted,
humbly, to move a vote of thanks to the meritorious Mr.
Joseph Cundall.

The mere sight of the little books published by Mr.
Cundall—of which some thirty now lie upon my table—
is as good as a nosegay. Their actual covers are as brilliant
as a bed of tulips, and blaze with emerald, and orange, and
cobalt, and gold, and crimson. I envy the feelings of the
young person for whom (after having undergone a previous
critical examination) this collection of treasures is destined. Here are fairy tales, at last, with real pictures to
them. What a library!—what a picture-gallery! Which
to take up first is the puzzle. I can fancy that perplexity
and terror seizing upon the small individual to whom all
these books will go in a parcel, when the string is cut, and
the brown paper is unfolded, and all these delights appear.
Let us take out one at hazard: it is the "History of Tom
Hickathrift the Conqueror."

He is bound in blue and gold: in the picture Mr. Frederick Tayler has represented Tom and a friend slaughter-
ing wild beasts with prodigious ferocity. Who was Tom
Hickathrift the Conqueror? Did you ever hear of him?

Fielding mentions him somewhere, too; but his history has passed away out of the nursery annals, and this is the first time his deeds have ever come under my cognizance. D:d Fielding himself write the book? The style is very like that of the author of Joseph Andrews. Tom lived in the Isle of Ely in Cambridgeshire, the story says, in the reign of William the Conqueror; his father, who was a laborer, being dead, "and his mother being tender of their son, maintained him by her own labor as well as she could; but all his delight was in the corner, and he ate as much at once as would serve six ordinary men. At ten years old he was six feet high and three feet thick; his hand was like a shoulder of mutton, and every other part proportionate; but his great strength was yet unknown."

The idea of latent strength here is prodigious. How strong the words are, and vigorous the similes! His hand was like a shoulder of mutton. He was six feet high, and three feet thick: all his delight was in the corner, and he ate as much as six men. A man six feet high is nothing, but a fellow three feet thick is tremendous. All the images heap up and complete the idea of Thomas's strength. His gormandizing indicates, his indolence exaggerates, the Herculean form. Tom first showed his strength by innocently taking away from a farmer, who told him he might have as much straw as he could carry, a thousand weight of straw. Another offering him and telling him to choose a stick for his mother's fire, Thomas selected a large tree, and went off with it over his shoulder, while a cart and six horses were tugging at a smaller piece of timber behind. The great charm of his adventures is, that they are told with that gravity and simplicity which only belong to real truth: —

"Tom's fame being spread, no one durst give him an angry word. At last a brewer at Lynn, who wanted a lusty man to carry beer to the Marsh and to Wisbeach, hearing of him, came to hire him; but he would not be hired, till his friends persuaded him, and his master promised him a new suit of clothes from top to toe, and that he should eat and drink of the best. At last Tom consented to be his man, and the master showed him which way he was to go; for there was a monstrous giant kept part of the Marsh, and none dared to go that way, for if the giant found them, he would either kill or make them his servants.

"But to come to Tom and his master. Tom did more in

one day than all the rest of his men did in three; so that his master, seeing him so tractable and careful in his business, made him his head man, and trusted him to carry beer by himself, for he needed none to help him. Thus he went each day to Wisbeach, a journey of near twenty miles.

"But going this way so often, and finding the other road that the giant kept was nearer by the half, Tom having increased his strength by good living, and improved his courage by drinking so much strong ale, resolved one day, as he was going to Wisbeach, without saying anything to his master, or to his fellow-servants, to take the nearest road or lose his life; to win the horse or lose the saddle; to kill or be killed, if he met with the giant.

"This resolved, he goes the nearest way with his cart, flinging open the gates in order to go through; but the giant soon espied him, and seeing him a daring fellow, vowed to stop his journey, and make a prize of his beer: but Tom cared not a fig for him; and the giant met him like a roaring lion, as though he would swallow him up.

"'Sirrah,' said he, 'who gave you authority to come this way? Do you not know, that I make all stand in fear of me? And you, like an impudent rogue, must come and fling open my gate at pleasure! Are you so careless of your life, that you do not care what you do? I will make you an example to all rogues under the sun. Dost thou not see how many heads of those that have offended my laws hang upon yonder tree? Thine shall hang above them all!'

"'None of your prating!' said Tom; 'you shall not find me like them.'

"'No!' said the giant.

"'Why you are but a fool, if you come to fight me, and bring no weapon to defend thyself!' cries Tom. 'I have got a weapon here shall make you know I am your master.'

"'Say you so, sirrah?' said the giant; and then ran to his cave to fetch his club, intending to dash his brains out at a blow.

"While the giant was gone for his club, Tom turned his cart upside down, and took the axletree and wheel for his sword and buckler; and excellent weapons they were, on such an emergency.

"The giant coming out again began to stare at Tom, to see him take the wheel in one of his hands, and the axletree in the other.

"'Oh, oh!' said the giant, 'you are like to do great things with those instruments; I have a twig here that will beat thee, thy axletree and wheel, to the ground!'

"Now that which the giant called a twig, was as thick as a mill-post; and with this the giant made a blow at him with such force, as made his wheel crack. Tom, nothing daunted, gave him as brave a blow on the side of the head, which made him reel again.

"'What,' said Tom, 'have you got drunk with my small-beer already?'

"But the giant, recovering, made many hard blows at him, which Tom kept off with his wheel, so that he received but very little hurt.

"In the mean time, Tom plied the giant so well with blows, that the sweat and blood ran together down his face, who, being almost spent with fighting so long, begged Tom to let him drink, and then he would fight him again.

"'No, no,' said he, 'my mother did not teach me such wit;' and, finding the giant growing weak, he redoubled his blows, till he brought him to the ground.

"The giant, finding himself overcome, roared hideously, and begged Tom to spare his life, and he would perform anything he should desire — even yield himself unto him, and be his servant.

"But Tom, having no more mercy on him than a bear upon a dog, laid on him till he found him breathless, and then cut off his head; after which he went into his cave, and there found great store of gold and silver, which made his heart leap for joy."

This must surely be Fielding: the battle is quite like the Fielding-Homer. Tom, "having increased his strength by good living, and improved his courage by drinking strong ale," is a phrase only to be written by a great man. It indicates a lazy strength, like that of Tom himself in the corner. "The giant roared hideously, but Tom had no more mercy on him than a bear upon a dog." If anybody but Harry Fielding can write of a battle in this way, it is a pity we had not more of the works of the author. He says that for this action, Tom, who took possession of the giant's cave and all his gold and silver, "was no longer called plain Tom, but Mister Hickathrift!"

With the aid of a valorous opponent, who was a tinker, and who being conquered in battle by Tom became his fast friend ever after, Tom overcame 10,000 disaffected, who had gathered in the Isle of Ely (they must have been 10,000 of the refugee Saxons, under Hereward the Saxon, who fled from the tyranny of the Conqueror, and are mentioned by Mr. Wright in his lately published, learned, and ingenious essays, — and, indeed, it was a shame that one of the German name of Hickathrift should attack those of his own flesh and blood); but for this anti-national feat Tom was knighted, and henceforth appeared only as Sir Thomas Hickathrift.

"News was brought to the king, by the commons of Kent, that a very dreadful giant was landed on one of the islands, and had brought with him a great number of bears, and also young lions, with a dreadful dragon, upon which he always rode; which said monster and other ravenous beasts had much frightened all the inhabitants of the island. And, moreover, they said, if speedy course was not taken to suppress them, they would destroy the country.

"The king, hearing of this relation, was a little startled; yet he persuaded them to return home, and make the best defence they could for the present, assuring them that he would not forget them, and so they departed.

"The king, hearing these dreadful tidings, immediately sat in council, to consider what was best to be done.

"At length, Tom Hickathrift was pitched upon, as being a bold, stout subject; for which reason it was judged best to make him governor of that island, which place of trust he readily accepted, and accordingly went down with his wife and family to take possession of the same, attended by a hundred and odd knights and gentlemen, at least.

"Sir Thomas had not been there many days, when, looking out of his own window, he espied this giant mounted on a dreadful dragon, and on his shoulder he bore a club of iron; he had but one eye, which was in the middle of his forehead, and was as large as a barber's basin, and seemed like flaming fire; the hair of his head hung down like snakes, and his beard like rusty wire.

"Lifting up his eyes, he saw Sir Thomas, who was reviewing him from one of the windows of the castle. The giant then began to knit his brow, and breathe out some threatening word to the governor, — who, indeed, was a little surprised at the approach of such a monstrous and ill-favored brute.

"The giant finding that Tom did not make much haste

to get down to him, he alighted from his dragon, and chained him to an oak-tree; then marched to the castle, setting his broad shoulders against the corner of the wall, as if he intended to overthrow the whole bulk of the building at once. Tom perceiving it, said, —

" 'Is this the game you would be at? faith, I will spoil your sport, for I have a delicate tool to pick your tooth with.' Then taking the two-handed sword which the king gave him, and flinging open the gate, he there found the giant, who, by an unfortunate slip in his thrusting, was fallen all along, and lay not able to help himself.

" 'How now,' said Tom, 'do you come here to take up your lodging?' and with that, he ran his long sword between the giant's shoulders, which made the brute groan as loud as thunder.

"Then Sir Thomas pulled out his sword again, and at six or seven blows smote off his head; and then turning to the dragon, which was all this while chained to the tree, without any further words, but with four or five blows, cut off the head of that also."

Once and again this must be Harry Fielding. The words of the narrative are of immense strength and simplicity. When Tom runs his long sword through the giant, it only "makes the brute groan as loud as thunder." An inferior hand would have spoiled all by trying a dying speech. One recognizes Fielding's cudgel-style by the force and simplicity of the blow; and the greatness of Hickathrift is only increased by the conclusion of his history. He is left singing a song at a very noble and splendid feast, to which he invited all his friends and acquaintances, when he made them the following promise: —

> "My friends, while I have strength to stand,
>   Most manfully I will pursue
> All dangers till I clear the land
>   Of lions, bears, and tigers too."

And that is all. How fine the conclusion is! The enormous champion does not die, but lapses into silence. He may be alive yet somewhere in the fens drinking mutely. A health to him! The day was a good day which brought the acquaintance of Tom Hickathrift.

Patient Grissell and the babes in the wood are dressed by Mr. Cundall in scarlet and gold — attired in glorious raiment after their death and sufferings as a reward for martyrdom in life. As for Grissell, I have always had my opinion about her. She is so intolerably patient as to provoke any husband, and owed a great deal of her ill-treatment to the shameful meekness with which she bore it. · But the babes in the wood must awaken the sympathy of any but an ogre, and every man, woman, or child who has a heart for poetry must feel himself stirred by the lines which tell their sad story : —

> " He took the children by the hand,
>   Tears standing in their eye,
> And bade them straightway follow him ;
>   And look, they did not cry.
> And two long miles he led them on,
>   While they for food complain.
> ' Stay here,' quoth he, ' I'll bring you bread
>   When I come back again.'
>
> These pretty babes, with hand in hand,
>   Went wandering up and down,
> But never more could see the man
>   Approaching from the town.
> Their pretty lips with blackberries
>   Were all besmeared and dyed,
> And when they saw the darksome night
>   They sat them down and cried.
>
> Thus wandered these poor innocents
>   Till death did end their grief ;
> In one another's arms they died,
>   As wanting due relief.
> No burial this pretty pair
>   Of any man receives,
> Till Robin Redbreast piously
>   Did cover them with leaves."

Sweet little martyrs ! Poetry contains nothing more touching than their legend. They have lain for hundreds of years embalmed in it. Time has not spoiled the smile of their sweet faces, nestling cheek by cheek under the yellow leaves. Robins have become sacred birds for the good deed they did. They will be allowed to sing in Paradise for that.

"Bevis of Hampton," that famous knight, is not a warrior much to the taste of the present times. He kills a great deal too much, and without any sense of humor and without inspiring any awe; but "Guy of Warwick" is a true knight. After the steward's son has done great deeds, and by his valor and virtue has won the hand of fair Felice, and with it her father's title of Earl of Warwick, the famous warrior is smitten with a sense of the vanity of all earthly things, even of married love and of fair Felice, who consents, like a pious soul as she is, that he should take the cross and go to Palestine.

"While Guy was in this repenting solitude," the legend says, "fair Felice, like a mourning widow, clothed herself in sable attire, and vowed chastity in the absence of her beloved husband. Her whole delight was in divine meditations and heavenly consolations, praying for the welfare of her beloved Lord Guy. And, to show her humility, she sold all her jewels and costly robes, and gave the money to the poor."

Years and years after her lord was gone, there used to come for alms to her castle-gate an old pilgrim, whom the fair Felice relieved with hundreds of other poor. At last, this old hermit, feeling his death drawing nigh, took a ring from his hand and sent it to fair Felice, and she knew by that token it was her lord and husband, and hastened to him. And Guy soon after died in the arms of his beloved Felice, who, having survived him only fifteen days, was buried in the same grave. So ends the story of Guy, the bold baron of price, and of the fair maid Felice. A worthy legend. His bones are dust, and his sword is rust, and his soul is with the saints, I trust. Mr. Tayler supplies two noble illustrations to Sir Bevis and Sir Guy.

We must pass over the rest of the Gammer Gurton library with a brief commendation. The ballads and stories are good, the pictures are good, the type is good, the covers are fine; and the price is small. The same may be said of the " Home-Treasury," edited by the benevolent Felix Summerly. This "Home-Treasury " contains a deal of pleasant reading and delightful pictures. The fairy tales are skilfully recast, and charmingly illustrated with colored prints (perhaps all prints for children ought to have pretty colors, by the way) by some of the good-natured artists before mentioned. The delightful drawings for Little Red Riding-hood are supplied by Mr. Webster. Mr. Townshend nobly illustrates Jack and the Bean-Stalk ; while the pretty love-tale of Beast and the Beauty is delineated by Mr. Redgrave. In the book of " Fairy Tales and Ballads " Cope, Redgrave, and Tayler vie with each other which shall most show skill and recreate youth. For the "Story-Books of the Seasons" and "Mrs. Harriet-Myrtle Series" Mr. Absolon has supplied a profusion of designs, which are all, without exception, charming. The organ of love of children as developed on that gentleman's cranium must be something prodigious, and the bump of benevolence quite a mountain. Blessed is he whose hat is enlarged by them!

Let a word be said, in conclusion, regarding the admirable story of the Good-natured Bear, one of the wittiest, pleasantest, and kindest of books that I have read for many a long day. Witness this extract, which contains the commencement of the bear's autobiography : —

"'I am a native of Poland, and was born in one of the largest and most comfortable caves in the forest of Towski-pouski. My father and mother were greatly respected by all the inhabitants of the forest, and were, in fact, regarded, not only by all their own species, but by every other animal, as persons of some consequence. I do not mention this little circumstance from any pride, but only out of filial affection for their memory.

"'My father was a man of a proud and resentful — my father, I meant to say, was a person of a proud and resentful disposition, though of the greatest courage and honor; but my mother was one in whom all the qualities of the fairer, or at least, the softer sex, were united. I shall never forget the patience, the gentleness, the skill, and the firmness with which she first taught me to walk alone. I mean to walk on all fours, of course; the upright manner of my present walking was only learned afterwards. As this infant effort, however, is one of my very earliest recollections, I have mentioned it before all the rest, and if you please, I will give you a little account of it.'

"'Oh! do, Mr. Bear,' cried Gretchen; and no sooner had she uttered the words, than all the children cried out at the same time, 'Oh! please do, sir!' The bear took several long whiffs at his pipe, and thus continued : —

"'My mother took me to a retired part of the forest, where few animals ever came; and telling me that I must now stand alone, extended both paws, and slowly lowered me towards the earth. The height, as I looked down, seemed terrible, and I felt my legs kick in the air with fear of, I did not know what, till suddenly I felt four hard things, and no motion. It was the fixed earth beneath my four infant legs. "Now," said my mother, "you are what is called standing alone ! " But what she said I heard as in a dream. With my back in the air, as though it rested on a wooden trestle, with my nose poking out straight, snuffing the fresh breeze, and the many scents of the woods, my ears pricking and shooting with all sorts of new sounds, to wonder at, to want to have, to love, or to tumble down at, — and my eyes staring before me full of light, and confused gold, and dancing things, I seemed to be in a condition over which I had no power to effect the least change, and in which I must remain fixed until some wonderful thing happened. But the firm voice of my mother came to my assistance, and I heard her tell me to look upon the earth beneath me, and see where I was. First I looked up among the boughs, then sideways at my shoulder, then I squinted at the tip of my nose — all by mistake and innocence — at last, I bent my nose in despair, and saw my fore-paws standing, and this of course was right. The first thing that caught my attention, being the first thing I saw distinctly, was a little blue flower with a bright jewel in the middle, which I afterwards found was a drop of dew. Sometimes I thought this little blue darling was so close that it almost touched my eyes, and certainly the odor of it was up in my head; sometimes I thought it was deep down, a long way off. When I bent my face towards it to give it a kiss, it seemed just where it was, though I had not done what I had thought to do.

" 'The next thing I saw upon the ground was a soft-looking little creature, that crawled along with a round ball upon the middle of its back, of a beautiful white color, with brown and red curling stripes. The creature moved very, very slowly, and appeared always to follow the opinion and advice of two long horns on its head, that went feeling about on all sides. Presently it slowly approached my right fore-paw, and I wondered how I should feel, or smell, or hear it, as it went over my toes; but the instant one of the horns touched the hair of my paw both horns shrunk into nothing, and presently came out again, and the creature slowly moved away in another direction. While I was wondering at this strange proceeding — for I never thought of hurting the creature, not knowing how to hurt anything, and what should have made the horn fancy otherwise ? — while, then, I was wondering at this, my attention was suddenly drawn to a tuft of moss on my right near a hollow tree trunk. Out of this green tuft looked a pair of very bright, round, small eyes, which were staring up at me.

"'If I had known how to walk, I should have stepped back a few steps when I saw those bright little eyes, but I never ventured to lift a paw from the earth, since my mother had first set me down, nor did I know how to do so, or what were the proper thoughts or motions to begin with. So I stood looking at the eyes; and presently I saw that the head was yellow, and all the face and throat yellow, and that it had a large mouth. "What you have just seen," said my mother, "we call a snail; and what you now see is a frog." The names, however, did not help me at all to understand. Why the first should have turned from my paw so suddenly, and why this creature should continue to stare up at me in such a manner, I could not conceive. I expected, however, that it would soon come slowly crawling forth, and then I should see whether it would also avoid me in the same manner. I now observed that its body and breast were double somehow, and that its paws were very large for its size, but had no hair upon them, which I thought was probably occasioned by its slow crawling having rubbed it all off. I had scarcely made these observations and reflections, when a beam of bright light breaking through the trees, the creature suddenly gave a great hop right up under my nose, and I, thinking the world was at an end, instantly fell flat down on one side, and lay there waiting!'"

Those who wish to know more about him, and to see Mr. Tayler's admirable likenesses of him, must buy the book for themselves. For it must be kept away from its right owners no longer, and must be consigned to brown paper and bound up with twine along with its beautiful comrades, never to see the light again until the packet opens under the astonished eyes of A. H. T.

M. A. TITMARSH.

A GRUMBLE ABOUT THE CHRISTMAS BOOKS.

BY MICHAEL ANGELO TITMARSH.

[*Fraser's Magazine, January,* 1847.]

My dear Mr. Yorke, — When, in an unguarded moment, I complied with your request to look through the Christmas books of the season and report progress upon that new branch of English literature, we had both the idea that the occupation would be exceedingly easy, jovial and pleasant; that we should be able to make an agreeable lecture upon an amusing subject; that critics, authors, and readers, would be brought together in the most enticing and amiable manner possible; and we should finish off an article with kind hearts, friendly greetings, merry Christmas, and that sort of things, — a perfect prize paper, streaky with benevolence, and larded with the most unctuous human kindness, with an appropriate bit of holly placed in its hinder quarter.

Sir, we have both of us made a most dismal mistake. Had it been strong meat which you set before me for a Christmas feast, the above metaphor (which I took from Mr. Slater's shop at Kensington) might have applied. Beef might have invigorated the critic; but, ah, sir! what is that wretch to do who finds himself surfeited with mince-pies? I have read Christmas books until I have reached a state of mind the most deplorable. "Curses on all fairies!" I gasp out; "I will never swallow another one as long as I live! Perdition seize all Benevolence! Be hanged to the Good and the True! Fling me every drop of the milk of human kindness out of the window! — horrible, curdling slops, away with them! Kick old Father Christmas out of doors, the abominable old impostor! Next year I'll go to the Turks, the Scotch, or other Heathen who don't keep Christmas. Is all the street to come for a Christmas box? Are the waits to be invading us by millions, and yelling all night? By my soul, if anybody offers me plum pudding again this season, I'll fling it in his face!"

The fair writer of one of these volumes, "A Christmas in the Seventeenth Century" (I may have read something very like this tale in Vandevelde's novels, but it is a pretty story, and just as good for little dears as if it were quite new), mentions in the preface the rueful appearance of a Parisian friend of hers at Christmas, who was buying bon-bons as if he was doing penance, and cursed the odious custom of the *jour de l'an* which compelled him to spend a great part of his quarter's allowance in sugar-plums, to be presented to his acquaintance. The French gentleman was right: the sugar-plum system in France has become a nuisance, and in Protestant England the Christmas-book system is bidding fair to be another. Sir, it was wisely regulated that Christmas should come only once a year, but that does not mean that it is to stay all the year round. Do you suppose that any man could read through all these books and retain his senses? I have swallowed eight or nine out of the five and twenty or thirty volumes. I am in a pitiable condition. I speak with difficulty out of my fulness.

"Miss Smith, my love, what is our first Christmas pie? That in the green and gold dish, if you please."

Miss Smith. — "The dish is Mrs. Gore's, the plates are Mr. Cruikshank's, and very pretty plates they are. He, he, he!"

M. A. T. — "No trifling, madam, if you please. Read on."

Miss Smith reads as follows: —

"'Can you read, my boy? and are you sharp enough to undertake errands?' said a young officer of the Guards, on whose well-fitting uniform little George had fixed a wistful eye, one summer morning at the corner of St. James's Street, as he was lounging near Sam's shop, on pretence of looking at the engravings of a fashionable annual.

"'I can read, sir,' replied the boy, longing to add, 'and if you will employ me for a message, I will do my best to give you satisfaction,' for the handsome countenance of the young officer captivated his fancy. But the often repeated injunction of his grandmother, that, betide what might, he was never to derogate from the habits of life of a gentleman's son, forbade his endeavoring to earn a shilling, a coin that rarely found its way into the palm of his hand.

"'You have an honest face of your own,' added the officer, after casting a hasty glance around, to ascertain that no one was at hand to overhear or notice their colloquy.

'Do you think you could make out Belgrave Street, Belgrave Square?'

" ' To be sure I could, sir.'

" ' In that case, my lad, here's half a crown for you, to make the best of your way to number seven, where you will leave this letter,' continued he, placing one in his hand; 'and, remember, should any questions be asked by the servants, you are to say that it was given you by a lady you never saw before, and of whom you don't know the name.'

" ' If I'm to say that, sir, I'm afraid I can't oblige you,' replied the child, returning the money and the letter; 'and, at all events, I should not have accepted the half-crown. I am not an errand boy, sir; I am a gentleman's son!'

" ' You are a confounded little ass, I suspect,' returned the officer, nettled and surprised. 'What on earth can it signify whether you receive the letter from a gentleman or lady?'

" ' Not the least, sir. It signifies only that I should not say the one, when the other is the case. But I will undertake to carry your letter safe and speedily, and give no explanations at all, however much questioned, if that would suit you.'

" ' I fancy I can trust you, my lad,' replied the officer, more and more surprised by the tone and bearing of the child. 'But I should be glad to learn, on your return, how you have prospered in your errand.'

" ' You are on guard, I think, sir!' said George, glancing at his gay accoutrements. 'I shall be in Belgrave Street and back in less than twenty minutes. You can manage, perhaps, to remain hereabouts till then?'

" And the appointment once made, George did not allow the grass to grow under his feet. Fresh from a first perusal of 'Paul and Virginia,' he seemed to understand (on perceiving that the letter about which the young captain appeared so anxious was addressed to a 'Miss Hallet') why he was so anxious concerning the delivery.

" ' I left it safe, sir, at number seven. No questions were asked,' said he, a little out of breath, as soon as he came within hail of the scarlet coat.

" ' So far, so good,' observed the young man, turning towards a friend on whose arm he was leaning. 'I think I may be sure, this time, that it will reach her hand.'

" And as George had now fully discharged his commission, he was making off towards home, when the officer suddenly called him back.

"'Hillo, my lad! we mustn't part in this way,' said he. 'You've done me better service than you think for; and though you don't choose to be paid for it, you must have something to keep in remembrance of my gratitude.'

"The whole party were now opposite the shop of Palmer the cutler, into which the apparently overjoyed letter-sender ordered his prompt messenger to follow him; and, in a moment, a tray of many-bladed knives — knives after a boy's own heart — glittered before the eyes of George.

"'Make your choice, youngster!' said the officer, who, by the obsequiousness of the shopman, was apparently well known and highly considered. 'You seem steady enough to be trusted with sharp implements.'

"'Recollect, my dear Wroxton,' interrupted his companion, good-humoredly, 'that a knife is the most unlucky keepsake in the world!'

"'Ay, between lovers!' retorted the young guardsman, pointing out to his *protégé* a handsome four-bladed knife with a mother-of-pearl handle, which he seemed to recommend. 'But in this case, all I want is to remind this trusty Pacolet of mine that I am in existence; and that he will often find me on the same spot, waiting to engage him for the same service he executed so well just now.'

"Scarcely knowing in what words to express his gratitude for the generous manner in which his trifling assistance was requited, poor George thankfully acquiesced in the shopman's suggestion that his initials should be engraved on the silver escutcheon ornamenting the handle of the knife. It could be finished in a few hours. On the morrow, George was to call for it at Palmer's.

"'And mind you don't disappoint the little fellow,' said his new friend, preparing to leave the shop. 'It is impossible for me to send my own servants to Sir Jasper's,' continued he, addressing his companion, as they proceeded down the steps to resume their lounge in St. James's Street; 'and this boy is precisely the sort of messenger not to excite suspicion.'"

. What an agreeable vivacity there is about this description! Sparkling, easy, stylish, and so like nature. I think that incident of a knife — a four-bladed knife with a mother-of-pearl handle — from Palmer's, in St. James's Street, is *impayable*. You fancy the scene: the young bucks in scarlet — Palmer himself — the Conservative Club opposite, with the splendid dandies in the bow-window —

the red-jackets who hold the horses — the cab-stand — St. James's Gate and clock. Que sçais-je ? How deftly in a few strokes a real artist can bring out a picture.

The picture is taken from New Year's Day, by Mrs. Gore. This book has nothing earthly in it about New Year's Day. The plot and mystery are as follows : —

There was once a hectoring young Turk of a captain of foot, who married a young woman of inferior rank, and, singular to state, ill-used her. By this lady, Captain Hallet had a little son: he bullied and ill-used this little son too in such a manner that the lad threatened to drown himself; and his coat and cap were all that were found of the young fellow by the side of the poluphlois-boiothalasses, into the deep bosom of which he had committed himself.

The mother's heart broke in twain at the calamity; so did John Talbot's, the captain's man (so far as male hearts can be said to break, for this sort mends again almost as good as new commonly) : the captain became an altered man too, and no wonder. A couple of murders on his conscience could not make a captain of foot very cheerful.

The Peninsular War breaking out at this juncture, Captain Jasper Hallet joined the heroic Major-General Sir Arthur Wellesley, at present F. M. the Duke of Wellington, K. G. etc. Assaults, scaladoes, ambuscadoes, hurrahs, cut-and-thrust, fire away, run-you-through-the-body, Give it 'em, boys ! became the captain's chief delight ; and forlorn hopes were his principal diversions. Wounded he was a great deal, as men will be in this sort of sport; and we picture him to ourselves as devilled and scarred like the leg of that turkey which has stood the assault of Christmas-day. But no friendly ball laid low the capting — as how should it ? otherwise Mrs. Gore's story could never have been written — on the contrary, he rose to be a major — a colonel — to clasps and ribbons innumerable — to command a brigade in the unlucky campaigns of New Orleans, and a division at the attack of Bhurtpore. And I leave you to imagine that his portion of the swag (as the Hindostan phrase is for plunder) must have been considerable, when I state that it amounted to 400,000*l.* Mrs. Gore is a noble creature, and makes the money fly about, that is the truth.

And don't you see when a man has 400,000*l.* how we get to like him in spite of a murder or two ? Our author yields

with charming *naïveté* to the general impression.   He is a
good fellow, after all; but he has four hundred thousand;
he has repented of his early brutalities; his claret is
famous, etc., etc.   Lieutenant-General Sir Jasper Hallet,
K. C. B., Belgrave Square, with his niece, the lovely Mira,
to whom it was known he had given 20,000*l.*, and on whom
many of the old fogies at the United Service Club were
looking as eligible partners for their own sons.   The
United Service — que dis-je ? — the Guards' Club had an
eye on her too; and no less a young fellow than my Lord
Wroxton (the rogue !) was smitten by her.

One day as Miss Hallet was driving in her uncle's elegant chariot with the grays, and Johns behind, and Robert
the coachman in the silver wig on the dickey — as Robert
was cutting in and out among the carriages like — blazes, I
was going to say, but why use an expression so familiar ?
— it chanced that he cut over a child — a poor boy — a
fair-haired delicate boy — a bright-eyed thing — cut him
over, and very nearly sent the wheels over him.   The little
cherub was rescued from the chariot-wheel; but before the
lovely but naturally flustered Mira had found out his name,
he was gone.

Now, my dears, do you begin to be on the scent ?   Who
can that fair-haired, blue-eyed, bright-eyed thing be ?   Is
it a baker's boy, is it a charity boy, a doctor's boy, or any
other ditto ?   My heart tells me that that child is not what
he seems.   But of that anon.

In a court off St. James's Street — for if we can't be
always genteel we'll be always near it — in a dreary room,
having spent her money, pawned her spoons, exhausted the
little store which misfortune had left her, lives a grumbling
old woman, by the name of Mrs. Lawrie.   She is an American, and as such the grandmother of the bright-eyed child
whose acquaintance we have just had the honor to make.

Yes, but who was his father ?   His father was Colonel
Jasper Foreman (mark the Jasper, S. V. P !).   Coming to
this country, his own native place, with ingots of gold
packed in chests, on board the Antelope packet, at only
three days from shore, and just when the captain, after
some conversations with him, had begun to treat Colonel
"Jasper Foreman" with much more respect than a mere
Yankee colonel could expect — at three days off port, the
ship went down, with the captain, with Colonel Foreman,
all his money, all his papers, everything except the boy,

and his grandmother, and her dozen silver spoons and forks. It's a mercy the old lady was in the habit of carrying them about with her, or what would the pair have done on reaching Albion's shore?

They went to live in the court off St. James's Street, melting away the spoons one by one, and such other valuables as had escaped the shipwreck. The old lady's health was impaired, and her temper · abominable. How like a little angel did young George tend that crabbed old grandmother! George had a little bird — a poor little bird, and loved the little warbler as boyhood will love. The old hunx grumbled at the little bird, and said it ate them out of house and home. He took it into St. James's Park (the keepers let him pass, for George, though poor, mended his clothes most elegantly, and always managed to look genteel, bless him), and he let loose the little bird in the Park: there's a picture of it, with the towers of Westminster Abbey, and the bird, and a lady and gent walking in the distance. He parted from his darling bird, and went home to his grandmamma. He went home and made her gruel. "Bitterly did the old lady complain of the over-sugaring of the gruel." There is a picture of that too. George is bringing her that gruel in a basin; there's a cow on the chimneypiece, a saucepan in the fender, a cup and a parcel (of Embden groats, probably) on the table. Tears — sweet, gushing tears, sobs of heart-breaking yet heart-soothing affection, break from one over this ravishing scene. I am crying so, I can hardly write. The printers will never sure decipher this blotted page. So she complained of the over-sugaring of the gruel, did she? Dear child! The scene, I feel, is growing too tender.

    .   .   .   .   .

As I describe this harrowing tale of innocence and woe, I protest I get so bewildered with grief as to lose the power of coherently continuing the narrative. This little George — this little diddle-iddle darling, walking in St. James's Street, was accosted by Lord Wroxton, who gave him a letter to carry — a letter to Belgrave Street, to no other than Miss Mira Hallet. The name of the owner of the house, Sir Jasper Hallet, excited in the boy a thousand tumultuously mysterious emotions. Jasper! his papa's name was Jasper! Were the two Jaspers related anyhow? The scoffing menials thrust away the child who asked the question; but still he was hovering about the place — still watching Miss Hallet and following her carriage, and one day, in a chase after it, he received the upset which opens the story.

Well, well, a little boy knocked down in the very first page of a story of course gets up again — of course he finds his parents — of course his grandfather makes him a present of at least half the four hundred thousand ? No such thing: the little boy sickens all through the volume. Grandpapa goes abroad. Comic business takes place — such dreary comic business ! — about the lovers of Miss Mira. In the midst of the comic business at Ems, grandpapa receives a letter, — his boy is found. It is Jasper's son, who, instead of drowning himself then (the cheerful catastrophe arriving later), only went to sea. Old John Talbot, the faithful servant, has found him starving in a garret. Away, away ! — post haste, treble *drink-gelt, vite postillon !* Sir Jasper arrives, and Mira, *essoufflée,* to find the little boy — just dead. There's a picture of him. A white sheet covers him over — old John Talbot is sobbing at the bedside — enter the general, as from his post-chaise. Horror, horror ! Send for the undertaker ! It is all up with poor little Georgy !

And I declare I have not the slightest compunctions for his demise. The book ought to be bound in crape, and printed on black-edged paper. This is a Christmas-book ! Where's merry Christmas going ? Of all, all deadly liveliness — of all maudlin ululations — of all such grandmothers, grandsons, and water-gruel, let us be delivered ! — My love, hand me, if you please, the sky-blue-covered book, January Eve, by George Soane, B.A.

I have my doubts whether anybody has a right to compose a story, certainly no one is authorized to write a Christmas story, whereof the end is not perfectly comfortable to all parties — to the readers first, to the heroes and heroines subsequently, and all the minor characters according to their deserts or beyond them. Why, poor rogues in her majesty's very jails are served with beef and pudding, and mercifulness and hospitality, at this season of the year ; and wherefore are you and I, my dear Miss Smith — not ill-natured persons in the main ; good-natured, at any rate when we are pleased — to be made miserable at the conclusion of a history, by being called upon to sympathize with the sickness, the premature demise, or otherwise undeserved misfortune, of certain honest personages with whose adventures we are made acquainted? That is why, madam, I was so wroth anon with Mrs. Gore. I won't show mercy unto her. Why should I to a lady who has just been so unmerciful to a poor little Whatdyecallem — the General Thingumgig's grandson, I mean — who died most miserably just as he was coming into his estate? Mrs. Gore had the fate of the little fellow perfectly in her hands : there is no earthly reason why he should not have got well of the carriage running over him. Why should not Mr. M'Cann, of Parliament Street, for instance, have been passing by, as he always is in the newspapers, and set the little chap's shoulder in a twinkling? or why was not my friend Doctor Quinton, of Arlington Street, driving down St. James's Street at the period of the accident? He would have stepped out of his carriage, popped in the little lad, carried him to his grandmother, cured that abominable old woman of her lumbago and her ill-humor, without ever so much as thinking of a fee, and made all straight and pleasant by the time Sir Jasper Whatisit had arrived from Wiesbaden. It was just as easy for Mrs. Gore to save that child and make it perfectly well and hearty, as to throttle it, and go off to the undertaker's with a religious reflection. None of your Herodian stories for me. No, no! I am not jolly at a funeral. I confess it does not amuse me. I have no taste for murders, or measles, or poison, or black jobs of any sort. We will have a word or two with Sir Edward Lytton-Bulwer, Bart., presently, by the way, who, for his infamous and murderous propensities, as lately shown in his most appalling and arsenical novel of Lucretia, deserves to be brought up with a tight hand. But of this anon.

We spake but now of Mrs. Gore going to the undertaker's. When the excellent Mrs. Hubbard went to the undertaker's and got a coffin, what was the upshot of that funereal transaction? Why, as we all know, when she came back her favorite was laughing. As, of course, he should be.

That's your proper sort of pantomime business — that's the right way in Christmas books. Haven't you seen Clown in the play; his head cut off by the butcher and left on the block before all beholders ; his limbs severally mangled, and made into polonies, and yet, in two minutes, he says, "How are you?" (the droll dog!) as lively as ever? Haven't we seen Pantaloon killed before our very eyes, put pitilessly into his mother's mangle, brought from that instrument utterly dead, and stretched eighteen feet in length — and are we hurt, are our feelings outraged? No; we know Harlequin will have him alive again in two minutes by a quiver of his stick, and the old rascal will be kittling Columbine under the chin, while that spangled maniac, her lover, is waggling his head in his frill (as if it were a pudding in a dish), and dancing the most absurd, clumsy hornpipe in the back scene. And as in pantomimes so I say in Christmas stories, those fireside Christmas pantomimes, which are no more natural than Mother Goose or Harlequin Gulliver. Kill your people off as much as you like; but always bring 'em to life again. Belabor your villains as you please. As they are more hideous than mortals, pummel them more severely than mortals can bear. But they must always amend, and you must be reconciled to them in the last scene, when the spangled fairy comes out of the revolving star, and, uttering the magic octosyllabic incantations of reconcilement, vanishes into an elysium of blue fire. Sweet, kindly, eight-syllabled incantations, pleasant fantastic fairy follies, charming mystery, wherein the soul is plunged, as the gentle curtain descends, and covers those scenes of beloved and absurd glory! Do you suppose the people who invented such were fools, and wanted to imitate great blundering realities to inculcate great stupid, moral apophthegms? — anybody can do that — anybody can say that "Evil communications corrupt good manners," or that "Procrastination is the thief of time," or what not: but a poet does not take his inspirations from the copy-book or his pictures from the police-office. Is there any moralizing in Titania, Ariosto, or Undine?

All this is *apropos* of the sky-blue story-book by George Soane, B.A. Now this sky-blue story-book (whereof the flavor somewhat perhaps resembles the beverage of academic youth) has great merits. First, it is improbable; secondly, it is pretty and graceful; thirdly, it has many pleasant pastoral descriptions, and kindly ballet groups and dances; fourthly, the criminals are reformed, the dead come to life again, and the devil is not the devil — to which, by the way, I take exception.

The rich uncle from India is the key of the story — (*mon Dieu*, how I wish I had one coming from that quarter!) — the conduct of a beggar on horseback, the theme of satire. Tom Starlight, the poacher, drinking with his club at the Black Lion, and inveighing against the tyranny

of a scoundrelly aristocracy, finds himself converted all of a
sudden into Squire Starlight, of Taunton Hall. The squire
gives up the doctrines of the poacher : he is the strictest of
game preservers in all the county, the most severe of all
landlords and arrogant of men. Honest Jack Lint, the sur-
geon, was going to marry Tom's sister when he was in low
life ; but, become a nobleman, Tom says she shall marry old
Lord Rheumatiz ; and so the poor girl all but breaks her
heart. Stella breaks hers outright. She is the blind old
schoolmaster's daughter, old Elias Birch — a dear, impossible old gentleman, with pink cheeks, red stockings, and
cotton hair, such as you see come out of the canvas cottage
in the ballet and bless the lassies and lads (with their shirt
sleeves tied up with ribbon) before the ballet begins.

"At this critical moment, when the question was on his
lips, which, if spoken, might perhaps have averted no common calamity, he was interrupted by a chorus of boyish
voices, so close and so unexpected as almost to startle him.

> " ' Te, magister, salutamus ;
>   Te, magister, nunc laudamus,
>   Semper, semper sis beatus,
>   Felix dies quo tu natus,
>   Hurrah ! '

" ' Why, it's the boys from the free school ! ' exclaimed
the old man ; ' I did not know it was a holiday.'

" No, dear Elias, nor was it a holiday, according to the
school-rubric ; but it is good sometimes to be merry, even
though it is not so set down in the calendar ; and this was
your birthday — the first since blindness had compelled
you to give up the *ferula*, which you had wielded so gently
over the urchins, and in many instances over their fathers
and even grandfathers before them. Here they were,
grateful little fellows, with full hands, and fuller hearts,
come to say, ' We do love you so, kind old master ! ' And,
to use a common phrase, though not in a common sense,
there was no love lost between them, for Elias could
scarcely have taken a livelier interest in their welfare had
they really been his own children.

" In they tumbled, thronging, talking, laughing, till as
many had crowded into the cottage-parlor as it would well
hold, when the younger and weaker fry, who were thus
ousted by their seniors, clambered up to the window-sill,
where they clustered like a swarm of bees. The new

schoolmaster, quite astounded at such a jubilee, would fain
have re-established order among them. — Order! silly fellow! what are you thinking of? is order better than those
merry faces, all hope and sunshine? is order better than
all that mass of happiness, which laughs, and shouts, and
climbs, and hustles, and is not to be purchased at any price?
leave them alone, for goodness' sake. And he did leave
them alone, for he was not a bad fellow, that new master,
though he was far from being an Elias Fairfield. Somehow, too, he was beginning to laugh, and be exceedingly
merry himself, without exactly knowing why — perhaps it
was for company's sake.

"But the head-boy had a grand Latin speech to deliver,
a thing of his own concoction, and made expressly for the
occasion. Of course he was in a hurry to begin — most
orators are — and his influence, assisted by a hint from
Stella that the noise was almost too much for her grandfather, effected a temporary lull. A proud moment was it
for the young Cicero, and with infinite complacency did the
sightless old man listen to his harangue, only throwing in
an occasional correction — he could not entirely forget
former habits — when the orator blundered in his grammar,
as would now and then happen.

"Then came the presentation of gifts, in which each
young holiday-maker acted for himself, and in a few minutes the cottage table was covered with nosegays, for as
early as the season was — primroses, crocuses, both yellow
and purple, polyanthuses, pansies, and I know not what
besides. One little fellow, having nothing better within
his means, tied together a bunch of daisies, which he presented amidst the jeers of his schoolmates — 'a pretty
gift for any one! on a birthday too!' and again the laugh
went round. But the old man caught the child to his
bosom, and kissing him tenderly, while the tears ran down
his furrowed cheeks, bade Stella take especial care of the
daisies.

"'Put them in water directly, love, and don't fling them
away, either, when they die — mind that. You can lay
them between the leaves of my great Bible, and then I
shall always have them near me.'

"What next? — the orator again steps forward. No more
Latin speeches, I hope — oh no! not the least fear of that.
He is supported as they say of other deputations, by a
dozen of the eldest boys, who for the last two months have

clubbed together their weekly allowances to buy a silver goblet for their dear old master. It was second-hand, but just as good as new; the dents and bruises had been carefully hammered out, and it had been polished up both inside and outside, as only a silversmith can do these things. Indeed, their own funds had not sufficed for so magnificent an undertaking, and so they had been helped out by fathers, or brothers, or uncles, who in their day had been scholars of Elias, and were now grown up into substantial yeomen, or thriving shopkeepers.

"What next? — a deputation of young girls from the neighboring villages, with fowls, and eggs, and bacon. Why, surely, they must fancy the cottage in a state of siege, and badly off for provisions!

"What next? — Sir Edward's gamekeeper with a hare, and his kind remembrance to his old master — will call himself before the day's over."

This is as it should be: your proper, pleasant, rouged, grinning, junketing, pantomimic business. It is not intended to be natural — only pretty and kind-hearted — pleasing to the eye — cheerfully ticklesome to the senses — mildly festive, benevolent, and brisk. I doubt, after all, if there is any need for an artist to make his portraits like. What you want is not to be struck by the resemblance, but to be impregnated with the idea. For instance, when the thunderstorm comes, as in Beethoven's Pastoral Symphony, you don't think of putting up your umbrella: when you read young Mr. S. Roger's pretty verses —

> "Mine be a cot beside a hill,
> A beehive's hum salute my," etc.

you are not led to suppose that they contain a real picture of rural life and felicity; but they fill the mind with sweet, pleasant, countrified, hay-smelling, hawthorn-flowering, tree-whispering, river-babbling, breeze-blowing, rural perceptions, wherein lie the reader's delight and the poet's charm and mystery. As the mesmerists' giving a glass of cold water to their lucky patients can make the liquor assume any taste, from Johannisberg to ginger-beer — it is water still, but it has the effect of wine: so a poet mesmerizes you with his magical tap, and — but for the tenth time we are straying from the point in hand, which is, Why Stella Birch broke her heart.

She broke her heart, then, because Tom Starlight broke it — that is, he ill-used her — that is, he promised her. Well, well, she jumped into the mill-stream with a shriek and a plunge; and that brute Tom, not contented with the ruin of one poor girl, must endeavor to perpetrate the destruction of another, his sister, by marrying her to the before-mentioned Lord Lumbago.   Fancy the fury of poor Jack Pills — Fanny perishing away — the bells actually ringing for her marriage with Lord Sciatica — the trembling victim led to the altar, and Bob Sawyer about to poison himself with the most excruciating black doses in his establishment.   When, presto! the fairy in the revolving car appears.   The old gentleman is not the devil who gave Tom the estate, but Tom's uncle from India who wishes to try him. Tom is not Squire Starlight of Taunton Hall, but a dumb, penniless, detected, young scapegrace, to be handed over to the castigators.   Viscount Chalkstones shall not marry poor dear little Fanny, who, on the contrary, shall bless Tom Tourniquet with her hand and twenty thousand pounds administered by the uncle in India.   Stella is not dead any more than you are.   She jumped into the water, I own; but the miller heard the plop and fished her out and kept her safe, and now she comes back, and of course Tom Starlight makes an honest woman of her.   The only person who dies is old Elias Rodwell, the schoolmaster; but then he is so old, so very old, and his hair so very cottony, that his death is rather a pleasure than otherwise; and you fancy his life was only a sort of make-believe. And so everybody is happy, and the light-blue entertainment of Mr. Soane closes.   It is a good, cheap, easy, and profitable Christmas pastime.

I take the Brothers Mayhew to be a couple of good-natured hermits, living out of the world in practices of asceticism, and yet having a kindly recollection of that scene of strife and struggle which they have left behind them.   They write, from their monastery, a work of prodigious benevolence, stupendous moralization, frequent wisdom, and rather a clumsy and doubtful fancy and humor.   To say of a "good genius" that he "turns everything into gold," is, perhaps, an undeserved, though not an unprecedented compliment to bullion.   It is an homage to specie.   The proposition stands thus: a good genius turns everything into gold; therefore gold is a good genius.   And the fable is wrought in the following manner: —

Silvio, a forester in a goatskin jacket, having lost his paternal hut by a sudden inundation, finds himself in his native wood with no resource but his hatchet and a piece of bread, his last refreshment. In the wood Silvio finds a hive of honey. The houseless and penniless youth is about to give a relish to his last piece of bread with the honey so discovered, when a sentimental objection suddenly makes him pause. "No," says he (but in the finest language), "I will not deprive these innocent bees of the produce of their labor; that which they have gathered, as they roamed from flower to flower, let them enjoy in dignified otiosity; I will dip my crust into the stream, content myself with that wholesome repast, and not rob them of the results of their industry."

This unexampled benevolence touches the Queen Bee, who is a fairy in disguise. She suddenly appears before Silvio in her character of Fairy Bee-queen — bids him to state in what manner she can be serviceable to him — and, in fact, fulfils every possible wish that the young Silvio can form. "Only come out in that goatskin jacket," says she, "so that I may know you, and anything you like shall be yours."

First, he wishes to have his cottage restored to him; the Good Genius instantly re-instates him in that tenement. The Princess of the Country calls upon him, and is dissatisfied with the accommodation. Silvio, of course, finds out that it is no longer convenient. He demands a neat little villa, whither the Princess too follows him. Encouraged by her visit, the audacious young man proposes marriage to her. "What! you," says she, "a mere country householder, wish to marry the likes of me?" And she leaves him in a huff. "Make me a prince," says Silvio to his fairy patroness, "so that I may be her equal;" and immediately the Queen Bee erects a principality and city for him. Silvio marries the Princess, and — they live happy ever after, you would imagine?

Not so. Prince Silvio plunges into idleness and debaucheries; he is driven out of his capital by his indignant subjects. He loses his goatskin jacket, the great talisman of his fortune. He is plunged into misfortunes, which he bears with great philosophy and most eloquent benevolence; but finally finding his goatskin again, his kingdom is restored, his prosperity returns, and he and his princess and daughter are doubtless happy to this very day.

The history is interspersed with some comic business. Silvio's barber, in fact, gets hold of the goatskin jacket when the prince makes his precipitate flight from his dominions — enjoys unintelligible property whilst wearing this article; and goes mad upon losing it when Silvio comes back to his own again.   I protest against the whole affair — against the fable — against the jacket — against the bee — against Silvio — against his bad fortune and his good — against the fairy turning everything into money, etc.

If a man wants to make a mere fantastic tale, nobody calls upon him to be tight and close in his logic.   If he wants to moralize, his proposition should be neat and clear, as his argument is correct.   I am reconciled now to the wolf eating up Red Riding Hood (though I was sceptical in my childhood on this point), because I have given up believing that this is a moral tale altogether, and am content to receive it as a wild, odd, surprising, and not unkindly fairy story.   But if gentlemen set out professing a laborious moral, inculcating the beauties of industry, and how it turns everything into gold or pinchbeck, as the matter may be, I and other little children have a right to demand a pure fable along with all this didactic solemnity. "Brothers Mayhew," I exclaim, "if you are going to amuse me, do so.   Awaken my wonder — my laughter — my sense of pleasure; excite me by sweet rural pictures, or brilliant fairy colors, or jovial grotesque perplexities: but if you would instruct, in the name of Justice let us have the real sort of morals.   Sermons and snapdragon do not go well together.   Plum-pudding is good in its way; but a dose of brandy is better with it than a brimming ladleful of virtue.   If there were really your sort of good genius in the world, Socrates ought to have driven off from his trial in a coach-and-six to Xantippe, the loveliest and best-natured of women ; and yet we know to the contrary.   She was a shrew, and her husband was hanged.   A banker's account is a fine thing when properly organized, and the balance agreeably preponderating upon your side ; but there are other accounts we have to settle, and if they look at this sublunary sphere, *mes frères*, and the misfortunes of the good and the prosperity of their opposites — at Genius and Virtue in neglect and penury, and Dulness blundering into success, and Knavery filching Reputation, how can sublime moralists talk about goodness and gold together?   Whatever we may do privately as individuals, let us sublime moralists never publicly worship twopence halfpenny. I, for my part (as one of the aforesaid), will always make an uproar when I meet with any apologue conveying such a foolish signification; and I wish that some Christmas story-tellers would make us a few tales, in which all the rogues should prosper, and all the honest men go to jail, just to correct the present odious tendency of the guides of public taste.

The truth is, that the book of the Brothers Mayhew has so much merit, and is written often with so much brilliancy, and frequently with such dulness, — is so wise at times, and so unsatisfactory in the main, that it seems to me to be the critical office to abuse and deny it altogether, — the which I cordially do; and I warn the public, firstly, that under pretence of giving him a fairy story, the authors of the Good Genius that Turned Everything into, etc., inveigle the reader into a sermon, — that the sermon is quite unsatisfactory, but that the teachers have a plenty of brains to supply their abundance of doctrine.

A very able and complimentary review of this book appeared under the title of "Fairy Politics;" for be it known that Silvio and the fairy discuss a prodigious deal of political ethics together. If any fairy presumes to talk any such nonsense to me, I will do my best from my place in the pit to hiss him off the stage. Had it been any the best known and dearest author — had it been Dickens himself, we should assume the privilege of replying to him with the cat-call, or other Protestant instrument, until the policeman ordered us off the premises.

"To see the faults of a great master, look at his imitators," Reynolds says in his Discourses; and the sins of Mr. Dickens's followers must frighten that gentleman not a little. Almost every one of the Christmas carollers are exaggerating the master's own exaggerations, and caricaturing the face of Nature most shamelessly. Every object in the world is brought to life, and invested with a vulgar knowingness and outrageous jocularity. Winds used to whistle in former days, and oaks to toss their arms in the storm. Winds are now made to laugh, to howl, to scream, to triumph, to sing choruses; trees to squint, to shiver, to leer, to grin, to smoke pipes, dance hornpipes, and smoke those of tobacco. When the Brothers Mayhew wish to be funny and in the fashion, they say, —

"The bright eye of day was now fast getting blood-shot

with the coming cold of night." "A bee goes singing past him, merry as though he had taken a flower cup too much." "Aurora had just begun to light her fire in the grate of the East, and the old Sun was still snug under the blankets of the horizon." "The king thanked his stars that he was not always called upon to leave his bed until the sun had passed his bright copper warming-pan over the damp clouds, and properly aired the atmosphere for his reception."

What clumsy joking this is! what dreary buffooning! by men who can write, too, as well as this! It must be premised that the Princess Amaranth, Silvio's wife, is longing to see her father, the old king, and she breaks her wish to her husband in the Eastern manner by an allegory: —

"'It is related that the Sea-shell was the favorite daughter of the Wave; and that he watched over her with love, shielding her from injury: and folded her in his bosom, and cherished her as his best beloved, ever whispering the music of affection in her ear. Now the Sea-shell loved the noble Rock upon the shore; but the Wave and the Rock were enemies, battling with each other; so that when the haughty Wave found out the love of his rosy-lipped child, he spoke in a voice of rage to her thus: "If thou sighest to wed with yonder Rock, I will cast thee from my bosom, and turn from thee. Go where thou wilt, my anger shall haunt thee, and ever ring in thy ear!" But the Shell loved on, and the swelling Wave dashed her from him. And though the steadfast Rock cherished his ocean Bride with every kindness, and kept her always by his side, still the Shell pined in sorrow; for, as her white-haired sire had said, the anger of the Wave kept ever haunting her, and ringing in her ear.'"

A Fairy lecturer: —

"And so saying the fairy hummed the following charm:—

> "'Quick! let him read the Rocks! and see
> In them Earth's biography!
> Discover Stars beyond the sight!
> Weigh them! and time the speed of Light!
> Within the dew-drop's tiny sphere
> Let Animalcule Worlds appear!
> Each puny Monster let him scan,
> Then mark the Animalcule Man!
> And tracing use in great and small,
> Sees Good in each, and God in all!'

"Then Silvio was lifted up in the air, and carried by winged spirits far into the realms of space, until the world beneath him dwindled into a star, and the stars above him swelled into worlds. And as he flew past them, and they past him, he saw systems rise after systems, and suns upon suns, whose light had never yet reached the eyes of men. And still, as he looked before him, the stars lay thick as sands in the blue sea of the heavens; while, as he travelled on, that which in the distance appeared only one brilliant mass of confusion, separated as he advanced, into new worlds, threading with wondrous order the glittering maze, and spinning in their lightning course, until the air vibrated again, and the universe was melodious with the hum of their motion.

"Suddenly Silvio was on the earth again, with the fairy bee at his side. Then, waving her wand, she showed him a little universe in every atom — a busy world in every drop; and how each grain of the earth was itself a globe teeming with life, and peopled with a manikin race, whose structure was as wonderful and as perfect as his own.

"Then she took him down with her deep into the earth, and turning over with her wand the layers of rocks, as though they were the leaves of a mighty volume, Silvio read within them the Wondrous Tale of Creation. And instantly he lived in the time when man was yet unborn, and monster beasts roamed through the giant forests, the undisputed monarchs of a desert world.

"And again ascending to the surface, the fairy opened to him the affinities of things, showing him how the air he breathed made metals moulder and fires burn; and how the black charcoal was the parent of the glittering diamond; and how the water he drank sprang from the burning of gases that he could neither feel, taste, smell, nor see; and how the atmosphere around him consisted of the selfsame ingredients as the acid, which scarcely any metal could withstand.

"Then she disclosed to him all the mysteries of herbs and minerals, showing him their good and evil powers, and how a little flower or a few small crystals might save or take a life.

"And, lastly, laying bare to him the mechanism of his own mysterious frame, she showed Silvio how the bread he ate became the blood of his arteries and veins; and how the sanguine stream meandered through his body like a ruby river, giving life and vigor to all within its course; and how thin nerves, like threads, worked his puppet limbs, and running to his brain, became the conduits of his will and feelings, and the cords which linked his immortal spirit to the world without.

"Bewildered with wonder, and with his brain aching with the knowledge he had learned, Silvio returned home."

Honest and fine as this writing is, surely it is out of place, and little to be understood by children. I protest against neither pantomimes nor against Walker's Orrery, but I protest against Walker's Orrery in a pantomime. And this is my ground for grumbling against this wise, this ingenious, this clever, but this clumsy and ponderous allegory of the Brothers Mayhew.

But the personification-mania of the Mayhew Brothers is as nothing compared to the same malady in the author of the Yule Log, Mr. A. Chamerovzow, who has summoned the admirable George Cruikshank to his aid, and produced his Christmas legend with gilt leaves and cover; in which there is the usual commodity of fairies, and a prize rustic, who, impelled by the demon of avarice, neglects his friends, knocks down his blessed angel of a wife, turns his seduced daughter out of doors, and is on the point of being murdered by his eldest son; but just at the critical moment of throttling he wakes up and finds it all a dream! Isn't this a novelty? Isn't this a piece of ingenuity? Take your rustic, your fairies, your nightmare, finish off with a plum-pudding and a dance under the holly-bush, and a benign invocation to Christmas, kind hearts, and what not. Are we to have this sort of business forever? *Mon Dieu!* will people never get tired of reading what they know, and authors weary of inventing what everybody has been going on inventing for ages past?

Read the following specimen of the style of Mr. Chamerovzow, and say, Is not the animated landscape nuisance becoming most tolerable, and no longer to be endured? —

"Still the years rolled on, and still the sturdy Beech mocked and braved the Tempest as boldly as ever. In the dingle it stood, unmolested and respected; almost venerated: for now it was known to be haunted, nobody durst expose himself to the fury of the Spirits by attempting to fell it. Nevertheless, some half-dozen times it was tried; but, invariably, the Woodman renounced the task in despair, after he had blunted his best axes, without cutting even through the bark.

"At length, Time beat the tree hollow : it was a long race, notwithstanding, and the gallant old Beech stood it out bravely, and proved itself game to the last; for though its inside was growing weaker and weaker, it still kept up a good appearance; so that one might have taken odds it would never give in, for all that its leaves showed later than they used, and fell earlier. Then its giant foot, which covered no end of ground, grew gouty; and large wooden corns and bunions spread all over it; its trunk, lately so solid and hale, began to crack, and peel, and to come out in broad, unhealthy-looking blotches; let alone that it wheezed asthmatically when the Wind blew; its massive limbs, too, betrayed rheumatic symptoms, and creaked and groaned at every puff.

"And now it was the Wind's turn to laugh at and buffet the Beech, that had for so many years mocked its power, and set its rage at defiance: every time it got a chance, away it swept with a branch, amputating it at one blow, and flinging the disabled member back into its teeth with savage malignity; then it would catch hold of its noble head, and tear, and tug, and pull, and twist it, until obliged to give over from sheer exhaustion; and all to loosen its roots, that it might enjoy the satisfaction of knocking the tree down and trampling upon it: still the old fellow fought hard, and did his best to roar and laugh at his ancient enemy as he used of yore; though anybody might have perceived the difference with only half an eye."

See in the second paragraph what happens to the beech : —

1. He is running a race with Time, who beats him.
2. He is brave and game.
3. His inside is getting weak.
4. His feet are gouty.
5. He has corns and bunions.
6. His body comes out in blotches.
7. He wheezes asthmatically.
8. He has the rheumatism.

There's a collection of cheerful ideas for you! There's a jolly, rollicking, buniony, wheezy, gouty, rheumatic, blotchy Christmas metaphor! Is this the way a gentleman takes to make himself pleasant? Is it ingenious? Is it poetical, or merely foolish, in a word? I believe it to be the easiest and silliest kind of composition in which any poetaster can indulge. I will engage to vivify my tailor's bill; to make a romance out of the heart of my boot-jack; to get up a tender interest for mashed turnips and boiled mutton; to invest my breeches with pathos; to communicate an air of mystery to my coat (dash its buttons!); to make my waistcoat split its sides with jocularity; or so to treat and degrade with clumsy joking, anything natural or supernatural; to make a farce of a thunder storm, or a tragedy of a teapot: but shall we do so? No! in the name of honest humor, no! Suppose Leslie (I take him as the finest humorous artist in England) were to make the chairs and tables in his pictures to squint at you, and set the tongs and pokers grinning, would Sancho and Don Quixote be rendered more funny by these foolish tricks? Suppose when Mr. and Mrs. Keeley want to make you laugh in a comedy, they were to order all the supernumeraries to rush on to the stage and squint and grin; to have all the scenes painted with goggle-eyed caricatures; and all the fiddlers imitating the squeaking of pigs, the braying of donkeys, or what not, on their instruments, would the story and the fun of the play be more comprehensible for this insane interruption? A comic artist, as I take it, has almost the entire range of thought to play upon; the maddest foolery at times becomes him perfectly as the deepest pathos; but this systematic fooling, this dreary cur-and-dry fancy, this grinning without fun, makes my gorge rise, my dear Mr. Yorke; and I protest, for the honor of the Trade. Mr. Merryman in the ring is not a humorist, but a poor, half-witted impostor: I have my own opinion of a fellow who deliberately cuts sham jokes. They should come from a humorist's heart, or they are but acts of dishonesty on his part and forgeries on the public.

In respect to the Drawing-Room Scrap-Book. As the seaman in real life and Cooper's novels knows, by the peculiar gaff in her binnacle, the luff in her topsail-halyards, or what not, his old ship, the "Lively Sally," though the "Mary Anne".is now painted on her stern, so old critical hands, in taking up Mr. Fisher's book, recognize old friends with new titles among the prints — old pictures with wonderful subjects marvellously gathered together from all quarters. Pictorially, the Drawing-Room Scrap-Book is a sea-pie, made up of scraps that have been served at many tables before. Her Majesty, in company with

Richard Cobden and Charles Villiers; the Chinese necromancers; Lord Hardinge welcoming in the spring; Sir Robert Sale at a Spanish bull-fight in the Mocenigo Palace. A rich and wonderful hash indeed!

The fair editor, Mrs. Norton, has been painted by two artists in the present volume; by Mr. Carrick on ivory, and by Sir Edward Lytton Bulwer Lytton in a kind of verses, against which we put a strenuous protest. Sir Bulwer calls her a radiant Stranger — a spirit of the Star, and a daughter of the Beam, with a large B, meaning that there is something quite unearthly in the appearance of the fair editor of the Drawing-Room Scrap-Book; that it is clear to Sir Lytton's perceptions that she belongs to another orb, in which he, Sir Edward (being possibly likewise of an angelical supernaturality himself), has made her acquaintance. He states, that while mere mortals have changes of comfort and care in life, to supernatural beings, like the Honorable Mrs. Norton, our very air is silent pain — a heavy pain; in fact, that they are doomed to a perpetual sadness, under the never-ending domination of the Old Blue Devil.

Let us hope that the statement is erroneous, and the pedigree not also correct. Over the very verses in which Sir Edward Bulwer Lytton makes the above extraordinary assertions, some downright prose writer says the Hon. Mrs. Norton is "Second daughter of Thomas Sheridan, Esq. (son of the Right Hon. R. B. Sheridan and his first wife, the celebrated Miss Lindley) and Caroline Henrietta Callander, daughter of Colonel Callander, of Craigforth, and Lady Elizabeth MacDonnell." How can a man, in the face of such a genealogy, declare that Mrs. Norton's parent was a Beam, with a large B? Isn't the prose-tree a sufficient pedigree? Had Genius ever a directer descent? "No human beauty," says the baronet, —

> " No human beauty ever bore
>   An aspect thus divine :
> The crown the brows of seraphs wear,
>   Hath left its mark on thine, —
> The unconscious glories round thee, bear
>   The stamp divine
>   Of One divine,
> Who trod the spheres of yore."

Come, come, Sir Bulwer, how can you talk to a lady so to her face? Whereabouts have you seen seraphs and their

crowns ?   When made acquaintance with ones divine ?
What are all these attitudes, platitudes, beatitudes ?   Isn't
a woman good enough for you that inherits Sheridan's
genius and sweet Cecilia's eyes and voice, but you must
assume an inspired air, and declare she is a stray angel ?
In the picture of the lady, she has a black velvet band
round her forehead, and buttons on her dress.   Fancy an
angel in buttons !   No ! no !   There's some error in the
Bard's (or, to speak more correctly, the Bart's) description.
This sort of writing, this flimsy, mystical, namby pamby,
we hold to be dangerous to man and reprehensible in
Barts.   When Irreverence puts on a sanctified look, when
Mayfair begins to have revelations, when — but let us restrain our beautiful and outraged feelings, and return to
the matter in hand.

The fact is, then (while strenuously denying the Beam
in Mrs. Norton's family-tree — indeed it is the big B buzzing about it that roused the critical peevishness), that
though we fearlessly assert Mrs. Norton to be only a
woman, and always a woman, Mr. Carrick's picture no more
represents her magnificent beauty than Mr. Joseph Hume
resembles Apollo.   To have seen it is to have seen something in history.   Would you not like to have seen Helen
or Cleopatra, Marie Antoinette (about whose beauty we
doubt whether the late Mr. Burke did not make exaggerated statements), Fair Rosamond, or the Queen of
Prussia, or Fox's Duchess of Devonshire, or that sweet
ancestor of Mrs. Norton's own, who smiles on Reynold's
canvas with such ravishing, delicious purity — the charming, charming Lindley ?   As good as this a man may haply
see, this very season, at the French play.   There these eyes
beheld it ; not a daughter of a Beam — not a spirit of a Star,
but a woman in black, with buttons — those very buttons
probably — only a woman.   Is it not enough, Sir Lytton ?
Stars and Beams ! — buttons and buttonhooks !   Quando
invenies parem ?   In our presence no man shall call such a
woman a Spirit without a word in his ear.

And now to speak of the moral part, the soul above buttons.   Of all the genuine poets I ever — but perhaps we
had best not.   When he has a mind to pick a hole in a
man's coat, who so active and mischievous as your humble
servant ?   When he wishes to address a person in terms of
unbounded laudation and respect, this present critic stut-
ters and bungles most awkwardly — makes a dash for his

hat, and a rush out of the room, perfectly overpowered by modesty. What a charming characteristic and confession! But did we pray and criticise, dear Miss S., in early days, when we went to hear Pasta sing? Hearken to this sad tale of false love and broken vows : —

" He remembers the light of her smile, — of that smile, in itself a
    caress,
So warmly and softly it fell, on the heart it was willing to bless;
He remembers the touch of her hand, as it lay gently clasped in his
    own,
And he crushes the flowers which she gave, and bows down his head
    with a groan.
How oft in the twilight of eve, — how oft in the glory of day, —
Hath she leaned on his bosom and vowed — the vows she has lived
    to betray.
Oh! lovely as angels above, — oh! false as the devils below,
Oh! hope that seemed more than divine, — oh! fountain of fathom-
    less woe,
How couldst thou forsake me! — Return, — return, still beloved, as
    thou art:
Wide open yet standeth the door of thy home in this desolate heart:
Return! — We will bury the past, — and the light on my eyelids shall
    beam
With the rapture of one who at dawn breaks the spell of a terrible
    dream!
In vain: even now, while I reel, — blind, helpless, and faint with
    despair —
Thou bendest with triumphs to hear the new voice that whispers
    thee fair.
Oh! fickle, and shallow, and cold — in all but thy fever of blood —
Unfit, from thy nature, to cling to aught that was earnest and good:
Thy love was an instinct of sex; it palled, when thy passion was o'er,
Like a wild bird that answers in spring the mate it remembers no
    more.
I shame that a creature so light should bid me thus quiver and
    bleed, —
I shame to have leaned and been pierced by my trust in so brittle a
    reed, —
I scorn thee! Go forth to the world, a parade of thy beauty to
    make;
Thrill, fever, and madden more hearts; — let them pine, — let them
    die, — for thy sake!
Let them yield up their manhood of soul, and adore their ideal in
    thee.
I laugh, as thou breathest false vows, — to break them again, as
    with me;
I laugh, as they anchor their hopes, where the quicksand forbids
    them to live;
Will they glean from the dregs of thy heart what the fresh faith of
    youth could not give ?
Let them sink, let them perish, — like me, — of thy smiles and thy
    glances bereft, —
Yet, if thou wert in sorrow and pain, — would I leave thee, — as I
    have been left ? "

Did we prate and criticise when. we heard Pasta sing ?
Didn't you, on the contrary, come closer and closer, and
sit quite silent, and listen with all your soul ?   And I'm
not sure that we applauded much when the song was over.
A great clapping of hands is but a coarse sort of sympathy.
We applaud in that way when a musical mountebank spins
down the scale, or leaps astonishingly over a bravura.   But
before a great artist we are silent.   And is not this a true
poet ?   What a mournful, artless beauty is here !   What a
brooding, tender woman's heart !

What has struck myself and Miss Smith with especial
admiration in these songs of Mrs. Norton and her accomplished sister, Lady Dufferin, is the spontaneity of them.
They sing without labor, like birds : as if it were their
nature : —

> " Pouring their full heart
> In profuse strains of unpremeditated art ! "

There is something surprising in the faculty ; and one
listens with charmed astonishment to the song, sometimes
gay, often sad, always tender and musical.

I have, I trust, been tolerably ill-humored hitherto ; but
what man can go on grumbling in the presence of such an
angelical spirit as Hans Christian Andersen ?   Seeing him
praised in the *Athenæum* journal, I was straight put away
from reading a word of Hans' other works ; and it was only
last night, when going to bed, perfectly bored with the
beef-fed English fairies, their hob-nailed gambols, and ele-
phantine friskiness, his Shoes of Fortune and his Wonderful Stories came under the eyes of your humble servant.
Heaven bless Hans Christian !   Here are fairies !   Here is
fancy, and graceful wit, and delicate humor, and sweet,
naïve kindness, flowing from the heart !   Here is frolic
without any labor.   Here is admirable fooling without any
consciousness or degradation !   Though we have no sort of
respect for a great, hulking, whiskered, red-faced, middle-
aged man, who dresses himself in a pinafore and affects to
frolic like a baby, may we not be charmed by the play
prattle of a child ?   And Hans Christian Andersen so affects me.

Every page of the volumes sparkles with delightful grace
and genial fancy.   Hans and you are friends for life after
an hour's talk with him.   I shake thy hands, Hans Christian, thou kindly prattler and warbler !   A happy Christ-

mas to thee, thou happy-minded Christian! You smile,
dear Miss Smith! When we become acquainted with so
delicate and charming a genius, have we no right to be
thankful? Yes: let us respect every one of those friends
whom Heaven has sent us, — those sweet Christian messen-
gers of peace and good-will.

Do you remember the dainty description of the Prioress
in Chaucer? It has lately been quoted in Leigh Hunt's
charming volume of Wit and Humor, and concludes with
an account of a certain talisman this delicate creature
wore, —

> " About hire arm a broche of golde ful shene,
> On which was first ywritten a crouned A,
> And after *Amor vincit omnia.*"

The works of the real humorist always have this sacred
press mark, I think. Try Shakespeare, first of all: Cervantes, Addison, poor Dick Steele, and dear Harry Fielding: the tender and delightful Jean Paul, Sterne, and
Scott, — and Love is the humorist's best characteristic, and
gives that charming ring to their laughter in which all the
good-natured world joins in chorus. Foremost of all, at
present, I think Mr. Dickens may assume the Amor and
Crown for his badge and cognizance. His humanity has
mastered the sympathy of almost all: of wise men, of dullards, of all sorts of honest people. He makes good jokes,
bad jokes, the best and the worst jokes indeed possible.
The critics fasten on the latter and sneer: the public sympathy kicks the flimsy barriers away, and pours on. The
kindly spirit melts all critical doubts. Can he be worthless, or a sceptic, in whom all the world is putting faith —
who has the ear of all England — who has done so much to
make the poor known to the rich, and reconcile each to the
other, as much as Hansard, ay, or Exeter Hall? Is this a
man to be railed at by his literary brethren? In the
American war (this is an historical allegory), the man who
sneered at Washington most, was that brave officer, and
spotless patriot, General Arnold.

If I judge Mr. Dickens's present volume rightly, it has
been the author's aim, not to produce a prose tale of
mingled fun and sadness, and a close imitation of life,
but a prose poem, designed to awaken emotions tender,
mirthful, pastoral, wonderful. As in some of Mr. Maclise's
charming designs to the book, the costume of this figure is

rather a hint of the costume of the last century than a portrait of it, so the writer's characters seem to me modified — prettified, so to speak. The action of the piece you see clearly enough, but the actors speak and move to measure and music. The drolls are more violently funny; the serious heroes and heroines more gracefully and faultlessly beautiful. Such figures are never seen among real country people. Nor more are Tityrus and Melibœus like, or Hermann and Dorothea like, or Taglioni; bounding through air in gauze, like a Scotch peasant girl. Tityre tu patulæ is a ballet in hexameters; the Sylphide, a poem performed on the toes; these charming little books of Mr. Dickens's are chorals for Christmas executed in prose.

Last year the critics were specially outraged by the famous clock-and-kettle overture of the Christmas piece. "Is this truth, is this nature?" cries the Cynic, growling from his tub. You might say, Is it the multiplication table, or is it the *pons asinorum?* It is not intended to be true or natural, as I hold; it is intended to be a brisk, dashing, startling caricature. The poet does not want you to believe him, he wants to provoke your mirth and wonder. He is appealing, not to your reason and feelings as in a prose narrative, but to your fancy and feelings. He peoples the familiar hearth with sprites, and the church-tower with goblins; all the commonest objects swarm with preternatural life. The haymaker has convulsions, the warming-pan is vivified, the chairs are ambulatory, and the poker writhes with life. In the midst of these wonders goes on a little, common, kind-hearted, tender, every-day story of poverty averted, true hearts rewarded, the poor loving one another, a tyrant grotesquely punished. It is not much. But in these performances the music is everything. The Zauberflöte or the Barbière are not like life; *mais ——— !*

That is why we lose patience or affect to have no respect for minor performers. Numbers of unknown fiddlers, hearing of the success of Mr. Dickens's opera, rush forward fiddle in hand, of the very same shape by the very same maker. "Come and hear our partition," they say; "see how we have set the Barber to music, and what tunes we make Papanego sing!" Away with your miserable fiddlesticks, misguided people! You play after such a master! You take a bad moment. We may have heard some indifferent music from this composer, and some very weak and bad music from him too; but we have had, likewise, strains so delightful and noble, specimens of skill so unapproachable by others, that we protest against all followers. The grumbling fit seizes on me again as I think of them, and I long for some one to devour.

Ha! what have we here? M. A. Titmarsh's Christmas Book — Mrs. Perkins's Ball. Dedicated to the Mulligan of Ballymulligan. Ballymulligan! Ballyfiddlestick! What, you, too, Mr. Titmarsh? You, you sneering wretch, setting up a Christmas book of your own? This, then, is the meaning of your savage feelings towards "the minor fiddlers!" Is your kit, sirrah, any bigger than theirs? You, who in the columns of this very Magazine have sneered at the works of so many painters, look at your own performances! Some of your folks have scarcely more legs than Miss Biffin; they have fins instead of hands — they squint almost every one of them!

All this is quite true. But see where we have come to! to the very last page of the very last sheet; and the writer is called upon to stop just at the very moment he was going to cut his own head off.

So have I seen Mr. Clown (in that Christmas drama which has been foremost in my thoughts during all the above meditations) set up the gallows, adjust the rope, try the noose curiously, and — tumble head over heels.

STRICTURES ON PICTURES.

A LETTER FROM MICHAEL ANGELO TITMARSH, ESQUIRE, TO
MONSIEUR ANATOLE VICTOR ISIDOR HYACINTHE ACHILLE
HERCULE DE BRICABRAC, PEINTRE D'HISTOIRE, RUE
MOUFFETARD, À PARIS.

[*Fraser's Magazine, June*, 1838.]

LORD'S HOTEL, NEW STREET, COVENT GARDEN:
Tuesday, 15th May.

I PROPOSE to be both learned and pleasant in my remarks
upon the exhibitions here; for I know, my dear Bricabrac,
that it is your intention to translate this letter into French,
for the benefit of some of your countrymen, who are anxious about the progress of the fine arts — when I say some,
I mean all, for, thanks to your Government patronage, your
magnificent public galleries, and, above all, your delicious
sky and sunshine, there is not a scavenger in your nation
who has not a feeling for the beauty of Nature, which is,
my dear Anatole, neither more nor less than Art.

You know nothing about art in this country — almost as
little as we know of French art. One Gustave Planche, who
makes visits to London, and writes accounts of pictures in
your reviews, is, believe me, an impostor. I do not mean
a private impostor, for I know not whether Planche is a
real or assumed name, but simply a quack on matters of
art. Depend on it, my dear young friend, that there is
nobody like Titmarsh: you will learn more about the arts
in England from this letter than from anything in or out
of print.

Well, then, every year, at the commencement of this
blessed month of May, wide open the doors of three picture
galleries, in which figure all the works of genius which our
brother artists have produced during the whole year. I
wish you could see my historical picture of "Heliogabalus
in the Ruins of Carthage," or the full-length of Sir Samuel
Hicks and his Lady, — sitting in a garden light, Lady H.
reading the "Book of Beauty," Sir Samuel catching a butterfly which is settling on a flower-pot. This, however, is

all egotism. I am not going to speak of *my* works, which are pretty well known in Paris already, as I flatter myself, but of other artists — some of them men of merit — as well as myself.

Let us commence, then, with the commencement — the Royal Academy. That is held in one wing of a little building like a gin-shop, which is near St. Martin's Church. In the other wing is our National Gallery. As for the building, you must not take *that* as a specimen of our skill in the fine arts; come down the Seven Dials, and I will show you many modern structures of which the architect deserves far higher credit.

But, bad as the place is — a pygmy abortion, in lieu of a noble monument to the greatest school of painting in the greatest country of the modern world (you may be angry, but I'm right in *both* cases) — bad as the outside is, the interior, it must be confessed, is marvellously pretty, and convenient for the reception and exhibition of the pictures it will hold. Since the old pictures have got their new gallery, and their new scouring, one hardly knows them. O Ferdinand, Ferdinand, that *is* a treat, that National Gallery, and no mistake! I shall write to you fourteen or fifteen long letters about it some day or other. The apartment devoted to the Academy exhibition is equally commodious: a small room for miniatures and aquarelles, another for architectural drawings, and three saloons for pictures — all very small, but well lighted and neat; no interminable passage, like your five hundred yards at the Louvre, with a slippery floor, and tiresome straggling cross-lights. Let us buy a catalogue, and walk straight into the gallery, however: — we have been a long time talking, *de omnibus rebus*, at the door.

Look, my dear Isidor, at the first names in the catalogue, and thank your stars for being in such good company. Bless us and save us, what a power of knights is here!

Sir William Beechey.
Sir Martin Shee.
Sir David Wilkie.
Sir Augustus Callcott.
Sir W. J. Newton.
Sir Geoffrey Wyattville.
Sir Francis Chantrey.
Sir Richard Westmacott.
Sir Michael Angelo Titmarsh —

not yet, that is; but I shall be, in course, when our little liege lady — Heaven bless her! — has seen my portrait of Sir Sam and Lady Hicks.

If all these gentlemen in the list of Academicians and Associates are to have titles of some sort or other, I should propose, —

1. Baron BRIGGS. (At the very least, he is out and out the best portrait-painter of the set.)

2. DANIEL, PRINCE MACLISE. (His Royal Highness's pictures place him very near to the throne indeed.)

3. Edwin, Earl of Landseer.

4. The Lord Charles Landseer.

5. The Duke of Etty.

6. Archbishop Eastlake.

7. His Majesty KING MULREADY.

King Mulready, I repeat, in double capitals; for if this man has not the crowning picture of the exhibition, I am no better than a Dutchman. His picture represents the "Seven Ages," as described by a poet whom you have heard of — one Shakespeare, a Warwickshire man: and there they are, all together; the portly justice and the quarrelsome soldier; the lover leaning apart, and whispering sweet things in his pretty mistress's ear; the baby hanging on her gentle mother's bosom; the schoolboy, rosy and lazy; the old man crabbed and stingy; and the old old man of all, *sans* teeth, *sans* eyes, *sans* ears, *sans* everything — but why describe them? You will find the thing better done in Shakespeare, or possibly translated by some of your Frenchmen. I can't say much about the drawing of this picture, for here and there are some queer-looking limbs; but — oh, Anatole! — the intention is godlike. Not one of those figures but has a grace and a soul of his own: no conventional copies of the stony antique; no distorted caricatures, like those of your "classiques," David, Girodet, and Co. (the impostors!) — but such expressions as a great poet would draw, who thinks profoundly and truly, and never forgets (he could not if he would) grace and beauty withal. The color and manner of this noble picture are neither of the Venetian school, nor the Florentine, nor the English, but of the Mulready school. Ah! my dear Floridor! I wish that you and I, ere we die, may have erected such a beautiful monument to hallow and perpetuate our names. Our children — my boy, Sebastian Piombo Titmarsh — will see this picture in his old age, hanging by the side of the

Raffaelles in our National Gallery. I sometimes fancy, in the presence of such works of genius as this, that my picture of Sir Sam and Lady Hicks is but a magnificent error after all, and that it will die away, and be forgotten.

To this, then, of the whole gallery, I accord the palm, and cannot refrain from making a little sketch, illustrative of my feelings.

I have done everything, you see, very accurately, except Mr. Mulready's face; for, to say truth, I never saw that gentleman, and have no idea of his personal appearance.

TITMARSH PLACING THE LAUREL-WREATH ON THE BROWS
OF MULREADY.

Near to "All the world's a stage" is a charming picture, by Archbishop Eastlake; so denominated by me, because the rank is very respectable, and because there is a certain purity and religious feeling in all Mr. Eastlake does, which eminently entitles him to the honors of the prelacy. In this picture, Gaston de Foix (he whom Titian painted, his mistress buckling on his armor) is parting from his mistress. A fair peaceful garden is round about them; and here his lady sits and clings to him, as though she would cling forever. But, look! yonder stands the page and the horse pawing; and, beyond the wall which bounds the quiet garden and flowers, you see the spears and pennons of knights, the banners of King Louis and De Foix, "the thunderbolt of Italy." Long shining rows of steel-clad men are marching stately by; and with them must ride Count Gaston — to conquer and die at Ravenna. You can read his history, my dear friend, in Lacretelle, or Brantôme; only, perhaps, not so well expressed as it has just been by me.

Yonder is Sir David Wilkie's grand picture, "Queen Victoria holding her First Council." A marvellous painting, in which one admires the richness of the color, the breadth of light and shadow, the graceful dignity and beauty of the principal figure, and the extraordinary skill with which all the figures have been grouped, so as to produce a grand and simple effect. What can one say more, but admire the artist who has made, out of such unpoetical materials as a table of red cloth, and fifty unoccupied middle-aged gentlemen, a beautiful and interesting picture? Sir David has a charming portrait, too, of Mrs. Maberly, in dark crimson velvet, and delicate white hat and feathers: a marvel of color, though somewhat askew in the drawing.

The Earl of Landseer's best picture, to my thinking, is that which represents her Majesty's favorite dogs and parrot. He has, in painting, an absolute mastery over

Κύνεσσιν
Οἰωνοῖσί τε πᾶσι —

that is, he can paint all manner of birds and beasts as nobody else can. To tell you a secret, I do not think he understands how to paint the great beast, man, quite so well; or, at least, to do what is the highest quality of an artist, to place *a soul* under the ribs as he draws them. They are, if you like, the most dexterous pictures that ever were painted, but not *great* pictures. I would much rather look at yonder rough Leslie than at all the wonderful painting of parrots or greyhounds, though done to a hair or a feather.

Leslie is the only man in this country who translates Shakespeare into form and color. Old Shallow and Sir Hugh, Slender and his man Simple, pretty Anne Page and the Merry Wives of Windsor, are here joking with the fat knight; who, with a monstrous gravity and profound brazen humor, is narrating some tale of his feats with the wild Prince and Poins. Master Brooke is offering a tankard to Master Slender, who will not drink, forsooth.

This picture is executed with the utmost simplicity, and almost rudeness; but is charming, from its great truth of effect and expression. Wilkie's pictures (in his latter style) seem to begin where Leslie's end; the former's men and women look as if *the bodies had been taken out of them*, and only the surface left. Lovely as the Queen's figure is, for instance, it looks like a spirit, and not a woman; one may almost see through her into the waistcoat of Lord Lansdowne, and so on through the rest of the transparent heroes and statesmen of the company.

Opposite the Queen is another charming performance of Sir David — a bride dressing, amidst a rout of bridesmaids and relations. Some are crying, some are smiling, some are pinning her gown; a back door is open, and a golden sun shines into the room which contains a venerable-looking bed and tester, probably that in which the dear girl is to — but *parlons d'autres choses*. The color of this picture is delicious, and the effect faultless: Sir David does everything for a picture nowadays but the *drawing*. Who knows? Perhaps it is as well left out.

Look yonder, down to the ground, and admire a most beautiful fantastic Ariel.

> "On the bat's back do I fly,
> After sunset merrily."

Merry Ariel lies at his ease, and whips with gorgeous peacock's feather his courser, flapping lazy through the golden evening sky. This exquisite little picture is the work of Mr. Severn, an artist who has educated his taste and his hand in the early Roman school. He has not the dash and dexterity of the latter which belong to some of our painters, but he possesses that solemn earnestness and simplicity of mind and purpose which make a religion of art, and seem to be accorded only to a few in our profession. I have heard a pious pupil of Mr. Ingres (the head of your academy at Rome) aver stoutly, that, in matters of art, Titian was Antichrist, and Rubens, Martin Luther. They came with their brilliant colors and dashing worldly notions, upsetting that beautiful system of faith in which art had lived hitherto. Portraits of saints and martyrs, with pure eyes turned heavenward; and (as all true sanctity will) making those pure who came within their reach, now gave way to wicked likenesses of men of blood, or dangerous, devilish, sensual portraits of tempting women. Before Titian, a picture was the labor of years. Why did this reformer ever come among us, and show how it might be done in a day? He drove the good angels away from painters' easels, and called down a host of voluptuous spirits instead, who ever since have held the mastery there.

Only a few artists of our country (none in yours, where the so-called Catholic school is a mere theatrical folly), and some among the Germans, have kept to the true faith, and eschewed the temptations of Titian and his like. Mr. Eastlake is one of these. Who does not recollect his portrait of Miss Bury? Not a simple woman — the lovely daughter of the authoress of "Love," "Flirtation," and other remarkable works — but a glorified saint. Who does not remember his Saint Sebastian; his body bare, his eyes cast melancholy down; his limbs, as yet untouched by the arrows of his persecutors, tied to the fatal tree? Those two pictures of Mr. Eastlake would merit to hang in a gallery where there were only Raffaelles besides. Mr. Severn is another of the school. I don't know what hidden and indefinable charm there is in his simple pictures; but I never can look at them without a certain emotion of awe — without that thrill of the heart with which one hears country children sing the Old Hundredth, for instance. The singers are rude, perhaps, and the voices shrill; but the melody is still pure and godlike. Some such majestic and pious harmony is there in these pictures of Mr. Severn. Mr. Mulready's mind has lately gained this same kind of inspiration. I know no one else who possesses it, except, perhaps, myself. Without flattery, I may say that my picture of "Heliogabalus at Carthage" is *not* in the popular taste, and has about it some faint odor of celestial incense.

Do not, my dear Anatole, consider me too great an ass for persisting upon this point, and exemplifying Mr. Severn's picture of the "Crusaders catching a First View of Jerusalem" as an instance. Godfrey and Tancred, Raymond and Ademar, Beamond and Rinaldo, with Peter and the Christian host, behold at length the day dawning.

> "E quando il sol gli aridi campi fiede
>   Con raggi assai ferventi, e in alto sorge;
> Ecco apparir Gerusalem si vede,
>   Ecce additar Gerusalem si scorge,
> Ecco da mille voci unitamente
> Gerusalemme salutar si sente!"

Well, Godfrey and Tancred, Peter, and the rest, look like little wooden dolls; and as for the horses belonging to the crusading cavalry, I have seen better in gingerbread. But, what then? There is a higher ingredient in beauty than mere form; a skilful hand is only the second artistical quality, worthless, my Anatole, without the first, which is *a great heart.* This picture is beautiful, in spite of its defects, as many women are. Mrs. Titmarsh is beautiful, though she weighs nineteen stone.

Being on the subject of religious pictures, what shall I say of Mr. Ward's ? Anything so mysteriously hideous was never seen before now; they are worse than all the horrors in your Spanish Gallery at Paris. As Eastlake's are of the Catholic, these may be called of the Muggletonian school of art; monstrous, livid, and dreadful as the dreams of a man in the scarlet fever. I would much sooner buy a bottled baby with two heads as a pleasing ornament for my cabinet; and should be afraid to sit alone in a room with " ignorance, envy, and jealousy filling the throat, and widening the mouth of calumny endeavoring to bear down truth ! "

Mr. Maclise's picture of "Christmas" you will find excellently described in the May number of a periodical of much celebrity among us, called *Fraser's Magazine.* Since the circulation of that miscellany is almost as extensive in Paris as in London, it is needless in this letter to go over beaten ground, and speak at length of the plot of this remarkable picture. There are five hundred merry figures painted on this canvas, gobbling, singing, kissing, carousing. A line of jolly serving men troop down the hall stairs, and bear the boar's head in procession up to the daïs, where sits the good old English gentleman, and his guests and family; a set of mummers and vassals are crowded round a table gorging beef and wassail; a bevy of blooming girls and young men are huddled in a circle, and play at hunt the slipper. Of course, there are plenty of stories told at the huge hall fire, and kissing under the glistening mistletoe-bough. But I wish you could see the wonderful accuracy with which all these figures are drawn, and the extraordinary skill with which the artist has managed to throw into a hundred different faces a hundred different characters and individualities of joy. Every one of these little people is smiling, but each has his own particular smile. As for the coloring of the picture, it is, between ourselves, atrocious; but a man cannot have all the merits at once. Mr. Maclise has for his share, humor such as few painters ever possessed, and a power of drawing such as never was possessed by *any other ;* no, not by one, from Albert Dürer downwards. His scene from the

"Vicar of Wakefield " is equally charming. Moses's shining grinning face; the little man in red who stands on tiptoe, and painfully scrawls his copy; and the youngest of the family of the Primroses, who learns his letters on his father's knee, are perfect in design and expression. What might not this man do, if he would read and meditate a little, and profit by the works of men whose taste and education were superior to his own.

Mr. Charles Landseer has two *tableaux de genre*, which possess very great merit. His characters are a little too timid, perhaps, as Mr. Maclise's are too bold; but the figures are beautifully drawn, the coloring and effect excellent, and the accessories painted with great faithfulness and skill. "The Parting Benison" is, perhaps, the more interesting picture of the two.

And now we arrive at Mr. Etty, whose rich, luscious pencil has covered a hundred glowing canvases, which every painter must love. I don't know whether the Duke has this year produced anything which one might have expected from a man of his rank and consequence. He is, like great men, lazy, or indifferent, perhaps, about public approbation; and also, like great men, somewhat too luxurious and fond of pleasure. For instance, here is a picture of a sleepy nymph, most richly painted; but tipsy-looking, coarse, and so naked as to be unfit for appearance among respectable people at an exhibition. You will understand what I mean. There are some figures without a rag to cover them, which look modest and decent for all that; and others, which may be clothed to the chin, and yet are not fit for modest eyes to gaze on. *Verbum sat* — this naughty " Somnolency " ought to go to sleep in her night-gown.

But here is a far nobler painting, — the Prodigal kneeling down lonely in the stormy evening, and praying to Heaven for pardon. It is a grand and touching picture; and looks as large as if the three-foot canvas had been twenty. His wan wretched figure and clasped hands are lighted up by the sunset; the clouds are livid and heavy; and the wind is howling over the solitary common, and numbing the chill limbs of the poor wanderer. A goat and a boar are looking at him with horrid obscene eyes. They are the demons of Lust and Gluttony, which have brought him to this sad pass. And there seems no hope, no succor, no ear for the prayer of this wretched, wayworn, miserable man who kneels there alone, shuddering. Only above, in the gusty blue sky, you see a glistening, peaceful silver star, which points to home and hope, as clearly as if the little star were a signpost, and home at the very next turn of the road.

Away, then, O conscience-stricken prodigal! and you shall find a good father, who loves you; and an elder brother, who hates you — but never mind that; and a dear, kind, stout, old mother, who liked you twice as well as the elder, for all his goodness and psalm-singing, and has a tear and a prayer for you night and morning; and a pair of gentle sisters, maybe; and a poor young thing down in the village, who has never forgotten your walks in the quiet nut-woods, and the birds' nests you brought her, and the big boy you thrashed, because he broke the eggs: he is squire now, the big boy, and would marry her, but she will not have him — not she! — her thoughts are with her dark-eyed, bold-browed, devil-may-care playmate, who swore she should be his little wife — and then went to college — and then came back sick and changed — and then got into debt — and then —— But never mind, man! down to her at once. She will pretend to be cold at first, and then shiver and turn red and deadly pale; and then she tumbles into your arms, with a gush of sweet tears, and a pair of rainbows in her soft eyes, welcoming the sunshine back to her bosom again! To her, man! — never fear, miss! Hug him, and kiss him, as though you would draw the heart from his lips.

When she has done, the poor thing falls stone-pale and sobbing on young Prodigal's shoulder; and he carries her quite gently, to that old bench where he carved her name fourteen years ago, and steals his arm round her waist, and kisses her hand, and soothes her. Then comes out the poor widow, her mother, who is pale and tearful too, and tries to look cold and unconcerned. She kisses her daughter, and leads her trembling into the house. "You will come to us to-morrow, Tom?" says she, as she takes his hand at the gate.

To-morrow! To be sure he will; and this very night, too, after supper with the old people. (Young Squire Prodigal never sups; and has found out that he must ride into town, to arrange about a missionary meeting with the Reverend Doctor Slackjaw.) To be sure Tom Prodigal will go: the moon will be up, and who knows but Lucy may be looking at it about twelve o'clock. At one, back trots the young squire, and he sees two people whispering at a window; and he gives something very like a curse, as he digs into the ribs of his mare, and canters, clattering, down the silent road.

Yes — but, in the mean time, there is the old housekeeper, with "Lord bless us!" and "Heaven save us!" and "Who'd have thought ever again to see his dear face? And master to forget it all, who swore so dreadful that he would never see him! — as for missis, she always loved him." There, I say, is the old housekeeper, logging the fire, airing the sheets, and flapping the feather beds — for Master Tom's room has never been used this many a day; and the young ladies have got some flowers for his chimney-piece, and put back his mother's portrait, which they have had in their room ever since he went away and forgot it, woe is me! And old John, the butler, coachman, footman, valet, factotum, consults with master about supper.

"What can we have?" says master; "all the shops are shut, and there's nothing in the house."

John. — "No, no more there isn't; only Guernsey's calf. Butcher kill'd'n yesterday, as your honor knowth."

Master. — "Come, John, a calf's enough. Tell the cook to *send us up that.*"

And he gives a hoarse haw! haw! at his wit; and Mrs. Prodigal smiles too, and says, "Ah, Tom Prodigal, you were always a merry fellow!"

Well, John Footman carries down the message to cook, who is a country wench, and takes people at their word; and what do you think she sends up?

Top Dish.

Fillet of veal, and bacon on the side-table.

Bottom Dish.

Roast ribs of veal.

In the Middle.

Calves'-head soup (*à la tortue*).
Veal broth.

Between.

Boiled knuckle of veal, and parsley sauce.
Stewed veal, with brown sauce and forced-meat balls.

Entremets.

Veal olives (for sauce, see stewed veal).
Veal cutlets (*panées, sauce piquante*).
Ditto (*en papillote*).
Scotch collops.
Fricandeau of veal (*piqué au lard à la chicorée*).
Minced veal.
Blanquet of veal.

Second Course.

Curry of calves'-head.
Sweetbreads.
Calves'-foot jelly.

See, my dear Anatole, what a world of thought can be conjured up out of a few inches of painted canvas.

And now we come to the great and crowning picture of the exhibition, my own historical piece, namely, "Heliogabalus in the Ruins of Carthage." In this grand and finished perform ——

. . . .

Mr. Titmarsh's letter stops, unfortunately, here. We found it, at midnight, the 15th–16th May, in a gutter of Saint Martin's Lane, whence a young gentleman had been just removed by the police. It is to be presumed that intoxication could be his only cause for choosing such a sleeping-place, at such an hour; and it had probably commenced as he was writing the above fragment. We made inquiries at Lord's Coffee House, of Mr. Moth (who, from being the active and experienced head waiter, is now the obliging landlord of that establishment), and were told that a gentleman unknown had dined there at three, and had been ceaselessly occupied in writing and drinking until a quarter to twelve, when he abruptly left the house. Mr. Moth regretted to add, that the stranger had neglected to pay for thirteen glasses of gin and water, half a pint of porter, a bottle of soda-water, and a plate of ham sandwiches, which he had consumed in the course of the day.

We have paid Mr. Moth (whose very moderate charges, and excellent stock of wines and spirits, cannot be too highly commended), and shall gladly hand over to Mr. Titmarsh the remaining sum which is his due. Has he any more of his rhapsody ? — O. Y.

A SECOND LECTURE ON THE FINE ARTS, BY MICHAEL ANGELO TITMARSH, ESQUIRE.

THE EXHIBITIONS.

[*Fraser's Magazine, June*, 1838.]

JACK STRAW'S CASTLE, HAMPSTEAD.

My dear Bricabrac, — You, of course, remember the letter on the subject of our exhibitions which I addressed to you this time last year. As you are now lying at the Hôtel Dieu, wounded during the late unsuccessful *émeute* (which I think, my dear friend, is the seventeenth you have been engaged in), and as the letter which I wrote last year was received with unbounded applause by the people here, and caused a sale of three or four editions of this Magazine, I cannot surely, my dear Bricabrac, do better than send you another sheet or two, which may console you under your present bereavement, and at the same time amuse the British public, who now know their friend Titmarsh as well as you in France know that little scamp Thiers.

Well, then, from "Jack Straw's Castle," an hotel on Hampstead's breezy heath, which Keats, Wordsworth, Leigh Hunt, F. W. N. Bayley, and others of our choicest spirits, have often patronized, and a heath of which every pool, bramble, furze-bush-with-clothes-hanging-on-it-to-dry, steep, stock, stone, tree, lodging-house, and distant gloomy background of London city, or bright green stretch of sunshiny Hertfordshire meadows, has been depicted by our noble English landscape-painter, Constable, in his own Constabulary way — at "Jack Straw's Castle," I say, where I at this present moment am located (not that it matters in the least, but the world is always interested to know where men of genius are accustomed to disport themselves), I cannot do better than look over the heap of picture-gallery catalogues which I brought with me from London, and communicate to you, my friend in Paris, my remarks thereon.

A man with five shillings to spare may at this present

moment half kill himself with pleasure in London town, and in the neighborhood of Pall Mall, by going from one picture gallery to another, and examining the beauties and absurdities which are to be found in each. There is first the National Gallery (entrance nothing), in one wing of the little gin-shop of a building so styled near Saint Martin's Church; in another wing is the exhibition of the Royal Academy (entrance, one shilling; catalogue, one ditto). After having seen this, you come to the Water-Color Exhibition in Pall Mall East; then to the Gallery in Suffolk Street; and, finally, to the New Water-Color Society in Pall Mall, — a pretty room, which formerly used to be a gambling-house, where many a bout of seven's-the-main, and iced champagne, has been had by the dissipated in former days. All these collections (all the modern ones, that is) deserve to be noticed, and contain a deal of good, bad, and indifferent wares, as is the way with all other institutions in this wicked world.

Commençons donc avec le commencement — with the exhibition of the Royal Academy, which consists, as everybody knows, of thirty-eight knight and esquire Academicians, and nineteen simple and ungenteel Associates, who have not so much as a shabby Mister before their names. I recollect last year facetiously ranging these gentlemen in rank according to what I conceived to be their merits, — King Mulready, Prince Maclise, Lord Landseer, Archbishop Eastlake (according to the best of my memory, for " Jack Straw," strange to say, does not take in *Fraser's Magazine*), and so on. At present, a great number of new-comers, not Associates even, ought to be elevated to these aristocratic dignities; and, perhaps, the order ought to be somewhat changed. There are many more good pictures (here and elsewhere) than there were last year. A great stride has been taken in matters of art, my dear friend. The young painters are stepping forward. Let the old fogies look to it; let the old Academic Olympians beware, for there are fellows among the rising race who bid fair to oust them from sovereignty. They have not yet arrived at the throne, to be sure, but they are near it. The lads are not so good as the best of the Academicians; but many of the Academicians are infinitely worse than the lads, and are old, stupid, and cannot improve, as the younger and more active painters will.

If you are particularly anxious to know what is the best

picture in the room, not the biggest (Sir David Wilkie's is the biggest, and exactly contrary to the best), I must request you to turn your attention to a noble river-piece by J. W. M. Turner, Esquire, R.A., "The Fighting *Téméraire*" — as grand a painting as ever figured on the walls of any Academy, or came from the easel of any painter. The old *Téméraire* is dragged to her last home by a little, spiteful, diabolical steamer. A mighty red sun, amidst a host of flaring clouds, sinks to rest on one side of the picture, and illumines a river that seems interminable, and a countless navy that fades away into such a wonderful distance as never was painted before. The little demon of a steamer is belching out a volume (why do I say a volume ? not a hundred volumes could express it) of foul, lurid, red-hot, malignant smoke, paddling furiously, and lashing up the water round about it; while behind it (a cold gray moon looking down on it), slow, sad, and majestic, follows the brave old ship, with death, as it were, written on her. I think, my dear Bricabrac (although, to be sure, your nation would be somewhat offended by such a collection of trophies), that we ought not, in common gratitude, to sacrifice entirely these noble old champions of ours, but that we should have somewhere a museum of their skeletons, which our children might visit, and think of the brave deeds which were done in them. The bones of the *Agamemnon* and the *Captain*, the *Vanguard*, the *Culloden*, and the *Victory*, ought to be sacred relics, for Englishmen to worship almost. Think of them when alive, and braving the battle and the breeze, they carried Nelson and his heroes victorious by the Cape of Saint Vincent, in the dark waters of Aboukir, and through the fatal conflict of Trafalgar. All these things, my dear Bricabrac, are, you will say, absurd, and not to the purpose. Be it so; but Bowbellites as we are, we Cockneys feel our hearts leap up when we recall them to memory; and every clerk in Threadneedle Street feels the strength of a Nelson, when he thinks of the mighty actions performed by him.

It is absurd, you will say (and with a great deal of reason), for Titmarsh, or any other Briton, to grow so poetically enthusiastic about a four-foot canvas, representing a ship, a steamer, a river, and a sunset. But herein surely lies the power of the great artist. He makes you see and think of a great deal more than the objects before you; he knows how to soothe or intoxicate, to fire or to depress by a few notes, or forms, or colors, of which we cannot trace the effect to the source, but only acknowledge the power. I recollect some years ago, at the theatre at Weimar, hearing Beethoven's "Battle of Vittoria," in which, amidst a storm of glorious music, the air of "God save the King" was introduced. The very instant it began, every Englishman in the house was bolt upright, and so stood reverently until the air was played out. Why so? From some such thrill of excitement as makes us glow and rejoice over Mr. Turner and his "Fighting *Téméraire;*" which I am sure, when the art of translating colors into music or poetry shall be discovered, will be found to be a magnificent national ode or piece of music.

I must tell you, however, that Mr. Turner's performances are for the most part quite incomprehensible to me; and that his other pictures, which he is pleased to call "Cicero at his Villa," "Agrippina with the Ashes of Germanicus," "Pluto carrying off Proserpina," or what you will, are not a whit more natural, or less mad, than they used to be in former years, since he has forsaken nature, or attempted (like your French barbers) to embellish it. *On n'embellit pas la nature,* my dear Bricabrac; one may make pert caricatures of it, or mad exaggerations like Mr. Turner in his fancy pieces. O ye gods! why will he not stick to copying her majestical countenance, instead of daubing it with some absurd antics and fard of his own? Fancy pea-green skies, crimson lake trees, and orange and purple grass — fancy cataracts, rainbows, suns, moons, and thunderbolts — shake them well up, with a quantity of gamboge, and you will have an idea of a fancy picture by Turner. It is worth a shilling alone to go and see "Pluto and Proserpina." Such a landscape! such figures! such a little red-hot coal-scuttle of a chariot! As Nat Lee sings —

> "Methought I saw a hieroglyphic bat
> Skim o'er the surface of a slipshod hat;
> While, to increase the tumult of the skies,
> A damned potato o'er the whirlwind flies."

If you can understand these lines, you can understand one of Turner's landscapes; and I recommend them to him, as a pretty subject for a piece for next year.

Etty has a picture on the same subject as Turner's "Pluto carrying off Proserpina;" and if one may complain that in the latter the figures are not indicated, one cannot at least lay this fault to Mr. Etty's door. His figures *are* drawn, and a deuced deal *too much* drawn. A great large curtain of fig-leaves should be hung over every one of this artist's pictures, and the world should pass on, content to know that there are some glorious colors painted beneath. His color, indeed, is sublime; I doubt if Titian ever knew how to paint flesh better — but his taste! Not David nor Girodet ever offended propriety so — scarcely ever Peter Paul himself, by whose side as a colorist and a magnificent heroic painter, Mr. Etty is sometimes worthy to stand. I wish he would take Ariosto in hand, and give us a series of designs from him. His hand would be the very one for those deep luscious landscapes, and fiery scenes of love and battle. Besides "Proserpine," Mr. Etty has two more pictures, "Endymion," with a dirty, affected, beautiful, slatternly Diana, and a portrait of the "Lady Mayoress of York," which is a curiosity in its way. The line of her ladyship's eyes and mouth (it is a front face) are made to meet at a point in a marabou feather which she wears in her turban, and close to her cheekbone; while the expression of the whole countenance is so fierce, that you would imagine it a Lady Macbeth, and not a lady mayoress. The picture has, nevertheless, some very fine painting about it — as which of Mr. Etty's pictures has not?

The artists say there is very fine painting, too, in Sir David Wilkie's great "Sir David Baird;" for my part, I think very little. You see a great quantity of brown paint; in this is a great flashing of torches, feathers, and bayonets. You see in the foreground, huddled up in a rich heap of corpses and drapery, Tippoo Sahib; and swaggering over him on a step, waving a sword for no earthly purpose, and wearing a red jacket and buckskins, the figure of Sir David Baird. The picture is poor, feeble, theatrical; and I would just as soon have Mr. Hart's great canvas of "Lady Jane Grey" (which is worth exactly twopence-halfpenny) as Sir David's poor picture of "Seringapatam." Some of Sir David's portraits are worse even than his historical compositions — they seem to be painted with snuff and tallow-grease: the faces are merely indicated, and without individuality; the forms only half-drawn, and almost always wrong. What has come to the hand that painted "The Blind Fiddler" and "The Chelsea Pensioners"? Who would have thought that such a portrait as that of "Master Robert Donne," or the composition entitled "The Grandfather," could ever have come from the author of "The Rent Day" and "The Reading of the Will"? If it be but a contrast to this feeble, flimsy, transparent figure of Master Donne, the spectator cannot do better than cast his eyes upwards, and look at Mr. Linnell's excellent portrait of "Mr. Robert Peel." It is real substantial nature, carefully and honestly painted, and without any flashy tricks of art. It may seem ungracious in "us youth" thus to fall foul of our betters; but if Sir David has taught us to like good pictures, by painting them formerly, we cannot help criticising if he paints bad ones now : and bad they most surely are.

From the censure, however, must be excepted the picture of "Grace before Meat," which, a little misty and feeble, perhaps, in drawing and substance, in color, feeling, composition, and expression is exquisite. The eye loves to repose upon this picture, and the heart to brood over it afterwards. When, as I said before, lines and colors come to be translated into sounds, this picture, I have no doubt, will turn out to be a sweet and touching hymn-tune, with rude notes of cheerful voices, and peal of soft melodious organ, such as one hears stealing over the meadows on sunshiny Sabbath-days, while waves under cloudless blue the peaceful golden corn. Some such feeling of exquisite pleasure and content is to be had, too, from Mr. Eastlake's picture of "Our Lord and the Little Children." You never saw such tender white faces, and solemn eyes, and sweet forms of mothers round their little ones bending gracefully. These pictures come straight to the heart, and then all criticism and calculation vanish at once, — for the artist has attained his great end, which is, to strike far deeper than the sight; and we have no business to quarrel about defects in form and color, which are but little parts of the great painter's skill.

Look, for instance, at another piece of Mr. Eastlake's, called, somewhat affectedly, "La Svegliarina." The defects of the painter, which one does not condescend to notice when he is filled with a great idea, become visible instantly when he is only occupied with a small one; and you see that the hand is too scrupulous and finikin, the drawing weak, the flesh chalky, and unreal. The very same objections exist to the other picture, but the subject and the genius overcome them.

Passing from Mr. Eastlake's pictures to those of a greater

genius, though in a different line, — look at Mr. Leslie's little pieces. Can anything be more simple — almost rude —than their manner, and more complete in their effect upon the spectator? The very soul of comedy is in them; there is no coarseness, no exaggeration; but they gladden the eye, and the merriment which they excite cannot possibly be more pure, gentlemanlike, or delightful. Mr. Maclise has humor, too, and vast powers of expressing it; but whiskey is not more different from rich burgundy than his fun from Mr. Leslie's. To our thinking, Leslie's little head of " Sancho " is worth the whole picture from "Gil Blas," which hangs by it. In point of workmanship, this is, perhaps, the best picture that Mr. Maclise ever painted; the color is far better than that usually employed by him, and the representation of objects carried to such an extent as we do believe was never reached before. There is a poached egg, which one could swallow; a trout, that beats all the trout that was ever seen; a copper pan, scoured so clean that you might see your face in it; a green blind, through which the sun comes; and a wall, with the sun shining on it, that De Hooghe could not surpass. This young man has the greatest power of hand that was ever had, perhaps, by any painter in any time or country. What does he want? Polish, I think; thought, and cultivation. His great picture of " King Richard and Robin Hood " is a wonder of dexterity of hand; but coarse, I think, and inefficient in humor. His models repeat themselves too continually. Allen-a-Dale, the harper, is the very counterpart of Gil Blas; and Robin Hood is only Apollo with whiskers: the same grin, the same display of grinders, — the same coarse luscious mouth, belongs to both. In the large picture, everybody grins, and shows his whole *râtelier;* and you look at them and say, " These people seem all very jolly." Leslie's characters do not laugh themselves, but they make *you* laugh; and this is where the experienced American artist beats the dashing young Irish one. We shall say nothing of the color of Mr. Maclise's large picture; some part appears to us to be excellent, and the whole piece, as far as execution goes, is worthy of his amazing talents and high reputation. Mr. Maclise has but one portrait; it is, perhaps, the best in the exhibition: sober in color, wonderful for truth, effect, and power of drawing.

In speaking of portraits, there is never much to say; and

they are fewer, and for the most part more indifferent, than usual. Mr. Pickersgill has a good one, a gentleman in a green chair; and one or two outrageously bad. Mr. Phillips's "Doctor Sheppard" is a finely painted head and picture; his Lady Dunraven, and her son, as poor, ill-drawn, and ill-colored a performance as can possibly be. Mr. Wood has a pretty head; Mr. Stone a good portrait of a very noble-looking lady, the Hon. Mrs. Blackwood; Mr. Bewick a good one; and there are, of course, many others whose names might be mentioned with praise or censure, but whom we will, if you please, pass over altogether.

The great advance of the year is in the small historical compositions, of which there are many that deserve honorable mention. Redgrave's "Return of Olivia to the Vicar" has some very pretty painting and feeling in it; "Quentin Matsys," by the same artist, is tolerably good. D. Cowper's "Othello relating his Adventures," really beautiful; as is Cope's "Belgian Family." All these are painted with grace, feeling, and delicacy; as is E. M. Ward's "Cimabue and Giotto" (there is in Tiepolo's etchings the self-same composition, by the way); and Herbert's elegant picture of the "Brides of Venice." Mr. Severn's composition from the "Ancient Mariner" is a noble performance; and the figure of the angel with raised arm awful and beautiful too. It does good to see such figures in pictures as those and the above, invented and drawn, — for they belong, as we take it, to the best school of art, of which one is glad to see the daily spread among our young painters.

Mr. Charles Landseer's "Pillage of a Jew's House" is a very well and carefully painted picture, containing a great many figures and good points; but we are not going to praise it: it wants vigor, to our taste, and what you call, *actualité*. The people stretch their arms and turn their eyes the proper way, but as if they were in a tableau and paid for standing there; one longs to see them all in motion and naturally employed.

I feel, I confess, a kind of delight in finding out Mr. Edwin Landseer in a bad picture; for the man paints so wonderfully well, that one is angry that he does not paint better, which he might with half his talent, and without half his facility. "Van Amburgh and the Lions" *is* a bad picture, and no mistake; dexterous, of course, but flat and washy: the drawing even of the animals is careless; that of the man bad, though the head is very like, and very smartly painted. Then there are other dog-and-man portraits; "Miss Peel with Fido," for instance. Fido is wonderful, and so are the sponges, and hair-brushes, and looking-glass, prepared for the dog's bath; and the drawing of the child's face, as far as the lines and expression go, is very good; but the face is covered with flesh-colored paint, and not flesh, and the child looks like a wonderful doll, or imitation child, and not a real young lady, daughter of a gentleman who was prime minister last week (by-the-by, my dear Bricabrac, did you ever read such a pretty Whig game as that, and such a nice *coup d'état?*). There, again, is the beautiful little Princess of Cambridge, with a dog, and a piece of biscuit: the dog and the biscuit are just perfection; but the princess is no such thing, — only a beautiful apology for a princess, like that which Princess Penelope *didn't* send the other day to the Lord Mayor of London.

We have to thank you (and not our Academy, which has hung the picture in a most scurvy way) for Mr. Scheffer's "Prêche Protestant." This fine composition has been thrust down on the ground, and trampled under foot, as it were, by a great number of worthless Academics; but it merits one of the very best places in the gallery; and I mention it to hint an idea to your worship, which only could come from a great mind like that of Titmarsh, — to have, namely, some day a great European congress of paintings, which might be exhibited at one place, — Paris, say, as the most central; or, better still, travel about, under the care of trusty superintendents, as they might, without fear of injury. I think such a circuit would do much to make the brethren known to one another, and we should hear quickly of much manly emulation, and stout training for the contest. If you will mention this to Louis Philippe the next time you see that *roi citoyen* (mention it soon, — for, egad! the next *émeute* may be successful; and who knows when it will happen?) — if you will mention this at the Tuileries, *we* will take care of St. James's; for I suppose that you know, in spite of the Whigs, her most sacred Majesty reads every word of *Fraser's Magazine*, and will be as sure to see this on the first of next month, as Lord Melbourne will be to dine with her on that day.

But let us return to our muttons. I think there are few more of the oil pictures about which it is necessary to speak; and besides them, there are a host of miniatures, difficult to expatiate upon, but pleasing to behold. There are Chalon's ogling beauties, half a dozen of them : and the skill with which their silks and satins are dashed in by the painter is a marvel to the beholder. There are Ross's heads, that to be seen must be seen through a microscope. There is Saunders, who runs the best of the miniature men very hard; and Thorburn, with Newton, Robertson, Rochard, and a host of others: and, finally, there is the sculpture-room, containing many pieces of clay and marble, and, to my notions, but two good things, a sleeping child (ridiculously called the Lady Susan Somebody), by West-macott; and the bust of Miss Stuart, by Macdonald: never was anything on earth more exquisitely lovely.

These things seen, take your stick from the porter at the hall door, cut it, and go to fresh picture galleries; but ere you go, just by way of contrast, and to soothe your mind, after the glare and bustle of the modern collection, take half an hour's repose in the National Gallery; where, before the "Bacchus and Ariadne," you may see what the magic of color is; before "Christ and Lazarus" what is majestic, solemn grace and awful beauty; and before the new "Saint Catherine" what is the real divinity of art. Oh, Eastlake and Turner! — Oh, Maclise and Mulready! you are all very nice men; but what are you to the men of old ?

. . . . . .

Issuing then from the National Gallery — you may step over to Farrance's by the way, if you like, and sip an ice, or bolt a couple of dozen forced-meat balls in a basin of mock-turtle soup — issuing, I say, from the National Gallery, and after refreshing yourself or not, as your purse or appetite permits, you arrive speedily at the Water-Color Exhibition, and cannot do better than enter. I know nothing more cheerful or sparkling than the first *coup d'œil* of this little gallery. In the first place, you never can enter it without finding four or five pretty women, that's a fact; pretty women with pretty pink bonnets peeping at pretty pictures, and with sweet whispers vowing that Mrs. Seyffarth is a dear delicious painter, and that her style is "so soft;" and that Miss Sharpe paints every bit as well as her sister; and that Mr. Jean Paul Frederick Richter draws the loveliest things, to be sure, that ever were seen. Well, very likely the ladies are right, and it would be un-polite to argue the matter; but I wish Mrs. Seyffarth's gentlemen and ladies were not so dreadfully handsome, with such white pillars of necks, such long eyes and lashes, and such dabs of carmine at the mouth and nostrils. I wish Miss Sharpe would not paint Scripture subjects, and Mr. Richter great goggle-eyed, red-cheeked, simpering wenches, whose ogling has become odious from its repetition. However, the ladies like it, and, of course, must have their way.

If you want to see *real* nature, now, real expression, real startling home poetry, look at every one of Hunt's heads. Hogarth never painted anything better than these figures, taken singly. That man rushing away frightened from the beer-barrel is a noble head of terror; that Miss Jemima Crow, whose whole body is a grin, regards you with an ogle that all the race of Richters could never hope to imitate. Look at yonder card-players; they have a penny pack of the devil's books, and one has just laid down the king of trumps! I defy you to look at him without laughing, or to examine the wondrous puzzled face of his adversary without longing to hug the greasy rogue. Come hither, Mr. Maclise, and see what genuine comedy is; you who can paint better than all the Hunts and Leslies, and yet not near so well. If I were the Duke of Devonshire, I would have a couple of Hunts in every room in all my houses; if I had the blue-devils (and even their graces are, I suppose, occasionally so troubled), I would but cast my eyes upon these grand good-humored pictures, and defy care. Who does not recollect "Before and After the Mutton Pie," the two pictures of that wondrous boy? Where Mr. Hunt finds his models, I cannot tell; they are the very flower of the British youth; each of them is as good as " Sancho ; " blessed is he that has his portfolio full of them.

There is no need to mention to you the charming landscapes of Cox, Copley Fielding, De Wint, Gastineau, and the rest. A new painter, somewhat in the style of Harding, is Mr. Callow; and better, I think, than his master or original, whose colors are too gaudy to my taste, and effects too glaringly theatrical.

Mr. Cattermole has, among others, two very fine drawings: a large one, the most finished and the best colored of any which have been exhibited by this fine artist; and a smaller one, "The Portrait," which is charming. The portrait is that of Jane Seymour or Anne Boleyn; and Henry VIII. is the person examining it, with the Cardinal at his side, the painter before him, and one or two attendants. The picture seems to me a perfect masterpiece, very simply colored and composed, but delicious in effect and tone, and telling the story to a wonder. It is much more gratifying, I think, to let a painter tell his own story in this way, than to bind him down to a scene of "Ivanhoe" or "Uncle Toby;" or, worse still, to an illustration of some wretched story in some wretched fribble Annual. Woe to the painter who falls into the hands of Mr. Charles Heath (I speak, of course, not of Mr. Heath personally, but in the Pickwickian sense — of Mr. Heath the Annual-monger); he ruins the young artist, sucks his brains out, emasculates his genius so as to make it fit company for the purchasers of Annuals. Take, for instance, that unfortunate young man, Mr. Corbould, who gave great promise two years since, painted a pretty picture last year, and now — he has been in the hands of the Annual-mongers, and has left well-nigh all his vigor behind him. Numerous Zuleikas and Lalla Rookhs, which are hanging about the walls of the Academy and the New Water-Color Gallery, give lamentable proofs of this: such handsome Turks and leering sultanas; such Moors, with straight noses and pretty curled beards! Away, Mr. Corbould! away while it is yet time, out of the hands of these sickly, heartless Annual sirens! and ten years hence, when you have painted a good, vigorous, healthy picture, bestow the tear of gratitude upon Titmarsh, who tore you from the lap of your crimson-silk-and-gilt-edged Armida.

Mr. Cattermole has a couple, we will not say of imitators, but of friends, who admire his works very much; these are, Mr. Nash and Mr. Lake Price; the former paints furniture and old houses, the latter old houses and furniture, and both very pretty. No harm can be said of these miniature scene-painters; on the contrary, Mr. Price's "Gallery at Hardwicke" is really remarkably dexterous; and the chairs, tables, curtains, and pictures are nicked off with extraordinary neatness and sharpness — and then? why then, no more is to be said. Cobalt, sepia, and a sable pencil will do a deal of work, to be sure; and very pretty it is, too, when done; and as for finding fault with it, that nobody will and can; but an artist wants something more than sepia, cobalt, and sable pencils, and the knowledge how to use them. What do you think, my dear Bricabrac, of a little *genius?* — *that's* the picture-painter, depend on it.

Being on the subject of water-colors, we may as well step into the New Water-Color Exhibition : not so good as the old, but very good. You will see here a large drawing by Mr. Corbould of a tournament, which will show at once how clever that young artist is, and how weak and *maniéré*. You will see some charming unaffected English landscapes by Mr. Sims; and a capital Spanish Girl by Hicks, of which the flesh-painting cannot be too much approved. It is done without the heavy white, with which water-color artists are now wont to belabor their pictures; and is, therefore, frankly and clearly painted, as all transparent water-color drawing must be. The same praise of clearness, boldness, and depth of tone must be given to Mr. Absolon, who uses no white, and only just so much stippling as is necessary; his picture has the force of oil, and we should be glad to see his manner more followed.

Mr. Haghe's "Town Hall of Courtray" has attracted, and deservedly, a great deal of notice. It is a very fine and masterly architectural drawing, rich and sombre in effect, the figures introduced being very nearly as good as the rest of the picture. Mr. Haghe, we suppose, will be called to the upper house of water-color painters, who might well be anxious to receive into their ranks many persons belonging to the new society. We hope, however, the latter will be faithful to themselves; there is plenty of room for two galleries, and the public must, ere long, learn to appreciate the merits of the new one. Having spoken a word in favor of Mr. Johnston's pleasing and quaintly colored South American sketches, we have but to bend our steps to Suffolk Street, and draw this discourse to a close.

Here is a very fine picture indeed, by Mr. Hurlstone, "Olympia attacked by Bourbon's Soldiers in Saint Peter's and flying to the Cross." Seen from the further room, this picture is grand in effect and color, and the rush of the armed men towards the girl finely and vigorously expressed. The head of Olympia has been called too calm by the critics; it seems to me most beautiful, and the action of the figure springing forward and flinging its arms round the cross nobly conceived and executed. There is a good deal of fine Titianic painting in the soldiers' figures (oh that Mr. Hurlstone would throw away his lampblack!), and the background of the church is fine, vast, and gloomy. This is the best historical picture to be seen anywhere this year; perhaps the worst is the one which stands at the other end of the room, and which strikes upon the eye as if it were an immense water-color sketch of a feeble picture by President West. Speaking of historical paintings, I forgot to mention a large and fine picture by Mr. Dyce, the "Separation of Edwy and Elgiva;" somewhat crude and odd in color, with a good deal of exaggeration in the countenances of the figures, but having grandeur in it, and unmistakable genius; there is a figure of an old woman seated, which would pass muster very well in a group of Sebastian Piombo.

A capitally painted head by Mr. Stone, called the "Swordbearer," almost as fresh, bright, and vigorous as a Vandyke, is the portrait, we believe, of a brother artist, the clever actor Mr. M'Ian. The latter's picture of "Sir Tristram in the Cave" deserves especial remark and praise; and is really as fine a dramatic composition as one will often see. The figures of the knight and the lady asleep in the foreground are novel, striking, and beautifully easy. The advance of the old king, who comes upon the lovers; the look of the hideous dwarf, who finds them out; and behind, the line of spears that are seen glancing over the rocks, and indicating the march of the unseen troops, are all very well conceived and arranged. The piece deserves engraving; it is wild, poetic, and original. To how many pictures, nowadays, can one apply the two last terms?

There are some more new pictures, in the midst of a great quantity of trash, that deserve notice. Mr. D. Cowper is always good; Mr. Stewart's "Grandfather" contains two excellent likenesses, and is a pleasing little picture. Mr. Hurlstone's "Italian Boy," and "Girl with a Dog," are excellent; and, in this pleasant mood, for fear of falling into an angry fit on coming to look further into the gallery, it will be as well to conclude. Wishing many remembrances to Mrs. Bricabrac, and better luck to you in the next *émeute*, I beg here to bid you farewell and entreat you to accept the assurances of my distinguished consideration.

M. A. T.

Au CITOYEN BRUTUS NAPOLÉON BRICABRAC, *Réfugié d'Avril, Blessé de Mai, Condamné de Juin, Décoré de Juillet, etc. etc. Hôtel Dieu, à Paris.*

I.

A PICTORIAL RHAPSODY BY MICHAEL ANGELO TITMARSH.

WITH AN INTRODUCTORY LETTER TO MR. YORKE.

[*Fraser's Magazine, June and July,* 1840.]

My dear Yorke, — Do you remember the orders which you gave me at the close of our dinner last week at the Clarendon ? — that dinner which you always provide upon my arrival in town from my country-seat; knowing full well that Titmarsh before he works must dine, and when he dines, must dine well ? Do you, I say, remember the remarks which you addressed to me ? Probably not; for that third bottle of Clos-Vougeot had evidently done your business, and you were too tipsy even to pay the bill.

Well, let bills be bills, and what care we ? There is Mr. James Fraser, our employer, master, publisher, purse-bearer, and friend, who has such a pleasure in paying that it is a pity to balk him ; and I never saw a man look more happy than he when he lugged out four five-pound notes to pay for that dinner of ours. What a scene it was ! You asleep with your head in a dish of melted raspberry-ice ; Mr. Fraser calm, beneficent, majestic, counting out the thirteens to the waiters ; the Doctor and Mr. John Abraham Heraud singing " Suoni la tromba intrepida," each clutching the other's hand, and waving a punch-ladle or a dessert-knife in the unemployed paw, and the rest of us joining in chorus when they came to " gridando liberta." — But I am wandering from the point : the address which you delivered to me on drinking my health was in substance this : —

" Mr. Michael Angelo Titmarsh, the splendid feast of which you have partaken, and the celebrated company of individuals whom you see around you, will show you in what estimation myself and Mr. Fraser hold your talents, — not that the latter point is of any consequence, as I am the sole editor of the Magazine. Sir, you have been called to the metropolis from a very distant part of the country, your coach hire and personal expenses have been defrayed, you have been provided with a suit of clothes that *ought* to become you, for they have been for at least six months the wonder of the town while exhibited on my own person; and you may well fancy that all these charges have not been incurred on our parts, without an expectation of some corresponding return from you. You are a devilish bad painter, sir; but never mind, Hazlitt was another, and old Peter Pindar was a miserable dauber; Mr. Alexander Pope, who wrote several pretty poems, was always busy with brush and palette, and made sad work of them. You, then, in common with these before-named illustrations, as my friend, Lady Morgan, calls them [Sir Charles returned thanks], are a wretched artist; but a tolerable critic — nay, a good critic — nay, let me say to your face, the best critic, the clearest, the soundest, the gayest, the most eloquent, the most pathetic, and, above all, the most honest critic in matters of art that is to be found in her Majesty's dominions. And, therefore, Mr. Titmarsh, for we must give the deuce his due, you have been brought from your cottage near John O'Groat's or Land's End, — I forget which, — therefore you have been summoned to London at the present season.

"Sir, there are at this moment no less than five public exhibitions of pictures in the metropolis; and it will be your duty carefully to examine every one of them during your residence here, and bring us a full and accurate report upon all the pieces exhibited which are remarkable for goodness, badness, or mediocrity."

I here got up; and, laying my hand on my satin waistcoat, looked up to heaven, and said, " Sir, I " —

"Sit down, sir, and keep your eternal wagging jaws quiet! Waiter! whenever that person attempts to speak, have the goodness to fill his mouth with olives or a damson cheese. — To proceed. Sir, and you, gentlemen, and you, O intelligent public of Great Britain! (for I know that every word I say is in some way carried to you) you must all be aware, I say, how wickedly, — how foully, basely, meanly — how, in a word, with-every-deteriorating-adverb that ends in *ly* — in *ly*, gentlemen [here Mr. Yorke looked round, and myself and Mr. Fraser, rather alarmed lest we should have let slip a pun, began to raise a low faint laugh]

— you have all of you seen how the world has been imposed upon by persons calling themselves critics, who, in daily, weekly, monthly prints, protrude their nonsense upon the town. What are these men? Are they educated to be painters? — No! Have they a taste for painting? — No! I know of newspapers in this town, gentlemen, which send their reporters indifferently to a police office or a picture gallery, and expect them to describe Correggio or a fire in Fleet Street with equal fidelity. And, alas! it must be confessed that our matter-of-fact public of England is itself but a dull appreciator of the arts, and is too easily persuaded by the dull critics who lay down their stupid laws.

"But we cannot expect, Mr. Titmarsh, to do any good to our beloved public by telling them merely that their instructors are impostors. Abuse is no argument, foul words admit of no pretence (you may have remarked that I never use them myself, but always employ the arts of gentlemanly persuasion), and we must endeavor to create a reform amongst the nations by simply preaching a purer and higher doctrine. Go you among the picture galleries, as you have done in former years, and prattle on at your best rate; don't philosophize, or define, or talk big, for I will cut out every line of such stuff, but speak in a simple natural way, — without fear, and without favor.

"Mark that latter word 'favor' well; for you are a great deal too tender in your nature, and too profuse of compliments. Favor, sir, is the curse of the critical trade; and you will observe how a spirit of *camaraderie* and partisanship prevails in matters of art especially. The picture critics, as I have remarked, are eminently dull — dull and loud; perfectly ignorant upon all subjects connected with art, never able to guess at the name of an artist without a catalogue and a number, quite unknowing whether a picture be well or ill drawn, well or ill painted; they must prate, nevertheless, about light and shade, warm and cool color, keeping, chiaroscuro, and such other terms, from the Painters' Cant Dictionary, as they hear bandied about among the brethren of the brush.

"You will observe that such a critic has ordinarily his one or two idols that he worships; the one or two painters, namely, into whose studios he has free access, and from whose opinions he forms his own. There is Dash, for instance, of the Star newspaper; now and anon you hear him discourse of the fine arts, and you may take your affi-

davit that he has just issued from Blank's *atelier:* all
Blank's opinions he utters — utters and garbles, of course;
all his likings are founded on Blank's dicta, and all his
dislikings: 'tis probable that Blank has a rival, one Asterisk, living over the way. In Dash's eye Asterisk is the
lowest of creatures. At every fresh exhibition you read
how 'Mr. Blank has transcended his already transcendent
reputation;' 'Myriads are thronging round his glorious
canvases;' 'Billions have been trampled to death while
rushing to examine his grand portrait of Lady Smigsmag;'
'His picture of Sir Claude Calipash is a gorgeous representation of aldermanic dignity and high chivalric grace!'
As for Asterisk, you are told, 'Mr. Asterisk has two or
three pictures — prétty, but weak, repetitions of his old
faces and subjects in his old namby-pamby style. The
Committee, we hear, rejected most of his pictures: the
Committee are very compassionate. How *dared* they reject
Mr. Blank's stupendous historical picture of So-and-so?'"

[Here, my dear sir, I am sorry to say that there was a
general snore heard from the guests round the table, which
rather disturbed the flow of your rhetoric. You swallowed
down two or three pints of burgundy, however, and continued.]

"But I must conclude. Michael Angelo Titmarsh, you
know your duty. You are an honest man [loud cheers, the
people had awakened during the pause]. You must ᵉgo
forth determined to tell the truth, the whole truth and
nothing but the truth; as far as you, a fallible creature
[cries of 'No, no!'], know it. If you see a good picture,
were it the work of your bitterest enemy — and you have
hundreds — praise it."

"I will," gasped I.

"Hold your tongue, sir, and don't be interrupting me
with your perpetual orations! If you see a bad picture,
were it the work of your dearest associate, your brother,
the friend of your bosom, your benefactor — cut, slash,
slaughter him without mercy. Strip off humbug, sir,
though it cover your best boon companion. Praise merit,
though it belong to your fiercest foe, your rival in the
affections of your mistress, the man from whom you have
borrowed money, or taken a beating in private!"

"Mr. Yorke," said I, clinching my fists and starting up,
"this passes endurance, were you not intox ——;" but two
waiters here seized and held me down, luckily for you.

"Peace, Titmarsh" (said you); "'twas but raillery. Be honest, my friend, is all that I would say; and if you write a decent article on the exhibitions, Mr. Fraser will pay you handsomely for your trouble; and, in order that you may have every facility for visiting the picture galleries, I myself will give you a small sum in hand. Here are ten shillings. Five exhibitions, five shillings; catalogues, four. You will have twelvepence for yourself, to take refresh· ments in the intervals."

I held out my hand, for my anger had quite disappeared.

"Mr. Fraser," said you, "give the fellow half a sovereign; and, for Heaven's sake, teach him to be silent when a gentleman is speaking!"

What passed subsequently need not be stated here, but the above account of your speech is a pretty correct one; and, in pursuance of your orders, I busied myself with the exhibitions on the following day. The result of my labors will be found in the accompanying report. I have the honor, sir, of laying it at your feet, and of subscribing myself,

With the profoundest respect and devotion,
Sir,
Your very faithful and obedient Servant,
MICHAEL ANGELO TITMARSH.

Moreland's Coffee House, Dean Street, Soho.

ΡΑΨΩιΑΙΑ ἡ ΓΡΑΜΜΑ Α'.

THE ROYAL ACADEMY.

HAD the author of the following paragraphs the pen of a Sir Walter Scott or a Lady Morgan, he would write something excessively brilliant and witty about the first day of the exhibition, and of the company which crowd the rooms upon that occasion. On Friday the queen comes (Heaven bless her Majesty!) attended by her courtiers and train; and deigns, with royal eyes, to examine the works of her Royal Academicians. Her, as we are given to understand, the president receives, bowing profoundly, awe-stricken; his gold chain dangles from his presidential bosom, and sweet smiles of respectful courtesy light up his venerable face. Walking by her Majesty's side, he explains to her the wonders of the show. "That, may it please your

Majesty, is a picture representing yourself, painted by the good knight, Sir David Wilkie: deign to remark how the robes seem as if they were cut out of British oak, and the figure is as wooden as the figurehead of one of your Majesty's men-of-war. Opposite is your Majesty's royal consort, by Mr. Patten. We have the honor to possess two more pairs of Pattens in this Academy — ha, ha! Round about you will see some of my own poor works of art. Yonder is Mr. Landseer's portrait of your Majesty's own cockatoo, with a brace of Havadavats. Please your Royal Highness to look at the bit of biscuit; no baker could have done it more natural. Fair maid of honor, look at that lump of sugar; couldn't one take an affidavit, now, that it cost elevenpence a pound? Isn't it a sweet? I know only one thing sweeter, and that's your ladyship's lovely face!"

In such lively conversation might we fancy a bland president discoursing. The queen should make august replies; the lovely smiling maids of honor should utter remarks becoming their innocence and station (turning away very red from that corner of the apartment where hang certain Venuses and Andromedas, painted by William Etty, Esquire); the gallant prince, a lordly, handsome gentleman, with a slight foreign accent, should curl the dark mustache that adorns his comely lip, and say, "Potztausend! but dat bigture of First Loaf by Herr von Mulready ist wunderschön!" and courtly chamberlains, prim goldsticks, and sly polonaises of the Court should take their due share in the gay scene, and deliver their portions of the dialogue of the little drama.

All this, I say, might be done in a very sprightly neat way, were poor Titmarsh an Ainsworth or a Lady Morgan; and the scene might be ended smartly with the knighting of one of the Academicians by her Majesty on the spot. As thus: — "The royal party had stood for three and twenty minutes in mute admiration before that tremendous picture by Mr. Maclise, representing the banquet in the hall of Dunsinane. 'Gory shadow of Banquo,' said Lady Almeria to Lady Wilhelmina, 'how hideous thou art!' 'Hideous! hideous yourself, marry!' replied the arch and lovely Wilhelmina. 'By my halidome!' whispered the seneschal to the venerable prime minister, Lord Melborough; — 'by cock and pie, Sir Count, but it seems me that yon Scottish kerne, Macbeth, hath a shrewd look of terror!'

'And a marvellous unkempt beard,' answered the Earl; 'and a huge mouth gaping wide for very terror, and a hand palsied with fear.' 'Hoot awa, mon!' cried an old Scots general, but the chield Macbeth (I'm descanded from him leeneally in the saxty-ninth generation) knew hoo to wield a guid claymore!' 'His hand looks as if it had dropped a hot potato!' whispered a roguish page, and the little knave's remark caused a titter to run through the courtly circle, and brought a smile upon the cheek of the President of the Academy; who, sooth to say, had been twiddling his chain of office between his finger and thumb, somewhat jealous of the praise bestowed upon his young rival.

"'My Lord of Wellington,' said her Majesty, 'lend me your sword.' The veteran, smiling, drew forth that trenchant sabre, — that spotless blade of battle that had flashed victorious on the plains of far Assaye, in the breach of storm-girt Badajoz, in the mighty and supreme combat of Waterloo! A tear stood in the hero's eye as he fell on his gartered knee; and, holding the blade between his finger and thumb, he presented the hilt to his liege lady. 'Take it, madam,' said he; 'sheathe it in this old breast, if you will, for my heart and sword are my sovereign's. Take it, madam, and be not angry if there is blood upon the steel —'tis the blood of the enemies of my country!' The queen took it; and as the young and delicate creature waved that tremendous war-sword, a gentleman near her remarked, that surely never lighted on the earth a more delightful vision. 'Where is Mr. Maclise?' said her Majesty. The blushing painter stepped forward. 'Kneel! kneel!' whispered fifty voices: and, frightened, he did as they ordered him. 'Sure she's not going to cut my head off?' he cried to the good knights, Sir Augustus Callcott and Sir Isaac Newton, who were standing. 'Your name, sir?' said the Ladye of England. 'Sure you know it's Maclise!' cried the son of Erin. 'Your Christian name?' shrieked Sir Martin Shee, in agony. 'Christian name, is it? Oh, then, it's Daniel Malcolm, your Majesty, and much at your service!' She waved the sword majestically over his head, and said, 'Rise up, Sir Malcolm Maclise!'

.   .   .   .   .   .

"The ceremony was concluded, the brilliant *cortège* moved away, the royal barouches received the illustrious party, the heralds cried, 'Largesse, Largesse!' and flung silver pennies among the shouting crowds in Trafalgar Square;

and when the last man-at-arms that accompanied the royal train had disappeared, the loud *vivas* of the crowd were heard no more, the shrill song of the silver clarions had died away, his brother painters congratulated the newly dubbed chevalier, and retired to partake of a slight collation of bread and cheese and porter in the keeper's apartments."

Were we, I say, inclined to be romantic, did we dare to be imaginative, such a scene might be depicted with considerable effect; but, as it is, we must not allow poor fancy to get the better of reason, and declare that to write anything of the sort would be perfectly uncalled for and absurd. Let it simply be stated that on the Friday her Majesty comes and goes. On the Saturday the Academicians have a private view for the great personages; the lords of the empire and their ladies, the editors of the newspapers and their friends; and, after they have seen as much as possible, about seven o'clock the Academicians give a grand feed to their friends and patrons.

In the arrangement of this banquet, let us say roundly that Messieurs de l'Académie are vastly too aristocratic. Why were *we* not asked? The dinner is said to be done by Gunter; and, though the soup and fish are notoriously cold and uncomfortable, we are by no means squeamish, and would pass over this gross piece of neglect. We long, too, to hear a bishop say grace, and to sit cheek by jowl with a duke or two. Besides, we could make some return; a good joke is worth a plateful of turtle; a smart brisk pun is quite as valuable as a bottle of champagne; a neat anecdote deserves a slice of venison, with plenty of fat and currant jelly, and so on. On such principles of barter we might be disposed to treat. But a plague on this ribaldry and beating about the bush! let us leave the plates, and come at once to the pictures.

Once or twice before, in the columns of this Magazine, we have imparted to the public our notions about Greek art, and its manifold deadly errors. The contemplation of such specimens of it as we possess hath always, to tell the truth, left us in a state of unpleasant wonderment and perplexity. It carries corporeal beauty to a pitch of painful perfection, and deifies the body and bones truly: but, by dint of sheer beauty, it leaves humanity altogether inhuman — quite heartless and passionless. Look at Apollo the divine: there is no blood in his marble veins, no warmth in his bosom, no fire or speculation in his dull awful eyes. Laocoön writhes and twists in an anguish that never can, in the breast of any spectator, create the smallest degree of pity. Diana,

> "La chasseresse
> Blanche, au sein virginal,
> Qui presse
> Quelque cerf matinal," *

may run from this till Doomsday; and we feel no desire to join the cold passionless huntress in her ghostly chase. Such monsters of beauty are quite out of the reach of human sympathy: they were purposely (by the poor benighted heathens who followed this error, and strove to make their error as grand as possible) placed beyond it. They seemed to think that human joy and sorrow, passion and love, were mean and contemptible in themselves. Their gods were to be calm, and share in no such feelings. How much grander is the character of the Christian school, which teaches that love is the most beautiful of all things, and the first and highest element of beauty in art!

I don't know, madam, whether I make myself clearly understood in saying so much; but if you will have the kindness to look at a certain little picture by Mr. Eastlake in this gallery, you will see to what the observation applies, and that out of a homely subject, and a few simple figures not at all wonderful for excessive beauty or grandeur, the artist can make something infinitely more beautiful than Medicean Venuses and sublimer than Pythian Apollos. Happy are you, Charles Lock Eastlake, Esquire, R.A.! I think you have in your breast some of that sacred fire that lighted the bosom of Raphael Sanctius, Esquire, of Urbino, he being a young man, — a holy kind of Sabbath repose — a calm that comes not of feeling, but of the overflowing of it — a tender yearning sympathy and love for God's beautiful world and creatures. Impelled by such a delightful sentiment, the gentle spirit of him in whom it dwells (like the angels of old, who first taught us to receive the doctrine that love was the key to the world) breathes always peace on earth and good will towards men. And though the privilege of enjoying this happy frame of mind is accorded to the humblest as well as the most gifted genuis, yet the latter must remember that the intellect can exercise

* Alfred de Musset.

itself in no higher way than in the practice of this kind of adoration and gratitude. The great artist who is the priest of nature is consecrated especially to this service of praise; and though it may have no direct relation to religious subjects, the view of a picture of the highest order does always, like the view of stars in a calm night, or a fair quiet landscape in sunshine, fill the mind with an inexpressible content and gratitude towards the Maker who has created such beautiful things for our use.

And as the poet has told us how, not out of a wide landscape merely, or a sublime expanse of glittering stars, but of any very humble thing, we may gather the same delightful reflections (as out of a small flower, that brings us "thoughts that do often lie too deep for tears") — in like manner we do not want grand pictures and elaborate yards of canvas so to affect us, as the lover of drawing must have felt in looking at the Raphael designs lately exhibited in London. These were little faint scraps, mostly from the artist's pencil — small groups, unfinished single figures, just indicated; but the divine elements of beauty were as strong in them as in the grandest pieces: and there were many little sketches, not half an inch high, which charmed and affected one like the violet did Wordsworth; and left one in that unspeakable, complacent, grateful condition, which, as I have been endeavoring to state, is the highest aim of the art.

And if I might be allowed to give a hint to amateurs concerning pictures and their merit, I would say look to have your *heart* touched by them. The best paintings address themselves to the best feelings of it; and a great many very clever pictures do not touch it at all. Skill and handling are great parts of a painter's trade, but heart is the first; this is God's direct gift to him, and cannot be got in any academy, or under any master. Look about, therefore, for pictures, be they large or small, finished well or ill, landscapes, portraits, figure-pieces, pen-and-ink sketches, or what not, that contain sentiment and great ideas. He who possesses these will be sure to express them more or less well. Never mind about the manner. He who possesses them not may draw and color to perfection, and yet be no artist. As for telling you what sentiment is, and what it is not, wherein lies the secret of the sublime, there, madam, we must stop altogether; only, after reading Burke "On the Sublime," you will find yourself exactly as wise as you were before. I cannot tell why a landscape by Claude or Constable should be more beautiful — it is certainly not more dexterous — than a landscape by Mr. —— or Mr. ——. I cannot tell why Raphael should be superior to Mr. Benjamin Haydon (a fact which one person in the world may be perhaps inclined to doubt); or why "Vedrai, carino," in "Don Juan," should be more charming to me than "Suoni la tromba," before mentioned. The latter has twice as much drumming, trumpeting, and thundering in it. All these points are quite undefinable and inexplicable (I never read a metaphysical account of them that did not seem sheer dulness and nonsense); but we can have no doubt about them. And thus we come to Charles Lock Eastlake, Esquire, from whom we started about a page since; during which we have laid down, first, that sentiment is the first quality of a picture; second, that to say whether this sentiment exists or no rests with the individual entirely, the sentiment not being capable of any sort of definition. Charles Lock Eastlake, Esquire, possesses, to my thinking, this undefinable arch-quality of sentiment to a very high degree. And, besides him, let us mention William Mulready, Esquire, Cope, Boxall, Redgrave, Herbert (the two latter don't show so much of it this year as formerly), and Richmond.

Mr. Eastlake's picture is as pure as a Sabbath hymn sung by the voices of children. He has taken a very simple subject — hardly any subject at all; but such suggestive points are the best, perhaps, that a painter can take; for with the illustration of a given subject out of a history or romance, when one has seen it, one has commonly seen all, whereas such a piece as this, which Mr. Eastlake calls, "The Salutation of the Aged Friar," brings the spectator to a delightful peaceful state of mind, and gives him matter to ponder upon long after. The story of this piece is simply this : — A group of innocent happy-looking Italian peasants are approaching a couple of friars ; a boy has stepped forward with a little flower, which he presents to the elder of these, and the old monk is giving him his blessing.

Now, it would be very easy to find fault with this picture, and complain of excessive redness in the shadows, excessive whiteness in the linen, of repetition in the faces, — the smallest child is the very counterpart of one in the "Christ and the Little Children" by the same artist last year — the women are not only copies of women before

painted by Mr. Eastlake, but absolutely copies of one
another; the drawing lacks vigor, the flesh-tints variety
(they seem to be produced, by the most careful stippling,
with a brilliant composition of lake and burnt sienna,
cooled off as they come to the edges with a little blue).
But though, in the writer's judgment, there are in the picture every one ôf these faults, the merits of the performance incomparably exceed them, and these are of the purely
sentimental and intellectual kinds. What a tender grace
and purity in the female heads! If Mr. Eastlake repeats
his model often, at least he has been very lucky in finding
or making her: indeed, I don't know in any painter, ancient or modern, such a charming character of female
beauty. The countenances of the monks are full of unction; the children, with their mild beaming eyes, are fresh
with recollections of heaven. There is no affectation of
middle-age mannerism, such as silly Germans and silly
Frenchmen are wont to call Catholic art; and the picture
is truly Catholic in consequence, having about it what the
hymn calls "solemn mirth," and giving the spectator the
utmost possible pleasure in viewing it. Now, if we might
suggest to Mr. Lane, the lithographer, how he might confer
a vast benefit upon the public, we would entreat him to
make several large copies of pictures of this class, execut-
ing them with that admirable grace and fidelity which are
the characteristics of all his copies. Let these be colored
accurately, as they might be, at a small charge, and poor
people for a few guineas might speedily make for themselves delightful picture galleries. The color adds amazingly to the charm of these pictures, and attracts the eye
to them. And they are such placid pious companions for a
man's study, that the continual presence of them could not
fail to purify his taste and his heart.

I am not here arguing, let it be remembered, that Mr.
Eastlake is absolute perfection; and will concede to those
who find fault with him that his works are deficient in
power, however remarkable for grace. Be it so. But, then,
let us admire his skill in choosing such subjects as are best
suited to his style of thinking, and least likely to show his
faults. In the pieces ordinarily painted by him, grace and
tender feeling are the chief requisites; and I don't recollect
a work of his in which he has aimed at other qualities.
One more picture besides the old Friar has Mr. Eastlake,
a portrait of that beautiful Miss Bury, whom our readers

must recollect in the old house, in a black mantle, a red gown, with long golden hair waving over her shoulders, and a lily in her hand. The picture was engraved afterwards in one of the Annuals; and was one of the most delightful works that ever came from Mr. Eastlake's pencil. I can't say as much for the present portrait: the picture wants relief, and is very odd and heavy in color.* The handsome lady looks as if she wanted her stays. O beautiful lily-bearer of six years since! you should not have appeared like a mortal after having once shone upon us as an angel.

And now we are come to the man whom we delight to honor, Mr. Mulready, who has three pictures in the exhibition that are all charming in their way. The first ("Fair Time," 116) was painted, it is said, more than a score of years since; and the observer may look into it with some payment for his curiosity, for it contains specimens of the artist's old and new manner. The picture in its first state is somewhat in the Wilkie style of that day (oh, for the Wilkie style of that day!), having many grays, and imitating closely the Dutchmen. Since then the painter has been touching up the figures in the foreground with his new and favorite lurid orange-color; and you may see how this is stippled in upon the faces and hands, and borrow, perhaps, a hint or two regarding the Mulreadian secret.

What is the meaning of this strange color? — these glowing burning crimsons, and intense blues, and greens more green than the first budding leaves of spring or the mignonette-pots in a Cockney's window at Brixton. But don't fancy that we are joking or about to joke at Mr. Mulready. These gaudy prismatic colors are wonderfully captivating to the eye: and, amidst a host of pictures, it cannot fail to settle on a Mulready in preference to all. But, for consistency's sake, a protest must be put in against the color; it is pleasant, but wrong; we never saw it in nature — not even when looking through an orange-colored glass. This point being settled, then, and our minds eased, let us look at the design and conception of "First Love;" and pray, sir, where in the whole works of modern artists will you find anything more exquisitely beautiful? I don't know what that young fellow, so solemn, so tender, is whispering into the ear of that dear girl (she is only fifteen now, but, *sapristi*, how beautiful she will be about three years hence!), who is folding a pair of slim arms round a little baby, and making believe to nurse it, as they three are

standing one glowing summer day under some trees by a
stile. I don't know, I say, what they are saying ; nor, if I
could hear, would I tell — 'tis a secret, madam. Recollect the
words that the Captain whispered in your ear that afternoon
in the shrubbery. Your heart throbs, your cheek flushes ;
the sweet sound of those words tells clear upon your ear,
and you say, " Oh, Mr. Titmarsh, how *can* you ? " Be not
afraid, madam — never, never will I peach ; but sing, in the
words of a poet who is occasionally quoted in the House of
Commons —

> " Est et fideli tuta silentio
> Merces. Vetabo qui Cereris sacrum
> Vulgarit arcanæ, sub isdem
> Sit trabibus, fragilemve mecum
> Solvat phaselum."

Which may be interpreted (with a slight alteration of the
name of Ceres for that of a much more agreeable goddess) —

> Be happy, and thy counsel keep,
> 'Tis thus the bard adviseth thee ;
> Remember that the silent lip
> In silence shall rewarded be.
> And fly the wretch who dares to strip
> Love of its sacred mystery.
>
> My loyal legs I would not stretch
> Beneath the same mahogany ;
> Nor trust myself in Chelsea Reach,
> In punt or skiff, with such as he.
> The villain who would kiss and peach,
> I hold him for mine enemy !

But, to return to our muttons, I would not give a fig for the
taste of the individual who does not see the exquisite
beauty of this little group. Our artist has more passion
than the before-lauded Mr. Eastlake, but quite as much
delicacy and tenderness ; and they seem to me to possess
the poetry of picture-making more than any other of their
brethren.

By the way, what is this insane yell that has been raised
throughout the public press about Mr. Mulready's other
performance, the postage cover, and why are the sages so
bitter against it ? The *Times* says it is disgraceful and
ludicrous ; the elegant writers of the *Weekly Dispatch* vow
it is ludicrous and disgraceful ; the same sweet song is
echoed by papers, Radical and Conservative, in London and
the provinces, all the literary gentlemen being alive, and

smarting under this insult to the arts of the country. Honest gentlemen of the press, be not so thin-skinned! Take my word for it, there is no cause for such vehement anger — no good opportunity here for you to show off that exquisite knowledge of the fine arts for which you are so celebrated throughout the world. Gentlemen, the drawing of which you complain is *not* bad. The commonest engravers, who would be ashamed to produce such a design, will tell you, if they know anything of their business, that they could not make a better in a hurry. Every man who knows what drawing is will acknowledge that some of these little groups are charmingly drawn; and I will trouble your commonest engravers to design the Chinese group, the American, or the West Indian, in a manner more graceful and more characteristic than that of the much-bespattered post envelope. I am not holding up the whole affair as a masterpiece — *pas si bête.* The "triumphant hallegory of Britannia ruling the waves," as Mathews used to call it, is a little stale, certainly, nowadays; but what would you have? How is the sublime to be elicited from such a subject? Let some of the common engravers, in their leisure moments, since the thing is so easy, make a better design, or the literary men who are so indignant invent one. The Government, no doubt, is not bound heart and soul to Mr. Mulready, and is willing to hear reason. *Fiat justitia, ruat cœlum:* though all the world shall turn on thee, O Government, in this instance Titmarsh shall stand by thee — ay, and without any hope of reward. To be sure, if my Lord Normanby absolutely insists — but that is neither here nor there. I repeat, the Post Office envelope is not bad, *quoad* design. That very lion, which some of the men of the press (the Daniels!) have been crying out about, is finely, carefully, and characteristically sketched; those elephants I am sure were closely studied, before the artist in a few lines laid them down on his wood-block; and as for the persons who are to imitate the engraving so exactly, let them try. It has been done by the best wood-engraver in Europe. Ask any man in the profession if Mr. Thompson is not at the head of it? He has bestowed on it a vast deal of time, and skill, and labor; and all who know the difficulties of wood-engraving — of outline wood-engraving — and of rendering faithfully a design so very minute as this, will smile at the sages who declare that all the world could forge it. There was one provincial paper which declared, in a style peculiarly elegant, that a man "with a block of wood and a *bread-and-cheese* knife could easily imitate the envelope;" which remark, for its profound truth and sagacity, the London journals copied.   For shame, gentlemen !   Do you think you show your knowledge by adopting such opinions as these, or prove your taste by clothing yourselves in the second-hand garments of the rustic who talks about bread and cheese ?   Try, Tyrotomos, upon whatever block thou choos-est to practise ; or, be wise, and with appropriate bread-and-cheese knife cut only bread and cheese.   Of bread, white and brown, of cheese, old, new, mouldy, toasted, the writer of the *Double-Gloster Journal,* the *Stilton Examiner,* the *Cheddar Champion,* and *North Wiltshire Intelligencer,* may possibly be a competent critic, and (with mouth replete with the delicious condiment) may no doubt eloquently speak.   But let us be cautious before we agree to and admiringly adopt his opinions upon matters of art.   Mr. Thompson is the first wood-engraver in our country — Mr. Mulready one of the best painters in our or any school; it is hard that such men are to be assailed in such language, and by such a critic !

This artist's picture of an interior is remarkable for the same exaggerated color, and for the same excellences.   The landscape seen from the window is beautifully solemn, and very finely painted, in the clear bright manner ·of Van Dyck and Cranach, and the early German school.

Mr. Richmond's picture of "Our Lord after the Resur-rection " deserves a much better place than it has in the little, dingy, newly discovered octagon closet; and leaves us to regret that he should occupy himself so much with water-color portraits, and so little with compositions in oil. This picture is beautifully conceived, and very finely and carefully drawn and painted.   One of the apostles is copied from Raphael, and the more is the pity : a man who could execute two such grand figures as the other two in the picture need surely borrow from no one.   A water-color group by the same artist (547, " The Children of Colonel Lindsay ") contains two charming figures of a young lady and a little boy, painted with great care and precision of design and color, with great purity of sentiment, and with-out the least affectation.   Let our aristocracy send their wives and children (the handsomest wives and children in the world) to be painted by this gentleman, and those who are like him.   Miss Lindsay, with her plain red dress and·

modest looks, is surely a thousand times more captivating than those dangerous smiling Delilahs in her neighborhood, whom Mr. Chalon has painted. We must not be understood to undervalue this latter gentleman, however; his drawings are miracles of dexterity; every year they seem to be more skilful and more brilliant. Such satins and lace, such diamond rings and charming little lapdogs, were never painted before, — not by Watteau, the first master of the *genre*, — nor by Lancret, who was scarcely his inferior. A miniature on ivory by Mr. Chalon, among the thousand prim, pretty little pictures of the same class which all the ladies crowd about, is remarkable for its brilliancy of color and charming freedom of handling; as is an oil sketch of masquerading figures, by the same painter, for the curious coarseness of the painting.

Before we leave the high-class pictures, we must mention Mr. Boxall's beautiful "Hope," which is exquisitely refined and delicate in sentiment, color, and execution. Placed close beneath one of Turner's magnificent tornadoes of color, it loses none of its own beauty. As Uhland writes of a certain king and queen who are seated in state side by side, —

" Der *Turner* furchtbar prächtig wie blut'ger Nordlichtschein,
Der *Boxall* süss und milde, als blickte Vollmond drein."

Which signifies in English that, —

" As beams the moon so gentle near the sun, that blood-red burner,
So shineth William Boxall by Joseph Mallord Turner."

In another part of the room, and contrasting their quiet grace in the same way with Mr. Turner's glaring colors, are a couple of delightful pictures by Mr. Cope, with mottoes that will explain their subjects. "Help thy father in his age, and despise him not when thou art in thy full strength;" and "Reject not the affliction of the afflicted, neither turn away thy face from a poor man." The latter of these pictures is especially beautiful, and the figure of the female charity as graceful and delicate as may be. I wish I could say a great deal in praise of Mr. Cope's large altar-piece: it is a very meritorious performance; but here praise stops, and such praise is worth exactly nothing. A large picture must either be splendid, or else naught. This "Crucifixion" has a great deal of vigor, feeling, grace; BUT

— the but is fatal; all minor praises are drowned in it.
Recollect, however, Mr. Cope, that Titmarsh, who writes
this, is only giving his private opinion; that he is mortal;
that it is barely possible that he should be in the wrong;
and with this confession, which I am compelled (for fear
you might overlook the circumstance) to make, you will, I
dare say, console yourself, and do well. But men must
gird themselves, and go through long trainings, before they
can execute such gigantic works as altar-pieces. Handel,
doubtless, wrote many little pleasing melodies before he
pealed out the "Hallelujah" chorus; and so painters will
do well to try their powers, and, if possible, measure and
understand them, before they use them. There is Mr.
Hart, for instance, who took in an evil hour to the making
of great pictures; in the present exhibition is a decently
small one; but the artist has overstretched himself in the
former attempts; as one hears of gentlemen on the rack,
the limbs are stretched one or two inches by the process,
and the patient comes away by so much the taller: but he
can't *walk* near so well as before, and all his strength is
stretched out of him.

Let this be a solemn hint to a clever young painter, Mr.
Elmore, who has painted a clever picture of "The Murder
of Saint Thomas à Becket," for Mr. Daniel O'Connell.
Come off your rack, Mr. Elmore, or you will hurt yourself.
Much better is it to paint small subjects, for some time at
least. "Non cuivis contingit adire Corinthum," as the
proverb says; but there is a number of pleasant villages in
this world beside, where we may snugly take up our
quarters. By the way, what is the meaning of Tom à
Becket's black cassock under his canonicals? Would John
Tuam celebrate mass in such a dress? A painter should
be as careful about his costumes as an historian about his
dates, or he plays the deuce with his composition.

Now, in this matter of costume, nobody can be more
scrupulous than Mr. Charles Landseer, whose picture of
Nell Gwynne is painted with admirable effect, and honest
scrupulousness. It is very good in color, very gay in
spirits (perhaps too refined — for Nelly never was such a
hypocrite as to look as modest as that); but the gentlemen
and ladies do not look as if they were accustomed to their
dresses, for all their correctness, but had put them on for
the first time. Indeed, this is a very small fault, and the
merits of the picture are very great: every one of the ac

cessories is curiously well painted, — some of the figures very spirited (the drawer is excellent) : and the picture one of the most agreeable in the whole gallery. Mr. Redgrave has another costume picture, of a rather old subject, from "The Rambler." A poor girl comes to be companion to Mr. and Mrs. Courtly, who are at piquet; their servants are bringing in tea, and the master and mistress are looking at the new-comer with a great deal of easy scorn. The poor girl is charming; Mrs. Courtly not quite genteel, but with a wonderful quilted petticoat; Courtly looks as if he were not accustomed to his clothes; the servants are very good; and as for the properties, as they would be called on the stage, these are almost too good, painted with a daguerréo-typical minuteness that gives this and Mr. Redgrave's other picture of " Paracelsus" a finikin air, if we may use such a disrespectful term. Both performances, however, contain very high merit of expression and sentiment; and are of such a character as we seldom saw in our schools twenty years ago.

There is a large picture by a Scotch artist, Mr. Duncan, representing "The Entry of Charles Edward into Edinburgh," which runs a little into caricature, but contains a vast deal of character and merit; and which, above all, in the article of costume, shows much study and taste. Mr. Duncan seems to have formed his style upon Mr. Allan and Mr. Wilkie — I beg his pardon — Sir David. The former has a pleasing brown picture likewise on the subject of the Pretender. The latter's Maid of Saragossa and Spaniard at the gun, any one may see habited as Irish peasants superintending " A Whiskey Still," in the middle room, No. 252.

This picture, I say, any one may see and admire who pleases : to me it seems all rags, and duds, and a strange, straggling, misty composition. There are fine things, of course; for how can Sir David help painting fine things ? In the "Benvenuto" there is superb color, with a rich management of lakes especially, which has been borrowed from no master that we know of. The Queen is as bad a likeness and picture as we have seen for many a day. "Mrs. Ferguson, of Raith," a magnificent picture indeed, as grand in effect as a Rubens or Titian, and having a style of its own. The little sketch from Allan Ramsay is delightful ; and the nobleman and hounds (with the exception of his own clumsy vermilion robe), as fine as the fellow-sized portrait mentioned before. Allan Ramsay has given a pretty subject, and brought us a pretty picture from another painter, Mr. A. Johnston, who has illustrated those pleasant quaint lines, —

> " Last morning I was gay, and early out ;
> Upon a dike I leaned, glow'ring about.
> I saw my Meg come linkan o'er the lea ;
> I saw my Meg, but Meggy saw na me."

And here let us mention with praise two small pictures in a style somewhat similar — " The Recruit," and " Hermann and Dorothea," by Mr. Poole. The former of these little pieces is very touching and beautiful. There is among the present exhibitioners no lack of this kind of talent; and we could point out many pictures that are equally remarkable for grace and agreeable feeling. Mr. Stone's "Annot Lyle" should not be passed over, — a pretty picture, very well painted, the female head of great beauty and expression.

Now, if we want to praise performances showing a great deal of power and vigor, rather than grace and delicacy, there are Mr. Etty's "Andromeda" and "Venus." In the former, the dim figure of advancing Perseus galloping on his airy charger is very fine and ghostly; in the latter, the body of the Venus, and indeed the whole picture, is a perfect miracle of color. Titian may have painted Italian flesh equally well; but he never, I think, could surpass the skill of Mr. Etty. The trunk of this voluptuous Venus is the most astonishing representation of beautiful English flesh and blood, painted in the grandest and broadest style. It is said that the Academy at Edinburgh has a room full of Etty's pictures; they could not do better in England than follow the example; but perhaps the paintings had better be kept *for the Academy only* — for the *profanum vulgus* are scarcely fitted to comprehend their peculiar beauties. A prettily drawn, graceful, nude figure is "Bathsheba," by Mr. Fisher, of the street and city of Cork.

The other great man of Cork is Daniel Maclise by name; and if in the riot of fancy he hath by playful Titmarsh been raised to the honor of knighthood, it is certain that here Titmarsh is a true prophet, and that the sovereign will so elevate him, one day or other, to sit with other cavaliers at the Academic round table. As for his pictures, — why, as for his pictures, madam, these are to be carefully reviewed in the next number of this Magazine;

for the present notice has noticed scarcely anybody, and yet stretched to an inordinate length. "Macbeth" is not to be hurried off under six pages; and for this June number, Mr. Fraser vows that he has no such room to spare.

We have said how Mr. Turner's pictures blaze about the rooms; it is not a little curious to hear how artists and the public differ in their judgment concerning them; the enthusiastic wonder of the first-named, the blank surprise and incredulity of the latter. "The new moon; or, I've lost my boat: you sha'n't have your hoop," is the ingenious title of one, — a very beautiful picture, too, of a long shining sea-sand, lighted from the upper part of the canvas by the above-named luminary of night, and from the left-hand corner by a wonderful wary boy in a red jacket — the best painted figure that we ever knew painted by Joseph Mallord Turner, Esquire.

He and Mr. Ward vie with each other in mottoes for their pictures. Ward's epigraph to the S——'s nest is wondrous poetic.

277. The S——'s Nest. S. Ward, R.A.

> "Say they that happiness lives with the great,
> On gorgeous trappings mixt with pomp and state ?
> More frequent found upon the simple plain,
> In poorest garb, with Julia, Jess, or Jane ;
> In sport or slumber, as it likes her best,
> Where'er she *lays* she finds it a S——'s nest."

Ay, and a S——'s eggs, too, as one would fancy, were great geniuses not above grammar. Mark the line, too,

> "On gorgeous trappings *mixt* with pomp and state,"

and construe the whole of this sensible passage.

Not less sublime is Mr. Ward's fellow-Academician : —

230. "Slavers throwing overboard the Dead and Dying: Typhoon coming on." J. M. W. Turner, R.A.

> "Aloft all hands, strike the topmasts and belay !
> Yon angry setting sun and fierce-edged clouds
> Declare the Typhoon's coming.
> Before it sweeps your decks, throw overboard
> The dead and dying — ne'er heed their chains.
> Hope, Hope, fallacious Hope !
> Where is thy market now ?"
> *MS. Fallacies of Hope.*

Fallacies of Hope, indeed: to a pretty mart has she brought her pigs! How should Hope be hooked on to the slaver? By the anchor, to be sure, which accounts for it. As for the picture, the R.A.'s rays are indeed terrific; and the slaver throwing its cargo overboard is the most tremendous piece of color that ever was seen; it sets the corner of the room in which it hangs into a flame. Is the picture sublime or ridiculous? Indeed I don't know which. Rocks of gamboge are marked down upon the canvas; flakes of white laid on with a trowel; bladders of vermilion madly spirted here and there. Yonder is the slaver rocking in the midst of a flashing foam of white lead. The sun glares down upon a horrible sea of emerald and purple, into which chocolate-colored slaves are plunged, and chains that will not sink; and round these are floundering such a race of fishes as never was seen since the *sæculum Pyrrhæ;* gasping dolphins, redder than the reddest herrings; horrid spreading polypi, like huge, slimy, poached eggs, in which hapless niggers plunge and disappear. Ye gods, what a "middle passage"! How Mr. Fowell Buxton must shudder! What would they say to this in Exeter Hall? If Wilberforce's statue downstairs were to be confronted with this picture, the stony old gentleman would spring off his chair, and fly away in terror!

And here, as we are speaking of the slave-trade, let us say a word in welcome to a French artist, Monsieur Biard, and his admirable picture. Let the friends of the negro forthwith buy this canvas, and cause a plate to be taken from it. It is the best, most striking, most pathetic lecture against the trade that ever was delivered. The picture is as fine as Hogarth; and the artist, who, as we have heard, right or wrong, has only of late years adopted the profession of painting, and was formerly in the French navy, has evidently drawn a great deal of his materials from life and personal observation. The scene is laid upon the African coast. King Tom or King Boy has come with troops of slaves down the Quorra, and sits in the midst of his chiefs and mistresses (one a fair creature, not much darker than a copper tea-kettle) bargaining with a French dealer. What a horrible callous brutality there is in the scoundrel's face, as he lolls over his greasy ledger, and makes his calculations. A number of his crew are about him; their boats close at hand, in which they are stowing their cargo. See the poor wretches, men and women, col-

lared together, drooping down. There is one poor thing
just parted from her child. On the ground in front lies a
stalwart negro; one connoisseur is handling his chest, to
try his wind; another has opened his mouth, and examines
his teeth, to know his age and soundness. Yonder is a
poor woman kneeling before one of the Frenchmen; her
shoulder is fizzing under the hot iron with which he brands
her; she is looking up, shuddering and wild, yet quite mild
and patient: it breaks your heart to look at her. I never
saw anything so exquisitely pathetic as that face. God
bless you, Monsieur Biard, for painting it! It stirs the
heart more than a hundred thousand tracts, reports, or sermons: it must convert every man who has seen it. You
British Government, who have given twenty millions
toward the good end of freeing this hapless people, give
yet a couple of thousand more to the French painter, and
don't let his work go out of the country, now that it is
here. Let it hang along with the Hogarths in the National
Gallery; it is as good as the best of them. Or, there is
Mr. Thomas Babington Macaulay, who has a family interest in the matter, and does not know how to spend all the
money he brought home from India; let the right honorable gentleman look to it. Down with your dust, right
honorable sir; give Monsieur Biard a couple of thousand
for his picture of the negroes, and it will be the best black
act you ever did in your life; and don't go for to be angry
at the suggestion, or fancy we are taking liberties. What
is said is said from one public man to another, in a Pickwickian sense, *de puissance en puissance,* — from Titmarsh,
in his critical *cathedra,* to your father's eminent son, rich
with the spoils of Ind, and wielding the bolts of war.

What a marvellous power is this of the painter's! how
each great man can excite us at his will! what a weapon
he has, if he knows how to wield it! Look for a while at
Mr. Etty's pictures and away you rush, your "eyes on fire,"
drunken with the luscious colors that are poured out for
you on the liberal canvas, and warm with the sight of the
beautiful sirens that appear on it. You fly from this (and
full time, too) and plunge into a green shady landscape of
Lee or Creswick, and follow a quiet stream babbling beneath whispering trees, and checkered with cool shade and
golden sunshine; or you set the world — nay, the Thames
and the ocean — on fire with that incendiary Turner; or
you laugh with honest kind-hearted Webster, and his

troops of merry children ; or you fall a-weeping with Monsieur Biard for his poor blacks; or you go and consult the priests of the place, Eastlake, Mulready, Boxall, Cope, and the like, and straightway your mind is carried off in an ecstasy,—happy thrilling hymns sound in your ears melodious,—sweet thankfulness fills your bosom. How much instruction and happiness have we gained from these men, and how grateful should we be to them!

[It is well that Mr. Titmarsh stopped here, and I shall take special care to examine any further remarks which he may think fit to send. Four-fifths of this would have been cancelled, had the printed sheets fallen sooner into our hands. The story about the "Clarendon" is an absurd fiction; no dinner ever took place there. I never fell asleep in a plate of raspberry ice; and though I certainly did recommend this person to do justice by the painters, making him a speech to that effect, my opinions were infinitely better expressed, and I would repeat them were it not so late in the month. — O. Y.]

II.

A PICTORIAL RHAPSODY. — Concluded.

AND FOLLOWED BY A REMARKABLE STATEMENT OF FACTS BY MRS. BARBARA.

[*Fraser's Magazine, July*, 1840.]

AND now, in pursuance of the promise recorded in the last number of this Magazine, and for the performance of which the public has ever since been in breathless expectation, it hath become Titmarsh's duty to note down his opinions of the remaining pictures in the Academy exhibition; and to criticise such other pieces as the other galleries may show.

In the first place, then, with regard to Mr. Maclise, it becomes us to say our say : and as the *Observer* newspaper, which, though under the express patronage of the royal family, devotes by far the noblest part of its eloquence to the consideration of dramatic subjects, and to the discussion of the gains, losses, and theatrical conduct of managers, — as, I say, the *Observer* newspaper, whenever Madame Vestris or Mr. Yates adopts any plan that concurs with the notions of the paper in question, does not fail to say that Madame Vestris or Mr. Yates has been induced so to reform in consequence of the *Observer's* particular suggestion; in like manner, Titmarsh is fully convinced that all the painters in this town have their eyes incessantly fixed upon his criticisms, and that all the wise ones regulate their opinions by his.

In the language of the *Observer*, then, Mr. Maclise has done wisely to adopt our suggestiou with regard to the moral treatment of his pictures, and has made a great advance in his art. Of his four pictures, let us dismiss the scene from " Gil Blas " at once. Coming from a second-rate man, it would be well enough; it is well drawn, grouped, lighted, shadowed, and the people all grin very comically, as people do in pictures called comic; but the soul of fun is wanting, as I take it, — the merry, brisk, good-humored spirit which in Le Sage's text so charms the reader.

"Olivia and Malvolio" is, on the contrary, one of the best and most spiritual performances of the artist. Nothing can be more elegant than the tender languid melancholy of Olivia, nor more poetical than the general treatment of the picture. The long clipped alleys and quaint gardens, the peacocks trailing through the walks, and vases basking in the sun, are finely painted and conceived. Examine the picture at a little distance, and the *ensemble* of the composition and color is extraordinarily pleasing. The details, too, are, as usual, wonderful for their accuracy. Here are flower-beds, and a tree above Olivia's head, of which every leaf is painted, and painted with such skill as not in the least to injure the general effect of the picture. Mr. Maclise has a daguerréotypic eye, and a feeling of form stronger, I do believe, than has ever been possessed by any painter before him.

Look at the portrait of Mr. Dickens, — well arranged as a picture, good in color, and light, and shadow, and as a likeness perfectly amazing; a looking-glass could not render a better fac-simile. Here we have the real identical man Dickens: the artist must have understood the inward Boz as well as the outward before he made this admirable representation of him. What cheerful intelligence there is about the man's eyes and large forehead! The mouth is too large and full, too eager and active, perhaps; the smile is very sweet and generous. If Monsieur de Balzac, that voluminous physiognomist, could examine this head, he would, no doubt, interpret every tone and wrinkle in it: the nose firm, and well placed; the nostrils wide and full, as are the nostrils of all men of genius (this is Monsieur Balzac's maxim). The past and the future, says Jean Paul, are written in every countenance. I think we may promise ourselves a brilliant future from this one. There seems no flagging as yet in it, no sense of fatigue, or consciousness of decaying power. Long mayest thou, O Boz! reign over thy comic kingdom; long may we pay tribute, whether of threepence weekly or of a shilling monthly, it matters not. Mighty prince! at thy imperial feet, Titmarsh, humblest of thy servants, offers his vows of loyalty, and his humble tribute of praise.

And now (as soon as we are off our knees, and have done paying court to sovereign Boz) it behooves us to say a word or two concerning the picture of "Macbeth," which occupies such a conspicuous place in the Academy gallery. Well, then, this picture of "Macbeth" has been, to our notion, a great deal too much praised and abused; only Titmarsh understands the golden mean, as is acknowledged by all who read his criticisms. Here is a very fine masterly picture, no doubt, full of beauties, and showing extraordinary power; but not a masterpiece, as I humbly take it, — not a picture to move the beholder as much as many performances that do not display half the power that is here exhibited. I don't pretend to lay down any absolute laws on the sublime (the reader will remember how the ancient satirist hath accused John Dennis of madness, for his vehement preaching of such rules). No, no; Michael Angelo T. is not quite so impertinent as that; but the public and the artist will not mind being told, without any previous definitions, that this picture is not of the highest order: the "Malvolio" is far more spiritual and suggestive, if we may so speak; it tells not only its own tale very charmingly, but creates for the beholder a very pleasant melancholy train of thought, as every good picture does in its kind, from a six-inch canvas by Hobbema or Ruysdael up to a thousand-foot wall of Michael Angelo. If you read over the banquet-scene in words, it leaves an impression far more dreadful and lively. On the stage, it has always seemed to us to fail; and though out of a trap-door in the middle of it Mr. Cooper is seen to rise very solemnly, — his face covered with white, and a dreadful gash of vermilion across his neck; though he nods and waggles his head about in a very quiet ghostlike manner; yet, strange to say, neither this scene, nor this great actor, has ever frightened us, as they both should, as the former does when we read it at home. The fact is, that it is quite out of Mr. Cooper's power to look ghostly enough, or, perhaps, to soar along with us to that sublime height to which our imagination is continually carrying us.

A large part of this vast picture Mr. Maclise has painted very finely. The lords are all there in gloomy state, fierce stalwart men in steel; the variety of attitude and light in which the different groups are placed, the wonderful knowledge and firmness with which each individual figure and feature are placed down upon the canvas will be understood and admired by the public, but by the artist still more, who knows the difficulty of these things, which

seem so easy, which are so easy, no doubt, to a man
with Mr. Maclise's extraordinary gifts. How fine is yonder group at the farthest table, lighted up by the reflected
light from the armor of one of them ! The effect, as far as
we know, is entirely new; the figures drawn with exquisite minuteness and clearness, not in the least interrupting
the general harmony of the picture. Look at the two
women standing near Lady Macbeth's throne, and those
beautiful little hands of one of them placed over the state-
chair : the science, workmanship, feeling in these figures
are alike wonderful. The face, bust, and attitude of Lady
Macbeth are grandly designed; the figures to her right,
with looks of stern doubt and wonder, are nobly designed
and arranged. The main figure of Macbeth, I confess, does
not please; nor the object which has occasioned the frightful convulsive attitude in which he stands. He sees not
the ghost of Banquo, but a huge, indistinct, gory shadow,
which seems to shake its bloody locks, and frown upon him.
Through this shade, intercepted only by its lurid transpar-
ency, you see the figures of the guests; they are looking
towards it, and *through* it. The skill with which this point
is made is unquestionable; there is something there, and
nothing. The spectators feel this as well as the painted
actors of the scene; there are times when, in looking at the
picture, one loses sight of the shade altogether, and begins
to wonder with Rosse, Lenox, and the rest.

The idea, then, so far as it goes, is as excellently worked
out as it is daringly conceived. But is it a just one ? I
think not. I should say it was a grim piece of comedy
rather than tragedy. One is puzzled by this piece of *dia-
blerie*, — not deeply affected and awe-stricken, as in the midst
of such heroical characters and circumstances one should be.

> " Avaunt, and quit my sight! Let the earth hide thee!
> Thy bones are marrowless — thy blood is cold;
> Thou hast no speculation in those eyes
> Which thou dost glare with."

Before the poet's eyes, at least, the figure of the ghost
stood complete — an actual visible body, with the life gone
out of it; an image far more grand and dreadful than the
painter's fantastical shadow, because more simple. The
shadow is an awful object, — granted; but the most sublime, beautiful, fearful sight in all nature is, surely, the
face of a man; wonderful in all its expressions of grief or

joy, daring or endurance, thought, hope, love, or pain.　How Shakespeare painted all these; with what careful thought and brooding were all his imaginary creatures made!

I believe we have mentioned the best figure-pieces in the exhibition; for, alas! the "Milton and his Daughters" of Sir Augustus Callcott, although one of the biggest canvases in the gallery, is by no means one of the best; and one may regret that this most *spirituel* of landscape-painters should have forsaken his old style to follow figure-drawing.　Mr. Hollins has a picture of "Benvenuto Cellini showing a Trinket to a Lady."　A subject of absorbing interest and passionate excitement, painted in a corresponding manner.　A prim lady sits smiling in a chair, by a table, on which is a very neat regular tablecloth, drawn at right angles with the picture-frame; parallel with the table is a chest of drawers, secrétaire, cabinet, or *bahut*.　Near this stands a waiting-maid, smiling archly; and in front you behold young Benvenuto, spick and span in his very best clothes and silk stockings, looking — as Benvenuto never did in his life. Of some parts of this picture, the color and workmanship are very pretty; but was there ever such a niminypiminy subject treated in such a niminypiminy way?　We can remember this gentleman's picture of "Margaret at the Spinning-wheel" last year, and should be glad to see and laud others that were equally pretty.　Mr. Lauder has, in the same room, a pleasing picture from Walter Scott, "The Glee-Maiden;" and a large sketch, likewise from Scott, by a French artist (who has been celebrated in this Magazine as the author of the picture "The Sinking of the 'Vengeur'"), is fine in effect and composition.

If Mr. Herbert's picture of "Travellers taking Refreshment at a Convent Gate" has not produced much sensation, it is because it is feeble in tone, not very striking in subject, and placed somewhat too high.　There is a great deal of beauty and delicacy in all the figures; and though lost here, amidst the glare and bustle of the Academy, it will be an excellent picture for the cabinet, where its quiet graces and merits will be better seen.

Mr. Webster's "Punch," before alluded to, deserves a great deal of praise.　The landscape is beautiful, the group of little figures assembled to view the show are delightfully gay and pretty.　Mr. Webster has the bump of philoprogenitiveness (as some ninny says of George Cruikshank in the *Westminster Review*); and all mothers of large families, young ladies who hope to be so one day or the other, and honest papas, are observed to examine this picture with much smiling interest. It is full of sunshine and innocent playful good-humor; all Punch's audience are on the grin. John, the squire's footman, is looking on with a protecting air; the old village folk are looking on, grinning with the very youngest; boys are scampering over the common, in order to be in time for the show; Punchman is tootooing on the pipes, and banging away on the drum; potboy has consigned to the earth his precious cargo, and the head of every tankard of liquor is wasting its frothy fragrance in the air; in like manner the pieman permits his wares to get cold; nurserymaids, schoolboys, happy children in go-carts, are employed in a similar way : indeed, a delightful little rustic comedy.

In respect of portraits, the prettiest, as I fancy, after Wilkie's splendid picture of Mrs. Ferguson, is one by Mr. Grant, of a lady with a scarf of a greenish color. The whole picture is of the same tone, and beautifully harmonious; nor are the lady's face and air the least elegant and charming part of it. The Duke has been painted a vast number of times, such are the penalties of glory; nor is it possible to conceive anything much worse than that portrait of him in which Colonel Gurwood is represented by his side, in a red velvet waistcoat, offering to his Grace certain despatches. It is in the style of the famous picture in the Regent Circus, representing Mr. Coleby the cigarist, an orange, a pineapple, a champagne-cork, a little dog, some decanters, and a yellow bandanna, — all which personages appear to be so excessively important that the puzzled eyes scarcely know upon which to settle. In like manner, in the Wellington-Gurwood testimonial, the accessories are so numerous, and so brilliantly colored, that it is long before one can look up to the countenances of the Colonel and his Grace; which, it is to be presumed, are the main objects of interest in the piece. And this plan has been not unartfully contrived, — for the heads are by no means painted up to the point of brilliancy which is visible in boots, clocks, bell-pulls, Turkey carpets, arm-chairs, and other properties here painted.

Now, if the artist of the above picture wishes to know how properties may be painted with all due minuteness, and yet conduce to the general effect of the picture, let him

examine the noble little portrait of Lord Cottenham, by
Leslie, — the only contribution of this great man to the
exhibition. Here are a number of accessories introduced,
but with that forethought and sense of propriety which, as
I fancy, distinguish all the works of Mr. Leslie. They are
not here for mere picturesque effect or ornamental huddle ;
but are made to tell the story of the piece, and indicate the
character of the dignified personage who fills the centre of
it. The black brocade drapery of the Chancellor's gown is
accurately painted, and falls in that majestic grave way in
which a chancellor's robe *should* fall. Are not the learned
lord's arms somewhat short and fin-like ? This is a query
which we put humbly, having never had occasion to remark
that part of his person.

Mr. Briggs has his usual pleasant well-painted portraits ;
and Mr. Patten a long full-length of Prince Albert that is
not admired by artists, it is said, but a good downright
honest *bourgeois* picture, as we fancy ; or, as a facetious
friend remarked, good plain *roast-and-boiled* painting. As
for the portrait opposite — that of her Majesty, it is a sheer
libel upon that pretty gracious countenance, an act of
rebellion for which Sir David should be put into York jail.
Parts of the picture are, however, splendidly painted. And
here, being upon the subject, let us say a word in praise
of those two delightful lithographic heads, after Ross,
which appear in the printshop windows. Our gracious
Queen's head is here most charming ; and that of the Prince
full of such manly frankness and benevolence as must make
all men cry "God bless him." I would much sooner
possess a copy of the Ross miniature of the Queen, than a
cast from her Majesty's bust by Sir Francis Chantrey, which
has the place of honor in the sculpture vault.

All Macdonald's busts deserve honorable notice. This
lucky sculptor has some beautiful subjects to model, and
beautiful and graceful all his marbles are. As much may
be said of Mr. M‘Dowell's girl, — the only piece of imaginative sculpture in the Academy that has struck us as
pleasing. Mr. Behnes, too, should receive many commen-
dations ; an old man's head particularly, that is full of
character and goodness ; and "The Bust of a Lady," which
may be called "A Lady with a Bust," — a beautiful bust,
indeed, of which the original and the artist have both good
right to be proud. Mr. Bell's virgin is not so pleasing in
the full size as in the miniature copy of it.

For the matter of landscapes, we confess ourselves to be no very ardent admirers of these performances, clever and dexterous as most of them are. The works of Mr. Stanfield and Mr. Roberts cannot fail to be skilful; and both of these famous artists show their wonderful power of drawing, as usual. But these skilful pictures have always appeared to us more pleasing in little on the sketching-board than when expanded upon the canvas. A couple of Martin's must be mentioned, — huge, queer, and tawdry to our eyes, but very much admired by the public, who is no bad connoisseur, after all; and also a fine Castle of Chillon, or Chalon, rudely painted, but very poetical and impressive.

[Here Titmarsh exchanges his check at the door for a valuable gingham umbrella, with a yellow horn-head, representing Lord Brougham or Doctor Syntax, and is soon seen, with his hat very much on one side, swaggering down Pall Mall East, to the Water-Color Gallery. He flings down eighteenpence in the easiest way, and goes upstairs.]

Accident, or what is worse, ill health, has deprived us of the two most skilful professors of the noble art of water-color painting; and, without the works of Messrs. Lewis and Cattermole, the gallery looks empty indeed. Those gentlemen are accustomed to supply the picture-lover with the *pièces de résistance* of the feast, with which, being decently satisfied, we can trifle with an old market-place by Prout, or six cows and four pigs by Hill, or a misty Downs by Copley Fielding, with some degree of pleasure. Discontented, then, with the absence of the substantials, it must be confessed that we have been examining the rest of the pictures in no very good humor. And so, to tell you a secret, I do not care a fig for all the old town-halls in the world, though they be drawn never so skilfully. How long are we to go on with Venice, Verona, Lago di Soandso, and Ponte di What-d'ye-call-'em? I am weary of gondolas, striped awnings, sailors with red night (or rather day) caps, cobalt distances, and posts in the water. I have seen so many white palaces standing before dark purple skies, so many black towers with gamboge atmospheres behind them, so many masses of rifle-green trees plunged into the deepest shadow, in the midst of sunshiny plains, for no other reason but because dark and light contrast together, that a slight expression of satiety may be permitted to me, and a longing for more simple nature. On a great staring theatre such pictures may do very well — you are obliged there to seek for these startling contrasts; and by the aid of blue lights, red lights, transparencies, and plenty of drums and appropriate music, the scene thus presented to one captivates the eye, and calls down thunder from the galleries.

But in little quiet rooms, on sheets of paper of a yard square, such monstrous theatrical effects are sadly painful. You don't mistake patches of brickdust for maidens' blushes, or fancy that tinfoil is diamonds, or require to be spoken to with the utmost roar of the lungs. Why, in painting, are we to have monstrous, flaring, Drury Lane tricks and claptraps put in practice, when a quieter style is, as I fancy, so infinitely more charming?

There is no use in mentioning the names of persons who are guilty of the above crimes; but let us say who is *not* guilty, and that is D. Cox, upon whose quiet landscapes, moist grass, cool trees, the refreshed eye rests with the utmost pleasure, after it has been perplexed and dazzled elsewhere. May we add an humble wish that this excellent painter will remain out of doors, amidst such quiet scenes as he loves, and not busy himself with Gothicism, middleageism, and the painting of quaint interiors? There are a dozen artists, of not a tithe of his genius, who can excel him at the architectural work. There is, for instance, Mr. Nash, who is improving yearly, and whose pictures are not only most dexterously sketched, but contain numberless little episodes, in the shape of groups of figures, that are full of grace and feeling. There is Mr. Haghe, too, of the lower house; but of him anon.

To show how ill and how well a man may paint at the same time, the public may look at a couple of drawings by J. Nash — one, the interior of a church; the other, a plain landscape: both of which are executed with excessive, almost childish rudeness, and are yet excellent, as being close copies of the best of all drawing-masters, Nature: and Mr. Barrett, who has lately written a book for students, tells them very sagaciously *not* to copy the manner of any master, however much he may be in the mode. Some there are, fashionable instructors in the art of water-coloring, of whom, indeed, a man had better not learn at any price; nay, were they to offer a guinea per lesson, instead of modestly demanding the same, the reader should be counselled not to accept of their instructions.

See in what a different school Mr. Hunt works, and what marvellous effects he produces! There is a small picture of an interior by him (to which the blue ticket having the pretty word SOLD written on it is not fixed) that, as a copy of nature, is a perfect miracle. No De Hooghe was ever better, more airy and sunshiny. And the most extraordinary part of this extraordinary picture is, that the artist has not produced his effect of excessive brilliancy by any violent contrasting darkness; but the whole picture is light; the sunshine is in every corner of the room; and this drawing remains unsold, while Dash, and Blank, and Asterisk have got off all theirs. The large head of the black girl is painted with wonderful power; in water-colors, we have scarcely seen anything so vigorous. The boys and virgins are, as usual, admirable; the lad with the bottle, he reading ballads in the barn, and the red, ragged, brick-dust-colored, brigand-looking fellow, especially good. In a corner is a most astonishing young gentleman with a pan of milk : he is stepping forward full in your face; and has seen something in it which has caused him to spill his milk and look dreadfully frightened. Every man, who is worth a fig, as he comes up to this picture, bursts out a-laughing — he can't help himself; you hear a dozen such laughs in the course of your visit. Why does this little drawing so seize hold of the beholder and cause him to roar? There is the secret : the painter has got the soul of comedy in him — the undefinable humorous genius. Happy is the man who possesses that drawing: a man must laugh if he were taking his last look at it before being hanged.

Mr. Taylor's flowing pencil has produced several pieces of delightful color; but we are led bitterly to deplore the use of that fatal white-lead pot, that is clogging and blackening the pictures of so many of the water-color painters nowadays. His large picture contains a great deal of this white mud, and has lost, as we fancy, in consequence, much of that liquid mellow tone for which his works are remarkable. The retreating figures in this picture are beautiful; the horses are excellently painted, with as much dexterous brilliancy of color as one sees in the oil pictures of Landseer. If the amateur wants to see how far transparent color will go, what rich effect may be produced by it, how little necessary it is to plaster drawings with flakes of white, let him examine the background of the design representing a page asleep on a chair, than which nothing can be more melodious in color, or more skilfully and naturally painted.

In the beauty gallery which this exhibition usually furnishes, there is Mr. Richter, who contributes his usual specimens; the fair Miss Sharpe, with those languishing-eyed charmers whom the world admires so much; and, still more to our taste, a sweet pretty lady, by Mr. Stone, in a hideous dress, with upper-Benjamin buttons; a couple of very graceful and delicate heads by Wright; and one beautiful head, a portrait evidently, by Cristall, that is placed very modestly in a corner near the ground — where such a drawing should be placed, of course, being vigorous, honest, natural, and beautiful. This artist's other drawing — a mysterious subject, representing primeval Scotchmen, rocks, waterfalls, a cataract of bulls, and other strange things, looks like a picture painted in a dream. Near it hangs Mr. Mackenzie's view of Saint Denis's Cathedral, that is painted with great carefulness, and is very true to nature. And having examined this, and Mr. Varley's fine gloomy sketches, you shall be no longer detained at this place, but walk on to see what more remains to be seen.

Of the New Water-Color Society, I think it may be asserted that their gallery contains neither such good nor such bad drawings as may be seen in the senior exhibition; unless, indeed, we except Mr. Haghe, a gentleman who in architectural subjects has a marvellous skill, and whose work deserves to be studied by all persons who follow the trade of water-coloring. This gentleman appears to have a profound knowledge (or an extraordinary instinct) of his profession as an architectural draughtsman. There are no tricks, no clumsy plastering of white, no painful niggling, nor swaggering affectation of boldness. He seems to understand every single tone and line which he lays down; and his picture, in my humble judgment, contains some of the very best qualities of which this branch of painting is capable. You cannot produce by any combination of water-colors such effects as may be had from oil, such richness and depth of tone, such pleasing variety of texture, as gums and varnishes will give; but, on the other hand, there are many beauties peculiar to the art, which the oil-painter cannot arrive at, — such as air, brightness, coolness, and flatness of surface; points which painters understand and can speak of a great deal better tham amateur writers and readers. Why will the practitioners, then, be so ambitious? Why strive after effects that are only to be got imperfectly at best, and at the expense of qualities far more valuable and pleasing? There are some aspiring individuals who will strive to play a whole band of music off a guitar, or to perform the broadsword exercise with a rapier, — monstrous attempts, that the moral critic must lift up his voice to reprehend. Valuable instruments are guitars and small-swords in themselves, the one for making pleasant small music, the other for drilling small holes in the human person; but let the professor of each art do his agreeable duty in his own line, nor strive with his unequal weapons to compete with persons who have greater advantages. Indeed, I have seldom seen the works of a skilful water-color painter of figures, without regretting that he had not taken to oil, which would allow him to put forth all the vigor of which he was capable. For works, however, like that of Mr. Haghe, which are not finished pictures, but admirable finished sketches, water is best; and we wish that his brethren followed his manner of using it. Take warning by these remarks, O Mr. Absolon! Your interiors have been regarded by Titmarsh with much pleasure, and deserve at his hands a great deal of commendation. Mr. Absolon, we take it, has been brought up in a French school — there are many traces of foreign manner in him; his figures, for instance, are better costumed than those of our common English artists. Look at the little sketch which goes by the laconic title of "Jump." Let Mrs. Seyffarth come and look at it before she paints Sir Roger de Coverley's figure again, and she will see what an air of life and authenticity the designer has thrown into his work. Several larger pieces by Mr. Absolon, in which are a face — is it the artist's own, by any chance? — (We fancy that we have a knack at guessing a portrait of an artist by himself, having designed about five thousand such in our own experience, — "Portrait of a Painter," "A Gentleman in a Vandyke Dress," "A Brigand," "A Turkish Costume," and so on: they are somehow always rejected by those cursed Academicians) — but to return to Absolon, whom we have left hanging up all this time on the branch of a sentence, he has taken hugely to the body-color system within the last twelve months, and small good has it done him. The accessories of his pictures are painted with much vigor and

feeling of color, are a great deal stronger than heretofore
— a great deal too strong for the figures themselves; and
the figures, being painted chiefly in transparent color, will
not bear the atmosphere of distemper by which they are
surrounded. The picture of "The Bachelor" is excellent
in point of effect and justness of color.

Mr. Corbould is a gentleman who must be mentioned
with a great deal of praise. His large drawing of the
"Canterbury Pilgrims at the Tabard" is very gay and
sparkling; and the artist shows that he possesses a genuine antiquarian or Walter-Scottish spirit. It is a pity that
his people are all so uncommon handsome. It is a pity
that his ladies wear such uncommonly low dresses — they
did not wear such (according to the best authorities) in
Chaucer's time; and even if they did, Mr. Corbould had
much better give them a little more cloth, which costs
nothing, and would spare much painful blushing to modest men like — never mind whom. But this is a moral
truth; nothing is so easy to see in a painter as a certain
inclination towards naughtiness, which we press-Josephs
are bound to cry fie at. Cover them up, Mr. Corbould —
muslin is the word; but of this no more. Where the
painter departs from his line of beauty, his faces have considerable humor and character. The whole of the pilgrim
group, as he has depicted it, is exceedingly picturesque.
It might be painted with a little more strength, and a good
deal less finical trifling with the pencil; but of these
manual errors the painter will no doubt get the better as
his practice and experience increase.

Here is a large and interesting picture by Mr. Warren,
of the Pasha of Egypt in the middle of the Nubian desert,
surrounded by pipe-bearers and camels, and taking his cup
of coffee. There is much character both in the figures and
scenery. A slight sketch by the same artist, "The King in
Thule," is very pretty, and would make a very good picture.

Mr. Bright is an artist of whom we do not before remember to have heard. His pictures are chiefly effects of sunset and moonlight; of too *criarde* a color as regards sun
and moon, but pretty and skilful in other points, and of a
style that strikes us as almost new. The manner of a
French artist, Monsieur Collignon, somewhat resembles
that of Mr. Bright. The cool parts of his pictures are excellent; but he has dangerous dealings with gamboge and
orange, pigments with the use of which a painter is bound

to be uncommonly cautious. Look at Mr. Turner, who has taken to them until they have driven him quite wild. If there be any Emperor of the Painters, he should issue " a special edict " against the gamboge-dealers : — 'tis a deleterious drug. " Hasten, hasten," Mr. Bright; " obey with trembling," and have a care of gamboge henceforth.

For the rest of the artists at this place, it may be said that Mr. Hicks has not been quite so active this year as formerly ; Mr. Boys has some delightful drawings in his style of art; and for the curious there is, moreover, a second-hand Cattermole, a sham Prout, a pseudo-Bentley, and a small double of Cox, whose works are to be seen in various parts of the room. Miss Corbould has a pretty picture. Mr. Duncan's drawings exhibit considerable skill and fidelity to nature. And here we must close our list of the juniors, whose exhibition is very well worth the shilling which all must pay who would enter their pretty gallery.

We have been through a number of picture galleries, and cannot do better than go and visit a gentleman who has a gallery of his own, containing only one picture. We mean Mr. Danby, with his " Deluge," now visible in Piccadilly. Every person in London will no doubt go and see this : artists, because the treatment and effect of the picture are extraordinarily skilful and broad ; and the rest of the world, who cannot fail of being deeply moved by the awful tragedy which is here laid before them. The work is full of the strongest dramatic interest ; a vast performance, grandly treated, and telling in a wonderful way its solemn awful tale. Mr. Danby has given a curious description of it to our hand ; and from this the reader will be able to understand what is the design and treatment of the piece.

[Here follows a long description of the picture.]

The episode of the angel is the sole part of the picture with which we should be disposed to quarrel ; but the rest, which has been excellently described in the queer wild words of the artist, is really as grand and magnificent a conception as ever we saw. Why Poussin's famous picture of an inundation has been called " The Deluge," I never could understand : it is only a very small and partial deluge. The artist has genius enough, if any artist ever had, to have executed a work far more vast and tremendous ; nor does his picture at the Louvre, nor Turner's Deluge, nor Martin's, nor any that we have ever seen, at all stand a competition with this extraordinary performance of Mr. Danby. He has painted *the* picture of "The Deluge;" we have before our eyes still the ark in the midst of the ruin floating calm and lonely, the great black cataracts of water pouring down, the mad rush of the miserable people clambering up the rocks; — nothing can be finer than the way in which the artist has painted the picture in all its innumerable details, and we hope to hear that his room will be hourly crowded, and his great labor and genius rewarded in some degree.

Let us take some rest after beholding this picture, and what place is cooler and more quiet than the Suffolk Street Gallery? If not remarkable for any pictures of extraordinary merit, it is at least to be praised as a place singularly favorable to meditation. It is a sweet calm solitude, lighted from the top with convenient blinds to keep out the sun. If you have an assignation, bid your mistress to come hither, there is only a dumb secretary in the room; and sitting, like the man in the "Arabian Nights," perpetually before a great book, in which he pores. This would be a grand place to hatch a conspiracy, to avoid a dun, to write an epic poem. Something ails the place! What is it? — what keeps the people away, and gives the moneytaker in his box a gloomy lonely sinecure? Alas, and alas! not even Mr. Haydon's "Samson Agonistes" is strong enough to pull the people in.

And yet this picture is worth going to see. You may here take occasion to observe the truth of Mr. Yorke's astute remark about another celebrated artist, and see how bad a painter is this great *writer* of historical paintings, Mr. Haydon. There is an account in some of the late papers — from America, of course — of a remarkably fat boy, three years old, five feet six high, with a fine bass voice, and a handsome beard and whiskers. Much such a hero is this Samson — a great red chubby-cheeked monster, looking at you with the most earnest, mild, dull eyes in the world, and twisting about a brace of ropes, as he comes sprawling forwards. Sprawling backwards is a Delilah — such a Delilah, with such an arm, with such a dress, on such a sofa, with such a set of ruffians behind her! The picture is perfectly amazing! Is this the author of the "Judgment of Solo-

mon " ? — the restorer or setter up of the great style of
painting in this country ?   The drawing of the figures is
not only faulty, but bad and careless as can be.   It never
was nor could be in nature ; and, such as it is, the drawing
is executed in a manner so loose and slovenly that one
wonders to behold it.   Is this the way in which a *chef
d'école* condescends to send forth a picture to the public ?
Would he have his scholars finish no more and draw no
better ?   Look at a picture of " Milton and his Daughters,"
the same subject which Sir A. Callcott has treated in the
Academy, which painters will insist upon treating, so profoundly interesting does it seem to be.   Mr. Haydon's
" Milton " is playing on the organ, and turning his blind
eyes towards the public with an expression that is absolutely laughable.   A buxom wench in huge gigot sleeves
stands behind the chair, another is at a table writing.   The
draperies of the ladies are mere smears of color ; in the
foreground lies a black cat or dog, a smudge of lamp-black,
in which the painter has not condescended to draw a figure.
The chair of the poetical organ-player is a similar lump of
red and brown ; nor is the conception of the picture, to our
thinking, one whit better than the execution.   If this be
the true style of art, there is another great work of the
kind at the " Saracen's Head," Snow Hill, which had better
be purchased for the National Gallery.

Mr. Hurlstone has, as usual, chosen this retired spot to
exhibit a very great number of pictures.   There is much
good in almost all of these.   The children especially are
painted with great truth and sweetness of expression, but
we never shall be able to reconcile ourselves to the extraordinary dirtiness of the color.   Here are ladies' dresses
which look as if they had served for May-day, and arms
and shoulders such as might have belonged to Cinderella.
Once in a way the artist shows he can paint a clean face,
such an one is that of a child in the little room ; it is
charming, if the artist did but know it, how much more
charming for being clean !   A very good picture of a subject somewhat similar to those which Mr. Hurlstone loves
to paint is Mr. Buckner's " Peasants of Sora in the Regno
di Napoli."   The artist has seen the works of Léopold
Robert, and profited evidently by the study of them.

Concerning other artists whose works appear in this gallery, we should speak favorably of Mr. O'Neill, who has
two pretty pictures ; of a couple of animal pieces, " A Pony

and Cows," by Mr. Sosi; and of a pretty picture by Mr.
Elmore, a vast deal better than his great Becket performance before alluded to.   Mr. Tomkins has some skilful
street scenes; and Mr. Holland, a large, raw, clever picture
of Milan Cathedral.   And so farewell to this quiet spot,
and let us take a peep at the British Gallery, where a whole
room is devoted to the exhibition of Mr. Hilton, the late
Academician.

A man's sketches and his pictures should never be exhibited together ; the sketches invariably kill the pictures ;
are far more vigorous, masterly, and effective.   Some of
those hanging here, chiefly subjects from Spenser, are excellent indeed ; and fine in drawing, color, and composition.
The decision and spirit of the sketch disappear continually
in the finished piece, as any one may see in examining the
design for "Comus," and the large picture afterwards, the
two "Amphitrites," and many others.   Were the sketches,
however, removed, the beholder would be glad to admit the
great feeling and grace of the pictures, and the kindly
poetical spirit which distinguishes the works of the master.
Besides the Hiltons, the picture-lover has here an opportunity of seeing a fine Virgin by Julio Romano, and a most
noble one by Sebastian del Piombo, than which I never saw
anything more majestically beautiful.   The simpering
beauties of some of the Virgins of the Raphael school
many painters are successful in imitating.   See, O ye
painters ! how in Michael Angelo strength and beauty are
here combined, wonderful chastity and grace, humility, and a
grandeur almost divine.   The critic must have a care as he
talks of these pictures, however, for his words straightway
begin to grow turgid and pompous ; and, lo ! at the end of his
lines, the picture is not a whit better described than before.

And now, having devoted space enough to the discussion
of the merits of these different galleries and painters, I am
come to the important part of this paper — viz. to my
Essay on the State of the Fine Arts in this Kingdom, my
Proposals for the General Improvement of Public Taste,
and my Plan for the Education of Young Artists.
In the first place, I propose that Government should
endow a college for painters, where they may receive the
benefits of a good literary education, without which artists
will never prosper.   I propose that lectures should be read,

examinations held, and prizes and exhibitions given to students; that professorships should be instituted, and — and a president or lord rector appointed, with a baronetcy, a house, and a couple of thousands a year. This place, of course, will be offered to Michael Angelo Tit——

Mr. Titmarsh's paper came to us exactly as the reader here sees it. His contribution had been paid for in advance, and we regret exceedingly that the public should be deprived of what seemed to be the most valuable part of it. He has never been heard of since the first day of June. He was seen on that day pacing Waterloo Bridge for two hours; but whether he plunged into the river, or took advantage of the steamboat and went down it only, we cannot state.

Why this article was incomplete, the following document will, perhaps, show. It is the work of the waiter at Moreland's Hotel, where the eccentric and unhappy gentleman resided.

STATEMENT BY MRS. BARBARA.

"On the evening of the 30th of May, Anay Domino 1840, Mr. Mike Titmash came into our house in a wonderful state of delarium, drest in a new coat, a new bloo satting hankysher, a new wite at, and polisht jipannd boots, all of which he'd bot sins he went out after dinner; nor did he bring any of his old cloves back with him, though he'd often said, 'Barbara,' says he to me, 'when Mr. Frasier pays me my money, and I git new ones, you shall have these as your requisites:' that was his very words, thof I must confess I don't understand the same.

"He'd had dinner and coughy before he went; and we all cumjectured that he'd been somewhere particklar, for I heer'd him barging with a cabman from Hollywell Street, of which he said the fair was only hatepence; but being ableeged to pay a shilling, he cust and swoar horrybill.

"He came in, ordered some supper, laft and joakt with the gents in the parlor, and shewed them a deal of money, which some of the gentlemen was so good as to purpose to borry of him.

"They talked about literaryture and the fine harts (which is both much used by our gentlemen); and Mr. Mike was very merry. Specially he sung them a song, which he ancored hisself for twenty minutes; and ordered a bole of our punch, which is chocked against his skor to this very day.

"About twelve o'clock he went to bed, very comfortable and quiet, only he cooldnt stand on his legs very well, and cooldnt speak much, excep, 'Frasier forever!' 'All of a York!' and some such nonsense, which neither me nor George nor Mrs. Stoaks could understand.

"'What's the matter?' says Mrs. Stokes.   'Barbara,' says she to me, 'has he taken any thin?' says she.

"'Law bless you, mum!' says I (I always says, Law bless you), 'as I am a Christen woman, and hope to be married, he's had nothin out of common.'

"'What had he for dinner?' says she, as if she didn't know.

"'There was biled salmon,' says I, 'and a half-crown lobster in soss (bless us if he left so much as a clor or tisspunful!), boil pork and peace puddn, and a secknd course of beef steak and onions, cole plumpuddn, maccarony, and afterwards cheese and sallat.'

"'I don't mean that,' says she.   'What was his liquors, or bavyrage?'

"'Two Guineas's stouts; old Madeira, one pint; port, half a ditto; four tumlers of niggus; and three cole brandy and water, and sigars.'

"'He is a good fellow,' says Mrs. Stokes, 'and spends his money freely, that I declare.'

"'I wish he'd ony *pay* it,' says I to Mrs. Stokes, says I. 'He's lived in our house any time these fourteen years and never'—

"'Hush your imperence!' says Mrs. Stokes; 'he's a gentleman, and pays when he pleases. He's not one of your common sort.   Did he have any tea?'

"'No,' says I, 'not a drop; ony coughy and muffns.   I told you so — three on 'em; and growled preciously, too, because there was no more.   But I wasn't a going to fetch him any more, he whose money we'd never'—

"'Barbara,' says Mrs. Stokes, 'leave the room — do. You're always a suspecting every gentleman.   Well, what did he have at supper?'

"'You know,' says I, 'pickled salmon — that chap's a reglar devil at salmon' (those were my very words) — 'cold pork, and cold peace puddn agin; toasted chease this time; and such a lot of hale and rum-punch as I never saw —

nine glasses of heach, I do believe, as I am an honest woman.'

" 'Barbara,' says mistress, 'that's not the question. *Did he mix his liquors*, Barbara ? That's the pint.'

" 'No,' says I, 'Mrs. Stokes; that indeed he didn't.' And so we agread that he couldnt posbly be affected by drink, and that something wunderfle must have hapned to him, to send him to bed so quear like.

" Nex morning I took him his tea in bed (on the 4th flore back, No 104 was his number); and says he to me, 'Barbara,' says he, 'you find me in sperrits.'

" 'Find you in sperrits ! I believe we do,' says I; 'we've found you in 'em these fifteen year. I wish you'd find us in *money*,' says I; and laft, too, for I thought it was a good un.

" 'Pooh!' says he, 'my dear, that's not what I mean. You find me in spirits bycause my exlent publisher, Mr. Frasier, of Regent Street, paid me handsum for a remarkable harticle I wrote in his Magazine. He gives twice as much as the other publishers,' says he; 'though, if he didn't, I'd write for him just the same — rayther more, I'm so fond of him.'

" 'How much has he gave you ?' says I; 'because I hope you'll pay us.'

" 'Oh,' says he, after a bit, 'a lot of money. Here, you, you darling,' says he (he did; upon my word, he did), 'go and git me change for a five-pound note.'

" And when he got up and had his brekfast, and been out, he changed another five-pound note; and after lunch, another five-pound note; and when he came in to dine, another five-pound note, to pay the cabman. Well, thought we, he's made of money, and so he seemed: but you shall hear soon how it was that he had all them notes to change.

" After dinner he was a sitten over his punch, when some of our gents came in: and he began to talk and brag to them about his harticle, and what he had for it ; and that he was the best cricket * in Europe; and how Mr. Murray had begged to be introjuiced to him, and was so pleased with him, and he with Murray; and how he'd been asked to write in the *Quartly Review*, and in bless us knows what; and how, in fact, he was going to carry all London by storm.

---

* Critic, Mrs. Barbara means, an absurd monomania of Mr. Titmarsh.

"'Have you seen what the *Morning Poast* says of you?'
says Frank Flint, one of them hartist chaps as comes to
our house.

"'No,' says he, 'I aint. Barbara, bring some more
punch, do you hear? No, I aint; but that's a fashnable
paper,' says he, 'and always takes notice of a fashnable chap
like me. What *does* it say?' says he.

"Mr. Flint opened his mouth and grinned very wide;
and taking the *Morning Poast* out of his pocket (he was a
great friend of Mr. Titmarsh's, and, like a good-naterd
friend as he was, had always a kind thing to say or do) —
Frank pulls out a *Morning Poast*, I say (which had cost
Frank Phippens *): 'Here it is,' says he; 'read for yourself; it will make you quite happy.' And so he began to
grin to all the gents like winkin.

"When he red it, Titmarsh's jor dropt all of a sudn: he
turned pupple, and bloo, and violate; and then, with a
mighty effut, he swigg off his rum and water, and staggered
out of the room.

"He looked so ill when he went up stairs to bed, that
Mrs. Stokes insisted upon making him some grool for him
to have warm in bed; but, Lor bless you! he threw it in
my face when I went up, and rord and swor so dredfle,
that I rann down stairs quite frightened.

"Nex morning I knockt at his dor at nine — no anser.

"At ten, tried agin — never a word.

"At eleven, twelve, one, two, up we went, with a fresh
cup of hot tea every time. His dor was lockt, and not one
sillibaly could we git.

"At for we began to think he'd suasided hisself; and
having called in the policemen, bust open the dor.

"And then we beheld a pretty spactycle! Fancy him
in his gor, his throat cut from hear to hear, his white night-
gownd all over blood, his beautiful face all pail with hagny!
— well, no such thing. Fancy him hanging from the bed-
post by one of his pore dear garters! — well, no such thing.
Agin, fancy him flung out of the window, and dasht into
ten billium peaces on the minionet-potts in the fust floar;
or else a naked, melumcolly corpse, laying on the hairy
spikes! — not in the least. He wasn't dead, nor he wasn't
the least unwell, nor he wasn't asleep neither — he only
wasn't there; and from that day we have heard nothen

* Fivepence, Mrs. Barbara means.

about him. He left on his table the following note as follows : —

"'1st *June*, 1840. *Midnight*.

"'MRS. STOKES, — I am attached to you by the most disinterested friendship. I have patronized your house for fourteen years, and it was my intention to have paid you a part of your bill, but the *Morning Post* newspaper has destroyed that blessed hope forever.

"'Before you receive this I shall be — *ask not where:* my mind shudders to think where! You will carry the papers directed to Regent Street to that address, and perhaps you will receive in return a handsome sum of money ; but if the bud of my youth is blighted, the promise of a long and happy career suddenly and cruelly cut short, an affectionate family deprived of its support and ornament, say that the *Morning Post* has done this by its savage criticisms upon me, the last this day.

"'FAREWELL.'

"This is hall he said. From that day to this we have never seen the poor fellow — we have never heerd of him — we have never known any think about him. Being halarmed, Mrs. Stoks hadvertized him in the papers; but not wishing to vex his family, we called him by another name, and put hour address diffrent too. Hall was of no use ; and I can't tell you what a pang I felt in my busum when, on going to get change for the five-pound notes he'd given me at the public-house in Hoxford Street, the lan'lord laft when he saw them ; and said, says he, 'Do you know, Mrs. Barbara, that a queer gent came in here with five sovrings one day, has a glass of hale, and haskes me to change his sovrings for a note ? which I did. Then in about two hours he came back with five more sovrings, gets another note and another glass of hale, and so goes on four times in one blessed day ! It's my beleaf that he had only five pound, and wanted you to suppose that he was worth twenty, for you've got all his notes, I see !'

"And so the poor fellow had no money with him after all ! I do pity him, I do, from my hart; and I do hate that wicked *Morning Post* for so treating such a kind, sweet, good-nater'd gentleman !

(*Signed*) "BARBARA.

"MORLAND'S HOTEL: 15 *Jewin*, 1840."

This is conclusive. Our departed friend had many faults, but he is gone, and we will not discuss them now. It appears that, on the 1st of June, the *Morning Post* published a criticism upon him, accusing him of ignorance, bad taste, and gross partiality.   His gentle and susceptible spirit could not brook the rebuke; he was not angry; he did not retort; but *his heart broke!*

Peace to his ashes !   A couple of volumes of his works, we see by our advertisements, are about immediately to appear.

ON MEN AND PICTURES.

À PROPOS OF A WALK IN THE LOUVRE.

[*Fraser's Magazine*, July, 1841.]

PARIS, June, 1841.

IN the days of my youth I knew a young fellow that I shall here call Tidbody, and who, born in a provincial town of respectable parents, had been considered by the drawing-master of the place, and, indeed, by the principal tea-parties there, as a great genius in the painting line, and one that was sure to make his fortune.

When he had made portraits of his grandmother, of the house-dog, of the door-knocker, of the church and parson of the place, and had copied, *tant bien que mal*, most of the prints that were to be found in the various houses of the village, Harry Tidbody was voted to be very nearly perfect; and his honest parents laid out their little savings in sending the lad to Rome and Paris.

I saw him in the latter town in the year '32, before an immense easel, perched upon a high stool, and copying with perfect complacency a Correggio in the gallery, which he thought he had imitated to a nicety. No misgivings ever entered into the man's mind that he was making an ass of himself; he never once paused to consider that his copy was as much like the Correggio as my nose is like the Apollo's. But he rose early of mornings, and scrubbed away all day with his megilps and varnishes; he worked away through cold and through sunshine; when other men were warming their fingers at the stoves, or wisely lounging on the Boulevard, he worked away, and thought he was cultivating art in the purest fashion, and smiled with easy scorn upon those who took the world more easily than he. Tidbody drank water with his meals — if meals those miserable scraps of bread and cheese, or bread and sausage, could be called which he lined his lean stomach with; and voted those persons godless gluttons who recreated themselves with brandy and beef. He rose up at daybreak, and worked away with bladder and brush; he passed all night at life-academies, designing life-guardsmen with chalk and stump; he never was known to take any other recreation; and in ten years he had spent as much time over his drawing as another man spends in thirty. At the end of his second year of academical studies Harry Tidbody could draw exactly as well as he could eight years after. He had visited Florence, and Rome, and Venice, in the interval; but there he was as he had begun, without one single farther idea, and not an inch nearer the goal at which he aimed.

One day at the Life-academy in Saint Martin's Lane, I saw before me the back of a shock head of hair and a pair of ragged elbows, belonging to a man in a certain pompous attitude which I thought I recognized; and when the model retired behind the curtain to take his ten minutes' repose, the man belonging to the back in question turned round a little, and took out an old snuffy cotton handkerchief, and wiped his forehead and lank cheek-bones, that were moist with the vast mental and bodily exertions of the night. Harry Tidbody was the man in question. In ten years he had spent at least three thousand nights in copying the model. When abroad, perhaps, he had passed the Sunday evenings too in the same rigorous and dismal pastime. He had piles upon piles of gray paper at his lodgings, covered with worthless nudities in black and white chalk.

At the end of the evening we shook hands, and I asked him how the arts flourished. The poor fellow, with a kind of dismal humor that formed a part of his character, twirled round upon the iron heels of his old patched Blucher boots, and showed me his figure for answer. Such a lean, long, ragged, fantastical-looking personage, it would be hard to match out of the drawing-schools.

"Tit, my boy," said he, when he had finished his pirouette, "you may see that the arts have not fattened me as yet; and, between ourselves, I make by my profession something considerably less than a thousand a year. But, mind you, I am not discouraged; my whole soul is in my calling; I can't do anything else if I would; and I will be a painter, or die in the attempt."

Tidbody is not dead, I am happy to say, but has a snug place in the Excise of eighty pounds a year, and now only exercises the pencil as an amateur. If his story has been told here at some length, the ingenious reader may fancy that there is some reason for it. In the first place, there is so little to say about the present exhibition at Paris that your humble servant does not know how to fill his pages without some digressions; and, secondly, the Tidbodian episode has a certain moral in it, without which it never would have been related, and which is good for all artists to read.

It came to my mind upon examining a picture of sixty feet by forty (indeed, it cannot be much smaller), which takes up a good deal of space in the large room of the Louvre. But of this picture anon. Let us come to the general considerations.

Why the deuce will men make light of that golden gift of mediocrity which for the most part they possess, and strive so absurdly at the sublime ? What is it that makes a fortune in this world but energetic mediocrity ? What is it that is so respected and prosperous as good, honest, emphatic, blundering dulness, bellowing commonplaces with its great, healthy lungs, kicking and struggling with its big feet and fists, and bringing an awe-stricken public down on its knees before it ? Think, my good sir, of the people who occupy your attention and the world's. Who are they ? Upon your honor and conscience now, are they not persons with thews and sinews like your own, only they use them with somewhat more activity — with a voice like yours, only they shout a little louder — with the average portion of brains, in fact, but working them more ? But this kind of disbelief in heroes is very offensive to the world, it must be confessed. There, now, is the *Times* newspaper, which the other day rated your humble servant for publishing an account of one of the great humbugs of modern days, viz. the late funeral of Napoleon — which rated me, I say, and talked in its own grave roaring way about the flippancy and conceit of Titmarsh.

O you thundering old *Times!* Napoleon's funeral was a humbug, and your constant reader said so. The people engaged in it were humbugs, and this your Michael Angelo hinted at. There may be irreverence in this, and the process of humbug-hunting may end rather awkwardly for some people. But surely there is no conceit. The shamming of modesty is the most pert conceit of all, the *prē-cieuse* affectation of deference where you don't feel it, the sneaking acquiescence in lies. It is very hard that a man may not tell the truth as he fancies it, without being accused of conceit: but so the world wags. As has already been prettily shown in that before-mentioned little book about Napoleon (that is still to be had of the publishers), there is a ballad in the volume, which, if properly studied, will be alone worth two and sixpence to any man.

Well, the funeral of Napoleon *was* a humbug; and, being so, what was a man to call it? What do we call a rose? Is it disrespectful to the pretty flower to call it by its own innocent name? And, in like manner, are we bound, out of respect for society, to speak of humbug only in a circumlocutory way — to call it something else, as they say some Indian people do their devil — to wrap it up in riddles and charades? Nothing is easier. Take, for instance, the following couple of sonnets on the subject: —

> The glad spring sun shone yesterday, as Mr.
> M. Titmarsh wandered with his favorite lassie
> By silver Seine, among the meadows grassy —
> Meadows, like mail-coach guards new clad at Easter.
> Fair was the sight 'twixt Neuilly and Passy ;
> And green the field, and bright the river's glister.
>
> The birds sang salutations to the spring;
> Already buds and leaves from branches burst:
> "The surly winter time hath done its worst,"
> Said Michael; "Lo, the bees are on the wing!"
> Then on the ground his lazy limbs did fling.
> Meanwhile the bees passed by him with my *first*.
> My *second* dare I to your notice bring,
> Or name to delicate ears that animal accurst ?
>
>
> To all our earthly family of fools
> *My whole*, resistless despot, gives the law —
> Humble and great, we kneel to it with awe;
> O'er camp and court, the senate and the schools,
> Our grand invisible Lama sits and rules,
> By ministers that are its men of straw.
> Sir Robert utters it in place of wit,
> And straight the Opposition shouts "Hear, hear !"
> And, oh ! but all the Whiggish benches cheer
> When great Lord John retorts it, as is fit.
> In you, my *Press*,* each day throughout the year,
> On vast broad sheets we find its praises writ.
> O wondrous are the columns that you rear,
> And sweet the morning hymns you roar in praise of it !

* The reader can easily accommodate this line to the name of his favorite paper. Thus: —

"In you, my { *Times, Post,* } each day throughout the year."

Sacred word! it is kept out of the dictionaries, as if the great compilers of those publications were afraid to utter it. Well, then, the funeral of Napoleon was a humbug, as Titmarsh wrote; and a still better proof that it was a humbug was this, that nobody bought Titmarsh's book, and of the 10,000 copies made ready by the publisher not above 3,000 went off. It was a humbug, and an exploded humbug. Peace be to it! *Parlons d'autres choses;* and let us begin to discourse about the pictures without further shilly-shally.

I must confess, with a great deal of shame, that I love to go to the picture gallery of a Sunday after church, on purpose to see the thousand happy people of the working sort amusing themselves — not very wickedly, as I fancy — on the only day in the week on which they have their freedom. Genteel people, who can amuse themselves every day throughout the year, do not frequent the Louvre on a Sunday. You can't see the pictures well, and are pushed and elbowed by all sorts of low-bred creatures. Yesterday there were at the very least two hundred common soldiers in the place — little vulgar ruffians, with red breeches and three-halfpence a day, examining the pictures in company with fifteen hundred grisettes, two thousand liberated shop-boys, eighteen hundred and forty-one artist-apprentices, half a dozen of livery servants, and many scores of fellows with caps, and jackets, and copper-colored countenances, and gold earrings, and large ugly hands, that are hammering or weaving or filing all the week. *Fi donc!* what a thing it is to have a taste for low company! Every man of decent breeding ought to have been in the Bois de Boulogne, in white kid gloves and on horseback, or on hackback at least. How the dandies just now went prancing and curvetting down the Champs Elysées, making their horses jump as they passed the carriages, with their japanned boots glittering in the sunshine! The fountains were flashing and foaming, as if they, too,

Or: —

"In you, my $\left\{ ,\dfrac{Herald,}{Tiser,} \right\}$ daily through the year."

Or, in France: —

"In you, my *Galignani's Messengere* ;"

a capital paper, because you have there the very cream of all the others. In the last line, for "morning" you can read "evening," or "weekly," as circumstances prompt.

were in their best for Sunday; the trees are covered all
over with little twinkling bright green sprouts; numberless exhibitions of Punch and the Fantoccini are going on
beneath them; and jugglers and balancers are entertaining
the people with their pranks. I met two fellows the other
day, one with a barrel-organ, and the other with a beard, a
turban, a red jacket, and a pair of dirty, short, spangled,
white trousers, who were cursing each other in the purest
Saint Giles's English; and if I had had impudence or generosity enough, I should have liked to make up their quarrel over a chopin of Strasburg beer, and hear the histories
of either. Think of these fellows quitting our beloved
country, and their homes in some calm nook of Field Lane
or Seven Dials, and toiling over to France with their music
and their juggling-traps, to balance cart-wheels and swallow knives for the amusement of our natural enemies!
They are very likely at work at this blessed minute, with
grinning *bonnes* and conscripts staring at their skill. It is
pleasant to walk by and see the nurses and the children so
uproariously happy. Yonder is one who has got a halfpenny to give to the beggar at the crossing; several are
riding gravely in little carriages drawn by goats. Ah,
truly, the sunshine is a fine thing; and one loves to see
the little people and the poor basking in it, as well as the
great in their fine carriages, or their prancing cock-tailed
horses.

In the midst of sights of this kind, you pass on a fine
Sunday afternoon down the Elysian Fields and the Tuileries, until you reach the before-mentioned low-bred crowd
rushing into the Louvre.

Well, then, the pictures of this exhibition are to be
numbered by thousands, and these thousands contain the
ordinary number of *chefs d'œuvre;* that is to say, there may
be a couple of works of genius, half a dozen very clever
performances, a hundred or so of good ones, fifteen hundred very decent, good, or bad pictures, and the remainder
atrocious. What a comfort it is, as I have often thought,
that they are not all masterpieces, and that there is a good
stock of mediocrity in this world, and that we only light
upon genius now and then, at rare angel intervals, handed
round like tokay at dessert, in a few houses, and in very
small quantities only! Fancy how sick one would grow of
it, if one had no other drink.

Now, in this exhibition there are, of course, a certain

number of persons who make believe that they are handing you round tokay — giving you the real imperial stuff, with the seal of genius stamped on the cork. There are numbers of ambitious pictures, in other words, chiefly upon sacred subjects, and in what is called a severe style of art.

The severe style of art consists in drawing your figures in the first place very big and very neat, in which there is no harm; and in dressing them chiefly in stiff, crisp, old-fashioned draperies, such as one sees in the illuminated missals and the old masters. The old masters, no doubt, copied the habits of the people about them; and it has always appeared as absurd to me to imitate these antique costumes, and to dress up saints and virgins after the fashion of the fifteenth century, as it would be to adorn them with hoops and red heels such as our grandmothers wore; and to make a Magdalen, for instance, taking off her patches, or an angel in powder and a hoop.

It is, or used to be, the custom at the theatres for the gravedigger in "Hamlet" always to wear fifteen or sixteen waistcoats, of which he leisurely divested himself, the audience roaring at each change of raiment. Do the Denmark gravediggers always wear fifteen waistcoats? Let anybody answer who has visited the country. But the probability is that the custom on the stage is a very ancient one, and that the public would not be satisfied at a departure from the legend. As in the matter of grave-diggers, so it is with angels: they have — and Heaven knows why — a regular costume, which every "serious" painter follows; and which has a great deal more to do with serious art than people at first may imagine. They have large white wings, that fill up a quarter of the picture in which they have the good fortune to be; they have white gowns that fall round their feet in pretty fantastical draperies; they have fillets round their brows, and their hair combed and neatly pomatumed down the middle; and if they have not a sword, have an elegant portable harp of a certain angelic shape. Large rims of gold leaf they have round their heads always, — a pretty business it would be if such adjuncts were to be left out.

Now, suppose the legend ordered that every gravedigger should be represented with a gold-leaf halo round his head, and every angel with fifteen waistcoats, artists would have followed serious art just as they do now most probably, and looked with scorn at the miserable creature who ventured to scoff at the waistcoats. Ten to one but a certain newspaper would have called a man flippant who did not respect the waistcoats — would have said that he was irreverent for not worshipping the waistcoats.* But why talk of it? The fact is I have rather a desire to set up for a martyr, like my neighbors in the literary trade: it is not a little comforting to undergo such persecutions courageously. "O Socrate! je boirai la ciguë avec toi!" as David said to Robespierre. You too were accused of blasphemy in your time; and the world has been treating us poor literary gents in the same way ever since. There, now, is Bulw—

But to return to the painters. In the matter of canvas covering the French artists are a great deal more audacious than ours; and I have known a man starve all the winter through, without fire and without beef, in order that he might have the honor of filling five and twenty feet square of canvas with some favorite subject of his.

It is curious to look through the collection, and see how for the most part the men draw their ideas. There are caricatures of the late and early style of Raphael; there are caricatures of Masaccio; there is a picture painted in the very pyramidical form, and in the manner of Andrea del Sarto; there is a Holy Family, the exact counterpart of Leonardo da Vinci; and, finally, there is Achille Deveria — it is no use to give the names and numbers of the other artists, who are not known in England — there is Achille Deveria, who, having nothing else to caricature, has caricatured a painted window, and designed a Charity, of which all the outlines are half an inch thick.

Then there are numberless caricatures in color as in form. There is a violet Entombment — a crimson one, a green one; a light emerald and gamboge Eve; all huge pictures, with talent enough in their composition, but remarkable for this strange mad love of extravagance, which belongs to the nation. Titian and the Venetians have loved to paint lurid skies and sunsets of purple and gold: here, in consequence, is a piebald picture of crimson and yellow, laid on in streaks from the top to the bottom.

Who has not heard a great, comfortable, big-chested man, with bands round a sleek double chin, and fat white cush-

* Last year, when our friend published some article in this Magazine, he seemed to be agitated almost to madness by a criticism, and a very just one too, which appeared in the *Morning Post.* At present he is similarly affected by some strictures on a defunct work of his. — O. Y.

ion squeezers of hands, and large red whiskers, and a soft roaring voice, the delight of a congregation, preaching for an hour with all the appearance and twice the emphasis of piety, and leading audiences captive? And who has not seen a humble individual, who is quite confused to be conducted down the aisle by the big beadle with his silver staff (the stalwart "drum-major ecclesiastic"); and when in his pulpit, saying his say in the simplest manner possible, uttering what are very likely commonplaces, without a single rhetorical grace or emphasis?

The great, comfortable, red-whiskered, roaring cushion-thumper is most probably the favorite with the public. But there are some persons who, nevertheless, prefer to listen to the man of timid mild commonplaces, because the simple words he speaks come from *his* heart, and so find a way directly to yours; where, if perhaps you can't find belief for them, you still are sure to receive them with respect and sympathy.

There are many such professors at the easel as well as the pulpit; and you see many painters with a great vigor and dexterity, and no sincerity of heart; some with little dexterity, but plenty of sincerity; some one or two in a million who have both these qualities, and thus become the great men of their art. I think there are instances of the two former kinds in this present exhibition of the Louvre. There are fellows who have covered great swaggering canvases with all the attitudes and externals of piety; and some few whose humble pictures cause no stir, and remain in quiet nooks, where one finds them, and straightway acknowledges the simple kindly appeal which they make.

Of such an order is the picture entitled "La Prière," by Monsieur Trimolet. A man and his wife are kneeling at an old-fashioned praying-desk, and the woman clasps a little sickly-looking child in her arms, and all three are praying as earnestly as their simple hearts will let them. The man is a limner, or painter of missals, by trade, as we fancy. One of his works lies upon the praying-desk, and it is evident that he can paint no more that day, for the sun is just set behind the old-fashioned roofs of the houses in the narrow street of the old city where he lives. Indeed, I have had a great deal of pleasure in looking at this little quiet painting, and in the course of half a dozen visits that I have paid to it, have become perfectly acquainted with

all the circumstances of the life of the honest missal illu-
minator and his wife, here praying at the end of their day's
work in the calm summer evening.

Very likely Monsieur Trimolet has quite a different history for his little personages, and so has everybody else
who examines the picture. But what of that ? There is
the privilege of pictures. A man does not know all that
lies in his picture, any more than he understands all the
character of his children. Directly one or the other makes
its appearance in the world, it has its own private existence, independent of the progenitor. And in respect of
works of art, if the same piece inspire one man with joy
that fills another with compassion, what are we to say of it,
but that it has sundry properties of its own which its
author even does not understand ? The fact is, pictures
"are as they seem to all," as Mr. Alfred Tennyson sings in
the first volume of his poems.

Some of this character of holiness and devotion that I
fancy I see in Monsieur Trimolet's pictures is likewise
observable in a piece by Madame Juillerat, representing
Saint Elizabeth of Hungary leading a little beggar-boy into
her house, where the holy dame of Hungary will, no doubt,
make him comfortable with a good plate of victuals. A
couple of young ladies follow behind the princess, with demure looks, and garlands in their hair, that hangs straight on
their shoulders, as one sees it in the old illuminations. The
whole picture has a pleasant, mystic, innocent look; and
one is all the better for regarding it. What a fine instinct
or taste it was in the old missal illuminators to be so particular in the painting of the minor parts of their pictures !
the precise manner in which the flowers and leaves, birds
and branches, are painted, gives an air of truth and simplicity to the whole performance, and makes nature, as it
were, an accomplice and actor in the scene going on. For
instance, you may look at a landscape with certain feelings
of pleasure; but if you have pulled a rose, and are smelling it, and if of a sudden a blackbird in a bush hard by
begins to sing and chirrup, your feeling of pleasure is very
much enhanced most likely; the senses with which you
examine the scene become brightened as it were, and the
scene itself becomes more agreeable to you. It is not the
same place as it was before you smelt the rose, or before
the blackbird began to sing. Now, in Madame Juillerat's
picture of the Saint of Hungary and the hungry boy, if the

flowers on the young ladies' heads had been omitted, or not painted with their pleasing minuteness and circumstantiality, I fancy that the effect of the piece would have been by no means the same. Another artist of the mystical school, Monsieur Servan, has employed the same adjuncts in a similarly successful manner. One of his pictures represents Saint Augustin meditating in a garden; a great cluster of rose-bushes, hollyhocks, and other plants is in the foreground, most accurately delineated; and a fine rich landscape and river stretch behind the saint, round whom the flowers seem to keep up a mysterious waving and whispering that fill one with a sweet, pleasing, indescribable kind of awe — a great perfection in this style of painting.

In Monsieur Aguado's gallery there is an early Raphael (which all the world declares to be a copy, but no matter). This piece only represents two young people walking hand-in-hand in a garden, and looking at you with a kind of "solemn mirth" (the expression of old Sternhold and Hopkins has always struck me as very fine). A meadow is behind them, at the end of which is a cottage, and by which flows a river, environed by certain very prim-looking trees; and that is all. Well; it is impossible for any person who has a sentiment for the art to look at this picture without feeling indescribably moved and pleased by it. It acts upon you — how? How does a beautiful, pious, tender air of Mozart act upon you? What is there in it that should make you happy and gentle, and fill you with all sorts of good thoughts and kindly feelings? I fear that what Dr. Thumpcushion says at church is correct, and that these indulgences are only carnal, and of the earth earthy; but the sensual effort in this case carries one quite away from the earth, and up to something that is very like heaven.

Now the writer of this has already been severely reprehended for saying that Raphael at thirty had lost that delightful innocence and purity which rendered the works of Raphael at twenty so divine; and perhaps it may be the critic's fault, and not the painter's (I'm not proud, and will allow that even a magazine critic may be mistaken). Perhaps, by the greatest stretch of the perhaps, it may be that Raphael was every whit as divine at thirty as at eighteen; and that the very quaintnesses and imperfections of manner observable in his early works are the reason why they appear so singularly pleasing to me. At least among painters of the present day, I feel myself more disposed to recognize spiritual beauties in those whose powers of execution are manifestly incomplete, than in artists whose hands are skilful and manner formed. Thus there are scores of large pictures here, hanging in the Louvre, that represent subjects taken from Holy Writ, or from the lives of the saints, — pictures skilfully enough painted and intended to be religious, that have not the slightest effect upon me, no more than Dr. Thumpcushion's loudest and glibbest sermon.

Here is No. 1475, for instance — a "Holy Family," painted in the antique manner, and with all the accessories before spoken of, viz. large flowers, fresh roses, and white stately lilies; curling tendrils of vines forming fantastical canopies for the heads of the sacred personages, and rings of gold-leaf drawn neatly round the same. Here is the Virgin, with long, stiff, prim draperies of blue, red, and white; and old Saint Anne in a sober dress, seated gravely at her side; and Saint Joseph in a becoming attitude; and all very cleverly treated, and pleasing to the eye. But though this picture is twice as well painted as any of those before mentioned, it does not touch my heart in the least; nor do any of the rest of the sacred pieces. Opposite the "Holy Family" is a great "Martyrdom of Polycarp," and the catalogue tells you how the executioners first tried to burn the saint; but the fire went out, and the executioners were knocked down; then a soldier struck the saint with a sword, and so killed him. The legends recount numerous miracles of this sort, which I confess have not any very edifying effect upon me. Saints are clapped into boiling oil, which immediately turns cool; or their heads are chopped off, and their blood turns to milk; and so on. One can't understand why these continual delays and disappointments take place, especially as the martyr is always killed at the end; so that it would be best at once to put him out of his pain. For this reason, possibly, the execution of Saint Polycarp did not properly affect the writer of this notice.

Monsieur Laemlein has a good picture of the "Waking of Adam," so royally described by Milton, a picture full of gladness, vigor, and sunshine. There is a very fine figure of a weeping woman in a picture of the "Death of the Virgin;" and the Virgin falling in Monsieur Steuben's picture of "Our Saviour going to Execution" is very pathetic. The mention of this gentleman brings us to what is called the *bourgeois* style of art, of which he is one of the chief professors. He excels in depicting a certain kind of sentiment, and in the vulgar, which is often too the true, pathetic.

Steuben has painted many scores of Napoleons; and his picture of Napoleon this year brings numbers of admiring people round it. The Emperor is seated on a sofa, reading despatches; and the little King of Rome, in a white muslin frock, with his hair beautifully curled, slumbers on his papa's knee. What a contrast! The conqueror of the world, the stern warrior, the great giver of laws and ruler of nations, he dare not move because the little baby is asleep; and he would not disturb him for all the kingdoms he knows so well how to conquer. This is not art, if you please; but it is pleasant to see fat good-natured mothers and grandmothers clustered round this picture, and looking at it with solemn eyes. The same painter has an Esmeralda dancing and frisking in her night-gown, and playing the tambourine to her goat, capering likewise. This picture is so delightfully bad, the little gypsy has such a killing ogle, that all the world admires it. Monsieur Steuben should send it to London, where it would be sure of a gigantic success.

Monsieur Grenier has a piece much looked at, in the *bourgeois* line. Some rogues of gypsies, or mountebanks, have kidnapped a fine fat child, and are stripping it of its pretty clothes; and poor baby is crying; and the gypsy-woman holding up her finger and threatening; and the he-mountebank is lying on a bank, smoking his pipe, — the callous monster! Preciously they will ill-treat that dear little darling, if justice do not overtake them, — if, ay, *if*. But, thank Heaven! there in the corner come the police, and they will have that pipe-smoking scoundrel off to the galleys before five minutes are over.

1056. A picture of the galleys. Two galley-slaves are before you, and the piece is called "A Crime and a Fault." The poor "Fault" is sitting on a stone, looking very repentant and unhappy indeed. The great "Crime" stands grinning you in the face, smoking his pipe. The ruffian! That pipe seems to be a great mark of callosity in ruffians. I heard one man whisper to another, as they were looking at these galley-slaves, "*They are portraits,*" and very much affected his companion seemed by the information.

Of a similar virtuous interest is 705, by Monsieur Finart, "A Family of African Colonists carried off by Abd-el-Kader." There is the poor male colonist without a single thing on but a rope round his wrists. His silver skin is dabbled with his golden blood, and he looks up to heaven as the Arabs are poking him on with the tips of their horrid spears. Behind him come his flocks and herds, and other members of his family. In front, principal figure, is his angelic wife in her night-gown, and in the arms of an odious blackamoor on horseback. Poor thing — poor thing! she is kicking, and struggling, and resisting, as hard as she possibly can.

485. "The Two Friends." Debay.

"Deux jeunes femmes se donnent le gage le plus sacré d'une amitié sincère, dans un acte de dévoûment et de reconnaissance.

"L'une d'elles, faible, exténuée d'efforts inutilement tentés pour allaiter, découvre son sein tari, cause du dépérissement de son enfant. Sa douleur est comprise par son amie, à qui la santé permet d'ajouter au bonheur de nourrir son propre enfant, celui de rappeler à la vie le fils mourant de sa compagne."

Monsieur's Debay's pictures are not bad, as most of the others here mentioned as appertaining to the *bourgeois* class; but, good or bad, I can't but own that I like to see these honest hearty representations, which work upon good simple feeling in a good downright way; and if not works of art, are certainly works that can do a great deal of good, and make honest people happy. Who is the man that despises melodramas? I swear that T. P. Cooke is a benefactor to mankind. Away with him who has no stomach for such kind of entertainments, where vice is always punished, where virtue always meets its reward; where Mrs. James Vining is always sure to be made comfortable somewhere at the end of the third act; and if O. Smith is lying in agonies of death, in red breeches, on the front of the stage, or has just gone off in a flash of fire down one of the traps, I know it is only make-believe on his part, and believe him to be a good kind-hearted fellow, that would not do harm to mortal! So much for pictures of the serious melodramatic sort.

Monsieur Biard, whose picture of the "Slave-trade" made so much noise in London last year — and indeed it is as fine as Hogarth — has this year many comic pieces, and a series representing the present Majesty of France when Duke of Orleans, undergoing various perils by land and by water. There is much good in these pieces; but I mean no disrespect in saying I like the comic ones best. There is one entitled " Une Distraction." A National Guard is amusing himself by catching flies. You can't fail to laugh when you see it. There is " Le Gros Péché," and the biggest of all sins, no less than a drum-major confessing. You can't see the monster's face, which the painter has wisely hidden behind the curtain, as,beyond the reach of art; but you see the priest's, and murder! what a sin it must be that the big tambour has just imparted to him! All the French critics sneer at Biard, as they do at Paul de Kock, for not being artistical enough; but I do not think these gentlemen need mind the sneer; they have the millions with them, as Feargus O'Connor says, and they are good judges, after all.

A great comfort it is to think that there is a reasonable prospect that, for the future, very few more battle-pieces will be painted. They have used up all the victories, and Versailles is almost full. So this year, much to my happiness, only a few yards of warlike canvas are exhibited in place of the furlongs which one was called upon to examine in former exhibitions. One retreat from Moscow is there, and one storming of El Gibbet or El Arish, or some such place in Africa. In the latter picture, you see a thousand fellows in loose red pantaloons, rushing up a hill with base heathen Turks on the top, who are firing off guns, carabines, and other pieces of ordnance, at them. All this is very well painted by Monsieur Bollangé, and the rush of red breeches has a queer and pleasing effect. In the Russian piece you have frozen men and cattle; mothers embracing their offspring; grenadiers scowling at the enemy, and especially one fellow standing on a bank with his bayonet placed in the attitude for receiving the charge, and actually charged by a whole regiment of Cossacks, — a complete pulk, my dear madam, coming on in three lines, with their lances pointed against this undaunted warrior of France. I believe Monsieur Thiers sat for the portrait, or else the editor of the *Courrier Français*, — the two men in this belligerent nation who are the belligerentest. *A propos* of Thiers, the *Nouvelles à la Main* has a good story of this little sham Napoleon. When the second son of the Duke of Orleans was born (I forget his Royal Highness's title), news was brought to Monsieur Thiers. He was told the Princess was well, and asked the courier who brought the news,

"Comment se portait *le Roi de Rome?*" It may be said, in confidence, that there is not a single word of truth in the story. But what of that? Are not sham stories as good as real ones? Ask Monsieur Leullier; who, in spite of all that has been said and written upon a certain sea-fight, has actually this year come forward with his

1311. "Héroïsme de l'Equipage du Vaisseau le Vengeur, 4 Juin, 1794."

"Après avoir soutenu longtemps un combat acharné contre trois vaisseaux Anglais, le vaisseau le Vengeur avait perdu la moitié de son équipage, le reste était blessé pour la plupart; le second capitaine avait été coupé en deux par un boulet; le vaisseau était rasé par le feu de l'ennemi, sa mâture abattue, ses flancs criblés par les boulets étaient ouverts de toutes parts ; sa cale se remplissait à vue d'œil; il s'enfonçait dans la mer. Les marins qui restent sur son bord servent la batterie basse jusqu'à ce qu'elle se trouve au niveau de la mer; quand elle va disparaître, ils s'élancent dans la seconde, où ils répètent la même manœuvre; celle-ci engloutie, ils montent sur le pont. Un tronçon de mât d'artimon restait encore debout; leurs pavillons en lambeaux y sont cloués; puis, réunissant instinctivement leurs volontés en une seule pensée, ils veulent périr avec le navire qui leur a été confié. Tous, combattants, blessés, mourants se raniment: un cri immense s'élève, répété sur toutes les parties du tillac: *Vive la République! Vive la France!* . . . *Le Vengeur* coule . . . les cris continuent; tous les bras sont dressés au ciel, et ces braves, préférant la mort à la captivité, emportent triomphalement leur pavillon dans ce glorieux tombeau." — *France Maritime.*

I think Mr. Thomas Carlyle is in the occasional habit of calling lies wind-bags. *This* wind-bag, one would have thought, exploded last year; but no such thing. You *can't* sink it, do what you will; it always comes bouncing up to the surface again, where it swims and bobs about gayly for the admiration of all. This lie the Frenchman will believe; all the papers talk gravely about the affair of the "Vengeur," as if an established fact; and I heard the matter disposed of by some artists the other day in a very satisfactory manner. One has always the gratification, in all French societies where the matter is discussed, of telling the real story (or if the subject be not discussed, of bringing the conversation round to it, and then telling the real story); one has always this gratification, and a great, wicked, delightful one it is, — you make the whole company uncomfortable at once; you narrate the history in a calm, good-humored, dispassionate tone; and as you proceed, you see the different personages of the audience looking uneasily at one another, and bursting out occasionally

with a "Mais cependant;" but you continue your tale
with perfect suavity of manner, and have the satisfaction
of knowing that you have stuck a dagger into the heart of
every single person using it.

Telling, I say, this story to some artists who were examining Monsieur Leullier's picture, and I trust that many
scores of persons besides were listening to the conversation,
one of them replied to my assertion, that Captain Renaudin's letters were extant, and that the whole affair was a
humbug, in the following way.

"Sir," said he, "the sinking of the 'Vengeur' is an *established fact of history*. It is completely proved by the
documents of the time; and as for the letters of Captain
Renaudin of which you speak, have we not had an example
the other day of some pretended letters of Louis Philippe's
which were published in a newspaper here? And what,
sir, were those letters? *Forgeries!*"

Q. E. D. Everybody said sansculotte was right: and I
have no doubt that, if all the "Vengeur's" crew could rise
from the dead, and that English cox — or boat — swain,
who was last *on board the ship*,* of which he and his comrades had possession, and had to swim for his life, could
come forward, and swear to the real story, I make no doubt
that the Frenchmen would not believe it. Only one, I
know, my friend Julius, who, ever since the tale has been
told to him, has been crying it into all ears and in all societies, and vows he is perfectly hoarse with telling it.

As for Monsieur Leullier's picture, there is really a great
deal of good in it. Fellows embracing, and others lifting
up hands and eyes to Heaven; and in the distance an English ship, with the crew in *red coats*, firing away on the
doomed vessel. Possibly, they are only marines whom we
see; but as I once beheld several English naval officers in
a play habited in top-boots, perhaps the legend in France
may be that the navy, like the army, with us, is capari-
soned in scarlet. A good subject for another historical
picture would be Cambronne, saying, "La Garde meurt,
mais ne se rend pas." I have bought a couple of engravings of the "Vengeur" and Cambronne, and shall be glad
to make a little historical collection of facts similarly
authenticated.   •

Accursed, I say, be all uniform coats of blue or of red;

* The writer heard of this man from an English captain in the navy,
who had him on board his ship.

all ye epaulets and sabretashes; all ye guns, shrapnels, and musketoons; all ye silken banners embroidered with bloody reminiscences of successful fights: down — down to the bottomless pit with you all, and let honest men live and love each other without you! What business have I, forsooth, to plume myself because the Duke of Wellington beat the French in Spain and elsewhere; and kindle as I read the tale, and fancy myself of an heroic stock, because my uncle Tom was at the battle of Waterloo, and because we beat Napoleon there? Who are *we*, in the name of Beelzebub? Did we ever fight in our lives? Have we the slightest inclination for fighting and murdering one another? Why are we to go on hating one another from generation to generation, swelling up our little bosoms with absurd national conceit, strutting and crowing over our neighbors, and longing to be at fisticuffs with them again? As Aristotle remarks, in war there are always two parties; and though it often happens that both declare themselves to be victorious, it still is generally the case that one party beats and the other is beaten. The conqueror is thus filled with national pride, and the conquered with national hatred and a desire to do better next time. If he has his revenge and beats his opponent as desired, these agreeable feelings are reversed, and so Pride and Hatred continue *in sæcula sæculorum*, and ribbons and orders are given away, and great men rise and flourish. "Remember you are Britons!" cries our general; "there is the enemy, and, d—— 'em, give 'em the bayonet!" Hurrah! helter-skelter, load and fire, cut and thrust, down they go! "Soldats! dans ce moment terrible la France vous regarde! Vive l'Empereur!" shouts Jacques Bonhomme, and his sword is through your ribs in a twinkling. "Children!" roars Feld-marechal Sauerkraut, "men of Hohenzollernsigmaringen! remember the eyes of Vaterland are upon you!" and murder again is the consequence. Tomahee-tereboo leads on the Ashantees with the very same war-cry, and they eat all their prisoners with true patriotic cannibalism.

Thus the great truth is handed down from father to son that

A Briton,
A Frenchman,   } is superior to all the world;
An Ashantee,
A Hohenzollernsigmaringenite, etc.

and by this truth the dullards of the respective nations swear, and by it statesmen govern.

Let the reader say for himself, does he not believe himself to be superior to a man of any other country? We can't help it — in spite of ourselves we do. But if, by changing the name, the fable applies to yourself, why do you laugh?

Κυιδ ϱιδης; μυτατω νωμινε δη τη
Φαβυλα ναϱϱατυϱ,

as a certain poet says (in a quotation that is pretty well known in England, and therefore put down here in a new fashion). Why do you laugh, forsooth? Why do you *not* laugh? If donkeys' ears are a matter of laughter, surely we may laugh at them when growing on our own skulls.

Take a couple of instances from "actual life," as the fashionable novel-puffers say.

A little fat silly woman, who in no country but this would ever have pretensions to beauty, has lately set up a circulating library in our street. She lends the five-franc editions of the English novels, as well as the romances of her own country, and I have had several of the former works of fiction from her store: Bulwer's "Night and Morning," very pleasant kind-hearted reading; "Peter Priggins," an astonishing work of slang, that ought to be translated if but to give Europe an idea of what a gay young gentleman in England sometimes is; and other novels — never mind what. But to revert to the fat woman.

She sits all day ogling and simpering behind her little counter; and from the slow, prim, precise way in which she lets her silly sentences slip through her mouth, you see at once that she is quite satisfied with them, and expects that every customer should give her an opportunity of uttering a few of them for his benefit. Going there for a book, I always find myself entangled in a quarter of an hour's conversation.

This is carried on in not very bad French on my part; at least I find that when I say something genteel to the library-woman, she is not at a loss to understand me, and we have passed already many minutes in this kind of intercourse. Two days since, returning "Night and Morning" to the library-lady and demanding the romance of "Peter Priggins," she offered me instead "Ida," par Monsieur le Vicomte Darlincourt, which I refused, having already experienced some of his lordship's works; next she produced "Stella," "Valida," "Eloa," by various French ladies of literary celebrity; but again I declined, declaring respectfully that, however agreeable the society of ladies might be, I found their works a little insipid. The fact is, that after being accustomed to such potent mixtures as the French romancers offer you, the mild compositions of the French romancer-esses pall on the palate.*

"Madame," says I, to cut the matter short, "je ne demande qu'un roman Anglais, 'Peter Priggins:' l'avez-vous? oui ou non?"

"Ah!" says the library-woman, "Monsieur ne comprend pas notre langue, c'est dommage."

Now one might, at first sight, fancy the above speech an epigram, and not a bad one, on an Englishman's blundering French grammar and pronunciation; but those who know the library-lady must be aware that she never was guilty of such a thing in her life. It was simply a French bull, resulting from the lady's dulness, and by no means a sarcasm. She uttered the words with a great air of superiority and a prim toss of the head, as much as to say, "How much cleverer I am than you, you silly foreigner! and what a fine thing it is in me to know the finest language in the world!" In this way I have heard donkeys of our two countries address foreigners in broken English or French, as if people who could not understand a language when properly spoken could comprehend it when spoken ill. Why the deuce do people give themselves these impertinent stupid airs of superiority, and pique themselves upon the great cleverness of speaking their own language?

Take another instance of this same egregious national conceit. At the English pastry-cook's — (you can't readily find a prettier or more graceful woman than Madame Colombin, nor better plum-cake than she sells) — at Madame Colombin's, yesterday, a huge Briton, with sandy whiskers and a double chin, was swallowing patties and cherry-brandy, and all the while making remarks to a friend similarly employed. They were talking about English and French ships.

"Hang me, Higgins," says Sandy-whiskers, "if I'd ever go into one of their cursed French ships! I should be afraid of sinking at the very first puff of wind!"

---

* In our own country, of course, Mrs. Trollope, Miss Mitford, Miss Pardoe, Mrs. Charles Gore, Miss Edgeworth, Miss Ferrier, Miss Stickney, Miss Barrett, Lady Blessington, Miss Smith, Mrs. Austin, Miss Austen, etc., form exceptions to this rule; and glad am I to offer per favor of this note a humble tribute of admiration to those ladies.

What Higgins replied does not matter. But think what a number of Sandy-whiskerses there are in our nation, — fellows who are proud of this stupid mistrust, — who think it a mark of national spirit to despise French skill, bravery, cookery, seamanship, and what not. Swallow your beef and porter, you great fat-paunched man; enjoy your language and your country, as you have been bred to do; but don't fancy yourself, on account of these inheritances of yours, superior to other people of other ways and language. You have luck, perhaps, if you will, in having such a diet and dwelling-place, but no *merit*. . . . And with this little discursive essay upon national prejudices let us come back to the pictures, and finish our walk through the gallery.

In that agreeable branch of the art for which we have I believe no name, but which the French call *genre*, there are at Paris several eminent professors ; and as upon the French stage the costume-pieces are far better produced than with us, so also are French costume-pictures much more accurately and characteristically handled than are such subjects in our own country. You do not see Cimabue and Giotto in the costume of Francis I., as they appeared (depicted by Mr. Simpson, I think) in the Royal Academy Exhibition of last year; but the artists go to some trouble in collecting their antiquarian stuff, and paint it pretty scrupulously.

Monsieur Jacquard has some pretty small pictures *de genre ;* a very good one, indeed, of fat "Monks granting Absolution from Fasting ; " of which the details are finely and accurately painted, a task more easy for a French artist than an English one, for the former's studio (as may be seen by a picture in this exhibition) is generally a magnificent curiosity shop; and for old carvings, screens, crockery, armor, draperies, etc., the painter here has but to look to his own walls and copy away at his ease. Accordingly Jacquard's monks, especially all the properties of the picture, are admirable.

Monsieur Baron has "The Youth of Ribera," a merry Spanish beggar-boy, among a crowd of his like, drawing sketches of them under a garden wall. The figures are very prettily thought and grouped; there is a fine terrace, and palace, and statues in the background, very rich and luxurious; perhaps too pretty and gay in colors, and too strong in details.

But the king of the painters of small history subjects is Monsieur Robert Fleury ; a great artist indeed, and I trust heartily he may be induced to send one or two of his pieces to London, to show our people what he can do.   His mind, judging from his works, is rather of a gloomy turn; and he deals somewhat too much, to my taste, in the horrible. He has this year "A Scene in the Inquisition."   A man is howling and writhing with his feet over a fire; grim inquisitors are watching over him; and a dreadful executioner, with fierce eyes peering from under a mysterious capuchin, is doggedly sitting over the coals.   The picture is downright horror, but admirably and honestly drawn; and in effect rich, sombre, and simple.

"Benvenuto Cellini" is better still; and the critics have lauded the piece as giving a good idea of the fierce fantastic Florentine sculptor; but I think Monsieur Fleury has taken him in too grim a mood, and made his ferocity too downright.   There was always a dash of the ridiculous in the man, even in his most truculent moments; and I fancy that such simple rage as is here represented scarcely characterizes him.   The fellow never cut a throat without some sense of humor, and here we have him greatly too majestic to my taste.   "Old Michael Angelo watching over the Sick-bed of his Servant Urbino" is a noble painting; as fine in feeling as in design and color.   One can't but admire in all these the *manliness* of the artist.   The picture is painted in a large, rich, massive, vigorous manner; and it is gratifying to see that this great man, after resolute seeking for many years, has found the full use of his hand at last, and can express himself as he would.   The picture is fit to hang in the very best gallery in the world; and a century hence will no doubt be worth five times as many crowns as the artist asks or has had for it.

Being on the subject of great pictures, let us here mention

712. "Portrait of a Lady," by Hippolyte Flandrin.

Of this portrait all I can say is, that if you take the best portraits by the best masters — a head of Sebastian or Michael Angelo, a head of Raphael, or one of those rarer ones of Andrea del Sarto — not one of them, for lofty character and majestic nobleness and simplicity, can surpass this magnificent work.

This seems, doubtless, very exaggerated praise, and people reading it may possibly sneer at the critic who ventures to speak in such a way.   To all such I say, Come and see it. You who admire Sir Thomas and the "Books of Beauty" will possibly not admire it; you who give ten thousand guineas for a blowzy Murillo will possibly not relish Monsieur Flandrin's manner; but you who love simplicity and greatness come and see how an old lady, with a black mantilla and dark eyes, and gray hair and a few red flowers in her cap, has been painted by Monsieur Flandrin of Lyons. If I were Louis Philippe, I would send a legion-of-honor cross, of the biggest sort, to decorate the bosom of the painter who has executed this noble piece.

As for portraits (with the exception of this one, which no man in England can equal, not even Mr. Samuel Lawrence, who is trying to get to this point, but has not reached it yet) our English painters keep the lead still, nor is there much remarkable among the hundreds in the gallery. There are vast numbers of English faces staring at you from the canvases; and among the miniatures especially one can't help laughing at the continual recurrence of the healthy, vacant, simpering, aristocratic English type. There are black velvets and satins, ladies with birds of paradise, deputies on sofas, and generals and marshals in the midst of smoke and cannon-balls. Nothing can be less to my taste than a pot-bellied swaggering Marshal Soult, who rests his bâton on his stomach, and looks at you in the midst of a dim cloud of war. The Duchesse de Nemours is done by Monsieur Winterhalter, and has a place of honor, as becomes a good portrait; and, above all, such a pretty lady. She is a pretty, smiling, buxom blonde, with plenty of hair, and rather too much hands, not to speak disrespectfully; and a slice of lace which goes across the middle of her white satin gown seems to cut the picture very disagreeably in two. There is a beautiful head in a large portrait of a lad of eighteen, painted by himself; and here may be mentioned two single figures in pastel by an architect, remarkable for earnest *spirituel* beauty; likewise two heads in chalk by De Rudder; most charming sketches, full of delicacy, grace, and truth.

The only one of the acknowledged great who has exhibited this year is Monsieur Delacroix, who has a large picture relative to the siege of Constantinople that looks very like a piece of crumpled tapestry, but that has nevertheless its admirers and its merits, as what work of his has not?

His two smaller pieces are charming. "A Jewish Wedding at Tangiers" is brilliant with light and merriment; a

particular sort of merriment, that is, that makes you gloomy
in the very midst of the heyday : and his "Boat" is awful.
A score of shipwrecked men are in this boat, on a great,
wide, swollen, interminable sea — no hope, no speck of sail
— and they are drawing lots which shall be killed and eaten.
A burly seaman, with a red beard, has just put his hand
into the hat and is touching his own to the officer.   One
fellow sits with his hands clasped, and gazing — gazing into
the great void before him.   By Jupiter, his eyes are un-
fathomable !   he is looking at miles and miles of lead-
colored, bitter, pitiless brine !   Indeed one can't bear to
look at him long ; nor at that poor woman, so sickly, and
so beautiful, whom they may as well kill at once, or she
will save them the trouble of drawing straws ; and give up
to their maws that poor, white, faded, delicate, shrivelled
carcass.   Ah, what a thing it is to be hungry !   Oh, Eugenius
Delacroix !   how can you manage, with a few paint-bladders,
and a dirty brush, and a careless hand, to dash down such
savage histories as these, and fill people's minds with
thoughts so dreadful ?   Ay, there it is ; whenever I go
through that part of the gallery where Monsieur Delacroix's
picture is, I always turn away now, and look at a fat woman
with a paroquet opposite.   For what's the use of being
uncomfortable ?

Another great picture is one of about four inches square
— "The Chess-Players," by Monsieur Meissonier — truly an
astonishing piece of workmanship.   No silly tricks of effect,
and abrupt startling shadow and light, but a picture painted
with the minuteness and accuracy of a daguerreotype, and
as near as possible perfect in its kind.   Two men are playing at chess, and the chess-men are no bigger than pin-
heads ; every one of them an accurate portrait, with all the
light, shadow, roundness, character, and color belonging
to it.

Of the landscapes it is very hard indeed to speak, for
professors of landscape almost all execute their art well ;
but few so well as to strike one with especial attention, or
to produce much remark.   Constable has been a great
friend to the new landscape-school in France, who have laid
aside the slimy weak manner formerly in vogue, and perhaps have adopted in its place a method equally reprehensible — that of plastering their pictures excessively.
When you wish to represent a piece of old timber, or a
crumbling wall, or the ruts and stones in a road, this im-

pasting method is very successful; but here the skies are trowelled on; the light-vaporing distances are as thick as plum-pudding, the cool clear shadows are mashed-down masses of sienna and indigo. But it is undeniable that, by these violent means, a certain power is had, and noonday effects of strong sunshine are often dashingly rendered.

How much pleasanter is it to see a little quiet gray waste of David Cox than the very best and smartest of such works! Some men from Düsseldorf have sent very fine scientific faithful pictures, that are a little heavy, but still you see that they are portraits drawn respectfully from the great, beautiful, various, divine face of Nature.

In the statue-gallery there is nothing worth talking about; and so let us make an end of the Louvre, and politely wish a good-morning to everybody.

AN EXHIBITION GOSSIP.

BY MICHAEL ANGELO TITMARSH.

IN A LETTER TO MONSIEUR GUILLAUME, PEINTRE, A SON
ATELIER, RUE DE MONSIEUR, FAUBOURG ST. GERMAIN,
PARIS.

[*Ainsworth's Magazine, June, 1842.*]

Dear Guillaume, — Some of the dullest chapters that
ever were written in this world — viz., those on the History
of Modern Europe, by Russell, begin with an address to
some imaginary young friend, to whom the Doctor is supposed to communicate his knowledge. " Dear John,"
begins he, quite affectionately, " I take up my pen to state
that the last of the Carlovingians " — or, " Dear John, I
am happy to inform you that the aspect of Europe on the
accession of Henry VIII. was so and so." In the same
manner, and in your famous " *Lettres à Sophie,*" the history
of the heathen gods and goddesses is communicated to
some possible young lady; and this simple plan has, no
doubt, been adopted because the authors wished to convey
their information with the utmost simplicity possible, and
in a free, easy, honest, confidential sort of a way.

This (as usual), dear Guillaume, has nothing to do with
the subject in hand; but I have ventured to place a little
gossip concerning the Exhibition, under an envelope inscribed with your respectable name, because I have no right
to adopt the editorial *we,* and so implicate a host of illustrious authors, who give their names and aid to Mr. Ainsworth's Magazine, in opinions that are very likely not worth
sixpence; and because that simple upright I, which often
seems egotistical and presuming, is, I fancy, less affected
and pert than " we " often is. " I " is merely an individual;
whereas, " we " is clearly somebody else. " I " merely expresses an opinion; whereas, " we " at once lays down
the law.

Pardon, then, the continued use of the personal pronoun,
as I am sure, my dear friend, you will; because as you do

not understand a word of English, how possibly can you quarrel with my style ?

We have often had great battles together on the subject of our respective schools of art; and having seen the two Exhibitions, I am glad to be able to say that ours is the best *this* year, at least, though, perhaps, for many years past you have had the superiority. We have more good pictures in our 1400, than you in your 3000; among the good, we have more *very* good, than you have this year (none nobler and better than the drawings of M. Decamps); and though there are no such large canvases and ambitious subjects as cover the walls of your *salon*, I think our painters have more first-class pictures in their humble way.

They wisely, I think, avoid those great historical "parades" which cover so much space in the Louvre. A young man has sometimes a fit of what is called "historical painting;" comes out with a great canvas, disposed in the regular six-feet heroical order; and having probably half ruined himself in the painting of his piece, which nobody (let us be thankful for it!) buys, curses the decayed state of taste in the country, and falls to portrait-painting, or takes small natural subjects, in which the world can sympathize, and with which he is best able to grapple. We have no government museums like yours to furnish; — no galleries in chief towns of departments to adorn; — no painted chapels, requiring fresh supplies of saints and martyrs, which your artists do to order. Art is a matter of private enterprise here, like everything else: and our painters must suit the small rooms of their customers, and supply them with such subjects as are likely to please them. If you were to make me a present of half a cartoon, or a prophet by Michael Angelo, or a Spanish martyrdom, I would turn the picture against the wall. Such great things are only good for great edifices, and to be seen occasionally; — we want pleasant pictures, that we can live with — something that shall be lively, pleasing or tender, or sublime, if you will, but only of a moderate-sized sublimity. Confess, if you had to live in a huge room with the Last Judgment at one end of it, and the Death of Ananias at the other, would not you be afraid to remain alone — or, at any rate, long for a comfortable bare wall ? The world produces, now and then, one of the great daring geniuses who make those tremendous works of art; but they come only seldom — and Heaven be thanked for it! We have had one in our country — John Milton by name. Honestly confess now, was there not a fervor in your youth when you had a plan of an epic, or, at least, of an heroic Michael-Angelesque picture? The sublime rage fades as one grows older and cooler; and so the good, sensible, honest English painters, for the most part, content themselves with doing no more than they can.

But though we have no heroical canvases, it is not to be inferred that we do not cultivate a humbler sort of high art; and you painters of religious subjects know, from the very subjects which you are called upon to draw, that humility may be even more sublime than greatness. For instance, there is in almost everything Mr. Eastlake does (in spite of a little feebleness of hand and primness of mannerism) a purity which is to us quite angelical, so that we can't look at one of his pictures without being touched and purified by it. Mr. Mulready has an art, too, which is not inferior, and though he commonly takes, like the before-mentioned gentleman, some very simple, homely subject to illustrate, manages to affect and delight one, as much as painter can. Mr. Mulready calls his picture, "The Ford;" Mr. Eastlake styles his, "Sisters." The "Sisters" are two young ladies looking over a balcony; "The Ford" is a stream through which some boys are carrying a girl: and how is a critic to describe the beauty in such subjects as these? It would be easy to say these pictures are exquisitely drawn, beautifully colored, and so forth; but that is not the reason of their beauty: on the contrary, any man who has a mind may find fault with the drawing and coloring of both. Well, there is a charm about them seemingly independent of drawing and coloring: and what is it? There's no foot rule that I know of to measure it; and the very wisest lecturer on art might define and define, and be not a whit nearer the truth. I can't tell you why I like to hear a blackbird sing; it is certainly not so clever as a piping bullfinch.

I always begin with the works of these gentlemen, and look at them oftenest and longest; but that is only a simple expression of individual taste, and by no means an attempt at laying down the law, upon a subject which is quite out of the limits of all legislation. A better critic might possibly (I say "possibly," not as regards the correctness of my own opinion, but the unquestionable merit of the two admirable artists above named), another critic will possibly have other objects for admiration, and if such a person were to say, Pause — before you award pre-eminence to this artist or that, pause — for instance, look at those two Leslies, can anything in point of *esprit* and feeling surpass them ? — indeed the other critic would give very sound advice. Nothing can be finer than the comedy of the Scene from Twelfth Night, more joyous, frank, manly, laughter-moving; — or more tender, and grave, and naïf, than the picture of Queen Catherine and her attendant. The great beauty of these pieces is the total absence of affectation. The figures are in perfectly quiet, simple positions, looking as if they were not the least aware of the spectator's presence (a rare quality in pictures, as I think, of which little dramas, the actors, like those upon the living stage, have a great love of "striking an attitude," and are always on the look-out for the applause of the lookers-on), whereas Mr. Leslie's excellent little troop of comedians know their art so perfectly that it becomes the very image of nature, and the best nature, too. Some painters (skilled in the depicting of such knicknacks) overpower their pieces with "properties" — guitars, old armors, flower-jugs, curtains, and what not. The very chairs and tables in the picture of Queen Catherine have a noble, simple arrangement about them; they look sad and stately, and cast great dreary shadows — they will lighten up a little, doubtless, when the girl begins to sing.

You and I have been in the habit of accusing one of the cleverest painters of the country of want of poetry: no other than Mr. Edwin Landseer, who, with his marvellous power of hand, a sort of aristocrat among painters, has seemed to say — I care for my dog and my gun; I'm an English country gentleman, and poetry is beneath me. He has made us laugh sometimes, when he is in the mood, with his admirable humor, but has held off as it were from poetic subjects, as a man would do who was addressing himself in a fine ball-room to a party of fine people, who would stare if any such subjects were broached. I don't care to own that in former years those dogs, those birds, deer, wild-ducks, and so forth, were painted to such a pitch of desperate perfection as to make me quite angry — elegant, beautiful, well-appointed, perfect models for grace and manner; they were like some of our English dandies that one sees, and who never can be brought to pass the limits of a certain polite smile, and decorous, sensible insipidity.

The more one sees them, the more vexed one grows, for, be hanged to them, there is no earthly fault to find with them. This, to be sure, is begging the question, and you may not be disposed to allow either the correctness of the simile, or that dandies are insipid, or that field sports, or pictures thereof, can possibly be tedious; but, at any rate, it is a comfort to see that a man of genius, who is a poet, *will* be one sometimes, and here are a couple of noble poetical pieces from Mr. Landseer's pencil. The "Otter and Trout" has something awful about it; the hunted stag, panting through the water and startling up the wild-fowl, is a beautiful and touching poem. Oh, that these two pictures, and a few more of different English artists, could be carried across the Channel — say when Mr. Partridge's portrait of the Queen goes to act as a counterpoise to that work!

A few Etties might likewise be put into the same box, and a few delightful golden landscapes of Callcott. To these I would add Mr. Maclise's "Hamlet," about whose faults and merits there have been some loud controversies; but in every Exhibition for the last five years, if you saw a crowd before a picture, it was sure to be before his; and with all the faults people found, no one could go away without a sort of wonder at the prodigious talent of this gentleman. Sometimes it was mere wonder; in the present Exhibition it is wonder and pleasure too; and his picture of Hamlet is by far the best, to my thinking, that the artist has ever produced. If, for the credit of Old England (and I hereby humbly beg Mr. Maclise to listen to the suggestion), it could be transported to the walls of your *salon*, it would show French artists, who are accustomed to sneer at the drawing of the English school, that we have a man whose power of drawing is greater than that of any artist among you, — of any artist that ever lived, I should like to venture to say. An artist, possessing this vast power of hand, often wastes it — as Paganini did, for instance — in capriccios, and extravagances, and brilliant feats of skill, as if defying the world to come and cope with him. The picture of the play in "Hamlet" is a great deal more, and is a noble poetic delineation of the awful story. Here I am obliged to repeat, for the tenth time in this letter, how vain it is to attempt to describe such works by means of pen and ink. Fancy Hamlet, ungartered, lying on the ground, looking into the very soul of King Claudius, who writhes under the play of Gonzago. Fancy the Queen, perplexed and sad (she does not know of the murder), and poor Ophelia, and Polonius, with his staff, pottering over the tragedy; and Horatio, and all sorts of knights and ladies, looking wondering on. Fancy, in the little theatre, the king asleep; a lamp in front casts a huge forked fantastic shadow over the scene — a shadow that looks like a horrible devil in the background that is grinning and aping the murder. Fancy ghastly flickering tapestries of Cain and Abel on the walls, and all this painted with the utmost force, truth, and dexterity — fancy all this, and then you will have not the least idea of one of the most startling, wonderful pictures that the English school has ever produced.

Mr. Maclise may be said to be at the head of the young men; and though you and I, my dear Guillaume, are both old, and while others are perpetually deploring the past, I think it is a consolation to see that the present is better, and to argue that the future will be better still. You did not give up David without a pang, and still think Baron Gérard a very wonderful fellow. I can remember once, when Westall seemed really worth looking at, when a huge black exaggeration of Northcote or Opie struck me as mighty fine, and Mr. West seemed a most worthy President of our Academy. Confess now that the race who succeeded them did better than they; and indeed the young men, if I may be permitted to hint such a thing, do better still — not better than individuals — for Eastlake, Mulready, Etty, Leslie, are exhibiters of twenty years' standing, and the young men may live a thousand years and never surpass them; but a finer taste is more general among them than existed some thirty years back, and a purer, humbler, truer love of nature. Have you seen the "Deserted Village" of the "Etching Club"? What charming feeling and purity is there among most of the designs of these young painters, and what a credit are they to the English school!

The designers of the "Etching Club" seem to form a little knot or circle among themselves; and though the names of Cope, Redgrave, Herbert, Stone, have hardly reached you as yet in France, they will be heard of some day even there, where your clever people, who can appreciate all sorts of art, will not fail to admire the quiet, thoughtful, pious, delicate feeling which characterizes the works of this charming little school. All Mr. Cope's pictures, though somewhat feeble in hand, are beautifully tender and graceful. "The Hawthorn-bush, with seats beneath the shade, for talking age and whispering lovers made," is a beautiful picture for color, sentiment, and composition. The old people, properly garrulous, talking of old times, or the crops, or the Doctor's sermon; the lovers — a charming pair — loving with all their souls, kind, hearty, and tender. The Schoolmaster of one of his other pictures is an excellent awful portrait of Goldsmith's pedagogue. Mr. Redgrave's "Cinderella" is very pleasant, his landscape beautiful. Mr. Stone's "Advice" is full of tender sentiment, and contains some frank, excellent painting; but how vapid all such comments appear, and how can you, on the banks of the Seine, understand from these sort of vague, unsatisfactory praises, what are the merits or demerits of the pieces spoken about!

We have here a delightful, *naïf* artist, Mr. Webster by name, who has taken little boys under his protection, and paints them in the most charming comic way — in that best sort of comedy, which makes one doubt whether to laugh or to cry. His largest picture this year represents two boys bound for school. Breakfast is hurried over (a horrid early breakfast); the trunk is packed; papa is pulling on his boots; there is the coach coming down the hill, and the guard blowing his pitiless horn. All the little girls are gathered round their brothers: the elder is munching a biscuit, and determined to be a man; but the younger, whom the little sister of all has got hold of by the hand, can't bear the parting, and is crying his eyes out.

I quarrel with Mr. Webster for making one laugh at the boy, and giving him a comic face. I say no man who has experienced it has a right to laugh at such a sorrow. Did you ever, in France, look out for the diligence that was to take you to school, and hear a fatal conducteur blowing his horn as you waited by the hillside — as you waited with the poor mother, turning her eyes away — and slowly got off the old pony, which you were not to see for six months — for a century — for a thousand miserable years again? Oh, that first night at school! those bitter, bitter tears at night, as you lay awake in the silence, poor little lonely boy, yearning after love and home. Life has sorrows enough, God knows, but, I swear, none like that! I was thinking about all this as I looked at Mr. Webster's picture, and behold it turned itself into an avenue of lime-trees, and a certain old stile that led to a stubble-field; and it was evening, about the 14th of September, and after dinner (how that *last* glass of wine used to choke and burn in the throat!), and presently, a mile off, you heard, horribly distinct, the whirring of the well-known Defiance coach wheels. It was up in a moment — the trunk on the roof; and — bah! from that day I can't bear to see mothers and children parting.

This, to be sure, is beside the subject; but pray let Mr. Webster change the face of his boy.

Letters (except from young ladies to one another) are not allowed to go beyond a certain decent length; hence, though I may have a fancy to speak to you of many score of other good pictures, out of the fourteen hundred here exhibited, there are numbers which we must pass over without any notice whatever. It is hard to pass by Mr. Richmond's beautiful water-color figures, without a word concerning them; or Mr. Charles Landseer's capital picture of "Ladies and Cavaliers;" or not to have at least half a page to spare, in order to make an onslaught upon Mr. Chalon and his ogling beauties: he has a portrait of Mdlle. Rachel, quite curious for its cleverness and unlikeness, and one of the most chaste and refined of our actresses, Mrs. Charles Kean, who is represented as a killing coquette; and so Mr. Kean may be thankful that the portrait does not in the least resemble his lady.

There is scarce any need to say that the oil-portrait painters maintain their usual reputation and excellence; Mr. Briggs, Mr. Pickersgill, Mr. Grant, show some excellent canvases: the latter's ladies are beautiful, and his "Lord Cardigan" a fine painting and portrait; Mr. Briggs's "Archbishop" is a noble head and picture; Mr. Pickersgill has, among others, a full-length of a Navy Captain, very fine; Mr. Linnell's portraits are very fine; and Mr. S. Lawrence has one (the Attorney-General), excellently drawn, and fine in character. This year's picture of her Majesty is intended for *your* Majesty, Louis Philippe — perhaps the French court might have had a more favorable representation of the Queen. There is only one "Duke of Wellington" that I have remarked — (indeed it must be a weary task to the good-natured and simple old nobleman to give up to artists the use of his brave face, as he is so often called upon to do) — at present he appears in a group of red-coated brethren in arms, called the "Heroes of Water-

loo." The picture, from the quantity of requisite vermilion, was most difficult to treat, but is cleverly managed,
and the likeness very good. All the warriors assembled are
smiling, to a man; and in the background is a picture of
Napoleon, who is smiling too — and this is surely too great
a stretch of good nature.

What can I say of the Napoleon of Mr. Turner? called
(with frightful satire) the "Exile and the *Rock-limpet.*"
He stands in the midst of a scarlet tornado, looking at
least forty feet high.

Ah! says the mysterious poet, from whom Mr. Turner
loves to quote, —

> "Ah! thy tent-formed shell is like
> The soldier's nightly bivouac, alone
> Amidst a sea of blood ———
> —— *but you can join your comrades.*"
>
> FALLACIES OF HOPE.

These remarkable lines entirely explain the meaning of
the picture; another piece is described by lines from the
same poem, in a metre more regular: —

> "The midnight torch gleamed o'er the steamer's side,
> And *merit's corse* was yielded to the tide."

When the pictures are rehung, as sometimes I believe is
the case, it might perhaps be as well to turn these upside
down, and see how they would look *then;* the Campo
Santo of Venice, when examined closely, is scarcely less
mysterious; at a little distance, however, it is a most brilliant, airy, and beautiful picture. O for the old days,
before Mr. Turner had lighted on "The Fallacies," and
could see like other people!

Other landscape painters, not so romantic, are, as usual,
excellent. You know Mr. Stanfield and Mr. Roberts, in
France, as well as we do: I wish one day you could see the
hearty, fresh English landscapes of Lee and Creswick,
where you can almost see the dew on the fresh grass, and
trace the ripple of the water, and the whispering in the
foliage of the cool, wholesome wind.

.   .   .   .   .   .

There is not an inch more room in the paper; and a
great deal that was to be said about the Water-color Soci-

eties and Suffolk Street must remain unsaid for ever and ever. But I wish you could see a drawing by Miss Setchel, in the Junior Water-color Society, and a dozen by Mr. Absolon, which are delightful in grace and expression, and in tender, pathetic humor.

M. A. T.

LETTERS ON THE FINE ARTS.

I.—THE ART UNIONS.

FROM M. A. TITMARSH, ESQ., TO SANDERS M'GILP, ESQ.

[*Pictorial Times, March–May*, 1843.]

My dear Sanders, — I have always had the highest confidence in your judgment, and am therefore pretty certain that your picture is one of vast merit. The value, you say, is two hundred guineas, and you have, I hope, with laudable prudence, induced your relatives, your grandmother, your confiding aunts, the tradesmen with whom you have little accounts, and the friends with whom you are occasionally kind enough to go and dine, to subscribe to the Art Union, in hopes that one or other of them may gain the principal prize, when their taste, as well as their friendship (and where can friendship be better bestowed?), will induce them to purchase your work. To your relatives affection alone would dictate the acquisition of your picture; to your tradesmen you offer, if possible, a still stronger inducement. "I owe you 40*l*.," you can say to Mr. Snip, your respected tailor; "I cannot pay those 40*l*.;" but gain the first prize, and you have my picture for 200 guineas, which in reality is worth 500, plus the payment of your bill, the amount of which you can deduct from the sum due to myself." Thus Mr. Snooks gets

	£	s.	d.
A picture (valued at 500 guineas)	525	0	0
The payment of his bill	40	0	0
And costs of writ	2	2	0
	£567	2	0

in return for a single sovereign subscribed to the Union.

The advantage of Art Unions has never before, I believe, been considered in this light: and if every artist would but go round to his tradesmen and represent the truth to them as here laid down, no doubt great numbers of addi-

tional patrons would be found for the noble art you practise. How many a man, for instance, has not one but half
a dozen tailors in the category in which I have placed Mr.
Snip. Well; let them all subscribe ; — the more the
merrier. "If one win, gentlemen," you say, "remember
I am in a condition to pay all the rest their accounts."
And thus is an interest for Art brought home to the
bosoms and boards of six deserving families.

Is, or is not, the principle a good one? Are, or are
not, tradesmen to be paid? Are, or are not, artists to be
well clothed? And would, or would not, the diffusion of
their divine science enlarge the heart and soften the rude
manners of the million? What, on this head, does Hesiod
observe? The Teian bard nobly remarks,* —

Ινγενυας διδιχισσε φιδηλιτερ αρτης,
Ημολλιτ μωρης νεχ σινιτ κσσε φερως

And if the principle *be* a good one, I say it should be
universal. Say (as an encouragement) to the collector who
comes for your rate, "I'll pay you if you take a ticket in
the *Art Union !*" Remark to your butcher, in a pleasant
way, "Mr. Brisket, I desire from you, for your own advantage, one stake more." "From the loin, or where?" says
he. "No," say you, laughingly interrupting him, "a stake
in the *Art Union.*" And point out to your washerwoman
what an ennobling and glorious thing it would be — a holy
effluence, a bright and beaming radiance woven into the
dark chain of her existence — (or other words of might and
poesy suited to her capacity), point out, I say, what a
pleasure it would be to her to be able to exclaim, "I wash
Mr. M'Gilp's shirts — and look! one of his five hundred
guinea masterpieces hangs yonder, over my mangle."

It is in his power, it is in anybody's power. The very
Malay sweeper who shivers at the corner of your street and
acts as your model, may easily save money enough to take
a ticket, and have his portrait, as Othello, to decorate his
humble place of abode.

You may fancy, my friend, that there is some caricature

---

* We suspect that Mr. Titmarsh is here attempting to mystify the un-
learned reader. Anacreon, not Hesiod, was "the Teian bard," and it is
neither Hesiod nor Anacreon, but Ovid, who (in Latin not in Greek
verse) "remarks," —

———— ingenuas didicisse fideliter artes,
Emollit mores, nec sinit esse feros. ED.

in this, and possibly you are right. You will never stoop to Mr. Snip in the manner pointed out by me: you are above entreating your washerwoman, cutting jokes with your butcher, or cajoling the respectable gentleman who calls for your contributions once a quarter. Art, say you, is above paltry speculation and mean ideas of gain. An artist never stoops to intrigue, or chaffers for money. He is the priest of nature, called to worship at her glorious altar, by special vocation; one chosen out of the million, and called up to the high places; in short, you will make a speech, crammed with fine words, proving your disinterestedness and the awful poetical nature of your calling.

Psha! my good friend, let us have no more of this stale talk. You are a tradesman as well as my lord on the woolsack, or Mr. Smith selling figs, or General Sones breathing freely and at his ease in an atmosphere of cannon-balls. You each do your duty in your calling, and according to your genius, but you want to be paid for what you do. You want the best pay and the greatest share of reputation you can get. You will do nothing dishonest in the pursuit of your trade; but will you not yield a little "to the exigencies of the public service"? General Sones, though he may have his own opinion of the Chinese war, will attack mandarins without mercy; my Lord Chancellor has pleaded many a queer cause before he reposed on yonder woolsack; Smith has had recourse to many little harmless tricks to get a sale for his figs and treacle; and you (as I take it) are not a whit better than they. Did you ever paint a lady in her portrait handsomer than nature made her? Did you ever, when your immense genius panted to be at work on some vast historical piece, crush your aspirations so far as to sit down and depict a plain gentleman in a buff waistcoat and a watch chain, for the sake of the twenty guineas which were to be elicited from his ample pepper-and-salt pantaloons? You have done all this; and were quite right in doing it too. How else are the little M'Gilps to get their dinners, or your lady the means of discharging her weekly bills?

And now you will begin, I trust, to perceive that the ridicule cast upon the Art Union system in the first sentences of this letter, is not in reality so very severe: it is the sort of sneering language which the enemies of those establishments are in the habit of indulging in, though expressed as high, no doubt you will think in a far more satiric and witty manner than most of the Anti-Unionists have at command. Hear, for instance, the *Athenæum.* "So early," says that journal, "as 1837, we put on record our opinion that the Art Union would and must of necessity tend to the still further degradation of Art. Any man," we observed, "who purchases pictures may be presumed to have a love for, and this will in the end generate a knowledge of, Art. But there will be many subscribers who desire only a little gambling — to risk a pound for the chance of winning a hundred — and who would quite as soon join in a raffle for a horse, or a snuff-box, or a pipe of port wine, as for a picture. The motive of the subscriber is of no consequence, so long as others have to dispose of the money; but the Art Union proposes that each subscriber 'shall select for himself.' Now is it not certain that such patronage must tend to degrade Art? The scheme may be beneficial to the lowest class of artists, but utterly ruinous to Art itself. When every individual, be he *whom* he may, is allowed to follow his own judgment in the disposal of his prize-money, the best results can be but an irresponsible indulgence of individual whim and caprice — the worst and certain is the degradation of Art. Men who paint to live, instead of working with all their power, be it more or less, up to the best and highest judgments, must solicit the sweet voices of the uninformed, the chance prize-holders, and therefore purchasers of the Art Unions."

So writes the *Athenæum,* and you will at once perceive the truth of my previous assertions : — 1. That the *Athenæum's* arguments resemble those employed at the commencement of this letter. 2. That the arguments at the beginning of this letter are far more cleverly and wickedly put.

Let us now proceed to demolish the one and the other ; and we will, if you please, take the dicta of the *Athenæum* in the first place into consideration.

"Every man" (says the *Athenæum*) "who purchases pictures may be presumed to have a love for, and this will in the end generate a knowledge of, Art."

"But this Art Union is joined by many for the sake of gambling, and who would *quite as soon* join in a raffle for a horse, or a snuff-box, or a pipe of port wine, as for a picture."

Why quite as soon? A man who wants a pipe of port wine does not, we presume, raffle for a horse; or being excecdingly desirous of a snuff-mull, he does not raffle for a pipe of port wine. There are certainly in the world many "uninformed" persons, as the insinuating *Athenæum* remarks; let us say at once there are fools, but not such tremendous fools as our misanthropic contemporary would discover.

No, no. A man raffles for a horse because the dealers or the knackers will give him a price for it, or because his wife wishes to be driven out in the gig, or because he has a mind to cut a dash in the ring. A man raffles for a gold snuff-box because he is fond of Macabau, or because he likes to sport such a box after dinner, or because he wishes to make it a present to Mr. Boys when he brings out any more of his relative's lithographs, or for some other simple and equally apparent reason. And so for a pipe of port wine: a man risks his money in order to gain it, because he likes port wine, or because he can sell it, or because he wishes to present a few dozens to a friend.

I wish, for my part, I had a friend who desired to dispose of either of the three articles; but that is a mere personal ejaculation, and nothing to the point. The point is, that a man bids money for a horse because he wants it, and for a picture because he would like to have a picture. Common charity must admit so much good sense in the world.

Well, then, it is granted that a man joins in a raffle for a set of pictures because he is interested in pictures; that is, *he may be presumed to have a love for Art.* And a love for Art in the end, says the *Athenæum*, with much sagacity, *will generate a knowledge of Art.* Amen. In that case the excellence of Art Unions is established at once.

But no, says the philosopher who argues every week from under the columns of the temple of Minerva: this love which generates knowledge is only conceded to men who purchase pictures, not to those who raffle for them. Is not this a little hard? How much income tax must a man pay in order to have a decent love of Art; a love that shall be potent enough to become the father of a future knowledge? I may say, without exaggeration, that Sir Robert Peel is richer than I am; but does it follow that he loves Art better? It may be, or nòt; but, at least, the right honorable baronet's income does not establish the superiority of his taste. Let any gentleman go into a pastry-cook's and eat raspberry tarts; ten to one, pressed against the window of the shop you will see the blue nose of a penniless urchin, who is looking at the good things with all his might. Would one say that Dives, because he eats the tarts, loved them better than little Lazarus who yearned after them? No, even the *Athenæum* would not say that; the cruel, cruel *Athenæum*.

Now, suppose that round that shop window, and allured by the same charming prospect which has brought their comrade thither, other little Lazaruses should assemble: they love tarts; they are penniless; but still not altogether without coin. Say they have a farthing apiece; and clubbing together their wealth, or poverty rather, these rascally young gamblers make a lottery in the cap of one of them, and what is the consequence? the winner of the prize steps in and takes a raspberry tart from the very same tray at which great Dives himself has been gormandizing. It is gambling, certainly; but I suspect the pastry-cook (considering its result) will look upon the crime rather justly — she might never have sold her wares but for that TART UNION.

I shall resume this subject next week with philosophical considerations upon Polytechnic societies, upon the lunar prospectus (or that of Mr. Moon), and upon the puerile distribution (or that of Mr. Boys).

Meanwhile, dear M'Gilp, I remain,
Your very humble servant,
MICHAEL ANGELO TITMARSH.

II. — THE OBJECTIONS AGAINST ART UNIONS.

M. A. TITMARSH, ESQ., TO SANDERS M'GILP, ESQ.

My dear Sanders, — The Tart Union alluded to last week has been appreciated; and I am given to understand that several young gentlemen about Covent Garden and the foundation colleges in the city (where the youthful students wear leather breeches, and green coats, and caps famous for their similarity in shape to the muffin) have put the scheme into practice, and are very eager in borrowing or begging farthings for the pastry-cook's interest and their own.

That the scheme will benefit the former is clear: and should any of them be inclined, by way of gratitude, to forward to the office of the paper a *proof plate* of their tarts, there are several juvenile persons about the premises who will gladly give an opinion of their merits. One of the union or distribution schemes mentioned in our last has forwarded proofs of its claims to public favor, proofs of its puffs we would say, but that is a pun, and the truth must be told, let what will come of it, and we are now solemnly met, my brave M'Gilp, to discuss it.

The fact is, that the goodness or badness of the prints in question does not, at least for the sake of the argument, matter a fig. Suppose a man (by means of the electrotype of course) were enabled to reproduce a series of copies from the vignettes to Mr. Catnach's ballads, and charge a guinea, two guineas — a thousand pounds; three farthings, for whitey-brown proofs of the same. He is quite free to do so. Nobody need buy unless they like. Or suppose he could (always by means of the electrotype) produce India paper proof plates of all the Cartoons, and sell them for a halfpenny. He is quite as much at liberty to do the one as the other; and I do believe that the reason of fair dealing and moderate prices in the world has been not so much the honesty as the selfishness of our nature. We sell cheap because no one will buy else. We are honest because no one *will* trust us unless they *can* trust us. In a doubtful commerce with few concurrents and uncertain gains, men do not unfrequently cheat. But competition hustles roguery pretty quickly out of the market; the swaggering, swindling, lying impostor has no chance against the burly good sense of the public.

And I must confess, for my part, that if a man has a thirty-guinea watch to raffle for, and thirty persons are willing to subscribe so much amongst them, and try the chance of winning it, I see no much greater harm in this "union" than in many other speculations where (of course) chances exist of losing or winning. But to moralize on the Art Union case because of this little harmless peddling with guineas, and to say that it provokes a spirit of gambling, is too hard. Is it altogether sinful to play a rubber of whist at shilling points? Does it imply an abominable desire of gain and a frightful perversion in the individual who bets half a crown on the rubber? Are we basely cast down because we lose, or brutally exultant because we win, half a score shillings? If it be a deadly sin, Heaven help our grandfathers and grandmothers, who played cards every night of their lives, and must be anything but comfortable now. But let us hope that with regard to the criminality of the proceeding the *Athenæum* is wrong. Many of us have tried a raffle at Margate, and slept no worse for it. Once, at school, I drew lots with two other boys, and the prize was a flogging; and it does not much matter which of us won; but the others were not very sorry about it, depend on that. No; let this harmless little sin pass. As long as it provokes no very evil passions, as long as the pleasure of winning is great, and the pain of losing small, let gentlemen and ladies have their sport, and bet their bet, and our moralists not altogether despair. You cannot say that the Art Union supporters are actuated by a violent or unwholesome love of gambling; they don't injure their properties by the subscription of their guinea; they don't absent themselves from home, contract dissipated habits, bring their wives and families to ruin. They give a guinea, and are not much the better or the worse for the outlay. This is an encouragement of lotteries, the *Athenæum* may say, presently; but indeed the objection is not worth a fig. The old lotteries were undisguised robberies. The Art Unions are none. The old lotteries lived upon atrocious lies and puffs, encouraged silly people with exaggerated notions of gain. The Art Union offers but to purchase pictures with the aggregate of your money, and to distribute the pictures so bought. There are no falsehoods · told, and no absurd lying baits held out.

A country book-club is a lottery, a wicked, gambling transaction, in which squires and parsons take a part. A house or life assurance is a lottery. You take the odds there to win in a certain event; and may by very straitlaced moralists be accused of " gambling," for so providing against fortune; but the Parliament has sanctioned this gambling, and the State draws a considerable profit from it. An underwriter gambles when he insures a ship; calculating that he has a profit on the chances. A man gambles when he buys stock to sell afterwards, or a newspaper, or a house, or any other commodity upon which profit or loss may accrue. In the latter cases, perhaps, he gambles as he does at whist, knowing himself to be a good player, and trusting to skill and chance for his success. But in the former cases the underwriter of the ship or house has no security; it is sheer luck; dependent on a fire or a gale of wind, with the *pull* of the chances in his favor.

In a commercial country, then, where there is so much authorized gambling for profit, a little gambling for mere amusement's and kindness's sake may be tolerated. Let it be allowed at any rate that there is no great criminality in the Art Union species of gambling, and so quietly pass over the moral objection to the scheme. Then there has been lately mooted in the papers a legal objection; but that is not a very frightful one. Both of the learned gentlemen who have been consulted and have pronounced for and against Art Unions have allowed that there is no danger of prosecution, and that poor bugbear will frighten honest folks no more.

But the strong objection is that on the part of some artists of the old school, who say that the Art Union system deteriorates art; that it sets painters speculating upon fancy pieces to suit the tastes of the prize-holders; that they think this will be a taking two hundred guinea subject, or that a neat gaudy piece that will be sure to hook something; and they paint accordingly.

Now, let any man who has looked at English picture-galleries for the last ten or twenty years be called upon to say from his heart, whether there has not been a great, a noble improvement? — whether there is not infinitely more fancy, feeling, poetry, education among artists as a body now than then? Good Heavens! if they do paint what are called *subjects*, what is the harm? If people do like fancy pieces, where is the great evil? If I have no fancy to have my own portrait staring me in the face in the dining-room, and would rather have Mr. Stone's "one particular star," for instance (and it is a charming picture), am I such a degraded wretch? This is but cant on the part of humbugs on one side, and on the other ultra-ticklishness of too susceptible minds.

What does the charge amount to? That the artist tries by one means or other to consult the taste of the public. The public is ignorant; therefore its choice is bad: therefore the artists paint bad pictures: therefore the taste grows worse and worse: therefore the public and artist are degraded by a desperate helpless arithmetical progression, out of which as one fancies there is no escape.

But look what the real state of the case is, as it has been recited by a weekly paper (the *Age*) — that too moans over the degeneracy of its namesake, and prophesies a most pathetic future for Englishmen, because they have been lately seized with a love for illustrated books. First, says the *Age*, came the *Observer*, with its picture of Thurtell's cottage, then the *Hive*, then the *Mirror*, then this and that, then the *Illustrated London News*, then the *Pictorial Times*. Well, *après?* as the French say. The *Hive* was better than Thurtell's cottage, the *Mirror* was better than the *Hive*, the *News* better than the *Mirror*, and the *Times* better than the *News*, and (though the *Times* readers may fancy the thing impossible) the day will come when something shall surpass even the *Times*, and so on to the infinity of optimism. And so with pictures as with prints. The public is not used to having the former yet, but wait a while and it will take them; and take them better and better every day. The commercial energy of our hearty country is such that where there is a small demand dealers well know how to raise it to be a great one; and raise fresh wants by fresh supplies ingeniously insinuated, and by happy inventions in advance. As for GENIUS, that is not to be spoken of in this way; but Genius is rare; it comes to us but once in many, many years; and do you think the genius of painting less likely to flourish in our country because people are buying (by means of these Art Unions) five hundred little fancy pictures per annum, in addition to the ten thousand portraits they bought before?

As for aristocratic patronage of Art only let us ask in what state was Art here before Art Unions began? Did artists complain or not? Did they say that there was no opportunity to cultivate their poetical feelings, and that they must paint portraits to live? I am sure the people of England are likely to be better patrons of art than the English aristocracy ever were, and that the aristocracy have been tried and *didn't* patronize it; that they neither knew how to value a picture nor an artist: what artist ever got so good a place as a tenth-rate lawyer, or as a hundredth-rate soldier, or as a lucky physician, or as an alderman who had made a good speculation, or a country squire who had a borough? The aristocracy never acknowledged the existence of art in this country, for they never acknowledged the artist. They were the handsomest men and women in the world, and they had their simpering faces painted: but what have they done for art to honor it? No, no. *They* are not the friends of Genius: that day is over: its friends lie elsewhere: rude and uncultivated as yet, but hearty, generous, and eager. It may put up with rough fare; but it can't live in ante-chambers with lackeys, eating my lord's broken meat; equality is its breath, and *sympathy* the condition of its existence. What sympathy did my lords ever give it? No: the law, the sword, the alderman's consols, and the doctor's pill, they can stomach; they can reconcile these to their lordly nature, and infuse them into their august body.

But the POET had best come lower. What have their lordships to do with *him*? He has never been one of their intimates. In the old song of Schiller, Love bids the poet, now that the earth is partitioned among the strong and wealthy, to come to heaven in his distress, in which there will always be a place for him: but he has to try the people yet — the weak and poor: and they, whose union makes their strength, depend on it, have a shelter and a welcome for him.

And so, though the taste of the public might be better than it is now (of which there is no question), I think we have every right to hope that it *will* be better. There are a thousand men read and think to-day, for one who read on this same day of April, 1743. The poet and artist is called upon to appeal to the few no longer. His profit and fame are with the many; and do not let it be thought irreverence to put the profit and fame together. Nobody ever denies the Duke of Wellington's genius, because his Grace receives twenty thousand a year from his country in gratitude for the services rendered by him; and if the nation should take a fancy to reward poets in the same way, we have similarly no right to quarrel with the verdict.

The dukedoms, twenty-thousands-a-year, Piccadilly-palaces, and the like, are not, however, pleaded for here. Miss Coutts or Miss Rothschild have the like (or may, no doubt, for the asking), and nobody grudges the wealth, though neither ever were in the battle of Waterloo that I know of. But let us ask, as the condition of improvement in art, if not fame and honor, at least sympathy, from the public for the artist. The refinement of taste will come afterwards; and as every man a little conversant with the art of painting, or any other art, must know how his judgment improves, and how by degrees he learns to admire justly, so the public will learn to admire more and more wisely every day. The sixpenny prints they buy twenty years hence will be better than the sixpenny prints now : the Art Union pictures

they select better than those which frighten the despond-
ing susceptibilities of our philosophers nowadays. Away
with these prophets of ill, these timid old maids of Cassan-
dras, who lift up their crutches and croak, and cry, "Woe!"
It is the nature of the old bodies to despond, but let "us
youth" be not frightened by their prate. If any publisher
could find it worth his while to bring out a hundred beautiful engravings for a penny, depend on it art would not
retrograde in the country. If a hundred thousand people
chose to subscribe to the Art Union, the interest for art
would be so much the greater, the encouragement to artists
so much the greater; and if you interest the people and
encourage the artists, it is absurd to suppose that one or
the other would go back.

But this, as you will doubtless observe, has nothing to
do with the lunatic prospectus (or that of Mr. Moon), or
with the puerile distribution (or that of Mr. Boys). Let
us consider the sham Art Unions on another day. What I
wish to urge in the above sentences is, that the people are
the artist's best friends; that for his reputation and profit
henceforth he had best look to them; and rather than work
for a class of *patrons*, he had better rely for support on his
friends. If you have something that is worth the telling,—
something for the good of mankind, — it is better to be able
to take it to a hundred tailors or tinkers, than to one duke
or two dandies (speaking with perfect respect of both);
and as an actor would rather have a hundred people in the
pit for an audience than but one hearer who had paid ten
pounds for a private box, an artist need have no squeamish
objections to the same popularity, and will find a more sure
and lasting profit in it. · Many men of genius will say,
"No; we do not want the applause of the vulgar; give us
the opinion of the few." Who prevents them ? They *have*
these few as before; but because the artist of a lower walk
changes his patron, and, instead of catering for the private
boxes, appeals to the pit, there is no harm done. The pit,
it is my firm belief, knows just as much about the matter
in question as the boxes know; and now you have made
art one of the wants of the public, you will find the pro-
viders of the commodity and its purchasers grow more refined in their tastes alike; and the popular critic of a few
years hence calling for good pictures, when now bad ones
please him.

How should he know better as yet? His betters have

taught him to admire Books of Beauty, trashy, flashy, coronation pictures, and the like tawdry gimcracks, which please a feeble intellect and a debauched taste. Give him time, and he will learn to like better things. And for the artist himself, will he not gain by bringing to the public market the article which he was obliged before to prepare for individual patronage? He has made many more sacrifices to the latter, than ever he will be called upon to do for the former. His independence does not suffer by honest barter in the public place, any more than an author's does who takes his wares to the bookseller or newspaper, and asks and gets his price. The writer looks to my lord no longer, but has found a better and surer friend: and so for art; I would like to see Art Unions all over England, from London to Little Peddlington: every one of the subscribers become interested in a subject about which he has not thought hitherto, and which was kept as the exclusive privilege of his betters.

The *Spectator* has an excellent suggestion with regard to Art Unions, I think; which is, that a committee should purchase pictures with the funds of the Union, and that the prize-holder should then choose. Bad pictures would not, probably, be bought in this way, and the threatened degradation of art would then be averted. Perhaps the majority of the present Unionists, however, would not accede to this plan, and prefer to choose their pictures for themselves. Well: let them keep to the old plan, and let us have another Art Union as the new. The more the better — the more *real* Unions: as for the sham ones, we will discourse of these anon.   Yours, my dear M'Gilp,

                                          M. A. Titmarsh.

P.S. I hope your Cartoon is in a state of forwardness: we shall see in a month or two what the giants of art can do. But meanwhile do not neglect your little picture out of Gil Blas or the Vicar of Wakefield (of course it is from one or the other). Let those humble intellects which can only understand common feeling and every-day life have too their little gentle gratifications. Why should not the poor in spirit be provided for as well as the tremendous geniuses? If a child take a fancy to a penny theatrical print, let him have it; if a workman want a green parrot with a bobbing head to decorate his humble mantel-piece, let us not grudge it to him; and if an immense supereminent intelligence cannot satisfy his poetical craving with anything less sublime than Milton, or less vast than Michael Angelo, — all I can say for my part is, that I wish he may get it. The kind and beneficent Genius of Art has pleasures for all according to their degree; and spreads its harmless happy feast for big and little — for the Titanic appetite that can't be satisfied with less than a roasted elephant, as well as for the small humble cock-robin of an intellect that can sing its little grace and make its meal on a bread-crumb.

III. — THE ROYAL ACADEMY.

My dear M'Gilp, — I think every succeeding year shows a progress in the English school of painters. They paint from *the heart* more than of old, and less from the old heroic, absurd, incomprehensible, unattainable rules. They look at Nature very hard, and match her with the best of their eyes and ability. They do not aim at such great subjects as heretofore, or at subjects which the world is pleased to call great, viz., tales from Hume or Gibbon of royal personages under various circumstances of battle, murder, and sudden death. Lemprière, too, is justly neglected; and Milton has quite given place to Gil Blas and the Vicar of Wakefield.

The heroic, and peace be with it! has been deposed; and our artists, in place, cultivate the pathetic and the familiar. But a few, very few, worshippers of the old gods remain. There are only two or three specimens in the present exhibition of the grand historic style. There is a huge dun-colored picture in the large room, by an Academician probably; but I have neither the name nor the subject: there is Mr. Haydon's history-piece of the Maid of Saragossa — a great, coarse, vulgar, ill-drawn, ill-painted caricature; and an allegory or two by other artists, in the old-fashioned style.

The younger painters are content to exercise their art on subjects far less exalted: a gentle sentiment, an agreeable, quiet incident, a tea-table tragedy, or a bread-and-butter idyl, suffices for the most part their gentle powers. Nor surely ought one to quarrel at all with this prevalent mode. It is at least natural, which the heroic was not. Bread and butter can be digested by every man; whereas Prometheus on his rock, or Orestes in his strait-waistcoat, or Hector dragged behind Achilles' car, or "Britannia, guarded by

Religion and Neptune, welcoming General Tomkins in the Temple of Glory " — the ancient heroic, allegorical subjects — can be supposed deeply to interest very few of the inhabitants of this city or kingdom. We have wisely given up pretending that we were interested in such, and confess a partiality for more simple and homely themes.

The Exhibition rooms are adorned with numberless very pleasing pictures in this quiet taste. Mr. Leslie offers up to our simple household gods a Vicar of Wakefield; Mr. Maclise presents a Gil Blas; Mr. Redgrave gently depicts the woes of a governess who is reading a black-edged note, and the soft sorrows of a country lass going to service; Mr. Stone has the last appeal of a rustic lover; Mr. Charles Landseer has a party drinking comfortably under the trees; Mr. Macnee shows us a young person musing in a quiet nook, and thinking over her love.

All these subjects, it will be observed, are small subjects; but they are treated, for the most part, with extraordinary skill. As for Lady Blarney, in Mr. Leslie's picture, with that wonderful leer of her wicked, squinting, vacant eyes, she is as good as the very best Hogarth; her face is the perfection of comedy; and the honest primrose countenances round about, charming for their simplicity and rich, kindly humor. The Malade Imaginaire is no less excellent; more farcical and exaggerated in the arrangement; but the play is farcical and exaggerated; and the picture, as the play, is full of jovial, hearty laughter. No artist possesses this precious quality of making us laugh kindly, so much as Mr. Leslie. There is not the least gall or satire in it, only sheer, irresistible good humor.

Now in the tableau by Mr. Maclise, many of the principal personages are scowling, or ogling, or grinning, and showing their teeth, with all their might; and yet the spectator, as I fancy, is by no means so amused as by those more quiet actors in Mr. Leslie's little comedies. There is, especially in Mr. Maclise's company, one young fellow who ought to be hissed, or who should have humble parts to act, and not be thrust forward in the chief characters as he has been of late years, with his immense grinning mouthful of white teeth and knowing, leering eyes. The ladies we have seen, too, repeatedly, and it must be confessed they are not of the high comedy sort. The characters appear to be, as it were, performing a tableau from Gil Blas, not the actual heroes or heroines of that easy, jovial drama.

As for the "properties" of the piece, to use the dramatic phrase, they are admirably rich and correct. The painter's skill in representing them is prodigious. The plate, the carvings, the wine-flasks, the poor old melancholy monkey on his perch, the little parrots, the carpet, are painted with a truth and dexterity quite marvellous, and equal the most finished productions of the Dutch schools. Terburg never painted such a carpet; every bit of plate is a curiosity of truthful representation. This extraordinary power of minute representation is shown in another picture by Mr. Maclise, the Cornish Waterfall, round which every leaf in every tree is depicted, and in which the figure of the girl is a delightful specimen of the artist's graphic power.

Mr. Redgrave's "Going to Service" is not so well drawn as his pictures of former years. An old lady in an arm-chair, two young sisters embracing each other, a brother very stiff and solemn in a smock-frock, and a wagon waiting outside, tell the story of this little domestic comedy. It has a milk-and-watery pathos. The governess has her bread and butter by her side, too; but the picture is much better, the girl's figure extremely beautiful and graceful, and the adjuncts of the picture are painted with extreme care and skill.

Mr. Stone's "Last Appeal" is beautiful. It is evidently the finish of the history of the two young people who are to be seen in the Water-color Exhibition. There the girl is smiling and pleased, and there is some hope still for the pale, earnest young man who loves her with all his might. But between the two pictures, between Pall Mall and the Trafalgar Column, sad changes have occurred. The young woman has met a great big life-guardsman, probably, who has 'quite changed her views of things: and you see that the last appeal is made without any hope for the appellant. The girl hides away her pretty face and we see that all is over. She likes the poor fellow well enough, but it is only as a brother: her heart is with the life-guardsman, who is strutting down the lane at this moment with his laced cap on one ear, cutting the buttercups' heads off with his rattan cane. The whole story is told, without, alas! the possibility of a mistake, and the young fellow in the gray stockings has nothing to do but to jump down the wall, at the side of which he has been making his appeal.

The painting of this picture is excellent: the amateur will not fail to appreciate the beauty of the drawing, the care, and at the same time freedom, of the execution, and a number of excellences of method which are difficult to be described in print, except in certain technical terms that are quite unsatisfactory to the general reader.

Mr. Charles Landseer's Monks of Rubrosi is the best, perhaps, of his pictures. ·The scene is extremely cheerful, fresh, and brilliant; the landscape almost as good as the . figures, and these are all good. Two grave-looking, aristocratic fathers of the abbey have been fly-fishing; a couple of humbler brethren in brown are busy at a hamper of good things; a gallant young sportsman in green velvet lies on the grass and toasts a pretty lass that is somehow waiting upon their reverences. The picture is not only good, but has the further good quality of being *pleasant;* and some clever artist will do no harm in condescending so far to suit the general taste. There is no reason after all why a man should not humble himself to this extent, and make friends with the public patron.

For instance, take Mr. Poole's picture of Solomon Eagle and the plague of London. It is exceedingly clever; but who would buy such a piece? Figures writhe over the picture blue and livid with the plague—some are dying in agony—some stupid with pain. You see the dead-cart in the distance; and in the midst stands naked Solomon, with bloodshot eyes and wild, maniacal looks, preaching death, woe, and judgment. Where should such a piece hang? It is too gloomy for a hospital, and surely not cheerful enough for a dining-room. It is not a religious picture that would serve to decorate the walls of a church. A very dismal, gloomy conventicle might perhaps be a suitable abode for it; but would it not be better to tempt the public with something more good-humored?

Of the religious pieces Mr. Herbert's "Woman of Samaria" will please many a visitor to the Exhibition, on account of the beauty and dignity of the head and figure of the Saviour. The woman, as I thought, was neither beautiful nor graceful. Mr. Eastlake's "Hagar" is beautiful as everything else by this accomplished artist; but here, perhaps, the beauty is too great, and the pain not enough. The scene is not represented with its actual agony and despair; but this is, as it were, a sort of limning to remind you of the scene; a piece of mystical poetry with Ishmael and Hagar for the theme. I must confess that Mr. Linnell's "Supper at Emmaus" did not strike me as the least mystical or poetical, and that Mr. Etty's "Entombment" was anything but holy and severe. Perhaps the most pious and charming head in the whole Exhibition is that of the Queen, by Mr. Leslie, in his Coronation picture; it has a delightful modesty and a purity quite angelical.

Mr. Etty's pictures of the heathen sort are delightful; wonderful for a gorgeous flush of color, such as has belonged, perhaps, to no painter since Rubens. But of these we will discourse next week.

M. A. TITMARSH.

IV.—THE ROYAL ACADEMY (SECOND NOTICE).

My dear M'Gilp,—If Her Majesty is the purchaser of all the royal pictures by Parris, by Hayter, by Leslie, by Landseer,—of all the royal portraits, by these and a score more, in and out of the Academy,—there must be a pretty large gallery at Buckingham Palace by this time, and, let it be said with respect, a considerable sameness in the collection. The royal face is a very handsome one, and especially in the medallion shape, in gold. I would like to look at thousands of them every week for my part, and would never tire in extending my cabinet.

But confess, my dear sir, are we not beginning to have enough of royal-parade pictures? And are not the humbler classes somewhat tired of them? Only the publishers and the grandees, their enlightened patrons, still continue to admire. Dark rooms are still prepared for such; gas-jets and large subscription books artfully laid on and out. The Court Guide still goes to see Winterhalter's portrait of the Queen ("I wish they may get it," as the D—ch—ss of ————— observes; the picture is not painted by Winterhalter: but what do *they* know, whether it be good or bad?). The Court Guide still buys huge proofs of her Majesty's marriage, or the Princess's christening, or the real authorized Coronation picture (every one of the half-dozen are real authorized Coronation pictures), and is content therewith. Ah! Heaven bless that elegant aristocracy of England; that wise, that enlightened, that noble class of our betters! The subject of these pictures is worthy of their noble souls — fit for their vast comprehensions ; and as the poor workman buys his prints of the Prodigal Son's progress, the young cockney-buck his portrait of Mrs. Honey, or some other beauty with long ringlets and short petticoats, the sporting man his varnished hunting-piece, so the great have their likings, and we judge them by what they admire.

And what an admiration theirs is! There's her Majesty in state! what a lovely white satin! and the velvet, my dear, painted to the very life. Every single jewel's a portrait, I give you my honor; and Prince Albert's own star and garter sat to the artist; the archbishop's wig is done to a hair; and was there ever a more wonderful piece of art than that picture of the duke in his orders and his epaulets, and his white kerseymere pantaloons? Round the Sovereign are all the maids of honor; round the maids of honor all the officers of state; round the officers of state all the beef-eaters and gentlemen-at-arms: and on these magnificent subjects our best painters are continually employed. Noble themes for the exercise of genius! brilliant proofs of enlightened public taste! The court-milliners must be proud to think that their works are thus immortalized, and the descendants of our tailors will look at these pieces with a justifiable family pride.

Mr. Leslie has had to chronicle coats and satin-slips in this way, and has represented *his* sense in the drama of the coronation (how many more episodes of the same piece have been represented, and by how many more painters I don't know), and his picture is so finely done, so full of beauty and grandeur, that for once a court picture has been made interesting. I have remarked on the principal feature before — the exquisite grace and piety represented in the countenance and attitude of the Queen; but the judgment of the quality, as far as I have been able to gather it (and it is good to this end to play the spy's part, and overhear the opinions of the genteel personages who come to see the Exhibition), — the genteel judgment is decidedly against the painter, and his portraits are pronounced to be failures, and his picture quite inferior to many others by other hands. Let us hope the opinion will be so general, that this charming painter shall never be called upon to paint at court ceremony again. I would rather see honest Mrs. Primrose's portrait by him, than that of the loveliest lady of honor; and the depicting of uniforms, and lappets, and feathers left to those politer artists whose genius is suited to subjects so genteel.

There is no Prince Albert this year, I regret to say; but we have two portraits of her Majesty, in trains, velvets, arm-chairs, etc. — one by the President and one by Mr. Grant, and neither worth a crown-piece. One of the most exquisite and refined little sketches ever seen is the portrait of Lady Lyttelton by the latter artist; it is a delightful picture of a beautiful and high-bred maiden. Mr. Chalon's aristocracy does not ogle and simper quite so much as in former years; and their ladyships are painted with all the artist's accustomed skill. Mr. Richmond's heads are excellent as usual; and there is a rival to these gentlemen, who has given us a water-color portrait of the Bishop of Exeter, in which the amiable and candid features of that learned prelate are depicted with great fidelity and talent. Mr. Carrick's men-miniatures are perhaps the best among those pleasing performances: the likeness of a former secretary for Ireland will especially please those who know his lordship's countenance, and those who do not, by its resemblance to an eminent comedian whose absence from the stage all regret. Mr. Thornburn cultivates more, perhaps, than any other miniature painter the poetry of his art. The gallant knights Sir Ross and Sir Newton are as victorious as usual; and Mr. Lover's head of Mr. Lever deserves praiseworthy mention: it will be looked at with interest by Harry Lorrequer's English readers, and by those who had the opportunity of seeing him in the body, and hearing his manly and kind-hearted speech at the Literary Fund the other day.

Of Mr. Etty's color pieces what words can give an idea? Many lovers of Titian and Rubens will admit that here is an English painter who almost rivals them in his original way, and all will admire their magnificent beauty. Mr. Turner, our other colorist, is harder to be understood. The last time the gentle reader received a black eye at school, and for a moment after the delivery of the blow, when flashes of blue, yellow, and crimson lightning blazed before the ball so preternaturally excited, he saw something not unlike the Moses of Mr. Turner. His picture of Cleopatra meeting Alexander the Great at Moscow, the morning before the Deluge (perhaps this may not be the exact title, but it will do as well as another), is of the most transcendental sort. The quotations from the "Fallacies of Hope" continue still in great force: as thus —

> "The Ark stood firm on Ararat: the returning Sun
> Exhaled Earth's humid bubbles, and, emulous of light,
> Reflected her lost forms, each in prismatic guise,
> Hope's harbinger, ephemeral as the summer fly,
> Which rises, flits, expands, and dies."
>
> FALLACIES OF HOPE.

The artist has done full justice to these sweet lines.

We are given to understand by cognoscenti that the Italian skies are always of the bluest cobalt: hence many persons are dissatisfied with Mr. Stanfield's Italian landscapes as unfaithful, because deficient in the proper depth of ultramarine. On this subject let proper judges speak; but others less qualified will find the pictures beautiful, and more beautiful for their quiet and calm. Who can praise Mr. Creswick sufficiently? The Welsh girl will, one of these days, fetch a sum of money as great as ever was given for Hobbema or Ruysdael; and "Evening" is an English Claude. Mr. Lee's fresh country landscapes will find hundreds of admirers; and perhaps there are no two prettier little pictures in the gallery than Mr. Linton's "Sorrento" and Mr. Jutsum's "Tintern."

In walking round the vault in which the sculpture is entombed, I did not see anything especially worthy of mark, except a bust of Count d'Orsay, who has himself broken ground as an artist, and whose genius will one day no doubt make its way. Why have we not our common share of the admirable pictures of Mr. Edwin Landseer? It can't be that a man of his facility has painted but three pictures in a year, and picture lovers wonder where the rest are.

M. A. Titmarsh.

MAY GAMBOLS; OR, TITMARSH IN THE PICTURE GALLERIES.

[*Fraser's Magazine, June,* 1844.]

THE readers of this miscellany may, perhaps, have re-marked that always, at the May season and the period of the exhibitions, our eccentric correspondent Titmarsh seems to be seized with a double fit of eccentricity, and to break out into such violent fantastical gambols as might cause us to be alarmed did we not know him to be harmless, and in-duce us to doubt of his reason but that the fit is generally brief, and passes off after the first excitement occasioned by visiting the picture galleries. It was in one of these fits some years since, that he announced in this Magazine his own suicide, which we know to be absurd, for he has drawn many hundred guineas from us since: — on the same occasion he described his debts and sojourn at a respectable hotel, in which it seems he has never set his foot. But these hallucinations pass away with May, and next month he will, no doubt, be calmer, or, at least, not more absurd than usual. Some disappointments occurring to himself, and the refusal of his great picture of "Heliogabalus" in the year 1803 (which caused his retirement from practice as a painter), may account for his extreme bitterness against some of the chief artists in this or any other school or country. Thus we have him in these pages abus-ing Raphael; in the very last month he fell foul of Rubens, and in the present paper he actually pooh-poohs Sir Martin Shee and some of the Royal Academy. This is too much. "Cœlum ipsum," as Horace says, "petimus stultitiâ." But we will quote no more the well-known words of the Epicu-rean bard.

We only add that we do not feel in the least bound by any one of the opinions here brought forward, from most of which, except where the writer contradicts himself and so saves us the trouble, we cordially dissent; and perhaps the reader had best pass on to the next article, omitting all perusal of this, excepting, of course, the editorial notice of — O. Y.

JACK STRAW'S CASTLE, HAMPSTEAD, May 25.

THIS is written in the midst of a general desolation and discouragement of the honest practitioners who dwell in the dingy first floors about Middlesex Hospital and Soho. The long-haired ones are tearing their lanky locks; the velvet-coated sons of genius are plunged in despair; the law has ordered the suppression of Art-Unions, and the wheel of fortune has suddenly and cruelly been made to stand still. When the dreadful news came that the kindly harmless Art-lottery was to be put an end to, although Derby-lotteries are advertised in every gin shop in London, and every ruffian in the City may gamble at his leisure, the men of the brush and palette convoked a tumultuous meeting, where, amidst tears, shrieks, and wrath, the cruelty of their case was debated. Wyse of Waterford calmly presided over the stormy bladder-squeezers, the insulted wielders of the knife and maulstick. Wyse soothed their angry spirits with words of wisdom and hope. He stood up in the assembly of the legislators of the land and pointed out their wrongs. The painters' friend, the kind old Lansdowne, lifted up his cordial voice among the peers of England, and asked for protection for the children of Raphael and Apelles. No one said nay. All pitied the misfortune of the painters; even Lord Brougham was stilled into compassion, and the voice of Vaux was only heard in sobs.

These are days of darkness, but there is hope in the vista; the lottery-subscription lies in limbo, but it shall be released therefrom and flourish, exuberantly revivified, in future years. Had the ruin been consummated, this hand should have withered rather than have attempted to inscribe jokes concerning it. No, *Fraser* is the artists' friend, their mild parent. While his Royal Highness Prince Albert dines with the Academicians, the rest of painters, less fortunate, are patronized by her Majesty REGINA.

Yes, in spite of the Art-Union accident, there is hope for the painters. Sir Martin Archer Shee thinks that the Prince's condescension in dining with the Academy will do incalculable benefit to the art. Henceforth its position is assured in the world. This august patronage, the President says, evincing the sympathy of the higher classes, must awaken the interest of the low: and the public (the

ignorant rogues!) will thus learn to appreciate what they
have not cared for hitherto. Interested! Of course they
will be. O Academicians! ask the public to dinner, and
you will see how much interested they will be. We are
authorized to state that next year any person who will send
in his name will have a cover provided; Trafalgar Square
is to be awned in, plates are to be laid for 250,000, one of
the new basins is to be filled with turtle and the other with
cold punch. The President and the *élite* are to sit upon
Nelson's pillar, while rows of benches, stretching as far as
the Union Club, Northumberland House, and St. Martin's
Church, will accommodate the vulgar. Mr. Toole is to
have a speaking-trumpet; and a twenty-four-pounder to be
discharged at each toast.

There are other symptoms of awakening interest in the
public mind. The readers of newspapers will remark this
year that the leaders of public opinion have devoted an
unusually large space and print to reviews of the fine arts.
They have been employing critics who, though they contradict each other a good deal, are yet evidently better acquainted with the subject than critics of old used to be,
when gentlemen of the profession were instructed to report on a fire, or an Old Bailey trial, or a Greek play, or
an opera, or a boxing-match, or a picture gallery, as their
turn came. Read now the *Times*, the *Chronicle*, the *Post*
(especially the *Post*, of which the painting critiques have
been very good), and it will be seen that the critic knows
his business, and from the length of his articles it may be
conjectured that the public is interested in knowing what
he has to say. This is all, probably, from the Prince having dined at the Academy. The nation did not care for
pictures until then, — until the nobility taught us; gracious
nobility! Above all, what a compliment to the public!

As one looks round the rooms of the Royal Academy,
one cannot but deplore the fate of the poor fellows who
have been speculating upon the Art-Unions; and yet in the
act of grief there is a lurking satisfaction. The poor fellows can't sell their pieces; that is a pity. But why did
the poor fellows paint such fiddle-faddle pictures? They
catered for the *bourgeois*, the sly rogues! They know honest John Bull's taste, and simple admiration of namby-
pamby, and so they supplied him with an article that was
just likely to suit him. In like manner savages are supplied
with glass beads; children are accommodated with toys

and trash, by dexterous speculators who know their market.
Well, I am sorry that the painting speculators have had a
stop put to their little venture, and that the ugly law
against lotteries has stepped in and seized upon the twelve
thousand pounds, which was to furnish many a hungry
British Raphael with a coat and a beefsteak. Many a
Mrs. Raphael, who was looking out for a new dress, or a
trip to Margate or Boulogne for the summer, must forego
the pleasure, and remain in dingy Newman Street. Many
little ones will go back to Turnham Green academies and
not carry the amount of last half-year's bill in the trunk;
many a landlord will bully about the non-payment of the
rent; and a vast number of frame-makers will look wistfully at their carving and gilding as it returns after the exhibition to Mr. Tinto, Charlotte Street, along with poor
Tinto's picture from the "Vicar of Wakefield" that he
made sure of selling to an Art-Union prizeman. This is
the pathetic side of the question. My heart is tender, and
I weep for the honest painters peering dismally at the
twelve thousand pounds like hungry boys do at a tart-shop.

But — here stern justice interposes, and the MAN having
relented, the CRITIC raises his inexorable voice — but, I say,
the enemies of Art-Unions have had some reason for their
complaints, and I fear it is too true that the effect of those
institutions, as far as they have gone hitherto, has not been
mightily favorable to the cause of art. One day, by custom, no doubt, the public taste will grow better, and as the
man who begins by intoxicating himself with a glass of
gin finishes sometimes by easily absorbing a bottle; as the
law student, who at first is tired with a chapter of Black-
stone, will presently swallow you down with pleasure a
whole volume of Chitty; as EDUCATION, in a word, advances,
it is humbly to be hoped that the great and generous
British public will not be so easily satisfied as at present,
and will ask for a better article for its money.

Meanwhile, their taste being pitiable, the artists supply
them with poor stuff — pretty cheap tawdry toys and gimcracks in place of august and beautiful objects of art. It
is always the case. I do not mean to say that the literary
men are a bit better. Poor fellows of the pen and pencil!
we must live. The public likes light literature and we
write it. Here am I writing magazine jokes and follies,
and why? Because the public like such, will purchase no
other. Otherwise, as Mr. Nickisson and all who are ac-

quainted with M. A. Titmarsh in private know, my real inclinations would lead me to write works upon mathematics,
geology, and chemistry, varying them in my lighter hours
with little playful treatises on questions of political economy, epic poems, and essays on the Æolic digamma. So,
in fact, these severe rebukes with which I am about to
belabor my neighbor must be taken as they are given, in a
humble and friendly spirit; they are not actuated by pride,
but by deep sympathy. Just as we read in holy Mr. Newman's life of St. Stephen Harding, that it was the custom
among the godly Cistercian monks (in the good old times,
which holy Newman would restore) to assemble every morning in full chapter; and there, after each monk had made
his confession, it was free to — nay, it was strictly enjoined
on — any other brother to rise and say, "Brother So-and-so
hath not told all his sins; our dear brother has forgotten
that yesterday he ate his split-peas with too much gorman-
dize;" or, "This morning he did indecently rejoice over
his water-gruel," or what not — these real Christians were
called upon to inform, not only of themselves, but to be in-
formers over each other; and, the information being given,
the brother informed against thanked his brother the informer, and laid himself down on the desk, and was flag-
ellated with gratitude. Sweet friends! be you like the
Cistercians! Brother Michael Angelo is going to inform
against you. Get ready your garments and prepare for
flagellation. Brother Michael Angelo is about to lay on and
spare not.

Brother Michael lifts up his voice against the young
painters collectively in the first place, afterwards individually, when he will also take leave to tickle them with
the wholesome stripes of the flagellum. In the first place,
then (and my heart is so tender that, rather than begin
the operation, I have been beating about the bush for more
than a page, of which page the reader is cordially requested
to omit the perusal, as it is not the least to the purpose), I
say that the young painters of England, whose uprise this
Magazine and this critic were the first to hail, asserting
loudly their superiority over the pompous old sham classical big-wigs of the Academy — the young painters of
England *are not doing their duty.* They are going backwards, or, rather, they are flinging themselves under the
wheels of that great golden Juggernaut of an Art-Union.
The thought of the money is leading them astray; they

are poets no longer, but money-hunters. They paint down to the level of the public intelligence, rather than seek to elevate the public to them. Why do these great geniuses fail in their duty of instruction? Why, knowing better things, do they serve out such awful twaddle as we have from them? Alas! it is not for art they paint, but for the Art-Union.

The first dear brother I shall take the liberty to request to get ready for operation is brother Charles Landseer. Brother Charles has sinned. He has grievously sinned. And we will begin with this miserable sinner, and administer to him admonition in a friendly, though most fierce and cutting manner.

The subject of brother Charles Landseer's crime is this. The sinner has said to himself, "The British public likes domestic pieces. They will have nothing but domestic pieces. I will give them one, and of a new sort. Suppose I paint a picture that must make a hit. My picture will have every sort of interest. It shall interest the religious public; it shall interest the domestic public; it shall interest the amateur for the cleverness of its painting; it shall interest little boys and girls, for I will introduce no end of animals, camels, monkeys, elephants, and cockatoos; it shall interest sentimental young ladies, for I will take care to have a pretty little episode for them. I will take the town by storm, in a word." This is what I conceive was passing in brother Charles Landseer's sinful soul when he conceived and executed his NOAH'S ARK IN A DOMESTIC POINT OF VIEW.

Noah and his family (with some supplemental young children, very sweetly painted) are seated in the ark, and a port-hole is opened, out of which one of the sons is looking at the now peaceful waters. The sunshine enters the huge repository of the life of the world, and the dove has just flown in with an olive-branch, and nestles in the bosom of one of the daughters of Noah; the patriarch and his aged partner are lifting up their venerable eyes in thankfulness; the children stand around, the peaceful laborer and the brown huntsman each testifying his devotion after his fashion. The animals round about participate in the joyful nature of the scene, their instinct seems to tell them that the hour of their deliverance is near.

There, the picture is described romantically and in the best of language. Now let us proceed to examine the poe-

try critically, and to see what its claims are. Well, the
ark is a great subject. The history from which we have
our account of it, from a poet surely demands a reverent
treatment; a blacksmith roaring from the desk of a conventicle may treat it familiarly, but an educated artist
ought surely to approach such a theme with respect. The
point here is only urged æsthetically. As a matter of *taste*,
then (and the present humble writer has no business to
speak on any other), such a manner of treating the subject
is certainly reprehensible. The ark is vulgarized here
and reduced to the proportions of a Calais steamer. The
passengers are rejoicing: they are glad to get away.
Their live animals are about them no more nor less sublime
than so many cattle or horses in loose boxes. The parrots
perched on the hoop yonder have as little signification as a
set of birds in a cage at the Zoölogical Gardens; the very
dove becomes neither more nor less than the *pet* of the
pretty girl represented in the centre of the picture. All
the greatness of the subject is lost; and, putting the historical nature of the personages out of the question, they
have little more interest than a group of any emigrants in
the hold of a ship, who rouse and rally at the sound of
"Land ho!"

Why, if all great themes of poetry are to be treated in
this way, the art would be easy. We might have Hector
shaving himself before going out to fight Achilles, as, undoubtedly, the Trojan hero did; Priam in a cotton nightcap asleep in a four-poster on the night of the sack of
Troy, Hecuba, of course, by his side, with curl-papers, and
her *tour de tête* on the toilet-glass. We might have Dido's
maid coming after her mistress in the shower with pattens
and an umbrella; or Cleopatra's page guttling the figs in
the basket which had brought the asp that killed the mistress of Antony. Absurd trivialities, or pretty trivialities,
are nothing to the question; those I have adduced here are
absurd, but they are just as poetical as prettiness, not a
whit less degrading and commonplace. No painter has a
right to treat great historical subjects in such a fashion;
and though the public are sure to admire, and young ladies,
in raptures, look on at the darling of a dove, and little
boys in delight cry, "Look, papa, at the paroquets!"
"Law, ma, what big trunks the elephants have!" it yet
behooves the critic to say this is an unpoetical piece, and
severely to reprehend the unhappy perpetrator thereof.

I know brother Charles will appeal. I know it will be
pleaded in his favor that the picture is capitally painted,
some of the figures very pretty; two — that of the old
woman and the boy looking out — quite grand in drawing
and color; the picture charming for its silvery tone and
agreeable pleasantry of color. All this is true. But he
has sinned, he has greatly sinned; let him acknowledge
his fault in the presence of the chapter, and receive the
customary and wholesome reward thereof.

Frater Redgrave is the next malefactor whose sins deserve a reprobation. In the namby-pamby line his errors
are very sad. Has he not been already warned in this very
miscellany of his propensity to small sentiment? Has he
corrected himself of that grievous tendency? No: his
weakness grows more and more upon him, and he is now
more sinful than ever. One of his pictures is taken from
the most startling lyric in our language, the "Song of the
Shirt," a song as bitter and manly as it is exquisitely soft
and tender, a song of which the humor draws tears.*

Mr. Redgrave has illustrated everything except the humor, the manliness, and the bitterness of the song. He
has only depicted the tender good-natured part of it. It is
impossible to quarrel with the philanthropy of the painter.
His shirt-maker sits by her little neat bed, work, working
away. You may see how late it is, for the candle is nearly
burnt out, the clock (capital poetic notion!) says what
o'clock it is, the gray-streaked dawn is rising over the
opposite house seen through the cheerless casement, and
where (from a light which it has in its window) you may
imagine that another poor shirt-maker is toiling, too. The
one before us is pretty, pale, and wan; she turns up the
whites of her fine fatigued eyes to the little ceiling. She is
ill, as the artist has shown us by a fine stroke of genius — a
parcel of medicine-bottles on the mantel-piece! The picture is carefully and cleverly painted — extremely popular — gazed at with vast interest by most spectators. Is
it, however, a poetical subject? Yes, Hood has shown that
it can be made one, but by surprising turns of thought
brought to bear upon it, strange, terrible, unexpected lights
of humor which he has flung upon it. And to "trump"
this tremendous card, Mr. Redgrave gives us this picture;
his points being the clock, which tells the time of day, the

* How is it that none of the papers have noticed the astonishing poem
by Mr. Hood in the May number of his magazine, to which our language
contains no parallel? — M. A. T.

vials, which show the poor girl takes physic, and such other vast labors of intellect!

Mr. Redgrave's other picture, the "Marriage Morning," is also inspired by that milk and water of human kindness, the flavor of which is so insipid to the roast-beef intellect. This is a scene of a marriage morning; the bride is taking leave of her mamma after the ceremony, and that amiable lady, reclining in an easy-chair, is invoking benedictions upon the parting couple, and has a hand of her daughter and her son-in-law clasped in each of hers. She is smiling sadly, restraining her natural sorrow, which will break out so soon as the postchaise you see through the window, and on which the footman is piling the nuptial luggage, shall have driven off to Salt Hill, or Rose Cottage, Richmond, which I recommend. The bride's father, a venerable bald-headed gentleman, with a most benignant, though slow-coachish look, is trying to console poor Anna Maria, the unmarried sister, who is losing the companion of her youth. Never mind, Anna Maria, my dear, your turn will come, too; there is a young gentleman making a speech in the parlor to the health of the new-married pair, who, I lay a wager, will be struck by your fine eyes, and be for serving you as your sister has been treated. This small fable is worked out with great care in a picture in which there is much clever and conscientious painting, from which, however, I must confess, I derive little pleasure. The sentiment and color of the picture somehow coincide; the eye rests upon a variety of neat tints of pale drab, pale green, pale brown, pale puce color, of a sickly warmth, not pleasant to the eye. The drawing is feeble, the expression of the faces pretty but lackadaisical. The penance I would order Mr. Redgrave should be a pint of port wine to be taken daily, and a devilled kidney every morning for breakfast before beginning to paint.

A little of the devil, too, would do Mr. Frank Stone no harm. He, too, is growing dangerously sentimental. His picture, with a quotation from Horace, "Mæcenas atavis edite regibus," represents a sort of game of tender cross-purposes, very difficult to describe in print. Suppose two lads, Jocky and Tommy, and two lassies, Jenny and Jessamy. They are placed thus: —

		Tommy.
Jessamy.	Jenny.	Jocky.
	A dog.	

Now Jocky is making love to Jenny, in an easy, off-hand sort of way, and though, or, perhaps, *because*, he doesn't care for her much, is evidently delighting the young woman. She looks round, with a pleased smile on her fresh plump cheeks, and turns slightly towards heaven a sweet little *retroussé* nose, and twiddles her fingers (most exquisitely these hands are drawn and painted, by the way) in the most contented way. But, ah! how little does she heed Tommy, who, standing behind Jocky, reclining against a porch, is looking and longing for this light-hearted Jenny! And, oh! why does Tommy cast such sheep's eyes upon Jenny, when by her side sits *Jessamy*, the tender and romantic, the dark-eyed and raven-haired being, whose treasures of affection are flung at heedless Tommy's feet? All the world is interested in Jessamy; her face is beautiful, her look of despairing love is so exquisitely tender that it touches every spectator; and the ladies are unanimous in wondering how Tommy can throw himself away upon that simpering Jenny, when such a superior creature as Jessamy is to be had for the asking. But such is the way of the world, and Tommy will marry, simply because everybody tells him not.

Thus far for the sentiment of the picture. The details are very good; there is too much stippling and show of finish, perhaps, in the handling, and the painting might have been more substantial, and lost nothing. But the color is good, the group very well composed, and the variety of expression excellent. There is great passion, as well as charming delicacy, in the disappointed maiden's face; much fine appreciation of character in the easy smiling triumph of the rival; and, although this sentence was commenced with the express determination of rating Mr. Stone soundly, lo! it is finished without a word of blame. Well, let's vent our anger on the dog. That *is* very bad, and seems to have no more bones than an apple dumpling. It is only because the artist has been painting disappointed lovers a great deal of late, that one is disposed to grumble, not at the work, but at the want of variety of subject.

As a sentimental picture, the best and truest, to my taste, is that by Mr. Webster, the "Portraits of Mr. and Mrs. Webster," painted to celebrate their fiftieth wedding-day. Such a charming old couple were never seen. There is delightful grace, sentiment, and purity in these two gentle kindly heads; much more sentiment and grace than

even in Mr. Eastlake's "Héloïse," a face which the artist has painted over and over again; a beautiful woman,
but tiresome, unearthly, unsubstantial, and no more like
Héloïse than like the Duke of Wellington. If the late Mr.
Pope's epistle be correct, Eloisa was a most unmistakable
woman; this is a substanceless, passionless, solemn, mystical apparition; but I doubt if a woman be not the more
poetical being of the two.

   Being on the subject of sentimental pictures, Monsieur
Delaroche's great "Holy Family" must be mentioned here;
and, if there is reason to quarrel with the unsatisfactory
nature of English sentiment, in truth it appears that the
French are not much better provided with the high poetical quality. This picture has all the outside of poetry, all
the costume of religion, all the prettiness and primness of
the new German dandy-pietistical school. It is an agreeable compound of Correggio and Raphael, with a strong dash
of Overbeck; it is painted as clean and pretty as a tulip on
a dessert-plate, the lines made out so neatly that none can
mistake them; the drawing good, the female face as pretty
and demure as can be, her drapery of spotless blue, and the
man's of approved red, the infant as pink as strawberries
and cream, every leaf of the tree sweetly drawn, and the
trunk of the most delicate dove-colored gray. All these
merits the picture has; it is a well-appointed picture.
But is that all? Is that enough to make a poet? There
are lines in the Oxford prize poems, that are smooth as
Pope's; and it is notorious that, for coloring, there is no
painting like the Chinese. But I hope the French artists
have better men springing up among them than the President of the French Academy at Rome.

   Biard, the Hogarthian painter, whose slave-trade picture
was so noble, has sent us a couple of pieces, which both, in
their way, possess merit. The one is an Arabian caravan
moving over a brick-dust-colored desert, under a red arid
sky. The picture is lifelike, and so far poetical that it
seems to tell the truth. Then there is a steamboat disas-
ter, with every variety of sea-sickness, laughably painted.
Shuddering soldiery, sprawling dandies, Englishmen, Sa-
voyards, guitars, lovers, monkeys, — a dreadful confusion
of qualmish people, whose agonies will put the most misanthropic observer into good humor. Biard's "Havre
Packet" is much more praiseworthy in my mind than
Delaroche's "Holy Family;" for I deny the merit of fail-

ing greatly in pictures — the great merit is to succeed. There is no greater error, surely, than that received dictum of the ambitious to aim at high things; it is best to do what you mean to do: better to kill a crow than to miss an eagle.

As the French artists are sending in their works from across the water, why, for the honor of England, will not some of our painters let the Parisians know that here, too, are men whose genius is worthy of appreciation? They may be the best draughtsmen in the world, but they have no draughtsman like Maclise, they have no colorist like Etty, they have no painter like MULREADY, above all, whose name I beg the printer to place in the largest capitals, and to surround with a wreath of laurels. Mr. Mulready was crowned in this Magazine once before. Here again he is proclaimed. It looks like 'extravagance, or flattery, for the blushing critic to tell his real mind about the "Whistonian Controversy."

And yet, as the truth must be told, why not say it now at once? I believe this to be one of the finest cabinet pictures in the world. It seems to me to possess an assemblage of excellences so rare, to be in drawing so admirable, in expression so fine, in finish so exquisite, in composition so beautiful, in humor and· beauty of expression so delightful, that I can't but ask where is a good picture, if this be not one? And, in enumerating all the above perfections, I find I have forgotten the greatest of all, the color; it is quite original, this, — brilliant, rich, astonishingly luminous, and intense. The pictures of Van Eyck are not more brilliant in tone than this magnificent combination of blazing reds, browns, and purples. I know of no scheme of color like it, and heartily trust that time will preserve it; when this little picture, and some of its fellows, will be purchased as eagerly as a Hemlinck or a Gerard Douw is bought nowadays. If Mr. Mulready has a mind to the Grand Cross of the Legion of Honor, he has but to send this picture to Paris next year, and, with the recommendation of *Fraser's Magazine*, the affair is settled. Meanwhile, it is pleasant to know that the artist (although his work will fetch ten times as much money a hundred years hence) has not been ill rewarded, as times go, for his trouble and genius.

We have another great and original colorist among us, as luscious as Rubens, as rich almost as Titian — Mr.

Etty; and every year the exhibition sparkles with magnificent little canvases, the works of this indefatigable strenuous admirer of nude Beauty. The form is not quite so sublime as the color in this artist's paintings; the female figure is often rather too expansively treated, it swells here and there to the proportions of the Caffrarian, rather than the Medicean, Venus; but, in color, little can be conceived that is more voluptuously beautiful. This year introduces to us one of the artist's noblest compositions, a classical and pictorial *orgy*, as it were, — a magnificent vision of rich colors and beautiful forms, — a grand feast of sensual poetry. The verses from "Comus," which the painter has taken to illustrate, have the same character: —

> " All amidst the gardens fair
> Of Hesperus and his daughters three
> That sing about the golden tree,
> Along the crisped shades and bowers,
> Revels the spruce and jocund spring.
> Beds of hyacinths and roses,
> Where young Adonis oft reposes,
> Waxing well of his deep wound,
> In slumber soft and on the ground
> Sadly sits the Assyrian Queen;
> But far above in spangled sheen,
> Celestial Cupid, her famed son, advanced,
> Holds his dear Psyche sweet entranced."

It is a dream rather than a reality, the words and images purposely indistinct and incoherent. In the same way the painter has made the beautiful figures sweep before us in a haze of golden sunshine. This picture is one of a series to be painted in fresco, and to decorate the walls of a summer-house in the gardens of Buckingham Palace, for which edifice Mr. Maclise and Mr. Leslie have also made paintings.

That of Mr. Leslie's is too homely. He is a prose painter. His kind buxom young lass has none of the look of Milton's lady, that charming compound of the saint and the fine lady — that sweet impersonation of the chivalric mythology — an angel, but with her sixteen quarterings — a countess descended from the skies. Leslie's lady has no such high breeding, the Comus above her looks as if he might revel on ale; a rustic seducer, with an air of rude hobnailed health. Nor are the demons and fantastic figures introduced imaginative enough; they are fellows with masks, from Covent Garden. Compare the two figures at the sides of the picture with the two Cupids of Mr. Etty. In the former there is no fancy. The latter are two flowers of poetry; there are no words to characterize those two delicious little figures, no more than to describe a little air of Mozart, which, once heard, remains with you forever; or a new flower, or a phrase of Keats or Tennyson, which blooms out upon you suddenly, astonishing as much as it pleases. Well, in endeavoring to account for his admiration, the critic pumps for words in vain; if he uses such as he finds, he runs the risk of being considered intolerably pert and affected; silent pleasure, therefore, best beseems him; but this I know, that were my humble recommendations attended to at Court, when the pictures are put in the pleasure-house, her sacred Majesty, giving a splendid banquet to welcome them and the painter, should touch Mr. Etty on the left shoulder and say, "Rise, my knight of the Bath, for painting the left-hand Cupid;" and the Emperor of Russia (being likewise present) should tap him on the right shoulder, exclaiming, "Rise, my knight of the Eagle, for the right-hand Cupid."

Mr. Maclise's "Comus" picture is wonderful for the variety of its design, and has, too, a high poetry of its own. All the figures are here still and solemn as in a tableau; the lady still on her unearthly snaky chair, Sabrina still stooping over her. On one side the brothers, and opposite the solemn attendant spirit; round these, interminable groups and vistas of fairy beings, twining in a thousand attitudes of grace, and sparkling white and bloodless against a leaden blue sky. It is the most poetical of the artist's pictures, the most extraordinary exhibition of his proper skill. Is it true that the artists are only to receive three hundred guineas apiece for these noble compositions? Why, a print-seller would give more, and artists should not be allowed to paint simply for the honor of decorating a royal summer-house.

Among the poetical pictures of the exhibition should be mentioned with especial praise Mr. Cope's delightful "Charity," than the female figures in which Raphael scarce painted anything more charmingly beautiful. And Mr. Cope has this merit, that his work is no prim imitation of the stiff old Cimabue and Giotto manner, no aping of the crisp draperies and hard outlines of the missal illuminations, without which the religious artist would have us believe religious expression is impossible. It is pleasant, after seeing the wretched caricatures of old-world usages which stare us in the face in every quarter of London now — little dumpy Saxon chapels built in raw brick, spick and span *bandbox* churches of the pointed Norman style for Cockneys in zephyr coats to assemble in, new old painted windows of the twelfth century, tessellated pavements of the Byzantine school, gimcrack imitations of the Golden Legend printed with red letters, and crosses, and quaint figures stolen out of Norman missals — to find artists aiming at the Beautiful and Pure without thinking it necessary to resort to these paltry archæological quackeries, which have no Faith, no Truth, no Life in them; but which give us ceremony in lieu of reality, and insist on forms, as if they were the conditions of belief.

Lest the reader should misunderstand the cause of this anger, we beg him to take the trouble to cross Pall Mall to Saint James's Street, where objects of art are likewise exhibited; he will see the reason of our wrath. Here are all the ornamental artists of England sending in their works, and what are they? — All imitations. The Alhambra here; the Temple Church there; here a Gothic saint; yonder a Saxon altar-rail; farther on a sprawling rococo of Louis XV.; all worked neatly and cleverly enough, but with no originality, no honesty of thought. The twelfth century revived in Mr. Crockford's bazaar, forsooth! with examples of every century except our own. It would be worth while for some one to write an essay, showing how astonishingly Sir Walter Scott * has influenced the world; how he changed the character of novelists, then of historians, whom he brought from their philosophy to the study of pageantry and costume: how the artists then began to fall back into the middle ages and the architects to follow; until now behold we have Mr. Newman and his congregation of Littlemore marching out with taper and crosier, and falling down to worship Saint Willibald, and Saint Winnibald, and Saint Walberga the Saxon virgin. But Mr. Cope's picture is leading the reader rather farther than a critique about exhibitions has any right to divert him, and let us walk soberly back to Trafalgar Square.

Remark the beautiful figures of the children in Mr. Cope's picture (276), the fainting one, and the golden-

* Or more properly Goethe. " Goetz von Berlichingen " was the father of the Scottish romances, and Scott remained constant to that mode, while the greater artist tried a thousand others.

haired infant at the gate. It is a noble and touching
Scripture illustration. The artist's other picture, "Gene-
viève," is not so successful; the faces seem to have been
painted from a dirty palette, the evening tints of the sky
are as smoky as a sunset in Saint James's Park; the composition unpleasant, and not enough to fill the surface of
canvas.

Mr. Herbert's picture of "The Trial of the Seven Bishops" is painted with better attention to costume than most
English painters are disposed to pay. The characters in
our artists' history-pieces, as indeed on our theatres, do not
look commonly accustomed to the dresses which they assume; wear them awkwardly, take liberties of alteration
and adjustment, and spoil thereby the truth of the delineation. The French artists, on the canvas or the boards,
understand this branch of their art much better. Look at
Monsieur Biard's "Mecca Pilgrims," how carefully and
accurately they are attired; or go to the French play and
see Cartigny in a Hogarthian dress. He wears it as though
he had been born a hundred years back— looks the old
marquess to perfection. In this attention to dress Mr.
Herbert's picture is very praiseworthy; the men are quite
at home in their quaint coats and periwigs of James II.'s
time; the ladies at ease in their stiff long-waisted gowns,
their fans, and their queer caps and patches. And the picture is pleasing from the extreme brightness and cleanli-
ness of the painting. All looks as neat and fresh as Sam
Pepys when he turned out in his new suit, his lady in her
satin and brocade. But here the praise must stop. The
great concourse of people delineated, the bishops and the
jury, the judges and the sheriffs, the halberdiers and the
fine ladies, seem very little interested in the transaction in
which they are engaged, and look as if they were assembled rather for show than business. Nor, indeed, is the
artist much in fault. Painters have not fair play in these
parade pictures. It is only with us that Reform-banquets,
or views of the House of Lords at the passing of the Slop-
perton Railway Bill, or Coronation Processions, obtain
favor; in which vast numbers of public characters are
grouped unreally together, and politics are made to give
an interest to art.

Mr. Herbert's picture of "Sir Thomas More and his
Daughter, watching from the Prisoner's Room in the Tower
Four Monks led away to Execution," is not the most elabo·

rate, perhaps, but the very best of this painter's works. It is full of grace, and sentiment, and religious unction. You see that the painter's heart is in the scenes which he represents. The countenances of the two figures are finely conceived; the sorrowful anxious beauty of the daughter's face, the resigned humility of the martyr at her side, and the accessories or properties of the pious little drama are cleverly and poetically introduced; such as mystic sentences of hope and trust inscribed by former sufferers on the walls, the prisoner's rosary and book of prayers to the Virgin, that lie on his bed. These types and emblems of the main story are not obtruded, but serve to increase the interest of the action; just as you hear in a concerted piece of music a single instrument playing its little plaintive part alone, and yet belonging to the whole.

If you want to see a picture where costume is *not* represented, behold Mr. Lauder's "Claverhouse ordering Morton to Execution." There sits Claverhouse in the centre, in a Kean wig and ringlets, such as was never worn in any age of this world, except at the theatre, in 1816, and he scowls with a true melodramatic ferocity; and he lifts a signpost of a finger towards Morton, who forthwith begins to writhe and struggle into an attitude in the midst of a group of subordinate, cuirassed, buff-coated gentry. Morton is represented in tights, slippers, and a tunic; something after the fashion of Retzsch's figures in "Faust" (which are refinements of costumes worn a century and a half before the days when Charles disported at Tillietudlem); and he, too, must proceed to scowl and frown "with a flashing eye and a distended nostril," as they say in the novels, — as Gomersal scowls at Widdicomb before the combat between those two chiefs begins; and while they are measuring each other according to the stage wont, from the toe of the yellow boot up to the tip of the stage-wig. There is a tragedy heroine in Mr. Lauder's picture, striking her attitude, too, to complete the scene. It is entirely unnatural, theatrical, of the Davidgian, nay, Richardsonian drama, and all such attempts at effect must be reprehended by the stern critic. When such a cool practitioner as Claverhouse ordered a gentleman to be shot, he would not put himself into an attitude : when such a quiet gentleman as Morton received the unpleasant communication in the midst of a company of grenadiers who must overpower him, and of ladies to whom his resistance would be unpleasant, he would act like a man and go out quietly, not stop to rant and fume like a fellow in a booth. I believe it is in Mr. Henningsen's book that there is a story of Zumalacarreguy, Don Carlos's Dundee, who, sitting at the table with a Christino prisoner, smoking cigars and playing piquet very quietly, received a communication which he handed over to the Christino. "Your people," says he, "have shot one of my officers, and I have promised reprisals; I am sorry to say, my dear general, that I must execute you in twenty minutes!" And so the two gentlemen finished their game at piquet, and parted company — the one to inspect his lines, the other for the courtyard hard by, where a file of grenadiers was waiting to receive his excellency — with mutual politeness and. regret. It was the fortune of war. There was no help for it; no need of ranting and stamping, which would ill become any person of good breeding.

The Scotch artists have a tragic taste; and we should mention with especial praise Mr. Duncan's picture with the agreeable epigraph, "She set the bairn on the ground and tied up his head, and straightened his body, and covered him with her plaid, and laid down and wept over him." The extract is from Walker's "Life of Peden;" the martyrdom was done on the body of a boy by one of those bloody troopers whom we have seen in Mr. Lauder's picture carrying off poor shrieking Morton. Mr. Duncan's picture is very fine, — dark, rich, and deep in sentiment; the woman is painted with some of Rubens's swelling lines (such as may be seen in some of his best Magdalens), and with their rich tones of gray. If a certain extremely heavy Cupid poising in the air by a miracle be the other picture of Mr. Duncan's, it can be only said that his tragedy is better than his lightsome compositions — an arrow from yonder lad would bruise the recipient black and blue.

Another admirable picture of a Scotch artist is 427, "The Highland Lament," by Alexander Johnston. It is a shame to put such a picture in such a place. It hangs on the ground, almost invisible, while dozens of tawdry portraits are staring at you on the line. Could Mr. Johnston's picture be but seen properly, its great beauty and merit would not fail to strike hundreds of visitors who pass it over now. A Highland piper comes running forward, playing some wild lament on his dismal instrument; the women follow after, wailing and sad; the mournful procession winds over a dismal moor. The picture is as clever for its fine treatment and color, for the grace and action of the figure, as it is curious as an illustration of national manners.

In speaking of the Scotch painters, the Wilkie-like pictures of Mr. Fraser, with their peculiar *smeary* manner, their richness of tone, and their pleasant effect and humor, should not be passed over; while those of Mr. Geddes and Sir William Allan may be omitted with perfect propriety. The latter presents her Majesty and Prince Albert perched on a rock; the former has a figure from Walter Scott, of very little interest to any but the parties concerned.

Among the Irish painters we remark two portraits by Mr. Crowley, representing Mrs. Aikenhead, superior*ess* of the Sisters of Charity in Ireland, who gives a very favorable picture of the Society — for it is impossible to conceive an abbess more comfortable, kind, and healthy-looking; and a portrait of Dr. Murray, Roman Catholic Archbishop of Dublin, not a good picture of a fine, benevolent, and venerable head. We do not know whether the painter of 149, "An Irish Peasant awaiting her Husband's Return," Mr. Anthony, is an Irishman; but it is a pretty sad picture, which well characterizes the poverty, the affection, and the wretchedness of the poor Irish cabin, and tells sweetly and modestly a plaintive story. The largest work in the exhibition is from the pencil of an Irishman, Mr. Leahy, "Lady Jane Grey praying before Execution." One cannot but admire the courage of artists who paint great works upon these tragic subjects; great works quite unfitted for any private room, and scarcely suited to any public one. But, large as it is, it may be said (without any playing upon words) that the work grows upon estimation. The painting is hard and incomplete; but the principal figure excellent: the face especially is finely painted and full of great beauty. Also, in the Irish pictures may be included Mr. Solomon Hart's Persian gentleman smoking a *calahan*, — a sly hint at the learned Sergeant member for Cork, who has often done the same thing.

Mr. Maclise's little scene from "Undine" does not seem to us German in character, as some of the critics call it, because it is clear and hard in line. What German artist is there who can draw with this astonishing vigor, precision, and variety of attitude? The picture is one of admirable and delightful fancy. The swarms of solemn little fairies crowding round Undine and her somewhat theatrical lover may keep a spectator for hours employed in pleasure and wonder. They look to be the real portraits of the little people, sketched by the painter in some visit to their country. There is, especially, on a branch in the top corner of the picture, a conversation going on between a fairy and a squirrel (who is a fairy too), which must have been taken from nature, or Mother Bunch's delightful super-nature. How awful their great glassy blue eyes are ! How they peer out from under grass, and out of flowers, and from twigs and branches, and swing off over the tree-top, singing shrill little fairy choruses ! We must have the Fairy Tales illustrated by this gentleman, that is clear ; he is the only person, except Tieck, of Dresden, who knows anything about them. — Yes, there *is* some one else ; and a word may be introduced here in welcome to the admirable young designer whose hand has lately been employed to illustrate the columns of our facetious friend (and the friend of everybody) *Punch*. This young artist (who has avowed his name, a very well-known one, that of Doyle) has poured into *Punch's* columns a series of drawings quite extraordinary for their fancy, their variety, their beauty and fun. It is the true genius of fairyland, of burlesque which never loses sight of beauty. Friend *Punch's* very wrapper is quite a marvel in this way, at which we can never look without discovering some new little quip of humor or pleasant frolic of grace.

And if we have had reason to complain of Mr. Leslie's "Comus" as deficient in poetry, what person is there that will not welcome "Sancho," although we have seen him before almost in the same attitude, employed in the same way, recounting his adventures to the kind smiling duchess as she sits in state ? There is only the sour old duenna who refuses to be amused, and nothing has ever amused her these sixty years. But the ladies are all charmed, and tittering with one another; the black slave who leans against the pillar has gone off in an honest fit of downright laughter. Even the little dog, the wonderful little Blenheim, by the lady's side, would laugh if she could (but, alas ! it is impossible), as the other little dog is said to have done on the singular occasion when "the cow jumped over the moon." * The glory of dulness is in Sancho's face. I don't believe there is a man in the world — no, not even in

* " Qualia prospiciens Catulus ferit æthera risu
  Ipsaque trans lunæ cornua Vacca salit." — LUCRETIUS.

the House of Commons — so stupid as that. On the Whig side there is, certainly, — but no, it is best not to make comparisons which fall short of the mark. This is, indeed, the Sancho that Cervantes drew.

Although the editor of this magazine had made a solemn condition with the writer of this notice that no pictures taken from the " Vicar of Wakefield " or " Gil Blas " should, by any favor or pretence, be noticed in the review; yet, as the great picture of Mr. Mulready compelled the infraction of the rule, rushing through our resolve by the indomitable force of genius, we must, as the line is broken, present other Vicars, Thornhills, and Olivias, to walk in and promenade themselves in our columns, in spite of the vain placards at the entrance, " VICARS OF WAKEFIELD NOT ADMITTED." In the first place let the Reverend Dr. Primrose and Miss Primrose walk up in Mr. Hollins's company. The Vicar is mildly expostulating with his daughter regarding the attentions of Squire Thornhill. He looks mild, too mild; she looks ill-humored, very sulky. Is it about the scolding, or the Squire ? The figures are very nicely painted; but they do not look accustomed (the lady especially) to the dresses they wear. After them come Mrs. Primrose, the Misses and the young Masters Primrose, presented by Mr. Frith in his pretty picture (491). Squire Thornhill sits at his ease, and recounts his town adventures to the ladies; the beautiful Olivia is quite lost in love with the slim red-coated dandy; her sister is listening with respect; but, above all, the old lady and children hearken with wonder. These latter are charming figures, as indeed are all in the picture. As for Gil Blas — but we shall be resolute about *him.* Certain Gil Blas there are in the exhibition eating olla-podridas, and what not. Not a word, however, shall be said regarding any one of them.

Among the figure-pieces Mr. Ward's " Lafleur " must not be forgotten, which is pleasant, lively, and smartly drawn and painted; nor Mr. Gilbert's "Pear-tree Well," which contains three graceful classical figures, which are rich in effect and color; nor Mr. MacInnes's good picture of Luther listening to the sacred ballad (the reformer is shut up in the octagon-room); nor a picture of Oliver Goldsmith on his rambles, playing the flute at a peasant's door, in which the color is very pretty; the character of the French peasants not French at all; and the poet's figure easy, correct, and well drawn.

Among more serious subjects may be mentioned with praise Mr. Dyce's two fierce figures, representing King Joash shooting the arrow of deliverance, which if the critic call "French," because they are well and carefully drawn, Mr. Dyce may be proud of being a Frenchman. Mr. Lauder's "Wise and Foolish Virgins" is a fine composition; the color sombre and mysterious; some of the figures extremely graceful, and the sentiment of the picture excellent. This is a picture which would infallibly have had a chance of a prize, if the poor dear Art-Union were free to act.

Mr. Elmore's "Rienzi addressing the People" is one of the very best pictures in the gallery. It is well and agreeably colored, bright, pleasing, and airy. A group of people are gathered round the tribune, who addresses them among Roman ruins under a clear blue sky. The grouping is very good; the figures rich and picturesque in attitude and costume. There is a group in front of a mother and child who are thinking of anything but Rienzi and liberty; who, perhaps, ought not to be so prominent, as they take away from the purpose of the picture, but who are beautiful wherever they are. And the picture is further to be remarked for the clear, steady, and honest painting which distinguishes it.

What is to be said of Mr. Poole's "Moors beleaguered in Valencia"? A clever hideous picture in the very worst taste; disease and desperation characteristically illustrated. The Spaniards beleaguer the town, and everybody is starving. Mothers with dry breasts unable to nourish infants; old men, with lean ribs and bloodshot eyes, moaning on the pavement; brown young skeletons pacing up and down the rampart, some raving, all desperate. Such is the agreeable theme which the painter has taken up. It is worse than last year, when the artist only painted the Plague of London. Some *did* recover from that. All these Moors will be dead before another day, and the vultures will fatten on their lean carcasses, and pick out their red-hot eyeballs. Why do young men indulge in these horrors? Young poets and romancers often do so, and fancy they are exhibiting "power;" whereas nothing is so easy. Any man with mere instinct can succeed in the brutal art. The coarse fury of Zurbaran and Morales is as far below the sweet and beneficent calm of Murillo as a butcher is beneath a hero. Don't let us have any more of these hideous exhibitions — these ghoul festivals. It may be remembered that Amina in the "Arabian Nights," who liked church-yard suppers, could only eat a grain of rice when she came to natural food. There is a good deal of sly satire in the apologue which might be applied to many (especially French) literary and pictorial artists of the convulsionary school.

We must not take leave of the compositions without mentioning Mr. Landseer's wonderful "Shoeing" and Stag; the latter the most poetical, the former the most dexterous, perhaps, of the works of this accomplished painter. The latter picture, at a little distance, expands almost into the size of nature. The enormous stag by the side of a great blue northern lake stalks over the snow down to the shore, whither his mate is coming through the water to join him. Snowy mountains bend round the lonely landscape, the stars are shining out keenly in the deep icy blue overhead; in a word, your teeth begin to chatter as you look at the picture, and it can't properly be seen without a great-coat. The donkey and the horse in the shoeing picture are prodigious imitations of nature; the blacksmith only becomes impalpable. There is a charming portrait in the great room by the same artist in which the same effect may be remarked. A lady is represented with two dogs in her lap; the dogs look real; the lady a thin unsubstantial vision of a beautiful woman. You ought to see the landscape through her.

Amongst the landscape-painters, Mr. Stanfield has really painted this year better than any former year — a difficult matter. The pictures are admirable, the drawing of the water wonderful, the look of freshness and breeze and motion conveyed with delightful skill. All Mr. Creswick's pictures will be seen with pleasure, especially the delicious " Summer Evening; " the most airy and clear, and also the most poetical of his landscapes. The fine "Evening Scene " of Danby also seems to have the extent and splendor, and to suggest the solemn feelings of a vast mountain-scene at sunset. The admirers of Sir Augustus Callcott's soft golden landscapes will here find some of his most delightful pieces. Mr. Roberts has painted his best in his Nile scene, and his French architectural pieces are of scarce inferior merit. Mr. Lee, Mr. Witherington, and Mr. Leitch have contributed works, showing all their well-known qualities and skill. As for Mr. Turner, he has out-prodigied almost all former prodigies. He has made a picture with real rain, behind which is real sunshine, and you expect a rainbow every minute. Meanwhile, there comes a train down upon you, really moving at the rate of fifty miles an hour, and which the reader had best make haste to see, lest it should dash out of the picture, and be away up Charing Cross through the wall opposite. All these wonders are performed with means not less wonderful than the effects are. The rain, in the astounding picture called "Rain — Steam — Speed," is composed of dabs of dirty putty *slapped* on to the canvas with a trowel; the sunshine scintillates out of very thick smeary lumps of chrome yellow. The shadows are produced by cool tones of crimson lake, and quiet glazings of vermilion. Although the fire in the steam-engine *looks* as if it were red, I am not prepared to say that it is not painted with cobalt and pea-green. And as for the manner in which the "*Speed*" is done, of that the less said the better, — only it is a positive fact that there is a steam-coach going fifty miles an hour. The world has never seen anything like this picture.

In respect of the portraits of the exhibition, if Royal Academicians will take the word of the *Morning Post*, the *Morning Chronicle*, the *Spectator*, and, far above all, of *Fraser's Magazine*, they will pause a little before they hang such a noble portrait as that of W. Conyngham, Esquire, by Samuel Lawrence, away out of sight, while some of their own paltry canvases meet the spectator nose to nose. The man with the gloves of Titian in the Louvre has evidently inspired Mr. Lawrence, and his picture is so far an imitation; but what then? it is better to imitate great things well than to imitate a simpering barber's dummy, like No. 10,000, let us say, or to perpetrate yonder horrors, — weak, but, oh! how heavy, smeared, flat, pink and red, grinning, ill-drawn portraits (such as Nos. 99,999 and 99,999*d*) which the old Academicians perpetrate! You are right to keep the best picture in the room out of the way, to be sure; it would sternly frown your simpering unfortunates out of countenance; but let us have at least a chance of seeing the good pictures. Have one room, say, for the Academicians, and another for the clever artists. Diminish your number of exhibited pictures to six, if you like, but give the young men a chance. It is pitiful to see their works pushed out of sight, and to be offered what you give us in exchange.

This does not apply to all the esquires who paint portraits; but with regard to the names of the delinquents, it is best to be silent, lest a showing up of them should have a terrible effect on the otherwise worthy men, and drive them to an untimely desperation. So I shall say little about the portraits, mentioning merely that Mr. Grant has one or two, a small one especially, of great beauty and ladylike grace; and one very bad one such as that of Lord Forrester. Mr. Pickersgill has some good heads; the little portrait of Mr. Ainsworth by Mr. Maclise is as clever and like as the artist knows how to make it. Mr. Middleton has some female heads especially beautiful. Mrs. Carpenter is one of the most manly painters in the exhibition; and if you walk into the miniature-room, you may look at the delicious little gems from the pencil of Sir William Ross, those still more graceful and poetical by Mr. Thorburn, and the delightful coxcombries of Mr. Chalon. I have found out a proper task for that gentleman, and hereby propose that he should illustrate "Coningsby."

In the statue-room, Mr. Gibson's classic group attracts attention and deserves praise; and the busts of Parker, Macdonald, Behnes, and other well-known portrait-sculptors, have all their usual finish, skill, and charm.

At the Water-color Gallery the pleased spectator lingers as usual delighted, surrounded by the pleasant drawings and the most genteel company. It requires no small courage to walk through that avenue of plush breeches with which the lobby is lined, and to pass two files of whiskered men, in canes and huge calves, who contemptuously regard us poor fellows with Bluchers and gingham umbrellas. But these passed, you are in the best society. Bishops, I have remarked, frequent this gallery in venerable numbers; likewise dignified clergymen with rosettes; Quakeresses, also, in dove-colored silks meekly changing color; squires and their families from the country; and it is a fact that you never can enter the Gallery without seeing a wonderfully pretty girl. This fact merits to be generally known, and is alone worth the price of this article.

I suspect that there are some people from the country who admire Mr. Prout still; those fresh, honest, unalloyed country appetites! There are the Prout Nurembergs and Venices still; the awnings, the water-posts, and the red-capped bargemen drawn with a reed pen; but we *blasés* young *roués* about London get tired of these simple dishes, and must have more excitement. There, too, are Mr. Hill's stags with pink stomachs, his spinach pastures and mottled farmhouses; also innumerable windy downs and heaths by Mr. Copley Fielding: — in the which breezy flats I have so often wandered before with burnt-sienna ploughboys, that the walk is no longer tempting.

Not so, however, the marine pieces of Mr. Bentley. That gentleman, to our thinking, has never painted so well. Witness his "Indiaman towed up the Thames" (53), his "Signalling the Pilot" (161), and his admirable view of "Mont Saint Michel" (127), in which the vessel quite dances and falls on the water. He deserves to divide the prize with Mr. Stanfield at the Academy.

All the works of a clever young landscape-painter, Mr. G. A. Fripp, may be looked at with pleasure; they show great talent, no small dexterity, and genuine enthusiastic love of nature. Mr. Alfred Fripp, a figure-painter, merits likewise very much praise; his works are not complete as yet, but his style is thoughtful, dramatic, and original.

Mr. Hunt's dramas of one or two characters are as entertaining and curious as ever. His "Outcast" is amazingly fine, and tragic in character. His "Sick Cigar-boy," a wonderful delineation of nausea. Look at the picture of the toilet, in which, with the parlor-tongs, Betty, the housemaid, is curling little miss's hair: there is a dish of yellow soap in that drawing, and an old comb and brush, the fidelity of which makes the delicate beholder shudder. On one of the screens there are some "bird's-nests," out of which I am surprised no spectator has yet stolen any of the eggs — you have but to stoop down and take them.

Mr. Taylor's delightful drawings are even more than ordinarily clever. His "Houseless Wanderers" is worthy of Hogarth in humor; most deliciously colored and treated. "The Gleaner" is full of sunshine; the larder quite a curiosity, as showing the ease, truth, and dexterity with which the artist washes in his flowing delineations from nature. In his dogs, you don't know which most to admire, the fidelity with which the animals are painted, or the ease with which they are done.

This gift of facility Mr. Cattermole also possesses to an amazing extent. As pieces of effect, his "Porch" and "Rook-shooting" are as wonderful as they are pleasing. His large picture of "Monks in a Refectory" is very fine; rich, original, and sober in color; excellent in sentiment and general grouping; in individual attitude and drawing

not sufficiently correct. As the figures aie much smaller
than those in the refectory, these faults are less visible in
the magnificent "Battle for the Bridge," a composition,
perhaps, the most complete that the artist has yet produced.
The landscape is painted as grandly as Salvator; the sky
wonderfully airy, the sunshine shining through the glades
of the wood, the huge trees rocking and swaying as the
breeze rushes by them; the battling figures are full of
hurry, fire, and tumult. All these things are rather indicated by the painter than defined by him; but such hints
are enough from such a genius. The charmed and captivated imagination is quite ready to supply what else is
wanting.

Mr. Frederick Nash has some unpretending, homely,
exquisitely faithful scenes in the Rhine country, "Bop-
part," "Bacharach," etc., of which a sojourner in those
charming districts will always be glad to have a reminiscence. Mr. Joseph Nash has not some of the cleverest of
his mannerisms, nor Mr. Lake Price the best of his smart,
dandified, utterly unnatural exteriors. By far the best
designs of this kind are the Windsor and Buckingham
Palace sketches of Mr. Douglas Morison, executed with
curious fidelity and skill. There is the dining-hall in
Buckingham Palace, with all the portraits, all the candles
in all the chandeliers; the China gimcracks over the
mantelpiece, the dinner-table set out, the napkins folded
mitrewise, the round water-glasses, the sherry-glasses, the
champagne ditto, and all in a space not so big as two pages
of this Magazine. There is the Queen's own chamber at
Windsor, her Majesty's piano, her royal writing-table, an
escritoire with pigeon-holes, where the august papers are
probably kept; and very curious, clever, and ugly all these
pictures of furniture are too, and will be a model for the
avoidance of upholsterers in coming ages.

Mr. John William Wright's sweet female figures must
not be passed over; nor the pleasant Stothard-like drawings of his veteran namesake. The "Gypsies" of Mr.
Oakley will also be looked at with pleasure; and this gentleman may be complimented as likely to rival the Rich-
monds and the Chalons " in another place," where may be
seen a very good full-length portrait drawn by him.

The exhibition of the New Society of Water-color Painters
has grown to be quite as handsome and agreeable as that

of its mamma, the old Society in Pall Mall East. Those who remember this little band of painters, to whom the gates of the elder Gallery were hopelessly shut, must be glad to see the progress the younger branch has made; and we have every reason to congratulate ourselves that, instead of one pleasant exhibition annually, the amateur can recreate himself now with two. Many of the pictures here are of very great merit.

Mr. Warren's Egyptian pictures are clever, and only need to be agreeable where he takes a pretty subject, such as that of the "Egyptian Lady" (150); his work is pretty sure to be followed by that welcome little ticket of emerald green in the corner, which announces that a purchaser has made his appearance. But the eye is little interested by views of yellow deserts and sheikhs, and woolly-headed warriors with ugly wooden swords.

And yet mere taste, grace, and beauty won't always succeed; witness Mr. Absolon's drawings, of which few — far too few — boast the green seal and which are one and all of them charming. There is one in the first room from the "V-c-r of W-kef—ld" (we are determined not to write that name again), which is delightfully composed, and a fresh, happy picture of a country *fête.* "The Dartmoor Turf-gatherers" (87) is still better; the picture is full of air, grace, pretty drawing, and brilliant color, and yet no green seal. "A Little Sulky;" "The Devonshire Cottage-door;" "The Widow on the Stile;" "The Stocking-knitter;" are all, too, excellent in their way, and bear the artist's *cachet* of gentle and amiable grace. But the drawings, in point of execution, do not go far enough; they are not sufficiently bright to attract the eyes of that great and respectable body of amateurs who love no end of cobalt, carmine, stippling, and plenty of emerald green and vermilion; they are not made out sufficiently in line to rank as pictures.

Behold how Mr. Corbould can work when he likes — how *he* can work you off the carmine stippling! In his large piece, "The Britons deploring the Departure of the Romans," there is much very fine and extraordinary cleverness of pencil. Witness the draperies of the two women, which are painted with so much cleverness and beauty that, indeed, one regrets that one of them has not got a little drapery more. The same tender regard pervades the bosom while looking at that of Joan of Arc, "While engaged in the servile offices of her situation as a menial at an inn, ruminating upon the distressing state of France." Her "servile situation" seems to be that of an ostler at the establishment in question, for she is leading down a couple of animals to drink; and as for the "distressing state of France," it ought not, surely, to affect such a fat little comfortable simple-looking undressed body. Bating the figure of Joan, who looks as pretty as a young lady out of the last novel, bating, I say, baiting Joan, who never rode horses, depend on't, in that genteel way, the picture is exceedingly skilful, and much better in color than Mr. Corbould's former works.

Mr. Wehnert's great drawing is a failure, but an honorable defeat. It shows great power and mastery over the material with which he works. He has two pretty German figures in the foreroom: "The Innkeeper's Daughter" (38); and "Perdita and Florizel" (316). Perhaps he is the author of the pretty arabesques with which the Society have this year ornamented their list of pictures; he has a German name, and *English* artists can have no need to be copying from Düsseldorf's embellishments to decorate the catalogues.

Mr. Haghe's great drawing of the "Death of Zurbaran" is not interesting from any peculiar fineness of expression in the faces of the actors who figure in this gloomy scene; but it is largely and boldly painted, in deep sombre washes of colors, with none of the niggling prettinesses to which artists in water-colors seem forced to resort in order to bring their pictures to a high state of finish. Here the figures and the draperies look as if they were laid down at once with a bold yet careful certainty of hand. The effect of the piece is very fine, the figures grandly grouped. Among all the water-color painters we know of none who can wield the brush like Mr. Haghe, with his skill, his breadth, and his certainty.

Mr. Jenkins's beautiful female figure in the drawing called "Love" (123) must be mentioned with especial praise; it is charming in design, color, and sentiment. Another female figure, "The Girl at the Stile," by the same artist, has not equal finish, roundness, and completeness, but the same sentiment of tender grace and beauty.

Mr. Bright's landscape drawings are exceedingly clever, but there is too much of the drawing-master in the handling, too much dash, skurry, sharp cleverness of execution.

Him Mr. Jutsum follows with cleverness not quite equal, and mannerism still greater. After the performance of which the eye reposes gratefully upon some pleasant evening scenes by Mr. Duncan (3, 10); and the delightful "Shady Land" of Mr. Youngman. Mr. Boys's pictures will be always looked at and admired for the skill and correctness of a hand which, in drawing, is not inferior to that of Canaletto.

As for Suffolk Street, that delicious retreat may or may not be still open. I have been there, but was frightened from the place by the sight of Haydon's Napoleon, with his vast head, his large body, and his little legs, staring out upon the indigo sea, in a grass-green coat. Nervous people avoid that sight, and the Emperor remains in Suffolk Street as lonely as at Saint Helena.

PICTURE GOSSIP: IN A LETTER FROM MICHAEL ANGELO TITMARSH.

ALL' ILLUSTRISSIMO SIGNOR, IL MIO SIGNOR COLENDISSIMO, AUGUSTO HA ARVÉ, PITTORE IN ROMA.

[*Fraser's Magazine, June,* 1845.]

I AM going to fulfil the promise, my dear Augusto, which I uttered, with a faltering voice and streaming eyes, before I stepped into the jingling old courier's vehicle, which was to bear me from Rome to Florence. Can I forget that night — that parting? Gaunter stood by so affected, that for the last quarter of an hour he did not swear once; Flake's emotion exhibited itself in audible sobs; Jellyson said naught, but thrust a bundle of Torlonia's four-baiocchi cigars into the hand of a departing friend; and you your-self were so deeply agitated by the event, that you took four glasses of absinthe to string up your nerves for the fatal moment. Strange vision of past days! — for vision it seems to me now. And have I been in Rome really and truly? Have I seen the great works of my Christian namesake of the Buonarotti family, and the light arcades of the Vatican? Have I seen the glorious Apollo, and that other divine fiddle-player whom Raphael painted? Yes — and the English dandies swaggering on the Pincian Hill! Yes — and have eaten woodcocks and drunk Orvieto hard by the huge broad-shouldered Pantheon Portico, in the comfortable parlors of the "Falcone." Do you recollect that speech I made at Bertini's in proposing the health of the Pope of Rome on Christmas-day? — do you remem-ber it? *I* don't. But his Holiness, no doubt, heard of the oration, and was flattered by the compliment of the illustrious English traveller.

I went to the exhibition of the Royal Academy lately, and all these reminiscences rushed back on a sudden with affecting volubility; not that there was anything in or out of the gallery which put me specially in mind of sumptu-ous and liberal Rome; but in the great room was the picture of a fellow in a broad Roman hat, in a velvet Roman coat, and large yellow mustachios, and that prodigious scowl which young artists assume when sitting for their portraits — he was one of our set at Rome; and the scenes of the winter came back pathetically to my mind, and all the friends of that season, — Orifice and his sentimental songs; Father Giraldo and his poodle, and MacBrick the trump of bankers. Hence the determination to write this letter; but the hand is crabbed, and the postage is dear, and, instead of despatching it by the mail, I shall send it to you by means of the printer, knowing well that *Fraser's Magazine* is eagerly read at Rome, and not (on account of its morality) excluded in the *Index Expurgatorius.*

And it will be doubly agreeable to me to write to you regarding the fine arts in England, because I know, my dear Augusto, that you have a thorough contempt for my opinion — indeed, for that of all persons, excepting, of course, one whose name is already written in this sentence. Such, however, is not the feeling respecting my critical powers in this country; *here* they know the merit of Michael Angelo Titmarsh better, and they say, " He paints so badly, that, hang it ! he *must* be a good judge; " in the latter part of which opinion, of course, I agree.

You should have seen the consternation of the fellows at my arrival ! — of our dear brethren who thought I was safe at Rome for the season, and that their works, exhibited in May, would be spared the dreadful ordeal of my ferocious eye. When I entered the club-room in Saint Martin's Lane, and called for a glass of brandy and water like a bomb-shell, you should have seen the terror of some of the artists assembled ! They knew that the frightful projectile just launched into their club-room must *burst* in the natural course of things. Who would be struck down by the explosion ? was the thought of every one. Some of the hypocrites welcomed me meanly back, some of the timid trembled, some of the savage and guilty muttered curses at my arrival. You should have seen the ferocious looks of Daggerly, for example, as he scowled at me from the supper-table, and clutched the trenchant weapon with which he was dissevering his toasted cheese.

From the period of my arrival until that of the opening of the various galleries, I maintained with the artists every proper affability, but still was not too familiar. It is the custom of their friends, before their pictures are sent in to the exhibitions, to visit the painters' works at their private studios, and there encourage them by saying, "Bravo, Jones" (I don't mean Jones, R.A., for I defy any man to say bravo to *him*, but Jones in general) ! "Tomkins, this is your greatest work !" "Smith, my boy, they must elect you an Associate for this !" — and so forth. These harmless banalities of compliment pass between the painters and their friends on such occasions. I, myself, have uttered many such civil phrases in former years under like circumstances. But it is different now. Fame has its privations as well as its pleasures. The friend may see his companions in private, but the JUDGE must not pay visits to his clients. I stayed away from the *ateliers* of all the artists (at least, I only visited one, kindly telling him that he didn't count as an artist at all), and would only see their pictures in the public galleries, and judge them in the fair race with their neighbors. This announcement and conduct of mine filled all the Berners Street and Fitzroy Square district with terror.

As I am writing this, after having had my fill of their works as publicly exhibited, in the country, at a distance from catalogues, my only book of reference being an orchard whereof the trees are now bursting into full blossom, — it is probable that my remarks will be rather general than particular, that I shall only discourse about those pictures which I especially remember, or, indeed, upon any other point suitable to my humor and your delectation.

I went round the galleries with a young friend of mine, who, like yourself at present, has been a student of "High Art" at Rome. He had been a pupil of Monsieur Ingres, at Paris. He could draw rude figures of eight feet high to a nicety, and had produced many heroic compositions of that pleasing class and size, to the great profit of the paper-stretchers both in Paris and Rome. He came back from the latter place a year since, with his beard and mustachios of course. He could find no room in all Newman Street and Soho big enough to hold him and his genius, and was turned out of a decent house because, for the purpose of art, he wished to batter down the partition-wall between the two drawing-rooms he had. His great cartoon last year (whether it was "Caractacus before Claudius," or a scene from the "Vicar of Wakefield," I won't say) failed somehow. He was a good deal cut up by the defeat, and went into the country to his relations, from whom he returned after a while, with his mustachios shaved, clean linen, and other signs of depression. He said (with a hollow laugh) he should not commence on his great canvas this year, and so gave up the completion of his composition of "Boadicea addressing the Iceni:" quite a novel subject, which, with that ingenuity and profound reading which distinguish his brethren, he had determined to take up.

Well, sir, this youth and I went to the exhibitions together, and I watched his behavior before the pictures. At the tragic, swaggering, theatrical-historical pictures, he yawned; before some of the grand flashy landscapes, he stood without the least emotion; but before some quiet scenes of humor or pathos, or some easy little copy of nature, the youth stood in pleased contemplation, the nails of his highlows seemed to be screwed into the floor there, and his face dimpled over with grins.

"These little pictures," said he, on being questioned, "are worth a hundred times more than the big ones. In the latter you see signs of ignorance of every kind, weakness of hand, poverty of invention, carelessness of drawing, lamentable imbecility of thought. Their heroism is borrowed from the theatre, their sentiment is so maudlin that it makes you sick. I see no symptoms of thought or of minds strong and genuine enough to cope with elevated subjects. No individuality, no novelty, the decencies of costume " (my friend did not mean that the figures we were looking at were naked, like Mr. Etty's, but that they were dressed out of all historical propriety) "are disregarded; the people are striking attitudes, as at the Coburg. There is something painful to me in this *naïve* exhibition of incompetency, this imbecility that is so unconscious of its own failure. If, however, the aspiring men don't succeed, the modest do ; and what they have really seen or experienced, our artists can depict with successful accuracy and delightful skill. Hence," says he, "I would sooner have So-and-so's little sketch ('A Donkey on a Common') than What-d'ye-call-'em's enormous picture ('Sir Walter Manny and the Crusaders discovering Nova Scotia'), and prefer yonder unpretending sketch, 'Shrimp Catchers, Morning' (how exquisitely the long and level sands are touched off ! how beautifully the morning light touches the countenances of the fishermen. and illumines the rosy features of the

shrimps !), to yonder pretentious illustration from Spenser,
'Sir Botibol rescues Una from Sir Uglimore in the Cave of
the Enchantress Ichthyosaura.'"

I am only mentioning another's opinion of these pictures,
and would not of course, for my own part, wish to give
pain by provoking comparisons that must be disagreeable
to some persons. But I could not help agreeing with my
young friend and saying, "Well, then, in the name of
goodness, my dear fellow, if you only like what is real, and
natural, and unaffected — if upon such works you gaze with
delight, while from more pretentious performances you
turn away with weariness, why the deuce must *you* be in
the heroic vein ? Why don't you *do* what you like ? " The
young man turned round on the iron heel of his highlows,
and walked downstairs clinking them sulkily.

There is a variety of classes and divisions into which
the works of our geniuses may be separated. There are
the heroic pictures, the theatrical-heroic, the religious, the
historical-sentimental, the historical-familiar, the namby-
pamby, and so forth.

Among the heroic pictures of course Mr. Haydon's ranks
the first, its size and pretentions call for that place. It
roars out to you as it were with a Titanic voice from among
all the competitors to public favor, " Come and look at me."
A broad-shouldered, swaggering, hulking archangel, with
those rolling eyes and distending nostrils which belong to
the species of sublime caricature, stands scowling on a
sphere from which the devil is just descending bound earth-
wards. Planets, comets, and other astronomical phenomena
roll and blaze round the pair and flame in the new blue
sky. There is something burly and bold in this resolute
genius which will attract only enormous subjects, which
will deal with nothing but the epic, something respectable
even in the defeats of such characters. I was looking the
other day at Southampton at a stout gentleman in a green
coat and white hat, who a year or two since fully believed
that he could walk upon the water, and set off in the presence of a great concourse of people upon his supermarine
journey. There is no need to tell you that the poor fellow
got a wetting and sank amidst the jeers of all his beholders.
I think somehow they should not have laughed at that
honest ducked gentleman, they should have respected the
faith and simplicity which led him unhesitatingly to venture upon that watery experiment; and so, instead of

laughing at Haydon, which you and I were just about to
do, let us check our jocularity and give him credit for his
great earnestness of purpose. I begin to feel the world
growing more pathetic daily, and laugh less every year of
my life. Why laugh at idle hopes, or vain purposes, or
utter blundering self-confidence? Let us be gentle with
them henceforth; who knows whether there may not be
something of the sort *chez nous?* But I am wandering
from Haydon and his big picture. Let us hope somebody
will buy. Who, I cannot tell: it will do for a chapel; it is
too big for a house. I have it — it might answer to hang
up over a caravan at a fair, if a travelling orrery were exhibited inside.

This may be sheer impertinence and error; the picture
may suit some tastes — it does the *Times* for instance,
which pronounces it to be a noble work of the highest art;
whereas the *Post* won't believe a bit, and passes it by with
scorn. What a comfort it is that there are different tastes
then, and that almost all artists have thus a chance of
getting a livelihood somehow! There is Martin, for another instance, with his brace of pictures about Adam and
Eve, which I would venture to place in the theatrical-
heroic class. One looks at those strange pieces and wonders how people can be found to admire, and yet they do.
Grave old people, with chains and seals, look dumfounded
into those vast perspectives, and think the apex of the
sublime is reached there. In one of Sir Bulwer Lytton's
novels there is a passage to that effect. I forget where,
but there is a new edition of them coming out in single
volumes, and I am positive you will find the sentiment
somewhere; they come up to his conceptions of the sublime, they answer to his ideas of beauty, or the Beautiful
as he writes it with a large B. He is himself an artist
and a man of genius. What right have we poor devils to
question such an authority? Do you recollect how we used
to laugh in the Capitol at the Domenichino Sibyl which
this same author praises so enthusiastically? a wooden,
pink-faced, goggle-eyed, ogling creature, we said it was, with
no more beauty or sentiment than a wax doll. But this
was our conceit, dear Augusto. On subjects of art, perhaps, there is no reasoning after all: or who can tell why
children have a passion for lollipops, and this man worships
beef while t'other adores mutton? To the child lollipops
may be the truthful and beautiful, and why should not

some men find Martin's pictures as much to their taste as Milton?

Another instance of the blessed variety of tastes may be mentioned here advantageously: while, as you have seen, the *Times* awards the palm to Haydon, and Sir Lytton exalts Martin as the greatest painter of the English school, the *Chronicle*, quite as well informed, no doubt, says that Mr. Eddis is the great genius of the present season, and that his picture of Moses's mother parting with him before leaving him in the bulrushes is a great and noble composition.

This critic must have a taste for the neat and agreeable, that is clear. Mr. Eddis's picture is nicely colored; the figures in fine clean draperies, the sky a bright clean color; Moses's mother is a handsome woman; and as she holds her child to her breast for the last time, and lifts up her fine eyes to heaven, the beholder may be reasonably moved by a decent *bourgeois* compassion; a handsome woman parting from her child is always an object of proper sympathy; but as for the greatness of the picture as a work of art, that is another question of tastes again. This picture seemed to me to be essentially a prose composition, not a poetical one. It tells you no more than you can see. It has no more wonder of poetry about it than a police-report or a newspaper paragraph, and should be placed, as I take it, in the historic-sentimental school, which is pretty much followed in England — nay, as close as possible to the namby-pamby quarter.

Of the latter sort there are some illustrious examples; and as it is the fashion for critics to award prizes, I would for my part cheerfully award the prize of a new silver tea-spoon to Mr. Redgrave, the champion of suffering female innocence, for his "Governess." That picture is more decidedly *spoony* than, perhaps, any other of this present season: and the subject seems to be a favorite with the artist. We have had the "Governess" one year before, or a variation of her under the name of the "Teacher," or *vice versâ.* The Teacher's young pupils are at play in the garden, she sits sadly in the schoolroom; there she sits, poor dear! — the piano is open beside her, and (oh, harrowing thought!) "Home, sweet home!" is open in the music-book. She sits and thinks of that dear place, with a sheet of black-edged note-paper in her hand. They have brought her her tea and bread and butter on a tray. She has drunk the tea, *she has not tasted the bread and butter.* There is pathos for you! there is art! This is, indeed, a love for lollipops with a vengeance, a regular babyhood of taste, about which a man with a manly stomach may be allowed to protest a little peevishly, and implore the public to give up such puling food.

There is a gentleman in the Octagon Room who, to be sure, runs Mr. Redgrave rather hard, and should have a silver papspoon at any rate, if the teaspoon is irrevocably awarded to his rival. The Octagon Room prize is a picture called the "Arrival of the Overland Mail." A lady is in her bedchamber, a portrait of her husband, Major Jones (cherished lord of that bridal apartment, with its drab-curtained bed), hangs on the wainscot in the distance, and you see his red coat and mustachios gleaming there between the wardrobe and the washhandstand. But where is his lady? She is on her knees by the bedside, her face has sunk into the feather-bed; her hands are clasped agonizingly together; a most tremendous black-edged letter has just arrived by the overland mail. It is all up with Jones. Well, let us hope she will marry again, and get over her grief for poor J..

Is there not something *naïve* and simple in this downright way of exciting compassion? I saw people looking at this pair of pictures evidently with yearning hearts. The great geniuses who invented them have not, you see, toiled in vain. They can command the sympathies of the public, they have gained Art-Union prizes, let us hope, as well as those humble imaginary ones which I have just awarded, and yet my heart is not naturally hard, though it refuses to be moved by such means as are here employed.

If the simple statement of a death is to harrow up the feelings, or to claim the tributary tear, *mon Dieu!* a man ought to howl every morning over the newspaper obituary. If we are to cry for every governess who leaves home, what a fund of pathos the *Times* advertisements would afford daily; we might weep down whole columns of close type. I have said before I am growing more inclined to the pathetic daily, but let us in the name of goodness make a stand somewhere, or the namby-pamby of the world will become unendurable; and we shall melt away in a deluge of blubber. This drivelling hysterical sentimentality it is surely the critic's duty to grin down, to shake any man roughly by the shoulder who seems dangerously affected by it, and, not sparing his feelings in the least, tell him he is a fool for his pains; to have no more respect for those who invent it, but expose their error with all the downrightness that is necessary.

By far the prettiest of the maudlin pictures is Mr. Stone's "Premier Pas." It is that old, pretty, rococo, fantastic Jenny and Jessamy couple, whose loves the painter has been chronicling any time these five years, and whom he has spied out at various wells, porches, etc. The lad is making love with all his might, and the maiden is in a pretty confusion — her heart flutters, and she only seems to spin. She drinks in the warm words of the young fellow with a pleasant conviction of the invincibility of her charms. He appeals nervously, and tugs at a pink which is growing up the porch-side. It is that pink, somehow, which has saved the picture from being decidedly namby-pamby. There is something new, fresh, and delicate about the little incident of the flower. It redeems Jenny, and renders that young prig Jessamy bearable. The picture is very nicely painted, according to the careful artist's wont. The neck and hands of the girl are especially pretty. The lad's face is effeminate and imbecile, but his velveteen breeches are painted with great vigor and strength.

This artist's picture of the "Queen and Ophelia" is in a much higher walk of art. There may be doubts about Ophelia. She is too pretty to my taste. Her dress (especially the black bands round her arms) too elaborately conspicuous and coquettish. The Queen is a noble dramatic head and attitude. Ophelia seems to be looking at us, the audience, and in a pretty attitude expressly to captivate us. The Queen is only thinking about the crazed girl, and Hamlet, and her own gloomy affairs, and has quite forgotten her own noble beauty and superb presence. The color of the picture struck me as quite new, sedate, but bright and very agreeable; the checkered light and shadow is made cleverly to aid in forming the composition; it is very picturesque and good. It is by far the best of Mr. Stone's works, and in the best line. Good-by, Jenny and Jessamy; we hope never to see you again — no more rococo rustics, no more namby-pamby; the man who can paint the Queen of "Hamlet" must forsake henceforth such fiddle-faddle company.

By the way, has any Shakspearian commentator ever remarked how fond the Queen really was of her second husband, the excellent Claudius? How courteous and kind the latter was always towards her? So excellent a family-man ought to be pardoned a few errors in consideration of his admirable behavior to his wife. He *did* go a little far, certainly, but then it was to possess a jewel of a woman.

More pictures indicating a fine appreciation of the tragic sentiment are to be found in the exhibition. Among them may be mentioned specially Mr. Johnson's picture of "Lord Russell taking the Communion in Prison before Execution." The story is finely told here, the group large and noble. The figure of the kneeling wife, who looks at her husband meekly engaged in the last sacred office, is very good indeed; and the little episode of the jailer, who looks out into the yard indifferent, seems to me to give evidence of a true dramatic genius. In "Hamlet," how those indifferent remarks of Guildenstern and Rosencrantz, at the end, bring out the main figures and deepen the surrounding gloom of the tragedy.

In Mr. Frith's admirable picture of the "Good Pastor," from Goldsmith, there is some sentiment of a very quiet, refined, Sir Roger-de-Coverley-like sort — not too much of it — it is indicated rather than expressed. "Sentiment, sir," Walker of the "Original" used to say — "sentiment, sir, is like garlic in made dishes: it should be felt everywhere and seen nowhere."

Now, I won't say that Mr. Frith's sentiment is like garlic, or provoke any other savory comparison regarding it; but say, in a word, this is one of the pictures I would like to have sent abroad to be exhibited at a European congress of painters, to show what an English artist can do. The young painter seems to me to have had a thorough comprehension of his subject and his own abilities. And what a rare quality is this, to know what you can do! An ass will go and take the grand historic walk, while, with lowly wisdom, Mr. Frith prefers the lowly path where there are plenty of flowers growing, and children prattling along the walks. This is the sort of picture that is good to paint nowadays — kindly, beautiful, inspiring delicate sympathies, and awakening tender good-humor. It is a comfort to have such a companion as that in a study to look up at when your eyes are tired with work, and to refresh you with its gentle quiet good-fellowship. I can see it now, as I shut my eyes, displayed faithfully on the camera obscura of the brain — the dear old parson with his congregation of old and young clustered round him; the little ones plucking him by the gown, with wondering eyes, half roguery, half terror; the smoke is curling up from the cottage chimneys in a peaceful Sabbath sort of way; the three village quid-nuncs are chattering together at the churchyard stile; there's a poor girl seated there on a stone, who has been crossed in love evidently, and looks anxiously to the parson for a little doubtful consolation. That's the real sort of sentiment—there's no need of a great, clumsy, black-edged letter to placard her misery, as it were, after Mr. Red-grave's fashion; the sentiment is only the more sincere for being unobtrusive, and the spectator gives his compassion the more readily because the unfortunate object makes no coarse demands upon his pity.

The painting of this picture is exceedingly clever and dexterous. One or two of the foremost figures are painted with the breadth and pearly delicacy of Greuze. The three village politicians, in the background, might have been touched by Teniers, so neat, brisk, and sharp is the execution of the artist's facile brush.

Mr. Frost (a new name, I think, in the catalogue) has given us a picture of "Sabrina," which is so pretty that I heartily hope it has not been purchased for the collection from "Comus," which adorns the Buckingham Palace summer-house. It is worthy of a better place and price than our royal patrons appear to be disposed to give for the works of English artists. What victims have those poor fellows been of this awful patronage! Great has been the commotion in the pictorial world, dear Augusto, regard-ing the fate of those frescos which royalty was pleased to order, which it condescended to purchase at a price that no poor amateur would have the face to offer. Think of the greatest patronage in the world giving forty pounds for pictures worth four hundred—condescending to buy works from humble men who could not refuse, and paying for them below their value! Think of august powers and principalities ordering the works of such a great man as Etty to be hacked out of the palace wall—that was a slap in the face to every artist in England; and I can agree with the conclusion come to by an indignant poet of *Punch's* band, who says, for his part:—

> " I will not toil for Queen and crown,
>   If princely patrons spurn me down;
>   I will not ask for royal job—
>   Let my Mæcenas be A SNOB !"

This is, however, a delicate, an awful subject, over which loyal subjects like you and I had best mourn in silence; but the fate of Etty's noble picture of last year made me tremble lest Frost should be similarly nipped: and I hope more genuine patronage for this promising young painter. His picture is like a mixture of a very good Hilton and Howard raised to a state of genius. There is sameness in the heads, but great grace and beauty — a fine sweeping movement in the composition of the beautiful fairy figures, undulating gracefully through the stream, while the lilies lie gracefully overhead. There is another submarine picture of "Nymphs cajoling Young Hylas," which contains great deal of very clever imitations of Boucher.

That youthful Goodall, whose early attempts promised so much, is not quite realizing those promises, I think, and is cajoled, like Hylas before mentioned, by dangerous beauty. His "Connemara Girls going to Market" are a vast deal too clean and pretty for such females. They laugh and simper in much too genteel a manner; they are washing such pretty white feet as I don't think are common about Leenane or Ballynahinch, and would be better at ease in white satin slippers than trudging up Croaghpatrick. There is a luxury of geographical knowledge for you! I have not done with it yet. Stop till we come to Roberts's "View of Jerusalem," and Muller's pictures of "Rhodes," and "Xanthus," and "Telmessus." This artist's sketches are excellent; like nature, and like Decamps, that best of painters of Oriental life and colors. In the pictures the artist forgets the brilliancy of color which is so conspicuous in his sketches, and "Telmessus" looks as gray and heavy as Dover in March.

Mr. Pickersgill (not the Academician, by any means) deserves great praise for two very poetical pieces; one from Spenser, I think (Sir Botibol, let us say, as before, with somebody in some hag's cave); another called the "Four Ages," which has still better grace and sentiment. This artist, too, is evidently one of the disciples of Hilton; and another, who has also, as it seems to me, studied with advantage that graceful and agreeable English painter, Mr. Hook, whose "Song of the Olden Time" is hung up in the Octagon Closet, and makes a sunshine in that exceedingly shady place. The female figure is faulty, but charming (many charmers have their little faults, it is said); the old bard who is singing the song of the olden time, a most venerable, agreeable, and handsome old minstrel. In Alnaschar-like moods a man fancies himself a noble patron, and munificent rewarder of artists; in which case I should like to possess myself of the works of these two young men, and give them four times as large a price as the —— gave for pictures five times as good as theirs.

I suppose Mr. Eastlake's composition from "Comus" is the contribution in which *he* has been mulcted, in company with his celebrated brother artists, for the famous Buckingham Palace pavilion. Working for nothing is very well: but to work for a good, honest, remunerating price is, perhaps, the best way, after all. I can't help thinking that the artist's courage has failed him over his "Comus" picture. Time and pains he has given, that is quite evident. The picture is prodigiously labored, and hatched, and tickled up with a Chinese minuteness; but there is a woful lack of *vis* in the work. That poor laborer has kept his promise, has worked the given number of hours; but he has had no food all the while, and has executed his job in a somewhat faint manner. This face of the lady is pure and beautiful; but we have seen it at any time these ten years, with its red transparent shadows, its mouth in which butter wouldn't melt, and its beautiful brown-madder hair. She is getting rather tedious, that sweet, irreproachable creature, that is the fact. She may be an angel; but sky-blue, my wicked senses tell me, is a feeble sort of drink, and men require stronger nourishment.

Mr. Eastlake's picture is a prim, mystic, cruciform composition. The lady languishes in the middle; an angel is consoling her, and embracing her with an arm out of joint; little rows of cherubs stand on each side the angels and the lady, — wonderful little children, with blue or brown beady eyes, and sweet little flossy, curly hair, and no muscles or bones, as becomes such supernatural beings, no doubt. I have seen similar little darlings in the toy-shops in the Lowther Arcade for a shilling, with just such pink cheeks and round eyes, their bodies formed out of cotton wool, and their extremities veiled in silver paper. Well; it is as well, perhaps, that Etty's jovial nymphs should not come into such a company. Good Lord! how they would astonish the weak nerves of Mr. Eastlake's *précieuse* young lady!

Quite unabashed by the squeamishness exhibited in the highest quarter (as the newspapers call it), Mr. Etty goes on rejoicing in his old fashion. Perhaps he is worse than

ever this year, and despises *nec dulces amores nec choreas,*
because certain great personages are offended. Perhaps,
this year, his ladies and Cupids are a little *hasardés ;* his
Venuses expand more than ever in the line of Hottentot
beauty; his drawing and coloring are still more audacious
than they were; patches of red shine on the cheeks of his
blowzy nymphs; his idea of form goes to the verge of
monstrosity. If you look at the pictures closely (and, considering all things, it requires some courage to do so), the
forms disappear; feet and hands are scumbled away, and
distances appear to be dabs and blotches of lake and brown
and ultramarine. It must be confessed that some of these
pictures would *not* be suitable to hang up everywhere — in
a young ladies' school, for instance. But how rich and
superb is the color! Did Titian paint better, or Rubens as
well? There is a nymph and child in the left corner of
the Great Room, sitting, without the slightest fear of catching cold, in a sort of moonlight, of which the color appears
to me to be as rich and wonderful as Titian's best — "Bacchus and Ariadne," for instance — and better than Rubens's.
There is a little head of a boy in a blue dress (for once in
a way) which kills every picture in the room, out-stares
all the red-coated generals, out-blazes Mrs. Thwaites and
her diamonds (who has the place of honor); and has that
unmistakable, inestimable, indescribable mark of the GREAT
painter about it, which makes the soul of a man kindle up
as he sees it, and owns that there is Genius. How delightful it is to feel that shock, and how few are the works of
art that can give it!

The author of that sibylline book of mystic rhymes, the
unrevealed bard of the " Fallacies of Hope," is as great as
usual, vibrating between the absurd and the sublime, until
the eye grows dazzled in watching him, and can't really tell
in what region he is. If Etty's color is wild and mysterious, looking here as if smeared with the finger, and there
with the palette-knife, what can be said about Turner?
Go up and look at one of his pictures, and you laugh at
yourself and at him, and at the picture, and that wonderful
amateur who is invariably found to give a thousand pounds
for it, or more — some sum wild, prodigious, unheard-of,
monstrous, like the picture itself. All about the author of
the " Fallacies of Hope " is a mysterious extravaganza:
price, poem, purchaser, picture. Look at the latter for a
little time, and it begins to affect you too, — to mesmerize

you. It is revealed to you; and as it is said in the East the magicians make children see the sultans, carpet-bearers, tents, etc., in a spot of ink in their hands, so the magician Joseph Mallord makes you see what he likes on a board that to the first view is merely dabbed over with occasional streaks of yellow, and flicked here and there with vermilion. The vermilion blotches become little boats full of harpooners and gondolas with a deal of music going on on board. That is not a smear of purple you see yonder, but a beautiful whale, whose tail has just slapped a half-dozen whaleboats into perdition; and as for what you fancied to be a few zig-zag lines spattered on the canvas at haphazard, look! they turn out to be a ship with all her sails; the captain and his crew are clearly visible in the ship's bows: and you may distinctly see the oil-casks getting ready under the superintendence of that man with the red whiskers and the cast in his eye; who is, of course, the chief mate. In a word, I say that Turner is a great and awful mystery to me. I don't like to contemplate him too much, lest I should actually begin to believe in his poetry as well as his paintings, and fancy the " Fallacies of Hope " to be one of the finest poems in the world.

Now Stanfield has no mysticism or oracularity about him. You can see what he means at once. His style is as simple and manly as a seaman's song. One of the most dexterous, he is also one of the most careful of painters. Every year his works are more elaborated, and you are surprised to find a progress in an artist who had seemed to reach his acme before. His battle of frigates this year is a brilliant sparkling pageant of naval war; his great picture of the " Mole of Ancona," fresh, healthy, and bright as breeze and sea can make it. There are better pieces still by this painter, to my mind; one in the first room, especially, — a Dutch landscape, with a warm sunny tone upon it, worthy of Cuyp and Callcott. Who is G. Stanfield, an exhibiter, and evidently a pupil of the Royal Academician? Can it be a son of that gent? If so, the father has a worthy heir to his name and honors. G. Stanfield's Dutch picture may be looked at by the side of his father's.

Roberts has also distinguished himself and advanced in skill, great as his care had been and powerful his effects before. " The Ruins of Karnac " is the most poetical of this painter's works, I think. A vast and awful scene of gloomy Egyptian ruin! the sun lights up tremendous lines of edifices, which were only parts formerly of the enormous city of the hundred gates; long lines of camels come over the reddening desert, and camps are set by the side of the glowing pools. This is a good picture to gaze at, and to fill your eyes and thoughts with grandiose ideas of Eastern life.

This gentleman's large picture of "Jerusalem" did not satisfy me so much. It is yet very faithful; anybody who has visited this place must see the careful fidelity with which the artist has mapped the rocks and valleys, and laid down the lines of the buildings; but the picture has, to my eyes, too green and trim a look; the mosques and houses look fresh and new, instead of being mouldering, old, sun-baked edifices of glaring stone rising amidst wretchedness and ruin. There is not, to my mind, that sad fatal aspect, which the city presents from whatever quarter you view it, and which haunts a man who has seen it ever after with an impression of terror. Perhaps in the spring for a little while, at which season the sketch for this picture was painted, the country round about may look very cheerful. When we saw it in autumn, the mountains that stand round about Jerusalem were not green, but ghastly piles of hot rock, patched here and there with yellow weedy herbage. A cactus or a few bleak olive-trees made up the vegetation of the wretched gloomy landscape; whereas in Mr. Roberts's picture the valley of Jehoshaphat looks like a glade in a park, and the hills, up to the gates, are carpeted with verdure.

Being on the subject of Jerusalem, here may be mentioned with praise Mr. Hart's picture of a Jewish ceremony, with a Hebrew name I have forgotten. This piece is exceedingly bright and pleasing in color, odd and novel as a representation of manners and costume, a striking and agreeable picture. I don't think as much can be said for the same artist's "Sir Thomas More going to Execution." Miss More is crying on papa's neck, pa looks up to heaven, halberdiers look fierce, etc.: all the regular adjuncts and property of pictorial tragedy are here brought into play. But nobody cares, that is the fact; and one fancies the designer himself cannot have cared much for the orthodox historical group whose misfortunes he was depicting.

These pictures are like boys' hexameters at school. Every lad of decent parts in the sixth form has a knack of turning out great quantities of respectable verse, without blunders, and with scarce any mental labor; but these verses are not the least like poetry, any more than the great Academical paintings of the artists are like great painting. You want something more than a composition, and a set of costumes and figures decently posed and studied. If these were all, for instance, Mr. Charles Landseer's picture of "Charles I. before the Battle of Edge Hill" would be a good work of art. Charles stands at a tree before the inn-door, officers are round about, the little princes are playing with a little dog, as becomes their youth and innocence, rows of soldiers appear in red coats, nobody seems to have anything particular to do, except the royal martyr, who is looking at a bone of ham that a girl out of the inn has hold of.

Now this is all very well, but you want something more than this in an historic picture, which should have its parts, characters, varieties, and climax like a drama. You don't want the *Deus intersit* for no other purpose than to look at a knuckle of ham; and here is a piece well composed and (bating a little want of life in the figures) well drawn, brightly and pleasantly painted, as all this artist's works are, all the parts and accessories studied and executed with care and skill, and yet meaning nothing—the part of Hamlet omitted. The King in this attitude (with the bâton in his hand, simpering at the bacon aforesaid) has no more of the heroic in him than the pork he contemplates, and he deserves to lose every battle he fights. I prefer the artist's other still-life pictures to this. He has a couple more, professedly so called, very cleverly executed and capital cabinet pieces.

Strange to say, I have not one picture to remark upon taken from the "Vicar of Wakefield." Mr. Ward has a very good Hogarthian work, with some little extravagance and caricature, representing Johnson waiting in Lord Chesterfield's antechamber, among a crowd of hangers-on and petitioners, who are sulky, or yawning, or neglected, while a pretty Italian singer comes out, having evidently had a very satisfactory interview with his lordship, and who (to lose no time) is arranging another rendezvous with another admirer. This story is very well, coarsely, and humorously told, and is as racy as a chapter out of Smollett. There is a yawning chaplain, whose head is full of humor; and a pathetic episode of a widow and pretty child, in which the artist has not succeeded so well.

There is great delicacy and beauty in Mr. Herbert's picture of "Pope Gregory teaching Children to Sing." His Holiness lies on his sofa languidly beating time over his book. He does not look strong enough to use the scourge in his hands, and with which the painter says he used to correct his little choristers. Two ghostly aides-de-camp in the shape of worn, handsome, shaven, ascetic friars, stand behind the pontiff demurely; and all the choristers are in full song, with their mouths as wide open as a nest of young birds when the mother comes. The painter seems to me to have acquired the true spirit of the middle-age devotion. All his works have unction; and the prim, subdued, ascetic face, which forms the charm and mystery of the missal-illuminations, and which has operated to convert some imaginative minds from the new to the old faith.

And, by way of a wonder, behold a devotional picture from Mr. Edwin Landseer, "A Shepherd praying at a Cross in the Fields." I suppose the Sabbath church-bells are ringing from the city far away in the plain. Do you remember the beautiful lines of Uhland? —

> " Es ist der Tag des Herrn:
> Ich bin allein auf weitern Flur,
> Noch eine Morgenglocke nur,
> Und Stille nah und fern.
>
> Anbetend knie ich hier.
> O süsses Graun, geheimes Wehn,
> Als knieeten Viele ungesehn
> Und beteten mit mir.''

Here is a noble and touching pictorial illustration of them — of Sabbath repose and *recueillement* — an almost endless flock of sheep lies around the pious pastor: the sun shines peacefully over the vast fertile plain; blue mountains keep watch in the distance; and the sky above is serenely clear. I think this is the highest flight of poetry the painter has dared to take yet. The numbers and variety of attitude and expression in that flock of sheep quite startle the spectator as he examines them. The picture is a wonder of skill.

How richly the good pictures cluster at this end of the room! There is a little Mulready, of which the color blazes out like sapphires and rubies; a pair of Leslies — one called the "Heiress" — one a scene from Molière —

both delightful: — these are flanked by the magnificent nymphs of Etty, before mentioned. What school of art in Europe, or what age, can show better painters than these in their various lines ? The young men do well, but the eldest do best still. No wonder the English pictures are fetching their thousands of guineas at the sales. They deserve these great prices as well as the best works of the Hollanders.

I am sure that three such pictures as Mr. Webster's "Dame's School" ought to entitle the proprietor to pay the income tax. There is a little caricature in some of the children's faces; but the schoolmistress is a perfect figure, most admirably natural, humorous, and sentimental. The picture is beautifully painted, full of air, of delightful harmony and tone.

There are works by Creswick that can hardly be praised too much. One particularly, called "A Place to be Remembered," which no lover of pictures can see and forget. Danby's great "Evening Scene" has portions which are not surpassed by Cuyp or Claude; and a noble landscape of Dee's, among several others — a height with some trees and a great expanse of country beneath.

From the fine pictures you come to the class which are very nearly being fine pictures. In this I would enumerate a landscape or two by Collins; Mr. Leigh's "Polyphemus," of which the landscape part is very good, and only the figure questionable; and let us say Mr. Elmore's "Origin of the Guelf and Ghibelline Factions," which contains excellent passages, and admirable drawing and dexterity, but fails to strike as a whole somehow. There is not sufficient purpose in it, or the story is not enough to interest, or, though the parts are excellent, the whole is somewhere deficient.

There is very little comedy in the exhibition, most of the young artists tending to the sentimental rather than the ludicrous. Leslie's scene from Molière is the best comedy. Collins's "Fetching the Doctor" is also delightful fun. The greatest farce, however, is Chalon's picture with an Italian title, "B. Virgine col," etc. Impudence never went beyond this. The infant's hair has been curled into ringlets, the mother sits on her chair with painted cheeks and a Haymarket leer. The picture might serve for the oratory of an opera-girl.

Among the portraits, Knight's and Watson Gordon's are

the best. A "Mr. Pigeon" by the former hangs in the place of honor usually devoted to our gracious Prince, and is a fine rich state picture. Even better are there by Mr. Watson Gordon: one representing a gentleman in black silk stockings, whose name has escaped the memory of your humble servant; another, a fine portrait of Mr. De Quincey, the opium-eater. Mr. Lawrence's heads, solemn and solidly painted, look out at you from their frames, though they be ever so high placed, and push out of sight the works of more flimsy but successful practitioners. A portrait of great power and richness of color is that of Mr. Lopez by Linnell. Mr. Grant is a favorite; but a very unsound painter to my mind, painting like a brilliant and graceful amateur rather than a serious artist. But there is a quiet refinement and beauty about his female heads, which no other painter can perhaps give, and charms in spite of many errors. Is it Count d'Orsay, or is it Mr. Ainsworth, that the former has painted? Two peas are not more alike than these two illustrious characters.

In the miniature-room, Mr. Richmond's drawings are of so grand and noble a character, that they fill the eye as much as full-length canvases. Nothing can be finer than Mrs. Fry and the gray-haired lady in black velvet. There is a certain severe, respectable, Exeter-Hall look about most of this artist's pictures, that the observer may compare with the Catholic physiognomies of Mr. Herbert: see his picture of Mr. Pugin, for instance; it tells of chants and cathedrals, as Mr. Richmond's work somehow does of Clapham Common and the May Meetings. The genius of Mayfair fires the bosom of Chalon — the tea-party, the quadrille, the hairdresser, the tailor, and the flunky. All Ross's miniatures sparkle with his wonderful and minute skill; Carrick's are excellent; Thorburn's almost take the rank of historical pictures. In his picture of two sisters, one has almost the most beautiful head in the world; and his picture of Prince Albert, clothed in red and leaning on a turquoise sabre, has ennobled that fine head, and given his Royal Highness's pale features an air of sunburnt and warlike vigor. Miss Corbaux, too, has painted one of the loveliest heads ever seen. Perhaps this is the pleasantest room of the whole, for you are sure to meet your friends here; kind faces smile at you from the ivory; and features of fair creatures, oh! how ——

[Here the eccentric author breaks into a rhapsody of thirteen pages regarding No. 2576, Mrs. Major Blogg, who was formerly Miss Poddy of Cheltenham, whom it appears that Michael Angelo knew and admired. The feelings of the Poddy family might be hurt, and the jealousy of Major Blogg aroused, were we to print Titmarsh's rapturous description of that lady; nor, indeed, can we give him any further space, seeing that this is nearly the last page of the Magazine. He concludes by a withering denunciation of most of the statues in the vault where they are buried; praising, however, the children, Paul and Virginia, the head of Baily's nymph, and M'Dowall's boy. He remarks the honest character of the English countenance as exhibited in the busts, and contrasts it with Louis Philippe's head by Jones, on whom, both as a sculptor and a singer, he bestows great praise. He indignantly remonstrates with the committee for putting by far the finest female bust in the room, No. 1434, by Powers of Florence, in a situation where it cannot be seen; and, quitting the gallery finally, says he must go before he leaves town and give one more look at Hunt's "Boy at Prayers," in the Water-color Exhibition, which he pronounces to be the finest serious work of the year.]

FITZ–BOODLE PAPERS.

PROFESSIONS BY GEORGE FITZ–BOODLE.

THIRD PROFESSION.

[*Fraser's Magazine, July*, 1842.]

THE last profession is one in all respects inferior to the two preceding; is merely temporary, whereas they are for life; but has this advantage, that it may be exercised by the vulgarest man in Europe, and requires not the least previous experience or education.

It is better, unluckily, for a foreigner than an Englishman; but the latter may easily adopt it, if he have any American relations, or if he choose to call himself a citizen of the great republic. In fact, this profession simply consists in being a foreigner.

You may be ever so illiterate and low-bred, and you are all the better for the profession. Your worst social qualities will stand you instead. You should, to practise properly, be curious, talkative, abominably impudent, and forward. You should never be rebuffed because people turn their backs on you, but should attack them again and again; and depend upon it that if you are determined to know a man, he will end, out of mere weariness, by admitting you to his acquaintance.

Say that you have met a person once at a café, or tavern, and you do not know one single Englishman in the world (except the tradesmen in the nameless quarter where you were born) but this, some young fellow from college probably, who is spending his vacation abroad. Well, you know this man, and it is enough. Ask him at once for letters of introduction; say that you are a young American (for I presume the reader is an Englishman, and this character he can therefore assume more readily than any other)

wishing to travel, and ask him for letters to his family in
England. He hums and ha's, and says he will send them.
Nonsense! call the waiter to bring pens, ink, and paper;
lay them laughingly before your friend; say that now is
the best time, and almost certainly you will have the letters. He can't abuse you in the notes, because you are
looking over his shoulder. The two or three first men
upon whom you make the attempt may say that you may go
to the deuce, and threaten to kick you out of the room; —
but 'tis against the chances, this sort of ferocity. Men are
rather soft than spirited, and if they be spirited you have
only to wait until you find a soft one.

It will be as well, perhaps, while making the demand
upon your friend in the café, to produce a series of letters
directed to the Marquess of L——e, the Duke of D——,
Mr. R—— the poet, Mr. C. K——, the eminent actor now
retired, and other distinguished literary or fashionable
persons, saying that your friends in America have already
supplied you with these, but that you want chiefly introductions to private families, to see "the homes of England;" and, as Englishmen respect lords (see the remarks
in Profession II.) most likely your young café acquaintance
will be dazzled by the sight of these addresses, and will
give you letters the more willingly, saying to himself,
"Who knows, egad, but that this American may get my
sisters to L—— House?" One way or the other, you will
be sure to end by having a letter — a real letter; and as
for those you have written, why, upon my honor, I do not
think that you can do better than present some of them on
the chance; for the duke and the marquess receive so many
people at their houses, that they cannot be expected to remember all their names. Write, then, bravely at once, —

To his Grace the Duke of Dorsetshire, K. G., London.

Twenty-one Street, Boston, May, 1842.

My dear Duke, — In the friendly hospitality which you exercised
towards me on my last visit to London, I am fain to hope that you
looked somewhat to my character as an individual, as well as to my
quality as a citizen of the greatest country of the world: I, for my part,
have always retained the warmest regard for you, and shall be happy
to see you any time you come our way.

Assuming, I am sure justifiably, that your repeated assurances of regard were sincere (for I do not consider you as false, as I found the
rest of the English nobility), I send, to be under your special protection whilst in London, my dear young friend, Nahum Hodge, distinguished among us as a patriot and a poet; in the first of which

capacities he burned several farmhouses in Canada last fall, and, in the latter, has produced his celebrated work, "The Bellowings of the Buffalo," printed at Buffalo, New York, by Messrs. Bowie and Cutler, and which are far superior to any poems ever produced in the old country. Relying upon our acquaintance, I have put down your name, my dear Duke, as a subscriber for six copies, and will beg you to hand over to my young friend, Nahum, twelve dollars — the price.

He is a modest, retiring young man, as most of our young republicans are, and will want to be urged and pushed forward into good society. This, my dear fellow, I am sure you will do for me. Ask him as often as you can to dinner, and present him at the best houses you can in London. I have written to the Marquess of Sandown, reminding him of our acquaintance, and saying that you will vouch for the respectability of young Nahum, who will take the liberty of leaving his card at Sandown House. I do not wish that he should be presented at your court; for I conceive that a republican ought not to sanctify by his presence any exhibition so degrading as that of the English levee.

Nahum Hodge will call on you at breakfast time; I have told him that is the best hour to find yourself and the dear duchess at home. Give my love to her and the children, and believe me, my dear friend,

Your Lordship's most faithful Servant,
EBENEZER BROWN.

Such a letter as this will pretty surely get you admission to his Grace; and, of course, you will be left to your own resources to make yourself comfortable in the house. Do not be rebuffed if the porter says, "Not at home;" say, "You liveried varlet and slave! Do you pretend to lie in the face of a free-born American republican? Take in that note, do you hear, or I'll wap you like one of my niggers!" Those fat, over-fed men, who loll in porters' chairs, are generally timid, and your card will be sure to be received.

While a servant has gone up-stairs with it, walk into the library at once,* look at all the papers, the seals, the books on the table, the addresses of all the letters, examine the pictures, and shout out, "Here, you fat porter, come and tell me who these tarnation people are!" The man will respectfully come to you; and whatever be your fate with the family up-stairs — whether the duke says he cannot see you, or that he knows nothing of you, at least you will have had an insight into his house and pictures, and may note down everything you see.

It is not probable that he will say he knows nothing of you. He is too polite and kind-hearted for that, — nay, possibly, may recall to his mind that he once did receive an American by the name of Brown. If he only says he

* Of course, you will select a house that is not *entre cour et jardin.*

cannot see you, of course you will call again till he does;
and be sure that the porter will never dare to shut the door
on you.

You will call and call so often, that he will end by inviting you to a party. Meanwhile, you will have had your
evenings pretty well filled by invitations from the sisters
of your friend whom you met in the café at Paris — agreeable girls — say their name is Smith, and they live in Mon-
tague Place, or near Blackheath. Be sure that you tell
them all that you know the Duke of Dorsetshire, that you
have been with his Grace that morning, and so on; and not
only good old Mr. Smith, but all his circle, will take care
to invite you to as many dinners as you can possibly
devour.

Your conduct at these repasts will be perfectly simple.
Keep your eyes open, and do pretty much as you see other
people do; but never acknowledge that you are in fault if
any one presumes to blame you. Eat peas with your knife;
and, if gently taken to task about this habit by Smith (a
worthy man, who takes an interest in his "son's friend"),
say, "Well, General Jackson eats peas with his knife: and
I ain't proud. I guess General Jackson can wap any Englishman." Say this sort of thing simply and unaffectedly,
and you will be sure not to be pestered as to your mode of
conveying your food to your mouth.

Take care at dinner not to admire anything; on the contrary, if they bring you Madeira, saying, "La bless you,
taste our Madeira. My father's got some that he gave fifty
dollars a bottle for; this here ain't fit to bile for puddns."
If there are ducks, ask everybody if they have tasted can-
vas-backed ducks; oysters, say the New York oyster will
feed six men; turtle, prefer terrapin, and so on.

And don't fancy that because you are insolent and disagreeable, people will be shy of you in this country. Sir,
they like to be bullied in England, as to be bullies when
abroad. They like a man to sneer at their dinners; it
argues that you are in the habit of getting better. I have
known the lowest-bred men imaginable pass for fine fellows
by following this simple rule. Remember through life that
a man will always rather submit to insolence than resist it.

Let this be your guide, then, in your commerce with all
ranks. You will dine, of course, with your friends about
Russell Square and Greenwich, until such time as you get
a fair entry into the houses of greater people (by the way,

you will find these much more shy of dinners, and more profuse with their tea-parties, than your humbler entertainers). But, if you don't dine with them, you must keep up your credit in the other quarter of the town — make believe to dine with them. You can get a dinner for eightpence on those days, and figure in the evening party afterwards.

At the great parties, make up to that part of the room where the distinguished people are, — not the great men of the land, but the wits, mark you, — and begin talking with them at once; they will all respect you in their hearts, as they respect themselves, for being at such a grand house as that of his Grace the Duke of Dorsetshire.

The wits will, after a little, take you to the Wits' Club, the Muffinæum, where you will enter gratis as a distinguished foreigner. You can breakfast there for a shilling, have the run of the letter-paper, and will, of course, take care to date your letters from thence.

Mind, then, once put your foot into a great house, and your fortune in society is easily made. You have but to attack, people will rather yield than resist. I once knew a Kentucky man who, hearing the Marquess of Carum Gorum talking of the likelihood of grouse that year, interposed, "My lord, it must be a wonderful sight for a stranger to see a grand meeting of the aristocrats of England in the heathery hills of Scotia. What would I not give to behold such an exhibition!" The marquess smiled, shrugged, and said, "Well, sir, if you come North, you must give me a day;" and then turned on his heel. This was in March: on the fourteenth of August, Kentuck appeared with a new shooting-jacket and a double-barrelled gun, got on credit, and stayed a fortnight at Mull House.

At last, he sent in a letter, before breakfast on Sabbath morning, to Lord Carum Gorum, saying, that he knew he was trespassing beyond all measure upon his lordship's patience, but that he was a stranger in the land, his remittances from America had somehow been delayed, and the fact was, that there he was, water-logged till they came.

Lord Carum Gorum enclosed him a ten-pound note in an envelope, with a notification that a gig would be ready for him after service, and Kentuck passed a very agreeable fortnight in Edinburgh, and published in the "Buffalo's Hump" a brilliant account of his stay at the noble lord's castle.

Then, again, if you see a famous beauty, praise every one of her points outrageously in your letter to the "Buffalo's Hump" as

ON THE LADY EMILY X——,

WHO LEFT DANCING AND CAME AND TALKED TO THE POET AT THE DÉJEUNER AT C—— LODGE.

Beneath the gold acacia buds
My gentle Nora sits and broods,
Far, far away in Boston woods,
          My gentle Nora!

I see the tear-drop in her e'e,
Her bosom's heaving tenderly;
I know — I know she thinks of me,
          My darling Nora!

And where am I? My love, whilst thou
Sit'st sad beneath the acacia bough,
Where pearl's on neck, and wreath on brow,
          I stand, my Nora!

'Mid carcanet and coronet,
Where joy-lamps shine and flowers are set —
Where England's chivalry are met,
          Behold me, Nora!

In this strange scene of revelry,
Amidst this gorgeous chivalry,
A form I saw was like to thee,
          My love — my Nora!

She paused amidst her converse glad;
The lady saw that I was sad,
She pitied the poor lonely lad, —
          Dost love her, Nora?

In sooth, she is a lovely dame,
A lip of red, an eye of flame,
And clustering golden locks, the same
          As thine, dear Nora!

Her glance is softer than the dawn's,
Her foot is lighter than the fawn's,
Her breast is whiter than the swan's,
          Or thine, my Nora!

Oh, gentle breast to pity me!
Oh, lovely Ladye Emily!
Till death — till death, I'll think of thee —
          Of thee and Nora!

This sort of thing, addressed to a thin, shrivelled person of five and forty (and I declare it is as easy to write such verses as to smoke a cigar), will be sure to have its effect; and, in this way, you may live a couple of years in England very fashionably and well. By impudence you may go from one great house to another — by impudence you may get credit with all the fashionable tradesmen in London — by impudence you may find a publisher for your tour; and if with all this impudence you cannot manage to pick up a few guineas by the way, you are not the man I take you for.

And this is my last profession. In concluding the sketch, of which it is of course not necessary for me to say that the little character I have drawn out is not taken from any particular individual. No, on my honor, far from it; it is, rather, an agreeable compound of many individuals, whom it has been our fortune to see here ; and as for the story of the Marquess of Carum Gorum, it is, like the noble marquess himself, a fiction. It is a possibility, that is all; an embodiment of a good and feasible way of raising money. Perhaps gentlemen in America, where our periodicals are printed régularly, as I am given to understand, may find the speculation worth their while ; and, accordingly, it is recommended to the republican press.

To the discriminating press of this country, how shall I express my obligations for the unanimous applause which hailed my first appearance ? It is the more wonderful as, I pledge my sacred word, I never wrote a document before much longer than a laundress's bill, or the acceptance of an invitation to dinner. But enough of this egotism ; thanks for praise conferred sound like vanity ; gratitude is hard to speak of, and at present it swells the full heart of   GEORGE SAVAGE FITZ-BOODLE.

P.S. — My memoirs, and other interesting works, will appear next month; the length necessary to a discussion of the promised " Professions," having precluded the possibility of their insertion in the present number. They are of thrilling interest.

MEN'S WIVES.

No. IV.

THE ——'S WIFE.

[*Fraser's Magazine, November*, 1843.]

WE lay down on a little mound at a half-league from the city gates in a pleasant grass besprinkled with all the flowers of summer. The river went shining by us, jumping over innumerable little rocks, and by the beds of waving, whispering rushes, until it reached the old city bridge with its dismantled tower and gate, under the shadow of which sat Maximilian in his eternal punt bobbing for gudgeon. Farther on you saw the ancient city walls and ramparts, with the sentinels pacing before the blue and yellow barriers, and the blue eagle of Pumpernickel over the gate. All the towers and steeples of the town rose behind the grim bastions, under the clear blue sky; the bells were ringing as they always are, the birds in the little wood hard by were singing and chirping, the garden-houses and taverns were full of students drinking beer, and resounded with their choruses. To the right was the old fortress, with its gables and pinnacles cresting the huge hill, up which a zig-zag path toiled painfully.

"It is easier," said I, with much wisdom, "to come down that hill than to mount it." I suppose the robber-knights who inhabited Udolf of old chose the situation for that reason. If they saw a caravan in the plain here, they came down upon it with an impetus that infallibly over-set the guards of the merchants' treasure. If the dukes took a fancy to attack it, the escaladers, when they reached the top of the eminence, were so out of wind that they could be knocked over like so many penguins, and were cut down before they had rallied breath enough to cry quarter. From Udolf you could batter the town to pieces in ten minutes. What a skurry there would be if a shell fell plump into the market-place, and what a deal of eggs and butter would be smashed there! Hark! there is a bugle.

"It is the mad trumpeter," said Schneertbart. "Half the fortress is given up now to the madmen of the principality, and the other half is for the felons. See! there is a gang of them at work on the road yonder."

"Is Udolf any relation of the Castle of Udolpho?"

"It has its mysteries," said Milchbrod, nodding his head solemnly, "as well as that castle which Lord Byron has rendered immortal. Was it not Lord Byron?"

"Caspar Milchbrod, I believe it was," answered I. "Do you know any of them? If you have a good horrid story of ghosts, robbers, cut-throats and murders, pray tell it; we have an hour yet to dinner, and murder is my delight!"

"I shall tell you the story of Angelica, the wife of the — Hum!" said he.

"Whose wife?"

"That is the point of the story. You may add it to your histories of 'Men's Wives,' that are making such a sensation all over England and Germany. Listen!"

Schneertbart, at the mention of the story, jumped up as if he would make off, but, being fat and of an indolent turn, he thought better of it, and, pulling the flap of his cap over his face, and sprawling out on his back, like the blue spread-eagle over the tower-gate, incontinently fell asleep.

Milchbrod, darting at him a look of scorn, began the following history : —

"In the time of Duke Bernard the Invincible, whose victory over Sigismund of Kalbsbratia obtained him the above well-merited title (for though he was beaten several times afterwards, yet his soul was encouraged to the end, and, therefore, he was denominated Invincible with perfect justice). In Duke Bernard's time the fortress of Udolf was much more strongly garrisoned than at present, though a prison then as now. The great hall, where you may now see the poor madmen of the duchy eating their humble broth from their wooden trenchers and spoons, was the scene of many a gallant feast, from which full butts of wine returned empty; fat oxen disappeared, all except the bone; at which noble knights got drunk by the side of spotless ladies, and were served off gold and out of jewelled flagons by innumerable pages and domestics in the richest of liveries. A sad change is it now, my friend. When I think the livery of the place is an odious red and yellow serge, that the servants of the castle have their heads shaved and a chain to their legs instead of round their necks, and when I think that the glories and festivities of Udolf are now passed away forever! Oh! golden days of chivalry, a descendant of the Milchbrods may well deplore you!

"The court where they beat hemp now was once a stately place of arms, where warriors jousted and knights ran at the ring. Ladies looked on from the windows of the great hall and from the castellan's apartments, and, though the castle was gay and lordly as a noble castle should be, yet were not the purposes of security and punishment forgotten; under the great hall were innumerable dungeons, vaults, and places of torture, where the enemies of our dukes suffered the punishment of their crimes. They have been bricked up now for the most part, for what I cannot but call a foolish philanthropy found these dungeons too moist and too dark for malefactors of the present day, who must, forsooth, have whitewashed rooms and dry beddings, whilst our noble ancestors were fain to share their cell with toads, serpents, and darkness; and sometimes instead of flock mattresses and iron bedsteads, to stretch their limbs on the rack. Civilization, my dear sir" —

Here a loud snort from Schneertbart possibly gave Milchbrod a hint that he was digressing too much; and, omitting his opinions about civilization, he proceeded.

"In Duke Bernard's time, then, this prison was in its most palmy and flourishing state. The pains of the rack and the axe were at that time much more frequent than at present, and the wars of religion in which Germany was plunged, and in which our good duke, according to his convictions, took alternately the Romanist and the Reformed side, brought numbers of our nobles into arms, into conspiracies and treasons, and consequently into prison and torture-chambers. I mention these facts to show, that as the prison was a place of some importance and containing people of rank, the guardianship was naturally confided to a person in whom the duke could place the utmost confidence. Have you ever heard of the famous Colonel Dolchenblitz?"

I confessed I had not.

"Dolchenblitz, as a young man, was one of the most illustrious warriors of his day; and, as a soldier, captain, and afterwards colonel of free companies, had served under every flag in every war and in every country in Europe. He,

under the French, conquered the Milanese; he then passed
over into the Spanish service, and struck down King
Francis at Pavia with his hammer-of-arms; he was the
fourth over the wall of Rome when it was sacked by the
constable, and having married and made a considerable
plunder there he returned to his native country, where he
distinguished himself alternately in the service of the Emperor and the Reformed princes. A wound in the leg pre-
vented him at length from being so active in the field as he
had been accustomed to be; and Duke Bernard the Invincible, knowing his great bravery, his skill, his unalterable
fidelity (which was indestructible as long as his engagement lasted), and his great cruelty and sternness, chose
him very properly to be governor of his state, fortress, and
prison.

"The lady whom Colonel Dolchenblitz married was a
noble and beautiful Roman, and his wooing of her, it would
appear, was somewhat short. 'I took the best method of
winning Frau Dolchenblitz's heart,' he would say. 'I am
an ugly old trooper, covered with scars, fond of drink and
dice, with no more manners than my battle-horse, and she,
forsooth, was in love with a young countlet who was as
smooth as herself, and as scented as a flower garden; but
when my black-riders dragged her father and brother into
the court-yard, and had ropes ready to hang them at the
gate, I warrant my Angelica found that she loved me better
than her scented lover; and so I saved the lives of my
father and brother-in-law, and the dear creature consented
to be mine.'

"Of this marriage there came but one child, a daughter;
and the Roman lady presently died, not altogether sound
in her senses, it was said, from the treatment to which her
rough husband subjected her. The widower did not pretend to much grief; and the daughter, who had seen her
mother sneered at, sworn at, beaten daily when her gallant
father was in liquor, had never had any regard for her
poor mother; and, in her father's quarrels with his lady,
used from her earliest years to laugh and rejoice and take
the old trooper's side. You may imagine from this," cried
Milchbrod, "that she was not brought up in a very amiable
school. Ah!" added the youth, with a blush, "how unlike
was she, in all respects but in beauty, to my Lischen!

"There is still in the castle gallery a picture of the
Angelica, who bore the reputation at eighteen of being one

of the most beautiful women in the world. She is represented in a dress of red velvet looped up at the sleeves and breast with jewels, her head is turned over her shoulder, looking at you, and her long yellow hair flows over her neck. Her eyes are blue, her eyebrows of an auburn color, her lips open and smiling; but that smile is so diabolical, and those eyes have such an infernal twinkle, that it is impossible to look at the picture without a shudder, and I declare, for my part, that I would not like to be left alone in a room with the portrait and its horrid glassy eyes always following and leering after you.

"From a very early age her father would always insist upon having her by his side at table, where, I promise you, the conversation was not always as choice as in a nunnery, and where they drank deeper than at a hermitage. After dinner the dice would be brought, and the little girl often called the mains and threw for her father, and he said she always brought him luck when she did so. But this must have been a fancy of the old soldier's, for, in spite of his luck, he grew poorer and poorer, all his plunder taken in the wars went gradually down the throat of the dice-box, and he was presently so poor that his place as governor of the prison was his only means of livelihood, and that he could only play once a month when his pay came in.

"In spite of his poverty and his dissolute life and his ill-treatment of his lady, he was inordinately proud of his marriage; for the truth is, the lady was of the Colonna family. There was not a princess of Germany who, in the matter of birth, was more haughty than Madame Angelica, the governor's daughter; and the young imp of Lucifer, when she and her father sat at drink and dice with the lance-knights and officers, always took the pas of her own father, and had a raised seat for herself, while her company sat on benches. The old soldier admired this pride in his daughter, as he admired every other good or bad quality she possessed. She had often seen the prisoners flogged in the court-yard, and never turned pale. 'Par Dieu!' the father would say, 'the girl has a gallant courage!' If she lost at dice she would swear in her shrill voice as well as any trooper, and the father would laugh till the tears ran down his old cheeks. She could not read very well, but she could ride like an Amazon; and Count Sprinboch (the court chamberlain, who was imprisoned ten years at Udolf for treading on the duchess-dowager's gouty toe), taking a fancy to the child, taught her to dance and to sing to the mandolin, in both of which accomplishments she acquired great skill.

"Such were the accomplishments of the Angelica, when, at about the sixteenth year of her age, the court came to reside in the town; for the Imperialists were in possession of our residence, and here, at a hundred miles away from them, Duke Bernard the Invincible was free from molestation. On the first public day the governor of the fort came down in his litter to pay his respects to the sovereign, and his daughter, the lovely Angelica, rode a white palfrey, and ambled most gracefully at his side.

"The appearance of such a beauty set all the court-gallants in a flame. Not one of the maids of honor could compare with her, and their lovers left them by degrees. The steep road up to the castle yonder was scarce ever without one or more cavaliers upon it pinked out in their best, as gay as chains and feathers could make them, and on their way to pay their court to the Lily of Udolf; the lily — the Tiger-lily, forsooth! But man, foolish man, only looked to the face, and not to the soul, as I did when I selected my Lischen.

"The drinking and dicing now went on more gayly than it had done for many years: for when young noblemen sit down to play with a lady we know who it is that wins, and Madame Angelica was, pardi, not squeamish in gaining their money. It was, 'Fair sir, I will be double or quits with you.' 'Noble baron, I will take you three to one.' 'Worthy count, I will lay my gold chain against your bay gelding.' And so forth. And by the side of the lovely daughter sat the old father, tossing the drink off, and flinging the dice, and roaring, swearing, and singing, like a godless old trooper as he was. Then, of mornings there would be hunting and hawking parties, and it was always who should ride by the Angelica's side, and who should have the best horse, and the finest doublet, and leap the biggest ditch, over which she could jump, I warrant you, as well as the best rider there. The staid matrons and ladies of the court avoided this siren, but what cared she so long as the men were with her? The duke did not like to see his young men thus on the road to ruin; but his advice and his orders were all in vain. The Erb Prinz himself, Prince Maurice, was caught by the infection, and having fallen desperately in love with the Angelica, and made her great presents of jewels and horses, was sent by his father to Wittenberg, where he was told to forget his love in his books.

"There was, however, in the duke's service, and an especial friend and favorite of the hereditary prince, a young gentleman by the name of Ernst von Waldberg, who, though sent back to the university along with the young duke, had not the heart to remain there, for, indeed, his heart was at Castle Udolf with the bewitching Angelica. This unlucky and simple Ernst was the most passionate of all the Angelica's admirers, and had committed a thousand extravagances for her sake. He had ridden into Hungary and brought back a Turkish turban for her, with an unbeliever's head in it, too. He had sold half his father's estate and bought a jewel with it, with which he presented her. He had wagered a hundred gold crowns against a lock of her hair, and, having won, caused a casket to be made with the money, on which was engraved an inscription by the court poet, signifying that the gold within the casket was a thousand times more valuable than the gold whereof it was made, and that one was the dross of the earth, whereas the other one came from an angel.

"An angel, indeed! If they had christened that Angelica Diabolica, they would have been nearer the mark; but the devils were angels once, and one of these fallen ones was Angelica.

"When the poor young fellow had well-nigh spent his all in presents and jewels for Angelica, or over the tables and dice with her father, he bethought him that he would ask the young lady in marriage, and so humbly proffered his suit.

"'How much land have you, my Lord Ernst?' she said, in a scornful way.

"'Alas! I am but a younger son. My brother Max has the family estate, and I but an old tower and a few acres, which came to me from my mother's family,' answered Ernst. But he did not say how his brother had often paid his debts and filled his purse, and how many of the elder's crowns had been spent over the dice-table and had gone to enrich Angelica and her father.

"'But you must have great stores of money,' continued she, 'for what gentleman of the court spends so gallantly as you?'

"'It is my brother's money,' said Ernst gloomily, 'and

I will ask him for no more of it. But I have enough left
to buy a horse and sword, and with these, if you will but
be mine, I vow to win fame and wealth enough for any
princess in Christendom.'

" 'A horse and sword!' cried Angelica; 'a pretty fortune, forsooth. Any one of my father's troopers has as
much! You win fame and wealth; you a fitting husband
for the best lady in Christendom ? Psha! Look at what
you have done as yet, Sir Ernst, and brag no more. You
had a property, and you spent it in three months upon a
woman you never saw before. I have no fancy to marry a
beggar, or to trust to an elder brother for charity, or to
starve in rags with the rats in your family tower. Away
with you, Sir Spendthrift, buy your horse and sword if you
will, and go and travel and keep yourself and your horse;
you will find the matter hard enough without having a
wife at your pillion.'

"And, so saying, she called her huntsmen and hawks,
and, with a gay train of gentlemen behind her, went out
into the woods, as usual, where Diana herself, had she been
out a-hunting that day, could not have been more merry,
nor looked more beautiful and royal.

"As for Ernst, when he found how vain his love was,
and that he had only been encouraged by Angelica in order
to be robbed and cast away, a deep despair took possession
of the poor lad's soul, and he went in anguish back to his
brother's house, who tried, but in vain, to console him;
for, having stayed a while with his brother, Ernst one
morning suddenly took horse and rode away never to return. The next thing that his weeping elder brother heard
of him was that he had passed into Hungary, and had
been slain by the Turk before Buda. One of his comrades
in the war brought back a token from Ernst to his brother
Max — it was the gold casket which contained the hair of
Angelica.

"Angelica no more wept at receiving this news than she
had done at Ernst's departure. She hunted with her gallants as before, and on the very night after she had heard
of poor young Ernst's death appeared at supper in a fine
gold chain and scarlet robe he had given her. The hard-
ness of her heart did not seem to deter the young gentlemen of Saxony from paying court to her, and her cruelty
only added to the universal fame of her beauty.

"Though she had so many scores of lovers, and knew

well enough that these do not increase with age, she had
never as yet condescended to accept of one for a husband,
and others, and of the noblest sort, might be mentioned,
who, as well as Ernst, had been ruined and forsaken by her.
A certain witch had told her that she should marry a nobleman who should be the greatest swordsman of his day.
Who was the greatest warrior of Germany? I am not
sure that she did not look for King Gustave to divorce his
wife and fall on his knees to her, or for dark Wallenstein
to conjure the death of his princess and make Angelica the
lady of Sagan. Thus time went on. Lovers went up the
hill of Udolf, and, in sooth! lovers came down: the lady
there was still the loveliest in the land, and when the
crown prince came home from Wittenberg she would still
have been disposed to exercise her wiles upon him, but that
it was now too late, for the wise duke, his highness's
father, had married the young lord to a noble princess of
Bavaria, in whose innocence he forgot the dangerous and
wicked Angelica. I promise you the lady of Udolf sneered
prettily at the new princess, and talked of his 'highness's
humpbacked Venus;' all which speeches were carried to
court, and inspired the duke with such a fury, that he was
for shutting up Angelica as a prisoner in her father's own
castle; but wise counsellors intervened, and it was thought
best to let the matter drop. For, indeed, comparisons between the royal princess and the lady of Udolf would have
been only unfavorable to the former, who, between ourselves, was dark of complexion and not quite so straight
either in the back as her rival.

"Presently there came to court Max, Ernst's elder
brother, a grave man, of a sharp and bitter wit, given to
books and studies, but, withal, gentle and generous to the
poor. No one knew how generous until he died, when
there followed, weeping, such crowds of the humbler sort
his body to the grave as never was known in that day, for
the good old nobles were rather accustomed to take than
to give, and the Lord Max was of the noblest and richest
of all the families in the duchy.

"Calm as he was, yet, strange to say, he too was speedily
caught in the toils of Angelica, and seemed to be as much
in love with her as his unfortunate brother had been. 'I
do not wonder at Ernst's passion for such an angelical
being,' he said, 'and can fancy any man dying in despair
of winning her.' These words were carried quickly to the

lady of Udolf, and the next court party where she met
Max she did not fail to look towards him with all the fas-
cinations of her wonderful eyes, from which Max, blushing
and bowing, retreated completely overcome. You might
see him on his gray horse riding up the mountain to Udolf
as often as his brother had been seen on his bay; and of
all the devoted slaves Angelica had in her court this unhappy man became the most subservient. He forsook his
books and calm ways of life to be always by the enchantress's side; he, who had never cared for sport, now, for
the pleasure of following Angelica, became a regular Nim-
rod of the chase; and although, up to the time of his acquaintance with her, he had abhorred wine and gaming, he
would pass nights now boozing with the old drunkard, and
playing at the dice with him and his daughter.

"There was something in his love for her that was quite
terrible. Common, light-minded gallants of the day do
not follow a woman as Max did, but, if rebuffed by one, fly
off to another; or, if overcome by a rival, wish him good
luck and betake themselves elsewhere. This ardent gentleman, loving for the first time, seemed resolved to have no
rival near him, and Angelica could scarcely pardon him for
the way in which he got rid of her lovers one after another.
There was Baron Herman, who was much in her good
graces, and was sent away to England by Max's influence
with the duke; there was Count Augustus, with whom he
picked a quarrel, and whom he wounded in a duel. All the
world deplored the infatuation of this brave gentleman,
and the duke himself took him to task for suffering himself to be enslaved by a woman who had already been so
fatal to his family.

"He placed himself as such a dragon before her gate
that he drove away all wavering or faint-hearted pretenders
to her hand; and it seemed pretty clear that Angelica, if
she would not marry him, would find it very difficult to
marry another. And why not marry him? He was noble,
rich, handsome, wise, and brave. What more could a lady
require in a husband? and could the proud Angelica herself expect a better fate? 'In my mother's lifetime,' Max
said, 'I cannot marry. She is old now, and was much
shaken by the death of Ernst, and she would go to the
grave with a curse on her lips for me did she think I was
about to marry the woman who caused my brother's death.'

"Thus, although he did not actually offer his hand to

her, he came to be considered generally as her accepted
lover; and the gallants who before had been ever around
her fell off one by one.   I am not sure whether Madame
Angelica was pleased with the alteration, and whether she
preferred the adoration of a single heart to the love of
many, to which she had been accustomed before.   Perhaps,
however, her reasoning was this: 'I am sure of Max; he is
a husband of whom any woman might be proud; and very
few nobles in Germany are richer or of better blood than
he.   He cannot marry for some time to come.   Well, I am
young, and can afford to wait; and if, meanwhile, there
present itself some better name, fortune, and person than
Max's, I am free to choose, and can fling him aside like his
brother before him.'   Meantime, thought she, I can dress
Max to the ménage of matrimony; which meant that, that
she could make a very slave of him, as she did; and he
was as obedient to her caprice and whims as her page or
her waiting-woman.

"The entertainments which were given at Castle Udolf
were rather more liked by the gentlemen than by the ladies,
who had little love for a person like Angelica, the daughter
of a man only ennobled yesterday — a woman who lived,
laughed, rode, gambled, in the society of men as familiarly
as if she had a beard on her chin and a rapier at her side;
and, above all, a woman who was incomparably handsomer
than the handsomest of her rivals.   Thus ladies' visits to
her were not frequent; nor, indeed, did she care much for
their neglect.   She was not born, she said, to spin flax;
nor to embroider cushions; nor to look after house-maids
and scullions, as ladies do.   She received her male guests
as though she were a queen, to whom they came to pay
homage, and little cared that their wives stayed at home.

"At one of her entertainments Max appeared with two
masks (it was the custom of those days for persons to go
so disguised; and you would see at a court-ball half the
ladies and men, especially the ugly of the former sex, so
habited); the one, coming up to Angelica, withdrew his
vizard, and she saw it was her ancient admirer the prince,
who stayed for a while, besought her, laughing, to keep his
visit a secret from the princess, and then left her to Max
and the other mask; but the other did not remove his covering, though winningly entreated thereto by Angelica.

"The mask and Max, after a brief conversation with the
lady of the castle, sat down to the tables to play at dice.

And Max called presently to Angelica to come and play for him, to which invitation, nothing loath, she acceded. . That dice-box has a temptation for woman as well as man, and woe to both if they yield to it !

" 'Who is the mask ? ' asked Angelica of Max. But Max answered that his name was for the present a mystery.

" 'Is he noble ? ' said the scornful lady.

" 'Did he not come hither with me and the prince ; and am I in the habit of consorting with other than nobles ? ' replied Max, as haughty as she. 'The mask is a nobleman, ay, and a soldier, who has done more execution in his time than any man in the army.' That he was rich was very clear: his purse was well filled ; whether he lost or won, he laughed with easy gayety ; and Angelica could see under his mask how all the time of the play his fierce, brilliant eyes watched and shone on her.

"She and Max, who played against the stranger, won from him a considerable sum. 'I would lose such a sum,' said he, 'every night, if you, fair lady, would but promise to win it from me ; ' and, asking for, and having been promised, a revenge, he gallantly took his leave.

"He came the next night, and the partners against him had the same good luck ; a third and a fourth night Angelica received him, and, as she always won, and as he was gay at losing as another is at winning, and was always ready to laugh and joke with her father, or to utter compliments to herself, Angelica began to think the stranger one of the most agreeable of men.

"She began to grudge, too, to Max, some of his winnings; or, rather, she was angry both that he should win and that he should not win enough: for Max would stop playing in the midst, as it seemed, of a vein of good luck ; saying that enough was won and lost for the night ; that play was the amusement of gentlemen, not their passion nor means of gain : whereon the mask would gather up his crowns ; and, greatly to the annoyance of Angelica, the play would cease.

" 'If I could play with him alone,' thought she, 'there is no end to the sums which I might win of this stranger; and money we want, Heaven knows ; for my father's pay is mortgaged thrice over to the Jews, and we owe ten times as much as we can pay.'

"She found no great difficulty in managing an interview with the stranger alone. He was always willing, he said,

to be at her side ; and Max being called at this time into
the country, the pair met by themselves, or in the company
of the tipsy old governor of Udolf, who counted for no
more than an extra flagon in the room, and who would have
let his daughter play for a million, or sit down to a match
with the foul fiend himself, were she so minded ; and here
the mask and Angelica used to pass many long evenings
together.

"But her lust of gain was properly punished ; for when
Max was gone, instead of winning, as she had been wont
to do in his company, Fortune seemed now to desert her,
and she lost night after night. Nor was the mask one of
the sort of players who could be paid off by a smile, as
some gallants had been ; or who would take a ringlet as a
receipt for a hundred crowns ; or would play on credit, as
Angelica would have done, had he been willing. 'Fair
lady,' said he, 'I am too old a soldier to play my ducats
against smiles, though they be from the loveliest lips in
the world ; that which I lose I pay ; that which I win I
take. Such is always the way with us in camp ; and
"donner und blitz ! " that is the way I like best.' So the
day Angelica proposed to play him on credit he put up his
purse, and, laughing, took his leave. The next day she
pawned a jewel, and engaged him again ; and, in sooth, he
went off laughing, as usual, his loud laugh, with the price
of the emerald in his pocket.

"When they were alone, it must be said that the mask
made no difficulty to withdraw his vizard, and showed a
handsome, pale, wild face ; with black, glaring eyes ; sharp
teeth, and black hair and beard. When asked what he
should be called, he said, 'Call me Wolfgang ; but, hist ! I
am in the imperial service. The duke would seize me were
he to know that I was here ; for,' added he, with a horrid
grin, 'I slew a dear friend of his in battle.' He always
grinned, did Herr Wolfgang ; he laughed a hundred times
a day, ay, and drank much, and swore more. There was
something terrible about him ; and he loved to tell terrible
stories of the wars, in which he could match for horror and
cruelty Col. Dolchenblitz himself.

"'This is the man I would have for thy husband, girl,'
said he to his daughter ; 'he is a thousand times better
than your puling courtiers and pale bookworms ; a fellow
that can drink his bottle, and does not fear the devil himself ; and can use his sword to carve out for himself any

fortune to which he may be minded. Thou art but a child
to him in play. See how he takes your ducats from you,
and makes the dice obey him. Cease playing with him,
girl, or he will ruin us else; and so fill me another cup of
wine.'

"It was in the bottom of the flagon that the last words
of the old man's speeches used commonly to end; and I
am not sure that Angelica was not prepared to think the
advice given a very good one; for it was in the nature of
this lovely girl to care for no man. But it seemed to her,
that in daring and wickedness this man was a match for
her; and she only sighed that he should be noble and rich
enough, and that then she might make him her own. For
he dazzled her imagination with stories of great leaders of
the day, the honors they won, and the wealth they obtained.
' Think of Wallenstein,' said he, ' but a humble page in a
lady's house; a prince now, and almost a sovereign. Tilly
was but a portionless Flemish cadet; and think of the
plunder of Magdeburg.'

" ' I wish I had shared it,' said Angelica.

" ' What! and your father a Protestant ? '

" ' Psha!' replied the girl. At which Herr Wolfgang and
her father would burst into a hoarse laugh, and swear, with
loud oaths, that she deserved to be a queen; and would so
drink her grace's health in many a bumper. And then
they would fall to the dice again; and Signor Wolfgang
would win the last crown-piece in the purse of either father
or daughter, and at midnight would take his leave. And a
wonder was, that no one knew whence he came or how he
left the castle; for the sentry at the gate never saw him
pass or enter.

"He would laugh when asked how. ' Psha!' he would
say, ' I am all mystery; and I will tell, as a secret, that when
I come or go I turn myself into a bird, and fly in and out.'

"And so, though he could not write his name, and had
no more manners than a trooper, and though he won every
penny of Angelica's money from her, the girl had a greater
respect and terror for him than for any man alive; and he
made more way in her heart in a fortnight than many a
sighing lover would do in ten years.

"Presently, Max returned from his visit to the country;
and Angelica began to make comparisons between his calm,
cold, stately, sneering manner and the honest daring of
Herr Wolfgang his friend. ' It is a pity,' thought she,

'that he should have the fine estate who could live on a
book and a crust. If Herr Wolfgang had Max's wealth, he
would spend it like a prince, and his wife would be the
first lady in Germany.'

"Max came to invite Angelica to his castle of Waldberg;
it was prepared to receive her as to receive a sovereign.
She had never seen anything more stately than the gardens,
or more costly than the furniture; and the lackeys in
Max's livery were more numerous and more splendid than
those who waited on the duke himself. He took her over
his farms and villages; it was a two-days' journey. He
showed her his stores of plate, and his cellars, the innumerable horses in the stables, and flocks and cattle in the
fields. As she saw all these treasures, her heart grew
colder towards Wolfgang; and she began to think that
Max would be a better husband for her. But Herr Wolfgang did not seem much cast down, though she bestowed
scarce a word upon him all day.

"'Would you take these lands and their lord, lady fair?'
whispered Max to Angelica, as they were riding home.

"'That would I!' cried she, smiling in triumph; and
holding out her hand to Max, who, kissing it very respectfully, never quitted her side that day.

"She had now only frowns for Herr Wolfgang, to whom
she had been so gracious hitherto; and at supper that day,
or at play afterwards, she scarce deigned to say a word to
him. But he laughed, and shouted, and drank his wine as
before. They played deep; but Max, the most magnificent
of hosts, had always a casket filled with gold by the side
of Angelica; who, therefore, little cared to lose.

"The next day she spent in going over the treasury of
the castle, and the various chambers in it. There was one
room which she passed, but did not enter. 'That was
Ernst's room,' said Max, looking very gloomy. 'My lord,
what a frown!' said Angelica; 'can I bear a husband who
frowns so?' and quickly passed into another chamber.
At the end of the day came the dice as usual. Angelica
could not live without them. They played, and Herr Wolfgang lost a very heavy sum, 5000 crowns. But he laughed,
and bade Max make out an order on his intendant, and
signed it with his name.

"'I can write no more than that,' said he; 'but 'tis
enough for a gentleman. To-morrow, Sir Max, you will
give me my revenge?'

" 'To-morrow,' said Max, 'I will promise not to balk you, and will play for any stake you will.' And so they parted.

"The day after many lords and ladies began to arrive, and in the evening, to supper, came over, from a hunting-lodge he had in the neighborhood, his highness the hereditary prince and his princess, who were served at a table alone, Max waiting on them. 'When this castle is mine,' said Angelica, 'I will be princess here, and my husband shall act the lackey to no duke in Christendom.'

"Dice and music were called as usual. 'Will your highness dance or play?' But his highness preferred dancing, as he was young and active; and her highness preferred dancing too, for she was crooked and out of shape. The prince led out Lady Angelica; she had never looked more beautiful, and swam through the dance in a royal style indeed.

"As they were dancing, people came to say, 'The Lord Max and Herr Wolfgang are at the dice, playing very heavy stakes.' And so it was; and Angelica, who was as eager for play as a Turk for opium, went presently to look at the players, around whom there was already a crowd wondering.

"But, much as she loved play, Angelica was frightened at the stakes played by Max and Wolfgang; for moderate as the Lord Max had been abroad, at home it seemed to be a point of honor with him to be magnificent, and he said he would refuse no stake that was offered to him.

" 'Three throws for 10,000 crowns,' said Wolfgang. 'Make out an order for my intendant if I lose, and I will sign it with my mark.'

" 'Three throws for 10,000 crowns! — Done!' answered Max. He lost. 'The order, Herr Wolfgang, must be on my intendant now, and your Austrian woods will not have to suffer. Give me my revenge!'

" 'Twenty thousand crowns against your farm and woods of Avenback.'

" 'They are worth only eighteen, but I said I would refuse you nothing, and cry done!' Max tossed, and lost the woods of Avenback.

" 'Have you not played enough, my lords, for to-day?' said Angelica, somewhat frightened.

" 'No!' shouted Wolfgang, with his roaring laugh. 'No! in the devil's name, let us go on. I feel myself in the vein, and have Lord Max's word that he will take any bet of mine. I will play you 20,000 crowns and your farm — my farm — against your barony and village Weinheim.'

"'Lord Max, I entreat — I command you not to play!' cried Angelica.

"'Done!' said Max. 'Weinheim against the crowns and the farm.' He lost again.

"In an hour this unhappy gentleman lost all the property that his forefathers had been gathering for centuries; his houses and lands, his cattle and horses, his plate, arms, and furniture. Laughing and shouting, Wolfgang still pressed him.

"'I have no more,' said Max, 'you have my all; — but stay,' said he, 'I have one thing more. Here is my bride, the Lady Angelica.'

"'A hundred thousand crowns against her!' shouted Wolfgang.

"'Fool!' said Angelica, turning scornfully on Max, 'do you think I will marry a beggar? I said I would take the lord of these lands,' added she, blushing, and gazing on Wolfgang.

"'He is at your feet, lady,' said Wolfgang, going down on his knee; and the prince at this moment coming into the room, Max said bitterly, 'I brought you, my lord, to be present at a marriage, and a marriage there shall be. Here is the lord of Waldberg who weds the Lady Angelica.'

"'Ho! a chaplain — a chaplain!' called the prince: and there was one at hand, and before almost Angelica could say ' yea' or 'nay,' she was given away to Herr Wolfgang, and the service was read, and the contract signed by the witnesses, and all the guests came to congratulate her.

"'As the friend of poor, dead Ernst,' said the prince, 'I thank you for not marrying Max.'

"'The humpbacked Venus congratulates you,' said the princess, with a courtesy and a sneer.

"'I have lost all, but have still a marriage-present to make to the Lady Angelica,' said Max; and he held out a gold casket, which she took. It was that one in which Ernst had kept her hair, and which he had worn at his death.

"Angelica flung down the casket in a rage.

"'Am I to be insulted in my own castle,' she said, 'and on my own marriage-day? Prince — Princess — Max of

Waldberg — beggar of Waldberg, I despise and scorn you all! When it will please you to leave this house, you are welcome. Its doors will gladly open to let you out. My Lord Wolfgang, I must trust to your sword to revenge any insults that may be passed on a woman who is too weak to defend herself.'

"'Any one who insults you insults me,' said Wolfgang, at which the prince burst into a laugh.

"'Coward!' said Angelica, 'your princedom saves your manhood. In any other country but your own you would not dare to act as you do.' And so saying, and looking as fierce as a boar at bay, glaring round at the circle of staring courtiers, and forgetting her doubts and fears in her courage and hatred, she left the room on Wolfgang's arm.

"'It is a gallant woman, by heaven!' said the prince.

"The old governor of Udolf had not been present at the festival, which had ended so unluckily for the feast-giver, Herr Max, and in Angelica's sudden marriage. Certain Anabaptist rogues, who had been making a disturbance in the duchy, had been taken prisoners of late, and after having been tortured and racked for some six months, had been sentenced to death, as became the dogs; and, meanwhile, until their execution, were kept, with more than ordinary precautions, in Castle Udolf, for many of their people were still in the country, and thoughts of a rescue apprehended. The day, at last, was fixed for their death, — some three days after the sudden wedding of the Lady Angelica.

"In those three days she had ridden again over the farm and orchards; she had examined all the treasures and furniture of her castle once more. At night she feasted with her spouse, sitting at the high table, which poor Max had prepared for the prince and princess, and causing the servants and pages to serve her upon bended knees.

"'Why do these menials look so cold upon their mistress and lord?' asked she.

"'Marry,' said Wolfgang, 'the poor devils have served the Waldberg family since they were born: they are only the more faithful for their sorrow.'

"'I will have yonder old scowling seneschal scourged by the huntsmen to-morrow,' said Angelica.

"'Do!' said Wolfgang, laughing wildly; 'it will be an

amusement to you, for you will be alone all to-morrow, sweet Angelica.'

" ' And why alone, sir ? ' said she.

" 'I am called to the city on urgent business.'

" ' And what is the business which calls you away alone ? '

" Her husband would not say. He said it was a state secret, which did not concern women. She replied that she was no child, and would know it. He only laughed, and laughed louder as she burst into a fury; and when she became quite white with rage, and clinched her little fists, and ground her teeth, and grasped at the knife she wore in her girdle, he lashed the knife out of her hand with a cut of his riding-rod, and bade her women carry her away. 'Look to my lady,' said he, 'and never leave her. Her mother was mad, and she has a touch of the malady.' And so he left her, and was off by break of day.

" At break of day Angelica was up too; and no sooner had her husband's horses left the court-yard of the castle, than she called for her own, and rode towards the city in the direction in which he had gone. Great crowds of people were advancing towards the town, and she remembered, for the first time, that an execution was about to take place. There had not been one for seven years, so peaceable was our country then; there was not even an executioner in the duke's service, for the old man had died, and no other had been found to take his place. 'I will see this at any rate,' said Angelica; for an execution was her delight, and she remembered every circumstance of the last with the utmost accuracy.

" As she was spurring onwards she overtook a company of horsemen. It was the young prince and his suite, among whom was riding Lord Max, who took off his cap and saluted her.

" ' Make way for the Lady Angelica ! ' cried one.

" 'Health to the blushing bride ! ' said the prince. ' What, so soon tired of billing and cooing at Waldberg ? '

" 'I hope your grace found the beds soft and the servants obedient,' said Max. 'They had my parting instructions.'

" 'They had the instructions of their own mistress,' replied Angelica. 'I pray you let me pass on to my husband, Lord Wolfgang.'

"'The Lord Wolfgang will be with you anon,' said the prince. 'We were here on the watch for you and him, and to pay our *devoirs* to the loveliest of brides.'

"' An execution is just such a festival as becomes your ladyship. Make way there! Place for the Lady Angelica! Here is the gallery from which you can see the whole ceremony. The people will be here anon.' And, almost in spite of herself, Angelica was led up into a scaffold from which the dismal preparations for the death-scene were quite visible.

"Presently the trumpets blew from Udolf. The men-at-arms and their victims came winding down the hills. Old Dolchenblitz leading the procession, armed, on his gray charger. 'Look at the victims,' said some one by Angelica's side, 'they are as calm as if they were going to a feast.' 'See, here comes the masked executioner,' said another, 'who bought his life upon these terms.'

"'He is a noble,' whispered Max to Angelica, 'and he is the greatest swordsman in Europe.' Angelica did not reply, but trembled very much.

"Singing their psalms, the Anabaptists mounted the scaffold. The first took his place in the chair, and the executioner did his terrible work. 'Here is the head of a traitor,' said the executioner.

"'You recognize your husband's voice, noble Lady Angelica,' said Max.

"She gave a loud scream and fell down as if shot. The people were too much excited by the spectacle to listen to her scream. The rest of the executions went on; but of these she saw nothing. She was carried home to Udolf raving mad. And so it was that Max of Waldberg revenged his brother's death. They say he was never the same man afterwards, and repented bitterly of his severity; but the Princess Ulrica Amelia Sophonisba Jacquelina vowed that the punishment was not a whit too severe for the traitress who had dared to call her the humpbacked Venus. I have shortened as far as possible the horrors of the *dénoûment* of this dismal drama. The executioner returned to Vienna with a thousand crowns and all he had won of Angelica in private. Max gave the father and his unhappy daughter a pension for their lives; but he never married himself, and his estates passed away into another branch of our family."

"What, are you connected with him, Milchbrod?" said I, "and is the story true?"

"True. The execution took place on the very spot where you are lying."

I jumped up rather nervously. And here you have the story of the "Brother's Revenge; or, the Executioner's Wife."

ODDS AND ENDS.

MEMORIALS OF GORMANDIZING.

IN A LETTER TO OLIVER YORKE, ESQUIRE, BY M. A.
TITMARSH.

[*Fraser's Magazine, June,* 1841.]

PARIS, *May,* 1841.

SIR, — The man who makes the best salads in London,
and whom, therefore, we have facetiously called Sultan
Saladin, — a man who is conspicious for his love and
practice of all the polite arts — music, to wit, architecture,
painting, and cookery — once took the humble personage
who writes this into his library, and laid before me two or
three volumes of manuscript year-books, such as, since he
began to travel and to observe, he has been in the habit of
keeping.

Every night, in the course of his rambles, his highness
the sultan (indeed, his port is sublime, as, for the matter
of that, are all the wines in his cellar) sets down with an
iron pen, and in the neatest handwriting in the world, the
events and observations of the day; with the same iron
pen he illuminates the leaf of his journal by the most
faithful and delightful sketches of the scenery which he
has witnessed in the course of the four and twenty hours;
and if he has dined at an inn or restaurant, gasthaus,
posada, albergo, or what not, invariably inserts into his
log-book the bill of fare. The sultan leads a jolly life — a
tall stalwart man, who every day about six o'clock in London and Paris, at two in Italy, in Germany and Belgium
at an hour after noon, feels the noble calls of hunger
agitating his lordly bosom (or its neighborhood, that is),
and replies to the call by a good dinner. Ah! it is wonderful to think how the healthy and philosophic mind can

accommodate itself in all cases to the varying circumstances of the time — how, in its travels through the world, the liberal and cosmopolite stomach recognizes the national dinner-hour! Depend upon it that, in all countries, nature has wisely ordained and suited to their exigencies THE DISHES OF A PEOPLE. I mean to say that olla podrida is good in Spain (though a plateful of it, eaten in Paris, once made me so dreadfully ill that it is a mercy I was spared ever to eat another dinner); I mean to say, and have proved it, that sauerkraut is good in Germany; and I make no doubt that whale's blubber is a very tolerable dish in Kamtschatka, though I have never visited the country. Cannibalism in the South Seas, and sheepsheadism in Scotland, are the only practices that one cannot, perhaps, reconcile with this rule — at least, whatever a man's private opinions may be, the decencies of society oblige him to eschew the expression of them upon subjects which the national prejudice has precluded from free discussion.

Well, after looking through three or four of Saladin's volumes, I grew so charmed with them, that I used to come back every day and study them. I declare there are bills of fare in those books over which I have cried; and the reading of them, especially about an hour before dinner, has made me so ferociously hungry, that, in the first place, the sultan (a kind-hearted generous man, as every man is who loves his meals) could not help inviting me to take potluck with him; and, secondly, I could eat twice as much as upon common occasions, though my appetite is always good.

Lying awake, then, of nights, or wandering solitary abroad on wide commons, or by the side of silent rivers, or at church when Dr. Snufflem was preaching his favorite sermon, or stretched on the flat of my back smoking a cigar at the club when X was talking of the corn-laws, or Y was describing that famous run they·had with the Z hounds — at all periods, I say, favorable to self-examination, those bills of fare have come into my mind, and often and often I have thought them over. "Titmarsh," I have said to myself, "if ever you travel again, do as the sultan has done, and *keep your dinner-bills.* They are always pleasant to look over; they always will recall happy hours and actions, be you ever so hard pushed for a dinner, and fain to put up with an onion and a crust; of the past fate cannot deprive you. Yesterday is the philosopher's

property ; and, by thinking of it and using it to advantage,
he may gayly go through to-morrow, doubtful and dismal
though it be. Try this lamb stuffed with pistachio-nuts ;
another handful of this pillau. Ho, you rascals ! bring
round the sherbet there, and never spare the jars of wine
— 'tis true Persian, on the honor of a Barmecide ! " Is
not that dinner in the " Arabian Nights " a right good
dinner ? Would you have had Bedreddin to refuse and
turn sulky at the windy repast, or to sit down grinning in
the face of his grave entertainer, and gayly take what
came ? Remember what came of the honest fellow's philosophy. He slapped the grim old prince in the face ; and
the grim old prince, who had invited him but to laugh at
him, did presently order a real and substantial repast to be
set before him — great pyramids of smoking rice and
pillau (a good pillau is one of the best dishes in the world),
savory kids, snow-cooled sherbets, luscious wine of Shiraz ;
with an accompaniment of moon-faced beauties from the
harem, no doubt, dancing, singing, and smiling in the most
ravishing manner. Thus should we,.my dear friends, laugh
at Fate's beard, as we confront him — thus should we, if
the old monster be insolent, fall to and box his ears. He
has a spice of humor in his composition ; and be sure he
will be tickled by such conduct.

Some months ago, when the expectation of war between
England and France grew to be so strong, and there was
such a talk of mobilizing national guards, and arming three
or four hundred thousand more French soldiers — when
such ferocious yells of hatred against perfidious Albion
were uttered by the liberal French press, that I did really
believe the rupture between the two countries was about
immediately to take place ; being seriously alarmed, I set
off for Paris at once. My good sir, what could we do without our Paris ? I came here first in 1815 (when the Duke
and I were a good deal remarked by the inhabitants) ; I
proposed but to stay a week ; stopped three months, and
have returned every year since. There is something fatal
in the place — a charm about it — a wicked one very likely
— but it acts on us all ; and perpetually the old Paris man
comes hieing back to his quarters again, and is to be found,
as usual, sunning himself in the Rue de la Paix. Painters,
princes, gourmands, officers on half-pay — serious old ladies
even acknowledge the attraction of the place — are more
at ease here than in any other place in Europe ; and back

they come, and are to be found sooner or later occupying their old haunts.

My darling city improves too, with each visit, and has some new palace, or church, or statue, or other gimcrack, to greet your eyes withal. A few years since, and lo! on the column of the Place Vendôme, instead of the shabby, tri-colored rag, shone the bronze statue of Napoleon. Then came the famous triumphal arch; a noble building indeed! — how stately and white, and beautiful and strong, it seems to dominate over the whole city! Next was the obelisk; a huge bustle and festival being made to welcome it to the city. Then came the fair asphaltum terraces round about the obelisk; then the fountains to decorate the terraces. I have scarcely been twelve months absent, and behold they have gilded all the Naiads and Tritons; they have clapped a huge fountain in the very midst of the Champs Elysées — a great, glittering, frothing fountain, that to the poetic eye looks like an enormous shaving-brush; and all down the avenue they have placed hundreds of gilded flaring gas-lamps, that make this gayest walk in the world look gayer still than ever. But a truce to such descriptions, which might carry one far, very far, from the object proposed in this paper.

I simply wish to introduce to public notice a brief dinner-journal. It has been written with the utmost honesty and simplicity of purpose; and exhibits a picture or table of the development of the human mind under a series of gastronomic experiments, diversified in their nature, and diversified, consequently, in their effects. A man in London has not, for the most part, the opportunity to make these experiments. You are a family man, let us presume, and you live in that metropolis for half a century. You have on Sunday, say, a leg of mutton and potatoes for dinner. On Monday you have cold mutton and potatoes. On Tuesday hashed mutton and potatoes; the hashed mutton being flavored with little damp triangular pieces of toast. which always surround that charming dish. Well, on Wednesday, the mutton ended, you have beef: the beef undergoes the same alternations of cookery, and disappears. Your life presents a succession of joints, varied every now and then by a bit of fish and some poultry. You drink three glasses of a brandyfied liquor called sherry at dinner; your excellent lady imbibes one. When she has had her glass of port after dinner, she goes upstairs with the children, and you fall asleep in your arm-chair. Some of the most pure and precious enjoyments of life are unknown to you. You eat and drink, but you do not know the *art* of eating and drinking; nay, most probably you despise those who do. "Give me a slice of meat," say you, very likely, "and a fig for your gourmands." You fancy it is very virtuous and manly all this. Nonsense, my good sir; you are indifferent because you are ignorant, because your life is passed in a narrow circle of ideas, and because you are bigotedly blind and pompously callous to the beauties and excellences beyond you.

Sir, RESPECT YOUR DINNER; idolize it, enjoy it properly. You will be by many hours in the week, many weeks in the year, and many years in your life the happier if you do.

Don't tell us that it is not worthy of a man. All a man's senses are worthy of employment, and should be cultivated as a duty. The senses are the arts. What glorious feasts does Nature prepare for your eye in animal form, in landscape, and painting! Are you to put out your eyes and not see? What royal dishes of melody does her bounty provide for you in the shape of poetry, music, whether windy or wiry, notes of the human voice, or ravishing song of birds! Are you to stuff your ears with cotton, and vow that the sense of hearing is unmanly? — you obstinate dolt you! No, surely; nor must you be so absurd as to fancy that the art of eating is in any way less worthy than the other two. You like your dinner, man; never be ashamed to say so. If you don't like your victuals, pass on to the next article; but remember that every man who has been worth a fig in this world, as poet, painter, or musician, has had a good appetite and a good taste. Ah, what a poet Byron would have been had he taken his meals properly, and allowed himself to grow fat — if Nature intended him to grow fat — and not have physicked his intellect with wretched opium pills and acrid vinegar, that sent his principles to sleep, and turned his feelings sour! If that man had respected his dinner, he never would have written "Don Juan."

Allons donc! enough sermonizing; let us sit down and fall to at once.

I dined soon after my arrival at a very pleasant Paris club, where daily is provided a dinner for ten persons, that is universally reported to be excellent. Five men in England would have consumed the same amount of victuals, as you will see by the bills of fare : —

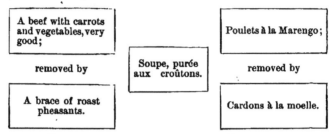

A beef with carrots and vegetables, very good;		Poulets à la Marengo;
removed by	Soupe, purée aux croûtons.	removed by
A brace of roast pheasants.		Cardons à la moelle.

Dessert of cheese, pears, and Fontainebleau grapes.
Bordeaux (red) and excellent Chablis at discretion.

This dinner was very nicely served. A venerable *maître d'hôtel* in black, cutting up neatly the dishes on a trencher at the side-table, and several waiters attending in green coats, red plush tights, and their hair curled. There was a great quantity of light in the room; some handsome pieces of plated ware; the pheasants came in with their tails to their backs; and the smart waiters, with their hair dressed and parted down the middle, gave a pleasant. lively, stylish appearance to the whole affair.

Now, I certainly dined (by the way, I must not forget to mention that we had with the beef some boiled kidney potatoes, very neatly dished up in a napkin) — I certainly dined, I say; and half an hour afterwards felt, perhaps, more at my ease than I should have done had I consulted my own inclinations, and devoured twice the quantity that on this occasion came to my share. But I would rather, as a man not caring for appearances, dine, as a general rule, off a beefsteak for two at the Café Foy, than sit down to take a tenth part of such a meal every day. There was only one man at the table besides your humble servant who did not put water into his wine; and he — I mean the other — was observed by his friends, who exclaimed, "Comment! vous buvez sec," as if to do so was a wonder. The consequence was, that half a dozen bottles of wine served for the whole ten of us; and the guests, having despatched their dinner in an hour, skipped lightly away from it, did not stay to ruminate, and to feel uneasy, and to fiddle about the last and penultimate waistcoat button, as we do after a house-dinner at an English club. What was it that made the charm of this dinner ? — for pleasant it was. It was the neat and comfortable manner in which it was served; the pheasant-tails had a considerable effect; that snowy napkin, coquettishly arranged round the kidneys, gave them a *distingué* air; the light and glittering service gave an appearance of plenty and hospitality that sent everybody away contented.

I put down this dinner just to show English and Scotch housekeepers what may be done, and for what price. Say,

		s.	d.
Soup and fresh bread, Beef and carrots } prime cost		2	6
Fowls and sauce		·3	6
Pheasants (hens)		5	0
Grapes, pears, cheese, vegetables		3	0
		14	0

For fifteenpence *par tête* a company of ten persons may have a dinner set before them, — nay, and be made to fancy that they dine well, provided the service is handsomely arranged, that you have a good stock of side-dishes, etc., in your plate-chest, and don't spare the spermaceti.

As for the wine, that depends on yourself. Always be crying out to your friends, " Mr. So-and-so, I don't drink myself, but pray pass the bottle. Tomkins, my boy, help your neighbor, and never mind me. What ! Hopkins, are there two of us on the doctor's list ? Pass the wine; *Smith* I'm sure won't refuse it;" and so on. A very good plan is to have the butler (or the fellow in the white waistcoat who "behaves as sich ") pour out the wine when wanted (in half-glasses, of course), and to make a deuced great noise and shouting, "John, John, why the devil, sir, don't you help Mr. Simkins to another glass of wine ? " If you point out Simkins once or twice in this way, depend upon it, *he* won't drink a great quantity of your liquor. You may thus keep your friends from being dangerous, by a thousand innocent manœuvres; and, as I have said before, you may very probably make them believe that they have had a famous dinner. There was only one man in our company of ten the other day who ever thought he had not dined; and what was he ? a foreigner, — a man of a discontented, inquiring spirit, always carping at things, and never satisfied.

Well, next day I dined *au cinquième* with a family (of Irish extraction, by the way), and what do you think was our dinner for six persons ? Why, simply,

Nine dozen Ostend oysters;
Soup à la mulligatawny;
Boiled turkey, with celery sauce;
Saddle of mutton rôti.
Removes: Plompouding; croûte de macaroni.
Vin: Beaune ordinaire, volnay, bordeaux, champagne,
    eau chaude, cognac.

I forget the dessert. Alas! in moments of prosperity and plenty, one is often forgetful: I remember the dessert at the Cercle well enough.

A person whom they call in this country an *illustration littéraire* — the editor of a newspaper, in fact — with a very pretty wife, were of the party, and looked at the dinner with a great deal of good-humored superiority. I declare, upon my honor, that I helped both the illustration and his lady twice to saddle of mutton; and as for the turkey and celery sauce, you should have seen how our host dispensed it to them! They ate the oysters, they ate the soup ("Diable! mais il est poivré!" said the illustration, with tears in his eyes), they ate the turkey, they ate the mutton, they ate the pudding; and what did our hostess say? Why, casting down her eyes gently, and with the modestest air in the world, she said, — "There is such a beautiful piece of cold beef in the larder; do somebody ask for a little slice of it."

Heaven bless her for that speech! I loved and respected her for it; it brought the tears to my eyes. A man who could sneer at such a sentiment could have neither heart nor good breeding. Don't you see that it shows

                Simplicity,
                Modesty,
                Hospitality?

Put these against

                Waiters with their hair curled,
                Pheasants roasted with their tails on,
                A dozen spermaceti candles.

Add them up, I say, oh candid reader, and answer in the sum of human happiness, which of the two accounts makes the better figure?

I declare, I know few things more affecting than that little question about the cold beef; and, considering calmly our national characteristics, balancing in the scale of quiet thought our defects and our merits, am daily more inclined

to believe that there is something in the race of Britons
which renders them usually superior to the French family.
This is but one of the traits of English character that has
been occasioned by the use of roast beef.

It is an immense question, that of diet.   Look at the two
bills of fare just set down; the relative consumption of
ten animals and six.   What a profound physical and
moral difference may we trace here!   How distinct, from
the cradle upwards, must have been the thoughts, feelings,
education of the parties who ordered those two dinners!
It is a fact which does not admit of a question, that the
French are beginning, since so many English have come
among them, to use beef much more profusely.   Everybody
at the restaurateur's orders beefsteak and pommes.   Will
the national character slowly undergo a change under the
influence of this dish?   Will the French be more simple?
broader in the shoulders? less inclined to brag about military glory and such humbug?   All this in the dark vista
of futurity the spectator may fancy is visible to him, and
the philanthropist cannot but applaud the change.   This
brings me naturally to the consideration of the manner of
dressing beefsteaks in this country, and of the merit of
that manner.

I dined on a Saturday at the Café Foy, on the Boulevard,
in a private room, with a friend.   We had

> Potage julienne, with a little purée in it;
> Two entrecôtes aux épinards;
> One perdreau truffé;
> One fromage roquefort;
> A bottle of nuits with the beef;
> A bottle of sauterne with the partridge.

And perhaps a glass of punch, with a cigar, afterwards:
but that is neither here nor there.   The insertion of the
purée into the julienne was not of my recommending; and
if this junction is effected at all, the operation should be
performed with the greatest care.   If you put too much
purée, both soups are infallibly spoiled.   A much better
plan it is to have your julienne by itself, though I will not
enlarge on this point, as the excellent friend with whom I
dined may chance to see this notice, and may be hurt at
the renewal in print of a dispute which caused a good deal
of pain to both of us.   By the way, we had half a dozen
sardines while the dinner was getting ready, eating them

with delicious bread and butter, for which this place is famous. Then followed the soup. Why the deuce *would* ·he have the pu—— but never mind. After the soup, we had what I do not hesitate to call the very best beefsteak I ever ate in my life. By the shade of Heliogabalus! as I write about it now, a week after I have eaten it, the old, rich, sweet, piquant, juicy taste comes smacking on my lips again; and I feel something of that exquisite sensation I then had. I am ashamed of the delight which the eating of that piece of meat caused me. G—— and I had quarrelled about the soup (I said so, and don't wish to return to the subject); but when we began on the steak, we looked at each other, and loved each other. We did not speak, — our hearts were too full for that; but we took a bit, and laid down our forks, and looked at one another, and understood each other. There were no two individuals on this wide earth, — no two lovers billing in the shade, — no mother clasping baby to her heart, more supremely happy than we. Every now and then we had a glass of honest, firm, generous Burgundy, that nobly supported the meat. As you may fancy, we did not leave a single morsel of the steak; but when it was done, we put bits of bread into the silver dish, and wistfully sopped up the gravy. I suppose I shall never in this world taste anything so good again. But what then? What if I *did* like it excessively? Was my liking unjust or unmanly? Is my regret now puling or unworthy? No. "Laudo manentem!" as Titmouse says. When it is eaten, I resign myself, and can eat a two-franc dinner at Richard's without ill humor and without a pang.

Any dispute about the relative excellence of the beefsteak cut from the filet, as is usual in France, and of the *entrecôte*, must henceforth be idle and absurd. Whenever, my dear young friend, you go to Paris, call at once for the *entrecôte;* the filet in comparison to it is a poor *fade* lady's meat. What folly, by the way, is that in England which induces us to attach an estimation to the part of the sirloin that is called the Sunday side, — poor, tender, stringy stuff, not comparable to the manly meat on the other side, handsomely garnished with crisp fat, and with a layer of horn! Give the Sunday side to misses and ladies' maids, for men be the Monday's side, or, better still, a thousand times more succulent and full of flavor—the *ribs of beef.* This is the meat I would eat were I going to do battle with **any**

mortal foe.   Fancy a hundred thousand Englishmen, after
a meal of stalwart beef ribs, encountering a hundred thousand Frenchmen who had partaken of a trifling collation
of soups, turnips, carrots, onions, and Gruyère cheese.
Would it be manly to engage at such odds ?   I say, no.

Passing by Véry's one day, I saw a cadaverous cook with
a spatula, thumping a poor beefsteak with all his might.
This is not only a horrible cruelty, but an error.   They not
only beat the beef, moreover, but they soak it in oil.
Absurd, disgusting barbarity !   Beef so beaten loses its
natural spirit; it is too noble for corporal punishment.
You may by these tortures and artifices make it soft and
greasy, but tender and juicy never.

The landlord of the Café Foy (I have received no sort of
consideration from him) knows this truth full well, and
follows the simple honest plan ; first, to have good meat,
and next to hang it a long time.   I have instructed him
how to do the steaks to a turn, not raw, horribly livid and
blue in the midst, as I have seen great flaps of meat (what
a shame to think of our fine meat being so treated !), but
cooked all the way through.   Go to the Café Foy then, ask
for a BEEFSTEAK À LA TITMARSH, and you will see what a
dish will be set before you.   I have dwelt upon this point
at too much length, perhaps, for some of my readers ; but
it can't be helped.   The truth is, beef is my weakness ; and
I do declare that I derive more positive enjoyment from
the simple viand than from any concoction whatever in the
whole cook's cyclopædia.

Always drink red wine with beefsteaks ; port, if possible ; if not, Burgundy, of not too high a flavor, — good
Beaune, say.   This fact, which is very likely not known to
many persons who, forsooth, are too magnificent to care
about their meat and drink, — this simple fact I take to be
worth the whole price I shall get for this article.

But to return to dinner.   We were left, I think, G——
and I, sopping up the gravy with bits of bread, and declaring that no power on earth could induce us to eat a morsel
more that day.   At one time, we thought of countermand-
ing the perdreau aux truffes, that to my certain knowledge
had been betruffed five days before.

Poor blind mortals that we were ; ungrateful to our
appetites, needlessly mistrustful and cowardly.   A man
may do what he dares ; nor does he know, until he tries,
what the honest appetite will bear.   We were kept waiting

between the steak and the partridge some ten minutes or so. For the first two or three minutes we lay back in our chairs quite exhausted indeed. Then we began to fiddle with a dish of toothpicks, for want of anything more savory; then we looked out of the window; then G—— got in a rage, rang the bell violently, and asked, "Pourquoi diable nous fait-on attendre si longtemps?" The waiter grinned. He is a nice good-humored fellow, Auguste; and I heartily trust that some reader of this may give him a five-franc piece for my sake. Auguste grinned and disappeared.

Presently, we were aware of an odor gradually coming towards us, something musky, fiery, savory, mysterious, — a hot drowsy smell, that lulls the senses, and yet inflames them, — the *truffes* were coming! Yonder they lie, caverned under the full bosom of the red-legged bird. My hand trembled as, after a little pause, I cut the animal in two. G—— said I did not give him his share of the truffes; I don't believe I did. I spilled some salt into my plate, and a little cayenne pepper — very little: we began, as far as I can remember, the following conversation: —

Gustavus. Chop, chop, chop.

Michael Angelo. Globlobloblob.

G. Gobble.

M. A. Obble.

G. Here's a big one.

M. A. Hobgob. What wine shall we have? I should like some champagne.

G. It's bad here. Have some Sauterne.

M. A. Very well. Hobgobglobglob, etc.

Auguste (opening the Sauterne). Cloo-oo-oo-oop! The cork is out; he pours it into the glass, glock, glock, glock.

Nothing more took place in the way of talk. The poor little partridge was soon a heap of bones — a very little heap. A trufflesque odor was left in the room, but only an odor. Presently, the cheese was brought: the amber Sauterne flask has turned of a sickly green hue; nothing, save half a glass of sediment at the bottom, remained to tell of the light and social spirit that had but one half-hour before inhabited the flask. Darkness fell upon our little chamber; the men in the street began crying, "*Messager! Journal du Soir!*" The bright moon rose glittering over the tiles of the Rue Louis le Grand, opposite, illuminating two glasses of punch that two gentlemen in a small room of

the Café Foy did ever and anon raise to their lips. Both
were silent; both happy; both were smoking cigars, — for
both knew that the soothing plant of Cuba is sweeter to
the philosopher after dinner than the prattle of all the
women in the world.   Women — pshaw !   The man who,
after dinner — after a good dinner — can think about driving home, and shaving himself by candlelight, and induing
a damp shirt, and a pair of tight glazed pumps to show his
cobweb stockings and set his feet in a flame; and, having
undergone all this, can get into a cold cab, and drive off to
No. 222 Harley Street, where Mrs. Mortimer Smith is at
home; where you take off your cloak in a damp dark back
parlor, called Mr. Smith's study, and containing, when you
arrive, twenty-four ladies' cloaks and tippets, fourteen
hats, two pairs of clogs (belonging to two gentlemen of the
Middle Temple, who walk for economy, and think dancing
at Mrs. Mortimer Smith's the height of enjoyment); — the
man who can do all this, and walk, gracefully smiling, into
Mrs. Smith's drawing-rooms, where the brown holland bags
have been removed from the chandeliers; a man from
Kirkman's is thumping on the piano, and Mrs. Smith is
standing simpering in the middle of the room, dressed in
red, with a bird of paradise in her turban, a tremulous fan
in one hand, and the other clutching hold of her little fat
gold watch and seals; — the man who, after making his
bow to Mrs. Smith, can advance to Miss Jones, in blue
crape, and lead her to a place among six other pairs of
solemn-looking persons, and whisper *fadaises* to her (at
which she cries, "Oh, fie, you naughty man ! how can
you ? "), and look at Miss Smith's red shoulders struggling
out of her gown, and her mottled elbows that a pair of
crumpled kid gloves leave in a state of delicious nature;
and, after having gone through certain mysterious quadrille
figures with her, lead her back to her mamma, who has just
seized a third glass of muddy negus from the black footman; — the man who can do all this may do it, and go
hang, for me !   And many such men there be, my Gustavus, in yonder dusky London city.   Be it ours, my dear
friend, when the day's labor and repast are done, to lie and
ruminate calmly; to watch the bland cigar smoke as it rises
gently ceiling-wards; to be idle in body as well as mind;
not to kick our heels madly in quadrilles, and puff and
pant in senseless gallopades : let us appreciate the joys of
idleness; let us give a loose to silence; and having enjoyed

this, the best dessert after a goodly dinner, at close of eve,
saunter slowly home.

. . . . .

As the dinner above described drew no less than three
five-franc pieces out of my purse, I determined to econo-
mize for the next few days, and either to be invited out to
dinner, or else to partake of some repast at a small charge,
such as one may have here. I had on the day succeeding
the truffled partridge a dinner for a shilling; viz., —

> Bifsteck aux pommes (heu quantum mutatus ab illo!)
> Galantine de volaille,
> Fromage de Gruyère,
> Demi-bouteille du vin très-vieux de Mâcon ou Chablis,
> Pain à discrétion.

This dinner, my young friend, was taken about half-past
two o'clock in the day, and was, in fact, a breakfast, — a
breakfast taken at a two-franc house, in the Rue Haute Vi-
vienne; it was certainly a sufficient dinner : I certainly was
not hungry for all the rest of the day. Nay, the wine was
decently good, as almost all wine is in the morning, if one
had the courage or the power to drink it. You see many
honest English families marching into these two-franc eating-houses, at five o'clock, and they fancy they dine in great
luxury. Returning to England, however, they inform their
friends that the meat in France is not good; that the fowls
are very small, and black; the kidneys very tough; the
partridges and fruit have no taste in them, and the soup is
execrably thin. A dinner at Williams's, in the Old Bailey,
is better than the best of these; and therefore had the
English Cockney better remain at Williams's than judge
the great nation so falsely.

The worst of these two-franc establishments is a horrid
air of shabby elegance which distinguishes them. At some
of them they will go the length of changing your knife and
fork with every dish; they have grand chimney-glasses, and
a fine lady at the counter, and fine arabesque paintings on
the walls; they give you your soup in a battered dish of
plated ware, which has served its best time, most likely,
in a first-rate establishment, and comes here to *étaler* its
second-hand splendor amongst amateurs of a lower grade.
I fancy the very meat that is served to you has undergone
the same degradation, and that some of the mouldy cutlets
that are offered to the two-franc epicures lay once plump
and juicy in Véry's larder. Much better is the sanded floor

and the iron fork! Homely neatness is the charm of poverty: elegance should belong to wealth alone. There is a very decent place where you dine for thirty-two sous in the Passage Choiseul. You get your soup in china bowls; they don't change your knife and fork, but they give you very fit portions of meat and potatoes, and mayhap a herring with mustard sauce, a dish of apple fritters, a dessert of stewed prunes, and a pint of drinkable wine, as I have proved only yesterday.

After two such banyan days, I allowed myself a little feasting; and as nobody persisted in asking me to dinner, I went off to the "Trois Frères" by myself, and dined in that excellent company.

I would recommend a man who is going to dine by himself here, to reflect well before he orders soup for dinner.

My notion is, that you eat as much after soup as without it, but you *don't eat with the same appetite.*

Especially if you are a healthy man, as I am — deuced hungry at five o'clock. My appetite runs away with me; and if I order soup (which is always enough for two), I invariably swallow the whole of it; and the greater portion of my *petit pain*, too, before my second dish arrives.

The best part of a pint of julienne, or purée à la Condé, is very well for a man who has only one dish besides to devour; but not for you and me, who like our fish and our *rôti* of game or meat as well.

Oysters you may eat. They do, for a fact, prepare one to go through the rest of a dinner properly. Lemon and cayenne pepper is the word, depend on it, and a glass of white wine braces you up for what is to follow.

French restaurateur dinners are intended, however, for two people, at least; still better for three; and require a good deal of thought before you can arrange them for one.

Here, for instance, is a recent *menu*: —

Trois Frères Provençaux.

	f.	c.
Pain	0	25
Beaune première	3	0
Purée à la Créci	0	75 .
Turbot aux capres	1	75
Quart poulet aux truffes	2	25
Champignons à la Provençale	1	25
Gelée aux pommes	1	25
Cognac	0	30
	10	80

A heavy bill for a single man; and a heavy dinner, too; for I have said before I have a great appetite, and when a thing is put before me I eat it. At Brussels I once ate fourteen dishes; and have seen a lady, with whom I was in love, at the table of a German grand-duke, eat seventeen dishes. This is a positive, though disgusting fact. Up to the first twelve dishes she had a very good chance of becoming Mrs. Titmarsh, but I have lost sight of her since.

Well, then, I say to you, if you have self-command enough to send away half your soup, order some; but you are a poor creature if you do after all. If you are a man, and have *not* that self-command, don't have any. The Frenchmen cannot live without it, but I say to you that you are better than a Frenchman. I would lay even money that you who are reading this are more than five feet seven in height, and weigh eleven stone; while a Frenchman is five feet four, and does not weigh nine. The Frenchman has after his soup a dish of vegetables, where you have one of meat. You are a different and superior animal — a French-beating animal (the history of hundreds of years has shown you to be so); you must have, to keep up that superior weight and sinew, which is the secret of your superiority — as for public institutions, bah! — you must have, I say, simpler, stronger, more succulent food.

Eschew the soup, then, and have the fish up at once. It is the best to begin with fish, if you like it, as every epicure and honest man should, simply boiled or fried in the English fashion, and not tortured and bullied with oils, onions, wine, and herbs, as in Paris it is frequently done.

Turbot with lobster-sauce is too much; turbot à la Hollandaise vulgar; sliced potatoes swimming in melted butter are a mean concomitant for a noble, simple, liberal fish: turbot with capers is the thing. The brisk little capers relieve the dulness of the turbot; the melted butter is rich, bland, and calm — it *should be,* that is to say; not that vapid watery mixture that I see in London; not oiled butter, as the Hollanders have it, but melted, with plenty of thickening matter: I don't know how to do it, but I know it when it is good.

They melt butter well at the "Rocher de Cancale," and at the "Frères."

Well, this turbot was very good; not so well, of course, as one gets it in London, and dried rather in the boiling; which can't be helped, unless you are a Lucullus or a

Cambacérès of a man, and can afford to order one for yourself. This *grandeur d'âme* is very rare; my friend Tom Willows is almost the only man I know who possessed it. Yes, ——, one of the wittiest men in London, I once knew to take the whole *intérieur* of a diligence (six places), because he was a little unwell. Ever since I have admired that man. He understands true economy; a mean extravagant man would have contented himself with a single place, and been unwell in consequence. How I am rambling from my subject, however! The fish was good, and I ate up every single scrap of it, sucking the bones and fins curiously. That is the deuce of an appetite, it *must* be satisfied; and if you were to put a roast donkey before me, with the promise of a haunch of venison afterwards, I believe I should eat the greater part of the long-eared animal.

A pint of purée à la Créci, a pain de gruau, a slice of turbot — a man should think about ordering his bill, for he has had enough dinner; but no, we are creatures of superstition and habit, and must have one regular course of meat. Here comes the poulet à la Marengo: I hope they've given me the wing.

No such thing. The poulet à la Marengo aux truffes is bad — too oily by far; the truffes are not of this year, as they should be, for there are cartloads in town: they are poor in flavor, and have only been cast into the dish a minute before it was brought to table, and what is the consequence? They do not flavor the meat in the least; some faint trufflesque savor you may get as you are crunching each individual root, but that is all, and that all not worth the having; for as nothing is finer than a good truffle, in like manner nothing is meaner than a bad one. It is merely pompous, windy, and pretentious, like those scraps of philosophy with which a certain eminent novelist decks out his meat.

A mushroom, thought I, is better a thousand times than these tough flavorless roots. I finished every one of them, however, and the fine fat capon's thigh which they surrounded. It was a disappointment not to get a wing, to be sure. They *always* give me legs; but, after all, with a little good-humor and philosophy, a leg of a fine Mans capon may be found very acceptable. How plump and tender the rogue's thigh is! his very drumstick is as fat as the calf of a London footman; and the sinews, which puzzle one so over the lean black hen-legs in London, are miraculously whisked away from the limb before me. Look at it now! Half a dozen cuts with the knife and yonder lies the bone — white, large, stark naked, without a morsel of flesh left upon it, solitary in the midst of a pool of melted butter.

How good the Burgundy smacks after it! I always drink Burgundy at this house, and that not of the best. It is my firm opinion that a third-rate Burgundy, and a third-rate claret — Beaune and Larose, for instance, are *better* than the best. The Bordeaux enlivens, the Burgundy invigorates; stronger drink only inflames; and where a bottle of good Beaune only causes a man to feel a certain manly warmth of benevolence — a glow something like that produced by sunshine and gentle exercise — a bottle of Chambertin will set all your frame in a fever, swell the extremities, and cause the pulses to throb. Chambertin should *never* be handed round more than twice; and I recollect to this moment the headache I had after drinking a bottle and a half of Romanée gelée, for which this house is famous. Somebody else *paid* for the — (no other than you, O Gustavus! with whom I hope to have many a tall dinner on the same charges) — but 'twas in our hot youth, ere experience had taught us that moderation was happiness, and had shown us that it is absurd to be guzzling wine at fifteen francs a bottle.

By the way, I may here mention a story relating to some of Blackwood's men, who dined at this very house. Fancy the fellows trying claret, which they voted sour; then Burgundy, at which they made wry faces, and finished the evening with brandy and *lunel!* This is what men call eating a French dinner. Willows and I dined at the "Rocher," and an English family there feeding ordered — mutton chops and potatoes. Why not, in these cases, stay at home? Chops are better chops in England (the best chops in the world are to be had at the Reform Club) than in France. What could literary men mean by ordering lunel? I always rather liked the descriptions of eating in the "Noctes." They were gross in all cases, absurdly erroneous in many; but there was manliness about them, and strong evidence of a great, though misdirected and uneducated, genius for victuals.

Mushrooms, thought I, are better than those tasteless truffles, and so ordered a dish to try. You know what a

Provençale sauce is, I have no doubt ? — a rich savory mixture of garlic and oil; which, with a little cayenne pepper and salt, impart a pleasant taste to the plump little mushrooms, that can't be described but may be thought of with pleasure.

The only point was, how will they agree with me tomorrow morning ? for the fact is, I had eaten an immense quantity of them, and began to be afraid! Suppose we go and have a glass of punch and a cigar! Oh, glorious garden of the Palais Royal! your trees are leafless now, but what matters ? Your alleys are damp, but what of that? All the windows are blazing with light and merriment; at least two thousand happy people are pacing up and down the colonnades; cheerful sounds of money chinking are heard as you pass the changers' shops; bustling shouts of "Garçon!" and "V'là, Monsieur!" come from the swinging doors of the restaurateurs. Look at that group of soldiers gaping at Véfour's window, where lie lobsters, pineapples, fat truffle-stuffed partridges, which make me almost hungry again. I wonder whether those three fellows with mustachios and a toothpick apiece have had a dinner, or only a toothpick. When the "Trois Frères" used to be on the first floor, and had a door leading into the Rue de Valois, as well as one into the garden, I recollect seeing three men with toothpicks mount the stair from the street, descend the stair into the garden, and give themselves as great airs as if they had dined for a napoleon a head. The rogues are lucky if they have had a sixteen-sous dinner; and the next time I dine abroad, I am resolved to have one myself. I never understood why Gil Blas grew so mighty squeamish in the affair of the cat and the hare. Hare is best, but why should not cat be good ?

Being on the subject of bad dinners, I may as well ease my mind of one that occurred to me some few days back. When walking in the Boulevard, I met my friend, Captain Hopkinson, of the half-pay, looking very hungry, and indeed going to dine. In most cases one respects the dictum of a half-pay officer regarding a dining-house. He knows as a general rule where the fat of the land lies, and how to take his share of that fat in the most economical manner.

"I tell you what I do," says Hopkinson; "I allow myself fifteen francs a week for dinner (I count upon being asked out twice a week), and so have a three-franc dinner at Richard's, where, for the extra francs, they give me an excellent bottle of wine, and make me comfortable."

"Why shouldn't they?" I thought. "Here is a man who has served his country, and no doubt knows a thing when he sees it." We made a party of four, therefore, and went to the Captain's place to dine.

We had a private room *au second ;* a very damp and dirty private room with a faint odor of stale punch, and dingy glasses round the walls.

We had a soup of purée aux croûtons; a very dingy dubious soup indeed, thickened, I fancy, with brown paper, and flavored with the same.

At the end of the soup, Monsieur Landlord came upstairs very kindly, and gave us each a pinch of snuff out of a gold snuff-box.

We had four portions of anguille à la Tartare, very good and fresh (it is best in these places to eat freshwater fish). Each portion was half the length of a man's finger. Dish one was despatched in no time, and we began drinking the famous wine that our guide recommended. I have cut him ever since. It was four-sous wine, — weak, vapid, watery stuff, of the most unsatisfactory nature.

We had four portions of gigot aux haricots — four flaps of bleeding tough meat, cut unnaturally (that is, with the grain: the French gash the meat in parallel lines with the bone). We ate these up as we might, and the landlord was so good as to come up again and favor us with a pinch from his gold box.

With wonderful unanimity, as we were told the place was famous for civet de lièvre, we ordered civet de lièvre for four.

It came up, but we couldn't — really we couldn't. We were obliged to have extra dishes, and pay extra. Gustavus had a mayonnaise of crayfish, and half a fowl; I fell to work upon my cheese, as usual, and availed myself of the discretionary bread. We went away disgusted, wretched, unhappy. We had had for our three francs bad bread, bad meat, bad wine. And there stood the landlord at the door (and be hanged to him!) grinning and offering his box.

We don't speak to Hopkinson any more now when we meet him. How can you trust or be friendly with a man who deceives you in this miserable way?

What is the moral to be drawn from this dinner? It is evident. Avoid pretence; mistrust shabby elegance; cut your coat according to your cloth; if you have but a few shillings in your pocket, aim only at those humble and honest meats which your small store will purchase. At the Café Foy, for the same money, I might have had

	f.	s.
A delicious entrecôte and potatoes	1	5
A pint of excellent wine	0	10
A little bread (meaning a great deal)	0	5
A dish of stewed kidneys	1	0
	3	0

Or at Paolo's:

A bread (as before)	0	5
A heap of macaroni, or raviuoli	0	15
A Milanese cutlet	1	0
A pint of wine	0	10

And ten sous for any other luxury your imagination could suggest. The raviuoli and the cutlets are admirably dressed at Paolo's. Does any healthy man need more?

These dinners, I am perfectly aware, are by no means splendid; and I might, with the most perfect ease, write you out a dozen bills of fare, each more splendid and piquant than the other, in which all the luxuries of the season should figure. But the remarks here set down are the result of experience, not fancy, and intended only for persons in the middling classes of life. Very few men can afford to pay more than five francs daily for dinner. Let us calmly, then, consider what enjoyment may be had for those five francs; how, by economy on one day, we may venture upon luxury the next; how, by a little forethought and care, we may be happy on all days. Who knew and studied this cheap philosophy of life better than old Horace before quoted? Sometimes (when in luck) he chirruped over cups that were fit for an archbishop's supper; sometimes he philosophized over his own *ordinaire* at his own farm. How affecting is the last ode of the first book: —

To his serving-boy.	*Ad Ministram.*
Persicos odi,	Dear Lucy, you know what my wish is, —
Puer, apparatus;	I hate all your Frenchified fuss;
Displicent nexæ	Your silly entrées and made dishes
Philyrâ coronæ:	Were never intended for us.
Mitte sectari	No footman in lace and in ruffles
Rosa quo locorum	Need dangle behind my arm-chair;
Sera moretur.	And never mind seeking for truffles,
	Although they be ever so rare.

Simplici myrto	But a plain leg of mutton, my Lucy,
Nihil allabores	I pr'ythee get ready at three:
Sedulus curæ:	Have it smoking, and tender, and juicy,
Neque te ministrum	And what better meat can there be?
Dedecet myrtus,	And when it has feasted the master,
Neque me sub arctâ	'Twill amply suffice for the maid;
Vite bibentem.	Meanwhile I will smoke my canaster,
	And tipple my ale in the shade.

Not that this is the truth entirely and forever. Horatius Flaccus was too wise to dislike a good thing; but it is possible that the Persian apparatus was on that day beyond his means, and so he contented himself with humble fare.

A gentleman, by the by, has just come to Paris to whom I am very kind; and who will, in all human probability, between this and next month, ask me to a dinner at the "Rocher de Cancale." If so, something may occur worth writing about; or if you are anxious to hear more on the subject, send me over a sum to my address, to be laid out for you exclusively in eating. I give you my honor I will do you justice, and account for every farthing of it.

One of the most absurd customs at present in use is that of giving your friend — when some piece of good luck happens to him, such as an appointment as Chief Judge of Owhyhee, or King's advocate to Timbuctoo — of giving your friend, because, forsooth, he may have been suddenly elevated from 200*l.* a year to 2,000*l.*, an enormous dinner of congratulation.

Last year, for instance, when our friend, Fred Jowling, got his place of Commissioner at Quashumaboo, it was considered absolutely necessary to give the man a dinner, and some score of us had to pay about fifty shillings apiece for the purpose. I had, so help me Moses! but three guineas in the world at that period; and out of this sum the *bienséances* compelled me to sacrifice five-sixths, to feast myself in company of a man gorged with wealth, rattling sovereigns in his pocket as if they had been so much dross, and capable of treating us all without missing the sum he might expend on us.

Jow himself allowed, as I represented the case to him, that the arrangement *was* very hard; but represented, fairly enough, that this was one of the sacrifices that a man of the world, from time to time, is called to make. "You, my dear Titmarsh," said he, "know very well that I don't care for these grand entertainments" (the rogue, he is a five-bottle man, and just the most finished *gourmet* of my acquaintance!) ; " you know that I am perfectly convinced of your friendship for me, though you join in the dinner or not, but — it would look rather queer if you backed out, — *it would look rather queer.*"   Jow said this in such an emphatic way, that I saw I must lay down my money ; and accordingly Mr. Lovegrove of Blackwall, for a certain quantity of iced punch, champagne, cider-cup, fish, flesh, and fowl, received the last of my sovereigns.

At the beginning of the year Bolter got a place too — Judge Advocate in the Topinambo Islands, of 3,000*l.* a year, which, he said, was a poor remuneration in consideration of *the practice* which he gave up in town.   He may have practised on his laundress, but for anything else I believe the man never had a client in his life.

However, on his way to Topinambo — by Marseilles, Egypt, the Desert, the Persian Gulf, and so on — Bolter arrived in Paris ; and I saw from his appearance, and. his manner of shaking hands with me, and the peculiar way in which he talked about the " Rocher de Cancale," that he expected we were to give him a dinner, as we had to Jowling.

There were four friends of Bolter's in the capital besides myself, and among us the dinner question was mooted : we agreed that it should be a simple dinner of ten francs a head, and this was the bill of fare : —

1.   Oysters (common), nice.
2.   Oysters, green of Marennes (very good).
3.   Potage, purée de gibier (very fair).

As we were English, they instantly then served us, —

4.   Sole en matelotte Normande (comme ça).
5.   Turbot à la crème au gratin (excellent).
6.   Jardinière cutlets (particularly seedy).
7.   Poulet à la Marengo (very fair, but why the deuce is one always to be pestered by it ?).
8.
9.   } (Entrées of some kind, but a blank in my memory.)
10.   A rôt of chevreuil.
11.   Ditto of ortolans (very hot, crisp, and nice).
12.   Ditto of partridges (quite good and plump).
13.   Pointes d'asperges.
14.   Champignons à la Provençale (the most delicious mushrooms I ever tasted).
15.   Pineapple jelly.
16.   Blanc, or red mange.

17. Pencacks. Let everybody who goes to the " Rocher " order these pancakes; they are arranged with jelly inside, rolled up between various *couches* of vermicelli, flavored with a *leetle* wine; and, by everything sacred, the most delightful meat possible.
18. Timbale of macaroni.

The jellies and sucreries should have been mentioned in the dessert, and there were numberless plates of trifles, which made the table look very pretty, but need not be mentioned here.

The dinner was not a fine one, as you see. No rarities, no truffles even, no mets de primeur, though there were peas and asparagus in the market at a pretty fair price. But with rarities no man has any business except he have a colossal fortune. Hothouse strawberries, asparagus, etc., are, as far as my experience goes, most *fade*, mean, and tasteless meats. Much better to have a simple dinner of twenty dishes, and content therewith, than to look for impossible splendors and Apician morsels.

In respect of wine. Let those who go to the " Rocher " take my advice and order Madeira. They have here some pale old East India very good. How they got it is a secret, for the Parisians do not know good Madeira when they see it. Some very fair strong young wine may be had at the Hôtel des Américains, in the Rue Saint Honoré; as, indeed, all West India produce — pineapple rum, for instance. I may say, with confidence, that I never knew what rum was until I tasted this at Paris.

But to the "Rocher." The Madeira was the best wine served; though some Burgundy, handed round in the course of dinner, and a bottle of Montrachet, similarly poured out to us, were very fair. The champagne was decidedly not good — poor, inflated, thin stuff. They say the drink we swallow in England is not genuine wine, but brandy-loaded and otherwise doctored for the English market; but, ah, what superior wine! *Au reste*, the French will not generally pay the money for the wine; and it therefore is carried from an ungrateful country to more generous climes, where it is better appreciated. We had claret and speeches after dinner; and very possibly some of the persons present made free with a jug of hot water, a few lumps of sugar, and the horrid addition of a glass of cognac. There can be no worse practice than this. After a dinner of eighteen dishes, in which you have drunk at least thirty-six glasses of wine — when the stomach is full, the brain heavy, the hands and feet inflamed — when the claret begins to pall — you, forsooth, must gorge yourself with brandy and water, and puff filthy cigars. For shame! Who ever does it? Does a gentleman drink brandy and water? Does a man who mixes in the society of the lovelier half of humanity befoul himself by tobacco-smoke? Fie, fie! avoid the practice. I indulge in it always myself; but that is no reason why you, a young man entering into the world, should degrade yourself in any such way. No, no, my dear lad, never refuse an evening party, and avoid tobacco as you would the upas plant.

By the way, not having my purse about me when the above dinner was given, I was constrained to borrow from Bolter, whom I knew more intimately than the rest; and nothing grieved me more than to find, on calling at his hotel four days afterwards, that he had set off by the mail post for Marseilles. Friend of my youth, dear dear Bolter! if haply this trifling page should come before thine eyes, weary of perusing the sacred rolls of Themis in thy far-off island in the Indian Sea, thou wilt recall our little dinner in the little room of the Cancalian Coffee-house, and think for a while of thy friend!

Let us now mention one or two places that the Briton, on his arrival here, should frequent or avoid. As a quiet dear house, where there are some of the best rooms in Paris — always the best meat, fowls, vegetables, etc. — we may specially recommend Monsieur Voisin's café, opposite the Church of the Assumption. A very decent and lively house of restauration is that at the corner of the Rue du Faubourg Montmartre, on the Boulevard. I never yet had a good dinner at Véfour's; *something* is always *manqué* at the place. The grand Vatel is worthy of note, as cheap, pretty, and quiet. All the English houses gentlemen may frequent who are so inclined; but though the writer of this has many times dined for sixteen sous at Catcomb's, cheek by jowl with a French chasseur or a laborer, he has, he confesses, an antipathy to enter into the confidence of a footman or groom of his own country.

A gentleman who purchases pictures in this town was lately waited upon by a lady, who said she had in her possession one of the greatest rarities in the world, — a picture admirable, too, as a work of art, — no less than an original portrait of Shakspeare, by his comrade, the famous John Davis. The gentleman rushed off immediately to

behold the wonder, and saw a head, rudely but vigorously painted on panel, about twice the size of life, with a couple of hooks drawn through the top part of the board, under which was written, —

THE WILLIAM SHAKSPEARE,

BY JOHN DAVIS.

"Voyez-vous, Monsieur," said the lady; "il n'y a plus de doute. Le portrait de Shakspeare, du célèbre Davis, et signé même de lui !"

I remember it used to hang up in a silent little street in the Latin quarter, near an old convent, before a quaint old quiet tavern that I loved. It was pleasant to see the old name written up in a strange land, and the well-known friendly face greeting one. There was a quiet little garden at the back of the tavern, and famous good roast beef, clean rooms, and English beer. Where are you now, John Davis? Could not the image of thy august patron preserve thy house from ruin, or rally the faithful around it? Are you unfortunate, Davis? Are you a bankrupt? Let us hope not. I swear to thee, that when, one sunny afternoon, I saw the ensign of thy tavern, I loved thee for thy choice, and doused my cap on entering the porch, and looked around, and thought all friends were here.

In the queer old pleasant novel of the "Spiritual Quixote" honest Tugwell, the Sancho of the story, relates a Warwickshire legend, which at the time Graves wrote was not much more than a hundred years old; and by which it appears that the owner of New Place was a famous jesting gentleman, and used to sit at his gate of summer evenings, cutting the queerest merriest jokes with all the passers-by. I have heard from a Warwickshire clergyman that the legend still exists in the country; and Ward's "Diary" says that Master Shakspeare died of a surfeit, brought on by carousing with a literary friend who had come to visit him from London. And wherefore not? Better to die of good wine and good company than of slow disease and doctors' doses. Some geniuses live on sour misanthropy, and some on meek milk and water. Let us not deal too hardly with those that are of a jovial sort, and indulge in the decent practice of the cup and the platter.

A word or two, by way of conclusion, may be said about the numerous pleasant villages in the neighborhood of

Paris, or rather of the eating and drinking to be found in
the taverns of those suburban spots.   At Versailles, Monsieur Duboux, at the Hôtel des Réservoirs, has a good cook
and cellars, and will gratify you with a heavier bill than is
paid at Véry's and the " Rocher."   On the beautiful terrace
of Saint Germain, looking over miles of river and vine-
yard, of fair villages basking in the meadows, and great
tall trees stretching wide round about, you may sit in the
open air of summer evenings, and see the white spires of
Saint Denis rising in the distance, and the gray arches of
Marly to the right, and before you the city of Paris with
innumerable domes and towers.

Watching these objects, and the setting sun gorgeously
illumining the heavens and them, you may have an excellent
dinner served to you by the *chef* of Messire Gallois, who
at present owns the pavilion where Louis XIV. was born.
The *maître d'hôtel* is from the "Rocher," and told us that
he came out to Saint Germain for the sake of the air.   The
only drawback to the entertainment is, that the charges
are as atrociously high in price as the dishes provided are
small in quantity; and dining in this pavilion on the 15th
of April, at a period when a *botte* of asparagus at Paris
cost only three francs, the writer of this and a chosen
associate had to pay seven francs for about the third part
of a *botte* of asparagus served up to them by Messire
Gallois.

Facts like these ought not to go unnoticed.   Therefore
let the readers of *Fraser's Magazine* who propose a visit to
Paris take warning by the unhappy fate of the person now
addressing them, and avoid the place or not, as they think
fit.   A bad dinner does no harm to any human soul, and
the philosopher partakes of such with easy resignation;
but a bad and dear dinner is enough to raise the anger of
any man, however naturally sweet-tempered, and he is
bound to warn his acquaintance of it.

With one parting syllable in praise of the "Marronniers"
at Bercy, where you get capital eels, fried gudgeons fresh
from the Seine, and excellent wine of the ordinary kind,
this discourse is here closed.   " En telle ou meilleure pensée, Beuueurs très illustres (car à vous non à aultres sont
dédiés ces escriptz), reconfortez vostre malheur, et beuuez
fraiz si faire se peult."

MEN AND COATS.

[*Fraser's Magazine, August,* 1841.]

THERE is some peculiar influence, which no doubt the reader has remarked in his own case, for it has been sung by ten thousand poets or versifying persons, whose ideas you adopt, if perchance, as is barely possible, you have none of your own — there is, I say, a certain balmy influence in the spring-time, which brings a rush of fresh dancing blood into the veins of all nature, and causes it to wear a peculiarly festive and sporting look. Look at the old Sun, — how pale he was all the winter through! Some days he was so cold and wretched he would not come out at all, — he would not leave his bed till eight o'clock, and retired to rest, the old sluggard! at four; but lo! comes May, and he is up at five, — he feels, like the rest of us, the delicious vernal influence; he is always walking abroad in the fresh air, and his jolly face lights up anew! Remark the trees; they have dragged through the shivering winter-time without so much as a rag to cover them, but about May they feel obligated to follow the mode, and come out in a new suit of green. The meadows, in like manner, appear invested with a variety of pretty spring fashions, not only covering their backs with a brand-new glossy suit, but sporting a world of little coquettish ornamental gimcracks that are suited to the season. This one covers his robe with the most delicate twinkling white daisies; that tricks himself out with numberless golden cowslips, or decorates his bosom with a bunch of dusky violets. Birds sing and make love; bees wake and make honey; horses and men leave off their shaggy winter clothing and turn out in fresh coats. The only animal that does not feel the power of spring is that selfish, silent, and cold-blooded beast, the oyster, who shuts himself up for the best months of the year, and with whom the climate disagrees.

Some people have wondered how it is that what is called "the season" in London should not begin until spring. What an absurd subject for wondering at! How *could* the London season begin at any other time? How could the great, black, bilious, overgrown city, stifled by gas, and fogs, and politics, ever hope to have a season at all, unless nature with a violent effort came to its aid about Eastertime, and infused into it a little spring blood? The town of London feels then the influences of the spring, and salutes it after its fashion. The parks are green for about a couple of months. Lady Smigsmag and other leaders of the *ton* give their series of grand parties; Gunter and Grange come forward with iced-creams and champagnes; ducks and green peas burst out; the river Thames blossoms with whitebait; and Alderman Birch announces the arrival of fresh lively turtle. If there are no birds to sing and make love, as in country places, at least there are coveys of opera-girls that frisk and hop about airily, and Rubini and Lablache to act as a couple of nightingales. "A lady of fashion remarked," says Dyson in the *Morning Post,* "that for all persons pretending to hold a position in genteel society," — I forget the exact words, but the sense of them remains indelibly engraven upon my mind, — "for any one pretending to take a place in genteel society two things are *indispensable.* And what are these? — a BOUQUET AND AN EMBROIDERED POCKET-HANDKERCHIEF." This is a self-evident truth. Dyson does not furnish the bouquets — he is not a market-gardener — he is not the goddess Flora; but, a town man, he knows what the season requires, and furnishes his contribution to it. The lilies of the field are not more white and graceful than his embroidered nose ornaments, and, with a little *eau des cent milles fleurs,* not more fragrant. Dyson knows that pocket-handkerchiefs are necessary, and has "an express from Longchamps" to bring them over.

Whether they are picked from ladies' pockets by Dyson's couriers, who then hurry breathless across the Channel with them, no one need ask. But the gist of Dyson's advertisement, and of all the preceding remarks, is this great truth, which need not be carried out further by any illustrations from geography or natural history, — that in the spring-time all nature renews itself. There is not a country newspaper published in England that does not proclaim the same fact. Madame Hoggin informs the nobility and gentry of Penzance that her new and gigantic stock of Parisian fashions has just arrived from London. Mademoiselle M'Whirter begs to announce to the *haut-ton* in the environs of John-o'-Groat's that she has this instant re-turned from Paris, with her dazzling and beautiful collection of spring fashions.

In common with the birds, the trees, the meadows, — in common with the Sun, with Dyson, with all nature, in fact, — I yielded to the irresistible spring impulse — *homo sum, nihil humani a me alienum,* etc. — I acknowledged the influence of the season, and ordered a new coat, waistcoat, and tr—— in short, a new suit. Now, having worn it for a few days, and studied the effect which it has upon the wearer, I thought that perhaps an essay upon new clothes and their influence might be attended with some profit both to the public and the writer.

One thing is certain. A man does not have a new suit of clothes every day; and another general proposition may be advanced, that a man in sporting a coat for the first time is either

> agreeably affected, or
> disagreeably affected, or
> not affected at all, —

which latter case I don't believe. There is no man, how-ever accustomed to new clothes, but must feel some senti-ment of pride in assuming them, — no philosopher, however calm, but must remark the change of raiment. Men con-sent to wear old clothes forever, — nay, feel a pang at parting with them for new; but the first appearance of a new garment is always attended with exultation.

Even the feeling of shyness, which makes a man ashamed of his splendor, is a proof of his high sense of it. What causes an individual to sneak about in corners and shady places, to avoid going out in new clothes of a Sunday, lest he be mistaken for a snob? Sometimes even to go the length of ordering his servant to powder his new coat with sand, or to wear it for a couple of days, and remove the gloss thereof? Are not these manœuvres proofs of the effects of new coats upon mankind in general?

As this notice will occupy at least ten pages (for a reason that may be afterwards mentioned), I intend, like the great philosophers who have always sacrificed themselves for the public good — imbibing diseases, poisons, and medi-cines, submitting to operations, inhaling asphyxiations, etc., in order that they might note in themselves the particular phenomena of the case, — in like manner, I say, I intend to write this essay in five several coats, viz. : —

1. My old single-breasted black frock-coat, with patches at the elbows, made to go into mourning for William IV.

2. My double-breasted green ditto, made last year but one, and still very good, but rather queer about the lining, and snowy in the seams.

3. My grand black dress-coat, made by Messrs. Sparding and Spohrer, of Conduit Street, in 1836. A little scouring and renovating having given it a stylish look even now; and it was always a splendid cut.

4. My worsted-net jacket that my uncle Harry gave me on his departure for Italy. This jacket is wadded inside with a wool like that one makes Welsh wigs of; and, though not handsome, amazing comfortable, with pockets all over.

5. MY NEW FROCK-COAT.

Now, will the reader be able to perceive any difference in the style of writing of each chapter? I fancy I see it myself clearly; and am convinced that the new frock-coat chapter will be infinitely more genteel, spruce, and glossy than the woollen-jacket chapter; which, again, shall be more comfortable than the poor, seedy, patched William-the-Fourth's black-frock chapter. The double-breasted green one will be dashing, manly, free and easy; and, though not fashionable, yet with a well-bred look. The grand black-dress chapter will be solemn and grave, devil-ish tight about the waist, abounding in bows and shrugs, and small talk; it will have a great odor of bohea and pound cake; perhaps there will be a faint whiff of negus; and the tails will whisk up in a quadrille at the end, or sink down, mayhap, on a supper-table bench before a quantity of trifles, lobster salads, and champagnes; and near a lovely blushing white satin skirt, which is continually crying out, "O you ojous creature!" or, "O you naughty satirical man, you!" "And do you really believe Miss Moffat dyes her hair?" "And have you read that sweet thing in the 'Keepsake' by Lord Diddle?" "Well, only one *leetle* leetle drop, for mamma will scold;" and "O you horrid Mr. Titmarsh, you have filled my glass, I declare!" Dear white satin skirt, what pretty shoulders and eyes you have! what a nice white neck, and bluish-mottled, round, innocent arms! how fresh you are and candid! and ah, my dear, what a fool you are!

I don't have so many coats nowadays as in the days of hot youth, when the figure was more elegant, and credit, mayhap, more plenty; and, perhaps, this accounts for the feeling of unusual exultation that comes over me as I assume this one. Look at the skirts how they are shining in the sun, with a delicate gloss upon them, — that evanescent gloss that passes away with the first freshness of the coat, as the bloom does from the peach. A friend meets you, — he salutes you cordially, but looks puzzled for a moment at the change in your appearance. "I have it!" says 'Jones. "Hobson, my boy, I congratulate you, — a new coat, and very neat cut, — puce-colored frock, brown silk lining, brass buttons and velvet collar, — quite novel, and quiet and genteel at the same time." You say, "Pooh, Jones! do you think so, though?" and at the same time turn round just to give him a view of the back, in which there is not a single wrinkle. You find suddenly that you must buy a new stock; that your old Berlin gloves will never do; and that a pair of three-and-sixpenny kids are absolutely necessary. You find your boots are cruelly thick, and fancy that the attention of the world is accurately divided between the new frock-coat and the patch on your great toe. It is very odd that that patch did not annoy you yesterday in the least degree, — that you looked with a good-natured grin at the old sausage-fingered Berlin gloves, bulging out at the end and concaved like spoons. But there *is* a change in the man, without any doubt. Notice Sir M—— O'D——: those who know that celebrated military man by sight are aware of one peculiarity in his appearance — his hat is never brushed. I met him one day with the beaver brushed quite primly; and, looking hard at the baronet to ascertain the cause of this phenomenon, saw that he had a new coat. Even his great spirit was obliged to yield to the power of the coat, — he made a genteel effort, — he awoke up from his habitual Diogenic carelessness; and I have no doubt, had Alexander, before he visited the cynic, ordered some one to fling a new robe into his barrel, but that he would have found the fellow prating and boasting with all the airs of a man of fashion, and talking of tilburies, opera-girls, and the last ball at Devonshire House, as if the brute had been used all his life to no other company. Fie upon the swaggering vulgar bully! I have always wondered how the Prince of Macedon, a gentleman by birth, with an excellent tutor to educate him, could have been imposed upon by the grovelling, obscene, envious tub-man, and could have uttered the speech we know of. It was a humbug, depend upon it, attributed to his Majesty by some maladroit *bon-mot* maker of the Court, and passed subsequently for genuine Alexandrine.

It is hardly necessary for the moralist earnestly to point out to persons moving in a modest station of life the necessity of not having coats of too fashionable and rakish a cut. Coats have been, and will be in the course of this disquisition, frequently compared to the flowers of the field; like them they bloom for a season, like them they grow seedy and they fade.

Can you afford always to renew your coat when this fatal hour arrives? Is your coat like the French monarchy, and does it never die? Have, then, clothes of the newest fashion, and pass on to the next article in the Magazine, — unless, always, you prefer the style of this one.

But while a shabby coat, worn in a manly way, is a bearable, nay, sometimes a pleasing object, reminding one of "a good man struggling with the storms of fate," whom Mr. Joseph Addison has represented in his tragedy of "Cato," — while a man of a certain character may look august and gentlemanlike in a coat of a certain cut, — it is quite impossible for a person who sports an ultra-fashionable costume to wear it with decency beyond a half-year, say. *My* coats always last me two years, and any man who knows me knows how *I* look; but I defy Count d'Orsay thus publicly to wear a suit for seven hundred and thirty days consecutively, and look respectable at the end of that time. In like manner I would defy, without any disrespect, the Marchioness of X——, or her Grace the Duchess of Z——, to sport a white satin gown constantly for six months and look decent. There is *propriety* in dress. Ah, my poor Noll Goldsmith, in your famous plum-colored velvet! I can see thee strutting down Fleet Street, and stout old Sam rolling behind as Maister Boswell pours some Caledonian jokes into his ear, and grins at the poor vain poet. In what a pretty condition will Goldy's puce-colored velvet be about two months hence, when it is covered with dust and grease, and he comes in his slatternly finery to borrow a guinea of his friend.

A friend of the writer's once made him a present of two very handsome gold pins; and what did the author of this notice do ? Why, with his usual sagacity, he instantly sold the pins for five and twenty shillings, the cost of the gold, knowing full well that he could not afford to live up to such fancy articles. If you sport handsome gold pins, you must have everything about you to match. Nor do I in the least agree with my friend Bosk, who has a large amethyst brooch, and fancies that, because he sticks it in his shirt, his atrocious shabby stock and surtout may pass muster. No, no! let us be all peacock, if you please; but one peacock's feather in your tail is a very absurd ornament, and of course all moderate men will avoid it. I remember, when I travelled with Captain Cook in the South Sea Islands, to have seen Quashamaboo with nothing on him but a remarkably fine cocked hat, his queen sported a red coat, and one of the princesses went frisking about in a pair of leather breeches, much to our astonishment.

This costume was not much more absurd than poor Goldsmith's, who might be very likely seen drawing forth from the gold-embroidered pocket of his plum-colored velvet a pat of butter wrapped in a cabbage-leaf, a pair of farthing rush-lights, an onion or two, and a bit of bacon.

I recollect meeting a great, clever, ruffianly boor of a man, who had made acquaintance with a certain set of very questionable aristocracy, and gave himself the air of a man of fashion. He had a coat made of the very pattern of Lord Toggery's — a green frock, a green velvet collar, a green lining: a plate of spring cabbage is not of a brisker, brighter hue. This man, who had been a shopkeeper's apprentice originally, now declared that every man who was a gentleman wore white kid gloves, and for a certain period sported a fresh pair every day.

One hot, clear, sunshiny July day, walking down the Haymarket at two o'clock, I heard a great yelling and shouting of blackguard boys, and saw that they were hunting some object in their front.

The object approached us, — it was a green object, — a green coat, collar, and lining, and a pair of pseudo-white kid gloves. The gloves were dabbled with mud and blood, the man was bleeding at the nose, and slavering at the mouth, and yelling some unintelligible verses of a song, and swaying to and fro across the sunshiny street, with the blackguard boys in chase.

I turned round the corner of Vigo Lane with the velocity of a cannon-ball, and sprang panting into a baker's shop.

It was Mr. Bludyer, our London Diogenes.   Have a care,
ye gay dashing Alexanders ! how ye influence such men by
too much praise, or debauch them by too much intimacy.
How much of that man's extravagance, and absurd aristocratic airs, and subsequent *roueries*, and cutting of old
acquaintance, is to be attributed to his imitation of Lord
Toggery's coat !

Actors of the lower sort affect very much braiding and
fur collars to their frock-coats; and a very curious and
instructive sight it is to behold these personages with pale
lean faces, and hats cocked on one side, in a sort of pseudo-
military trim.   One sees many such sauntering under
Drury Lane Colonnade, or about Bow Street, with sickly
smiles on their faces.   Poor fellows, poor fellows ! how
much of their character is embroidered in that seedy braiding of their coats !   Near five o'clock, in the neighborhood
of Rupert Street and the Haymarket, you may still occasionally see the old, shabby, manly, gentlemanly, half-pay
frock : but the braid is now growing scarce in London; and
your military man, with reason perhaps, dresses more like
a civilian; and, understanding life better, and the means of
making his half-crown go as far as five shillings in former
days, has usually a club to dine at, and leaves Rupert Street
eating-houses to persons of a different grade, — to some of
those dubious dandies whom one sees swaggering in Regent
Street in the afternoon, or to those gay spruce gentlemen
whom you encounter in St. Paul's Churchyard at ten minutes after five, on their way westward from the City.   Look
at the same hour at the Temple, and issuing thence and
from Essex Street you behold many scores of neat barristers, who are walking to the joint and half a pint of Marsala at the Oxford and Cambridge Club.   They are generally tall, slim, proper, well-dressed men, but their coats are
too prim and professionally cut.   Indeed, I have generally
remarked that their clerks, who leave chambers about the
same time, have a far more rakish and fashionable air; and
if, my dear madam, you will condescend to take a beefsteak
at the "Cock," or at some of the houses around Covent
Garden, you will at once allow that this statement is
perfectly correct.

I have always had rather a contempt for a man who, on
arriving at home, deliberately takes his best coat from his
back and adopts an old and shabby one.   It is a mean precaution.   Unless very low in the world indeed, one should

be above a proceeding so petty. Once I knew a French
lady very smartly dressed in a black velvet pelisse, a person
whom I admired very much, — and indeed for the matter
of that she was very fond of me, but that is neither here
nor there, — I say I knew a French lady of some repute
who used to wear a velvet pelisse, and how do you think
the back of it was arranged?

Why, pelisses are worn, as you know, very full behind;
and Madame de Tournuronval had actually a strip of black
satin let into the hinder part of her dress, over which the
velvet used to close with a spring when she walked or
stood, so that the satin was invisible. But when she sat
on a chair, especially one of the cane-bottomed species,
Euphemia gave a loose to her spring, the velvet divided on
each side, and she sat down on the satin.

Was it an authorized stratagem of millinery? Is a
woman under any circumstances permitted to indulge in
such a manœuvre? I say, No. A woman with such a
gown is of a mean deceitful character. Of a woman who
has a black satin patch behind her velvet gown, it is right
that one should speak ill behind the back; and when I saw
Euphemia Tournuronval spread out her wings (*non usitatæ
pennæ*, but what else to call them?) — spread out her skirts
and insure them from injury by means of this dastardly
ruse, I quitted the room in disgust, and never was intimate
with her as before. A widow I know she was; I am certain she looked sweet upon me; and she said she had a
fortune, but I don't believe it. Away with parsimonious
ostentation! That woman, had I married her, would either
have turned out a swindler, or we should have had *bouilli*
five times a week for dinner, — *bouilli* off silver, and hungry
lackeys in lace looking on at the windy meal!

The old coat plan is not so base as the above female
arrangement; but, say what you will, it is not high-minded
and honorable to go out in a good coat, to flaunt the streets
in it with an easy *dégagé* air, as if you always wore such,
and, returning home, assume another under pretext of dressing for dinner. There is no harm in putting on your old
coat of a morning, or in wearing one always. Common
reason points out the former precaution, which is at once
modest and manly. If your coat pinches you, there is no
harm in changing it; if you are going out to dinner, there
is no harm in changing it for a better. But I say the plan
of habitual changing is a base one, and only fit for a man at

last extremities; or for a clerk in the City, who hangs up his best garment on a peg, both at the office and at home; or for a man who smokes, and has to keep his coat for tea-parties, — a paltry precaution, however, this. If you like smoking, why shouldn't you? If you *do* smell a little of tobacco, where's the harm? The smell is not pleasant, but it does not kill anybody. If the lady of the house do not like it, she is quite at liberty not to invite you again. *Et puis?* Bah! Of what age are you and I? Have we lived? Have we seen men and cities? Have we their manners noted, and understood their idiosyncrasy? Without a doubt! And what is the truth at which we have arrived? This, — that a pipe of tobacco is many an hour in the day, and many a week in the month, a thousand times better and more agreeable society than the best Miss, the loveliest Mrs., the most beautiful Baroness, Countess, or what not. Go to tea-parties, those who will; talk fiddle-faddle, such as like; many men there are who do so, and are a little partial to music, and know how to twist the leaf of the song that Miss Jemima is singing exactly at the right moment. Very good. These are the enjoyments of dress-coats; but *men*, — are they to be put off with such fare forever? No! One goes out to dinner, because one likes eating and drinking; because the very act of eating and drinking opens the heart, and causes the tongue to wag. But evening parties! Oh, milk and water, bread and butter! No, no, the age is wiser! The manly youth frequents his club for common society, has a small circle of amiable ladies for friendly intercourse, his book and his pipe always.

Do not be angry, ladies, that one of your most ardent and sincere admirers should seem to speak disparagingly of your merits, or recommend his fellows to shun the society in which you ordinarily assemble. No, miss, I am the man who respects you truly, — the man who respects and loves you when you are most lovely and respectable, — in your families, my dears. A wife, a mother, a daughter, — has God made anything more beautiful? A friend, — can one find a truer, kinder, a more generous and enthusiastic one, than a woman often will be? All that has to do with your hearts is beautiful, and in everything with which they meddle a man must be a brute not to love and honor you.

But Miss Rudge in blue crape, squeaking romances at a

harp, or Miss Tobin dancing in a quadrille, or Miss Blogg twisting round the room in the arms of a lumbering Life-guardsman; — what are these? — so many vanities. With the operations here described the heart has nothing to do. Has the intellect? O ye gods! think of Miss Rudge's intellect while singing, —

> " Away, away to the mountain's brow,
>   Where the trees are gently waving;
> Away, away to the fountain's flow,
>   Where the streams are softly la-a-ving!"

These are the words of a real song that I have heard many times, and rapturously applauded too. Such a song, such a poem, — such a songster!

No, madam, if I want to hear a song sung, I will pay eight and sixpence and listen to Tamburini and Persiani. I will not pay, gloves, three and six; cab, there and back, four shillings; silk stockings every now and then, say a shilling a time: I will not pay to hear Miss Rudge screech such disgusting twaddle as the above. If I want to see dancing, there is Taglioni for my money; or across the water, Mrs. Serle and her forty pupils; or at Covent Garden, Madame Vedy, beautiful as a houri, dark-eyed and agile as a gazelle. I can see all these in comfort, and they dance a great deal better than Miss Blogg and Captain Haggerty, the great red-whiskered monster who always wears nankeens because he thinks his legs are fine. If I want conversation, what has Miss Flock to say to me, forsooth, between the figures of a cursed quadrille that we are all so gravely dancing? By heavens, what an agony it is! Look at the he-dancers, they seem oppressed with dreadful care. Look at the cavalier seul! if the operation lasted long the man's hair would turn white, — he would go mad! And is it for this that men and women assemble in multitudes, for this sorry pastime?

No! dance as you will, Miss Smith, and swim through the quadrille like a swan, or flutter through the galop like a sylphide, and have the most elegant fresh toilets, the most brilliantly polished white shoulders, the blandest eyes, the reddest, simperingest mouth, the whitest neck, the — in fact, I say, be as charming as you will, *that* is not the place in which, if you are worth anything, you are most charming. You are beautiful: you are very much *décollo-*

tée ; your eyes are always glancing down at a pretty pearl necklace, round a pearly neck, or on a fresh fragrant bouquet, stuck — fiddlestick ! What is it that the men admire in you ? — the animal, miss, — the white, plump, external Smith, which men with their eye-glasses, standing at various parts of the room, are scanning pertly and curiously, and of which they are speaking brutally. A pretty admiration, truly ! But is it possible that these men can admire anything else in you who have so much that is really admirable ? Cracknell, in the course of the waltz, has just time to pant into your ear, " Were you at Ascot Races ? " Kidwinter, who dances two sets of quadrilles with you, whispers to you, " Do you pwefer thtwawbewy ithe aw wathbewy ithe ? " and asks the name of " that gweat enawmuth fat woman in wed thatin and bird of pawadithe ? " to which you reply, " Law, sir, it's mamma ! " The rest of the evening passes away in conversation similarly edifying. What can any of the men admire in you, you silly creature, but the animal ? There is your mother, now, in red and a bird of paradise, as Kidwinter says. She has a large fan, which she flaps to and fro across a broad chest; and has one eye directed to her Amelia, dancing with Kidwinter before mentioned; another watching Jane, who is dancing *vis-à-vis* with Major Cutts; and a third complacently cast upon Edward, who is figuring with Miss Binx in the other quadrille. How the dear fellow has grown, to be sure ; and how like his papa at his age — heigh-ho ! There is mamma, the best woman breathing; but fat, and even enormous, as has been said of her. Does anybody gaze on *her ?* And yet she was once as slim and as fair as you, O simple Amelia !

Does anybody care for her ? Yes, one. Your father cares for her ; Smith cares for her; and in his eyes she is still the finest woman of the room; and he remembers when he danced down seven and forty couples of a country-dance with her, two years before you were born or thought of. But it was all chance that Miss Hopkins turned out to be the excellent creature she was. Smith did not know any more than that she was gay, plump, good-looking, and had five thousand pounds. Hit or miss, he took her, and has had assuredly no cause to complain; but she might have been a Borgia or Joan of Naples, and have had the same smiling looks and red cheeks and five thousand pounds, which won his heart in the year 1814.

The system of evening parties, then, is a false and absurd one. Ladies may frequent them professionally with
an eye to a husband, but a man is an ass who takes a wife
out of such assemblies, having no other means of judging
of the object of his choice. You are not the same person
in your white crape and satin slip as you are in your morning dress. A man is not the same in his tight coat and
feverish glazed pumps, and stiff white waistcoat, as he is
in his green double-breasted frock, his old black ditto, or
his woollen jacket. And a man is doubly an ass who is in
the habit of frequenting evening parties, unless he is forced
thither in search of a lady to whom he is attached, or unless
he is compelled to go by his wife. A man who loves dancing may be set down to be an ass; and the fashion is
greatly going out with the increasing good sense of the
age. Do not say that he who lives at home, or frequents
clubs in lieu of balls, is a brute, and has not a proper respect
for the female sex; on the contrary, he may respect it most
sincerely. He feels that a woman appears to most advantage, not among those whom she cannot care about, but
among those whom she loves. He thinks her beautiful
when she is at home making tea for her old father. He
believes her to be charming when she is singing a simple
song at her piano, but not when she is screeching at an
evening party. He thinks by far the most valuable part of
her is her heart; and a kind simple heart, my dears, shines
in conversation better than the best of wit. He admires
her best in her intercourse with her family and friends,
and detests the miserable twaddling slipslop that he is
obliged to hear from and utter to her in the course of a
ball; and avoids and despises such meetings.

He keeps his evening coat, then, for *dinners*. And if
this friendly address to all the mothers who read this miscellany may somewhat be acted upon by them; if heads of
families, instead of spending hundreds upon chalking floors,
and Gunter, and cold suppers, and Weippert's band, will
determine upon giving a series of plain, neat, nice dinners,
of not too many courses, but well cooked, of not too many
wines, but good of their sort, and according to the giver's
degree, they will see that the young men will come to them
fast enough; that they will marry their daughters quite as
fast, without injuring their health, and that they will make
a saving at the year's end. I say that young men, young
women, and heads of families should bless me for pointing

out this obvious plan to them, so natural, so hearty, so hospitable, so different to the present artificial mode.

A grand ball in a palace is splendid, generous, and noble, — a sort of procession in which people may figure properly. A family dance is a pretty and pleasant amusement; and (especially after dinner) it does the philosopher's heart good to look upon merry young people who know each other, and are happy, natural, and familiar. But a Baker Street hop is a base invention, and as such let it be denounced and avoided.

A dressing-gown has great merits, certainly, but it is dangerous. A man who wears it of mornings generally takes the liberty of going without a neckcloth, or of not shaving, and is no better than a driveller. Sometimes, to be sure, it is necessary, in self-defence, not to shave, as a precaution against yourself, that is to say; and I know no better means of insuring a man's remaining at home than neglecting the use of the lather and razor for a week, and encouraging a crop of bristles. When I wrote my tragedy, I shaved off for the last two acts my left eyebrow, and never stirred out of doors until it had grown to be a great deal thicker than its right-hand neighbor. But this was an extreme precaution, and unless a man has very strong reasons indeed for stopping at home, and a very violent propensity to gadding, his best plan is to shave every morning neatly, to put on his regular coat, and go regularly to work, and to avoid a dressing-gown as the father of all evil. Painters are the only persons who can decently appear in dressing-gowns; but these are none of your easy morning-gowns; they are commonly of splendid stuff, and put on by the artist in order to render himself remarkable and splendid in the eyes of his sitter. Your loose-wadded German schlafrock, imported of late years into our country, is the laziest, filthiest invention; and I always augur as ill of a man whom I see appearing at breakfast in one, as of a woman who comes downstairs in curl-papers.

By the way, in the third act of "Macbeth," Mr. Macready makes his appearance in the courtyard of Glamis Castle in an affair of brocade that has always struck me as absurd and un-Macbethlike. Mac in a dressing-gown (I mean 'Beth, not 'Ready), — Mac in list slippers, — Mac in a cotton nightcap, with a tassel bobbing up and down, — I say the thought is unworthy, and am sure the worthy thane would have come out, if suddenly called from bed, by any circumstance, however painful, in a *good stout jacket.* It is a more manly, simple, and majestic wear than the lazy dressing-gown; it more becomes a man of Macbeth's mountainous habits; it leaves his legs quite free, to run whithersoever he pleases, — whether to the stables, to look at the animals, — to the farm, to see the pig that has been slaughtered that morning, — to the garden, to examine whether that scoundrel of a John Hoskins has dug up the potato-bed, — to the nursery, to have a romp with the little Macbeths that are spluttering and quarrelling over their porridge, — or whither you will. A man in a jacket is fit company for anybody; there is no shame about it as about being seen in a changed coat; it is simple, steady, and straightforward. It is, as I have stated, all over pockets, which contain everything you want: in one, your buttons, hammer, small nails, thread, twine, and cloth-strips for the trees on the south wall; in another, your dog-whip and whistle, your knife, cigar-case, gingerbread for the children, paper of Epsom salts for John Hoskins's mother, who is mortal bad, — and so on: there is no end to the pockets, and to the things you put in them. Walk about in your jacket, and meet what person you will, you assume at once an independent air; and, thrusting your hands into the receptacle that flaps over each hip, look the visitor in the face, and talk to the ladies on a footing of perfect equality. Whereas, look at the sneaking way in which a man caught in a dressing-gown, in loose bagging trousers most likely (for the man who has a dressing-gown has, two to one, no braces), and in shuffling slippers, — see how he whisks his dressing-gown over his legs, and looks ashamed and uneasy. His lanky hair hangs over his blowzy, fat, shining, unhealthy face; his bristly dumpling-shaped double-chin peers over a flaccid shirt-collar; the sleeves of his gown are in rags, and you see underneath a pair of black wristbands, and the rim of a dingy flannel waistcoat.

A man who is not strictly neat in his person is not an honest man. I shall not enter into this very ticklish subject of personal purification and neatness, because this essay will be read by hundreds of thousands of ladies as well as men; and for the former I would wish to provide nothing but pleasure. Men may listen to stern truths; but for ladies one should only speak verities that are sparkling, rosy, brisk, and agreeable. A man who wears a dressing-gown is not neat in his appearance; his moral character takes invariably some of the slatternliness and looseness of his costume; he becomes enervated, lazy, incapable of great actions; a man IN A JACKET is a man. All great men wore jackets. Walter Scott wore a jacket, as everybody knows; Byron wore a jacket (not that I count a man who turns down his collars for much); I have a picture of Napoleon in a jacket at Saint Helena; Thomas Carlyle wears a jacket; Lord John Russell always mounts a jacket on arriving at the Colonial Office; and if I have a single fault to find with that popular writer, the author of —— never mind what, you know his name, as well as I, — it is that he is in the habit of composing his works in a large-flowered damask dressing-gown, and morocco slippers; whereas in a jacket he would write you off something, not so flowery, if you please, but of honest texture, — something, not so long, but terse, modest, and comfortable, — no great, long strealing tails of periods, — no staring peonies and hollyhocks of illustrations, — no flaring cords and tassels of episodes, — no great, dirty, wadded sleeves of sentiment, ragged at the elbows and cuffs, and mopping up everything that comes in their way, — cigar-ashes, ink, candle-wax, cold brandy and water, coffee, or whatever aids to the brain he may employ as a literary man; not to mention the quantity of tooth-powder, whisker-dye, soap-suds, and pomatum that the same garment receives in the course of the toilets at which it assists. Let all literary men, then, get jackets. I prefer them without tails; but do not let this interfere with another man's pleasure: he may have tails if he likes, and I for one will never say him nay.

Like all things, however, jackets are subject to abuse; and the pertness and conceit of those jackets cannot be sufficiently reprehended which one sees on the backs of men at watering-places, with a telescope poking out of one pocket, and a yellow bandanna flaunting from the other. Nothing is more contemptible than Tims in a jacket, with a blue bird's-eye neck-handkerchief tied sailor-fashion, puffing smoke like a steamer, with his great broad orbicular stern shining in the sun. I always long to give the wretch a smart smack upon that part where his coat-tails ought to be, and advise him to get into a more decent costume. There is an age and a figure for jackets; those who are of a certain build should not wear them in public.

Witness fat officers of the dragoon-guards that one has seen bumping up and down the Steyne, at Brighton, on their great chargers, with a laced and embroidered coat, a cartridge-box, or whatever you call it, of the size of a two-penny loaf, placed on the small of their backs, — if their backs may be said to have a small, — and two little twink-ling abortions of tails pointing downwards to the enormity jolting in the saddle. Officers should be occasionally meas-ured, and after passing a certain width should be drafted into other regiments, or allowed — nay, ordered — to wear frock-coats.

The French tailors make frock-coats very well, but the people who wear them have the disgusting habit of wearing stays, than which nothing can be more unbecoming the dignity of man. Look what a waist the Apollo has, not above four inches less in the girth than the chest is. Look, ladies, at the waist of the Venus, and pray, — pray do not pinch in your dear little ribs in that odious and unseemly way. In a young man a slim waist is very well; and if he looks like the Eddystone lighthouse, it is as nature intended him to look. A man of certain age may be built like a tower, stalwart and straight. Then a man's middle may expand from the pure cylindrical to the bar-rel shape; well, let him be content. Nothing is so horrid as a fat man with a band; an hour-glass is a most mean and ungracious figure. Daniel Lambert is ungracious, but not mean. One meets with some men who look in their frock-coats perfectly sordid, sneaking, and ungentleman-like, who if you see them dressed for an evening have a slim, easy, almost fashionable, appearance. Set these per-sons down as fellows of poor spirit and milksops. Stiff white ties and waistcoats, prim straight tails, and a gold chain will give any man of moderate lankiness an air of factitious gentility; but if you want to understand the in-dividual, look at him in the daytime; see him walking with his hat on. There is a great deal in the build and wearing of hats, a great deal more than at first meets the eye. I know a man who in a particular hat looked so ex-traordinarily like a man of property, that no tradesman on earth could refuse to give him credit. It was one of André's, and cost a guinea and a half ready money; but the person in question was frightened at the enormous charge, and afterwards purchased beavers in the City at the cost of seventeen and sixpence. And what was the consequence ?   He fell off in public estimation, and very soon after he came out in his City hat it began to be whispered abroad that he was a ruined man.

A blue coat is, after all, the best; but a gentleman of my acquaintance has made his fortune by an Oxford mixture, of all colors in the world, with a pair of white buckskin gloves.   He looks as if he had just got off his horse, and as if he had three thousand a year in the country.   There is a kind of proud humility in an Oxford mixture.   Velvet collars, and all such gimcracks, had best be avoided by sober people.   This paper is not written for drivelling dandies, but for honest men.   There is a great deal of philosophy and forethought in Sir Robert Peel's dress; he does not wear those white waistcoats for nothing,   I say that O'Connell's costume is likewise that of a profound rhetorician, slouching and careless as it seems.   Lord Melbourne's air of reckless, good-humored, don't-care-a-damn-ativenesss is not obtained without an effort.   Look at the Duke as he passes along in that stern little straight frock and plaid breeches; look at him, and off with your hat!   How much is there in that little gray coat of Napoleon's!   A spice of claptrap and dandyism, no doubt; but we must remember the country which he had to govern.   I never see a picture of George III., in his old stout Windsor uniform, without feeling a respect ; or of George IV., breeches and silk stockings, a wig, a sham smile, a frogged frock-coat and a fur collar, without that proper degree of reverence which such a costume should inspire.   The coat is the expression of the man, — οἷηπερ φύλλων, etc. ; and as the peach-tree throws out peach-leaves, the pear-tree pear ditto, as old George appeared invested in the sober old garment of blue and red, so did young George in oiled wigs, fur collars, stays, and braided surtouts, according to his nature.

.   .   .   .

Enough, — enough; and may these thoughts, arising in the writer's mind from the possession of a new coat, which circumstance caused him to think not only of new coats but of old ones, and of coats neither old nor new, — and not of coats merely, but of men, — may these thoughts so inspired answer the purpose for which they have been set down on paper, and which is not a silly wish to instruct mankind,— no, no; but an honest desire to pay a deserving tradesman whose confidence supplied the garment in question.

PENTONVILLE, April 25, 1841.

DICKENS IN FRANCE.

SEEING placarded on the walls a huge announcement that "Nicholas Nickleby, ou les Voleurs de Londres," was to be performed at the Ambigu-Comique Théâtre on the Boulevard, and having read in the *Journal des Débats* a most stern and ferocious criticism upon the piece in question, and upon poor Monsieur Dickens, its supposed author, it seemed to me by no means unprofitable to lay out fifty sous in the purchase of a stall at the theatre, and to judge with my own eyes of the merits and demerits of the play.

Who does not remember (except those who never saw the drama, and therefore of course cannot be expected to have any notion of it) — who does not, I say, remember the pathetic acting of Mrs. Keeley in the part of Smike, as performed at the Adelphi; the obstinate good-humor of Mr. Wilkinson, who, having to represent the brutal Squeers, was, according to his nature, so chuckling, oily, and kind-hearted, that little boys must have thought it a good joke to be flogged by him; finally, the acting of the admirable Yates in the kindred part of Mantalini? Can France, I thought, produce a fop equal to Yates? Is there any vulgarity and assurance on the Boulevard that can be compared to that of which, in the character of Mantalini, he gives a copy so wonderfully close to nature? Never then were fifty sous more cheerfully — nay, eagerly paid, than by your obedient servant.

After China, this is the most ignorant country, thought I, in the whole civilized world (the company was dropping into the theatre, and the musicians were one by one taking their seats); these people are so immensely conceited, that they think the rest of Europe beneath them; and though they have invaded Spain, Italy, Russia, Germany, not one in ten thousand can ask for a piece of bread in the national language of the countries so conquered. But see the force of genius; after a time it conquers everything, even the ignorance and conceit of Frenchmen! The name of Nicholas Nickleby crosses the Channel in spite of them. I shall see honest John Browdie and wicked Ralph once more, honest and wicked in French. Shall we have the Kenwigses, and their uncle, the delightful collector; and will he, in Portsmouth Church, make that famous marriage with Juliana Petowker? Above all, what will *Mrs.* Nickleby say? —the famous Mrs. Nickleby, who has lain undescribed until Boz seized upon her, and brought that great truth to light, and whom yet every man possesses in the bosom of his own family. Are there Mrs. Nicklebies — or, to speak more correctly, are there Mistresses Nickleby in France? We shall see all this at the rising of the curtain; and hark! the fiddlers are striking up.

Presently the prompter gives his three heart-thrilling slaps, and the great painted cloth moves upwards: it is always a moment of awe and pleasure. What is coming? First you get a glimpse of legs and feet; then suddenly the owners of the limbs in question in steady attitudes, looking as if they had been there one thousand years before; now behold the landscape, the clouds; the great curtain vanishes altogether, the charm is dissolved, and the disenchanted performers begin.

Act I.

You see a court of a school, with great iron bars in front, and a beauteous sylvan landscape beyond. Could you read the writing on the large board over the gate, you would know that the school was the " Paradis des Enfans," kept by Mr. Squeers. Somewhere by that bright river which meanders through the background is the castle of the stately Earl of Clarendon — no relation to a late ambassador at Madrid.

His lordship is from home; but his young and lovely daughter, Miss Annabella, is in Yorkshire, and at this very moment is taking a lesson of French from Mr. Squeers's *sous-maître*, Neekolass Neeklbee. Nicholas is, however, no vulgar usher; he is but lately an orphan; and his uncle, the rich London banker, Monsieur Ralph, taking charge of the lad's portionless sister, has procured for Nicholas this place of usher at a school in le Yorksheer.

A rich London banker procuring his nephew a place in a school at eight guineas per annum! Sure there must be some roguery in this; and the more so when you know that Monsieur Squeers, the keeper of the academy, was a few years since a vulgar rope-dancer and tumbler at a fair. But, peace! let these mysteries clear up, as, please Heaven, before five acts are over they will. Meanwhile Nicholas is happy in giving his lessons to the lovely Mees Annabel. Lessons, indeed! Lessons of what? Alack, alack! when two young, handsome, ardent, tender-hearted people pore over the same book, we know what may happen, be the book what it may. French or Hebrew, there is always one kind of language in the leaves, as those can tell who have conned them.

Meanwhile, in the absence of his usher, Monsieur Squeers keeps school. But one of his scholars is in the courtyard; a lad beautifully dressed, fat, clean, and rosy. A gentleman by the name of Browdie, by profession a drover, is with the boy, employed at the moment (for he is at leisure and fond of music) in giving him a lesson on *the clarinet*.

The boy thus receiving lessons is called facetiously by his master *Prospectus*, and why? Because he is so excessively fat and healthy, and well clothed, that his mere appearance in the courtyard is supposed to entice parents and guardians to place their children in a seminary where the scholars were in such admirable condition.

And here I cannot help observing, in the first place, that Squeers exhibiting in this manner a sample-boy, and pretending that the whole stock were like him (whereas they are a miserable, half-starved set), must have been an abominable old scoundrel; and, secondly (though the observation applies to the French nation merely, and may be considered more as political than general), that by way of a fat specimen, never was one more unsatisfactory than this. Such a poor shrivelled creature I never saw; it is like a French fat pig, as lanky as a greyhound! Both animals give one a thorough contempt for the nation.

John Browdie gives his lesson to Prospectus, who informs him of some of the circumstances narrated above; and, having concluded the lesson, honest John produces a piece of *pudding* for his pupil. Ah, how Prospectus devours it! for though the only well-fed boy in the school, he is, we regret to say, a gormandizer by disposition.

While Prospectus eats, another of Mr. Squeers's scholars is looking unnoticed on; another boy, a thousand times more miserable. See you poor shivering child, trembling over his book in a miserable hutch at the corner of the court! He is in rags, he is not allowed to live with the other boys; at play they constantly buffet him, at lesson-time their blunders are visited upon his poor shoulders.

Who is this unhappy boy? Ten years since a man by the name of Becher brought him to the Paradis des Enfans; and, paying in advance five years of his pension, left him under the charge of Monsieur Squeers. No family ever visited the child; and when at the five years' end the *instituteur* applied at the address given him by Becher for the further payment of his pupil's expenses, Monsieur Squeers found that Becher had grossly deceived him, that no such persons existed, and that no money was consequently forthcoming, hence the misfortunes which afterwards befell the hapless orphan. None cared for him — none knew him, 'tis possible that even the name he went by was fictitious. That name was Smike, pronounced Smeek.

Poor Smeek! he had, however, found one friend, — the kind-hearted *sous-maître* Neeklbee — who gave him half of his own daily pittance of bread and pudding, encouraged him to apply to his books, and defended him as much as possible from the assaults of the schoolboys and Monsieur Squeers.

John Browdie had just done giving his lesson of clarinet to Prospectus, when Neeklbee arrived at the school. There was a difference between John and Nicholas; for the former, seeing the young usher's frequent visits at Clarendon Castle, foolishly thought he was enamored of Mees Jenny, the fermier's daughter, on whom John too had fixed an eye of affection. Silly John! Nicholas's heart was fixed (hopelessly, as the young man thought) upon higher objects. However, the very instant that Nickleby entered the courtyard of the school, John took up his stick and set off for London, whither he was bound, with a drove of oxen.

Nickleby had not arrived a whit too soon to protect his poor friend, Smeek; all the boys were called into the courtyard by Monsieur Squarrs, and made to say their lessons; when it came to poor Smeek's turn, the timid lad trembled, hesitated, and could not do his spelling.

Inflamed with fury, old Squarrs rushed forward, and would have assommé his pupil, but human nature could bear this tyranny no longer. Nickleby, stepping forward, defended the poor prostrate child; and when Squeers raised his stick to strike — pouf! pif! un, deux, trois, et la! —

Monsieur Nicholas flanquéd him several coups de poing, and sent him bientôt grovelling à terre.

You may be sure that there was now a pretty hallooing among the boys; all jumped, kicked, thumped, bumped, and scratched their unhappy master (and serve him right, too!), and when they had finished their fun, vlan! flung open the gates of the Infants' Paradise and ran away home.

Neeklbee, seeing what he had done, had nothing left but to run away too: he penned a hasty line to his lovely pupil, Miss Annabel, to explain that though his departure was sudden his honor was safe, and seizing his stick quitted the school.

There was but one pupil left in it, and he, poor soul, knew not whither to go. But when he saw Nicholas, his sole friend, departing, he mustered courage, and then made a step forward — and then wondered if he dared — and then, when Nicholas was at a little distance from him, ran, ran, as if his life (as indeed it did) depended upon it.

This is the picture of Neeklbee and poor Smeek.* They are both dressed in the English fashion, and you must fancy the curtain falling amidst thunders of applause. [*End of Act I.*]

"Ah, ah, ah! ouf, pouf." — "Dieu, qu'il fait chaud!" — "Orgeat, limonade, bière!" — "L'Entracte, journal de tous les spectacles!" — "LA MARSEILLAI-AI-AISE!" —with such cries from pit and boxes the public wiles away the weary ten minutes between the acts. The three *bonnes* in the front boxes, who had been escorted by a gentleman in a red cap, and jacket, and earrings, begin sucking oranges with great comfort, while their friend amuses himself with a piece of barley-sugar. The *petite-maîtresse* in the private box smooths her *bandeaux* of hair and her little trim, white cuffs, and looks at her *chiffons*. The friend of the tight black velvet spencer, meanwhile, pulls his yellow kid gloves tighter on his hands, and looks superciliously round the house with his double-glass. Fourteen people, all smelling of smoke, all bearded, and all four feet high, pass over your body to their separate stalls. The prompter gives his thumps, whack — whack — whack! the music begins again, the curtain draws, and, lo! we have

---

* Referring to a sketch, the first of two sketches by the author, which accompanied this paper on its original appearance in *Fraser's Magazine*. — ED.

Act II.

The tavern of Les Armes du Roi appears to be one of the most frequented in the city of London. It must be in the Yorkshire road, that is clear; for the first person whom we see there is John Browdie; to whom presently comes Prospectus, then Neeklbee, then poor Smeek, each running away individually from the Paradis des Enfans.

It is likewise at this tavern that the great banker Ralph does his business, and lets you into a number of his secrets. Hither, too, comes Milor Clarendon, — a handsome peer, forsooth, but a sad reprobate, I fear. Sorrow has driven him to these wretched courses: ten years since he lost a son, a lovely child of six years of age; and, hardened by the loss, he has taken to gambling, to the use of *vins de France* which take the reason prisoner, and to other excitements still more criminal. He has cast his eyes upon the lovely Kate Nickleby (he, the father of Miss Annabel!) and asks the banker to sup with him, to lend him ten thousand pounds, and to bring his niece with him. With every one of these requests the capitalist promises to comply: the money he produces forthwith; the lady he goes to fetch. Ah, milor! beware — beware, your health is bad, your property is ruined, — death and insolvency stare you in the face, — but what cares Lor Clarendon? He is desperate; he orders a splendid repast in a private apartment, and while they are getting it ready, he and the young lords of his acquaintance sit down and crack a bottle in the coffee-room. A gallant set of gentlemen, truly, all in short coats with capes to them, in tights and Hessian boots, such as our nobility are in the custom of wearing.

"I bet you cinq cent guinées, Lor Beef," says Milor Clarendon (whom the wine has begun to excite), "that I will have the lovely Kate Nicklbee at supper with us to-night."

"Done!" says Lor Beef. But why starts yon stranger who has just come into the hotel? Why, forsooth? because he is Nicholas Nickleby, Kate's brother; and a pretty noise he makes when he hears of his lordship's project!

"You have Meess Neeklbee at your table, sir? You are a liar!"

All the lords start up.

"Who is this very strange person?" says Milor Clarendon, as cool as a cucumber.

"Dog! give me your name!" shouts Nicholas.

Ha! ha! ha!" says my lord scornfully.

"John," says Nickleby, seizing hold of a waiter, "tell me that man's name."

John the waiter looks frightened, and hums and ha's, when, at the moment, who should walk in but Mr. Ralph the banker, and his niece.

Ralph. "Nicholas! — confusion!"

Kate. "My brother!"

Nicholas. "Avaunt, woman! Tell me, sirrah, by what right you bring my sister into such company, and who is the villain to whom you have presented her?"

Ralph. "Lord *Clarendon.*"

Nicholas. "The father of Meess Annabel? Gracious heaven!"

What followed now need not be explained. The young lords and the bänker retire abashed to their supper, while Meess Kate, and Smike, who has just arrived, fall into the arms of Nicholas.

Such, ladies and gentlemen, is the second act, rather feeble in interest, and not altogether probable in action. That five people running away from Yorkshire should all come to the same inn in London, arriving within five minutes of each other, — that Mr. Ralph, the great banker, should make the hotel his place of business, and openly confess in the coffee-room to his ex-agent Becher that he had caused Becher to make away with or murder the son of Lord Clarendon, — finally, that Lord Clarendon himself, with an elegant town mansion, should receive his distinguished guests in a tavern, of not the first respectability,— all these points may, perhaps, strike the critic from their extreme improbability. But, bless your soul! if *these* are improbabilities, what will you say to the revelations of the

Third Act.

That scoundrel Squarrs before he kept the school was, as we have seen, a tumbler and *saltimbanque*, and, as such, member of the great fraternity of cadgers, beggars, *gueux,* thieves, that have their club in London. It is held in immense Gothic vaults under ground : here the beggars concert their plans, divide their spoil, and hold their orgies.

In returning to London Monsieur Squarrs instantly resumes his acquaintance with his old comrades, who appoint him, by the all-powerful interest of a *peculiar person,* head of the community of cadgers.

That person is no other than the banker Ralph, who, in secret, directs this godless crew, visits their haunts, and receives from them a boundless obedience. A villain himself, he has need of the aid of villany. He pants for vengeance against his nephew, he has determined that his niece shall fall a prey to Milor Clarendon, — nay, more, he has a dark suspicion that Smike — the orphan boy — the homeless fugitive from Yorkshire — is no other than the child who ten years ago — but, hush!

Where is his rebellious nephew and those whom he protects? The quick vigilance of Ralph soon discovered them; Nicholas, having taken the name of Edward Browne, was acting at a theatre in the neighborhood of the Thames. Haste, Squarrs, take a couple of trusty beggars with you, and hie thee to Wapping; seize young Smike and carry him to Cadger's Cavern, — haste, then! The mind shudders to consider what is to happen.

In Nicholas's room at the theatre we find his little family assembled, and with them honest John Browdie, who has forgotten his part on learning that Nicholas was attached, not to the *fermière*, but to the mistress; to them comes — gracious heavens! — Meess Annabel. "Fly!" says she, "fly! I have overheard a plot concocted between my father and your uncle; the sheriff is to seize you for the abduction of Smeek and the assault upon Squarrs," etc., etc., etc.

In short, it is quite impossible to describe this act, so much is there done in it. Lord Clarendon learns that he has pledged his life interest in his estates to Ralph.

His lordship *dies*, and Ralph seizes a paper, which proves beyond a doubt that young Smike is no other than Clarendon's long-lost son.

L'infame Squarrs with his satellites carry off the boy; Browdie pitches Squarrs into the river; the sheriff carries Nickleby to prison; and VICE TRIUMPHS in the person of the odious Ralph. But vice does not always triumph; wait a while and you will see. For in the

FOURTH ACT

John Browdie, determined to rescue his two young friends, follows Ralph like his shadow; he dogs him to a *rendez-vous* of the beggars, and overhears all his conversation with Squarrs. The boy is in the Cadger's Cavern, hidden a thou-

sand feet below the Thames; there is to be a grand jollifi-
cation among the rogues that night — a dance and a feast.
" *I,*" says John Browdie, " *will be there.*" And, wonderful
to say, who should pass but his old friend Prospectus, to
whom he gave lessons on the clarinet.

Prospectus is a cadger now, and is to play his clarinet
that night at Cadger's Hall. Browdie will join him, — he
is dressed up like a blind beggar, and strange sights, Heaven
knows, meet his eyes in Cadger's Hall.

Here they come trooping in by scores, — the halt and the
lame, black sweepers, one-legged fiddlers, the climber mots,
the fly-sakers, the kedgoree coves, — in a word, the rogues
of London, to their Gothic hall, a thousand miles below the
level of the sea. Squarrs is their nominal head; but their
real leader is the tall man yonder in the black mask, he
whom nobody knows but Browdie, who has found him out
at once, — 'tis Ralph!

"Bring out the prisoner," says the black mask; "he has
tried to escape — he has broken his oaths to the cadgers,
let him meet his punishment."

And without a word more, what do these cadgers do?
They take poor Smike and *bury him alive;* down he goes
into the vault, a stone is rolled over him, the cadgers go
away, — so much for Smike.

But in the mean time Master Browdie has not been idle.
He has picked the pocket of one of the cadgers of a portfolio containing papers that prove Smike to be Lord Clarendon beyond a doubt; he lags behind until all the cadgers
are gone, and with the help of Nicholas (who, by the by,
has found his way somehow into the place), he pushes away
the stone, and brings the fainting boy to the world.

These things are improbable you certainly may say, but
are they impossible? If they are possible, then they may
come to pass; if they may come to pass, then they may be
supposed to come to pass: and why should they not come
to pass? That is my argument: let us pass on to the

FIFTH ACT.

Aha! Master Ralph, you think you will have it all your
own way, do you? The lands of Clarendon are yours, provided there is no male heir, and you have done for *him.* The
peerage, to be sure (by the laws of England), is to pass to
the husband of Meess Annabella. Will she marry Ralph,

or not? Yes: then well and good; he is an earl for the future and the father of a new race of Clarendon. No: then, in order to spell her still more, he has provided amongst the beggars a lad who is to personate the young mislaid Lord Clarendon, who is to come armed with certain papers that make his right unquestionable, and who will be a creature of Ralph's, to be used or cast away at will.

Ralph pops the question; the lady repels him with scorn. "Quit the house, Meess," says he; "it is not yours, but mine. Give up that vain title which you have adopted since your papa's death; you are no countess, — your brother lives. Ho! John, Thomas, Samuel! introduce his lordship, the Comte de Clarendon."

And who slips in? Why, in a handsome new dress, in the English fashion, Smike to be sure — the boy whom Ralph has murdered — the boy who had risen from the tomb — the boy who had miraculously discovered the papers in Cadger's Hall and (by some underhand work that went on behind the scenes, which I don't pretend to understand) had substituted himself for the substitute which that wicked banker had proposed to bring forward! A rush of early recollections floods the panting heart of the young boy. Can it be? Yes — no; sure these halls are familiar to him? That conservatory, has he not played with the flowers there — played with his blessed mother at his side? That portrait! Stop! a—a—a—a—ah! it is — it is my sister Anna — Anna — bella!

Fancy the scene as the two young creatures rush with a scream into each other's arms. Fancy John Browdie's hilarity: he jumps for joy, and throws off his beggar's cloak and beard. Nicholas clasps his hands, and casts his fine eyes heavenward. But, above all, fancy the despair of that cursed banker Ralph as he sees his victim risen from the grave, and all his hopes dashed down into it. Oh! Heaven, Thy hand is here! How must the banker then have repented of his bargain with the late Lord Clarendon, and that he had not had his lordship's life insured! Perdition! to have been out-tricked by a boy and a country boor! Is there no hope? . . .

Hope? Psha! man, thy reign of vice is over, — it is the fifth act. Already the people are beginning to leave the house, and never more again canst thou expect to lift thy head.

"Monsieur Ralph," Browdie whispers, "after your pretty

doings in Cadger's Hall, had you not best be thinking of leaving the country, as Nicholas Nickleby's uncle, I would fain not see you, crick! You understand?" (pointing to his jugular).

"I do," says Ralph gloomily, "and will be off in two hours." And Lord Smike takes honest Browdie by one hand, gently pressing Kate's little fingers with the other, and the sheriff, and the footmen, and attendants form a tableau, and the curtain begins to fall, and the blushing Annabel whispers to happy Nicholas, — "Ah! my friend, I can give up with joy to my brother *ma couronne de comtesse*. What care I for rank or name with you? the name that I love above all others is that of LADY ANNABEL NICKLEBY." [*Exeunt omnes.*

The musicians have hurried off long before this. In one instant the stage lamps go out, and you see fellows starting forward to cover the boxes with canvas. Up goes the chandelier amongst the gods and goddesses painted on the ceiling. Those in the galleries, meanwhile, bellow out "SAINT ERNEST!" he it is who acted John Browdie. Then there is a yell of "SMEEK! SMEEK!" Blushing and bowing, Madame Prosper comes forward; by Heavens! a pretty woman, with tender eyes and a fresh, clear voice. Next the gods call for "CHILLY!" who acted the villain: but by this time you are bustling and struggling among the crowd in the lobbies, where there is the usual odor of garlic and tobacco. Men in sabots come tumbling down from the galleries; cries of "*Auguste, solo! Eugénie! prends ton parapluie.*" "*Monsieur, vous me marchez sur les pieds,*" are heard in the crowd, over which the brazen helmets of the Pompier's tower are shining. A cabman in the Boulevard, who opens his vehicle eagerly as you pass by, growls dreadful oaths when, seated inside, you politely request him to drive to the Barrière de l'Etoile. "*Ah, ces Anglais,*" says he, "*ça demeure dans les déserts — dans les déserts, grand Dieu! avec les loups; ils prennent leur* beauty-fine *thé avec leurs tartines le soir, et puis ils se couchent dans les déserts, ma parole d'honneur; commes des Arabes.*"

If the above explanation of the plot of the new piece of *Nicholas Nickleby* has appeared intolerably long to those few persons who have perused it, I can only say for their comfort that I have not told one-half of the real plot of the piece in question; nay, very likely have passed over all the most interesting part of it. There, for instance, was the assassination of the virtuous villain Becher, the dying scene with my lord, the manner in which Nicholas got into the Cadger's Cave, and got out again. Have I breathed a syllable upon any of these points? No; and never will to my dying day. The imperfect account of *Nicholas Nickleby* given above is all that the most impatient reader (let him have fair warning) can expect to hear from his humble servant. Let it be sufficient to know that the piece in itself contains a vast number of beauties entirely passed over by the unworthy critic, and only to be appreciated by any gentleman who will take the trouble to step across the Channel, and thence from his hotel to the ambiguously comic theatre. And let him make haste, too; for who knows what may happen? Human life is proverbially short. Theatrical pieces bloom and fade like the flowers of the field, and very likely long before this notice shall appear in print (as let us heartily, from mercenary considerations, pray that it will), the drama of *Nicholas Nickleby* may have disappeared altogether from the world's ken, like Carthage, Troy, Swallow Street, the Marylebone bank, Babylon, and other fond magnificences elevated by men, and now forgotten and prostrate.

As for the worthy Boz, it will be seen that *his* share in the piece is perfectly insignificant, and that he has no more connection with the noble geniuses who invented the drama than a peg has with a gold-laced hat that a nobleman may have hung on it, or a starting-post on the race-course with some magnificent thousand-guinea fiery horses who may choose to run from it. How poor do his writings appear after those of the Frenchman! How feeble, mean, and destitute of imagination! *He* never would have thought of introducing six lords, an ex-kidnapper, a great banker, an idiot, a schoolmaster, his usher, a cattle-driver, coming for the most part a couple of hundred miles, in order to lay open all their secrets in the coffee-room of the King's Arms hotel! He never could have invented the great subterraneous cavern, *cimetière et salle de bal*, as Jules Janin calls it! The credit of all this falls upon the French adapters of Monsieur Dickens's romance; and so it will be advisable to let the public know.

But as the French play-writers are better than Dickens, being incomparably more imaginative and poetic, so, in progression, is the French critic, Jules Janin, above named, a million times superior to the French playwrights, and, after Janin, Dickens disappears altogether. • He is cut up, disposed of, done for. J. J. has hacked him into small pieces, and while that wretched romancer is amusing himself across the Atlantic, and fancying, perhaps, that he is a popular character, his business has been done for ever and ever in Europe. What matters that he is read by millions in England and billions in America? that everybody who understands English has a corner in his heart for him? The great point is, *what does Jules Janin think?* and that we shall hear presently; for though I profess the greatest admiration for Mr. Dickens, yet there can be no reason why one should deny one's self the little pleasure of acquainting him that *some* ill-disposed persons in the world are inclined to abuse him. Without this privilege what is friendship good for?

Who is Janin? He is the critic of France. J. J., in fact, — the man who writes a weekly *feuilleton* in the *Journal des Débats* with such indisputable brilliancy and wit, and such a happy mixture of effrontery, and honesty, and poetry, and impudence, and falsehood, and impertinence, and good feeling, that one can't fail to be charmed with the compound, and to look rather eagerly for the Monday's paper; — Jules Janin is the man who, not knowing a single word of the English language, as he actually professes in the preface, *has helped to translate* the *Sentimental Journey.* He is the man who, when he was married (in a week when news were slack no doubt), actually *criticised his own marriage ceremony*, letting all the public see the proof-sheets of his bridal, as was the custom among certain ancient kings, I believe. In fact, a more modest, honest, unassuming, blushing, truth-telling, gentlemanlike J. J., it is impossible to conceive.

Well, he has fallen foul of Monsieur Dickens, this fat French moralist; he says Dickens is *immodest*, and Jules cannot abide immodesty; and a great and conclusive proof this is upon a question which the two nations have been in the habit of arguing, namely, which of the two is the purer in morals? and may be argued clear thus: —

1. We in England are accustomed to think Dickens modest, and allow our children to peruse his works.

2. In France, the man who wrote the history of *The Dead Donkey and the Guillotined Woman,** and afterwards

* Some day the writer meditates a great and splendid review of J. J.'s work.

his own epithalamium in the newspaper, is revolted by
Dickens.   •

3. Therefore Dickens *must* be immodest, and grossly
immodest, otherwise a person so confessedly excellent as
J. J. would never have discovered the crime.

4. And therefore it is pretty clear that the French morals
are of a much higher order than our own, which remark
will apply to persons and books and all the relations of
private and public life.

Let us now see how our fat Jules attacks Dickens. His
remarks on him begin in the following jocular way : —

"THÉÂTRE DE L'AMBIGU COMIQUE.
"NICOLAS NICKLEBY, MÉLODRAME, EN SIX ACTES.

" A genoux devant celui-là qui s'appelle Charles Dickens !
à genoux ! Il a accompli à lui seul ce que n'ont pu faire à
eux deux lord Byron et Walter Scott ! Joignez-y, si vous
voulez, Pope et Milton et tout ce que la littérature Anglaise
a produit de plus solennel et de plus charmant. Charles
Dickens ! mais il n'est question que de lui en Angleterre.
Il en est la gloire, et la joie, et l'orgueil ! Savez-vous com-
bien d'acheteurs possède ce Dickens ; j'ai dit *d'acheteurs*, de
gens qui tirent leur argent de leur bourse pour que cet
argent passe de leur main dans la main du libraire ? — Dix
mille acheteurs. Dix mille ? que disons-nous, dix mille !
vingt mille ! — Vingt mille ? Quoi ! vingt mille acheteurs ?
— Fi donc, vingt mille ! quarante mille acheteurs. — Et
quoi ! il a trouvé quarante mille acheteurs, vous vous moquez
de nous sans doute ? — Oui, mon brave homme, on se moque
de vous, car ce n'est pas vingt mille et quarante mille et
soixante mille acheteurs qu'a rencontrés ce Charles Dickens,
c'est cent mille acheteurs. Cent mille, pas un de moins.
Cent mille esclaves, cent mille tributaires, cent mille ! Et
nos grands écrivains modernes s'estiment bien heureux et
bien fiers quand leur livre le plus vanté parvient, au bout
de six mois de célébrité, à son huitième cent ! "

There is raillery for you ! there is a knowledge of English
literature, — of " Pope et Milton, si solennel et si charmant ! "   Milton, above all ; his little comédie *Samson
l'Agoniste* is one of the gayest and most graceful trifles that
ever was acted on the stage. And to think that Dickens
has sold more copies of his work than the above two eminent hommes-de-lettres, and Scott and Byron into the bar-

gain! It is a fact, and J. J. vouches for it. To be sure, J. J. knows no more of English literature than I do of hieroglyphics, — to be sure, he has not one word of English. N'importe: he has had the advantage of examining the books of Mr. Dickens's publishers, and has discovered that they sell of Boz's works "*cent mille, pas un de moins.*" Janin will not allow of one less. Can you answer numbers? And there are our grands écrivains modernes, who are happy if they sell eight hundred in six months. Byron and Scott doubtless, "le solennel Pope, et le charmant Milton," as well as other geniuses not belonging to the three kingdoms. If a man is an arithmetician as well as a critic, and we join together figures of speech and Arabic numerals, there is no knowing what he may not prove.

"*Or,*" continues J. J.: —

"Or, parmi les chefs-d'œuvre de sa façon que dévore l'Angleterre, ce Charles Dickens a produit un gros mélodrame en deux gros volumes, intitulé *Nicolas Nickleby.* Ce livre a été traduit chez nous par un homme de beaucoup d'esprit, qui n'est pas fait pour ce triste métier-là. Si vous saviez ce que peut être un pareil chef-d'œuvre, certes vous prendriez en pitié les susdits cent mille souscripteurs de Charles Dickens. Figurez-vous donc un amas d'inventions puériles, où l'horrible et le niais se donnent la main, dans une ronde infernale; ici passent en riant de bonnes gens si bons qu'ils en sont tout-à-fait bêtes; plus loin bondissent et blasphèment toutes sortes de bandits, de fripons, de voleurs et de misérables si affreux qu'on ne sait pas comment pourrait vivre, seulement vingt-quatre heures, une société ainsi composée. C'est le plus nauséabond mélange qu'on puisse imaginer de lait chaud et de bière tournée, d'œufs frais et de bœuf salé, de haillons et d'habits brodés, d'écus d'or et de gros sous, de roses et de pissenlits. On se bat, on s'embrasse, on s'injurie, on s'enivre, on meurt de faim. Les filles de la rue et les lords de la Chambre haute, les porte-faix et les poëtes, les écoliers et les voleurs, se promènent, bras dessus bras dessous, au milieu de ce tohubohu insupportable. Aimez-vous la fumée de tabac, l'odeur de l'ail, le goût du porc frais, l'harmonie que fait un plat d'étain frappé contre une casserole de cuivre non étamé? Lisez-moi consciencieusement ce livre de Charles Dickens. Quelles plaies! quelles pustules! et que de saintes vertus! Ce Dickens a réuni en bloc toutes les descriptions de Guzman d'Alfarache et tous les rêves de Grandisson. Oh!

qu'êtes-vous devenus, vous les lectrices tant soit peu prudes
des romans de Walter Scott ?   Oh ! qu'a-t-on fait de vous,
les lectrices animées de *Don Juan* et de *Lara ?*   O vous, les
chastes enthousiastes de la *Clarisse Harlowe,* voilez-vous
la face de honte !   A cent mille exemplaires le Charles
Dickens ! "

   To what a pitch of *dévergondage* must the English ladies
have arrived, when a fellow who can chronicle his own
marriage, and write *The Dead Donkey and the Guillotined
Woman,* — when even a man like that, whom nobody can
accuse of being squeamish, is obliged to turn away with
disgust at their monstrous immodesty !

J. J. is not difficult; a little harmless gallantry and
trifling with the seventh commandment does not offend
him, — far from it.   Because there are no love-intrigues in
Walter Scott, Jules says that Scott's readers are *tant soit
peu prudes!*   There *ought* to be, in fact, in life and in
novels, a little, pleasant, gentlemanlike, anti-seventh-com-
mandment excitement.   Read *The Dead Donkey and the
Guillotined Woman,* and you will see how the thing may
be agreeably and genteelly done.   See what he says of
Clarissa, — it is *chaste ;* of *Don Juan,* — it is not indecent,
it is not immoral, it is only ANIMÉE!   Animée! O ciel!
what a word !   Could any but a Frenchman have had the
grace to hit on it ?   "Animation" our Jules can pardon ;
prudery he can excuse, in his good-humored, contemptuous
way ; but Dickens — this Dickens, — O fie !   And, perhaps,
there never was a more succinct, complete, elegant, just, and
satisfactory account given of a book than that by our friend
Jules of *Nicholas Nickleby.*   "It is the most disgusting
mixture imaginable of warm milk and sour beer, of fresh
eggs and salt beef, of rags and laced clothes, of gold crowns
and coppers, of rose and dandelions."

There is a receipt for you! or take another, which is
quite as pleasant : —

II.

"The fumes of tobacco, the odor of garlic, the taste of
fresh pork, the harmony made by striking a pewter plate
against an untinned copper saucepan.   Read me conscien-
tiously this book of Charles Dickens; what sores! what
pustules !" etc.

Try either mixture (and both are curious), — for fresh

pork is an ingredient in one, salt beef in another; tobacco
and garlic in receipt No. 2 agreeably take the places of
warm milk and sour beer in formula No. 1; and whereas,
in the second prescription, a pewter plate and *untinned*
copper saucepan (what a devilish satire in that epithet
untinned !), a gold crown and a few half-pence answer in
the first. Take either mixture, and the result is a Dickens.
Hang thyself, thou unhappy writer of *Pickwick ;* or, blushing at this exposition of thy faults, turn red man altogether,
and build a wigwam in a wilderness, and live with 'possums
up gum-trees. Fresh pork and warm milk; sour beer and
salt b———. Faugh! how could you serve us so atrociously?

And this is one of the "chefs-d'œuvre *de sa façon* que
dévore l'Angleterre." The beastly country! How Jules
lashes the islanders with the sting of that epigram — *chefs-
d'œuvre de leur façon !*

.   .   .   .   .   .

Look you, J. J., it is time that such impertinence should
cease. Will somebody — out of three thousand literary
men in France, there are about three who have a smatter-
ing of the English — will some one of the three explain to
J. J. the enormous folly and falsehood of all that the fellow
has been saying about Dickens and English literature
generally? We have in England literary *chefs-d'œuvre de
notre façon,* and are by no means ashamed to devour the
same. "Le charmant Milton" was not, perhaps, very
skilled for making epigrams and chansons-à-boire, but,
after all, was a person of merit, and of his works have
been sold considerably more than eight hundred copies.
"Le solennel Pope" was a writer not undeserving of praise.
There must have been something worthy in Shakespeare, —
for his name has penetrated even to France, where he is not
unfrequently called "le Sublime Williams." Walter Scott,
though a prude, as you say, and not having the agreeable
laisser-aller of the author of the *Dead Donkey,* etc., could
still turn off a romance pretty creditably. He and "le
Sublime Williams" between them have turned your French
literature topsy-turvy; and many a live donkey of your
crew is trying to imitate their paces and their roars, and to
lord it like those dead lions. These men made *chefs-d'œuvre
de notre façon,* and we are by no means ashamed to acknowledge them.

But what right have you, O blundering ignoramus! to
pretend to judge them and their works, — you, who might

as well attempt to give a series of lectures upon the literature of the Hottentots, and are as ignorant of English as
the author of the *Random Recollections?* * Learn modesty,
Jules; listen to good advice; and when you say to other
persons, *lisez moi ce livre consciencieusement,* at least do the
same thing, O critic! before you attempt to judge and
arbitrate.

And I am ready to take an affidavit in the matter of this
criticism of *Nicholas Nickleby,* that the translator of
Sterne, who does not know English, has not read Boz in
the original — has not even read him in the translation,
and slanders him out of pure invention. Take these concluding opinions of J. J. as a proof of the fact: —

"De ce roman de *Nicolas Nickleby* a été tiré le mélodrame
qui va suivre. Commencez d'abord par entasser les souter-
rains sur les ténèbres, le vice sur le sang, le mensonge sur
l'injure, *l'adultère sur l'inceste,* battez-moi tout ce mélange,
et vous verrez ce que vous allez voir.

"Dans un comté Anglais, dans une école, ou plutôt dans
une horrible prison habitée par le froid et la faim, un
nommé Squeers entraîne, sous prétexte de les élever dans
la belle discipline, tous les enfans qu'on lui confie. Ce
misérable Squeers spécule tout simplement sur la faim, sur
la soif, sur les habits de ces pauvres petits. On n'entend
que le bruit des verges, les soupirs des battus, les cris des
battans, les blasphèmes du maître. C'est affreux à lire et à
voir. Surtout ce qui fait peur (je parle du livre en question), c'est la misère d'un pauvre petit nommé Smike, dont
cet affreux Squeers est le bourreau. Quand parut le livre de
Charles Dickens, on raconte que plus d'un maître de pension de l'Angleterre se récria contre la calomnie. Mais,
juste ciel! si la cent millième partie d'une pareille honte
était possible; s'il était vrai qu'un seul marchand de chair
humaine ainsi bâti pût exister le l'autre côté du détroit ce
serait le déshonneur d'une nation tout entière. Et si en
effet la chose est impossible, que venez-vous donc nous
conter, que le roman, tout comme la comédie, est la peinture
des mœurs?

"Or ce petit malheureux couvert de haillons et de plaies,
le jouet de M. Squeers, c'est tout simplement le fils unique
de Lord Clarendon, un des plus grands seigneurs de

---

* James Grant, whose book, entitled "Paris and its People," was very
caustically reviewed by Thackeray in *Fraser's Magazine,* December, 1843,
under the title of "Grant in Paris" (see vol. xx. of this series).

l'Angleterre. Voilà justement ce que je disais tout à l'heure. Dans ces romans qui sont le rebut d'une imagina-tion en délire, il n'y a pas de milieu. Ou bein vous êtes le dernier des mendians chargés d'une besace vide, ou bien, salut à vous! vous êtes duc et pair du royaume et chevalier de la Jarretière! Ou le manteau royal ou le haillon. Quelquefois, pour varier la thèse, on vous met par dessus vos haillons le manteau de pourpre. — Votre tête est pleine de vermine, à la bonne heure! mais laissez faire le roman-cier, il posera tout à l'heure sur vos immondes cheveux, la couronne ducale. Ainsi procèdent M. Dickens et le Capitaine Marryat et tous les autres."

Here we have a third receipt for the confection of *Nicholas Nickleby,* — darkness and caverns, vice and blood, incest and adultery, "*battez-moi tout ça,*" and the thing is done. Considering that Mr. Dickens has not said a word about darkness, about caverns, about blood (farther than a little harmless claret drawn from Squeers's nose), about the two other crimes mentioned by J. J., — is it not *de luxe* to put them into the Nickleby-receipt? Having read the romances of his own country, and no others, J. J. thought he was safe, no doubt, in introducing the last-named ingre-dients; but in England the people is still *tant soit peu prudes,* and will have none such fare. In what a luxury of filth, too, does this delicate critic indulge! *votre tête est pleine de vermine* (a flattering supposition for the French reader, by the way, and remarkable for its polite propriety). Your head is in this condition; but never mind; let the romancer do his work, and he will presently place upon *your filthy hair* (kind again) the ducal coronet. This is the way with Monsieur Dickens, Captain Marryat, and *the others.*

With whom, in Heaven's name? What has poor Dick-ens ever had to do with ducal crowns, or with the other ornaments of the kind which Monsieur Jules distributes to his friends? Tell lies about men, friend Jules, if you will, but not *such* lies. See, for the future, that they have a greater likelihood about them; and try, at least when you are talking of propriety and decency of behavior, to have your words somewhat more cleanly, and your own manners as little offensive as possible.

And with regard to the character of Squeers, the impos-sibility of it, and the consequent folly of placing such a portrait in a work that pretends to be a painting of man-

ners, that, too, is a falsehood like the rest.   Such a disgrace
to human nature not only existed, but existed in J. J.'s
country of France.   Who does not remember the history of
the Boulogne schoolmaster, a year since, whom the newspapers called the " French Squeers ; " and about the same
time, in the neighborhood of Paris, there was a case still
more atrocious, of a man and his wife who farmed some
score of children, subjected them to ill-treatment so horrible
that only J. J. himself, in his nastiest fit of indignation,
could describe it; and ended by murdering one or two, and
starving all.   The whole story was in the *Débats*, J. J.'s
own newspaper, where the accomplished critic may read it.

THE PARTIE FINE.

BY LANCELOT WAGSTAFF, ESQ.

[*Colburn's New Monthly Magazine, May and June*, 1844.]

COLONEL GOLLOP's dinner in Harley Street (the colonel is an East India director, and his Mulligatawny the best out of Bengal) was just put off, much to my disappointment, for I had no other engagement; Mrs. Wagstaff was out of town with her mother at Bognor; and my clothes had been brought down to the club to dress — all to no purpose.

I was disconsolately looking over the bill of fare, and debating between Irish stew and the thirteenth cut at a leg of lamb (of which seven barristers had partaken, each with his half-pint of Marsala), when Jiggins, the waiter, brought me in a card, saying that the gentleman was in the hall, and wished to see me.

The card was Fitzsimons's; — a worthy fellow, as I dare say my reader knows. I went out to speak to him. "Perhaps," thought I, "he is going to ask me to dine."

There was something particularly splendid in Fitz's appearance, as I saw at a glance. He had on a new blue and white silk neckcloth, so new that it had never been hemmed; his great gold jack-chain, as I call it, was displayed across his breast, showing off itself and a lace ruffle a great deal too ostentatiously, as I thought. He had lemon-colored gloves; French polished boots, with deuced high heels; his hair curled (it is red, but oils to a mahogany color); his hat extremely on one side; and his mustache lacquered up with, I do believe, the very same varnish which he puts to his boots. I hate those varnished boots, except for moderns, and Fitz is three and forty if he is a day.

However, there he stood, whipping his lacquered boots with a gold-headed stick, whistling, twirling his mustache, pulling up his shirt-collar, and giving himself confoundedly dandified airs in a word, before the hall-porter and the club message-boy in brass buttons.

"Wagstaff, my boy," says he, holding out a kid glove, in a most condescending manner, "I have something to propose to you."

"What is it, and what's your hour?" said I quite playfully.

"You've guessed it at once," answered he. "A dinner is what I mean — Mrs. Wagstaff is out of town, and" —

Here he whispered me.

.   .   .   .   .   .

Well? why not? — After all there may be some very good fun. If my mother-in-law heard of it she would be sure to make a row. But she is safe at Bognor (may she stay there forever!). It is much better that I should have some agreeable society than dine alone at the club, after the seven barristers, on the leg of lamb. Of course it was not to be an expensive dinner — of course not, Fitzsimons said, — no more it was to *him* — hang him — as you shall hear.

It was agreed that the dinner-hour should be seven: the place, Durognon's in the Haymarket; and as I rather pique myself on ordering a French dinner, that matter was to be consigned to me. I walked down to Durognon's, looked at the room, and ordered the dinner for four persons — the man asked how much champagne should be put in ice? which I considered rather a leading question, and giving a vague sort of reply to this (for I determined that Fitzsimons should treat us to as much as he liked), I walked away to while away the hour before dinner.

After all, I thought, I may as well dress: the things are ready at the club, and a man is right to give himself every personal advantage, especially when he is going to dine with — with LADIES. There — the secret is out. Fitz has invited me to make a fourth in a *petit diner* given to Madame Nelval of the French theatre, and her friend Mademoiselle Delval. I had seen Madame Nelval from a side-box a few evenings before — and, *parbleu homo sum;* I meant no harm; Gollop's dinner was off; Mrs. Wagstaff was out of town; and I confess I was very glad to have an opportunity of meeting this fascinating actress, and keeping up my French. So I dressed, and at seven o'clock walked back to Durognon's, whither it was agreed that Fitz was to bring the ladies in his Brougham; — the deuce knows how he gets the money to pay for it by the way, or to indulge in a hundred other expenses far beyond any moderate man's means.

As the St. James's clock struck seven, a gentleman — past the period of extreme youth it is true, but exhibiting a remarkably elegant person still in a very becoming costume, might have been seen walking by London House, and turning down Charles Street to the Haymarket. This individual, I need not say, was myself. I had done my white tie to a nicety, and could not help saying, as I gazed for a moment in the great glass in the club drawing-room — "*Corbleu*, Wagstaff, you are still as *distingué* a looking fellow as any in London." How women can admire that odious Fitzsimons on account of his dyed mustaches, I for one never could understand.

The dinner-table at Durognon's made a neat and hospitable appearance; the plated candlesticks were not more coppery than such goods usually are at taverns; the works of art on the walls were of tolerable merit; the window-curtains, partially drawn, yet allowed the occupant of the room to have a glimpse of the cab-stand opposite, and I seated myself close to the casement, as they say in the novels, awaiting Captain Fitzsimons's arrival with the two ladies.

I waited for some time — the cabs on the stand disappeared from the rank, plunged rattling into the mighty vortex of London, and were replaced by other cabs. The sun, which had set somewhere behind Piccadilly, was now replaced by the lustrous moon, the gas lamps, and the red and blue orbs that flared in the windows of the chemist opposite. Time passed on, but no Fitzsimons's Brougham made its appearance. I read the evening paper, half an hour was gone and no company come. At last, as the opera carriages actually began to thunder down the street, "a hand was on my shoulder," as the member for Pontefract * sings. I turned round suddenly from my reverie — that hand, that yellow kid-glove-covered hand was Fitzsimons's.

"Come along, my boy," says he, "we will go fetch the ladies — they live in Bury Street, only three minutes' walk."

I go to Bury Street? I be seen walking through St. James's Square, giving an arm to any other lady in Europe but my Arabella, my wife, Mrs. Wagstaff? Suppose her

* Richard Monckton Milnes. — ED.

uncle, the dean, is going to dine at the bishop's, and should see me? — me, walking with a French lady, in three-quarters of a bonnet! I should like to know what an opinion he would have of me, and where his money in the funds would go to?

"No," says I, "my dear Fitzsimons, a joke is a joke, and I am not more strait-laced than another; but the idea that Mr. Lancelot Wagstaff should be seen walking in St. James's Square with a young French actress, is a *little* too absurd. It would be all over the city to-morrow, and Arabella would tear my eyes out."

"You sha'n't walk with a French actress," said Fitz. "You shall give your arm to as respectable a woman as any in Baker Street — I pledge you my honor of this — Madame la Baronne de Saint Ménéhould, the widow of a General of the Empire — connected with the first people in France. Do you mean to say that she is not equal to any of your sugar-baking family?" I passed over Fitz's sneer regarding my family; and as it was a baroness, of course agreed to walk with Fitzsimons in search of the ladies.

"I thought you said Madame Delval this morning," said I.

"Oh, the baroness is coming too," answered Fitzsimons, and ordered a fifth cover to be laid. We walked to Bury Street, and presently after a great deal of chattering and clapping of doors and drawers, three ladies made their appearance in the drawing-room, and having gone through the ceremony of an introduction in an entire state of darkness, the order of march was given. I offered my arm to the Baroness de Saint Ménéhould, Fitz leading the way with the other two ladies.

We walked down Jermyn Street; my heart thumped with some uneasiness as we crossed by the gambling-house in Waterloo Place, lest any one should see me. There is a strong gas-lamp there, and I looked for the first time at my portly companion. She was fifty-five if a day — five years older than that Fitzsimons. This eased me, but somehow it didn't please me. I can walk with a woman of five and fifty any day — there's my mother-in-law, my aunts, and the deuce knows how many more I could mention. But I was consoled by the baroness presently saying, that she should, from my accent, have mistaken me for a Frenchman — a great compliment to a man who has been in Paris but once, and learned the language from a Scotch usher, never mind how many years ago, at Mr. Lord's Academy, Tooting, Surrey.

But I adore Paul de Kock's novels, and have studied them so rapturously that no wonder I should have made a proficiency in the language. Indeed Arabella has often expressed herself quite jealous as I lay on the sofa of an evening, laughing my waistcoat-strings off, over his delightful pages. (The dear creature is not herself very familiar with the language, and sings *Fluve dew Tage, Partong pour Syrie*, etc., with the most confirmed Clapham accent.) I say she has often confessed herself to be jealous of the effect produced on my mind by this dear, delightful, wicked, odious, fascinating writer, whose pictures of French society are so admirably ludicrous. It was through Paul de Kock that I longed to know something about Parisian life, and those charming *sémillantes, frétillantes, pétillantes* grisettes, whose manners he describes. "It's Paul de Kock in London, by Jove," said I to myself, when Fitz proposed the little dinner to me; "I shall see all their ways and their fun."—And *that* was the reason why, as Mrs. Wagstaff was out of town, I accepted the invitation so cordially.

Well; we arrived at Durognon's at a quarter-past eight, we five, and were ushered at length into the dining-room, where the ladies flung off their cloaks and bonnets, and I had an opportunity of seeing their faces completely.

Madame Delval's was as charming a face as I ever looked upon; her hair parted meekly over the forehead, which was rather low; the eyes and eyebrows beautiful; the nose such as Grecian sculptor scarce ever chipped out of Parian stone; the mouth small, and, when innocently smiling, displaying the loveliest pearly teeth, and calling out two charming attendant dimples on each fresh cheek; the ear a perfect little gem of an ear. (I adore ears — unadorned ears without any hideous ornaments dangling from them — pagodas, chandeliers, bunches of grapes, and similar monstrosities, such as ladies will hang from them — *entr' autres* my own wife, Mrs. W., who has got a pair of earrings her uncle, the dean, gave her, that really are as big as bootjacks almost.) She was habited in a neat, closely fitting silk dress of Parisian tartan silk, which showed off to advantage a figure that was perfect, and a waist that was ridiculously small. A more charming, candid, distinguished head it was impossible to see.

Mademoiselle Delval was a modest, clever, pleasing person, neatly attired in a striped something, I don't know the proper phrase; and Madame la Baronne was in a dress which I should decidedly call gingham.

When we sat down to the Potage Printanière, and I helped the baroness naturally first, addressing her respectfully by her title, the other two ladies began to laugh, and that brute, Fitzsimons, roared as if he was insane. "La Baronne de Saint Ménéhould!" cried out little Madame Delval; "o par exemple! c'est maman, mon cher monsieur!" On which (though I was deucedly nettled, I must confess), I said, that to be the mother of Madame Delval, was the proudest title any lady could have, and so sneaked out of my mortification with this, I flatter myself, not inelegant compliment. The ladies, one and all, declared that I spoke French like a Parisian, and so I ordered in the champagne ; and very good Durognon's Sillery is too.

Both the young ladies declared they detested it, but Madame Delval, the elder, honestly owned that she liked it; and indeed I could not but remark that, in our favor doubtless, the two younger dames forgot their prejudices, and that their glasses were no sooner filled than they were empty.

Ah, how charming it was to see the shuddering, timid, nervous way in which the lovely Delval, junior (let me call her at once by her Christian name of Virginie), turned away her little shrinking head as the waiter opened the bottles, and they went off with their natural exhilarating pop and fizz. At the opening of the first bottle, she flew into a corner; at the opening of the second, she ran to her mother's arms (*hinnuleo similis quærenti pavidam montibus aviis matrem,* as we used to say at Tooting), sweet sensibility! charming, timorous grace! but she took the liquor very kindly when it *was* opened, saying, as she turned up her fine eyes to Heaven, "Il n'y a rien qui m'agaçe les nerfs comme cela!" Agaçer les nerfs! What a delicate expression! The good old lady told her to be calm, and made light of her terror.

But though I had piqued myself on ordering the dinner, the little coquette soon set me down. She asked for the most wonderful things — for instance, she would have a salad of dandelion — the waiter was packed off to Covent Garden to seek for it. When the fish came, she turned to the waiter and said, "Comment? vous n'avez point de

moules ? " with the most natural air in the world, and as
if mussels were always served at Parisian dinners, which,
I suppose, is the case. And then at dessert, what must she
remark but the absence of asparagus, which, I must confess, I had not ordered.

"What," she said, turning round to my companion, "are
there no asparagus, monsieur ? — No asparagus! ah, monsieur! c'est ma vie, mon bonheur, que les asperges ! J'en
suis folle — des asperges. Je les adore — les asperges!
Je ne mange que cela, — il me les faut, Monsieur Fitzsimons. Vite, garçon ! des asperges — des asperges à
l'huile, entendez-vous ? "

We were both very much alarmed by this manifest excitement of Virginie's nerves ; and the asparagus was sent
for. O woman! you are some of you like the animals of
the field in so far as this, that you do not know your
power. Those who do can work wonders over us. No
man can resist them. We two were as timid, wretched,
and trembling, until the asparagus came, as any mortal
could be. It seemed as if we had committed a crime in not
ordering the asparagus that Virginie adored. If she had
proposed a pint of melted pearls, I think Fitz was the man
to send off to Storr and Mortimer's, and have the materials
bought. They (I don't mean the pearls, but the vegetables) came in about half an hour, and she ate them cold, as
she said, with oil and vinegar ; but the half-hour's pause
was a very painful one, and we vainly endeavored to fill
the odious vacuum with champagne. All the while, Fitzsimons, though he drank and kept nervously helping his
neighbors right and left, was quite silent and frightened.
I know which will be the better horse (as the phrase is)
if *he's* ever married. I was of course collected, and kept
putting in my jokes as usual, but I cannot help saying that I
wished myself out of the premises, dreading to think what
else Madame Virginie might ask for, and saying inwardly,
"What would my poor Arabella say if she knew her
scoundrel of a Lancelot was in such company ? "

Well — it may have been the champagne, or it may have
been the asparagus, — though I never, I confess, remarked
such a quality in the vegetable, — it may, I say, have been
the asparagus which created — what do you think? a
reconciliation between Virginie and Héloise — the Madame
Delval before mentioned. This is a delicate matter, but it
appeared the ladies had had a difference in the morning

about a ribbon, a fichu, or some such matter doubtless, and they had not spoken all dinner-time.

But after a bottle of sherry, four of Sillery (which we all took fairly, no flinching, no heel-taps, glass and glass about), after coffee and curaçoa, and after the asparagus, a reconciliation took place, Héloise looked at Virginie, Virginie looked at Héloise, the latter rose from her chair, tottered towards her friend, and they were in each other's arms in a minute. Old Madame Delval looked quite pleased at the scene, and said, smiling, to us, " *Elle a si bon cœur, ma fille!* " Oh those mothers! they are all the same. Not that she was wrong in this instance. The two young ladies embraced with the warmest cordiality, the quarrel about the ribbon was forgotten, the two young hearts were united once more; and though that selfish brute, Fitzsimons, who has no more heart than a bed-post, twiddled his eternal mustache, and yawned over the scene, I confess I was touched by this little outbreak of feeling, and this glimpse into the history of the hearts of the young persons, and drank a glass of curaçoa to old Madame Delval with a great deal of pleasure.

But, oh! fancy our terror, when all of a sudden Héloise, weeping on her friend's neck, began to laugh and to cry, and burst out shrieking into a fit of hysterics! When women begin hysterics a tremor seizes me — I become mad myself — I have had my wife and mother-in-law both in hysterics on the same rug, and I know what it is — the very sound of the whoo—oo—oo drives me wild. I have heard it imitated in theatres, and have rushed out in a frenzy. " Water! water! " gasped Virginie (we had somehow not had any all dinner-time), I tumbled out of the room, upsetting three waiters who were huddled at the door (and be hanged to them); " water," roared I, rushing downstairs, upsetting boots, and alarmed chamber-maids came panting in with a jug.

" What will they think of us? " thought I, trembling with emotion — " they will think we have murdered the poor young lady, and yet on my honor and conscience I — Oh why did I come — what *would* Arabella say if she knew? " I thought of the police coming in, of paragraphs in the paper beginning, " Two ruffians of gentlemanly exterior were brought before Mr. Jardine," etc., it was too horrible — if I had had my hat I would have taken a cab off the stand, and driven down to my wife at Bognor that minute; but I hadn't — so I went up to fetch it.

Héloise was lying on the sofa now, a little calmer; Madame Delval and the chamber-maid were being kind to her: as for that brute, Fitzsimons, he was standing in one of the windows, his legs asunder, his two fists thrust into the tail pockets of his brass-buttoned coat, whistling, "Suoni la Tromba," the picture of heartless, shameless indifference.

As soon as the maid was gone, and I was come in, Madame Virginie must of course begin hysterics too — they always do, these women. She turned towards me with an appealing look (she had been particularly attentive to me at dinner, much more than to Fitzsimons, whom she *boudéd* the whole time) — she gave me an appealing look — and struck up too.

I couldn't bear it. I flung myself down on a chair, and, beginning to bang my forehead, gasped out, "Oh Heavens! a cab, a cab!"

"We'll have a coach. Go back with them," said Fitz, coming swaggering up.

"*Go back* with them?" said I, "I'll never see them again as long as I live." No more I *would* go back with them. The carriage was called (the hysterics ceased the very moment Fitz flung open the window and the cab-stand opposite could hear) — the ladies went out. In vain good old Madame Delval looked as if she expected my arm. In vain Virginie cast her appealing look. I returned it them with the most stony indifference, and, falling back upon my chair, thought of my poor Arabella.

The coach drove off. I felt easier as the rattle of the departing wheels died away in the night, and I got up to go. "How glad I am it's over," thought I, on the stair; "if ever I go to a *partie fine* again may I" . . .

"I beg your parding, sir," said the waiter, touching my elbow just as I was at the hotel door.

"What is it?" says I.

"The bill, sir," says he, with a grin.

"The bill, sir?" I exclaimed; "why it's Captain Fitzsimons's dinner!"

"I beg your parding, sir; you ordered it," answered the man.

"But, good Heavens! you know Captain Fitzsimons?"

"We do, sir, precious well too. The capting owes mas-

moderate, but I had better have dined off that Irish stew at the club.

ARABELLA; OR, THE MORAL OF THE "PARTIE FINE."

WHEN the news came to Wagstaff that he had made a public appearance in the *New Monthly Magazine*, he affected to be in great wrath that his peccadilloes should have been laid bare to the whole nation; and was for sacrificing the individual who had held him up to ridicule. Luckily, that person was out of town for some days, so his anger had time to cool if it were real; but the truth must be told, that Lancelot Wagstaff was in heart quite delighted at being shown up for a *séducteur*, and has ordered some new waistcoats, and affects to talk very big about the French play, and has been growing a tuft to his chin ever since. Mrs. Wagstaff still continues at Bognor. Poor soul! *She* will never know whose was the portrait which figured last month in this Miscellany under the pseudonym of Wagstaff: it is only the coincidence of the new waistcoats and the sudden growth of that tuft that can by any possibility betray him.

Some critics have hinted that the scene described was immoral. So it was, there's not a doubt of it; but so is a great deal of life immoral: so are many of Hogarth's pictures immoral, if you don't choose to see their moral tendency; — nor indeed are critics to be very much blamed for not perceiving the moral of the brief tract called the Partie Fine, seeing, as it were, that it was not yet in sight. No: it was purposely kept back, as a surprise for the June number of the magazine. THIS is going to be the moral paper: and I hope to goodness that Mr. Colburn's editor will not refuse it, or I shall be set down, in spite of myself, as a writer of a questionable tendency. I solemnly demand the insertion of this paper, in order to set a well-meaning man right with a public he respects. Yes, ladies, you yourselves, if you peruse these few, these very few pages, will say, "Well, although he shocked us, the man *is* a moral man after all." He is, indeed he is. Don't believe the critics who say the contrary.

The former history described to you the conduct of Wagstaff abroad. Ah, ladies! you little knew that it was preparatory to showing the monster up when *at home.* You would not have understood the wretch had you not received this previous insight into his character. If *this* be not morality, I know not what is.

Those people who at the club and elsewhere are acquainted with **Mr. W.** declare he is the most generous and agreeable creature that ever turned out of the city. He arrives, his jolly face beaming with good nature. He has a good word for everybody, and every man a good word for him. Some Bachelor says, "Wag, my boy, there is a whitebait party at Greenwich; will you be one?" He hesitates. "I promised Mrs. Wagstaff to be home to dinner," says he; and when he says *that,* you may be sure he will go. If you propose to him a game of billiards in the afternoon, he will play till dinner, and make the most ludicrous jokes about his poor wife waiting till his return. If you ask him to smoke cigars, he will do so till morning, and goes home with a story to Mrs. W., which the poor soul receives with a desperate credulity. Once she used to sit up for him; but to continue that practice would have killed her. She goes to bed now, and Wagstaff reels in when he likes.

He is not ill-humored. Far from it. He never says an unkind word to the children, or to the cook, or to the boy who blacks his boots, or to his wife. She wishes he would. He comes downstairs exactly three minutes before office-time. He has his tea and his newspaper in bed. His eldest daughter brings the paper in, and his poor wife appears with the tea. He has a kind word for both, and scrubs the little girl's fresh cheek with his bristly beard, and laughs at the joke, and professes a prodigious interest in her lessons, and in knowing whether Miss Wiggles, the governess, is satisfied with her; and before she finishes her answer, he is deep in the folios of the *Times,* and does not care one farthing piece what the little girl says. He has promised to take the child to Astley's any time these four years. She could hardly speak when he promised it. She is a fine tall lass, and can read and write now: and though it was so long ago, has never forgotten the promise about Astley's.

When he is away from home, Wagstaff talks about his family with great affection. In the long, long days when

he is away, their mother, God help her! is telling them
what a good man their papa is — how kind and generous —
and how busy he is — what a pity! he is obliged to work
so hard and stay away from home! Poor creature, poor
creature! Sure Heaven will pardon her these lies if any
lies are pardonable. Whenever he says he will walk with
her, Arabella dresses herself in the gown he likes, and puts
on her pink bonnet, and is ready to the very minute, you
may be sure. How often is it that *he* is ready at the minute? How many scores and scores of times has he left the
heart-sick girl? — not forgetting her in the least — but
engaged elsewhere with a game of billiards, or a jolly friend
and a cigar — and perhaps wishing rather to be at home all
the time — but he is *so* good-natured, such a capital fellow!
Whenever he keeps his appointment — Heaven help us!
she brightens up as if it were Paradise coming to her.
She looks with a triumphant air at the servant who opens
the door, and round about at the neighbors' windows, as if
she would have all the world know that she is walking
with her husband. Every now and then as she walks (if
it is but twice or thrice in a year, for Wagstaff has his
business on week-days, and never gets up till one of a Sunday); every now and then as she walks with him, the
delighted creature gives a skip, and squeezes his arm, and
looks up in his face, she is so happy. And so is he too,
for he is as good-natured a fellow as ever breathed — and he
resolves to take her out the very next Sunday — only he
doesn't. Every one of these walk-days are noted down in
the poor soul's little Calendar of Home as saint's days.
She talks of them quite fondly; and there is not one of
her female friends whom she won't visit for weeks after,
and to whom she will not be sure to find some pretext for
recounting the wonderful walk.

Mon Dieu, ladies — all the time I was describing that
affair at Durognon's, those odious French women and their
chatter, and their ogling, and their champagne, I was thinking of Arabella far away in the distance and alone — I
declare, upon my honor, she was never out of my thoughts
for a single minute. *She* was the moral of the Partie Fine
— the simple, white-robed, spotless, meek-eyed angel of a
wife — thinking about her husband — and he among the
tawdry good-for-nothings, yonder! Fizz! there goes the
first champagne cork, Mr. Wagstaff is making a tender
speech to Madame Virginie.

At that moment Arabella is upstairs in the nursery, where the same moon is shining in, and putting her youngest boy to bed.

Bang! there goes the second cork. Virginie screams — Fitzsimons roars with laughter — Wagstaff hobnobs with the old lady, who gives a wink and a nod. They are taking away the fish and putting down the *entrées.*

At that moment Arabella has her second child between her knees (the little one is asleep with its thumb in its mouth, and the elder even is beginning to rub her eyes over her favorite fairy tale, though she has read it many scores of times). Arabella has the child between her knees, and just as Wag is clinking his glass with the old lady in London, his wife at Bognor says something to the child, who says after her, —

" *Dod bless my dear papa:* " and presently he is in bed too, and sleeps as soundly as his little sister.

And so it is that these pure blessings are sent — yearning after that fellow over his cups. Suppose they reach him? Why, the spotless things must blush and go out again from the company in which they find him. The drinking goes on, the jokes and fun get faster and faster. Arabella by this time has seen the eldest child asleep in her crib, and is looking out at the moon in silence as the children breathe round about her a soft chorus of slumber. Her mother is downstairs alone, reading "Blair's Sermons," — a high-shouldered, hook-nosed, lean, moral woman. She wonders her daughter don't come down to tea — there is her cup quite cold, with the cream stagnant on the surface, and her workbasket by its side, with a pair of man's slippers nearly done, and one lazy scrawl from her husband, four lines only, and ten days old. But Arabella keeps away thinking, thinking, and preferring to be alone. The girl has a sweet soft heart, and little sympathy with the mother's coarse, rigid, strong-minded nature. The only time they quarrel is, when the old lady calls her son-in-law a brute: *then* the young one fires up and defends her own like a little Amazon.

What is this secret of love? How does it spring? How is it that no neglect can kill it? In truth, its origin and endurance are alike utterly absurd and unreasonable. What secret power was it that made this delicate-minded young creature; who had been bred up upon the purest doctrines of the sainted Mrs. Chapone; who had never thought about love; who, simple soul, had been utterly absorbed in her little daily duties, her pianoforte practice, her French lesson, her use-of-the-globes, her canary bird, and her Mangnall's questions — what, I say, is it that makes this delicate girl all of a sudden expand into a passion of love for a young sugar-baker, simply because she meets him three times riding a gray mare on Clapham Common, and afterwards (the sly rogue!) on half a dozen occasions at her aunt's at tea? What is it that makes her feel that that young sugar-baker is the fatal man with whom her existence is bound up: go through fire and water to marry him: love him in spite of neglect and indifference: adore him so absurdly, that a half-hour's kindness from him more than balances a month's brutality? O, mystery of woman's heart! I declare all this lies in the moral of the *Partie Fine.*

Wagstaff, so splendid with his dinners and so generous on himself, is not so generous at home. He pays the bills with only a few oaths; but somehow he leaves his wife without money. He will give it to anybody rather than to her: a fact of which he himself is, very likely, unaware at this minute, or of the timidity of his wife in asking for it. In order to avoid this asking, the poor girl goes through unheard-of economies, and performs the most curious tricks of avarice. She dresses herself for nothing, and she dresses her children out of her own frocks. Certain dimities, caps, pinafores, and other fallals have gone through the family; and Arabella, though she sees ever such a pretty thing in a shop-window, will pass on with a sigh; whereas her Lancelot is a perfect devourer of waistcoats, and never sets his eyes on a flaring velvet that strikes his fancy, but you will be sure to behold him the next week swaggering about in the garment in Pall Mall. Women are ever practising these petty denials, about which the Lords of the Creation never think.

I will tell you what I once saw Arabella doing. She is a woman of very high breeding, and no inconsiderable share of family pride: well, one day on going to Wagstaff's house, who had invited a party of us to Blackwall, about a bet he had lost, I was, in the master's absence, ushered into the drawing-room, which is furnished very fine, and there sat the lady of the house at her work-table, with her child prattling at her knee.

I could not understand what made Mrs. Wagstaff blush so — look so entirely guilty of something or other — fidget, answer *à traverse,* and receive an old friend in this strange and inhospitable way.

She, the descendant of the Smiths of Smithfield, of the Browns of Brown Hall, the proud daughter of the aristocracy, *was making a pair of trousers for her eldest son.* She huddled them away hastily under a pillow — but bah! we have keen eyes — and from under that pillow the buttons peeped out, and with those buttons the secret — they were white ducks — Wagstaff's white ducks — his wife was making them into white ducklings for little Fred.

The sight affected me. I should like to have cried, only it is unmanly; and to cry about a pair of little breeches! — I should like to have seized hold of Mrs. Wagstaff and hugged her to my heart : but she would have screamed, and rung for John to show me downstairs; so I disguised my feelings by treading on the tail of her spaniel dog, whose squealing caused a diversion.

But I shall never forget those breeches. What! Wagstaff is flaunting in a coat of Nugee's, and his son has that sweet, humble tailor. Wagstaff is preparing for Blackwall, and here is his wife plying her gentle needle. Wagstaff feasts off plate and frothing wine; and Arabella sits down to cold mutton in the nursery, with her little ones ranged about her. Wagstaff enjoys, Arabella suffers. He flings about his gold; and she tries to stave off evil days by little savings of meek pence. Wagstaff sins and she forgives — and trusts, and loves, and hopes on in spite of carelessness, and coldness, and neglect, and extravagance, and — and *Parties Fines.*

This is the moral of the last story. O, ye Wagstaffs of this world, profit by it. O, ye gentle, meek angels of Arabellas, be meek and gentle still. If an angel can't reclaim a man, who can ? And I live in hopes of hearing that by the means of that charming mediation the odious Lancelot has become a reformed character.

TITMARSH.

GREENWICH — WHITEBAIT.

[*Colburn's New Monthly Magazine, July*, 1844.]

I WAS recently talking in a very touching and poetical strain about the above delicate fish to my friend Foozle and some others at the Club, and expatiating upon the excellence of the dinner which our little friend Guttlebury had given us; when Foozle, looking round about him with an air of triumph and immense wisdom, said, —

"I'll tell you what, Wagstaff, I'm a plain man, and despise all your gormandizing and kickshaws. I don't know the difference between one of your absurd made-dishes and another — give me a plain cut of mutton or beef. I'm a plain Englishman, I am, and no glutton."

Foozle, I say, thought this speech a terrible set-down for me — and indeed acted up to his principles — you may see him any day at six sitting down before a great reeking joint of meat; his eyes quivering, his face red, and he cutting great smoking red collops out of the beef before him, which he devours with corresponding quantities of cabbage and potatoes, and the other gratis luxuries of the club-table.

What I complain of is, not that the man should enjoy his great meal of steaming beef; let him be happy over that as much as the beef he is devouring was in life happy over oil-cakes or mangel-wurzel: but I hate the fellow's brutal self-complacency, and his scorn of other people who have different tastes from his. A man who brags regarding himself, that whatever he swallows is the same to him, and that his coarse palate recognizes no difference between venison and turtle, pudding or mutton-broth, as his indifferent jaws close over them, brags about a personal defect — the wretch — and not about a virtue. It is like a man boasting that he has no ear for music, or no eye for color, or that his nose cannot scent the difference between a rose and a cabbage — I say, as a general rule, set that man down as a conceited fellow who swaggers about not caring for his dinner.

Why shouldn't we care about it ?   Was eating not made to be a pleasure to us ?   Yes, I say, a daily pleasure : a sweet solamen : a pleasure familiar, yet ever new, the same and yet how different !   It is one of the causes of domesticity : the neat dinner makes the husband pleased, the housewife happy, the children consequently are well brought up and love their papa and mamma.   A good dinner is the centre of the circle of the social sympathies — it warms acquaintanceship into friendship — it maintains that friendship comfortably unimpaired : enemies meet over it and are reconciled.   How many of you, dear friends, has that late bottle of claret warmed into affectionate forgiveness, tender recollections of old times, and ardent glowing anticipations of new !   The brain is a tremendous secret.   I believe some chemist will arise anon, who will know how to doctor the brain as they do the body now, as Liebig doctors the ground.   They will apply certain medicines, and produce crops of certain qualities that are lying dormant now for want of intellectual guano.   But this is a subject for future speculation — a parenthesis growing out of another parenthesis.   What I would urge especially here is a point which must be familiar with every person accustomed to eat good dinners — viz. the noble and friendly qualities that they elicit.   How is it we cut such jokes over them ?   How is it we become so remarkably friendly ?   How is it that some of us, inspired by a good dinner, have sudden gusts of genius unknown in the quiet unfestive state ?   Some men make speeches, some shake their neighbor by the hand, and invite him or themselves to dine — some sing prodigiously — my friend, Saladin, for instance, goes home, he says, with the most beautiful harmonies ringing in his ears ; and I, for my part, will take any given tune, and make variations upon it for any given period of hours, greatly, no doubt, to the delight of all hearers. These are only temporary inspirations given us by the jolly genius, but are they to be despised on that account ?   No. Good dinners have been the greatest vehicles of benevolence since man began to eat.

A taste for good living, then, is praiseworthy in moderation — like all the other qualities and endowments of man. If a man were to neglect his family or his business on account of his love for the fiddle or the fine arts — he would commit just the crime that the dinner-sensualist is guilty of : but to enjoy wisely is a maxim of which no man need

be ashamed. But if you cannot eat a dinner of herbs as
well as a stalled ox, then you are an unfortunate man —
your love for good dinners has passed the wholesome boun‹
dary, and degenerated into gluttony.

Oh, shall I ever forget the sight of the only City dinner
I ever attended in my life! at the hall of the Right Worshipful Company of Chimney-sweepers — it was in May,
and a remarkably late pea-season. The hall was decorated
with banners and escutcheons of deceased *chummies* —
martial music resounded from the balconies as the Master
of the Company and the great ones marched in. We sat
down, grace was said, the tureen covers removed, and instantly a silence in the hall — a breathless silence — and
then a great gurgle! — grwlwlwlw it sounded like. The
worshipful Company were sucking in the turtle! Then
came the venison, and with it were two hundred quarts of
peas, at five and twenty shillings a quart — oh, my heart
sank within me, as we devoured the green ones! as the old
waddling, trembling, winking citizens held out their plates
quivering with anxiety, and, said Mr. Jones, "A little bit
of the f-f-fat, another spoonful of the p-p-pe-as" — and they
swallowed them down, the prematurely born children of
the spring — and there were thousands in London that day
without bread.

This is growing serious — and is a long grace before
whitebait to be sure — but at a whitebait dinner, haven't
you remarked that you take a number of dishes first? In
the first place, water-souchy, soochy, or soujy — flounder-
souchy is incomparably, exquisitely the best — perch is
muddy, bony, and tough; compared to it, slips are coarse;
and salmon — perhaps salmon is next to the flounder.
You hear many people exclaim against flounder-souchy — I
dined with Jorrocks, Sangsue, the Professor, and one or two
more, only the other day, and they all voted it tasteless.
Tasteless! It has an almost angelic delicacy of flavor: it
is as fresh as the recollections of childhood — it wants a
Correggio's pencil to describe it with sufficient tenderness.

"*If a flounder had two backs,*" Saladin said at the "Star
and Garter" the other day, "it would be divine!"

Foolish man, whither will your wild desires carry you?
As he is, a flounder is a perfect being. And the best reply
to those people who talk about its tastelessness, is to say
"Yes," and draw over the tureen to yourself, and never

leave it while a single slice of brown bread remains beside
it, or a single silver-breasted fishlet floats in the yellow
parsley-flavored wave.

About eels, salmon, lobsters, either *au gratin* or in cutlets, and about the variety of sauces — Genevese sauce,
Indian sauce (a strong but agreeable compound), etc., I
don't think it is necessary to speak. The slimy eel is found
elsewhere than in the stream of Thames (I have tasted him
charmingly matelotted with mushrooms and onions, at the
" Marronniers " at Passy), the lusty salmon flaps in other
waters — by the fair tree-clad banks of Lismore — by the
hospitable margin of Ballynahinch — by the beauteous
shores of Wye, and on the sandy flats of Scheveningen, I
have eaten and loved him. I do not generally eat him at
Greenwich. Not that he is not good. But he is not good
in such a place. It is like Mrs. Siddons dancing a hornpipe, or a chapter of Burke in a novel — the salmon is too
vast for Greenwich.

I would say the same, and more, regarding turtle. It
has no business in such a feast as that fresh and simple
one provided at the " Trafalgar " or the " Old Ship." It is
indecorous somehow to serve it in that company. A fine
large lively turtle, and a poor little whitebait by his side !
Ah, it is wrong to place them by each other.

At last we come to the bait — the twelve dishes of preparatory fish are removed, the Indian-sauced salmon has
been attacked in spite of our prohibition, the stewed eels
have been mauled, and the flounder-soup tureen is empty.
All those receptacles of pleasure are removed — eyes turned
eagerly to the door, and enter —

> Mr. Derbyshire (with a silver dish of whitebait).
> John (brown bread and butter).
> Samuel (lemons and cayenne).
> Frederick (a dish of whitebait).
> Gustavus (brown bread and butter).
> Adolphus (whitebait).
> A waiter with a napkin, which he flaps about the
>   room in an easy *dégagé* manner.

"There's plenty more to follow, sir," says Mr. D., whisk
ing off the cover. Frederick and Adolphus pass rapidly
round with their dishes; John and Gustavus place their
refreshments on the table, and Samuel obsequiously insin-
uates the condiments under his charge.

Ah! he must have had a fine mind who first invented

brown bread and butter with whitebait! That man was a kind, modest, gentle benefactor to his kind. We don't recognize sufficiently the merits of those men who leave us such quiet benefactions. A statue ought to be put up to the philosopher who joined together this charming couple. Who was it? Perhaps it was done by the astronomer at Greenwich, who observed it when seeking for some other discovery. If it were the astronomer — why, the next time we go to Greenwich we will go into the Park and ascend the hill, and pay our respects to the Observatory.

That, by the way, is another peculiarity about Greenwich. People leave town, and *say* they will walk in the Park before dinner. But we never do. We may suppose there is a Park from seeing trees; but we have never entered it. We walk wistfully up and down on the terrace before the Hospital, looking at the clock a great many times; at the brown old seamen basking in the sun; at the craft on the river; at the nursery-maids mayhap, and the gambols of the shrill-voiced Jacks-ashore on the beach. But the truth is, one's thinking of something else all the time. Of the bait. Remark how silent fellows are on steamboats going down to Greenwich. They won't acknowledge it, but they are thinking of what I tell you.

Well, when the whitebait does come, what is it, after all? Come now. Tell us, my dear sir, your real sentiments about this fish, this little, little fish about which we all make such a noise! There it lies. Lemon it, pepper it: pop it into your mouth — and what then? — a crisp crunch, and it is gone. Does it realize your expectations? Is it better than anything you ever tasted? Is it as good as raspberry open tarts used to be at school? Come, upon your honor and conscience now, is it better than a fresh dish of tittlebacks or gudgeons?

O fool, to pry with too curious eye into these secrets! O blunderer, to wish to dash down a fair image because it may be of plaster! O dull philosopher, not to know that pursuit is pleasure, and possession worthless without it! I, for my part, never will, as long as I live, put to myself that question about whitebait. Whitebait is a butterfly of the waters — and as the animal mentioned by Lord Byron invites the young pursuer near, and leads him through thy fields, Cashmere — as it carries him in his chase through a thousand agreeable paths scented with violets, sparkling with sunshine, with beauty to feast his eyes, and health in

the air — let the right-thinking man be content with the
pursuit, nor inquire too curiously about the object. How
many hunters get the brush of the fox, and what, when
gotten, is the worth of that tawny wisp of hair ?

Whitebait, then, is only a little means for acquiring a
great deal of pleasure. Somehow, it is always allied with
sunshine : it is always accompanied by jolly friends and
good-humor. You rush after that little fish, and leave the
cares of London behind you — the row and struggle, the
foggy darkness, the slippery pavement where every man
jostles you, striding on his way pre-occupied, with care
written on his brow. Look out of the window, the sky is
tinted with a thousand glorious hues, the ships pass silent
over the blue glittering waters — there is no object within
sight that is not calm, and happy, and beautiful. Yes !
turn your head a little, and there lie the towers of London
in the dim smoky sunset. There lie Care, Labor, To-
morrow. Friends, let us have another glass of claret, and
thank our luck that we have still to-day.

On thinking over the various whitebait dinners which
have fallen to our lot in the last month, somehow you are
sure to find the remembrance of them all pleasant. I have
seen some wretches taking whitebait and *tea*, which has
always inspired me with a sort of terror, and a yearning to
go up to the miserable objects so employed, and say, "My
good friend, here is a crown-piece; have a bottle of iced
punch, or a tankard of delicious cider-cup — but not tea,
dear sir; no, no, not tea; you can get that at home —
there's no exhilaration in Congo. It was not made to be
drunk on holidays." Those people are unworthy of the
"Ship" — I don't wish to quarrel with the enjoyments of
any man ; but fellows who take tea and whitebait should
not be allowed to damp the festive feelings of persons better engaged. They should be consigned to the smiling
damsels whom one meets on the walk to Mr. Derbyshire's,
who issue from dingy tenements no bigger than houses in
a pantomime, and who, whatever may be the rank of the
individual, persist in saying, "Tea, sir — I can accommodate your party — tea, sir, — srimps ? "

About the frequenters of Greenwich and the various
classes of ichthyophagi, many volumes might be written.
All classes of English Christians, with the exception of her
Majesty and Prince Albert (and the more is the pity that
their exalted rank deprives them of an amusement so

charming!), frequent the hospitable taverns — the most celebrated gormandizer and the very humble. There are the annual Ministerial Saturnalia, which, whenever I am called in by her Majesty, I shall have great pleasure in describing in these pages, and in which the lowest becomes the highest for the occasion, and Taper and Tadpole take just as high a rank as Lord Eskdale or Lord Monmouth. There are the private banquets in which Lord Monmouth diverts himself with his friends from the little French — but this subject has been already touched upon at much length. There are the lawyers' dinners, when Sir Frederick or Sir William is advanced to the honor of the bench or the attorney-generalship, and where much legal pleasantry is elicited. The last time I dined at the "Ship," hearing a dreadful Bacchanalian noise issuing from a private apartment, I was informed, "*It's the gentlemen of 'Punch,' sir.*" What would I not have given to be present at such an assembly of choice spirits! Even missionary societies and converters of the Quashimdoo Indians come hither for a little easy, harmless pleasuring after their labors, and no doubt the whitebait slips down their reverend throats, and is relished by them as well as by the profane crowd.

Then, in the coffee-room, let a man be by himself, and he is never lonely. Every table tells its little history. Yonder sit three City bucks, with all the elegant graces of the Custom-house and the Stock Exchange.

"That's a good glass of wine," says Wiggins.

"Ropy," said Figgins; "I'll put you in a pipe of that to stand you in three and twenty a dozen."

Once, in my presence, I heard a City "*gent*" speak so slightingly of a glass of very excellent brown sherry, that the landlord was moved almost to tears, and made a speech, of which the sorrow was only equalled by the indignation.

Sporting young fellows come down in great numbers, with cutaway coats and riding-whips, which must be very useful on the water. They discourse learnedly about Leander and Running Rein, and say, "I'll bet you three to two of that."

Likewise pink-faced lads from Oxford and Cambridge. Those from the former University wear lavender-colored gloves, and drink much less wine than their jolly comrades from the banks of Cam. It would be a breach of confidence to report their conversation: but I lately heard some very interesting anecdotes about the Master of Trinity, and one Bumpkins, a gyp there.

Of course there are foreigners. I have remarked many "Mosaic Arabs" who dress and drink remarkably smartly; honest, pudding-faced Germans, who sit sentimentally over their punch; and chattering little Frenchmen with stays, and whiskers, and canes, and little lacquered boots. These worthies drink ale for the most part, saying, "Je ne bois que l'ale, moi," or "Que la bière est bonne en Angleterre." "Et que le vin est mauvais," shrieks out the pygmy addressed, and so they club their sixpence, and remain faithful to the malt-and-hoppish liquor. It may be remarked that ladies and Frenchmen are not favorites with inn-waiters, coach-guards, cabmen, and such officials, doubtless for reasons entirely mercenary.

I could continue for many more pages, but the evening gray is tingeing the river; the packet-boat bells are ringing; the sails of the ships look grayer and more ghostlike as they sweep silently by. It is time to be thinking of returning, and so let us call for the bill, and finish with a moral. My dear sir, it is this. The weather is beautiful. The white-bait singularly fine this season. You are sure to be happy if you go to Greenwich. Go, then; and, above all, TAKE YOUR AMIABLE LADY WITH YOU.

Ah! if but ten readers will but follow this advice, Lancelot Wagstaff has not written in vain, and has made ten charming women happy!

THE CHEST OF CIGARS.

BY LANCELOT WAGSTAFF, ESQ.

[*The New Monthly Magazine, July*, 1845.]

"Not smoke?" said the gentleman near me.

We had the honor of dining at my Lord Hobanob's, who "smokes" after dinner, as all the world knows. The person who spoke was called the general by the company assembled.

"Not smoke?" says he.

"Why — I — that is — what would Mrs. Caudle say?" replied I, with a faint effort to be pleasant, "for the fact is, though my wife doesn't like cigars, I was once very fond of them."

"Is your lady a sentimental woman?" said the general.

"Extremely sentimental."

"Of a delicate turn?"

"Very much so; this is the first time I have been permitted — I mean that I have had any wish to dine out since my marriage," said the reader's humble servant.

"If I can prove to her that the happiness of a virtuous family was secured by cigars; that an admirable woman was saved from ruin by smoking; that a worthy man might have been driven to suicide but for Havanas; do you think, sir, that then, the respected lady who owns you would alter her opinion regarding the immorality of smoking?"

And so saying, the general handed me his box, and sent a puff so fragrant into my face, that I must own I took a cigar as he commenced his romantic tale in the following words : —

"When our army was in Holland, in the time of the lamented Duke of York, the 56th Hussars (Queen Charlotte's Own Slashers, as we were called from our tremendous ferocity) were quartered in the romantic vicinity of Vaterzouchy. A more gallant regiment never fought, conquered, or ran away, and we did all in that campaign. A better fellow than our colonel never existed — a dearer friend than Frederick Fantail, who was lieutenant in the troop I had the honor to command, mortal never had."

Here my informant the general's fine eye (he had but one remaining) filled with tears, and he gave a deep sigh through the lung which had not been perforated at the battle of Salamanca.

"Fantail had one consuming passion besides military glory — this was smoking. His pipe was never out of his lips from morning till night — till night? What did I say? He never went to bed without this horrible companion, and I have seen this misguided young man, seated on a barrel of gunpowder in the batteries, smoking as calmly as if death were not close under his coat-tails.

"To these two passions my friend speedily added another: a love for the charming daughter of Burgomaster van Slappenbroch, whom he met one day in his rambles.

"'I should never probably have remarked her, Goliah,' he would say to me, 'but for the circumstance that her father smoked a peculiar fine canaster. I longed to know him from that circumstance, and as he always moved about with his pipe and his daughter, from getting to admire one I began to appreciate the other, and soon Amelia occupied my whole soul. My figure and personal beauty soon attracted her attention;

'In fact,
She saw and loved me, who could resist
Frederick Fantail?'

"Amelia, sir, soon became Mrs. Fantail, but I shall spare you the details of the courtship at which I was not present; for having at the battle of Squeltersluys (so creditable to our arms) had the good fortune to run through a French field-marshal, and to receive a wound in the knee-pan, I was ordered home with the account of the victory, to lay the baton I had taken at the feet of my sovereign, and to have my left leg amputated by the late eminent Sir Everard Home. 'Twas whilst recovering from this little accident, that my friend, Fred Fantail, wooed and won his Amelia.

"Of course he described her in his letters as everything a heart could wish; but I found on visiting his relations in Baker Street, that she was by no means what they could wish. When I mentioned the name of his son, the brow of Sir Augustus Fantail grew black as thunder. Her ladyship looked sad and faint; Anna Maria turned her lovely, imploring eyes upon me beseeching me to silence, and I saw a gleam of fiendish satisfaction twinkling in the mean green squinters of Simon Fantail, Fred's younger brother, which plainly seemed to say, 'Fred is disinherited, I shall come in for 300,000*l.* now.' Sir Augustus had that sum in the family, and was, as you all know, an eminent City man.

"I learned from the lovely Anna Maria (in the embrasure of the drawing-room window, whither somehow we retired for a little conversation which does not concern you), I learned that Sir Augustus's chief rage against Fred arose from his having married the daughter of a Dutch sugar-baker. As the knight had been a dry-salter himself, he would not overlook this insult to his family, and vowed he would cut off forever the child who had so dishonored him.

"Nor was this all.

"'Oh, major,' said Anna Maria to me, putting into my hands a little purse, containing the amount of all her savings, 'give him—give him this. My poor Frederick wants money. He ran away with Amelia—how could they do such a naughty, naughty thing? He has left the army. Her father has discarded her; and I fear they are starving.'

"Here the dear child's beautiful hyacinthine eyes filled with tears, she held out her little hand with the little purse. I took one—both—I covered the one with kisses, and, putting the other into my bosom, I promised to deliver it to the person for whom its affectionate owner intended it.

"Did I do so? No! I kept that precious relic with thirteen little golden guineas twinkling in its meshes; I wore it long, long, in my heart of hearts, under my waistcoat of waistcoats, and as for Fred, I sent him an order on Cox and Greenwood's for five hundred pounds, as the books of that house will show.

"I did more than this; knowing his partiality for cigars, I bought two thousand of the best from Davis in the Quadrant, and despatched them to my poor friend.

"'A wife,' said I, 'is a good companion, no doubt; but why should he not,' I added sportively, 'have Don Amigos too in his troubles?'

"Davis did not laugh at this joke, not understanding Spanish; but you, my dear friend, I have no doubt, will at once perceive its admirable point.

"Thus it stood then. Amelia was disinherited for running away with Fred; Fred was discarded for running away with Amelia. They were penniless. What could my paltry thousand do for a fellow in the 56th Hussars, where our yearly mess bill came to twelve hundred pounds, and our undress boots cost ninety-three guineas a pair? You are incredulous? I have Hoby's bills, sir, and you can see them any day you call in Grosvenor Square.

"To proceed. My imprudent friend was married; and was, as I suspect you are yourself, sir, henpecked. My present of cigars was flung aside as useless. I got letters from Fred saying that his Amelia was a mighty fine lady; that though she had been bred up in a tobacco warehouse all her life, she abominated cigars — in fine, that he had given up the practice altogether. My little loan of a couple of thousand served to keep them going for some time, and they dashed on as if there was no end to that small sum. Ruin ensued, sir, but I knew not of the misfortune of my friend. I was abroad, sir, serving my sovereign in the West Indies, where I had the yellow fever seventeen times.

"Soldiers are bad correspondents, sir. I did not write to Fred Fantail or hear of him, except through a brother officer, Major de Boots, of ours, who joined us in the West Indies, and who told me the sad news. Fred had incurred debts of course — sold out — gone to pieces: 'And fanthy my dithgutht, my dear cweature,' said De Boots (you don't know him? he lisps confoundedly), 'at finding Fwed at Bwighton giving lethonth in dwawing, and hith wife, be-cause she wath a Dutchwoman, teaching Fwench! The fellow wanted to bowow money of me.'

"'And you gave him some, I hope, De Boots?' said I.

"'Not thickthpenth, by jingo,' said the heartless hussar, whom I called out the next morning and shot for his want of feeling.

"I returned to England to recruit my strength, which had been somewhat exhausted by the repeated attacks of fever, and one day as I was taking a tumbler at the great pump-room, Cheltenham, imagine, sir, my astonishment when an enormously stout lady, with yellow hair, and a pea-green satin dress, came up to me, gazed hard for a moment, gave an hysteric juggle in her throat, and flung her arms round my neck! I have led ninety-eight forlorn hopes, sir, but I give you my honor I never was so flustered as by this tremendous phenomenon.

"'For Heaven's sake, madam,' said I, 'calm yourself. Don't scream, — let me go. Who are you?'

"'O my bresairfer!' said the lady, still screeching, and in a foreign accent. 'Don't you know me? I am Amelia Vandail.'

"'Amelia Vandail?' says I, more perplexed than ever.

"'Amelia van Slappenbroch dat vas. Your friend Vrederick's vife. I am stouder now dan I vas vhen I knew you in Holland.'

"Stouder, indeed! I believe she was stouter! She was sixteen stone, or sixteen ten, if she weighed a pound: I got her off my shoulders and led her to a chair. Presently her husband joined us, and I need not tell you the warmth of my meeting with my old friend.

"'But what,' said I to Fantail, 'procured me such a warm greeting from your lovely lady?'

"'Don't you know that you are our benefactor — our blessing — the cause of our prosperity?'

"'Oh! the five hundred pounds!' said I, 'a mere bagatelle.'

"'No, my dearest friend, it was not your money, but your cigars, saved us. You know what a fine lady my wife was when we were first married, and to what straits our mutual imprudence soon drove us. Who would have thought that the superb Mrs. Fantail, who was so fine that she would not allow her husband to smoke a cigar, would be brought so low as to be obliged to sing in the public streets for bread? — that the dashing Fred Fantail should be so debased by poverty as (here my friend's noble features assumed an expression of horrible agony) as to turn a mangle, sir.

"'But away with withering recollections,' continued Fred. 'We were so poor, so wretched, that we resolved on suicide. My wife and I determined to fling ourselves off Waterloo Bridge, and, kissing our nine innocent babes as they slumbered, hastened wildly thither from the New Cut, Lambeth, where we were residing; but we forgot, we had no money to pay the toll — we were forced to come back, to pass our door again: and we determined to see the dear ones once more and then — away to Westminster!

"'There was a smell — a smell of tobacco issuing from the door of our humble hut as we came up. "Good Heavens! Mealy," said I to my beloved one, as we arrived at the door, and the thought flashed across me — "there is still hope — still something left — the cigars I received as a gift on my marriage. I had forgotten them! they are admirable! — they will sell for gold." And I hugged the innocent partner of my sufferings to my bosom. Thou wert thinner then, dearest, than thou art now,' said Fantail, with a glance of ineffable affection towards his lady.

" ' Well, sir, what do you think those cigars were worth to me ? ' continued he.

" ' I gave forty pounds for them : say you sold them for twenty.'

" ' Twenty ! my dear fellow — no ! Those cigars were worth Six Hundred Thousand Pounds to me ! as you shall hear. I said there was a smell of cigar smoke issuing from our humble cot — and why ? because somebody was smoking cigars. And who was that somebody ? Amelia's father, the burgomaster, Van Slappenbroch. His heart had partially relented towards his only child. He determined to see her. He found out our wretched abode in our absence — saw our unconscious infants sleeping there, huddled on the straw in the desolate chamber. The only article of furniture left was your chest of cigars. Van Slappenbroch opened it — tried one — 'twas excellent; a second — delicious ! a third ! — his daughter entered — the father and the tobacconist melted at once, and as she fainted in his arms he was reconciled to us forever ! '

"The rest of Fantail's story, my dear sir, you may easily imagine. Directly they heard in Baker Street that the Dutchman had pardoned his daughter, and had given her his fortune, of course old Fantail came down with his, and disinherited that squinting traitor, Simon. 'And, my dear fellow,' said Fred, ' if you will drive down with me to Fantail Castle, I will repay you the ten thousand pounds you lent me, and introduce you to a lady — my sister Anna Maria, who is very, very anxious to renew her acquaintance with you.'

"That lady is now my wife, sir," the general said, getting up to go away — "and she never objects to smoking."

"Who is the general ? " said I to our host, when the teller of the above singular story had left the room.

"Don't you know him ? " replied my Lord Hobanob, with a smile ; " you may believe every word he says. That is General Sir Goliah Gahagan."

BOB ROBINSON'S FIRST LOVE.

BY LANCELOT WAGSTAFF, ESQ.

[*Colburn's New Monthly Magazine, August*, 1845.]

CLERGYMEN who take private pupils upon small livings in the west of England, and prepare young gentlemen for the universities or for public life, ought to be obliged by law to destroy their female offspring as certain Indian people do — or at least there should be convents or hospitals for the daughters of the tutorizing clergy, where, until their papas had left off "coaching" (as the Oxford phrase was — it is perhaps changed since our time), these virgins should be carefully immured.

For it is next to impossible that lads of eighteen years of age should be put in the daily presence of a rosy-fingered young creature, who makes breakfast every morning in a pink frock; who trips across the common with good things in her basket for the suffering poor people of papa's parish; and who plays the most ravishing tunes on the piano in the evening after tea, when mathematics and the Greek plays are no longer thought of, when papa solaces himself with the *St. James's Chronicle;* when Smith and Jones amuse themselves at chess; and Robinson, who is musically inclined, accompanies Eliza on the flute: — it is next, I say, to impossible that something should not happen from the presence of such a young woman in a tutor's family — something delightful at its commencement, but often productive of woe, perplexity, and family annoyance ere its conclusion. Dear madam or miss! I will not insult you by naming it — you have often inspired that something, and many a manly heart has suffered because you were inevitably fair!

So, too, was Miss Griggs, daughter of the clergyman under whose charge several of us completed our education. He took a limited number of young men of distinguished family to prepare for the universities. He had a son at

Cambridge, whose extravagance he would hint was the cause of his taking pupils, and his lovely daughter, Eliza, kept his house. When parents and guardians would remark on the comeliness of the young woman, and hint that her presence might be dangerous to the peace of mind of the pupils, old Griggs would fling his eyes up to Heaven and say, "I consider that dear girl, sir, to be married. She is engaged to her cousin, the Reverend Samuel Butts, fellow and tutor of Maudlin, and when the first living falls vacant — alas! my Eliza will leave me. Would you have me part with her now? And yet, were she not engaged, she should not live under my roof, but reside, as she used to do previous to her engagement, with her angel mother's family." Here old Griggs's white handkerchief would come out, and as with a trembling voice he uttered these words, his bald forehead, white head, hook nose, and white neckcloth, never failed to impose respect upon his hearers; and parents thought their children lucky under the care of such a man.

But Butts was absent: we saw nothing of him save occasionally in vacation time, when he made his appearance in the shape of a dumpy little flaccid-faced man, who wore high-lows, and no straps to his trousers. He made but a poor figure by the side of the brilliant young bucks at Griggs's, who dressed for dinner, had their clothes from Clifford Street, and wore yellow kid gloves at church on Sundays. I think Miss G. (we did not like to call her Miss Griggs somehow) must have seen the disadvantage under which her Samuel labored in the company of young men of the world. But he was an honest man, great at the digamma, and Miss G. had been engaged to him years ago; before her brother's extravagance at college had compelled pa to take pupils. She wore a lock of his sandy hair in a seven-shilling brooch round her neck; and there was a sticking-plaster full-length of him in his cap and gown, done by the fellow from Brighton, who had hit off to a nicety his little bunch of a nose, and his dumpy, pudgy figure and high-lows, hanging up in the dining-room. Robinson (he who played the flute) used to look at that black figure with violent rage and disgust, shake his fist at it, utter tremendous comminations against Butts as a snob, and wish that either one were dead or the other had never been born, for his soul was consumed with passion for Eliza Griggs, and his heart was scorched with the flames of a first love.

Do not be alarmed for the consequences, madam; don't expect any harrowing romance — wir haben auch geliebt und gelebet — we have endured and survived it as other people do. It is like the small-pox diminished in virulence, and doesn't carry off half as many people as it used according to old accounts.

"They have been engaged for seven years," Robinson used to say, making us confidants of his love, and howling and raging about it as young men of his ardent temperament will do, "but she can't care about him; I know she can't; look how the brute squints; and see him eat peas with his knife — I could thwottle him."

It was quite true; Butts had that obliquity, and consumed his vegetables with the aid of the implement in question. Another day he would come out with, "She was a child when the engagement was made. He is a brute to hold her to it. He might have married her years ago, but he is waiting for the 1200*l.* a year great living, which may never fall in. The selfish scoundrel ought to release her from her engagement. But he didn't. The promise was there. The locket hung round her neck. I confide these things to you as a friend — a brother — Eliza would say. But let me submit to my destiny. What are you men but selfish? all, all selfish? Unfortunate Eliza!"

Don't imagine I am going to say anything disrespectful of her — don't fancy I would hint she was unfaithful to her Butts — in love matters women are never in fault. I never heard of a coquette in my life — nor of a woman playing with a man's affections, and heartlessly flinging him off — nor of a woman's marrying for money — nor of a sly mother who coaxed and wheedled a young fellow, until somehow Jemima was off her hands. No, no, the women are always right, and the author of "Mrs. Caudle's Lectures" ought to be pulled to pieces, like Orpheus, for vilifying the sex.

Eliza, then, did not give the least encouragement to young Robinson, though somehow they were always together. You couldn't go into the garden and see the pink frock among the gooseberry-bushes, but Robinson's green shooting-jacket was seen sauntering by — in the evening their flute and piano were always tweedledeedling in concert — and they never stopped until they had driven us out of the room with their music, when unaccountably the duet would cease; how was it that when miss was on the landing-place, Robinson was always coming upstairs? So it

was though.   They were talking about Mr. Butts probably.
What was that lock of hair Robinson kept in his desk? It
may have been his sister's, his grandmother's.   Were there
not many people with black hair besides Eliza?   And yet
the ill-natured might have fancied that some mercenary
motives influenced the pure heart of Miss Eliza.   Robinson,
though eight years younger than herself, was perhaps a
catch in a pecuniary point of view.   He was the son of the
famous banking-house of Hobbs, Dobbs, and Robinson; and
when arrived at five and twenty (for as for Hobbs and Dobbs
they were myths like Child, Coutts, and others), would take
his seat as head-partner of the house.   His widowed mother
was a Miss Rolfe, daughter of Admiral Rolfe, and sister of
General Sir Hugh Rolfe, K.C.B.   Mr. Rolfe Robinson our
young friend was called, being not a little proud of his
double-barrelled name.   By us he was denominated Rich
Robinson, Kid Robinson, or Band-box Robinson, alluding
to the wealth to which he was heir, and the splendor of his
person — or finally, in compliment to a hesitation in his
speech which he possessed — Staggering Bob.   He was, between ourselves, a weak, fair-haired, vapid, good-natured
fellow: at Eton he was called Miss Robinson.   Every one
of his nicknames justly characterized some peculiarity about
the honest fellow.

Huffle (belonging to the firm), Rolfe, his uncle, and his
mother, were joint guardians of this interesting heir.   His
lady mother spent her jointure in a stately way, occupying
a great house in Portman Square, and giving grand parties
in the season, whereof the *Morning Post* made mention.
Royal dukes, ambassadors, never less than three marquises;
Griggs, our tutor, never failed to read the names of these
guests, to talk about them at dinner — and I think felt
proud at having Mrs. Robinson's son in his house, who entertained such exalted company.   He always helped Bob
first in consequence, and gave him the wings of the fowls,
and the outside of the fillet of veal.

However, Mrs. Robinson had many daughters older than
Bob; and though she lived so splendidly, and though Bob
was to be chief of the banking-house, the young man himself was not very well supplied with cash by his mother.
But he did not want for friends elsewhere, and there was a
certain old clerk in the bank who furnished his young master with any sums that he required — "out of regard for
his dear father" the before-mentioned clerk used to say —

of course never expecting to be paid back again, or to curry favor with his young principal so soon as he took the direction of affairs. From this man Robinson used to get down chests of cigars and cases of liquors and champagne which he consumed in secret, at a certain cottage in the village. Nokes it was who provided surreptitious funds for the hiring of tandems, which, in our youthful days, we delighted to drive. Many a man at Griggs's, who had only his own father's purse to draw upon, envied Robinson such an invaluable friend as Nokes.

Well, this youth was in love with Miss Eliza Griggs. Her father was quite ignorant of the passion of course — never dreamed of such a thing. Fathers are so proverbially blind!

Young Griggs, the Cambridge man, seldom came down among us, except to bleed the governor. A wild and impetuous young man he was; not respectable, and of a bad set — but we lads respected him because he was a man, and had rooms of his own, and told us stories about Proctors and Newmarket; and had a cutaway green coat and large whiskers — to all of which honors we one day hoped to come.

One Easter vacation when young Griggs came down, however, we observed he watched his sister and Robinson very keenly; spoke harshly to the former, at which the latter would grow very angry; and finally, one day after dinner, when, as usual after the second glass of port, Griggs had given the signal for retiring, touched Robinson on the shoulder as we were quitting the dining-room, and said, "Mr. Robinson, I would wish to have a word with you on the lawn." At this summons I observed Robinson turn as red as a carrot, and give a hurried glance at Eliza, who very nearly dropped the bottle she was locking up of old Griggs's fiery port wine.

The particulars of the interview between the two gentlemen Robinson narrated to me that very evening (indeed he told everybody everything concerning himself). "Griggs" (says he) "has been asking me what my intentions are with regard to Eliza. He says my attentions to her are most remarkable; that I must have known she was already an engaged person, though he didn't care to confess that the engagement was one into which his sister had been forced, and which had never been pleasing to her — but that it was impossible that my attentions should continue, or the poor girl's affections be tampered with any further."

"Tampered with! says I" (continued Robinson, speaking for himself), "I tamper with the affections of Miss Griggs!"

"By Jove, sir, do you mean to say that you have not? Haven't you given her a pearl bracelet and a copy of Thomas Moore's poems? Haven't you written copies of verses to her, three in English and one in Latin Alcaics? Do you suppose, sir, as a man of honor, I can allow my sister's feelings to be played with, and you an inmate under my unsuspecting father's roof? No, sir, things can't end here. You must either declare yourself or — you know the alternative."

Here he gave a tremendous scowl, and his eyes flashed so, and his bushy whiskers curled round his face so fiercely, that Robinson, a timid man, — as almost all men who play on the flute are, — felt no small degree of perturbation.

"But I do declare myself," said the young gentleman. "I declare that I love your sister with all the ardor of a young heart; that she is the object of my daily thoughts and my nightly sighs — my soul's pole star — my — my" —

"Never mind any more, sir," replied young Griggs, somewhat appeased; "you have said all this in your poetry already." As Robinson confessed indeed he had.

The result of the interview between the young men was, that Robinson fully declared himself the adorer of Eliza, and promised to marry her immediately on the consent of his mother and guardians, if not now, upon his coming of age, and entering into the banking business which he was heir to.

"I may consider myself authorized on your part, then, to make this proposal to my sister?" said Griggs.

To which Bob agreed, and as Griggs thought the offer had best come in writing, Robinson and he retired to the former's room, where a paper was drawn out at Griggs's direction, and signed by the lover of Eliza.

But the strange part of the story, and the proof of what I before advanced, viz., that Eliza was perfectly innocent and unconscious of the effects produced by her fatal beauty — was that when George Griggs, her brother, carried her the offer, she vowed she had never been so surprised in her life — had never given Mr. Robinson the least encouragement — had, it is true, received presents of books from him and verses, which she regarded as mere proofs of schoolboy friendship, a frolic — liked him very much certainly as a brother, a younger brother, in whose welfare she should ever feel the tenderest interest, for whose happiness she should ever pray —but she was already engaged to Mr. Butts.

Bob professed to be broken-hearted by this sentence of Eliza's, but we all saw there was hope for him, and that if the engagement with Butts could be broken, he might then aspire to the bliss which he desiderated. As for checking him in his desires, or pointing out the folly of his marriage at eighteen with a young lady of four and twenty, that was a point which struck none of us — on the contrary, our pleasure was to suppose that old Griggs would refuse consent, that an elopement would take place in consequence, which Bob's friends would have the fun of arranging; and we even inspected the post-chaise at the Green Dragon, and ascertained the condition of the posters kept there in anticipation of such a romantic event — not that Eliza would have consented, of course not — I would not suppose that she or any other woman would do such a thing, and mention this as an instance, not of her indiscretion, but of our youthful folly.

Meanwhile, Mr. George Griggs returned to the university, having made an unsuccessful application, he said, upon the governor's feelings, to induce him to break off his sister's marriage with Butts.

"The old gentleman's honor was bound," his son said ; "he wished it were otherwise, but having pledged his word he could not withdraw it : and as soon as Butts pleased he might claim his bride. The living Butts desires must soon fall in," he added. "Hicky has had two fits of apoplexy already. Give him a third, and it will be too late."

With this intimation George Griggs departed, informing his young friend at the same time, that although he would gladly have shaken his hand as a brother-in-law, that relationship appeared now to be impossible; and• that if he heard of the least further communication between Bob and his sister, he should be obliged to return from Cambridge in a character most painful to him.

"Why, why," said he, "did you come into our house and bring wretchedness into our peaceful family ? Before she saw you my sister was happy — contented at least with her lot — now she only looks forward to it with terror, and I dread to think of the consequences — that match will kill her, sir — I know Eliza's heart — she will die, sir — and, mind me, there must be other victims if she do ! "

I don't know whether Bob was touched, or terrified, or delighted by this announcement — delighted to be the possessor of such charms — touched by the cruel havoc they caused — or terrified at the consequences which might ensue to himself from the exercise of his fatal power to please; however, he determined Miss Griggs should not die.

He accordingly wrote off the following letter to his correspondent: —

" *My dear Nokes,*—Send me down fifty pounds, and a case of pistols, and put them down to my account. Counting upon receiving your parcel and remittance per coach, Wednesday, I shall leave this on Wednesday evening at eleven, drive through London to the Angel, Islington, and be there probably at five o'clock in the morning. Have a carriage and four waiting for me there, and you may as well bring fifty pounds more, for posting is dear, and I am going to the North. Don't fail me at this most critical juncture of my life, and count upon the eternal gratitude of

"Robert Rolfe Robinson."

When the faithful Nokes received this letter, he for some time could not understand the nature of its contents, until at last the real nature flashed upon him that his young master was going to run away with some lady, and ruin his own and Nokes's prospects for life.

We made it all right meanwhile about the horses at the Green Dragon, which were to be ready at eleven o'clock on Wednesday evening; and in the afternoon of that day, walked down to Puddley Heath, two miles from our parsonage, where the London coach passed, and we made sure of finding our parcel.

Instead of the parcel it was little Nokes himself who jumped off the box, and, giving Robinson a squeeze of the hand, and a nod of the head, pointed significantly to the carpet-bag, which the hostler was handing down, and which, no doubt, contained the money and the pistols. What the deuce we wanted with pistols, I have never been able to ascertain — it was Tolmash, our comrade at Griggs's, who suggested the pistols, as we sat in conspiracy over the affair (for we delighted in it, and had hours and hours of consultation every night concerning it), it was, I say, Tolmash suggested the pistols, taking a hint from a picture in " Tom and Jerry," in which a fellow is represented as running away to Gretna Green, and pointing the " barkers " at the governor, who is just galloping up.

Bob was so impatient to see these weapons that it was with great difficulty Nokes could restrain him from examining them on the high-road, but we waited until we got a private room at the Green Dragon, where the weapons were shown, and where Bob explained at full length and with great eloquence his purpose of abduction.

"There was a gal, a beufle gal, whose heart was bweaking for him, and whose pawents wouldn't let him marwy — he was determined to run away with her if he couldn't get her — to blow his bwains out," etc., etc.

All this Bob told with great sputtering and emotion over a glass of brandy and water. Nokes looked grave.

"I suppose it's the parson's daughter you wrote me about, that I sent the necklace down for. I thought that would have been enough for her. Lord, Lord, what fools you young men are, Mr. Bob!"

"Fools! if you call me a fool, or bweathe a word against Eliza, I'll kick you wound the woom," roared Bob, who didn't seem to have much regard for his father's old friend.

"Well, well — stop — you'll regret it in after life; and remember the words of poor old faithful Jack Nokes; but never mind that. I can take a hard word from your father's son. Here are the pistols; you'd best not take them to the house, as you'll get into the carriage here, I presume. Here's the money — please just acknowledge it — I wash my hands of the business — kick Jack Nokes round the room, indeed!"

Bob seized Mr. Nokes's hand with eagerness, swore he was his best and deawest fwiend, as he should find when he came into Lombard Street; and then, being armed with the sinews of war, the chaise was ordered at eleven, and we all departed for the vicarage.

I repeat I have nothing to say against Miss Griggs — she wouldn't have come very likely — she would have spurned the proposition with scorn, and refused to run away altogether, even if — even if a circumstance had not happened which rendered that measure impossible.

At about nine o'clock — the moon was rising beautifully over the old church — Bob was packing his portmanteau for the expedition and laboriously striving to thrust in a large dressing-case full of silver saucepans, gold razors, etc., which must have been particularly useful to him, as he had no beard as yet. We were making ready for the start, I say, when a letter was brought for R. Rolfe Robinson, Esquire, in the well-known commercial running-hand of Mr. Nokes.

"*Sir*, — Though I may lose your friendship forever, I am determined to prevent this mad step on your part. I have written to Mr. Griggs, warning him solemnly, and threatening him with law proceedings and ruin, from which I am confident I have saved you. I was at school with your father, and saved him too, and devote myself to the son as to him.

"I have taken the post-chaise and the pistols back to town with me. Yours respectfully,

"JOHN NOKES."

Bob was bursting out in an oath, when the door opened, and our respected tutor, the Reverend Frederic Griggs, made his awful appearance, candle in hand, and with a most agitated countenance.

"What is this that I hear, Mr. Robinson?" he exclaimed. "What news, sir, is this for a tutor and a-a f-f-f-ather? Have I been harboring a traitor in my bosom — a serpent that would sting my innocent child — so young and so corrupted! Oh, heavens!"

And he proceeded into an oration which I pretermit, and which lasted for a quarter of an hour. Griggs had a flux of words, and which imposed greatly upon parents and guardians during a first visit or two, but became intolerably tedious to us who were forced to hear it every day. He left us after the oration, saying he was about to retire, and pray for the misguided young men, who had entered into a conspiracy against a fond father's peace.

Robinson was wild. He talked of suicide, but the pistols were gone, and he didn't think of using the gold razors in the grand new dressing-case. We sat with him, and tried to pacify him with philosophy, and a bottle of cherry-brandy. We left him at three o'clock, and he told us afterwards that he rushed frantically out of the room, to Miss Griggs's bedroom, and cried out passionately, "Eliza, Eliza!" The door was locked, of course, he could hear sobbing from within, accompanied by the heavy snore of Mrs. West, the housekeeper, who was placed as dragon over the weeping virgin. Poor soul! she did not come down in her pink frock to breakfast next morning.

But about that hour, up drove General Sir Hugh Rolfe, an apoplectic, goggle-eyed, white-whiskered little general, tightly girthed round the waist, with buckskin gloves, and a bamboo cane, at whose appearance, as he rolled out of the yellow post-chaise, poor Bob turned ashy pale.

We presently heard the general swearing in the passage, and the voice of the Reverend Mr. Griggs raised in meek expostulation.

"Fetch down his things — don't humbug me, sir — infamous swindle, sir. Bring down Mr. Robinson's bags — d——d impostor, sir," and so on. Volleys of oaths were let off by the fiery little man, which banged and exploded in our little hall like so many Vauxhall crackers.

Our friend was carried off. Our own relatives caused us to be removed speedily from Griggs's, under the plea that his daughter was a dangerous inmate of a tutor's house, and that he might take a fancy to make her run away with one of us. Nokes even said that the old gentleman had gone so far as to offer to make it worth his while if he would allow the *enlèvement* to take place — but the Reverend Frederic Griggs replied triumphantly to these calumnies, by marrying his daughter to the Reverend Samuel Butts (who got his living by the death of the apoplectic incumbent), and she is the mother of many children by him, and looks at that angel face of his with a fond smile, and asks, "Who but you, love, could ever have touched the heart of Eliza?"

THE DIGNITY OF LITERATURE.

[*To the Editor of the Morning Chronicle.*]

SIR, — In a leading article of your journal of Thursday, the 3d instant, you commented upon literary pensions and the status of literary men in this country, and illustrated your arguments by extracts from the story of *Pendennis*, at present in course of publication. You have received my writings with so much kindness, that, if you have occasion to disapprove of them or the author, I can't question your right to blame me, or doubt for a moment the friendliness and honesty of my critic; and however I might dispute the justice of your verdict in my case, I had proposed to submit to it in silence, being indeed very quiet in my conscience with regard to the charge made against me.

But another newspaper of high character and repute takes occasion to question the principles advocated in your article of Thursday, arguing in favor of pensions for literary persons as you argued against them; and the only point upon which the *Examiner* and the *Chronicle* appear to agree, unluckily, regards myself, who am offered up to general reprehension in two leading articles by the two writers: by the latter for " fostering a baneful prejudice " against literary men; by the former for " stooping to flat- ter " this prejudice in the public mind, and " condescend- ing to caricature (as is too often my habit) my literary fellow-laborers, in order to pay court to the non-literary class."

The charges of the *Examiner* against a man who has never, to his knowledge, been ashamed of his profession, or (except for its dulness) of any single line from his pen, grave as they are, are, I hope, not proven. " To stoop to flatter " any class is a novel accusation brought against my writings; and as for my scheme " to pay court to the non- literary class by disparaging my literary fellow-laborers," it is a design which would exhibit a degree not only of baseness but of folly upon my part of which, I trust, I am not capable. The editor of the *Examiner* may perhaps occasionally write, like other authors, in a hurry, and not be aware of the conclusions to which some of his sentences may lead. If I stoop to flatter anybody's prejudices for some interested motives of my own, I am no more nor less than a rogue and a cheat; which deductions from the *Examiner's* premisses I will not stoop to contradict, because the premisses themselves are simply absurd.

I deny that the considerable body of our countrymen described by the *Examiner* as the "non-literary class" has the least gratification in witnessing the degradation or disparagement of literary men. Why accuse the "non-literary class" of being so ungrateful? If the writings of an author give the reader pleasure or profit, surely the latter will have a favorable opinion of the person who benefits him. What intelligent man, of whatsoever political views, would not receive with respect and welcome that writer of the *Examiner* of whom your paper once said that "he made all England laugh and think"? Who would deny to that brilliant wit, that polished satirist, his just tribute of respect and admiration? Does any man who has written a book worth reading — any poet, historian, novelist, man of science — lose reputation by his character for genius or for learning? Does he not, on the contrary, get friends, sympathy, applause — money, perhaps? — all good and pleasant things in themselves, and not ungenerously awarded as they are honestly won. That generous faith in men of letters, that kindly regard in which the whole reading nation holds them, appear to me to be so clearly shown in our country every day, that to question them would be absurd, as, permit me to say for my part, it would be ungrateful. What is it that fills mechanics' institutes in the great provincial towns when literary men are invited to attend their festivals? Has not every literary man of mark his friends and his circle, his hundreds or his tens of thousands of readers? And has not every one had from these constant and affecting testimonials of the esteem in which they hold him? It is of course one writer's lot, from the nature of his subject or of his genius, to command the sympathies or awaken the curiosity of many more readers than shall choose to listen to another author; but surely all get their hearing. The literary profession is not held in disrepute; nobody wants to disparage it, no man loses his social rank, whatever it may be, by practising it. On the contrary; the pen gives a place in the world to men who had none before, a fair place, fairly achieved by their genius, as any other degree of eminence is by any other kind of merit. Literary men need not, as it seems to me, be in the least querulous about their position any more, or want the pity of anybody. The money-prizes which the chief among them get are not so high as those which fall to men of other callings — to bishops, or to judges, or to opera-singers and actors, nor have they received stars and garters as yet, or peerages and governorships of islands, such as fall to the lot of military officers. The rewards of the profession are not to be measured by the money stand- ard, for one man may spend a life of learning and labor on a book which does not pay the printer's bill; and another gets a little fortune by a few light volumes. But putting the money out of the question, I believe that the social estimation of the man of letters is as good as it de- serves to be, and as good as that of any other professional man.

With respect to the question in debate between you and the *Examiner*, as to the propriety of public rewards and honors to literary men, I don't see why men of letters should not cheerfully coincide with *Mr. Examiner*, in accepting all the honors, places, and prizes which they can get. The amount of such as will be awarded to them will not, we may be pretty sure, impoverish the country much; and if it is the custom of the State to reward by money, or titles of honor, or stars and garters of any sort, individuals who do the country service; and if individuals are gratified by having Sir, or my Lord, appended to their names, or stars and ribbons hooked on to their coats and waistcoats, as men most undoubtedly are, and as their wives, families, and relations are — there can be no reason why men of letters should not have the chance, as well as men of the robe or the sword; or why, if honor and money are good for one profession, they should not be good for another. No man in other callings thinks himself degraded by receiv- ing a reward from his government; nor surely need the literary man be more squeamish about pensions, and rib- bons, and titles, than the ambassador, or general, or judge. Every European state but ours rewards its men of lettters; the American government gives them their full share of

its small patronage; and if Americans, why not Englishmen? If Pitt Crawley is disappointed at not getting a
ribbon on retiring from his diplomatic post at Pumpernickel; if General O'Dowd is pleased to be called Sir Hector O'Dowd, K.C.B., and his wife at being denominated my
Lady O'Dowd — are literary men to be the only persons
exempt from vanity, and is it to be a sin in them to covet
honor?

And now with regard to the charge against myself of
fostering baneful prejudices against our calling — to which
I no more plead guilty than I should think Fielding would
have done, if he had been accused of a design to bring the
Church into contempt by describing Parson Trulliber —
permit me to say, that before you deliver sentence it would
be as well to have waited to hear the whole of the argument. Who knows what is coming in the future numbers
of the work which has incurred your displeasure and the
Examiner's, and whether you, in accusing me of prejudice,
and the *Examiner* (alas!) of swindling and flattering the
public, have not been premature? Time and the hour may
solve this mystery, for which the candid reader is referred
to "our next."

That I have a prejudice against running into debt, and
drunkenness, and disorderly life, and against quackery and
falsehood in my profession, I own; and that I like to have
a laugh at those pretenders in it who write confidential
news about fashion and politics for provincial *gobemouches;*
but I am not aware of feeling any malice in describing this
weakness, or of doing anything wrong in exposing the
former vices. Have they never existed amongst literary
men? Have their talents never been urged as a plea for
improvidence, and their very faults adduced as a consequence of their genius? The only moral that I, as a
writer, wished to hint in the descriptions against which you
protest was, that it was the duty of a literary man, as well
as any other, to practise regularity and sobriety, to love
his family, and to pay his tradesmen. Nor is the picture I
have drawn "a caricature which I condescend to," any
more than it is a wilful and insidious design on my part to
flatter "the non-literary class." If it be a caricature, it is
the result of a natural perversity of vision, not of an artful
desire to mislead; but my attempt was to tell the truth,
and I meant to tell it not unkindly. I have seen the bookseller whom Bludyer robbed of his books; I have carried

money, and from a noble brother man-of-letters, to some one
not unlike Shandon in prison, and have watched the beautiful devotion of his wife in that place. Why are these
things not to be described, if they illustrate, as they appear
to me to do, that strange and awful struggle of good and
wrong which takes place in our hearts and in the world? It
may be that I work out my moral ill, or it may possibly be
that the critic of the *Examiner* fails in apprehension. My
effort as an artist came perfectly within his province as a
censor; but when *Mr. Examiner* says of a gentleman that
he is "stooping to flatter the public prejudice," which public prejudice does not exist, I submit that he makes a
charge which is as absurd as it is unjust, and am thankful
that it repels itself.

And instead of accusing the public of persecuting and
disparaging us as a class, it seems to me that men of letters
had best silently assume that they are as good as any other
gentlemen; nor raise piteous controversies upon a question
which all people of sense must take as settled. If I sit at
your table, I suppose that I am my neighbor's equal, and
that he is mine. If I begin straightway with a protest of
"Sir, I am a literary man, but I would have you to know
that I am as good as you," which of us is it that questions
the dignity of the literary profession — my neighbor who
would like to eat his soup in quiet, or the man of letters
who commences the argument? And I hope that a comic
writer, because he describes one author as improvident,
and another as a parasite, may not only be guiltless of a
desire to vilify his profession, but may really have its
honor at heart. If there are no spendthrifts or parasites
among us, the satire becomes unjust; but if such exist, or
have existed, they are as good subjects for comedy as men
of other callings. I never heard that the Bar felt itself
aggrieved because *Punch* chose to describe Mr. Dump's
notorious state of insolvency, or that the picture of Stiggins, in "Pickwick," was intended as an insult to all Dis-
senters; or that all the attorneys in the empire were indignant at the famous history of the firm of "Quirk, Gammon,
and Snap." Are we to be passed over because we are
faultless, or because we cannot afford to be laughed at?
And if every character in a story is to represent a class,
not an individual — if every bad figure is to have its obliged
contrast a good one, and a balance of vice and virtue is to
be struck — novels, I think, would become impossible, as

they would be intolerably stupid and unnatural; and there would be a lamentable end of writers and readers of such compositions. Believe me, sir, to be your very faithful servant,

W. M. THACKERAY.

REFORM CLUB, Jan. 8, 1850.

CAPERS AND ANCHOVIES.

[*To the Editor of the Morning Chronicle.*]

"SIR, — I hope no Irish gentleman will be insulted at my recalling a story, venerable for its antiquity, of the Irish officer who, having stated that he had seen anchovies growing in profusion upon the rocks of Malta, called out and shot an Englishman who doubted his statement. As the unhappy Saxon fell writhing from his wound, the Irishman's second remarked, 'Look, Sir Lucius! you have made him cut capers!' 'Bedad, it's capers I mane!' the gallant and impetuous O'Trigger remarked, and instantly apologized in the handsomest terms to his English antagonist for his error. It was capers he had seen, and not anchovies, growing on the rocks; the blunder was his, but the bullet was in the Englishman's leg, who went away grumbling because the other had not thought of the truth before.

"Sir, three Irish newspapers, and an Irish Member of Parliament in his place in the Rotunda, have delivered their fire into me through a similar error. Every post brings me letters containing extracts from Irish papers, sent to me by friends, and one of them, who is most active in my behalf, informs me that there is a body of Irish gentlemen who are bent upon cudgelling me, and who are very likely waiting at my door whilst I write from the club, where, of course, I have denied myself. It is these, while it is yet time, whom I wish to prevent; and as many of them will probably read your journal to-morrow morning, you may possibly be the means of saving my bones, valuable to me and my family, and which I prefer before any apology for breaking them. The blunder of which I am the victim is at once absurd and painful, and I am sorry to be obliged to have recourse to the press for explanation.

"Ten years ago I wrote a satirical story in *Fraser's Magazine*, called 'Catherine,' and founded upon the history of the murderess, Catherine Hayes. The tale was intended to ridicule a taste then prevalent for making novel-heroes of Newgate malefactors. Every single personage in my story was a rascal, and hanged, or put to a violent death; and the history became so atrocious that it created a general dissatisfaction, and was pronounced to be horribly immoral. While the public went on reading the works which I had intended to ridicule, 'Catherine' was, in a word, a failure, and is dead, with all its heroes.

"In the last number of the story of *Pendennis* (which was written when I was absent from this country, and not in the least thinking about the opera here), I wrote a sentence to the purport that the greatest criminals and murderers — Bluebeard, George Barnwell, Catherine Hayes — had some spark of human feeling, and found some friends, — meaning thereby to encourage minor criminals not to despair. And my only thought in producing the last of these instances was about Mrs. Hayes, who died at Tyburn, and subsequently perished in my novel, and not in the least about an amiable and beautiful young lady now acting at Her Majesty's Theatre. I quite forgot her existence. I was pointing my moral, such as it was, with quite a different person, and never for a single instant, I declare on my word of honor, remembering the young lady, nor knowing anything regarding her engagement at the Haymarket.

"From this unlucky sentence in *Pendennis* my tribulations begin, and my capers are held up as the most wicked anchovies to indignant Ireland. Vindex writes to the *Freeman's Journal*, saying that I have an intention to insult the Irish nation in the person of an accomplished and innocent young lady, whom I class with murderers and cut-throats, whereby I damn myself to everlasting infamy. The *Freeman's Journal*, in language intelligible always, if not remarkable for grammatical or other propriety, says I am 'the Big Blubberman, the hugest humbug ever thrust on the public,' that I am guilty of unmanly grossness and cowardly assault, and that I wrote to ruin Miss Hayes, but did not succeed. The *Freeman* adds, in a concluding paragraph, that there may have been some person happening to bear a name coincident with that of the *Freeman's* accomplished countrywoman; and that if I have this very simple and complete defence to make, I shall hasten to offer it. I don't take in the *Freeman's Journal*, — I am not likely to be very anxious about reading it, — but the *Freeman* never gives me any notice of the attack which I am to hasten to defend, and, calling me coward and ruffian, leaves me. It is the anchovy-caper question settled in the approved manner.

"The *Mail*, assuming that I intended insult and injury, remarks on the incriminated sentence thus: 'Its brutality is so far neutralized by its absurdity as to render it utterly harmless.' No. 2.

"No. 3. The *Packet*, speaking on the judgment of both of its contemporaries, says admirably, —

"'This prompt and chivalrous espousal of a lady's cause is just what we should have expected from our brethren of the Irish press, and will be no doubt a source of much gratification to Miss Hayes. But . . . we only think it fair to state that he has not been guilty of the 'incredibly gross act' of associating our pure and amiable Catherine with the murderers and tyrants about whom he has written so nonsensically.'

"And then follows the revelation of the mystery about the real Catherine, the writer remarking that I am neither a fool nor a madman, and that I would not outrage Miss Hayes, lest some Saxon should kick me.

"Sir, if some pictures of the Irish, drawn by foreign hands, are caricatures, what are they compared to pictures of the Irish drawn by themselves? Would any man — could any man out of Ireland — invent such an argument as the last? It stands thus: —

"1. I have not intended to injure, nor have I in the least injured, Miss Hayes.

"2. The people who have abused me for injuring her have acted with chivalrous promptitude, and, no doubt, have greatly gratified Miss Hayes. Poor young lady! she is to be gratified by seeing a man belabored who never thought of her or meant her a wrong.

"3. But if I had injured Miss Hayes, many Saxon boot-toes would have taught me decency; that is, capers not being anchovies, gentlemen would have acted with much chivalry in shooting me; and if capers had been anchovies, I should richly have merited a kicking. Comfortable dilemma!

"I should not have noticed this charge except in Ireland, believing that it must be painful to the young lady whose name has been most innocently and unfortunately brought forward; but I see the case has already passed the Channel, and that there is no help for all parties but publicity.

I declare upon my honor, then, to Miss Hayes, that I am grieved to have been the means of annoying her, if I have done so; and I need not tell any gentleman — what gentleman would question me ? — that I never for a moment could mean an insult to innocence, and genius, and beauty.

"I am, sir, your very faithful servant,

"W. M. THACKERAY."

"GARRICK CLUB, April 11, 1850."

MR. THACKERAY IN THE UNITED STATES.

[*To the Editor of Fraser's Magazine, January*, 1853.]

You may remember, my dear sir, how I prognosticated a warm reception for your Mr. Michael Angelo Titmarsh in New York — how I advised that he should come by a Collins rather than a Cunard liner — how that he must land at New York rather than at Boston — or, at any rate, that he mustn't dare to begin lecturing at the latter city, and bring "cold joints" to the former one. In the last particular he has happily followed my suggestion, and has opened with a warm success in the chief city. The journals have been full of him. On the 19th of November, he commenced his lectures before the Mercantile Library Association (young ardent commercialists), in the spacious New York church belonging to the flock presided over by the Reverend Mr. Chapin; a strong row of ladies — the cream of the capital — and an "unusual number of the distinguished literary and professional celebrities." The critic of the *New York Tribune* is forward to commend his style of delivery as "that of a well-bred gentleman, reading with marked force and propriety to a large circle in the drawing-room." So far, excellent. This witness is a *gentleman* of the press, and is a credit to his order. But there are some others who have whetted the ordinary American appetite of inquisitiveness with astounding intelligence. Sydney Smith excused the national curiosity as not only venial, but laudable. In 1824, he wrote — " Where men live in woods and forests, as is the case, of course, in remote American settlements, it is the duty of every man to gratify the inhabitants by telling them his name, place, age, office, virtues, crimes, children, fortune, and remarks." It is not a matter of surprise, therefore, that this percontatorial foible has grown with the national growth.

You cannot help perceiving that the lion in America is public property and confiscate to the common weal. They trim the creature's nails, they cut the hair off his mane and tail (which is distributed or sold to his admirers), and they draw his teeth, which are frequently preserved with much the same care as you keep any memorable grinder whose presence has been agony and departure delight.

Bear-leading is not so much in vogue across the Atlantic as at your home in England; but the lion-leading is infinitely more in fashion.

Some learned man is appointed Androcles to the new arrival. One of the familiars of the press is despatched to attend the latest attraction, and by this reflecting medium the lion is perpetually presented to the popular gaze. The guest's most secret self is exposed by his host. Every action — every word — every gesture is preserved, and proclaimed — a sigh — a nod — a groan — a sneeze — a cough — or a wink — is each written down by this recording minister, who blots out nothing. No *tabula rasa* with him. The portrait is limned with the fidelity of Parrhasius, and filled up with the minuteness of the Daguerre process itself. No bloodhound or Bow Street officer can be keener or more exact on the trail than this irresistible and unavoidable spy. 'Tis in Austria they calotype criminals: in the far West the public press prints the identity of each notorious visitor to its shores.

In turn, Mr. Dickens, Lord Carlisle, Jenny Lind, and now Mr. Thackeray, have been lionized in America.

"They go to see, themselves a greater sight than all."

In providing for a gaping audience, narrators are disposed rather to go beyond reality. Your famous Oriental lecturer at the British and Foreign Institute had a wallet of personal experience, from which Lemuel Gulliver might have helped himself. With such hyperbole one or two of "our own correspondents" of American journals tell Mr. Thackeray more about his habits than he himself was cognizant of. Specially I have selected from the *Sachem* and *Broadway Delineator* (the latter-named newspaper has quite a fabulous circulation) a pleasant history of certain of the peculiarities of your great humorist at which I believe he himself must smile.

Mr. Thackeray's person, height, breadth, hair, complexion, voice, gesticulation, and manner are, with a fair enough accuracy, described.

Anon, these recorders, upon which we play, softly whisper, —

"One of his most singular habits is that of making rough sketches for caricatures on his finger-nails. The phosphoretic ink he originally used has destroyed the entire nails, so his fingers are now tipped with horn, on which he draws his portraits. The Duke of Marlboro' (under Queen Anne), General O'Gahagan (under Lord Lake), together with Ibrahim Pasha (at the Turkish Ambassador's), were thus taken. The celebrated engravings in the 'Paris Sketch Book,' ' Esmond,' etc., were made from these sketches. He has an insatiable passion for snuff, which he carries loose in his pockets. At a ball at the Duke of Northumberland's, he set a whole party sneezing, in a polka, in so convulsive a manner that they were obliged to break up in confusion. His pockets are all lined with tea-lead, after a fashion introduced by the late Lord Dartmouth.

"Mr. T. has a passion for daguerreotypes, of which he has a collection of many thousands. Most of these he took unobserved from the outer gallery of Saint Paul's. He generally carries his apparatus in one of Sangster's alpaca umbrellas, surmounted with the head of Doctor Syntax. (This umbrella, we believe, remained with the publishers of *Fraser's Magazine*, after the article on the London Exhibitions, in which it was alluded to.) He has been known to collar a beggar boy in the streets, drag him off to the nearest pastrycook's, and exercise his photographic art without ceremony. In London he had a tame laughing hyena presented to him, on the breaking up of the Tower menagerie, which followed him like a dog, and was much attached to his master, though totally blind from confinement, deaf, and going on three legs and a wooden one. He was always surrounded by pets and domestic animals in his house; two owls live in the ivy-tod of the summer-house in the garden. His back sitting-room has an aviary. Monkeys, dogs, parrots, cats, and guinea-pigs swarm in the chambers. The correspondent of the *Buffalo Revolver*, who stayed three weeks with Mr. Thackeray during the Great Exhibition, gave us these particulars.

"His papers on the 'Greater Petty Chaps' or 'Garden Warbler (*Sylva hortensis*),' ' the Fauvette,' created an immense sensation when Madame Otto Goldschmidt was last in London. The study is at the end of the garden. The outside is richly covered with honeysuckle, jasmine, and Virginia creepers. Here Mr. T. sits in perfect solitude, 'chewing the cud of sweet and bitter fancy.' Being an early riser, he is generally to be found there in the morning, whence he can watch the birds. His daily costume is a hanging chlamys, or frock-coat, which he closely buttons, to avoid the encumbrance of a waist-coat. Hence the multiplicity of his coat-pockets, whose extreme utility to him during his lecture has been remarked elsewhere. He wears no braces, but his nether garments are sustained by a suspensory belt or bandage of hemp round his loins. Socks or stockings he despises as effeminate, and has been heard to sigh for the days of the *Solea* or σανδάλιον. A hair-shirt close to the skin as Dejanira's robe, with a changeable linen front of the finest texture; a mortification, or penance, according to his cynical contempt and yet respect for human vanity, is a part of his ordinary apparel. A gibus hat and a pair of bluchers complete his attire. By a contrivance borrowed from the disguises of pantomimists, he undresses himself in the twinkling of a bed-post; and can slip into bed while an ordinary man is pulling off his coat. He is awaked from his sleep (lying always on his back in a sort of mesmeric trance) by a black servant (Joe's domestic in 'Vanity Fair'), who enters the bed-room at four o'clock precisely every morning, winter or summer, tears down the bed-clothes, and literally saturates his master with a can of cold water drawn from the nearest spring. As he has no whiskers, he never needs to shave, and he is used to clean his teeth with the feather end of the quill with which he writes in bed. (In this free and enlightened country he will find he need not waste his time in cleaning his teeth at all.) With all his excessive simplicity, he is as elaborate in the arrangement of his dress as Count d'Orsay or Mr. Brummel. His toilet occupies him after matin studies till mid-day. He then sits down to a substantial 'bever,' or luncheon of 'tea, coffee, bread, butter, salmon-shad, liver, black puddings, and sausages.' At the top of this he deposits two glasses of ratafia and three-fourths of a glass of rum-shrub. Immediately after the meal his horses are brought to the door; he starts at once in a mad gallop, or coolly commences a gentle amble, according to the character of the work, fast or slow, that he is engaged upon.

"He pays no visits and, being a solitudinarian, frequents not even a single club in London. He dresses punctiliously for dinner every day. He is but a sorry eater, and avoids all vegetable diet, as he thinks it dims the animal spirits. Only when engaged on pathetic subjects does he make a hearty meal; for the body macerated by long fasting, he says, cannot unaided contribute the tears he would shed over what he writes. Wine he abhors, as a true Mussulman. Mr. T.'s favorite drink is gin and toast and water, or cider and bitters, cream and cayenne.

.   .   .   .

"In religion a Parsee (he was born in Calcutta), in morals a Stagirite, in philosophy an Epicurean; though nothing in his conversation or manners would lead one to surmise that he belonged to either or any of these sects. In politics an unflinching Tory; fond of the Throne, admiring the Court, attached to the peerage, proud of the army and navy; a thick and thin upholder of Church and State, he is for tithes and taxes as in Pitt's time. He wears hair powdered to this day, from his entire reliance on the wisdom of his forefathers. Besides his novels, he is the author of the 'Vestiges of Creation,' the 'Errors of Numismatics,' 'Junius's Letters,' and 'Ivanhoe.' The sequel to this last he published three or four years ago. He wrote all Louis Napoleon's works, and Madame H.'s exquisite love letters; and whilst secretary to that prince in confinement at Ham, assisted him in his escape, by knocking down the sentry with a ruler with which he had been ruling accounts. Mr. T. is very fond of boxing, and used to have an occasional set-to with Ben Caunt, the Tipton Slasher, and young Sambo. He fences admirably, and ran the celebrated Bertrand through the lungs twice, at an *assaut d'armes* in Paris. He is an exquisite dancer, he founded Laurent's Casino (was a pupil of Old Grimaldi, surnamed *Iron Legs*), and played Harlequin in 'Mother Goose' pantomime once, when Ella, the regular performer, was taken ill and unable to appear.

"He has no voice, ear, or fancy even, for music, and the only instruments he cares to listen to are the Jew's-harp, the bagpipes, and the 'Indian drum.'

"He is disputatious and loquacious to a degree in company; and at a dinner at the Bishop of Oxford's, the discussion with Mr. Macaulay respecting the death of Mausolus, the husband of Zenobia, occupied the disputants for thirteen hours ere either rose to retire. Mr. Macaulay was found exhausted under the table. He has no acquaintance with modern languages, and his French, which he freely uses throughout his writings, is furnished by the Parisian governess in the Baron de B.'s establishment. In the classics he is superior to either Professor Sedgwick or Blackie (*vide* his 'Colloquies on Strabo,' and the 'Curtian Earthquake'). He was twice senior opt. at Magdalen College, and three times running carried off Barnes's prize for Greek Theses and Cantate," κ. τ. λ.

   .   .   .   .   .   .

Happily these delicate attentions have not ruffled Mr. Thackeray's good temper and genial appreciation of the high position occupied by literary men in the United States. Let me avow that this position not only reflects credit on the country which awards it, but helps to shed its lustre on the men of letters who become the guests of its hospitality. Mr. Thackeray's last lecture of the series, on the 7th ult., gracefully conceded this in the following tribute:—

"In England it was my custom, after the delivery of these lectures, to point such a moral as seemed to befit the country I lived in, and to protest against an outcry, which some brother authors of mine most imprudently and unjustly raise, when they say that our profession is neglected and its professors held in light esteem. Speaking in this country, I would say that such a complaint could not only not be advanced, but could not be even understood here, where your men of letters take their manly share in public life; whence Everett goes as Minister to Washington, and Irving and Bancroft to represent the republic in the old country. And if to English authors the English public is, as I believe, kind and just in the main, can any of us say, will any who visit your country not proudly and gratefully own, with what a cordial and generous greeting you receive us? I look round on this great company. I think of my gallant young patrons of the Mercantile Library Association, as whose servant I appear before you, and of the kind hands stretched out to welcome me by men famous in letters, and honored in our country as in their own, and I thank you and them for a most kindly greeting and a most generous hospitality. At home, and amongst his own people, it scarce becomes an English writer to speak of himself: his public estimation must depend upon his works; his private esteem on his character and his life. But here, among friends newly found, I ask leave to say that I am thankful; and I think with a grateful heart of those I leave behind me at home, who will be proud of the welcome you hold out to me, and will benefit, please God, when my days of work are over, by the kindness which you show to their father."

JOHN SMALL.

A LEAF OUT OF A SKETCH-BOOK.

[*The Victoria Regia, edited by Adelaide A. Procter, 1861.*]

IF you will take a leaf out of my sketch-book, you are welcome. It is only a scrap, but I have nothing better to give. When the fishing-boats come in at a watering-place, have'n't you remarked that though these may be choking with great fish, you can only get a few herrings or a whiting or two? The big fish are all bespoken in London. As it is with fish, so it is with authors, let us hope. Some Mr. Charles, of Paternoster Row, some Mr. Grove, of Cornhill (or elsewhere), has agreed for your turbots and your salmon, your soles and your lobsters. Take one of my little fish, — any leaf you like out of the little book, — a battered little book: through what a number of countries, to be sure, it has travelled in this pocket!

The sketches are but poor performances, say you. I don't say no; and value them no higher than you do, except as recollections of the past. The little scrawl helps to fetch back the scene which was present and alive once, and is gone away now, and dead. The past resurges out of its grave; comes up — a sad-eyed ghost sometimes — and gives a wan ghost-like look of recognition, ere it pops down under cover again. Here's the Thames, an old graveyard, an old church, and some old chestnuts standing behind it. Ah! it was·a very cheery place, that old graveyard; but what a dismal, cut-throat, cracked-windowed, disreputable residence was that "charming villa on the banks of the Thames," which led me on the day's excursion! Why, the "capacious stabling" was a ruinous wooden old barn, the garden was a mangy potato patch overlooked by the territories of a neighboring washerwoman. The housekeeper owned that the water was constantly in the cellars and ground-floor rooms in winter. Had I gone to live in that place, I should have perished like a flower in spring, or a young gazelle, let us say, with dark blue eyes. I had spent a day and hired a fly at ever so much charges, misled by an unveracious auctioneer, against whom I have no remedy for pubas in a little castle, were —— well, I never saw such a queer little crockery merchant.

Him and his little chair, boots, *képi*, crockery, you can see in the sketch, — but I see, nay, hear, a great deal more. At the end of the quiet little old, old street, which has retired out of the world's business as it were, being quite too aged, feeble, and musty to take any part in life, — there is a great braying and bellowing of serpents and bassoons, a nasal chant of clerical voices, and a pattering of multitudinous feet. We run towards the market. It is a Church *fête* day. Banners painted and gilt with images of saints are flaming in the sun. Candles are held aloft, feebly twinkling in the noon-tide shine. A great procession of children with white veils, white shoes, white roses, passes, and the whole town is standing with its hat off to see the religious show. When I look at my little merchant, then, I not only see him, but that procession passing over the place; and as I see those people in their surplices, I can almost see Eustache de Saint Pierre and his comrades walking in their shirts to present themselves to Edward and Philippa of blessed memory. And they stand before the wrathful monarch, — poor fellows, meekly shuddering in their chemises, with ropes round their necks; and good Philippa kneels before the royal conqueror, and says, "My King, my Edward, my hear; Sire! Give these citizens their

I suppose other pen and pencil sketchers have the same feeling. The sketch brings back, not only the scene, but the circumstances under which the scene was viewed. In taking up an old book, for instance, written in former days by your humble servant, he comes upon passages which are outwardly lively and facetious, but inspire their writer with the most dismal melancholy. I lose all cognizance of the text sometimes, which is hustled and elbowed out of sight by the crowd of thoughts which throng forward, and which were alive and active at the time that text was born. Ah, my good sir! a man's books mayn't be interesting (and I could mention other authors' works besides this one's which set me to sleep), but if you knew *all* a writer's thoughts, how interesting his book would be! Why, a grocer's day-book might be a wonderful history, if alongside of the entries of cheese, pickles, and figs, you could read the circumstances of the writer's life, and the griefs, hopes, joys, which caused the heart to beat, while the hand was writing and the ink flowing fresh. Ah memory! ah the past, ah the sad sad past! Look under this waistcoat, my dear madam. There. Over the liver. Don't be frightened. You can't see it. But there, at this moment, I assure you, there is an enormous vulture gnawing, gnawing.

Turn over the page. You can't deny that this is a nice little sketch of a quaint old town, with city towers, and an embattled town gate, with a hundred peaked gables, and rickety balconies, and gardens sweeping down to the river wall, with its toppling ancient summer-houses under which the river rushes; the rushing river, the talking river, that murmurs all day, and brawls all night over the stones. At early morning and evening, under this terrace which you see in the sketch—it is the terrace of the Steinbock or Capricorn Hotel—the cows come; and there, under the walnut-trees before the tannery, is a fountain and pump where the maids come in the afternoon, and for some hours make a clatter as noisy as the river. Mountains gird it around, clad in dark green firs, with purple shadows gushing over their sides, and glorious changes and gradations of sunrise and setting. A more picturesque, quaint, kind, quiet little town than this of Coire in the Grisons, I have seldom seen; or a more comfortable little inn than this of the Steinbock or Capricorn, on the terrace of which we are standing. But quick, let us turn the page. To look at it makes one horribly melancholy. As we are on the inn-terrace one of our party lies ill in the hotel within. When will that doctor come? Can we trust to a Swiss doctor in a remote little town away at the confines of the railway world? He is a good, sensible, complacent doctor, *laus Deo*, — the people of the hotel as kind, as attentive, as gentle, as eager to oblige. But oh, the gloom of those sunshiny days; the sickening languor and doubt which fill the heart as the hand is making yonder sketch and I think of the invalid suffering within!

Quick, turn the page. And what is here? This picture, ladies and gentlemen, represents a steamer on the Alabama River, plying (or *which plied*) between Montgomery and Mobile. See, there is a black nurse with a cotton handkerchief round her head, dandling and tossing a white baby. Look in at the open door of that cabin, or "stateroom" as they call the crib yonder. A mother is leaning by a bedplace; and see, kicking up in the air, are a little pair of white fat legs, over which that happy young mother is bending in such happy tender contemplation. That gentleman with a forked beard and a slouched hat, whose legs are sprawling here and there, and who is stabbing his mouth and teeth with his penknife, is quite good-natured, though he looks so fierce. A little time ago, as I was reading in the cabin, having one book in my hand and another at my elbow, he affably took the book at my elbow, read in it a little, and put it down by my side again. He meant no harm. I say he is quite good-natured and kind. His manners are not those of Mayfair, but is not Alabama a river as well as Thames? I wish that other little gentleman were in the cabin who asked me to liquor twice or thrice in the course of the morning, but whose hospitality I declined, preferring not to be made merry by wine or strong waters before dinner. After dinner, in return for his hospitality, I asked *him* if he would drink? "No, sir, I have dined," he answered with very great dignity, and a tone of reproof. Very good. Manners differ. I have not a word to say.

Well, my little Mentor is not in my sketch, but he is in my mind as I look at it: and this sketch, ladies and gentlemen, is especially interesting and valuable, because *the steamer blew up on the very next journey:* blew up, I give you my honor, — burst her boilers close by my stateroom, so that I might, had I but waited for a week, have witnessed a celebrated institution of the country, and had the full benefit of the boiling.

I turn a page, and who are these little men who appear on it? JIM and SADY are two young friends of mine at Savannah in Georgia. I made Sady's acquaintance on a first visit to America, — a pretty little brown boy with beautiful bright eyes, — and it appears that I presented him with a quarter of a dollar, which princely gift he remembered years afterwards, for never were eyes more bright and kind than the little man's when he saw me, and I dined with his kind masters on my second visit. Jim at my first visit had been a little toddling tadpole of a crea

ture, but during the interval of the two journeys had developed into the full-blown beauty which you see. On the day after my arrival these young persons paid me a visit, and here is a humble portraiture of them, and an accurate account of a conversation which took place between us, as taken down on the spot by the elder of the interlocutors.

Jim is five years old : Sady is seben : only Jim is a great deal fatter. Jim and Sady have had sausage and hominy for breakfast. One sausage, Jim's, was the biggest. Jim can sing, but declines on being pressed, and looks at Sady and grins. They both work in de garden. Jim has been

licked by Master, but Sady never. These are their best
clothes. They go to church in these clothes. Heard a fine
sermon yesterday, but don't know what it was about.
Never heard of England, never heard of America. Like
orangees best. Don't know any old woman who sells
orangees. (*A pecuniary transaction takes place.*) Will give
that quarter-dollar to Pa. That was Pa who waited at
dinner. Are hungry, but dinner not cooked yet. Jim all
the while is revolving on his axis, and when begged to
stand still turns round in a fitful manner.

    [*Exeunt Jim and Sady with a cake apiece which the
      housekeeper gives them. Jim tumbles downstairs.*

In his little red jacket, his little — his little ? — his immense red trousers.

On my word the fair proportions of Jim are not exaggerated, — such a queer little laughing blackamoorkin I
have never seen. Seen ? I see him now, and Sady, and a
half-dozen more of the good people, creeping on silent bare
feet to the drawing-room door when the music begins, and
listening with all their ears, with all their eyes. Good-
night, kind, warm-hearted little Sady and Jim ! May peace
soon be within your doors, and plenty within your walls !
I have had so much kindness there, that I grieve to think
of friends in arms, and brothers in anger.

LECTURE.

CHARITY AND HUMOR.*

SEVERAL charitable ladies of this city, to some of whom I am under great personal obligation, having thought that a Lecture of mine would advance a benevolent end which they had in view, I have preferred, in place of delivering a Discourse, which many of my hearers no doubt know already, upon a subject merely literary or biographical, to put together a few thoughts which may serve as a supplement to the former Lectures, if you like, and which have this at least in common with the kind purpose which assembles you here, that they rise out of the same occasion, and treat of charity.

Besides contributing to our stock of happiness, to our harmless laughter and amusement, to our scorn for falsehood and pretension, to our righteous hatred of hypocrisy, to our education in the perception of truth, our love of honesty, our knowledge of life, and shrewd guidance through the world, have not our humorous writers, our gay and kind week-day preachers, done much in support of that holy cause which has assembled you in this place; and which you are all abetting — the cause of love and charity, the cause of the poor, the weak, and the unhappy; the

* This lecture was first delivered in New York on behalf of a charity at the time of Mr. Thackeray's visit to America in 1852, when he had been giving his series of lectures on the English Humorists. It was subsequently repeated with slight variations in London (once under the title of "Week-day Preachers") for the benefit of the families of Angus B. Reach and Douglas Jerrold. The lecture on behalf of the Jerrold Fund was given on July 22, 1857, the day after the declaration of the poll in the Oxford election, when Mr. Thackeray was a candidate for Parliament, and was defeated by Mr. Cardwell. The *Times*, in its account of the lecture, says: "The opening words of the discourse, uttered with a comical solemnity, of which Mr. Thackeray alone is capable, ran thus: — 'Walking yesterday in the High Street of a certain ancient city.' So began the lecturer, and was interrupted by a storm of laughter that deferred for some moments the completion of the sentence."

sweet mission of love and tenderness and peace and good will towards men ? That same theme which is urged upon you by the eloquence and example of good men to whom you are delighted listeners on Sabbath days, is taught in his way and according to his power by the humorous writer, the commentator on every-day life and manners.

And as you are here assembled for a charitable purpose, giving your contributions at the door to benefit deserving people who need them, I like to hope and think that the men of our calling have done something in aid of the cause of charity, and have helped, with kind words and kind thoughts at least, to confer happiness and to do good. If the humorous writers claim to be week-day preachers, have they conferred any benefit by their sermons ? Are people happier, better, better disposed to their neighbors, more inclined to do works of kindness, to love, forbear, forgive, pity, after reading in Addison, in Steele, in Fielding, in Goldsmith, in Hood, in Dickens? I hope and believe so, and fancy that in writing they are also acting charitably, contributing with the means which Heaven supplies them to forward the end which brings you too together.

A love of the human species is a very vague and indefinite kind of virtue, sitting very easily on a man, not confining his actions at all, shining in print, or exploding in paragraphs, after which efforts of benevolence the philanthropist is sometimes said to go home, and be no better than his neighbors. Tartuffe and Joseph Surface, Stiggins and Chadband, who are always preaching fine sentiments, and are no more virtuous than hundreds of those whom they denounce and whom they cheat, are fair objects of mistrust and satire; but their hypocrisy, the homage, according to the old saying, which vice pays to virtue, has this of good in it, that its fruits are good: a man may preach good morals, though he may be himself but a lax practitioner; a Pharisee may put pieces of gold into the charity-plate out of mere hypocrisy and ostentation, but the bad man's gold feeds the widow and the fatherless as well as the good man's. The butcher and baker must needs look, not to motives, but to money, in return for their wares.

I am not going to hint that we of the Literary calling resemble Monsieur Tartuffe or Monsieur Stiggins, though there may be such men in our body, as there are in all.

A literary man of the humoristic turn is pretty sure to

be of a philanthropic nature, to have a great sensibility, to
be easily moved to pain or pleasure, keenly to appreciate
the varieties of temper of people round about him, and
sympathize in their laughter, love, amusement, tears.
Such a man is philanthropic, man-loving by nature, as
another is irascible, or red-haired, or six feet high. And
so I would arrogate no particular merit to literary men for
the possession of this faculty of doing good which some of
them enjoy. It costs a gentleman no sacrifice to be benevolent on paper; and the luxury of indulging in the most
beautiful and brilliant sentiments never makes any man a
penny the poorer. A literary man is no better than another, as far as my experience goes; and a man writing a
book, no better nor worse than one who keeps accounts in
a ledger, or follows any other occupation. Let us, however,
give him credit for the good, at least, which he is the
means of doing, as we give credit to a man with a million
for the hundred which he puts into the plate at a charity-
sermon. He never misses them. He has made them in a
moment by a lucky speculation, and parts with them,
knowing that he has an almost endless balance at his bank,
whence he can call for more. But in esteeming the bene-
faction, we are grateful to the benefactor, too, somewhat;
and so of men of genius, richly endowed, and lavish in
parting with their mind's wealth, we may view them at
least kindly and favorably, and be thankful for the bounty
of which Providence has made them the dispensers.

I have said myself somewhere, I do not know with what
correctness (for definitions never are complete), that humor
is wit and love; I am sure, at any rate, that the best
humor is that which contains most humanity, that which
is flavored throughout with tenderness and kindness. This
love does not demand constant utterance or actual expression, as a good father, in conversation with his children or
wife, is not perpetually embracing them, or making protes-
tations of his love; as a lover in the society of his mistress
is not, as far as I am led to believe, forever squeezing her
hand or sighing in her ear, "My soul's darling, I adore
you!" He shows his love by his conduct, by his fidelity,
by his watchful desire to make the beloved person happy;
it lightens from his eyes when she appears, though he may
not speak it; it fills his heart when she is present or
absent; influences all his words and actions; suffuses his
whole being; it sets the father cheerily to work through

the long day, supports him through the tedious labor of the weary absence or journey, and sends him happy home again, yearning towards the wife and children. This kind of love is not a spasm, but a life. It fondles and caresses at due seasons, no doubt; but the fond heart is always beating fondly and truly, though the wife is not sitting hand in hand with him, or the children hugging at his knee. And so with a loving humor: I think, it is a genial writer's habit of being; it is the kind gentle spirit's way of looking out on the world — that sweet friendliness, which fills his heart and his style. You recognize it, even though there may not be a single point of wit, or a single pathetic touch in the page; though you may not be called upon to salute his genius by a laugh or a tear. That collision of ideas, which provokes the one or the other, must be occasional. They must be like papa's embraces, which I spoke of anon, who only delivers them now and again, and cannot be expected to go on kissing the children all night. And so the writer's jokes and sentiment, his ebullitions of feeling, his outbreaks of high spirits, must not be too frequent. One tires of a page of which every sentence sparkles with points, of a sentimentalist who is always pumping the tears from his eyes or your own. One suspects the genuineness of the tear, the naturalness of the humor; these ought to be true and manly in a man, as everything else in his life should be manly and true; and he loses his dignity by laughing or weeping out of place, or too often.

When the Reverend Laurence Sterne begins to sentimentalize over the carriage in Monsieur Dessein's courtyard, and pretends to squeeze a tear out of a rickety old shandry-dan; when, presently, he encounters the dead donkey on his road to Paris, and snivels over that asinine corpse, I say: "Away, you drivelling quack: do not palm off these grimaces of grief upon simple folk who know no better, and cry misled by your hypocrisy." Tears are sacred. The tributes of kind hearts to misfortune, the mites which gentle souls drop into the collections made for God's poor and unhappy, are not to be tricked out of them by a whimpering hypocrite, handing round a begging-box for your compassion, and asking your pity for a lie. When that same man tells me of Lefevre's illness and Uncle Toby's charity; of the noble at Rennes coming home and reclaiming his sword, I thank him for the generous emotion which, springing genuinely from his own heart, has caused mine to admire benevolence and sympathize with honor; and to feel love, and kindness, and pity.

If I do not love Swift, as, thank God, I do not, however immensely I may admire him, it is because I revolt from the man who placards himself as a professional hater of his own kind; because he chisels his savage indignation on his tombstone, as if to perpetuate his protest against being born of our race—the suffering, the weak, the erring, the wicked, if you will, but still the friendly, the loving children of God our Father: it is because, as I read through Swift's dark volumes, I never find the aspect of nature seems to delight him; the smiles of children to please him; the sight of wedded love to soothe him. I do not remember in any line of his writing a passing allusion to a natural scene of beauty. When he speaks about the families of his comrades and brother clergymen, it is to assail them with gibes and scorn, and to laugh at them brutally for being fathers and for being poor. He does mention in the Journal to Stella a sick child, to be sure — a child of Lady Masham, that was ill of the small-pox — but then it is to confound the brat for being ill, and the mother for attending to it, when she should have been busy about a Court intrigue, in which the Dean was deeply engaged. And he alludes to a suitor of Stella's, and a match she might have made, and would have made, very likely, with an honorable and faithful and attached man, Tisdall, who loved her, and of whom Swift speaks in a letter to this lady in language so foul that you would not bear to hear it. In treating of the good the humorists have done, of the love and kindness they have taught and left behind them, it is not of this one I dare speak. Heaven help the lonely misanthrope! be kind to that multitude of sins, with so little charity to cover them!

Of Mr. Congreve's contributions to the English stock of benevolence, I do not speak; for, of any moral legacy to posterity, I doubt whether that brilliant man ever thought at all. He had some money, as I have told, every shilling of which he left to his friend the Duchess of Marlborough, a lady of great fortune and the highest fashion. He gave the gold of his brains to persons of fortune and fashion, too. There is no more feeling in his comedies than in as many books of Euclid. He no more pretends to teach love for the poor, and good will for the unfortunate, than a dancing master does; he teaches pirouettes and flic-flacs; and how to bow to a lady, and to walk a minuet. In his private life Congreve was immensely liked — more so than any man of his age almost; and, to have been so liked, must have been kind and good-natured. His good-nature bore him through extreme bodily ills and pain, with uncommon cheerfulness and courage. Being so gay, so bright, so popular, such a grand seigneur, be sure he was kind to those about him, generous to his dependants, serviceable to his friends. Society does not like a man so long as it liked Congreve, unless he is likable; it finds out a quack very soon; it scorns a poltroon or a curmudgeon: we may be certain that this man was brave, good-tempered, and liberal; so, very likely, is Monsieur Pirouette, of whom we spoke; he cuts his capers, he grins, bows, and dances to his fiddle. In private he may have a hundred virtues; in public, he teaches dancing. His business is cotillons, not ethics.

As much may be said of those charming and lazy Epicureans, Gay and Prior, sweet lyric singers, comrades of Anacreon, and disciples of love and the bottle. "Is there any moral shut within the bosom of a rose?" sings our great Tennyson. Does a nightingale preach from a bough, or the lark from his cloud? Not knowingly; yet we may be grateful, and love larks and roses, and the flower-crowned minstrels, too, who laugh and who sing.

Of Addison's contributions to the charity of the world I have spoken before, in trying to depict that noble figure; and say now, as then, that we should thank him as one of the greatest benefactors of that vast and immeasurably spreading family which speaks our common tongue. Wherever it is spoken, there is no man that does not feel, and understand, and use the noble English word "gentleman." And there is no man that teaches us to be gentlemen better than Joseph Addison. Gentle in our bearing through life; gentle and courteous to our neighbor; gentle in dealing with his follies and weaknesses; gentle in treating his opposition; deferential to the old; kindly to the poor, and those below us in degree; for people above us and below us we must find, in whatever hemisphere we dwell, whether kings or presidents govern us; and in no republic or monarchy that I know of, is a citizen exempt from the tax of befriending poverty and weakness, of respecting age, and of honoring his father and mother. It has just been whispered to me — I have not been three months in the country, and, of course, cannot venture to express an opinion of my own — that, in regard to paying this latter tax of respect and honor to age, some very few of the republican youths are occasionally a little remiss. I have heard of young Sons of Freedom publishing their Declaration of Independence before they could well spell it; and cutting the connection with father and mother before they had learned to shave. My own time of life having been stated, by various enlightened organs of public opinion, at almost any figure from forty-five to sixty, I cheerfully own that I belong to the fogy interest, and ask leave to rank in, and plead for, that respectable class. Now a gentleman can but be a gentleman, in Broadway or the backwoods, in Pall Mall or California; and where and whenever he lives, thousands of miles away in the wilderness, or hundreds of years hence, I am sure that reading the writings of this true gentleman, this true Christian, this noble Joseph Addison, must do him good. He may take Sir Roger de Coverley to the Diggings with him, and learn to be gentle and good-humored, and urbane, and friendly in the midst of that struggle in which his life is engaged. I take leave to say that the most brilliant youth of this city may read over this delightful memorial of a bygone age, of fashions long passed away; of manners long since changed and modified; of noble gentlemen, and a great and a brilliant and polished society; and find in it much to charm and polish, to refine and instruct him, a courteousness which can be out of place at' no time, and under no flag, a politeness and simplicity, a truthful manhood, a gentle respect and deference, which may be kept as the unbought grace of life, and cheap defence of mankind, long after its old artificial distinctions, after periwigs, and small-swords, and ruffles, and red-heeled shoes, and titles, and stars and garters have passed away. I will tell you when I have been put in mind of two of the finest gentlemen books bring us any mention of. I mean *our* books (not books of history, but books of humor). I will tell you when I have been put in mind of the courteous gallantry of the noble knight, Sir Roger de Coverley of Coverley Manor, of the noble Hidalgo Don Quixote of La Mancha; here in your own omnibus carriages and railway cars, when I have seen a woman step in, handsome or not, well-dressed or not, and a workman in hobnail shoes, or a dandy in the height of fashion, rise up and give her his place. I think

Mr. Spectator, with his short face, if he had seen such a deed of courtesy, would have smiled a sweet smile to the doer of that gentleman-like action, and have made him a low bow from under his great periwig, and have gone home and written a pretty paper about him.

I am sure Dick Steele would have hailed him, were he dandy or mechanic, and asked him to a tavern to share a bottle, or perhaps half a dozen. Mind, I do not set down the five last flasks to Dick's score for virtue, and look upon them as works of the most questionable supererogation.

Steele, as a literary benefactor to the world's charity, must rank very high indeed, not merely from his givings, which were abundant, but because his endowments are prodigiously increased in value since he bequeathed them, as the revenues of the lands, bequeathed to our Foundling Hospital at London, by honest Captain Coram, its founder, are immensely enhanced by the houses since built upon them. Steele was the founder of sentimental writing in English, and how the land has been since occupied, and what hundreds of us have laid out gardens and built up tenements on Steele's ground! Before his time, readers or hearers were never called upon to cry except at a tragedy, and compassion was not expected to express itself otherwise than in blank verse, or for personages much lower in rank than a dethroned monarch, or a widowed or a jilted empress. He stepped off the high-heeled cothurnus, and came down into common life; he held out his great hearty arms, and embraced us all; he had a bow for all women; a kiss for all children; a shake of the hand for all men, high or low; he showed us heaven's sun shining every day on quiet homes; not gilded palace-roofs only, or Court processions, or heroic warriors fighting for princesses, and pitched battles. He took away comedy from behind the fine lady's alcove, or the screen where the libertine was watching her. He ended all that wretched business of wives jeering at their husbands, of rakes laughing wives, and husbands, too, to scorn. That miserable, rouged, tawdry, sparkling, hollow-hearted comedy of the Restoration fled before him, and, like the wicked spirit in the Fairy books, shrank, as Steele let the daylight in, and shrieked, and shuddered, and vanished. The stage of humorists has been common life ever since Steele's and Addison's time; the joys and griefs, the aversions and sympathies, the laughter and tears of nature.

And here, coming off the stage, and throwing aside the motley-habit, or satiric disguise, in which he had before entertained you, mingling with the world, and wearing the same coat as his neighbor, the humorist's service became straightway immensely more available; his means of doing good infinitely multiplied; his success, and the esteem in which he was held, proportionately increased. It requires an effort, of which all minds are not capable, to understand "Don Quixote;" children and common people still read "Gulliver" for the story merely. Many more persons are sickened by "Jonathan Wild" than can comprehend the satire of it. Each of the great men who wrote those books was speaking from behind the satiric mask I anon mentioned. Its distortions appall many simple spectators; its settled sneer or laugh is unintelligible to thousands, who have not the wit to interpret the meaning of the vizored satirist preaching from within. Many a man was at fault about Jonathan Wild's greatness, who could feel and relish Allworthy's goodness in "Tom Jones," and Dr. Harrison's in "Amelia," and dear Parson Adams and Joseph Andrews. We love to read — we may grow ever so old, but we love to read of them still — of love and beauty, of frankness, and bravery, and generosity. We hate hypocrites and cowards; we long to defend oppressed innocence, and to soothe and succor gentle women and children. We are glad when vice is foiled and rascals punished; we lend a foot to kick Blifil downstairs; and as we attend the brave bridegroom to his wedding on the happy marriage day, we ask the groomsman's privilege to salute the blushing cheek of Sophia. A lax morality in many a vital point I own in Fielding, but a great hearty sympathy and benevolence; a great kindness for the poor; a great gentleness and pity for the unfortunate; a great love for the pure and good; these are among the contributions to the charity of the world with which this erring but noble creature endowed it.

As for Goldsmith, if the youngest and most unlettered person here has not been happy with the family at Wakefield; has not rejoiced when Olivia returned, and been thankful for her forgiveness and restoration; has not laughed with delighted good humor over Moses's gross of green spectacles; has not loved with all his heart the good Vicar, and that kind spirit which created those charming figures, and devised the beneficent fiction which speaks to us so tenderly — what call is there for me to speak? In this place, and on this occasion, remembering these men, I claim from you your sympathy for the good they have done, and for the sweet charity which they have bestowed on the world.

When humor joins with rhythm and music, and appears in song, its influence is irresistible, its charities are countless, it stirs the feelings to love, peace, friendship, as scarce any moral agent can. The songs of Béranger are hymns of love and tenderness; I have seen great whiskered Frenchmen warbling the "Bonne Vieille," the "Soldats, au pas, aux pas," with tears rolling down their mustachios. At a Burns Festival I have seen Scotchmen singing Burns, while the drops twinkled on their furrowed cheeks; while each rough hand was flung out to grasp its neighbor's; while early scenes and sacred recollections, and dear and delightful memories of the past came rushing back at the sound of the familiar words and music, and the softened heart was full of love and friendship and home. Humor! if tears are the alms of gentle spirits, and may be counted, as sure they may, among the sweetest of life's charities, — of that kindly sensibility, and sweet sudden emotion, which exhibits itself at the eyes, I know no such provocative as humor. It is an irresistible sympathizer; it surprises you into compassion: you are laughing and disarmed, and suddenly forced into tears. I heard a humorous balladist not long since, a minstrel with wool on his head, and an ultra-Ethiopian complexion, who performed a negro ballad that I confess moistened these spectacles in the most unexpected manner. They have gazed at dozens of tragedy-queens, dying on the stage, and expiring in appropriate blank verse, and I never wanted to wipe them. They have looked up, with deep respect be it said, at many scores of clergymen in pulpits, and without being dimmed; and behold a vagabond with a corked face and a banjo sings a little song, strikes a wild note which sets the whole heart thrilling with happy pity. Humor! humor is the mistress of tears; she knows the way to the *fons lachrymarum,* strikes in dry and rugged places with her enchanting wand, and bids the fountain gush and sparkle. She has refreshed myriads more from her natural springs than ever tragedy has watered from her pompous old urn.

Popular humor, and especially modern popular humor, and the writers, its exponents, are always kind and chivalrous, taking the side of the weak against the strong. In our plays, and books, and entertainments for the lower classes in England, I scarce remember a story or theatrical piece in which a wicked aristocrat is not bepummelled by a dashing young champion of the people. There was a book which had an immense popularity in England, and I believe has been greatly read here, in which the Mysteries of the Court of London were said to be unveiled by a gentleman who, I suspect, knows about as much about the Court of London as he does of that of Pekin. Years ago I treated myself to sixpennyworth of this performance at a railway station, and found poor dear George IV., our late most religious and gracious king, occupied in the most flagitious designs against the tradesmen's families in his metropolitan city. A couple of years after, I took sixpennyworth more of the same delectable history: George IV. was still at work, still ruining the peace of tradesmen's families; he had been at it for two whole years, and a bookseller at the Brighton station told me that this book was by many, many times the most popular of all periodical tales then published, "because," says he, "it lashes the aristocracy!" Not long since I went to two penny theatres in London; immense eager crowds of people thronged the buildings, and the vast masses thrilled and vibrated with the emotion produced by the piece represented on the stage, and burst into applause or laughter, such as many a polite actor would sigh for in vain. In both these pieces there was a wicked Lord kicked out of the window — there is always a wicked Lord kicked out of the window. First piece — "Domestic drama — Thrilling interest! — Weaver's family in distress! — Fanny gives away her bread to little Jacky, and starves! — Enter wicked Lord: tempts Fanny with offer of Diamond Necklace, Champagne Suppers, and coach to ride in! — Enter sturdy Blacksmith. — Scuffle between Blacksmith and Aristocratic minion: exit wicked Lord out of the window." Fanny, of course, becomes Mrs. Blacksmith.

The second piece was a nautical drama, also of thrilling interest, consisting chiefly of hornpipes, and acts of most tremendous oppression on the part of certain Earls and Magistrates towards the people. Two wicked Lords were in this piece the atrocious scoundrels: one Aristocrat, a deep-dyed villain, in short duck trousers and Berlin cotton gloves; while the other minion of wealth enjoyed an eyeglass with a blue ribbon, and whisked about the stage with

a penny cane. Having made away with Fanny Forester's
lover, Tom Bowling, by means of a press-gang, they meet
her all alone on a common, and subject her to the most op-
probrious language and behavior : "Release me, villains!"
says Fanny, pulling a brace of pistols out of her pockets,
and crossing them over her breast so as to cover wicked
Lord to the right, wicked Lord to the left; and they might
have remained in that position ever so much longer (for the
aristocratic rascals had pistols too), had not Tom Bowling
returned from sea at the very nick of time, armed with a
great marlinespike, with which — whack! whack! down goes
wicked Lord No. 1 — wicked Lord No. 2.   Fanny rushes
into Tom's arms with an hysterical shriek, and I dare say
they marry, and are very happy ever after.   Popular fun is
always kind: it is the champion of the humble against the
great.   In all popular parables, it is Little Jack that conquers, and the Giant that topples down.   I think our popular authors are rather hard upon the great folks.   Well,
well! their lordships have all the money, and can afford to
be laughed at.

In our days, in England, the importance of the humorous
preacher has prodigiously increased : his audiences are
enormous; every week or month his happy congregations
flock to him; they never tire of such sermons.   I believe
my friend Mr. Punch is as popular to-day as he has been
any day since his birth ; I believe that Mr. Dickens's readers are even more numerous than they ever have been since
his unrivalled pen commenced to delight the world with its
humor.   We have among us other literary parties; we have
Punch, as I have said, preaching from his booth; we have
a Jerrold party very numerous, and faithful to that acute
thinker and distinguished wit; and we have also — it must
be said, and it is still to be hoped — a Vanity-Fair party,
the author of which work has lately been described by the
London *Times* newspaper as a writer of considerable parts,
but a dreary misanthrope, who sees no good anywhere, who
sees the sky above him green, I think, instead of blue, and
only miserable sinners round about him.   So we are; so is
every writer and every reader I ever heard of; so was every
being who ever trod this earth, save One.   I cannot help
telling the truth as I view it, and describing what I see.
To describe it otherwise than it seems to me would be falsehood in that calling in which it has pleased Heaven to
place me; treason to that conscience which says that men

are weak; that truth must be told; that fault must be owned; that pardon must be prayed for; and that love reigns supreme over all.

I look back at the good which of late years the kind English Humorists have done; and if you are pleased to rank the present speaker among that class, I own to an honest pride at thinking what benefits society has derived from men of our calling. That "Song of the Shirt," which *Punch* first published, and the noble, the suffering, the melancholy, the tender Hood sang, may surely rank as a great act of charity to the world, and call from it its thanks and regard for its teacher and benefactor. That astonishing poem, which you all know, of the "Bridge of Sighs," who can read it without tenderness, without reverence to Heaven, charity to man, and thanks to the beneficent genius which sang for us nobly?

I never saw the writer but once; but shall always be glad to think that some words of mine, printed in a periodical of that day, and in praise of these amazing verses (which, strange to say, appeared almost unnoticed at first in the magazine in which Mr. Hood published them) — I am proud, I say, to think that some words of appreciation of mine reached him on his death-bed, and pleased and soothed him in that hour of manful resignation and pain.

As for the charities of Mr. Dickens, multiplied kindnesses which he has conferred upon us all; upon our children; upon people educated and uneducated; upon the myriads here and at home, who speak our common tongue; have not you, have not I, all of us reason to be thankful to this kind friend, who soothed and charmed so many hours, brought pleasure and sweet laughter to so many homes; made such multitudes of children happy; endowed us with such a sweet store of gracious thoughts, fair fancies, soft sympathies, hearty enjoyments? There are creations of Mr. Dickens's which seem to me to rank as personal benefits; figures so delightful, that one feels happier and better for knowing them, as one does for being brought into the society of very good men and women. The atmosphere in which these people live is wholesome to breathe in; you feel that to be allowed to speak to them is a personal kindness; you come away better for your contact with them; your hands seem cleaner from having the privilege of shaking theirs. Was there ever a better charity sermon preached in the world than Dickens's "Christmas Carol"? I believe

it occasioned immense hospitality throughout England; was
the means of lighting up hundreds of kind fires at Christ-
mas-time; caused a wonderful outpouring of Christmas good
feeling; of Christmas punch-brewing; an awful slaughter
of Christmas turkeys, and roasting and basting of Christmas beef. As for this man's love of children, that amiable
organ at the back of his honest head must be perfectly
monstrous. All children ought to love him. I know two
that do, and read his books ten times for once that they
peruse the dismal preachments of their father. I know one
who, when she is happy, reads "Nicholas Nickleby;" when
she is unhappy, reads "Nicholas Nickleby;" when she is
tired, reads "Nicholas Nickleby;" when she is in bed,
reads "Nicholas Nickleby;" when she has nothing to do,
reads "Nicholas Nickleby;" and when she has finished the
book, reads "Nicholas Nickleby" over again. This candid
young critic, at ten years of age, said, "I like Mr. Dickens's
books much better than your books, papa;" and frequently
expressed her desire that the latter author should write a
book like one of Mr. Dickens's books. Who can? Every
man must say his own thoughts in his own voice, in his
own way; lucky is he who has such a charming gift of
nature as this, which brings all the children in the world
trooping to him, and being fond of him.

I remember, when that famous "Nicholas Nickleby"
came out, seeing a letter from a pedagogue in the North of
England, which, dismal as it was, was immensely comical.
"Mr. Dickens's ill-advised publication," wrote the poor
schoolmaster, "has passed like a whirlwind over the schools
of the North." Dotheboys Hall was a cheap school. He
was a proprietor of a cheap school; there were many such
establishments in the northern counties. Parents were
ashamed that never were ashamed before until the kind
satirist laughed at them; relatives were frightened; scores
of little scholars were taken away; poor schoolmasters had to
shut their shops up; every pedagogue was voted a Squeers,
and many suffered, no doubt unjustly; but afterwards
schoolboys' backs were not so much caned; schoolboys'
meat was less tough and more plentiful; and schoolboys'
milk was not so sky-blue. What a kind light of benevolence it is that plays round Crummles and the Phenomenon,
and all those poor theatre people in that charming book!
What a humor! and what a good humor! I coincide
with the youthful critic, whose opinion has just been men-

tioned, and own to a family admiration for "Nicholas
Nickleby."

One might go on, though the task would be endless and
needless, chronicling the names of kind folk with whom
this kind genius has made us familiar. Who does not love
the Marchioness, and Mr. Richard Swiveller? Who does
not sympathize, not only with Oliver Twist, but his admirable young friend the Artful Dodger? Who has not the
inestimable advantage of possessing a Mrs. Nickleby in his
own family? Who does not bless Sairey Gamp and wonder at Mrs. Harris? Who does not venerate the chief of
that illustrious family who, being stricken by misfortune,
wisely and greatly turned his attention to "coals," the accomplished, the Epicurean, the dirty, the delightful Mi-
cawber?

I may quarrel with Mr. Dickens's art a thousand and a
thousand times, I delight and wonder at his genius; I recognize in it — I speak with awe and reverence — a commission from that Divine Beneficence, whose blessed task we
know it will one day be to wipe every tear from every eye.
Thankfully I take my share of the feast of love and kindness which this gentle, and generous, and charitable soul
has contributed to the happiness of the world. I take and
enjoy my share, and say a Benediction for the meal.

PUBLIC SPEECHES.

LITERATURE versus POLITICS.

1848.

IF the approbation which my profession receives is such as Mr. Adolphus is pleased to say it has been (he had just been speaking of the very high importance of this branch of literature, and of Mr. Thackeray as one of its most distinguished ornaments), I can only say that we are nearly as happy in this country as our brother literary men are in foreign countries; and that we have all but arrived at the state of dethroning you all. I don't wish that this catastrophe should be brought about for the sake of personal quiet; for one, I am desirous to read my books, write my articles, and get my money. I don't wish that that should take place; but if I survey mankind, not "from China to Peru," but over the map of Europe, with that cursory glance which novel-writers can afford to take, I see nothing but literary men who seem to be superintending the affairs of the Continent, and only our happy island which is exempt from the literary despotism. Look to Italy, towards the boot of which I turn my eyes, and first, I find that a great number of novelists and literary men are bouleversing the country from toe to heel, turning about Naples, and kicking Rome here and there, and causing a sudden onward impetus of the monarchy of the great Carlo Alberto himself. If I go to France, I find that men, and more particularly men of my own profession and Mr. James's profession, are governing the country; I find that writers of fiction and authors in general are ruling over the destinies of the empire; that Pegasus is, as it were, the charger of the first citizen of the Republic. But arriving at my own country. I beseech you to remember that there was a time, a little time ago, on the "10th of April last," when a great novelist — a great member of my profession — was standing upon Kennington Common in the van of liberty, prepared to assume any responsibility, to take upon himself any direction of government, to decorate himself with the tricolor sash, or the Robespierre waistcoat; and but for the timely, and I may say "special" interposition of many who are here present, you might have been at present commanded by a president of a literary republic, instead of by our present sovereign. I doubt whether any presidents of any literary republics would contribute as much to the funds of this society. I don't believe that the country as yet requires so much of our literary men; but in the mean while, I suppose it must be the task and endeavor of all us light practitioners of literature to do our best, to say our little say in the honestest way we can, to tell the truth as heartily and as simply as we are able to tell it, to expose the humbug, and to support the honest man.

THE REALITY OF THE NOVELIST'S CREATION.
1849.

I SUPPOSE, Mr. Chairman, years ago when you had a duty to perform, you did not think much about, or look to, what men of genius and men of eloquence in England might say of you; but you went and did your best with all your power, and what was the result? You determined to do your best on the next occasion. I believe that is the philosophy of what I have been doing in the course of my life; I don't know whether it has tended to fame or to laughter, or to seriousness; but I have tried to say the truth, and, as far as I know, I have tried to describe what I saw before me, as well as I best might, and to like my neighbor as well as my neighbor would let me like him. All the rest of the speech which I had prepared has fled into thin air; the only part of it which I remember was an apology for, or rather, an encomium of, the profession of us novelists, which, I am bound to say, ought to rank with the very greatest literary occupations. Why should historians take precedence of us? Our personages are as real as theirs. For instance, I maintain that our friends Parson Adams and Dr. Primrose are characters as authentic as Dr. Sacheverell, or Dr. Warburton, or any reverend personage of their times. Gil Blas is quite as real and as good a man as the Duke of Lerma, and I believe, a great deal more so.

I was thinking, too, that Don Quixote was to my mind as real a man as Don John or the Duke of Alva; and then I was turning to the history of a gentleman of whom I am particularly fond — a school-fellow of mine before Dr. Russell's time. I was turning to the life and history of one with whom we are all acquainted, and that is one Mr. Joseph Addison, who, I remember, was made Under-Secretary of State at one period of his life, under another celebrated man, Sir Charles Hedges, I think it was, but it is now so long ago, I am not sure; but I have no doubt Mr. Addison was much more proud of his connection with Sir Charles Hedges, and his place in Downing Street, and his red box, and his quarter's salary, punctually and regularly paid; I dare say he was much more proud of these, than of any literary honor which he received, such as being the author of the "Tour of Italy," and the "Campaign." But after all, though he was indubitably connected with Sir Charles Hedges, there was another knight with whom he was much more connected, and that was a certain Sir Roger de Coverley, whom we have always loved, and believed in a thousand times better than a thousand Sir Charles Hedges. And as I look round at this my table, gentlemen, I cannot but perceive that the materials for my favorite romances are never likely to be wanting to future authors. I don't know that anything I have written has been generally romantic; but if I were disposed to write a romance, I think I should like to try an Indian tale, and I should take for the heroes of it, or for some of the heroes of it — I would take the noble lord whom I see opposite to me (Lord Napier) with the Sutlej flowing before him, and the enemy in his front, and himself riding before the British army, with his little son Arthur and his son Charles by his side. I am sure, in all the regions of romance, I could find nothing more noble and affecting than that story, and I hope some of these days, some more able novelist will undertake it.

AUTHORS AND THEIR PATRONS.

1851.

LITERARY men are not by any means, at this present time, that most unfortunate and most degraded set of people whom they are sometimes represented to be. If foreign gentlemen should by any chance go to see "The Rivals" represented at one of our theatres, they will see Captain Absolute and Miss Lydia Languish making love to one another, and conversing, if not in the custom of our present day, or such as gentlemen and ladies are accustomed to use, at any rate in something near it; whereas, when the old father Sir Anthony Absolute comes in, nothing will content the stage but that he should appear with red heels, large buckles, and an immense Ramilies wig. This is the stage tradition: they won't believe in an old man, unless he appears in this dress, and with this wig; nor in an old lady, unless she comes forward in a quilted petticoat and high-heeled shoes; nor in Hamlet's gravedigger, unless he wears some four and twenty waistcoats; and so on. In my trade, in my especial branch of literature, the same tradition exists; and certain persons are constantly apt to bring forward, or to believe in the existence at this moment, of the miserable old literary hack of the time of George the Second, and bring him before us as the literary man of this day. I say that that disreputable old phantom ought to be hissed out of society. I don't believe in the literary man being obliged to resort to ignoble artifices and mean flatteries, to get places at the tables of the great, and to enter into society upon sufferance. I don't believe in the patrons of this present day, except such patrons as I am happy to have in you, and as any honest man might be proud to have, and shake by the hand and be shaken by the hand by. Therefore I propose from this day forward, that the oppressed literary man should disappear from among us. The times are altered; the people don't exist; "the patron and the jail," praise God, are vanished from out our institutions. It may be possible that the eminent Mr. Edmund Curl stood in the pillory in the time of Queen Anne, who, thank God, is dead; it may be, that in the reign of another celebrated monarch of these realms, Queen Elizabeth, authors who abused the .persons of honors would have their arms cut off on the first offence, and be hanged on the second. Gentlemen, what would be the position of my august friend and patron, Mr. Punch, if that were now the case? Where would be his hands, and his neck, and his ears, and his bowels? He would be disembowelled, and his members cast about the land. We don't want patrons, we want friends; and, I thank God, we have them. And as for any idea that our calling is despised by the world, I do for my part protest against and deny the whole statement. I have been in all sorts of society in this world, and I never have been despised that I know of. I don't believe there has been a literary man of the slightest merit, or of the slightest mark, who did not greatly advance himself by his literary labors. I see along this august table gentlemen whom I have had the honor of shaking by the hand, and gentlemen whom I should never have called my friends, but for the humble literary labors I have been engaged in. And, therefore, I say, don't let us be pitied any more. As for pity being employed upon authors, especially in my branch of the profession, if you will but look at the novelists of the present day, I think you will see it is altogether out of the question to pity them. We will take in the first place, if you please, a great novelist who is the head of a great party in a great assembly in this country. When this celebrated man went into his county to be proposed to represent it, and he was asked on what interest he stood, he nobly said, "he stood on his head." And who can question the gallantry and brilliancy of that eminent crest of his, and what man will deny the great merit of Mr. Disraeli? Take next another novelist, who writes from his ancestral hall, and addresses John Bull in letters on matters of politics, and John Bull buys eight editions of those letters. Is not this a prospect for a novelist? There is a third, who is employed upon this very evening, heart and hand, heart and voice, I may say, on a work of charity. And what is the consequence? The Queen of the realm, the greatest nobles of the empire, all the great of the world, will assemble to see him and do him honor. I say, therefore, don't let us have pity. I don't want it till I really do want it. Of course it is impossible for us to settle the mere prices by which the works of those who amuse the public are to be paid. I am perfectly aware that Signor Twankeydillo, of the Italian Opera, and Mademoiselle Petitpas, of the Haymarket, will get a great deal more money in a week, for the skilful exercise of their chest and toes, than I, or you, or any gentleman, shall be able to get by our brains and by weeks of hard labor. We cannot help these differences in payment, we know there must be high and low payments in our trade as in all trades; that there must be gluts of the market, and over-production, that there must be successful machinery, and rivals, and brilliant importations from foreign countries; that there must be hands out of employ, and tribulation of workmen. But these ill winds which afflict us blow fortunes to our successors. These are natural evils. It is the progress of the world, rather than any evil which we can remedy, and that is why I say this society acts most wisely and justly in endeavoring to remedy, not the chronic distress, but the temporary evil; that it finds a man at the moment of the pinch of necessity, helps him a little, and gives him a "God-speed," and sends him on his way. For my own part I have felt that necessity, and bent under that calamity; and it is because I have found friends who have nobly, with God's blessing, helped me at that moment of distress, that I feel deeply interested in the ends of a society which has for its object to help my brethren in similar need.

THE NOVELIST'S FUTURE LABORS.

1852.

WE, from this end of the table [on occasion of the Royal Literary Fund Dinner], speak humbly and from afar. We are the usefuls of the company, who over and over again perform our little part, deliver our little messages, and then sit down; whereas, you, yonder, are the great stars of the evening; you are collected with much care, and skill, and ingenuity, by the manager of this benefit performance; you perform Macbeth and Hamlet, we are the Rosencrantzes and Guildensterns; we are the Banquos, — as I know a Banquo who has shaken his gory old wig at Drury Lane, at a dozen Macbeths. We resemble the individual in plush, whom gentlemen may have seen at the opera, who comes forward and demurely waters the stage, to the applause of the audience — never mind who is the great Taglioni, or the Lind, or the Wagner, who is to receive all the glory. For my part, I am happy to fulfil that humble office, and to make my little spurt, and to retire, and leave the place for a greater and more able performer. How like British charity is to British valor! It always must be well fed before it comes into action! We see before us a ceremony of this sort, which Britons always undergo with pleasure. There is no tax which the Briton pays so cheerfully as the dinner-tax. Every man here, I have no doubt, who is a little acquainted with the world, must have received, in the course of the last month, a basketful of tickets, inviting him to meet in this place, for some purpose or other. We have all rapped upon this table, either admiring the speaker for his eloquence, or, at any rate, applauding him when he sits down. We all of us know — we have had it a hundred times — the celebrated flavor of the old Freemasons' mock-turtle, and the celebrated Freemasons' sherry; and if I seem to laugh at the usage, the honest, good old English usage, of eating and drinking, which brings us all together, for all sorts of good purposes — do not suppose that I laugh at it any more than I would at good old honest John Bull, who has under his good, huge, boisterous exterior, a great deal of kindness and goodness at the heart of him. Our festival may be compared with such a person; men meet here and shake hands, kind hearts grow kinder over the table, and a silent almoner issues forth from it, the festival over, and gratifies poor people, and relieves the sufferings of the poor, which would never be relieved but for your kindness. So that there is a grace that follows after your meat and sanctifies it. We have heard the historians and their calling worthily exalted just now; but it seems to me that my calling will be the very longest and the last of those of all the literary gentlemen I see before me. Long after the present generation is dead — of readers and of authors of books — there must be kindness ·and generosity, and folly and fidelity, and love and heroism, and humbug in the world; and, as long as they last, my successors, or the successors of the novelists who come long after us, will have plenty to do, and plenty of subjects to write upon. There may chance to be a time when wars will be over, and the "decisive battles" of the world will not need a historian. There may arrive a time when the Court of Chancery itself will be extinguished; and, as perhaps your Lordship is aware, there is a certain author of a certain work called "Bleak House," who, for the past three months, has been assaulting the Court of Chancery in a manner that I cannot conceive that ancient institution will survive. There may be a time when the Court of Chancery will cease to exist, and when the historian of the "Lives of the Lord Chancellors" will have no calling. I have often speculated upon what the successors of the novelists in future ages may have to do; and I have fancied them occupied with the times and people of our own age. If I could fancy a man so occupied hereafter, and busied we will say with a heroic story, I

would take the story which I heard hinted at the other
night by the honored, the oldest, the bravest and greatest
man in this country — I would take the great and glorious
action of Cape Danger, when, striking to the powers above
alone, the Birkenhead went down! When, with heroic
courage and endurance, the men remained on the decks,
and the women and children were allowed to go away safe,
as the people cheered them, and died doing their duty! I
know of no victory so sublime in any annals of the feats of
English valor; — I know of no story that could inspire a
great author or novelist better than that. Or, suppose we
should take the story of an individual of the present day,
whose name has been already mentioned; we might have a
literary hero, not less literary than Mr. David Copperfield,
or Mr. Arthur Pendennis, who is defunct: we might have a
literary hero who, at twenty years of age, astonished the
world with his brilliant story of "Vivian Grey," who, in a
little time afterwards, and still in the youthful period of
his life, amazed and delighted the public with " The Wondrous Tale of Alroy;" who, presently following up the
course of his career, and the development of his philosophical culture, explained to a breathless and listening world
the great Caucasian mystery; who, quitting literature, then
went into politics; met, faced, and fought, and conquered
the great political giant, and great orator of those days;
who subsequently led thanes and earls to battle, and
caused reluctant squires to carry his lance; and who, but
the other day, went in a gold coat to kiss the hand of his
Sovereign, as Leader of the House of Commons and Chancellor of Her Majesty's Exchequer. What a hero that will
be for some future novelist, and what a magnificent climax
for the third volume of his story.

ON LEAVING ENGLAND FOR AMERICA.

1855.

I know great numbers of us here present have been invited to a neighboring palace, where turtle, champagne, and
all good things are as plentiful almost as here, and where
there reigns a civic monarch with a splendid court of
officers, etc. The sort of greeting that I had myself to-day
— this splendor, etc. — the bevy in the ante-room — have
filled my bosom with an elation with which no doubt Sir

Francis Graham Moon's throbs. I am surrounded by respectful friends, etc., — and I feel myself like a Lord Mayor. To his Lordship's delight and magnificence there is a drawback. In the fountain of his pleasure there surges a bitter. He is thinking about the ninth of November, and I about the thirteenth of October.

Some years since, when I was younger and used to frequent jolly assemblies, I wrote a Bacchanalian song, to be chanted after dinner, etc. I wish some one would sing that song now to the tune of the "Dead March in Saul," etc., not for me — I am miserable enough, — but for you, who seem in a great deal too good spirits. I tell you I am not — all the drink in Mr. Bathe's cellar won't make me. There may be sherry there five hundred years old : Columbus may have taken it out from Cadiz with him when he went to discover America : and it won't make me jolly, etc. ; and yet, entirely unsatisfactory as this feast is to me, I should like some more. Why can't you give me some more ? I don't care about them costing two guineas a head. It is not the turtle I value. Let us go to Simpson's fish ordinary, or to Bertolini's, or John O'Groat's, etc., — I don't want to go away — I cling round the mahogany tree.

In the course of my profound and extensive reading, I have found it is the habit of the English nation to give dinners to the unfortunate. I have been living lately with some worthy singular fellows 150 or 160 years old. I find that upon certain occasions the greatest attention was always paid them. They might call for anything they liked for dinner. My friend Simon Fraser, Lord Lovat, about 109 years since, I think, partook very cheerfully of minced veal and sack before he was going on his journey. — Lord Ferrers (Rice). I could tell you a dozen jolly stories about feasts of this sort. I remember a particularly jolly one at which I was present, and which took place at least 900 years ago. My friend, Mr. Macready, gave it at Forres Castle, North Britain, Covent Garden. That was a magnificent affair indeed. The tables were piled with most splendid fruits ; gorgeous dish-covers glittered in endless perspective ; — Macbeth — Macready, I mean, — taking up a huge gold beaker, shining with enormous gems that must have been worth many hundred millions of money, filled it out of a gold six-gallon jug, and drank courteously to the general health of the whole table. Why did he put it down ? What made him, in the midst of that jolly party, appear so haggard and melancholy ? It was because he saw before him the ghost of John Cooper, with chalked face, and an immense streak of vermilion painted across his throat! No wonder he was disturbed. In like manner I have before me at this minute the horrid figure of a steward, with a basin perhaps, or a glass of brandy and water, which he will press me to drink and which I shall try and swallow, and which won't make me any better — I know it won't.

Then there's the dinner, which we all of us must remember in our schoolboy days, and which took place twice or thrice a year at home, on the day before Dr. Birch expected his young friends to re-assemble at his academy, Rodwell Regis. Don't you remember how the morning was spent ? — how you went about taking leave of the garden, and the old mare and foal, and the paddock, and the pointers in the kennel ? — and how your little sister wistfully kept at your side all day ? and how you went and looked at the confounded trunk which old Martha was packing with the new shirts, and that heavy cake packed up in the play-box ? and how kind "the governor" was all day ; and how at dinner he said "Jack, or Tom, pass the bottle," in a very cheery voice : and how your mother had got the dishes she knew you liked best, and how you had the wing instead of the leg, which used to be your ordinary share ? and how that dear, delightful, hot raspberry roly-poly pudding, good as it was, and fondly beloved by you, yet somehow had the effect of the notorious school stickjaw and choked you and stuck in your throat ? and how the gig came, and then how you heard the whirl of mail-coach wheels and the tooting of the guard's horn, as, with an odious punctuality, the mail and the four horses came galloping over the hill. Shake hands! good-by. God bless everybody! Don't cry, sister! and to-morrow we begin with Dr. Birch and six months at Rodwell Regis.

But after six months came the holidays again, etc.

COMMERCE AND LITERATURE.

1857.

I FEEL it needful for me to be particularly cautious whenever I come to any meeting in the city which has to deal with money and monetary affairs. It is seldom that I

appear at all in these regions, unless, indeed, it be occasionally to pay a pleasing visit to Messrs. Bradbury and Evans, in Bouverie Street, or to Messrs. Smith and Co., of Cornhill.   But I read my paper like every good Briton, and from that I gather a lesson of profound caution in speaking to mercantile men on subjects of this kind.   Supposing, for instance, that I have shares in the Bundelcund Banking Company, or in the Royal British Diddlesex Bank: I come down to a meeting of the shareholders, and hear an honored treasurer and an admirable president make the most flourishing reports of the state of our concern, showing to us enormous dividends accompanied with the most elegant bonuses; and proving to us that our funds are invested in the most secure way at Bogleywallak, Bundelcund, and Branksea Castle.   I go away delighted at the happy prospect before my wife and family, feeling perfect confidence that those innocent beings will be comfortable for the rest of their lives. What, then, is my horror, when, in one brief fortnight after, instead of those enormous dividends and elegant bonuses, I am served with a notice to pay up a most prodigious sum; when I find that our estates at Bundelcund and Bogleywallak have been ravaged by the Bengal tiger; that the island of Branksea is under water; that our respected president is obliged to go to Spain for the benefit of his health, and our eloquent treasurer cannot abide the London fog.   You see I must be a little careful.   But, granted that the accounts we hear have not, like our dinner, been subjected to an ingenious culinary process; granted that you have spent, as I read in your report, £25,000 in raising a noble school and grounds ; that you have collected around you the happy juvenile faces which I see smiling on yonder benches, to be the objects of your Christian kindness; granting all this to be true, then, gentlemen, I am your most humble servant, and no words that I can find can express my enthusiastic admiration for what you have done.   I sincerely wish, on behalf of my own class, the literary profession, that we could boast of anything as good.   I wish that we had an institution to which we could confide our children, instead of having to send them about to schools as we do, at an awful cost. When the respected Mr. Squeers of Do-the-boys Hall announces that he proposes to take a limited number of pupils — I should rather say a number of very limited pupils — it is not because he is in love with the little darlings that he does it, but because he designs to extract a profit

out of them. It always pains me to think of the profits
to be screwed out of the bellies of the poor little innocents.
Why have we not, as men of letters, some such association
as that which you have got up? I appeal to my literary
brethren, if any of them are present, whether we, the men
of the line, cannot emulate the men of the road? A week
ago a friend engaged in my own profession, making his
£1,000 a year, showed me his half-yearly account of his two
little boys at school. These little heroes of six and seven,
who are at a very excellent school, where they are well
provided for, came home with a little bill in their pocket
which amounted to the sum of £75 for the half-year.
Now think of this poor Paterfamilias earning his moderate
£1,000 a year, out of which he has his life assurance, his
income tax, and his house rent to pay, with three or four
poor relations to support — for doubtless we are all blessed
with those appendages — with the heavy bills of his wife
and daughters for millinery and mantua-making to meet,
especially at their present enormous rates and sizes. Think
of this over-burdened man having to pay £75 for one-half
year's schooling of his little boys! Let the gentlemen of
the press, then, try to devise some scheme which shall
benefit them, as you have undoubtedly benefited by what
you have accomplished for yourselves. We are all travellers
and voyagers who must embark on life's ocean; and before
you send your boys to sea you teach them to swim, to navi-
gate the ship, and guide her into port. The last time I
visited America, two years ago, I sailed on board the Africa,
Captain Harrison. As she was steaming out of Liverpool
one fine blowy October day, and was hardly over the bay,
when, animated by those peculiar sensations not uncommon
to landsmen at the commencement of a sea voyage, I was
holding on amidships [a laugh], up comes a quick-eyed
shrewd-looking little man, who holds on to the next rope
to me, and says, " Mr. Thackeray, I am the representative
of the house of Appleton and Co., of Broadway, New York
— a most liberal and enterprising publishing firm, who will
be most happy to do business with you." I don't know that
we then did any business in the line thus delicately hinted
at, because at that particular juncture we were both of us
called, by a heavy lurch of the ship, to a casting-up of
accounts of a far less agreeable character.

LETTERS.

TO MACVEY NAPIER, Esq.

[EDITOR OF THE EDINBURGH REVIEW.]

St. James's Street, July 16, 1845.

My Dear Sir,— I am glad to comply with your request that I should address you personally, and thank you for the letters which you have written to Mr. Longman regarding my contributions to the *Edinburgh Review*.

Eugène Sue has written a very great number of novels. beginning with maritime novels in the Satanic style, so to speak, full of crime and murder of every description. He met in his early works with no very great success. He gave up the indecencies of language, and astonished the world with *Mathilde* three years since, which had the singular quality among French novels of containing no improprieties of expression. In my mind, it is one of the most immoral books in the world. The *Mysteries of Paris* followed with still greater success, and the same extreme cleverness of construction, and the same sham virtue. It has been sold by tens of thousands in London in various shapes, in American editions, and illustrated English translations. To go through a course of Sue's writings would require, I should think, more than a short article, and the subject has been much dealt with in minor periodicals here. The *Glances at Life* is a very kindly and agreeable little book by a Cockney philosopher: could it be coupled in an article with N. P. Willis's *Dashes at Life*, which Messrs. Longman now advertise? A pleasant short paper might be written, I fancy, commenting on the humors of the pair. Should the subject meet with your approval, perhaps you will give me notice, and state what space the *Review* can afford. Should you not approve, I will look through *Lady*

474

Hester Stanhope, and hope to be able to treat it to your satisfaction. I am bringing out a little book about the Mediterranean myself, which I hope shortly to have the pleasure of sending you.

Your very obedient servant,

W. M. THACKERAY.

OCTOBER 16, 1845.

MY DEAR SIR, — I have just received and acknowledge with many thanks your banker's bill. From them or from you, I shall always be delighted to receive communications of this nature. From your liberal payment I can't but conclude that you reward me not only for laboring, but for being mutilated in your service. I assure you I suffered cruelly by the amputation which you were obliged to inflict upon my poor dear paper. I mourn still — as what father can help doing for his children ? — for several lovely jokes and promising facetiæ, which were born and might have lived but for your scissors urged by ruthless necessity. I trust however there are many more which the future may bring forth, and which will meet with more favor in your eyes. I quite agree with your friends who say Willis was too leniently used. Oh, to think of my pet passages gone forever!

Very faithfully yours,

W. M. THACKERAY.

TO WILLIAM EDMONDSTOUNE AYTOUN.

13 YOUNG STREET, KENSINGTON, January 2, 1847.

MY DEAR AYTOUN, — I hope The Maclosky received the Mulligan present. I ought to have written before, answering your kind, hearty letter, but business, you know, and weariness of quill-driving after business hours, etc. I don't write to anybody, that's the fact, unless I want something of them, and perhaps that's the case at this present.

I think I have never had any ambition hitherto, or cared what the world thought my work, good or bad; but now the truth forces itself upon me, if the world will once take to admiring Titmarsh, all his guineas will be multiplied by ten. Guineas are good. I have got children, only ten years more to the fore, say, etc.; now is the time, my lad, to make your A when the sun at length has begun to shine.

Well, I think if I can make a push at the present minute — if my friends will shout, Titmarsh forever! — hurrah for, etc., I may go up with a run to a pretty fair place in my trade, and be allowed to appear before the public as among the first fiddles. But my tunes must be heard in the streets, and organs must grind them. Ha! Now do you read me?

Why don't Blackwood give me an article? Because he refused the best story I ever wrote? Colburn refused the present *Novel without a Hero,* and if any man at Blackwood's or Colburn's, and if any man since — fiddle-de-dee. Upon my word and honor, I never said so much about myself before: but I know this, if I had the command of *Blackwood* and a humoristical person like Titmarsh should come up and labor hard and honestly (please God) for ten years, I would give him a hand. Now try, like a man, revolving these things in your soul, and see if you can't help me. . . . And if I can save a little money, by the Lord! I'll try and keep it.

Some day when less selfish I will write to you about other matters than the present ego. The dining season has begun in London already, I am sorry to say, and the Christmas feeding is frightfully severe. . . . I have my children with me, and am mighty happy in that paternal character — preside over legs of mutton comfortably — go to church at early morning and like it — pay rates and taxes, etc. Between this line and the above, a man had brought me the *Times* on *The Battle of Life* to read. Appy Dickens! But I love Pickwick and Crummles too well to abuse this great man. Aliquando bonus. And you, young man, coming up in the world full of fight, take counsel from a venerable and peaceable old gladiator who has stripped for many battles. Gad, sir, this caution is a very good sign. Do you remember how complimentary Scott and Goethe were? I like the patriarchal air of some people. Have you ever any snow in Scotland?

(Here follows an admirable drawing of a dustman singing beside his cart, with snow deep in the street.)

As I was walking in just now I met this fellow singing "I Dreamt that I Dwelt in Marble Halls," driving a dust-cart. I burst out laughing, and so did he. He is as good as Leech's boy in the last *Punch.* How good Leech is, and what a genuine humor! And Hans Christian Andersen, have you read him? I am wild about him, having

only just discovered that delightful, delicate, fanciful crea-
°ture. Good-by, my dear Aytoun. I wish you a merry
Christmas, and to honest Johnny Blackwood. Thank him
for the Magazine. I shall enjoy it in bed to-morrow morning, when I've left orders not to be called for church.

Yours ever,

W. M. T.

13 YOUNG STREET, KENSINGTON, Monday Night.
January 13, 1847.

MY DEAR AYTOUN, — The copy of Mrs. Perkins which
was sent by the Mulligan to the other chieftain has met
with a mishap. It travelled to Edinburgh in the portmanteau of a friend of mine, who arrived at ten o'clock at
night and started for Inverness the next morning at six.
Mrs. P. went with him. He forgot her at Inverness, and
came back to London, whither Mrs. Perkins was sent after
him at a cost of 4s. 10d. for carriage. She is not worth
that money either for you or me to pay, and waits in my
room till you come to town in spring.

I have been thinking of the other matter on which I un-
bosomed myself to you, and withdraw my former letter.
Puffs are good, and the testimony of good men; but I don't
think these will make a success for a man, and he ought to
stand as the public chooses to put him. I will try, please
God, to do my best, and the money will come, perhaps,
some day! Meanwhile a man so lucky as myself has no
reason to complain. So let all puffing alone, although, as
you know, I am glad if I can have and deserve your private
good opinion. The women like *Vanity Fair* I find, very
much, and the publishers are quite in good spirits regarding that venture.

This is all I have to say — in the solitude of midnight —
with a quiet cigar and the weakest gin and water in the
world, ruminating over a child's ball, from which I have
just come, having gone as chaperon to my little girls. One
of them had her hair plaited, in two tails, the other had ringlets (here follows a sketch of the children), and the most
fascinating bows of blue ribbon. It was very merry and
likewise sentimental. We went in a fly quite genteel, and,
law! what a comfort it was when it was over. Adyou.

Yours sincerely,

W. M. THACKERAY.

TO G. H. LEWES.*

LONDON, April 28, 1855.

DEAR LEWES, — I wish I had more to tell you regarding Weimar and Goethe. Five and twenty years ago, at least a score of young English lads used to live at Weimar for study, or sport, or society : all of which were to be had in the friendly little Saxon capital. The Grand Duke and Duchess received us with the kindliest hospitality. The Court was splendid, but yet most pleasant and homely. We were invited in our turns to dinners, balls, and assemblies there. Such young men as had a right appeared in uniforms, diplomatic and military. Some, I remember, invented gorgeous clothing; the kind old Hof-Marschall of those days, Monsieur de Spiegel (who had two of the most lovely daughters eyes ever looked on), being in no wise difficult as to the admission of these young Englanders. Of the winter nights we used to charter sedan-chairs, in which we were carried through the snow to those pleasant Court entertainments. I for my part had the good luck to purchase Schiller's sword, which formed a part of my Court costume, and still hangs in my study, and puts me in mind of days of youth the most kindly and delightful.

We knew the whole society of the little city, and but that the young ladies, one and all, spoke admirable English, we surely might have learned the very best German. The society met constantly. The ladies of the Court had their evenings. The theatre was open twice or thrice in the week, where we assembled, a large family party. Goethe had retired from the direction, but the great traditions remained still. The theatre was admirably conducted; and besides the excellent Weimar company, famous actors and singers from various parts of Germany performed " Gastrolle " † through the winter. In that winter I remember we had Ludwig Devrient in Shylock, *Hamlet*, *Falstaff*, and the *Robbers*, and the beautiful Schröder in *Fidelio*.

After three and twenty years' absence I passed a couple of summer days in the well-remembered place, and was fortunate enough to find some of the friends of my youth. Madame de Goethe was there, and received me and my

* This letter was written by Mr. Thackeray in answer to a request from G. H. Lewes for some account of his recollections of Goethe.
† What in England are called " starring engagements."

daughters with the kindness of old days. We drank tea in
the open air at the famous cottage in the Park,* which still
belongs to the family, and has been so often inhabited by
her illustrious father.

In 1831, though he had retired from the world, Goethe
would nevertheless very kindly receive strangers. His
daughter-in-law's tea-table was always spread for us. We
passed hours after hours there, and night after night, with
the pleasantest talk and music. We read over endless
novels and poems in French, English, and German. My
delight in those days was to make caricatures for children.
I was touched to find that they were remembered, and some
even kept until the present time; and very proud to be
told, as a lad, that the great Goethe had looked at some of
them.

He remained in his private apartments, where only a
very few privileged persons were admitted; but he liked
to know all that was happening, and interested himself
about all strangers. Whenever a countenance struck his
fancy, there was an artist settled in Weimar who made a
portrait of it. Goethe had quite a gallery of heads, in
black and white, taken by this painter. His house was all
over pictures, drawings, casts, statues, and medals.

Of course I remember very well the perturbation of
spirit with which, as a lad of nineteen, I received the long-
expected intimation that the Herr Geheimrath would see
me on such a morning. This notable audience took place
in a little ante-chamber of his private apartments, covered
all round with antique casts and bas-reliefs. He was habited in a long gray or drab redingote, with a white neckcloth and a red ribbon in his button-hole. He kept his
hands behind his back, just as in Rauch's statuette. His
complexion was very bright, clear, and rosy. His eyes ex-
traordinarily dark,† piercing and brilliant. I felt quite
afraid before them, and recollect comparing them to the
eyes of the hero of a certain romance called "Melmoth the
Wanderer," which used to alarm us boys thirty years ago;
eyes of an individual who had made a bargain with a Certain Person, and at an extreme old age retained these eyes
in all their awful splendor. I fancy Goethe must have
been still more handsome as an old man than even in the

* The *Gartenhaus.*
† This must have been the effect of the position in which he sat with
regard to the light. Goethe's eyes were dark brown, but not very dark.

days of his youth. His voice was very rich and sweet He asked me questions about myself, which I answered as best I could. I recollect I was at first astonished, and then somewhat relieved, when I found he spoke French with not a good accent.

Vidi tantum. I saw him but three times. Once walking in the garden of his house in the *Frauenplan;* once going to step into his chariot on a sunshiny day, wearing a cap and a cloak with a red collar. He was caressing at the time a beautiful little golden-haired granddaughter, over whose sweet fair face the earth has long since closed too.

Any of us who had books or magazines from England sent them to him, and he examined them eagerly. *Fraser's Magazine* had lately come out, and I remember he was interested in those admirable outline portraits which appeared for a while in its pages. But there was one, a very ghastly caricature of Mr. Rogers, which, as Madame de Goethe told me, he shut up and put away from him angrily. "They would make me look like that," he said: though in truth I can fancy nothing more serene, majestic, and *healthy*-looking than the grand old Goethe.

Though his sun was setting, the sky round about was calm and bright, and that little Weimar illumined by it. In every one of those kind *salons* the talk was still of Art and Letters. The theatre, though possessing no very extraordinary actors, was still conducted with a noble intelligence and order. The actors read books, and were men of letters and gentlemen, holding a not unkindly relationship with the *Adel.* At Court the conversation was exceedingly friendly, simple, and polished. The Grand Duchess (the present Grand Duchess Dowager), a lady of very remarkable endowments, would kindly borrow our books from us, lend us her own, and graciously talk to us young men about our literary tastes and pursuits. In the respect paid by this Court to the Patriarch of letters, there was something ennobling, I think, alike to the subject and sovereign. With a five-and-twenty-years' experience since those happy days of which I write and an acquaintance with an immense variety of human kind, I think I have never seen a society more simple, charitable, courteous, gentlemanlike, than that of the dear little Saxon city where the good Schiller and the great Goethe lived and lie buried.

Very sincerely yours,
W. M. THACKERAY.

TO ANTHONY TROLLOPE.

36 ONSLOW SQUARE, S. W., October 28, 1859.

MY DEAR MR. TROLLOPE, — Smith and Elder have sent you their proposals; and the business part done, let me come to the pleasure, and say how very glad indeed I shall be to have you as a co-operator in our new magazine. And looking over the annexed programme, you will see whether you can't help us in many ways besides tale-telling. Whatever a man knows about life and its doings, that let us hear about. You must have tossed a good deal about the world, and have countless sketches in your memory and your portfolio. Please to think if you can furbish up any of these besides a novel. When events occur, and you have a good lively tale, bear this in mind. One of our chief objects in this magazine is the getting out of novel spinning, and back into the world. Don't understand me to disparage our craft, especially your wares. I often say I am like the pastrycook, and don't care for tarts, but pre-fer bread and cheese; but the public love the tarts (luckily for us), and we must bake and sell them. There was quite an excitement in my family one evening when Pater-familias (who goes to sleep on a novel almost always when he tries it after dinner) came upstairs into the drawing-room wide awake and calling for the second volume of *The Three Clerks.* I hope the *Cornhill Magazine* will have as pleasant a story. And the Chapmans, if they are the hon-est men I take them to be, I've no doubt have told you with what sincere liking your works have been read by yours very faithfully,

W. M. THACKERAY.

TO HENRY WADSWORTH LONGFELLOW.

36 ONSLOW SQUARE, LONDON, November 16, 1859.

MY DEAR MR. LONGFELLOW, — Has Hiawatha ever a spare shaft in his quiver, which he can shoot across the Atlantic? How proud I should be if I could have a con-tribution or two from you for our *Cornhill Magazine.*

I should like still better to be driving to Cambridge in the snow, and expecting a supper there. Two or three months ago I actually thought such a scheme was about to

come off.   I intended to shut up my desk for a year, — not
write a line, — and go on my travels.   But the gods willed
otherwise.   I am pressed into the service of this Magazine,
and engaged to write ever so much more for the next three
years.   Then, if I last so long, I shall be free of books and
publishers; and hope to see friends to whose acquaintance
I look back with — I can't tell you how much gratitude
and kind feeling.

I send my best regards to Tom Appleton, and beg him
to back my petition to his brother-in-law.

Always sincerely yours,
W. M. Thackeray.

THE HISTORY OF DIONYSIUS DIDDLER.*

LADIES AND GENTLEMEN, — Many thousand years ago, in the reign of Chrononhotonthologos, King of Brentford, there lived a young gentleman whose history is about to be laid before you.

He was sixty years of age, and his name was Dionysius Diddler; no relation of any other Dionysius, nor, indeed, a Brentfordian by birth; for (though the Diddlers are very numerous in Brentford) this was a young fellow from Pat-land, which country he quitted at a very early age.

He was by trade a philosopher, — an excellent profession in Brentford, where the people are more ignorant and more easily humbugged than any people on earth; — and no doubt he would have made a pretty fortune by his philoso-phy, but the rogue longed to be a man of fashion, and spent all his money in buying clothes, and in giving treats to the ladies, of whom he was outrageously fond. Not that they were very partial to *him*, for he was not particularly handsome — especially without his wig and false teeth, both of which, I am sorry to say, this poor Diddler wore.

Well, the consequence of his extravagance was, that, although by his learning he had made himself famous (there was his Essay on the Tea-Kettle, his Remarks on Pumps, and his celebrated Closet Cyclopædia, that every one has heard of) — one day, after forty years of glory, Diddler found himself turned out of his lodging, without a penny, without his wig, which he had pawned, without even his teeth, which he had pawned too, seeing he had no use for them.

And now befell a series of adventures that you shall all hear; and so take warning, ye dashing blades of the town, by the awful fate of DIONYSIUS.

* First published in the *Autographic Mirror*, 1864. The drawings were made about 1838.

This is Dionysius Diddler! young, innocent, and with a fine head of hair, — when he was a student in the University of Ballybunion. — That is Ballybunion University, in the hedge.

Here he is, after forty years of fame, and he thinks upon dear Ballybunion. "I'm femous," says he, "all the world over: but what's the use of riputetion? Look at me with all me luggage at the end of me stick — all me money in me left-hand breeches pocket — and it's oh! but I'd give all me celebrity for a bowl of butther-milk and potaties."

He goes to call on Mr. Shortman, the publisher of the "Closet Cyclopædia," and sure and ouns! Mr. Shortman gives him three sovereigns and three five-pound notes.

The first thing he does is to take his wig out of pawn.

"And now," says he, "I'll go take a sthroll to the Wist Ind, and call on me frind, Sir Hinry Pelham."

He pays a visit to Sir Henry Pelham.

"Fait!" says Diddler, "the what d'ye-call-'ems fit me like a glove."

"And upon me honor and conshience, now I'm dthressed, but I look intirely ginteel."

In Pelham's coat, hat, boots, and pantaloons,
Forth issues Diddler from the Baronet's house,
In famed Red Lion's fashionable square,
And was it strange that Hodge, Sir Henry's groom,
Mistook the dandy Doctor for his master?
And while he for his foot the stirrup held,

Said reverently, "Master, will you mount?"
This Dionysius did, and rode away,—
But fear then seized upon the soul of Hodge,
Says he, "That genman cannot be my master,
For as he rode away, he gave me sixpence,
And my dear master never gives me nothen."

GENERAL INDEX TO THACKERAY'S WORKS.

ILLUSTRATIONS

IN THE STANDARD LIBRARY EDITION OF THE
WORKS OF W. M. THACKERAY.

[The 22 volumes of this edition contain about 1750 illustrations. Many of them were made by the author himself, but several well-known artists are represented, and in the following list the work of each is designated.]

A Little Dinner at Timmins's.

The initials on pages 364, 374, and 380 are by W. M. Thackeray.
The initials on pages 349, 355, 359, and 369 are by J. P. Atkinson.
The text illustrations are by W. M. Thackeray.

The Fatal Boots.

The initials are by J. P. Atkinson.
The full-page illustrations are by George Cruikshank.

Little Travels and Roadside Sketches.

The initials and text illustrations are by Thomas R. Macquoid.

Volume VI., BURLESQUES.

The frontispiece photogravure of W. M. Thackeray is from a bust in
1822 by J. Devile.

Novels by Eminent Hands.

The initials on pages 1, 15, 29, 44, 79, and 88 are by E. J. Wheeler.
The initial on page 67 is by W. M. Thackeray.
The text illustrations are by W. M. Thackeray.

The Diary of C. Jeames de la Pluche, Esq., with His Letters.

The initials on pages 95 and 101 are by J. P. Atkinson.
The initial on page 146 is by W. M. Thackeray.
The text illustrations are by W. M. Thackeray.

The Tremendous Adventures of Major Gahagan.

The text illustrations are by H. Furniss.

A Legend of the Rhine.

The initial and the text illustrations are by George Cruikshank.

Rebecca and Rowena.

All the illustrations are by Richard Doyle.

The History of the next French Revolution.

The initial on page 369 is by J. P. Atkinson.
The text illustrations are by W. M. Thackeray.

Cox's Diary.

The initials are by J. P. Atkinson.

Volume VII., THE HISTORY OF SAMUEL TITMARSH, Etc.

The frontispiece photogravure is by W. M. Thackeray.

The History of Samuel Titmarsh.

The initials are by J. P. Atkinson.
The text illustrations are by W. M. Thackeray.

Men's Wives.

The initials are by E. J. Wheeler.
The text illustrations are by Luke Fildes, A. R. A.

The Book of Snobs.

The initials on pages 361, 378, 430, 461, 466, 486, 504, and 508 are by
J. P. Atkinson.
All other initials are by W. M. Thackeray.
The text illustrations are by W. M. Thackeray.

Volume VIII., THE MEMOIRS OF BARRY LYNDON, Esq.

The frontispiece photogravure of W. M. Thackeray is from a drawing in 1833 by D. Maclise.

Barry Lyndon.

The initials are by W. Ralston.

The text illustrations on pages 7, 35, 46, 75, 99, 123, 186, 239, and 303 are by W. Ralston.

The text illustrations on pages 13, 18, 222, and 305 are by J. E. Millais, R. A.

Denis Duval.

The initials on pages 313 and 360 are by W. M. Thackeray.

The initials on pages 393 and 424 are by Frederick Walker.

The initials on pages 320, 343, 376, and 409 are by W. Ralston.

The text illustrations are by Frederick Walker.

Volume IX., THE NEWCOMES, I.

· The frontispiece photogravure and all other illustrations are by Richard Doyle.

Volume X., THE NEWCOMES, II.

The frontispiece photogravure and all other illustrations are by Richard Doyle.

Volume XI., THE PARIS SKETCH BOOK, Etc.

The frontispiece photogravure is by W. M. Thackeray.

The Paris Sketch Book.

The initials on pages 157 and 208 are by W. M. Thackeray.

All the other initials are by J. P. Atkinson.

The text illustrations on pages 12, 18, 43, 63, 74, 87, 92, 113, 119, 121, 139, 290, and 303 are by W. M. Thackeray.

The text illustrations on pages 3, 28, 66, 102, 153, 161, 178, 211, 228, 294, and 315 are by J. P. Atkinson.

The full-page illustrations are by W. M. Thackeray.

Eastern Sketches.

The initials are by W. J. Webb.

The text illustrations on pages 344, 394, 428, and 442 are by W. J. Webb.

The other text illustrations and the full page illustrations are by W. M. Thackeray.

Volume XII., THE IRISH SKETCH BOOK, Etc.

The frontispiece photogravure of W. M. Thackeray is from his last photograph taken in 1863.

The Irish Sketch Book.

The initials are by M. Fitzgerald.

The text illustrations on pages 3, 57, 73, 129, 161, 216, 246, 269, and 355 are by M. Fitzgerald.

The text illustration on page 337 is by John Collier.

The other text illustrations are by W. M. Thackeray.

CHARACTER SKETCHES.
The illustrations are by J. P. Atkinson.

VOLUME XIII., THE FOUR GEORGES, ETC.
The frontispiece photogravure is by W. M. Thackeray.

THE FOUR GEORGES.
The initials are by W. M. Thackeray.
The text illustration on page 28 is by W. M. Thackeray.
The text illustrations on pages 17, 30, 41, 63, 78, and 96 are by Frank Dicksie.
The text illustration on page 34 is copied by Thackeray from a contemporary caricature.
The text illustrations on pages 70 and 71 are copied by Thackeray from drawings by Gilray.
The text illustrations on pages 82, 83, and 102 are copied by Thackeray from contemporary prints.

THE ENGLISH HUMORISTS.
The initials on pages 113, 150, 186, and 296 are by F. Barnard.
The initial on page 222 is by Linley Sambourne.
The initial on page 263 is by E. J. Wheeler.
The text illustrations on pages 119, 155, 181, 198, 303, and 327 are by F. Barnard.
The text illustration on page 218 is by W. M. Thackeray.
The text illustrations on pages 233 and 253 are by Linley Sambourne.

SKETCHES AND TRAVELS IN LONDON.
The initial on page 343 is by Richard Doyle.
The initials on pages 367, 434, 474, 489, 501, and 506 are by J. P. Atkinson.
The other initials are by W. M. Thackeray.
The text illustrations are by W. M. Thackeray.

VOLUME XIV., THE HISTORY OF HENRY ESMOND, ESQ.
The frontispiece photogravure, Thackeray in his Study, is from a painting in 1854 by E. M. Ward.
The initials are by J. P. Atkinson.
The text illustrations are by George du Maurier.

VOLUME XV., THE VIRGINIANS, I.
The frontispiece photogravure and all other illustrations are by W. M. Thackeray.

VOLUME XVI., THE VIRGINIANS, II.
The frontispiece photogravure and all other illustrations are by W. M. Thackeray.

VOLUME XVII., THE ADVENTURES OF PHILIP, I.
The frontispiece photogravure of W. M. Thackeray is from a photograph in 1852.

A SHABBY GENTEEL STORY.
The illustrations are by R. B. Wallace.

THE ADVENTURES OF PHILIP.

The initials are by W. M. Thackeray.

The text illustrations on pages 140, 145, 179, and 211 are by W. M. Thackeray.

The text illustrations on pages 244, 286, 314, 357, 377, and 412 are by Frederick Walker.

VOLUME XVIII., THE ADVENTURES OF PHILIP, II.

The frontispiece photogravure is by W. M. Thackeray.

THE ADVENTURES OF PHILIP, II.

The initials are by Thackeray.

The text illustrations are by Frederick Walker.

CATHERINE: A STORY.

The initials are by F. A. Fraser.

The text illustrations are by W. M. Thackeray.

VOLUME XIX., ROUNDABOUT PAPERS, ETC.

The frontispiece photogravure is by George Cruikshank.

ROUNDABOUT PAPERS.

The initials on pages 1, 8, 29, 37, 47, 54, 88, 152, 192, and 201 are by Charles Keene.

The other initials are by W. M. Thackeray.

The text illustrations on pages 13, 31, 43, 58, 99, 131, and 194 are by Charles Keene.

The text illustrations on pages 4, 30, 38, 60, 71, 79, 93, 130, 153, 184, and 203 are by W. M. Thackeray.

The text illustration on page 24 is from a photograph.

The text illustration on page 52 is from a water-color drawing by W. M. Thackeray.

The text illustration on page 71 is copied by W. M. Thackeray from a drawing by George Cruikshank.

THE SECOND FUNERAL OF NAPOLEON.

The illustrations are by M. Fitzgerald.

CRITICAL REVIEWS.

The illustrations in "George Cruikshank" are by George Cruikshank.

The illustrations in "John Leech's Pictures" are by John Leech, except the one on page 421, which is by George Cruikshank.

VOLUME XX., CHRISTMAS STORIES, BALLADS, POEMS, ETC.

The frontispiece photogravure and all the other illustrations are by W. M. Thackeray.

VOLUME XXI., CONTRIBUTIONS TO PUNCH.

The frontispiece photogravure of W. M. Thackeray is after a drawing in 1854 by Samuel Laurence.

The other illustrations are by W. M. Thackeray.

VOLUME XXII., MISCELLANEOUS PAPERS AND SKETCHES.

The frontispiece steel engraving of W. M. Thackeray is from a photograph about 1851.

The other illustrations are by W. M. Thackeray.

Lightning Source UK Ltd.
Milton Keynes UK
UKHW020001100223
416721UK00001B/70